Mastering
Visual Basic .NET Database
Programming

Mastering™
Visual Basic® .NET Database Programming

Evangelos Petroutsos

Asli Bilgin

San Francisco   London

Associate Publisher: Richard Mills

Acquisitions and Developmental Editor: Denise Santoro Lincoln

Editor: Sharon Wilkey

Production Editor: Elizabeth Campbell

Technical Editors: John Godfrey, Martin Reid

Graphic Illustrator: Tony Jonick

Electronic Publishing Specialist: Judy Fung

Book Designer: Maureen Forys, Happenstance Type-O-Rama

Proofreaders: Emily Hsuan, Nelson Kim, Dave Nash, Laurie O'Connell, Nancy Riddiough

Indexer: Ted Laux

CD Coordinator: Dan Mummert

CD Technician: Kevin Ly

Cover Designer: Design Site

Cover Illustrator: Sergie Loobkoff

Acknowledgments

WRITING A BOOK IS something that you certainly can't do on your own. If you have an author in your life, there's something you should realize about them: Even though it may seem as if they fell off the face of the Earth, while they are writing furiously, realize that they are always extremely aware of the support, love and tolerance from their loved ones. Without this love and support, there's no way this book could ever be written and I extend my deepest thanks for the following people for enabling me to reach my goals.

Thanks to all the editors and contributors to this book. There's absolutely no way that this book would be here if it weren't for the compassion of Denise Santoro Lincoln (who found me in the first place) whose phone calls during difficult times made everything seem better. To Elizabeth Campbell, whose never-ending patience served as sheer motivation. To Sharon Wilkey for "enabling," not "allowing" me to write a quality book and for all her "great catches" — she should be a fisherman. To Evangelos Petroutsos for writing the previous version of this book, as well as chapters 16, 17, and the Appendix of this book.. Thanks to Mike Gunderloy for chapter 15. I'd also like to thank John Godfrey and Martin Reid, for their technical editing, Richard Mills for the sweet card, Judy Fung for laying out the chapters, and Carl Montgomery for writing the promotional text for the cover. Be sure to contribute all the quality of writing to the phenomenal team at Sybex — and I'll take the credit for all errors and bad jokes.

Writing a book about a product that hasn't come out yet is certainly challenging, and there's really no way to do it without vast amounts of technical support. Huge, tremendous thanks to Rob Howard for answering all my endless Qs and for hooking me up with the right people and being such a great friend, and great birthday song singer. To Mike Pizzo for enhancing the quality of the parts of this book about ADO.NET. To Barton Friedland for support both personally and technically, and being such a *tatli kelebek*. To Susan Warren for letting me pick her brain on Windows Forms and User Controls. To Scott Berry for clarification with data binding and Michael Harsh for user control tips. Many thanks to Marty Wasznicky for sharing great recipes, Ronan Sorensen and Scott Jamison both for sagely author advice.

For my dearest Jay Punk, who just never stops being an amazing person and keeps me real. To Arthur Brost, for always making me look good, for curious conversations and providing technical waterproofing. To Frank Johnson-Suglia for witty *bon-mots* and unusual interpretations. Without the latter three there's no way I could have delivered a project while writing this book. To Marc Raderman, for his incredible patience, concern and warmth that you can see in his eyes. To Bob Hoog, for providing me with fantastic opportunities, and of course, Stef Daskalakis, for introducing me to all these great people and inviting me to Plural in the first place. *Efharisto*.

Black and white is certainly no medium to even begin to express the shades of emotion I have for my friends and family that tolerated my (temporary) drop off the face of the Earth. First and foremost, to my family for tolerating the time when all our conversations just began with "what chapter are you on." To my dearest *Anne*, Aybeniz Bilgin, who is my best friend in the world, whose unselfishness is matched only by her enthusiasm, a heart of pure *altın* and *joie-de-vivre*. To my amazing *Baba*, Özkan Bilgin, whose magnanimity knows no bounds, and thankfully whose thirst for knowledge is contagious. To my sweet sister Nesli, who is a ray of sunshine in everyone's lives, whose compassion is breathtaking. Thank you to the Bilgin and Apak *aileler* for the great genes.

And of course, to "The Family" (and extended family) and Black Sheep members Samantha Panella (and Mike), Drennan Lane (and Mike, Duke too), Shamsi (and Mike) Gravel, Sonya Fleur (and Chris — not Mike — and Sophia) Powers, Julie (and Bob — not Mike — and Katrina) Wieschusen. Thanks to Sam for not calling the Roommate Finder's Assistance Agency when I "lost time" and for saying "I got time" and for giving me the most amazing and astounding friendship — I have never seen, read, nor heard about any type of friendship that could ever compare to ours. You'll always be the greatest balloon day dancer of them all. And yes, I officially now give you credit for the quote "The station wagon is the minivan of the nineties." To Drennan, who cooks a good chicken, no longer hoods, and really does have distinguishing features — the most distinct being the trueness of her friendship to me, when she fought that Nam battalion to fly up for my birthday, even though she didn't sit in the jump seat. Shamsi, for her Irish twinkle, while teaching me Mandarin, the adventures in Hong Kong, and giving me the motivation to knit a Winnebago. Julie Dredlocks, for teaching me how I like apples (I guess I never really knew) and for hanging my messed up nose painting. Sonya Fleur, what can I say Onion? Your intellect and introspection have always been an inspiration and I'll always be the Young O.

And of course, for those "Who-dropped-off-the-face-of-the-Earth / Who-we-haven't-seen-since-Nam." RJ Leneweaver — where have you been? We have your mail. Spraga, we have to play doubles one day. Exclusive, we found your car! Barney — Come on, you always knew when to show up….What about Little Tommy who got lost in traffic.....where is he anyways? Maybe with RJ Leneweaver and Mary O'Leary sitting with Martin at the Erin Pub looking for Amanda Huginkiss. What about the Gold Merc, did he find Wolfie and Cecil and the GL-10? And I have to really, really thank Brett "Alarmclock" Petersen for Otis P. Wilson, who's a big part of this book, who I haven't seen since Nam and whose presence I truly miss.

To Daryl Gaitan a.k.a. FB, for being a wonderful copilot in European adventures and introducing me to his fantastic family (big David, Irma, David, Stephanie, Monique, Kelly, Barbara, Dana, Asia). Now I know where he gets his warmth, love and laughter. To Danielle Adams for her sweet inquires on my progress and being an almost, part-time roommate. To Nicole Sapnar, for being a roommate even she was supposed to be scared. The Two-Brown-Shoe and Going-to-the-Hairdresser stories kept me going when I misplaced my laughter. To Jeremiah Stone, Kristin Brooks, and Patty Martins for all their visits and words of support. To Matt Nunn, for the "Almost Famous" tour and believing in me and octopi. "So long and thanks for all the fish." To Chris Kunicki, for unprecedented encouragement and morale. To Keith and Amanda Credendino, who were single when the book began and married when the book was over. To William Hurt, David Broome, B.J. Jones - my motivation and inspiration and my backboard for bouncing ideas – now is that anticlimactic or anticlimactic? To Darrell Legault and Kevin Watson for teaching me how to pronounce "grease" and "eaves trough". And last, but certainly not least, Bryan with a Y, Patrick with an I, Mulberry, (brother of Mike) — for being a rockstar, superstar and keeping me sane.

—*Asli Bilgin*

Many people contributed to this book, and I would like to thank them all. I guess I should start with the programmers at Microsoft, for their commitment to Visual Basic. Visual Basic has evolved from a small, limited programming environment to a first-class development tool.

Special thanks to the talented people at Sybex--to all of them and to each one individually.

—Evangelos Petroutsos

Foreword

ARE YOU BUILDING VISUAL Basic .NET applications that interact with a database? If so, this book is an essential guide to understanding how to program and use databases for real world applications. It covers a vast array of topics, useful for both beginners and experts. Don't let this book leave your side.

Asli Bilgin is a technical architect, writer and speaker with the global solution provider Plural. Evangelos Petroutsos has written several books on Microsoft technologies. The authors share their knowledge and expertise of real world database programming. They provide valuable insights not only into the programming model, but into theory and architecture as well.

This book goes beyond telling you "how" to program using Microsoft Visual Basic .NET, but explains the "why" behind the code, The authors provide real-world examples, such as a shopping cart system, that you can use as a foundation for your own systems. By understanding why you should design applications in a certain way, you can design more efficient and scalable systems. Throughout the book, Asli and Evangelos point out tips and tricks for your application design to improve performance, reusability and scalability.

Part I of the book begins with a whirlwind tour of database concepts starting with a brief discussion of what a database is and an overview of various Microsoft data access technologies. The book then provides an overview of basic concepts in relational databases, such as common database objects and normalization. Part I then continues with discussions of visual tools you can use to aid in the database planning and development process and a final chapter on Structure Query Language (SQL), the language used to communicate with a database.

In Part II the authors introduce programming concepts building upon the foundation established in part I. The first chapter is dedicated to programming on the data tier using Microsoft SQL Server's Transaction SQL (T-SQL). You will learn how to program stored procedures, functions, triggers, and transactions in T-SQL, and how these features can improve application performance and scalability. For example, Asli and Evangelos go into detail discussing why you should use stored procedures in your application.

After discussing programming the data tier, the discussion turns to ADO.NET, the class libraries provided by the .NET Framework for programming data resources. The authors start by introducing ADO.NET with an example and quickly moves into a more technical discussion of the object model and classes you will use on a daily basis when programming with ADO.NET. A through discussion of several important classes, such as Connection, Command, DataReader, and DataSet will leave you with the knowledge and tips necessary for using the classes successfully in your own application. In the subsequent chapter, ADO.NET Programming, the authors provide clarity as to how these classes are applied to real world programming and application designs, examples such as filtering, searching, and calling stored procedures are just a few of the gems covered.

Part III begins the more advanced topics, covering threading issues, XML integration, programming the middle tier, as well as discussing some of advanced Microsoft SQL Server 2000 topics.

The book concludes with Part IV, a practical set of chapter that discuss how to manage and work with data aware web applications built with ASP.NET. Asli and Evangelos discuss the use of ASP.NET Web Services to connect and share data via XML interfaces using SOAP, and also discuss aspects of ASP.NET Page and application design, covering topics such as the caching functionality built into ASP.NET.

Overall, this book provides the reader with a tremendous amount of useful perspectives and information, applicable for the beginner or the expert. If you want to build better databases applications using the .NET Framework, this book is for you!

Rob Howard
ASP.NET Program Manager
.NET Framework Team
Microsoft Corporation

Contents at a Glance

Contents

Introduction

IN THE PAST, WHEN you thought about database programming with Visual Basic, what did you envision? An Access database with some Windows forms slapped onto it, wired together with some data-bound DAO controls? This type of application definitely wasn't uncommon back in VB5, and even as late as VB6. What was wrong with these applications? Nothing, really. Most often, they served their purpose for their time and environment; however, they certainly didn't take into consideration the proliferation of the Internet, nor the importance of scalability. Generally, these applications would assume a stateful environment and maintain a persistent connection to the back-end database. This tight coupling between the front- and back-ends led to systems that are difficult to maintain. When you changed your data model, you would affect the front-end, and vice versa. If you changed any business logic, both ends would be affected. More and more people are realizing that the applications built today might still be around tomorrow. That means that they better scale well. Additionally, the assumption of a stateful environment is no longer a valid assumption in today's environment of disconnected users. Disconnected users are more common, not merely because of the prevalence of the Internet (which users browse from their desktop), but also because of the spread of wireless devices, such as cell phones and PDAs.

For those of you who have read the previous editions of this book, realize that this edition is almost a complete rewrite. DAO, RDO, and (to some extent) ODBC have all hung up their letters and retired. You can barely discern the faint visage of ADO reflected in the libraries of ADO.NET. XML is now the Big Man on Campus. Altogether, data access under the auspices of the .NET Framework takes on a new meaning, both conceptually and technically.

Conceptually, the .NET Framework forces you to reconsider how you design, build, and test your data access systems. The importance of understanding distributed logic becomes even more vital with the .NET Framework. A disconnected user-base calls for a need to separate the representation of data from the data itself. This requirement is clearly manifested within the philosophy behind XML. The XML schema is clearly distinguished from the actual data itself. This loose coupling is promoted by ADO.NET, as well—after all, XML is at its core. The ADO.NET objects for data access are completely distinct from those used for data storage or representation.

When you are building on the .NET Framework, you should extend this philosophy and ensure that your applications separate the data access logic from the business logic. Encapsulate the business logic in the middle tier. Use stored procedures for easier maintainability and faster performance. If you want your application to scale well, it's imperative that you design your classes to work in a distributed environment, especially if you are deploying them as web services.

The role of data is different in a distributed environment. Most often, you must rely on outdated snapshots. Yes, outdated, because as soon as the data leaves the database, it gets old quickly. Because of this, you'll have to understand how to work with data caching, streams, and synchronization. We cover all these concepts in this book.

On a technical level, how you design and write your data access code has changed. The VB runtime has been replaced by a unified Common Language Runtime. More than likely, you'll be working with the .NET base classes and .NET data providers, rather than ADO or OLE DB. You'll need to understand how to program with XML and its satellite technologies, such as XPath and XSLT. Relational data is not the only way to store your data; both relational and hierarchical data schemas play a vital role.

Mastering Visual Basic .NET Database Programming is the book for VB developers (past and present) who wish to move into database programming. If you want to understand the strategies and concepts, as well as practical implementations behind technologies such as VB .NET and XML, this is the book for you. Don't think of this as a merely a reference manual. You'll find interesting design discussions and strategies peppered throughout the book. On the other hand, don't view this book as an abstract, theoretical exploration—that's certainly not the case. Every chapter contains code samples and walk-throughs that contain practical examples of how you can work with databases by using VB .NET.

Today, Visual Basic .NET is still the most popular programming language and it's ideal for building database applications. Visual Studio .NET comes with an array of tools for building database applications, the visual database tools, that make it the best environment for developing distributed and autonomous systems.

Who Should Read This Book

This book is addressed to Visual Basic .NET and ASP.NET programmers who are interested in developing database applications. You'll definitely get more out of the book if you have programming experience with previous versions of Visual Basic, only because in some places we make comparisons between classic VB and VB .NET. Additionally, you'll find your VB experience helpful when you build ASP.NET applications. This is because ASP.NET supports compiled languages, such as VB .NET. However, newcomers to VB will not feel at all daunted by the topics addressed in the book. All the code walk-throughs provide detailed steps on what to type and where to type it.

Although it helps if you're familiar with Visual Basic, this book requires no knowledge of databases. Database programming is a very broad subject, so we had to make certain choices as to the topics covered in the book. As much as we would have liked to cover every aspect of database programming, there was simply no room. This book focuses on the technologies around SQL Server 2000, VB .NET, ADO.NET, XML, XSLT, and ASP.NET.

SQL Server is fully integrated into the VS .NET environment, and there are many SQL Server–specific tools that you can use to perform data access. This book doesn't assume knowledge of SQL Server, and it doesn't show you how to get started with SQL Server either. The only SQL Server topics discussed in detail here are Transact-SQL (T-SQL), stored procedures, and XML integration. T-SQL is SQL Server's built-in programming language. T-SQL complements Visual Basic .NET (or any other language that can access SQL Server databases). Stored procedures contain SQL code that keeps your data access code centralized and optimized. SQL Server 2000's integration with XML has made great progress since previous versions. SQL Server now enables you to submit XML-based commands to SQL via HTTP and SQL OLE DB, as well as submit XPath queries.

VB .NET has also made great strides with XML integration, building upon the base classes of the .NET Framework. The focus of this book is on the `System.Data` and `System.Xml` libraries, which are your key players for data access and storage. The ADO.NET classes can be found within the `System.Data` namespace and can be used with either COM-based OLE DB drivers or the new .NET data providers.

This book provides applications for both ASP.NET and Windows-based interfaces. For the most part, you'll find that the tools and data access code are interchangeable between the two types of systems. Server-side controls have certainly come a long way in ASP.NET and help bridge the gap between visual development within Windows and web applications.

The visual tools for data access in VS .NET are quite powerful and really can expedite your delivery time. However, they do come with limitations in terms of flexibility. Throughout the book, we try to point out these limitations and provide scenarios using both visual and programmatic data access. This way, you can have a better idea of when and where the point-and-click tools should be used, and when you need to roll up your sleeves and start typing.

What's Covered in This Book

This book is organized in four parts. It starts with the basics: the principles of database design, Visual Studio .NET's visual database tools, and Structured Query Language. As the book progresses, it delves deeper into database programming, covering the T-SQL language, the ADO.NET object model, XML, and VB .NET data aware controls. Toward the end of the book, you will find complex topics such as threading, exception handling, asynchronous operations, XSL Transformations, XPath queries, and ADO.NET events. Additionally, you'll touch upon database administration with SQL Server 2000, using such tools as the SQL Profiler and the Index Tuning Wizard. Finally, the last section of the book shows you how to build and deploy Web Services and ASP.NET projects.

PART 1: DATABASE CONCEPTS

The first part of this book discusses the basics of databases: how to design them, how to manipulate them with SQL, and how to use Transact-SQL (a programming language built into SQL Server).

In the first few chapters of the book, you'll read about the structure of relational databases and how to design them. Chapter 1, "Database Access: Architectures and Technologies," is a great chapter because it provides a strategic overview of what the .NET Framework is and how it affects the world of data access. In the following chapters, you'll find detailed discussions of SQL and the sample databases you're going to use in later chapters. We don't limit our topics to SQL Server 2000. You'll also find an extensive, yet high-level, overview of the many visual database tools within Visual Studio .NET. This will pave the way for working with the examples later in the book.

A good deal of the first part of the book is devoted to SQL and T-SQL. As a database programmer, you can't afford to skip these topics. SQL enables you to access any database; T-SQL will help you make the most of SQL Server.

PART 2: DATABASE PROGRAMMING

The second part of the book continues your exploration of SQL, specifically honing in on the T-SQL language. At this point, now that you've learned the fundamental principles of designing relational databases, you will move on to writing code to manipulate the data and database objects. T-SQL is used by SQL Server to generate DML statements and stored procedures. You'll see the advantage of using stored procedures over ad hoc SQL statements by actually creating and testing sample business rules using stored procedures. You'll also learn new SQL Server 2000 features, such as user-defined functions and enhanced trigger functionality.

ADO.NET is the fundamental data access engine for relational stores such as SQL Server. You'll learn how to leverage the ADO.NET object model to retrieve results in both relational and hierarchical form. You'll see how XML fits into Microsoft's data access strategy. Additionally, you'll understand the different models for retrieving data: cached and streamed. For those of you who have worked with previous versions of ADO, you'll see the differences between classic ADO and ADO.NET, as well as gain insight whether migration to ADO.NET is right for you. You'll walk through tangible examples of retrieving and updating data by using ADO.NET, as well as working with the new relational model between ADO.NET DataTables. You'll learn about more advanced features of ADO.NET, such as filtering, searching, and working with the DataView object.

In Part 2, you'll work closely with the DataSet object, building schemas on the fly, as well as leveraging the data binding techniques with .NET user interface controls. You'll examine and manipulate the components of the DataSet, such as the DataTable, DataRow, and DataColumn objects. By the end of this part, you'll have a solid understanding of what you can do with ADO.NET and should have no problem designing and building your own ADO.NET applications.

Finally, you'll also begin exploring XML's role in the .NET paradigm. You'll see practical examples of retrieving data and schema by using ADO.NET and manipulating them by using the VS .NET XML Designer. You'll explore the `System.Xml` namespace and understand how to load data not only from relational databases, but from XML data files as well. Chapter 10, "The Role of XML," explores the strategic role of XML within disconnected architecture and examines the new XML-related SQL Server 2000 features.

PART 3: ADVANCED DATA SERVICES

The first two parts of the book provide the material you need to design and create a database system by using the .NET platform. In Part 3, you will build upon this foundation by learning the advanced feature-sets within the .NET Framework.

You will learn how to secure the quality of your systems with efficient exception handling. You'll understand how asynchronous operations work by using the `System.Threading` namespace. For those of you who have worked with classic ADO, you'll realize that the landscape for asynchronous operations has changed quite dramatically. Even if you've never worked with threaded applications, you'll see the importance of understanding the event model in the .NET Framework, with ADO.NET as a classic example.

Part 3 of the book also expands upon your knowledge of XML, which was introduced in Part 2. You'll learn about the satellite technologies that surround XML, such as the XPath query language and XSL Transformations. You'll see quite amazing stuff, such as how you can query a SQL Server 2000 database by simply using XML and HTTP via a browser.

Part 3 brings together the pieces of the jigsaw puzzle by introducing and outlining the middle tier. For those of you who are new to the .NET Framework, you'll learn important .NET architectural considerations, such as assemblies and manifests.

Additionally, you'll learn about advanced SQL Server 2000 functionality, such as replication, SQL Profiler, Query Optimizer and the Index Tuning Wizard. All these considerations will not only help you design, but also tune your database for maximum performance and efficiency.

PART 4: DATA ACCESS FROM THE WEB

Each day, more and more companies are making use of the Internet, either building commercial sites or designing web applications that allow employees to access the corporate database through the Web.

In the fourth part of this book, you'll learn how to build web applications that access a database by using ADO.NET. You'll learn how to build web-based front-ends as well as Web Services in the middle tier. You'll learn how to work with server-side controls such as the DataGrid and DataList controls. No VB .NET book would be complete without an explanation of how you would deploy your application. You'll learn about the robust deployment projects available in VS .NET, as well as understand the implications of building distributed database systems.

What's on the CD

This book is accompanied by a CD containing the code for all the example projects discussed in the book. You'll find the projects in the SRC folder, and each chapter's projects are in their own folder, named after the project. For example, the Customers project in Chapter 5, "Transact-SQL" is stored in the SRC\CH05\CUSTOMERS folder. All the files needed to open the project and run it in the Visual Basic IDE are stored in this folder.

We suggest that you use the installation software on the CD to copy all projects to your hard disk, duplicating the structure of the SRC folder on your disk. You can run the projects off of the CD, but you can't save them on the CD after editing them. To edit a project, you must copy the project's folder to your hard disk and then open the project. Notice that the files copied off the CD have their Read-Only attribute set. To edit any projects you copied manually to your hard disk from the CD, follow these steps:

1. Select all files with the mouse; then right-click your selection.

2. From the shortcut menu, choose Properties to open the Properties dialog box.

3. In the Attributes section, clear the Read-Only box.

Using the Book's Projects

All the projects in this book use either the Northwind or Pubs sample databases. These databases ship with SQL Server 2000. To use these databases, you'll need a valid connection to them based on your environment settings. You have two choices when you are creating the Connection object in .NET. First, you can do so declaratively by using the visual tools provided with Visual Studio .NET or SQL Server 2000. These visual tools enable you to specify the database you want to connect to with point-and-click operations and prepare the appropriate Connection object for you. Alternately, you can opt to create the Connection object programmatically. We provide details on how to do both later in the book. Just realize that when you use the code examples throughout the book, you'll have to modify the connection settings to match your environment. Additionally, to keep the examples simple and easily accessible, we don't specify unique security credentials for our connections, which you should always specify if you are deploying a production system. Again, just be sure to change these security settings on your connections as well.

The projects that use SQL Server databases assume that SQL Server is running on the same machine you're using to test them. However, if you're using a database server on a network, you can still use the connections; just change your connection settings accordingly. All you have to do is change the name of the database server from `local` to the name of the machine on which SQL Server is running, and set the account name and password.

How to Reach the Authors

Despite our best efforts, a book this size sometimes contains errors. If you have any problems with the text or applications in this book, you can contact Asli Bilgin directly at `asli@mindspring.com`.

Although we can't promise a response to every question, we will try to address any problem in the text or examples and will provide updated versions. We would also like to hear any comments you might have about the book regarding topics you liked or disliked, as well as how useful you found the examples. Your comments will help us revise the book in future editions.

Updates

It's quite likely that a Service Pack for Visual Studio .NET will be released. Any changes and/or additions that affect the projects of the book will be posted at the book's section on the Sybex web site at `www.sybex.com`. To access this information, simply locate the Mastering Visual Basic .NET Database Programming title (or do a search for 2878) and follow the link to the Updates section.

Part 1

Database Concepts

In this section:

Chapter 1

Database Access: Architectures and Technologies

- ◆ Databases and database management systems
- ◆ Microsoft data access technologies
- ◆ From ADO to ADO.NET
- ◆ From client-server to distributed architecture
- ◆ How distributed applications work
- ◆ SQL Server 2000

THE FIRST CHAPTER IN a typical computer book is an introduction to the book's topic. So you might think that this chapter would be merely an introduction to databases—but it isn't. We supplement our introduction to database programming with conceptual design topics, such as distributed architecture and Microsoft data access strategies.

Databases are the broadest and most diverse area of computer programming. Before you can understand how to design and develop database systems, you must first understand the big picture behind data access technology. You should then be able to use this knowledge to anticipate design considerations before you type a line of code.

This chapter provides a high-level conceptual overview of data access technology and distributed architecture. This chapter is for those of you not familiar with such acronyms as *OLE DB*, *ADO*, *DBMS*, and *UDA*. You should read this chapter if you are not quite sure what *n-tier* means or are unfamiliar with designing distributed systems. Additionally, this chapter provides a historical glance back at Microsoft's data access evolution, from classic ADO/OLE DB to ADO.NET within the .NET Framework.

Databases and Database Management Systems

A *database* is a system for storing structured information, which is organized and stored in a way that allows its quick and efficient retrieval. You need to put a lot of effort into designing a database so that you can retrieve the data easily.

The information is broken into *tables,* as shown in Figure 1.1. Each table stores different entities (one table stores customer information, another table stores invoice information, and so on). You break the information into smaller chunks so that you can manage it easily (divide and conquer). You can design rules to protect the database against user actions and ask a special program to enforce these rules (for example, reject customers without a name). These rules apply to all the items stored in the Customers table; the same rules don't apply to the Products table and the Orders table, of course.

FIGURE 1.1

Sample tables

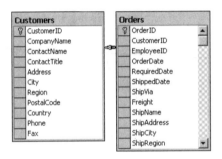

In addition to tables, you define *relationships* between tables. Relationships enable users to combine information from multiple tables. As you can see in Figure 1.1, the Customers table and the Orders table relate to each another. The thing that they have in common is a customer ID. Because a *customer* places *orders,* each order must relate to a customer. By establishing a relationship between the two tables, you can quickly retrieve the orders issued to a specific customer. Without such a relationship, you would have to scan the entire Orders table to isolate the desired orders. This view of a database, made up of tables related to one another, is a *conceptual* view of the database. And a database that relies on relationships between tables is called *relational* and can be represented in visual diagrams, as shown in Figure 1.1. You will learn more about relational diagrams later in this chapter.

Tables and relationships, along with other database entities, make up the design of the database. You can separate the design into two categories: logical design and physical design. A *logical design* is based on the conceptual view of how your data is stored in the system: a schema or an entity-relationship diagram can represent the logical design of your data on the system. The *physical design* of the database on the disk is quite different. In fact, you might not have any idea how data is stored in the database (and you should be thankful for this). The information is physically stored in and recalled from the database by a special program known as a *database management system (DBMS).* The DBMS provides a service that enables you to communicate between your logical and physical database design. Later in this chapter, you will see how this separation of physical and logical relates to designing .NET systems.

DBMSs are among the most complicated applications, and a modern DBMS can instantly locate a record in a table with several million records. While the DBMS maintains all the information in the database, applications can access this information through statements made in *Structured Query Language (SQL)*, a language for specifying high-level operations. These operations are called *queries*, and there are two types of queries: *selection queries*, which extract information from the database, and *action queries*, which update the database. How the DBMS maintains, updates, and retrieves this information is something that the application doesn't have to deal with.

Specifically, a DBMS provides the following functions:

◆ A DBMS enables applications to use SQL statements to define the structure of a database. The subset of SQL statements that define or edit this structure is called *Data Definition Language (DDL)*. Although all DBMSs use a visual interface with simple point-and-click operations to define the structure of the database, these tools translate the actions of the user into the appropriate DDL statements. SQL Server, for example, enables you to create databases by using a visual tool, the Enterprise Manager, but it also generates the equivalent DDL statements and stores them in a special file, called a script.

◆ A DBMS enables applications to use SQL statements to manipulate the information stored in the database. The subset of SQL statements that manipulate this information is known by another acronym: *DML*, which stands for *Data Manipulation Language*. Let's come up with our own acronym to represent the basic DML operations: QUAD (query, update, add, and delete records).

◆ A DBMS protects the integrity of the database by enforcing certain rules, which are incorporated into the design of the database. You can specify default values, prohibit certain fields from being empty, prevent the deletion of records that are linked to other records, and so on. Referential integrity enables you to build relationships between discrete data items. The relationships tie the data together, so that when data activity occurs, the related information is also affected. For example, you can tell the DBMS not to remove a customer if the customer is linked to one or more invoices. If you could remove the customer, that customer's invoices would be "orphaned." Referential integrity prevents orphaned records and undesirable deletions.

◆ In addition, the DBMS is responsible for the security of the database (it protects the database from access by unauthorized users). The DBMS can provide security in many ways. It could integrate with the underlying operating system security, use the DBMS security model, or allow you to build your own custom security model.

SQL Server is a database management system and not a database. An *SQL Server database* is a database maintained by SQL Server. *SQL* is a universal language for manipulating databases and is supported by most DBMSs—you'll examine it in detail in Chapter 4, "Structured Query Language." SQL retrieves selected records from the database and returns them to the client. Additionally, the language is capable of manipulating records—adding, updating, or deleting information within the database.

NOTE *A trial version of SQL Server 2000 is available from Microsoft at* www.microsoft.com/sql.

You aren't limited only to SQL to access your data. Microsoft provides a programming model called *ActiveX Data Objects (ADO)* that provides an easy-to-use, object-oriented interface for data access. *ADO.NET* is the latest incarnation of ADO, providing backward compatibility with the classic ADO interface. DataSets and DataReaders comprise the heart of ADO.NET. *DataSets* provide memory-resident copies of the data you need, along with the relationships and rules that surround that data. *DataReaders* provide fast access to forward-only, read-only data. You'll learn more about ADO.NET soon, but first let's discuss Microsoft's view of data access. After you understand Microsoft's data access strategy, you can apply it to the design and architecture of your systems.

Microsoft Data Access Technologies

Microsoft's approach to data access hinges on the concept of distributed architecture. One of Microsoft's long-term goals is the propagation of a common data store, and the advent of Universal Data Access (UDA) makes this possible. The advances made with ADO.NET extend this philosophy, in that the new data access model strongly supports interoperability, more than ever. Our intent in this section is to step through Microsoft's data access technologies and then to identify how they fit into a distributed architecture.

Windows DNA

Windows DNA (WinDNA) stands for *Distributed interNet Architecture*, and it's a methodology for building distributed applications. A methodology is a set of rules, or suggestions, rather than a blueprint for developing applications; in other words, it's a recommendation on how to build distributed applications. A *distributed application* is one made up of multiple components that run on different machines. WinDNA is an umbrella-term for distributed system methodology based on the Windows platform. WinDNA applications revolve around component-based architecture, specifically COM and COM+. Component-based architecture gives you great flexibility in many ways. You don't have to build everything from scratch, as components offer black-box reuse. Components offer greater scalability, which comes from the modular, Lego-like capability of components to plug and play into evolving functional systems. This modularity provides adaptability so that your application can change as business needs change. Finally, components make it easier to build distributed systems, enabling you to take advantage of processing power on other machines.

WinDNA makes it easier to build distributed applications. We discuss distributed architecture in detail later in this chapter; however, realize that these different machines do not have to be limited to a single LAN; they can be spread throughout many networks. Because the Internet consists of multiple machines spread throughout the world, the Internet is a logical backbone for WinDNA applications. So, in effect, WinDNA is about building applications for the Internet.

Interoperability plays a vital role in building efficient WinDNA applications. Interoperability comes from two levels: *data* and *services*. Microsoft addresses data interoperability issues with UDA, which was first introduced with WinDNA and matures with .NET. Microsoft addresses service interoperability with the .NET Framework. Although this book concentrates primarily on data architecture, you cannot build quality applications without understanding the services model introduced with .NET.

The .NET Framework

WinDNA uses an organic metaphor, with components representing the "cells" of a system. Each "cell" is responsible for a specific activity. Altogether, the "cells" can be viewed as a single entity, as a single system or "organism." Under the WinDNA paradigm, it was difficult for organisms to communicate with one another. The .NET Framework provides the infrastructure, or nervous system, for organisms to talk to one another by using services. These services leverage the communication channels and formats that are already in place—the Internet and Extensible Markup Language (XML).

Both WinDNA and the .NET Framework architectures are similar in the sense that they address distributed systems. However, there is one glaring difference between the two models: WinDNA is designed for tightly coupled component architecture, whereas the .NET Framework is designed for loosely coupled services. WinDNA components are strongly tied to their native applications, making remote access between systems a challenge. The .NET Framework lifts the wall between balkanized WinDNA components, liberating architecture for better communication between sites, services, and components.

The Microsoft .NET platform evolves WinDNA, by addressing the system interoperability problem. Microsoft resolves this problem by extending the WinDNA component-based architecture to a services-based model. Although many companies have Internet systems, it is difficult for these systems to talk to one another. The services-based model presented with .NET enables heterogeneous applications services to talk by using these channels (see Table 1.1). Notice that all the technologies that .NET leverages are ubiquitous and nonproprietary. Figure 1.2 shows the evolution of distributed architecture from WinDNA to the .NET Framework.

FIGURE 1.2

From WinDNA to .NET

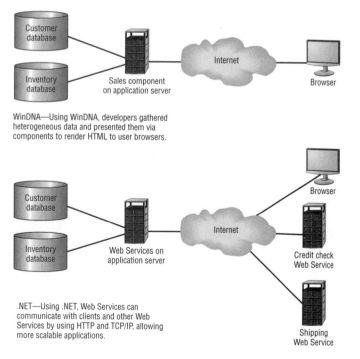

WinDNA—Using WinDNA, developers gathered heterogeneous data and presented them via components to render HTML to user browsers.

.NET—Using .NET, Web Services can communicate with clients and other Web Services by using HTTP and TCP/IP, allowing more scalable applications.

TABLE 1.1: TECHNOLOGIES USED WITH THE .NET FRAMEWORK

TECHNOLOGY	WHAT IT IS	ORGANIC MODEL
HTTP	Transport protocol	Circulatory system
WebServices	Service contracts	Synapses
XML	Data presentation and data transfer standard	DNA
The Internet	The delivery mechanism for WebServices	Nervous system

WHAT ARE WEBSERVICES?

In today's web architecture, you build components that join DBMS and operating system functionality, along with custom business logic. These components emit HTML to browsers. They are not designed for communication between sites. The components of each site live in their own world, and many times developers resort to "screen-scraping" the HTML results, rather than calling the components directly. Microsoft WebServices provide a mechanism that enables intra-site communication using industry-accepted standards.

Although WebServices are beginning to crop up for many technologies, Microsoft had not formalized the design, implementation, and delivery of their own WebServices until the release of the .NET Framework. Microsoft WebServices were introduced with the .NET platform as a way of publishing application logic as services via the Internet.

Microsoft's vision for WebService distribution and discovery will revolutionize the way we think about Internet architecture. Instead of trying to figure out how to access the functionality in external websites, you will be able to go to a centralized repository (`http://www.uddi.org`) that contains all the published WebServices. All you have to do is select one for your application to use. Instead of messy Distributed Component Object Model (DCOM) code and type-libraries, all you have to do is simply point to the WebService of your choice and begin using it.

We don't get into too much detail here; suffice it to say that WebServices serve as modular contracts for communication between local and remote resources. WebServices use two ubiquitous standards—Hypertext Transfer Protocol (HTTP) and XML. These are both standard ways of communicating on the Internet.

HOW DOES .NET FIT INTO DATA ACCESS?

The data access services that come with .NET have matured quite considerably since Microsoft's first introduction of UDA. The advancements in .NET data access center around the new Common Language Runtime (CLR) data types, .NET Framework base classes, and specifically the redesign of ADO into a more robust disconnected model.

Data types have changed dramatically since Visual Basic 6 (VB6). The CLR houses a universal type system called the *Common Type System (CTS)*, which is accessible by .NET-compliant languages.

WARNING *Some features of the CLR are not supported by every language. For example, VB .NET does not understand the concept of unsigned integers. If you want to ensure cross-language support for your code, follow the guidelines in the Common Language Specification (CLS), which serves as a language-neutral subset of the CLR. The CLS extrapolates the common denominators between languages for support within the .NET Framework.*

XML is visible throughout the .NET data access libraries, not just as a supported technology, but as a cornerstone of the .NET Framework. Not only are XML functionalities housed in their own XML library, but they also are also a core foundation within the ADO.NET libraries. Table 1.2 shows some of the data access libraries within the `System` namespace that are shipped with the .NET Framework.

TABLE 1.2: NEW DATA ACCESS LIBRARIES IN THE .NET FRAMEWORK

DATA ACCESS LIBRARY	DESCRIPTION
System.Data	The main data access library for ADO.NET.
System.Data.OleDb	This library houses the components that provide access via an OLE DB provider.
System.Data.SqlClient	This library houses the data access components that are optimized for SQL Server.
System.Xml	This library contains the XML components.

XML fits into this model insofar as these libraries can bring back data in the form of XML. You can use these libraries to build .NET WebServices. WebServices enable you to aggregate data from all over the Web, pulled from many devices. The client-server metaphor for data access is extinguished as we move to an environment where anything can be a data "server." A client can now both consume and produce WebServices. So a client can be a server, and a server can be a client. Confused yet? It will all come together as you read through this book.

In addition, .NET provides robust support for a disconnected environment. In fact, Microsoft completely redesigned ADO.NET, taking the best from ADO and tossing the rest. Because ADO had strong ties to a connected history, it never fully supported the disconnected environment. Microsoft developers followed a natural evolution from ADO 2.*x*. As WinDNA applications matured, developers began to see patterns of how applications used data. Developers began to build more-complex distributed applications, which caused speed to become a driving factor in design. Disconnected RecordSets enhanced that speed. Hence, the .NET model fully supports disconnected environments with ADO.NET DataSets completely separated from the database access engine. We explain this concept further as we get deeper into ADO.NET in Chapter 6, "A First Look at ADO.NET."

IMPACT ON BUSINESS PROCESS

Microsoft .NET is the third generation of distributed development architecture, embracing not only a new code base, but also a new software architecture philosophy. This philosophy uses the concept of the Internet as a grouping of services, rather than sites. Strategically, this could lead to an evolution of the Internet from a free, *laissez-faire* enterprise to a worldwide rental services agency. How would this happen? With the emergence of Web Services, enterprises will have a much tighter reign on who can access their services. If they want to, they could enforce "licensing" or "rental" models upon their WebServices.

In terms of business, this model effectively serves companies by enabling them to take advantage of one another's services, rather than reinventing the wheel. For example, Amazon has a phenomenal purchasing system. Say your mother wants to sell her buttons online. She could create a website that "rents" the Amazon purchasing WebServices, rather than build her own.

IMPACT ON TECHNICAL ARCHITECTURE

.NET will have the most impact on the Application layer architecture within a distributed system. .NET evolves the object-oriented paradigm by providing developers with a language-independent, CLR-based framework of libraries. The libraries are fully viewable and extensible, similar in concept to Java libraries. This replaces the "black-box" concept you had in VB6, with a transparent, "glass-box" model in .NET. In addition, Microsoft addresses the issues of interoperability between languages and applications, by embracing industry-accepted standards such as XML and HTTP as well as providing backward compatibility with COM.

With all this in mind, you must be careful about how you architect .NET solutions. Although this new platform helps resolve a good number of problems, it also introduces new issues for consideration. Debugging and testing take on a new outlook in a live WebServices environment. Optimal performance architecture must be taken into consideration, because WebServices do not necessarily have to be precompiled, nor do you always know the location of the WebService you are calling. Granted, we live in an environment where 24/7 connectivity is not unusual; however, latency will still be an issue as infrastructures mature. .NET presents robust support of a disconnected environment, and architecture must be designed to acknowledge this. Concurrency, queuing, and locking will be focal points in this new world order. Security becomes more crucial as WebServices are created and published on the Internet. No longer will we have components talking to one another internally, but organizations communicating externally.

This doesn't mean that you have to toss all your current design documents in the vertical file. If you design your application well by using WinDNA, it is safe to say that it will be a good design in .NET as well. Also, remember, Microsoft developers designed .NET for robust interoperability. WinDNA COM applications can peacefully coexist with .NET applications and can share functionality with them, using the interoperability services of .NET. This means that you don't have to port your entire system to .NET at once. If you have a well-designed Lego-like component model in WinDNA, you can easily port COM components to .NET services on an as-needed basis.

From ADO to ADO.NET

Data interoperability begins with the realization that not all information is stored in databases. When most of us are talking about data, we think of databases, rows, and columns—well-structured data that can be easily retrieved. However, not all information can be stored in databases. A lot of information is stored in e-mail folders, text documents, spreadsheets, even audio and video files. The ultimate data access technology is one that can access any information, from anywhere, whether it is a database, an electronic mailbox, a text file, or even a handheld device. Ideally, you should be able to access information in a uniform way, no matter where this information resides. And you should also be able to access it from anywhere, meaning the Internet.

Microsoft introduced the term *Universal Data Access (UDA)* to describe this idea. The premise of Universal Data Access is to allow applications to efficiently access data where it resides, through a common protocol.

At a high level, Microsoft's data access architecture can be visualized as shown in Figure 1.3. *Data providers*, or *data stores*, store information, and their job is to expose the data through data services. *Data consumers* receive and process the data. Finally, *business services*, which act as *data validators*, provide common services that extend the native functionality of the data providers.

FIGURE 1.3

Microsoft Universal Data Access

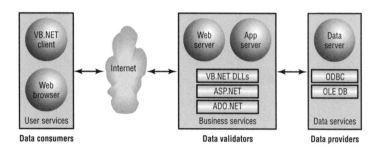

The key point of UDA is that it enables you to access data transparently, regardless of where it "lives." A data provider can be just about anything—an SQL Server database, a flat file, a message store, or a file system. UDA architecture resolved the problem of heterogeneous data access by providing a thin data access layer that could communicate with any OLE DB–compliant data provider. As long as your data provider is compliant with the core UDA technologies (OLE DB, ODBC, and ADO), you can readily transport and expose data through your data services.

Microsoft extends the concepts introduced with UDA by incorporating Internet standards into the .NET Framework's data access strategy. In addition to the core standards such as XML and HTTP, .NET also provides a rich base library for you to build data services. The .NET data providers give you two models to work with; the `SqlClient` or the `OleDb` libraries provide an object-oriented, relational way of viewing data and schemas. In addition, the native XML support in these libraries provides a hierarchical presentation of data and schemas. We discuss these technologies later in this section.

NOTE   *At this time, VS .NET ships with two .NET data providers:* `SqlClient` *and* `OleDb`. *However, you can download additional .NET data providers, such as ODBC.NET, from Microsoft's website (*www.microsoft.com*).*

In this book, data access consists of data providers and data consumers. Although we use a DBMS, SQL Server 2000, for our examples, you can substitute any other .NET-compliant data provider that you wish. The *data consumer* is any application that uses the data. A consumer of data services is often called a *client* application, because it is being served by the data provider. The client application makes requests to the DBMS, and the DBMS carries out the requests. The data consumer need not be a typical client application with a visible interface. In this book, you'll learn how to build different types of client applications, those that interact directly with the users and those that talk directly to other applications. We will show you how to leverage WebServices, enabling "clients" to be exposed as "servers" that other clients can consume.

In addition to data providers and consumers, we cover the transformation layer between the two. Generally, there are always rules to transform the data on its way in and out by using business validation logic, transformation, or consistency checks. Considering the exposure you get with WebServices, you should ensure that your data goes through the appropriate business rules and security when accessed by external systems.

To summarize, Universal Data Access was introduced with WinDNA as a platform for developing distributed database applications that can access a diverse variety of data sources across an intranet or the Internet. .NET extends this platform by using Internet standards such as HTTP and XML as its data delivery and storage mechanisms. The XML and ADO.NET libraries further extend your capabilities with data access. Now let's explore some of the main technologies used with Microsoft data access.

ADO and OLE DB

In WinDNA, the two cornerstones of Universal Data Access were ActiveX Data Objects (ADO) and object linking and embedding for databases (OLE DB). OLE DB is a layer that sits on top of the database. ADO sits on top of OLE DB by using a thin IDispatch overlay, which offers a simplified view of the database. These technologies were introduced to make it easier for programmers to write code to access databases.

Before WinDNA, each database exposed its functionality with its own set of application programming interface (API) functions. This made it difficult to access each database through its native interface, because you'd have to learn the specifics of each database (low-level, technical details). Porting the application to another database would be a major undertaking. To write applications that talk to two databases at once (SQL Server and Oracle, for instance), you'd have learn two APIs and discover the peculiarities of each database, unless you used OLE DB and ADO.

OLE DB offers a unified view of different data providers. Each database has its own set of OLE DB service providers, which provide a uniform view of the database by following common specifications. ADO hides the peculiarities of each database and gives developers a simple, conceptual view of the underlying database. The difference between ADO and OLE DB is that OLE DB gives you more control over the data access process, because it's a low-level interface. However, keep in mind that when you are using ADO, you are really using OLE DB. This could be a valid reason why the Microsoft development team renamed the base class data library from `System.Data.ADO` to `System.Data.OleDb`.

Figure 1.4 shows how your application can access various databases. The most efficient method is to get there directly through OLE DB. This also happens to be the most difficult route, and it's typically not what Visual Basic (VB) programmers do. The next most efficient method is to go through ADO, which makes the OLE DB layer transparent to the application. You can also access the database through Open Database Connectivity (ODBC), which is similar to OLE DB, but it's an older technology. If you can program ODBC, then you can program OLE DB, and there's no reason to use ODBC drivers, unless an OLE DB driver doesn't exist for your data source. Many of you are already familiar with Data Access Objects (DAO) and Remote Data Objects (RDO). These are older technologies for accessing databases through ODBC. In a way, they are equivalent to ADO. These components, however, have been deprecated, and you should use them only if you're supporting legacy database applications that already use DAO or RDO.

FIGURE 1.4

How client applications communicate with databases

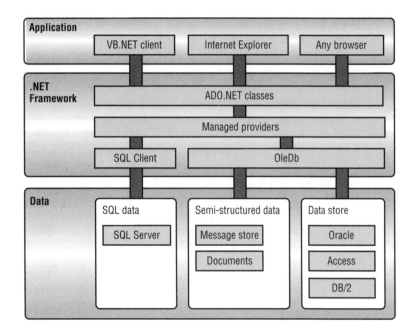

ADO.NET

ADO.NET takes the existing ADO architecture model and extends it by offering several advantages over previous versions of ADO and over other data access components. OLE DB and ADO solved the problems of transparency and redundancy with data access. ADO.NET addresses the problems with interoperability, performance, and maintainability.

ADO.NET provides interoperability by closely integrating with XML. In fact, any component that can read XML can take advantage of ADO.NET functionality. Although you could hook up to heterogeneous data sources with ADO 2.x, they still had to be OLE DB compliant. XML far outweighs OLE DB in industry acceptance, making it a logical choice for interoperability.

ADO.NET enhances the old model by providing higher degrees of maintainability and performance. It does this by leveraging the XML model of a separate Presentation and Data layer. In addition, ADO.NET treats the data access engine and the data itself as two distinct entities, unlike ADO. With ADO 2.x, disconnected RecordSets were marshaled within the constraints of COM's architectural overhead. XML is a simple text-based protocol, which greatly reduces the overhead of transmitting disconnecting data, vastly improving performance, and providing programmers with more maintainable code. Because ADO.NET tightly integrates with XML, you no longer have to deal with the expensive cost of converting ADO RecordSets to other data types.

Scalability is an important factor in ADO.NET design. This is achieved with the enforcement of a disconnected environment, ensuring that you can't hold lengthy database locks or persistent connections that would tie up your database server's resources. ADO.NET advances in scalability by using XML and HTTP as its foundation. XML plays a vital role with remoting technology standards, specifically with SOAP. *Simple Object Access Protocol (SOAP)* is yet another technology that leverages XML at its core.

SOAP replaces proprietary and binary DCOM by using XML and HTTP to make remote calls. Unlike DCOM, SOAP transports data in a text-based format. This makes it easier for data transport between firewalls, because many firewalls block COM marshalling.

ADO.NET provides a stronger programming model, integrating closely with the CLR. This makes it easy to integrate your data access code with the native services offered by the CLR, such as COM+ or Windows functionalities. In addition, programmability becomes more intuitive because ADO.NET uses XML's self-describing nature, rather than tables, columns and rows. In addition, by separating its in-memory cache from its actions, you have more control over how ADO.NET handles the actions you request. This could come in handy, for example, when you update a DataSet and you would like to have separate update logic for each of your heterogeneous data sources. Just try to do this in ADO 2.x; it's not fun, we assure you.

Although ADO.NET has many benefits, you must be judicious in your choice to migrate to ADO.NET. Porting from unmanaged to managed code requires careful design considerations. Unmanaged code uses the COM engine and traditional registration. Managed code leverages the CLR and is self-describing. In this book, we provide information that will help you decide whether to port your code. This information will enable you to port your unmanaged code intelligently, in a way that's best for your system needs.

THE ADO.NET OBJECTS

Let's switch our attention to the ADO.NET objects. You'll find all the information you need about ADO.NET in the following chapters, so this brief overview simply shows you how the ADO.NET object model reflects the basic operations performed on databases. A client application performs the following when retrieving data:

1. Establishes a connection to the database

2. Executes commands against the database

3. Maps database properties to data results

4. Stores data results

ADO.NET's basic objects correspond to these operations, and they are appropriately named Connection, Command, and DataAdapter. Both DataSets and DataReaders store or relay data results, respectively. We cover the differences between these two in a moment.

NOTE *You have two choices when you opt to connect to a database:* `System.Data.SqlClient` *or* `System.Data.OleDb`. *These choices serve as namespaces within the* `System.Data` *.NET library. You will learn more about* `System.Data` *later in this book; suffice it to say that a namespace is a unique way to group related sets of functionality within the .NET Framework. If you are working with an SQL database, you should use the* `System.Data` `.SqlClient` *namespace, whose objects are optimized for SQL Server access. Alternately, you can use the* `System.Data.OleDb` *namespace, which supports other OLE DB–compliant data sources, such as Oracle or Microsoft Access.*

Connection Object

Let's begin with the ADO.NET Connection object, which represents the connection to the database. After you create the Connection object, use the `ConnectionString` property to point to the data provider that you wish to use and then call the `Open()` method to actually establish the connection. We discuss the connection string in more detail later in this book; as you can see, it provides information regarding the data source, such as its name and security context.

New! ADO.NET provides a handy feature for passing the connection string with the constructor, as in:

```
Dim objConn as New System.Data.SqlClient.SqlConnection
("data source=XPDEMO2;initial catalog=Northwind;integrated
    security=SSPI;persist security info=False;workstation
    id=XPDEMO2;packet size=4096")
```

.NET enables you to override constructors by passing input parameters as you instantiate an object. You can see the power of constructors, enabling you to use a single line of code in lieu of three.

You have two choices when you are creating the Connection object in .NET. You can do so declaratively by using the visual tools provided with Visual Studio .NET or SQL Server 2000. These visual tools enable you use point-and-click operations to specify the database you want to connect to, and they prepare the appropriate Connection object for you. Alternately, you can opt to create the Connection object programmatically. We provide details on how to do both later in the book.

Command Object

After you've established a connection to the database, you can execute commands against it. A command can be an SQL statement or the name of a stored procedure.

New! Visual Studio .NET now enables you to create a stored procedure on the fly when you are creating your Command object. It uses a query builder that might seem familiar to those of you who have worked with Access. This is another great feature of Visual Studio that helps you stay within a single integrated development environment (IDE).

Stored procedures are applications written in Transact-SQL (T-SQL, the programming language of SQL Server) and often contain *arguments*, which are also known as *parameters*. Microsoft advocates the use of stored procedures to perform actions against your database. Especially when you are working with multiple tables, this is the quickest way to return data, because stored procedures optimize your code for the fastest performance. By storing all your statements in one stored procedure, SQL Server can analyze and optimize all your logic into a single execution plan. This single analysis isn't possible with a series of individual SQL statements, because a separate plan would be generated for each one, which might not be the most efficient for the series as a whole.

DataAdapter Object

New! To execute an SQL statement or a stored procedure, you must set up Command and DataAdapter objects. You pass the Command object the SQL statement or the name of the stored procedure as well as the required arguments. In addition, you have to create the DataAdapter object, regardless of whether you are using the `SqlClient` or `OleDb` namespace. The DataAdapter serves as the ambassador between the data source and the data itself. To retrieve data, you call the `Fill()` method of the DataAdapter object, passing it the reference to the DataSet object you wish to use. Realize that it might be more economical for you to use the DataReader object instead of a DataSet. Using the DataReader can be faster than populating the DataSet, and would be appropriate in situations when you need read-only data.

The most important point to remember is that ADO.NET splits the data source mapping (DataAdapter) from the data (DataSet). Keep in mind, the DataSet object is disconnected by nature and has no knowledge of the data provider. In addition, the DataSet also separates out its presentation from the data itself. Like XML, DataSets store data as XML, and schema as XML Schema Definition (XSD) files.

DataReader Object

New! The DataReader object is the heart of ADO.NET, and we cover it in detail later in the book. Suffice it to say that although the DataReader is similar in concept to the ADO 2.x RecordSet, its design and implementation is vastly different. It enables you to do more with complex data structures, because it's not limited to a tabular format as are RecordSets. One of the most convenient features of DataReader objects is that they replace the sequential indexing you had with RecordSets, with an array-like indexing. This way, you can directly go to the row you want, without the tedious `MoveNext()` statement. Additionally, DataReaders stream data, rather than retrieving it from an in-memory cache as do DataSets.

DataSet Object

New! The DataSet object works like an in-memory database. It generally contains a subset of the data source(s) to manipulate. Beneath the covers, the DataSet object is populated via the DataReader object, extending it to allow more robust data manipulation functionality. If you are working with large result sets, DataSets might consume a lot of resources, and you might be better off with the DataReader object. We help you decide which is the best choice for you when we cover ADO.NET in Chapter 6.

SHOULD YOU USE ACCESS?

Many readers are probably wondering whether they should develop applications with Access. Access is not an ideal production database server. When you contact Access and open a table, the entire table is uploaded to the client computer's memory. (If the table is large, it's uploaded in segments, but the processing takes place on the client.) If five users on the network are all accessing the same information, then five copies of the same table(s) are on the clients, plus the original. To describe Access applications, the term *file-based database* is used, but we prefer the (older) term *desktop database*.

One of the most important differences between Access and SQL Server is how they handle concurrency. SQL Server maintains a single copy of the data. Because all clients must go through the DBMS, SQL Server knows when a record is being edited and prevents other users from deleting it or even reading it. Access must compare the changes made on the client to the original and then decide whether other users can access a row. If a user opens a table and selects a row to edit, no other user can edit the same row. This is a nice feature, unless the user gets an important call or goes out to lunch. Then the row will remain locked indefinitely. As the number of users grows, the overhead is overwhelming, and it's time to upsize the database to SQL Server.

Continued on next page

SHOULD YOU USE ACCESS? *(continued)*

You have another option for lightweight database storage. Microsoft has released the Microsoft Data Engine (MSDE) component, which is a client-server data engine. MSDE is fully compatible with SQL Server; it's actually based on the same data engine as SQL Server, but it's designed for small workgroups. You can optionally install MSDE with four sample tutorials from your Visual Studio .NET installation, by selecting Start ➢ Program Files ➢ Microsoft .NET SDK Framework ➢ Samples and QuickStart Tutorials. If you don't want to, or have the space to install the samples, you can install just MSDE from the command line by calling `C:\Program Files\Microsoft.NET\FrameworkSDK\Samples>setup\settings setup.ini\ Isql2000.msi\qr`. You can also use MSDE to develop client-server applications with Access 2002, which comes with Office XP and Visio (or VB, for that matter) that can "see" SQL Server databases. MSDE applications are fully compatible with SQL Server and will work with SQL Server if you change the connection information to point to the MSDE database.

XML

The Internet has changed the way we access data. We see a trend of distributed architecture replacing traditional client-server applications, slowly but surely. XML has emerged as the *lingua franca* for the next generation of data access applications. Although many might feel that XML might not be the best format or the most efficient protocol for universal data format, it is certainly the most widely accepted. Acceptance weighs more heavily than pure technical merit when it comes to a technology's success.

However, this isn't to say that XML is not a viable technical solution. Many system architects would agree that XML has made their lives much easier. Before XML, data transfer was pretty much ad hoc, with electronic data interchange (EDI), proprietary agreements, and many other technologies linking heterogeneous data. There was no universal support for a single data format. This forced you to write a lot of "plumbing" code, transforming data from its native format to one that you could use. With XML, companies can now agree upon a standard that eliminates the need for the extra translation. Now you can focus more on the business needs, rather than the data format. Look at the diagram in Figure 1.5 to see the effect of XML on distributed architecture.

Not only does XML centralize the format of data that you send, it also standardizes the structure of the data you view and receive. You can customize these structures, or *schemas*, for each business, or vertical or horizontal service. XML's beauty lies in its capability to be flexible and customizable. Although XML adheres to a standard, you can still adapt within that standard. This enables you to define certain *elements* that are specific to your business needs. The best part about XML is that it enables you to separate the presentation from the data, enabling a higher degree of data reuse. You'll soon see how .NET, specifically ADO.NET, embraces this separation model.

Keep in mind that the practical world is not perfect, and you can't expect every organization to agree to an industry standard on how they want to define their data. That's where XSL Transformations (XSLT) language comes into play. XSLT provides a mechanism for describing the transformation between one XSD file to another. This way, organizations can map their schemas to one another, without a communications breakdown.

FIGURE 1.5

How XML
integrates systems

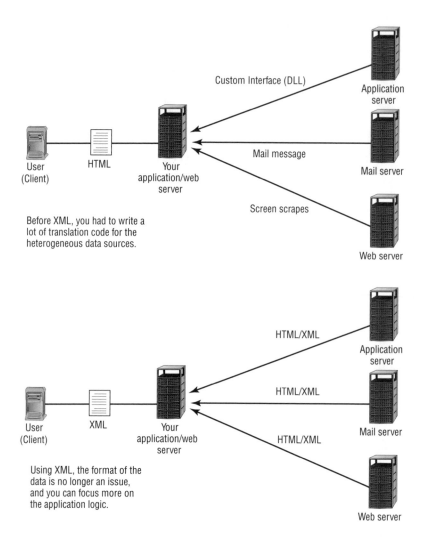

To summarize, with XML, it doesn't matter how data comes across the wire. XML isn't revolutionary. The reason why it's so important is that it is universally accepted. As .NET applications continue to mushroom, XML specifications will continue to grow within Microsoft's data access technologies. XML is an essential part of SQL Server 2000 and ADO.NET.

Data access isn't the only place for XML. Microsoft intertwines XML support in both its web browsers and web servers. In addition, Microsoft not only embraces XML in the Application layer, but also extends it, using XML to form the backbone of the .NET WebServices.

Now that you've seen how an application communicates with the database, you're ready to turn your attention to the evolution of Microsoft architecture with database applications. As you walk through how data access works with different architectures throughout history, you can get a solid

However, the client-server model didn't necessarily draw a distinct line between logical layers. Because developers were accustomed to programming linear code, they ended up splitting this monolithic code onto different processing machines without much logical partitioning. A separate layer for business logic didn't often exist at this stage of evolution. On top of that, developers did not always separate data from presentation logic. It wasn't unusual to find two copies of a database—one on the server, to handle heavy processing and storage, and another read-only cached copy (usually an .mdb file) sitting on the client, in order to optimize performance, as shown in Figure 1.7. The primary difference between client-server and two-tier applications was that two-tier applications actually split the presentation from the data.

FIGURE 1.7

Client-server architecture with cached data source

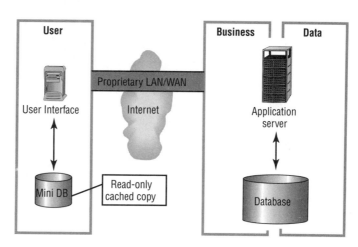

Client-Server Model (Cached)

The Two-Tier Model

The first tier of a client-server application is the client tier, or *presentation tier*, which runs on the client. This tier contains code that presents data and interacts with the user, such as a VB .NET application. You can also build client tiers that run in a browser—these are web applications that contain controls, which are similar to the basic VB .NET controls and enable the user to interact with the database.

Figure 1.8 shows a simple client application for browsing orders for a specific customer. This is VB .NET Windows Form that uses DataGrid controls to display the current customer's order will see how to create this application in Chapter 8, "Data-Aware Controls."

Client-server applications aren't limited to non-web applications. Figure 1.9 shows detail form, only this one is a Web Form and it's displayed on the browser. The W new server-side controls that come with ASP.NET, which allow for data bind the DataGrid control, which automatically displays the customer data by The DataGrid control enables you to bind to ADO.NET DataSets, a Windows Form. These are two of the applications you'll develop in

understanding of the advantages and disadvantages of each paradigm. Rememb(
.NET is interoperability, and this applies to legacy architectures as well. Your .N.
communicate with non-.NET architectures. Although distributed architecture is i
commonplace, it doesn't mean client-server architecture has gone away. Client-serv
might be appropriate to the system that you are designing. However, before you dec
through the evolution of data access architecture.

From Client-Server to Distributed Architecture

To understand the importance of distributed systems, you need to understand their evc
should comprehend the problem statements solved with each evolution. Understanding
quacies of one architecture will enable you to take advantage of the benefits of the next,
ing the pitfalls of the last.

In this section, we explain how distributed architecture evolved and how .NET fits into
tion (or revolution as some people call it). We take a unique approach, by applying the arch
of the past to the technologies of the present. This way, you can unify your perspective of t
ent models and realize that each of them might still be applicable depending on your require
We begin with the client-server model, although different applications models existed before

The Client-Server Model

In client-server architecture, the application is broken into two distinct components, which wor
together for a common goal. This is illustrated in Figure 1.6. Client-server architecture emerged
before the advent of the Web, and replaced a monolithic application structure. The beauty of cli(
server architecture was that it distributed systems onto different physical machines. This allowed f(
optimized hardware—one machine could have more powerful processing speed, and the other cou
have larger storage capacities.

FIGURE 1.6

Client-server
architecture

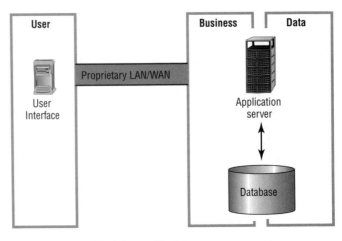

Client-Server Model

FIGURE 1.8

A VB .NET Windows Form client application for viewing and editing customers

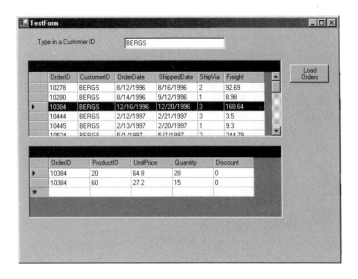

FIGURE 1.9

Master/detail form as a Web Form

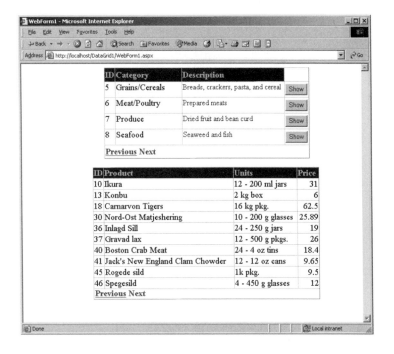

The client application requests data from the database and displays it on one or more Windows Forms or Web Forms. After the data is on the client computer, your application can process it and present it in many ways. The client computer is quite capable of manipulating the data locally by using DataSets while the server remains uninvolved in the process due to the disconnected nature of DataSets. If the user edits the fields, the client posts a request via ADO.NET to update the database. Because the client directly instantiates its connections to the data source, you have tightly coupled communication between the client and the database server.

The second tier is the *database server*, or the DBMS. This tier manipulates a complex object, the database, and offers a simplified view of the database through ADO.NET. Clients can make complicated requests, such as "Show me the names of the customers who have placed orders in excess of $100,000 in the last three months," or "Show me the best-selling products in the state of California." The DBMS receives many requests of this type from the clients, and it must service them all. Obviously, the DBMS can't afford to process and present the data before passing it to the client. One client might map the data on a graph, another client might display the same data on a ListBox control, and so on. The server's job is to extract the required data from the tables and furnish them to the client in the form of a disconnected DataSet. It simply transmits the DataSet to the client and lets the client process the information. The more powerful the client, the more it can do with the data. (As you will see later in this chapter, in the discussion of stored procedures, certain operations that are performed frequently or that require the manipulation of a very large number of rows to the client should be carried out by the server.)

By splitting the workload between clients and servers, you allow each application to do what it can do best. The DBMS runs on one of the fastest machines on the network, with the most storage capacity. The clients don't have to be as powerful. In fact, there are two types of clients: thin and fat clients.

Thin clients *Thin clients* are less-powerful interfaces that do very little processing on their own. A browser is a thin client, with its presentation capabilities determined by its current version or flavor. The benefits of thin clients are their cost (all you need to install is a browser) and their location transparency (they can access the database server from anywhere). Thin clients are easy to maintain too, because most of the logic resides on a server, a fact that can lower the cost of deployment of the application.

Fat clients A *fat client* usually runs on a desktop computer and leverages rich presentation features. Because client applications that run on fat clients are far more flexible and powerful, they require more expensive computers to run, and their proprietary interfaces often can't be standardized. You can make them as elaborate as the available hardware and software language permits.

The Three-Tier Model

The two-tier model is an efficient architecture for database applications, but not always the best choice, because the architecture limits scalability. Most programmers develop two-tier applications that run on small local area networks. A more advanced form of database access is one that involves three tiers.

Two-tiered modeling was popular until the emergence of the Internet, which introduced other physical tiers—the web and the application servers. As more and more developers ported logic to these servers, developers began to view this physical layer in a more logical way. This led to a vision of an Application layer as a distinct entity. The client-server model unfurled into a three-layer logical model (also referred to as the three-tier model).

NOTE   *In this book, we make a distinction between layers and tiers. For simplicity, a layer refers to a logical separation (for example, business, data, user). A tier refers to a physical separation (for example, DBMS, web server, stored procedures, DLL). Often, there is confusion about what n-tier really means. For the purposes of this book, n-tier is the physical distribution of tiers, which juxtaposes itself across the three logical layers. In the three-tier model, each logical layer corresponds to a one-to-one mapping with the physical tiers.*

In two-tier, or client-server, architecture, the client talks directly to the database server. An application that directly connects to a data provider and retrieves some information, such as customer names or product prices, is a client-server application. The role of the database server is to access and update the data. Everything else is left to the client. In other words, the client is responsible for presenting the data to the user, parsing user input, preparing the appropriate requests for the database server, and, finally, implementing the business rules. A *business rule* is a procedure specific to an entity, such as a corporation, industry or application. Your corporation, for example, might have rules for establishing the credit line of its customers. These rules must be translated into code, which is generally executed on the client in a two-tier model.

Business rules change often, as they reflect business practices. New rules are introduced, and existing ones are revised. This means that the code that implements them is subject to frequent changes. If you implement business rules on the client, you must distribute new executables or libraries to the workstations and make sure all users are using the latest version of the client software (that is, your application). This is an awkward and inefficient delivery mechanism. If business rules are implemented on the database server, you avoid the problem of redistributing the application, but you place an additional burden on the database server, tying it to the processor with calculations that could better be performed on another machine.

This leads naturally to the introduction of a third tier: the middle tier. The middle tier is a layer that sits between the client application and the server, as depicted in Figure 1.10. Generally a component-based layer (in WinDNA), it exposes methods and properties that isolate the client from the server. If many clients need to calculate insurance premiums, you can implement the calculations in the middle tier. Client applications can call the methods of the objects that reside on the middle tier and get the results. The client application need not know how premiums are calculated or whether the calculations require any database access. All they need to know is the name of one or more methods of the objects that runs on the middle tier.

FIGURE 1.10

The three logical layers

The main advantage of the middle tier is that it isolates the client from the server and centralizes the business rules. The client no longer directly accesses the database. Instead, it calls the methods exposed by the objects in the middle tier. A client application will eventually add a new customer to the database. Even this simple operation requires some validation. Is there a customer with the same key already in the database? Did the user fail to supply values for the required fields (you can't add a customer without a name, for example)? Adding orders to a database requires even more complicated validation. Do you have enough items of each product in stock to fill the order? And what do you do if you can fill only part of the order?

A well-structured application implements these operations in the middle tier. The client application doesn't have to know how each customer is stored in the database if it can call the `Customer .AddNew()` method, passing the values of the fields (customer name, address, phone numbers, and so on) as arguments. The middle tier will pass the information along to the Data layer, which will insert the new information to the database or raise an error if an error occurred.

Likewise, the client application can pass all the information of the invoice to the middle-tier component and let it determine the insertion of the new invoice. This action involves many tables. You might have to update the inventory, the customer's balance, possibly update a list of best-selling products, and so on. The middle-tier component will take care of these operations for the client. As a result, the development of the client application is greatly simplified. The client will call the `Invoice.AddNew()` method and pass the ID of the customer who placed the order, the products and quantities ordered, and (optionally) the discount. Or, you might leave it up to the middle tier to calculate the discount based on the total amount or the items ordered.

The `Invoice.AddNew()` method must update multiple tables in a *transaction*. In other words, it must make sure that all the tables were updated, or none of them. If the program updates the customer's balance, but fails to update the stock of the items ordered (or it updates the stock of only a few items), then the database will be left in an inconsistent state. The program should make sure that either all actions succeed or they all fail. You can execute transactions from within your client-side code, but it's a good idea to pass the responsibility of the transaction to a middle-tier component or the database server.

The middle tier forces you to design your application before you start coding. If you choose to implement business rules as a middle tier, you must analyze the requirements of the application, implement and debug the middle-tier components, and then start coding the client application. By taking the time to do careful design in the middle-tier, you will find that those efforts will naturally transfer to designing a solid front end and back end, as well. Time spent in the early planning phases will not only save you hours of debugging effort, but will enable your application to have a longer lifetime.

The middle tier can also save you a good deal of work when you decide to move the application to the Web. If the middle tier is already in place, you can use its components with a web interface. Let's describe a component you will develop later in the book. A client application needs a function to retrieve books based on title keywords and/or author name(s). If you specify which of the search arguments are title keywords and which ones are author names, the operation is quite simple. As we're sure you know, all electronic bookstores on the Web provide a box where you can enter any keyword and then search the database. The database server must use the keywords intelligently to retrieve the titles you're interested in. If you think about this operation, you'll realize that it's not trivial. Building the appropriate SQL statement to retrieve the desired titles is fairly complicated. Moreover, you might have to revise the search algorithm as the database grows.

Imagine that the same functionality is required from within both a client application that runs on the desktop and a client application that runs on the Internet (a web application). If you implement the `SearchTitles()` method as a middle-tier component, the same functionality will be available to all clients, whether they run on the desktop or the Web. You might wish to extend the search to multiple databases. You can easily handle this new case, by revising the code in a single place, the middle tier, and all the clients will be able to search all databases with the existing code. As long as you don't add any new arguments to the `SearchTitles()` method, the client will keep calling the same old function and be up to date.

It is possible to write client applications that never connect to the database and are not even aware that they're clients to a database server. If all the actions against the database take place through the middle tier, then the client's code will not need to contain any database structures. As you can understand, it's not feasible to expect that you can write a "database application without a database," but the middle tier can handle many of the complicated tasks of accessing the database and greatly simplify the coding of the client application.

THREE-TIER APPLICATIONS ON THE WEB

The best example of a three-tier application is a web application. Web applications are highly scalable, and the back-end tiers of the application can run on the same computer (the client tier runs on a separate machine, obviously).

Figure 1.11 shows a web application that runs in a browser and contacts a web server and a database server to interact with the user. The first tier—the Presentation layer—is the browser, which interacts with the user through HTML documents (web pages). A web page might contain controls where the user can enter information and submit it to the server. The web page, therefore, is the equivalent of a VB .NET Windows Form. Whereas your VB .NET application can read the controls' values the moment they're entered, the values of the controls on a web page must be passed to the server before they can be processed. (It is possible to do some processing on the client, but client-side scripting is beyond the scope of this book.)

FIGURE 1.11

A web application is a typical example of a three-tier application.

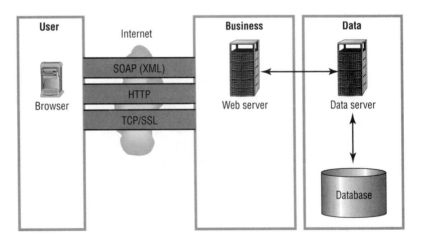

All requests are channeled by the browser to the web server. Internet Information Server (IIS) is Microsoft's web server and requires Windows NT, Windows 2000, or Windows .NET Server editions. The material in Part IV of this book, "Data Access for the Web," applies only to IIS. IIS resides in the middle tier (the Application layer). In WinDNA, the web server's role is to generate HTML documents and send them to the client. If the web server needs to access a database, it must contact a DBMS through a *dynamic link library (DLL)* by using a data provider such as OLE DB. The code on the web server runs as Active Server Pages, which can be written in any .NET-compatible language, such as VB .NET, C#, or JScript.

The DBMS, finally, is the Data layer of the application. Stored procedures, constraints, and triggers reside in this layer, working with the data as it goes in and out of the database.

Notice that the tiers of a web system need not reside and execute on different machines. The DBMS might be running on the same machine as the web server. Although they can run on the same machine, you should still consider them separate physical tiers. For testing purposes, you can run all three tiers on the same computer, but when you deploy the application, you should distribute the application across dedicated servers that are optimized for their specific task. As the site grows, you might have to *cluster* your database, and/or run as a *web farm* or *web garden* by using multiple web servers or processes. We provide more details on clustering and farming later in this book.

NOTE *You might be wondering how n-tier fits into this model. We cover that later in this chapter when we talk about distributed architecture.*

.NET Model

What benefits does .NET offer? As you know, before you begin building your application, you must first sit down and design it. Any well-designed distributed system should acknowledge four important points, which we refer to as the "abilities" of an application:

- Interoperability
- Scalability
- Reusability
- Extensibility

The Microsoft .NET platform was designed to address these four design considerations, more robustly than WinDNA. Let's discuss the problem statements that led to the evolution of .NET architecture.

NOTE *Although we focus more on distributed architecture in this section, be aware that .NET is fully capable of supporting existing architecture such as client-server. After all, interoperability is one of the key points of .NET.*

As depicted in Figure 1.12, WinDNA solidifies the distributed architecture model by allowing for a distinct logical and physical separation of system functions. For example, let's say you get a request to create a website that enables users to see their most recent orders. Behind the scenes, you need to access two heterogeneous data sources: a customer database and a sales database. Each of these databases are created by different project teams within your organization. To make it easier for other services to access their databases, DLLs are created that encapsulate the business rules for accessing data from the databases. To bring back this data to your website, you would write an order DLL to present this information back to the browser via Active Server Pages (ASP).

This architecture provides elegance in that the order DLL can be reused to present data to a variety of clients. However, generally it isn't that easy to have your DLL communicate with other server-side applications.

FIGURE 1.12

Architecture with WinDNA

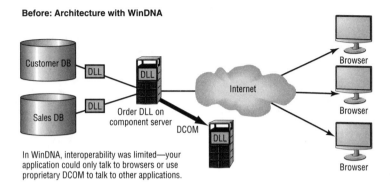

In WinDNA, interoperability was limited—your application could only talk to browsers or use proprietary DCOM to talk to other applications.

Although the WinDNA paradigm solved many problems with scalability and extensibility, new problem statements emerged. Integration and interoperability between different platforms and code bases was a challenge, at best. Maintenance and versioning became a consideration as applications matured. .NET seeks to address these problems by presenting an advanced archetype for designing systems.

Interoperability is the most important hurdle that .NET overcomes. What if the customer DLL was written in C++ while the sales DLL was written in VB and the developers used incompatible data types? You would still have to write "plumbing" code to unify these code bases within your order DLL. Although WinDNA provided all these wonderful reusable components, you would still have to leash them all together with a good amount of adaptive code, which was often proprietary for each component technology you would be using. Consider type compatibility between different languages. You had to know how VB and C++ differed when handling strings, and translate between the different types.

Thus, there emerged a need to agree on a common set of specifications about how applications and languages will talk to one another. .NET addresses this with the CLR.

Another challenge was trying to get sites to talk to one another. Consider the scenario in Figure 1.12. What would you do if the customer DLL and the order DLL sat behind firewalls? Tunneling TCP/IP via DCOM would be an option, but firewalls could still filter this out, preventing you from communicating. Often you end up reinventing the wheel because you can't access the code due to firewall or performance limitations. Worse yet, you might not even know that the code exists! This obstacle arises from the inability to discover services that might be useful to you. All these reasons spur the move from a component-based model to a services-based model. In .NET, you still build components, but now release them as WebServices. The point of WebServices is to provide the ability for external, trusted clients to discover and use your services. Figure 1.13 shows how .NET changes the WinDNA architecture.

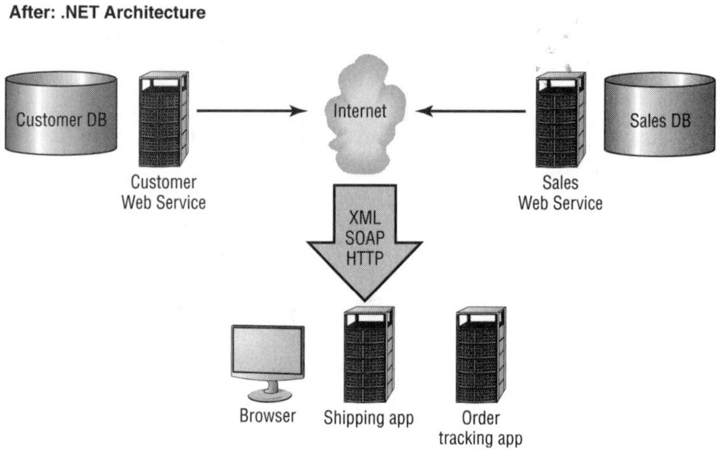

FIGURE 1.13

Architecture
with .NET

.NET provides greater scalability. As the WinDNA era matured, we also saw a definitive shift from a stateful model to a stateless model. We began moving away from a stateful, connected model because it just couldn't scale well. Any type of connection (for example, DCOM, Common Object Request Broker Architecture—CORBA, or connected RecordSets) has the potential to hog up resources for a long time. Microsoft developers did a complete redesign to create the .NET architecture in a disconnected fashion. The current remote connection model (DCOM) was too tightly coupled and proprietary. Although ADO 2.x supported disconnected RecordSets, it wasn't originally written for stateless environments. .NET was designed with the stateless model in mind in order to optimize scalability by using industry-accepted standards and protocols.

.NET also extends the concept of reusability. It uses the psychology of XML and the Internet as its foundation. WinDNA relied heavily on a binary and proprietary model, unlike the flexible framework provided with XML and the Internet. The main thing to remember about .NET's reusability is that XML provides the contractual model, and the Internet provides the distribution mechanism. The Internet provides a more ubiquitous connection protocol, which transforms sites into reusable application logic by extending the component model to the Web, which uses the new services model. As you can see from Figure 1.13, your DLLs now can be relayed to other server applications, as well as client browsers, by using SOAP, HTTP, and TCP/IP.

.NET provides extensibility in the way that it addresses the problem of deployment. The release mechanism changes with .NET: components can now release as services. These services no longer have to go through the Registry in order to be referenced. A simple Uniform Resource Locator (URL) reference is all that is necessary to use services. Geared to simply the deployment model (and to get rid of DLL Hell), .NET provides an easy way to upgrade WinDNA components or run them side by side with .NET components without interference from one another.

How Distributed Applications Work

What is a distributed application, and how does your database fit into the picture? Distributed systems consist of three logical layers and multiple physical tiers, as you can see in Figure 1.14. The term *n-tier* represents a system that has multiple physical tiers, distributed across the three logical layers.

FIGURE 1.14

Overlay of logical with physical

Distributed Architecture

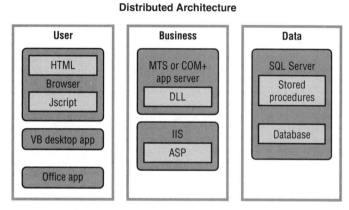

Logical Layers

There are three logical layers to any system: User, Business, and Data. Even client-server applications could use the three-layer metaphor, although with a lot of them, you would have a hard time trying to decipher and distinguish the layers within the code. Client-server applications often blurred the lines between these logical layers.

The *User layer* represents the presentation or user interface. The *Business layer* equates to the application logic that is specific to each business. The *Data layer* consists of both the storage and structure of data. If you think of the logical layers as "services," this analogy will come handy later, when we discuss WebServices. Take a look at the three logical layers first, and then you'll learn how the physical tiers juxtapose themselves on top of these layers.

Presentation layer   This layer handles user interaction and is primarily used for displaying information to the user. Frequently, we refer to this presentation layer as *user services*. By the way, user services are not trivial. They can include advanced data-bound controls and, in many cases, custom data-bound controls.

Application layer   This layer equates to the Business layer and contains the logic of the application. It simplifies the client's access to the database by isolating the business services from the Database and Presentation layers. The components of the Application or Business layer are frequently called *business services*.

Data layer   This layer is the data access layer, or *data services*. In a three-tier model, this would represent the database server. The requests are usually queries, for example, "Return all titles published by Sybex in 2002" or "Show the total of all orders placed in the first quarter of 2000 in California." Other requests might update the database by inserting new customers, orders, and so on. The database server must update the database and at the same time protect its integrity (for example, it will refuse to delete a customer if there are invoices issued to that specific customer).

Physical Tiers

You can overlay the physical distribution of your system across the three logical layers. The easiest way to understand the logical layers is to relate them to the physical architecture in a simplistic model. By relating these logical layers in a one-to-one relationship with the physical tiers, you will get the three-tier model. A lot of times there is confusion between three-tier and *n*-tier, as the two terms are often used interchangeably. *Three-tier* is a one-to-one relation between the logical layers and physical tiers of a system, whereas *n-tier* implies more than three physical tiers.

You can split the User layer across multiple tiers in an *n*-tier model. For example, you could have some presentation logic sitting in client-side script, and the rest of it residing in server-side ASP.NET logic, which renders out as HTML to the User layer. This is illustrated in Figure 1.14.

With *n*-tier architecture, you can distribute the Application layer across VB .NET and T-SQL code. In this scenario, you store business logic across two physical tiers, but still within the same logical layer.

Finally, when using *n*-tier architecture, the Data layer is not just relegated to the database itself. For example, you can have data logic sitting in a custom OLE DB wrapper, which you store in a DLL. In addition, you could physically distribute your Data layer logic across heterogeneous database systems.

SQL Server 2000

SQL Server is Microsoft's main Relational Database Management System (RDBMS). Since the release of SQL 7's intuitive user-interface, more and more developers have been taking advantage of the power of SQL Server to support multiple and concurrent users, large database sizes, and scalability. SQL Server's upgrading wizard also eased the burden on many DBAs to migrate over to SQL Server from Access.

SQL Server 2000's IDE makes many advances in usability, especially with the new Object Browser within the Query Analyzer, which we discuss later in this chapter. Those of you familiar with the VB6 IDE will find the Object Browser a reassuring touch of familiarity.

SQL Server 2000 also offers more programmability, such as giving you more control with their trigger model by using AFTER triggers, as well as tight integration with XML, giving you the ability to access SQL Server through a URL.

NOTE *Nearly all of this book's examples will work on a stand-alone computer running Windows 2000 Professional Edition. When you are building enterprise systems, we recommend using Windows 2000 Server.*

SQL Server has a few unique features that you can't ignore. To begin with, SQL Server has its own programming language, called T-SQL, which we mentioned earlier. T-SQL is an extension of SQL and it's so powerful that it can do just about everything you can do with VB .NET code. T-SQL supports many data-manipulation functions and flow-control statements. Not only it is capable of manipulating data, it can also manipulate a database schema. This ability to manipulate both data and schema fits in nicely with the separation of data and structure you see in XML.

NOTE *SQL Server 2000 is strongly tied to the .NET evolution, evidenced by its consideration as a .NET server. Like .NET, it uses the Web as a fortifier, supporting Internet standards such as HTTP for data transfer, XML to store data, and XSD for data schema. For those of you already familiar with SQL Server 7, it might be interesting to note the new features available in SQL 2000. We point these out throughout the book.*

You can do many of the things you do with VB .NET with T-SQL. However, VB .NET code generally runs on the client or application server, depending on your architecture. The advantage of T-SQL is that data manipulation code executes locally on the database server, which optimizes your performance, because it's closer to the actual data. To do the same with VB .NET code alone, you'd have to move data from the database server to the application layer and process it there. Stored procedures are faster than the equivalent VB .NET code and they centralize your data access code, because all clients will call the same procedure to carry out a task.

WRITE BETTER APPLICATIONS WITH STORED PROCEDURES

For many years, there has been a debate about whether business logic should be physically split between the application and database servers. In theory, it is nice to keep your business logic in one physical location, such as the application server. However, practice will show you that that you gain the best performance and scalability with business logic that is split. This distributes your business logic into T-SQL stored procedures on the database server and VB .NET code on the application server. Sometimes it is difficult to determine where the code should be physically placed, but a good rule of thumb to follow is that if it needs to query the database multiple times to process the business logic, it best belongs in T-SQL stored procedures.

In effect, it's quite acceptable to implement business rules as stored procedures. Chapter 6 discusses how to take advantage of stored procedures from within your VB code. Stored procedures become part of the database and can be used by multiple applications, not just the client application.

If you implement the NewInvoice stored procedure to add new invoices to a database, then you can call this stored procedure from within any VB .NET application that needs to add invoices to the database. If you implement the same operation as a method of a middle-tier component, then you can call this method from within any application—including the Office applications. You will write a stored procedure in Chapter 13 that searches for titles, and then you'll write a middle-tier component that uses this stored procedure. Because middle-tier components can be implemented as WebServices, they can be called from any HTTP- and SOAP-compliant application. In simple terms, this means that every programming language that supports the industry-accepted Internet standards can call methods of the middle-tier component. You will see how to create a script to add orders to the database. If you distribute the application, users don't have to go through the visible interface of the application to add new invoices. They can write a short script to automate the process.

In addition to stored procedures, SQL Server also uses triggers. A *trigger* is a special stored procedure that is executed when certain actions take place. For example, you can write a trigger to keep track of who has deleted a record and when. You can add triggers to individual tables, and the triggers can be invoked by three actions: insertions, deletions, and updates. SQL Server 2000 extends the trigger model to indicate when a trigger is executed by using the AFTER and INSTEAD OF expressions.

We discuss stored procedures and triggers in Chapter 5, "Transact-SQL," and you'll see how you can simplify your VB .NET code by implementing certain operations as stored procedures.

Installation

SQL Server 2000 comes with many installation editions. Be sure to choose one that is right for you and your operating system. Although we use Windows 2000 Advanced Server as our operating system, you can run Windows 2000 Server to use the SQL Server 2000 Enterprise, Standard, and Developer editions. If you have Windows 2000 Professional, you should run Evaluation or Developer editions. We use SQL Server Developer edition for our examples. However, the Enterprise and Standard editions should work just fine with the examples in this book. When you go through the installation wizard, make sure you install both Server and Client Tools.

WHAT'S THE BEST EDITION OF SQL SERVER 2000 FOR YOUR NEEDS?

Although we recommend the Developer edition for the purposes of this book, the Enterprise edition of SQL Server 2000 will offer you the most robust feature-set. If you use an edition other than Enterprise, keep in mind the following caveats:

◆ The Developer edition is not licensed to be a production server.

◆ The Evaluation edition is limited to only 120 days (so you better read this book fast).

◆ The CE edition limits database size to 2GB.

◆ The Personal edition cannot do transactional replication and has a limited workload. Do not use the SQL Server 2000 Desktop Engine. It is the successor to Microsoft Data Engine (MSDE) 1 and is not a DBMS. This means it does not include graphical management tools, which are relied upon heavily in this book. However, if you must use MSDE, install it with another edition of SQL Server, which will enable you to manipulate the MSDE through the traditional graphic interface. Keep in mind that Desktop Engine also limits database size to 2GB and has a limited workload. In addition, it doesn't support the full T-SQL language set.

To keep it simple, install SQL Server on the same machine you will use to develop your applications in the course of reading this book. However, you can opt to install SQL on a remote server. Because the application you design to use SQL Server is location independent, it doesn't matter where you put your SQL Server. However, make sure you consult your network administrator or database administrator (DBA) before installing SQL Server on your network.

After you install SQL Server, a new command is added to the Programs menu under your Start button: SQL Server. You will see the various SQL Server tools within this group. We briefly review the more important tools next.

SQL Server Tools

Many of you might not be familiar with SQL Server, so this section introduces you to its basic tools. As we noted earlier, you can obtain more information on ordering SQL Server 2000 by visiting the Microsoft website.

SQL SERVER SERVICE MANAGER

This tool enables you to start and stop SQL Server. To start SQL Server, select Start ➤ Programs ➤ Microsoft SQL Server ➤ Service Manager, which opens a window where you can start and stop SQL Server. Ensure that the name of your SQL Server is selected in the Server box and that the SQL Server service is selected in the Services box, and then click the Start button. If you'd rather have SQL Server automatically start every time you turn on your computer, check the option Auto-Start Service When OS Starts.

After SQL is installed, you will see a small gray server icon in the system tray of your Windows taskbar. This enables you to easily see the state of the service; a green Play icon is displayed when it is running, and a red Stop icon if stopped. You can also open the Service Manager, start the service, stop the service, or set polling options by right-clicking this icon.

If you attempt to connect to SQL Server from within a client application while SQL Server is not running, you will get an error message indicating that there's a problem with your network. At this point, you must stop the application, start SQL Server through the Service Manager or system tray icon, and then restart the application. Alternately, you can control the service state through the services tree of the computer management console.

Enterprise Manager

The Enterprise Manager, shown in Figure 1.15, is a visual tool that enables you to view and edit all the objects of SQL Server. This is where you create new databases, edit tables, create stored procedures, and so on. You can also view both a table's design and data. Use caution when working with the design of an SQL Server table. Only the DBA should open tables and examine or edit their contents.

FIGURE 1.15

The SQL Server Enterprise Manager window

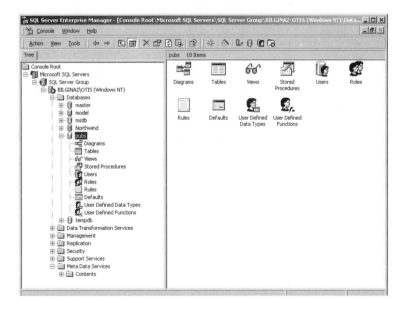

Microsoft VS .NET comes with the Server Explorer, which enables you to view different types of servers, including database servers. Using the Server Explorer, you can view the structure of your databases, create and edit tables, create and debug stored procedures, and more. You will explore these visual tools in Chapter 3, "The Visual Database Tools." Much of what you can do with Enterprise Manager can be done with the visual database tools, except for adding new users, setting user rights, and similar operations.

If you refer to Figure 1.15 in the left pane, you will see seven folders. Two of these folders, `Replication` and `Meta Data Services`, are new to SQL Server 2000.

DATABASES

This folder contains a subfolder for each database. If you select a database here, you will see a list of objects, described below, that are specific to that database.

Diagrams   A diagram is a picture of the database's structure, similar to the one shown in Figure 1.16. You can manipulate the very structure of the database from within this window, which shows how the various tables relate to each other. You can add new relationships, set their properties, add constraints for the various fields (for example, specify that certain fields must be positive), enforce referential integrity, and so on. Don't worry if you are not familiar with these terms; they are discussed in detail in the next few chapters of the book.

FIGURE 1.16

A database diagram shows the structure of its tables and the relationships between them.

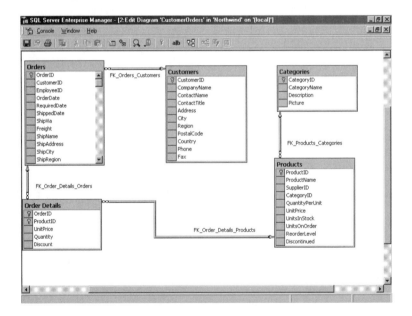

To create a new database diagram, right-click on the right window and choose New Diagram from the shortcut menu. A wizard prompts you to select the tables to include in the diagram, and then it generates the diagram by extracting the information it needs from the database itself. You will find more information on creating tables and diagrams in Chapter 3.

Tables   A table consists of rows and columns that store information. Databases have many tables, and each table has a specific structure. You can edit the columns of each table through the Design window, shown in Figure 1.17. To open the Design window of a table, right-click the table's name and choose Design Table from the shortcut menu. Alternately, you can just double-click the table's name to view the design properties of the table. This will not put you in the full design mode that you have when you select Design Table.

FIGURE 1.17

The Design window of the Customers table

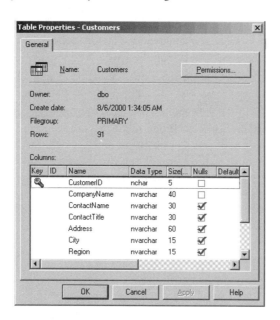

Views   A view is a section of a table, or a combination of multiple tables, and contains specific information needed by a client. If the Customers table contains salary information, you probably don't want every application to retrieve this information. You can define a view on the table that contains all the columns except for the salary-related ones. As far as the client application is concerned, the view is just another table. SQL Server's views are generated from SQL statements, and the data generated from a standard view is not uniquely stored in the database.

NOTE   *SQL Server 2000 (Developer and Enterprise editions) enhances views by now allowing you to create indexed views. Unlike standard views, which store only the source code, indexed views are actually stored as objects in the database.*

SQL Server 2000's new features enable you to create partitioned views, which can distribute data processing over multiple servers, and to index the view, which optimizes performance.

Most views are editable as long as you are updating only one of the base tables. To open a view, select Views in the left pane of the Enterprise Manager, then right-click the desired view's name in the right pane and choose Open View ➤ Return All Rows from the shortcut menu. The view's rows will appear on a grid, where you can edit their fields (if the view is updateable). To refresh the view, click the button with the exclamation mark in the action bar.

Stored procedures A stored procedure is analogous to a VB .NET function, only you write stored procedures in T-SQL, and they execute on the database server. In the Stored Procedures folder, you see the list of stored procedures attached to the database and their definitions. You can create new ones as well as edit and debug existing stored procedures. In addition, the Stored Procedure Properties window, which appears if you double-click a procedure's name, contains the definition of the procedure and a button labeled Check Syntax. If you click this button, the Enterprise Manager will verify the syntax of the stored procedure's definition. It points out the first mistake in the T-SQL code, so it doesn't really qualify as a debugging tool. SQL Server 2000 offers a richer debugging environment using an integrated T-SQL Debugger within the Query Analyzer. We discuss the Query Analyzer tool later in this chapter.

Users In this folder, you can review the users authorized to view and/or edit the selected database and add new users. By default, each database has two users: the owner of the database (user *dbo*) and a user with seriously limited privileges (user *guest*). To view the rights of a user, double-click their name. On that user's Properties dialog box, you can assign one or more *roles* to the selected user (instead of setting permissions one by one for individual users, you create roles and then assign these roles to the users). If you click the Permissions button, you will see the user's permissions for every object in the database, as shown in Figure 1.18. It's a good idea to create a user called *application* (or something similar) and use this ID to connect to the database from within your application. This user will impersonate your application, and you can give this user all the rights your application needs.

FIGURE 1.18

Setting user permissions for the various objects of a database

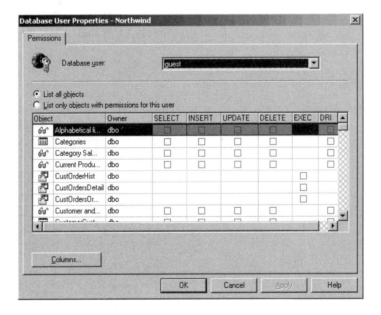

Roles When you select the Roles item in the right pane, you will see a list of the existing roles. A role is a set of permissions that you can use to apply to a group of users. If multiple users must have common privileges, create a new role, set permissions to this role, and then use it to specify the permissions of individual users. In both SQL Server 7 and SQL Server 2000, users can belong to multiple roles. Roles can be specific to an application, enabling you to encapsulate security specific to a database, rather than the server as a whole.

Rules   SQL Server enables you to specify rules for the values of individual fields of a table. These rules are called CHECK constraints and they are specified from within the Database Diagram window. There's no reason to use this window to specify rules, but it's included for compatibility reasons.

Defaults   Here you can define the default values for any field. The default values are used when the user, or the application, supplies no value for the specific field. It is simpler to specify defaults during the design of the table than to provide the code that checks the user-supplied value and supplies a default value if the user hasn't entered a value for a field.

User-defined data types   This is where the user-defined data types (UDTs) are specified. SQL Server doesn't allow the creation of arbitrary data structures as VB .NET does. A UDT must be based on one of the existing data types, but you can specify a length (for character and binary types) and, optionally, a default value. For example, you can create a UDT, name it ZCODE, and set its type to char and length to five. This is a shorthand notation, rather than a custom data type. UDTs are useful when you allow developers to create their own tables. You can create data types such as *FNAME, LNAME,* and so on, to make sure that all fields that store names, in all tables, have the same length. When you change the definition of a UDT, the table(s) change accordingly without any action on your part.

User-defined functions   The addition of user-defined functions (UDFs) is one of the most powerful benefits of using SQL Server 2000. UDFs give you flexibility and control over your SQL queries. You can also optimize the performance of your application by using them in lieu of temporary tables and views.

Keep in mind that the functions cannot return non-deterministic data. This means that the result from your UDF has to be a single, quantifiable value. For example, GETDATE() would not be a valid UDF to use, because it doesn't return a predictable result. You also cannot perform action queries (for example, update, insert) on a table or view. You will delve deeper into UDFs in Chapter 5.

DATA TRANSFORMATION SERVICES (DTS)

This folder contains the utilities for importing data into SQL Server and exporting data out of SQL Server. The DTS component of SQL Server enables you to import/export data and at the same time transform it.

MANAGEMENT

This folder contains the tools for managing databases. The most important tool is the Backup tool, which enables you to back up a database and schedule backup jobs. Because these tools are used for database administration rather than database programming, we do not discuss them in too much detail in this book. However, in order to design quality database systems, you should understand database administration.

REPLICATION

For those of you familiar with SQL Server 7, you will note that this is a new folder to the SQL Enterprise Manager. Because SQL Server 2000 boasts more robust replication features, the tools were upgraded to a more prominent location in the Enterprise Manager. SQL Server 2000 supports three replication types: Snapshot, Transaction, and Merge, as well as replication between heterogeneous data sources. You will explore replication in Chapter 14, "Advanced SQL Server 2000 Features."

SECURITY

Here's where the DBA creates new logins and assigns roles to users. We do not use these tools in this book.

SUPPORT SERVICES

This is where you configure two of SQL Server's support services: the Distributed Transaction Coordinator and SQL Server Mail. The Distributed Transaction Coordinator is a tool for managing transactions that span across multiple servers.

The SQL Server Mail service enables you to create mail messages from within SQL Server. You can schedule these messages to be created and transmitted automatically and to notify the database administrator about the success or failure of a task. You can attach log files and exception files to the message.

META DATA SERVICES

Meta Data Services are also a new feature to the SQL 2000 Enterprise Manager. This feature is used primary for data warehousing or online analytical processing (OLAP) processing. Its equivalent in SQL Server 7 was the OLAP Services Format, which can be upgraded to SQL Server 2000. We do not cover this feature in this book.

The Query Analyzer

If there's one tool you must learn well, this is it. The Query Analyzer is where you can execute SQL statements, batches, and stored procedures against a database. To start the Query Analyzer, select Start ➤ Programs ➤ Microsoft SQL Server ➤ Query Analyzer. Alternately, you can access it from the Enterprise Manager by selecting it from the Tools button in the action bar. The Query Analyzer has improved considerably from SQL Server 7 to SQL Server 2000, giving you a hierarchical, object-based view of your data, as opposed to a flattened view. The biggest change you will see is the Object Browser on the left side (you'll read more about that in just a bit.)

If you enter an SQL statement in the Query Analyzer window and click the Execute button (the button with the green arrow on the toolbar), or press Ctrl+E or F5, the window will split into two panes; the result of the query will appear in the lower pane—the Results pane—as shown in Figure 1.19. The statement executes against the database selected in the DB box at the top of the window, so make sure you've selected the appropriate database before you execute an

SQL statement for the first time. You can save the current statement to a text file with the File ➢ Save As command and open it later with the File ➢ Open command.

In addition to SQL statements, you can execute batches recognized by the `osql` and `isql` utilities and the Query Analyzer. A *batch* is a collection of T-SQL statements sent to these utilities. For example, you can enter multiple T-SQL statements and separate them with a `GO` statement. Each time a `GO` statement is reached, the Query Analyzer executes all the statements from the beginning of the file, or the previous `GO` statement. All the results will appear in the Results pane.

NOTE *SQL statements and batches are stored in text files with the extension* `.sql`. *All the SQL statements and stored procedures presented in this book can be found in a separate SQL file, each under the corresponding chapter's folder on the companion CD-ROM.*

FIGURE 1.19

Executing SQL statements with the Query Analyzer

By default, the Query Analyzer displays the row output produced by SQL Server: the results and any messages indicating the success or failure of the operation. The results display under the Grid tab, although it can be configured so that the results are shown in a plain text window or sent directly to a file, which you can see in Figure 1.19. The messages display within the Message tab, as shown in Figure 1.20.

NOTE *The Message tab will not appear when you display your results as text, because the messages will be listed below the text.*

FIGURE 1.20

The Query
Analyzer's
Message view

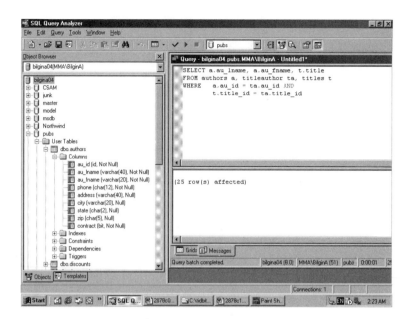

Object Browser

The Object Browser is a wonderful, new tool that comes with SQL Server 2000 and advances the SQL IDE to be more integrated with the other development platforms, such as Visual Studio .NET.

The Object Browser enables you to drill down into your databases in a hierarchical fashion, viewing the separate entities that belong to your database, such as stored procedures and tables. One of the features we like the best is the ability to separate system tables from user-defined tables, saving you the extra steps of having to configure this on your own every time.

As you can see in Figure 1.21, the Object Browser enables you to view not only database-related entities, but also the common tools associated with the DBMS, such as base data-types and various functions.

Object Search

The Object Search is a new SQL Server 2000 feature that enables you to perform advanced searches on the hierarchical object model presented by the Object Browser. As you can see in Figure 1.22, this powerful search engine is a useful feature, which is analogous to the Find Files feature in Windows Explorer. You can access this feature by selecting Tools ➢ Object Search from the drop-down list in the Query Analyzer.

FIGURE 1.21

Object Browser

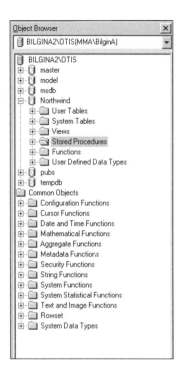

FIGURE 1.22

Object Search

Summary

This chapter is very broad indeed. It touches many topics, and it probably raises quite a few questions. The following chapters elaborate on all the topics discussed here. Starting with the next chapter, you'll learn how to design databases and how to manipulate them with SQL Server 2000. Then, you'll see how to use ADO.NET to write database applications that are almost independent of the DBMS you use. Although this book is geared toward SQL Server 2000, nearly all the ADO.NET code provided will work equally well with other OLE DB providers.

You're probably eager to see some VB .NET code that accesses databases. The next few chapters are not about VB .NET. Before you start writing VB .NET code, you should develop a good understanding of the structure of a database, the role of relationships and how they're used, and the T-SQL language. Unless you understand the available tools and what they do, you shouldn't jump into writing code. Even if you are familiar with relational concepts, you shouldn't skip Chapter 2, "Basic Concepts of Relational Databases," in its entirety, because it contains a good number of tips on designing databases with SQL Server. We provide a high-level overview on the new SQL Server 2000 features, such as cascading referential integrity, indexed views, and the new data types.

Chapter 2

Basic Concepts of Relational Databases

- ◆ Fundamentals of Database Design
- ◆ Database Objects
- ◆ Normalization Rules
- ◆ Database Integrity

HAVE YOU EVER HEARD of Nancy Davolio and Alfreds Futterkiste? If you have or if you have designed simple databases with Microsoft SQL Server, then you can safely skip this chapter and go on to Chapter 3, "The Visual Database Tools," which covers the new tools that come with Visual Studio .NET (VS .NET) and SQL Server 2000. If you haven't done any database programming, take the time to review this chapter. Before looking at any tools, it's important that you learn the basic principles of database design and familiarize yourself with the basic terms you'll see in the rest of the book: tables and indexes, relationships, primary and foreign keys, referential integrity, and a bunch of other goodies.

This chapter covers the principles of databases and the nature of relational databases, why you use a specific methodology to design them, and other related topics, including the normalization of databases. An important part of this chapter is the discussion of the structure of the Northwind and Pubs sample databases. These databases ship with SQL Server 2000, and we use them for our examples throughout the book.

TIP You can also install the Northwind and Pubs databases from a typical Visual Studio .NET installation by running the installation programs for the .NET QuickStart tutorials: select Programs ➤ Microsoft .NET Framework SDK ➤ Samples and QuickStart Tutorials from the Windows Start menu. Keep in mind that this doesn't install SQL Server, but the lightweight MSDE database server. Be warned that this version doesn't include the SQL Server IDE that we discuss throughout the book. Even if you already have SQL Server installed, you will still find these QuickStart tutorials useful because they contain many data access samples for using the .NET Framework.

Why examine the structure of existing databases instead of creating a new one from scratch? Because it's simpler to understand the structure of an existing database, especially a database designed by the people who designed the data engine itself. Besides, because we use these databases in the examples in the following chapters, you should make sure you understand their structures. Finally, the basic concepts of relational databases covered in this chapter provide stepping stones to the more advanced topics discussed later in this book.

Fundamentals of Database Design

In principle, designing databases is simple. More than anything else, it requires common sense and organization. The strength of any business lies in its ability to retrieve and store their information efficiently. As a database designer, you should consider certain principles before creating the actual database:

- ◆ Organization
- ◆ Integrity
- ◆ Optimization

First, a well-designed database system should always have well-organized data that is quick and easy to retrieve. In addition, the system should accurately record and store the data without corruption. Last, you must optimize the data and data manipulation code that you write. This way, your database management system (DBMS) can find and return the data in the least amount of time. Don't skip these steps, because any errors in the design of a database will surface later, when you try to extract its data. Let's consider these points in more detail:

Organization   If your data isn't well organized in the database, you won't be able to extract the data you want (or you'll have to extract a lot of unwanted information along with the useful data). Before you even begin working with any tools, you should first consider how you want to store your data. The easiest way to do this is to write down (or think about) what you want the system to do. Use no more than four or five sentences. Then, pick out all the nouns in those sentences. Generally, these nouns will correspond to the tables of your system. The next step is to get a paper and pen and to draw a pictorial representation of your data. Write down the nouns and draw boxes around them. Hang on to this sketch. You'll use it in just a bit, as you learn how to build relationships between these data items and create entity-relationship diagrams.

Integrity   Another important aspect of databases is integrity, which keeps your data accurate and consistent. Even the best-designed database can be incapacitated if it's populated with invalid data. The impact of corruption isn't a technical one. Rather, it's an impact on the business that relies on the database. Imagine the cost to a business if orders were lost and shipments delayed due to missing or invalid data. If you don't do something to maintain the integrity and consistency of your database, you might never be able to locate data. For instance, if you allow the users of a database to change the name of a company, how will you retrieve the invoices issued to the same company before its name was changed? For this reason, you can't rely on the users to maintain the integrity of the database. A modern DBMS provides built-in mechanisms to help you with this task. SQL Server, for example, can enforce the integrity of the relationships between data items. Say a customer places some orders. The DBMS should not allow you to remove the customer from the database, without first removing their associated orders. If a customer is deleted from the database, the corresponding orders will no longer refer to a valid customer. *Orphaning* describes the concept of broken relationships between associated sets of data. Later in this chapter, in the "Normalization Rules" section, you will see how to incorporate rules for maintaining the integrity. You can build these rules right into the database itself, in order to prevent orphaned records or other data corruption.

Optimization   After you incorporate organization and integrity into your database, you should think about tuning and optimization. Performance tuning isn't something you do after you have your database up and running. On the contrary, you should performance-tune your database throughout database design. Although SQL Server 2000 has made some serious advances in self-tuning, you still have to make sure you write solid data manipulation code to take advantage of these optimizations. Throughout this book, we provide you with tips and tricks to keep your database running like a well-oiled engine.

As you will see, the design of a database shouldn't be taken lightly. You can trace most problems in database applications back to the design of the database. You will find it difficult, if not impossible, to optimize a poorly designed database. The queries will be unnecessarily slow and, in many cases, unnecessarily complicated.

What Is a Database?

A database is one of those objects that is so hard to define, yet everyone knows what it is. Here's a simple definition, which even people with no prior programming experience will understand: A *database* is a system for storing complex, structured information. The same is true for a file, or even for the file system on your hard disk. What makes a database unique is that databases are designed for responsiveness. The purpose of a database is not so much the storage of information as its quick retrieval. In other words, you must structure your database so that it can be queried quickly and efficiently.

RELATIONAL DATABASES

The databases that we focus on in this book are *relational*, because they are based on relationships between the data they contain. The data is stored in tables, and tables contain related data, or *entities*, such as customers, products, orders, and so on. The idea is to keep the tables small and manageable; thus, separate entities are kept in their own tables. For example, if you start mixing customers and invoices, products and their suppliers in the same table, you'll end up repeating information—a highly undesirable situation. If there's one rule to live by as a database designer and programmer, this is it: Unless you are building a data warehouse, do not unnecessarily duplicate information. As we mentioned before, if you can name your table by using a single noun, then you are on the right track. So when we mention that duplicate data is not desirable, we do so in the context of OLTP systems.

OLAP VERSUS OLTP

How you design your database depends on the type of system you need. Database systems come in two distinct flavors: online analytical processing (OLAP) and online transaction processing (OLTP) systems. Each uses completely different design models, and you should never have a database that uses both models.

OLAP systems are often referred to as *data warehouses,* or *data mines.* These databases are generally read-only representations of volumes of data often used for reporting purposes. Thus, you'll often hear these systems called *decision support systems,* because they are often used to help high-level managers make business decisions. Their retrieval mechanism is quite different from that of OLTP systems. OLAP systems use the concept of cubes. *Cubes* are multidimensional representations of data, which you can think of like pivot tables in Excel. The storage also vastly differs from OLTP. In data warehouses, speed is the highest priority, so databases tend to be de-normalized, with lots of redundant data. We define *normalization* later in this chapter.

OLTP systems consist of users retrieving subsets of data based on specific criteria and manipulating single sets of data in an atomic process referred to as a "transaction." Because OLTP systems update data, considerations such as concurrency, locking, and archival have a higher priority than with data warehouses. OLTP systems attempt to reduce the amount of data that is stored so that SQL Server can process the data faster.

The systems that we are referring to in this book center around OLTP systems, rather than OLAP. However, we touch on OLAP a little bit in Chapter 14, "Advanced SQL Server 2000 Features."

Of course, entities are not independent of each other. Pull out the diagram you drew earlier with the boxes containing your nouns. Draw lines connecting the boxes that are related. For example, customers place orders, so the rows of a `Customers` table would link to the rows of an `Orders` table. Figure 2.1 shows a segment of a table with customers (top left) and the rows of a table with orders that correspond to one of the customers (bottom right). The lines that connect the rows of the two tables represent *relationships.* These databases are called *relational,* because they're based on relationships.

FIGURE 2.1

Linking customers
and orders with
relationships

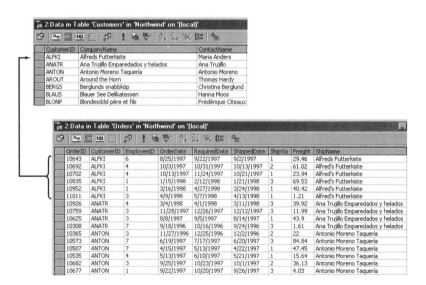

KEY FIELDS

As you can see in Figure 2.1, you implement relationships by inserting rows with matching values in the two related tables; the `CustomerID` column is repeated in both tables. The rows with a common value in their `CustomerID` field are related. In other words, the lines that connect the two tables simply indicate that there are two fields, one on each side of the relationship, with a common value. These two fields are called *key fields*. The `CustomerID` field of the `Customers` table is the *primary key*, because it identifies a single customer. The primary key must be unique and appear only in a single row of a table. The `CustomerID` field in the `Orders` table is the *foreign key* of the relationship, because it references another primary key. A foreign key can appear in multiple rows of a table. In this example, it will appear in as many rows of the `Orders` table as there are orders for the specific customer. (You'll read more about keys a bit later in this chapter.)

NOTE   This simple idea of linking tables based on the values of two columns that are common to both tables is at the heart of relational databases. It enables you to break your data into smaller units, the tables, yet be able to combine rows in multiple tables to retrieve and present the desired information.

Exploring the Northwind Database

So let's go back to the question we asked earlier: "Who are Nancy Davolio and Alfreds Futterkiste?" This is a great DBA interview question, and the answer lies in the Northwind database, which is a sample data database that ships with SQL Server. Nancy is the first record of the `Employees` table in Northwind. Alfreds is the first name that comes up in the `Customers` table. After you spend a lot of time working with Northwind, these names will inevitably come up over and over again. You'll get quite familiar with them by the time you finish this book. Before you examine the objects of databases in detail, let's look at the structure of the Northwind database. In the process, you'll develop a good feel for how relational databases are structured, and you'll find the discussion of the objects of a database easier to follow.

The Northwind database stores sales information: the customers and products of the Northwind Corporation and which products each customer has ordered, along with their prices, discounts, shipping information, and so on. Let's begin by examining the Northwind tables and their attributes. As you go through the tables, you'll learn the rationale that's used to help determine the Northwind database design. That way, you will have greater insight on both design and implementation.

The first step in database design is to break the information you want to store into smaller units, the tables, and establish relationships between them. To do so, you must identify the entities you want to store (products, customers, and so on) and create a table for each entity. As we've said, the best way to identify the entities is to find the nouns that represent your business case. More often than not, they will equate to the tables of your system.

For example, in the Northwind system, you need to track **orders** for your **customers** based on the **products** they choose. We've made the nouns bold for you, and as you can see, they correspond to the tables in the Northwind database.

You can picture a table as a grid: each row corresponds to a different item, but all items have the same structure. *Columns* (also known as *domains*) define the structure of the table, and each column represents an *attribute* of the entity stored in the table. You can think of attributes as terms that describe your nouns (tables). A table that stores products has a column for the product's name, another column for the product's price, and so on. As you can see, all these columns use terms that describe the product. Each product is stored in a different row. As you add or remove products from the table, the number of rows changes, but the number of columns remains the same; they determine the information you store about each product. This representation of columns in a table is also referred to as the table's *schema*. We provide more details about schemas throughout this book. Although it is possible to add and remove columns after you've added data to them, you should do your best to anticipate database use beforehand.

PRODUCTS TABLE

The Products table stores information about the products sold by the Northwind Corporation. This information includes the product's name, packaging information, price, and other relevant fields. Additionally, a unique, numeric ID number identifies each product in the table, as you can see in Figure 2.2.

Why not use the product name as the ID? Product names might be easier to remember, but you shouldn't use them because the product might not be unique and can change. Although SQL Server 2000 has new features (such as cascading updates) that can handle changes to the product name, each product name update would task the database with additional activity. Because the rows of the Products table are referenced by invoices, each product name change would entail a number of changes in the Order Details table (which is discussed later), as well. The product ID that identifies each product need not change; it's a numeric value used to reference a product. Thus, by using a unique numeric value to identify each product, you can change the product's name without affecting any other tables.

FIGURE 2.2

Each line in the Products table holds information about a specific product.

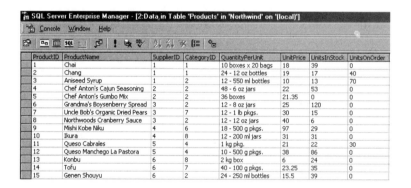

ProductID	ProductName	SupplierID	CategoryID	QuantityPerUnit	UnitPrice	UnitsInStock	UnitsOnOrder
1	Chai	1	1	10 boxes x 20 bags	18	39	0
2	Chang	1	1	24 - 12 oz bottles	19	17	40
3	Aniseed Syrup	1	2	12 - 550 ml bottles	10	13	70
4	Chef Anton's Cajun Seasoning	2	2	48 - 6 oz jars	22	53	0
5	Chef Anton's Gumbo Mix	2	2	36 boxes	21.35	0	0
6	Grandma's Boysenberry Spread	3	2	12 - 8 oz jars	25	120	0
7	Uncle Bob's Organic Dried Pears	3	7	12 - 1 lb pkgs.	30	15	0
8	Northwoods Cranberry Sauce	3	2	12 - 12 oz jars	40	6	0
9	Mishi Kobe Niku	4	6	18 - 500 g pkgs.	97	29	0
10	Ikura	4	8	12 - 200 ml jars	31	31	0
11	Queso Cabrales	5	4	1 kg pkg.	21	22	30
12	Queso Manchego La Pastora	5	4	10 - 500 g pkgs.	38	86	0
13	Konbu	6	8	2 kg box	6	24	0
14	Tofu	6	7	40 - 100 g pkgs.	23.25	35	0
15	Genen Shouyu	6	2	24 - 250 ml bottles	15.5	39	0

The SupplierID and CategoryID columns contain integer values that point to rows of two other tables, the Suppliers and Categories tables, respectively. These two tables contain information about the Northwind Corporation's suppliers and various product categories.

NOTE   *Supplier information can't be stored in the* **Products** *table, because the same supplier's name and address would be repeated for multiple products. The category name isn't stored in the* **Products** *table because storing a number takes up less space than the category name itself.*

SUPPLIERS TABLE

Each product in the Northwind database has a supplier. Because the same supplier might offer more than one product, the supplier information is stored in a different table, and a common field, the **SupplierID** field, is used to link each product to its supplier. For example, the products Mishi Kobe Niku and Ikura are purchased from the same supplier, Tokyo Traders. Their **SupplierID** fields point to the same row in the **Suppliers** table, as shown in Figure 2.3.

FIGURE 2.3

Linking products to their suppliers

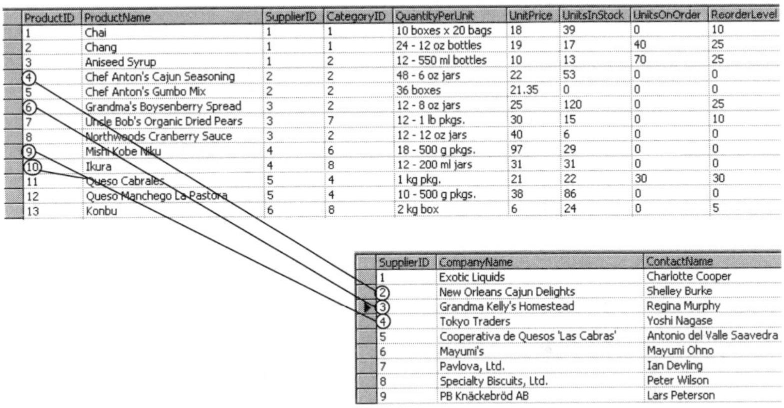

ProductID	ProductName	SupplierID	CategoryID	QuantityPerUnit	UnitPrice	UnitsInStock	UnitsOnOrder	ReorderLevel
1	Chai	1	1	10 boxes x 20 bags	18	39	0	10
2	Chang	1	1	24 - 12 oz bottles	19	17	40	25
3	Aniseed Syrup	1	2	12 - 550 ml bottles	10	13	70	25
4	Chef Anton's Cajun Seasoning	2	2	48 - 6 oz jars	22	53	0	0
5	Chef Anton's Gumbo Mix	2	2	36 boxes	21.35	0	0	0
6	Grandma's Boysenberry Spread	3	2	12 - 8 oz jars	25	120	0	25
7	Uncle Bob's Organic Dried Pears	3	7	12 - 1 lb pkgs.	30	15	0	10
8	Northwoods Cranberry Sauce	3	2	12 - 12 oz jars	40	6	0	0
9	Mishi Kobe Niku	4	6	18 - 500 g pkgs.	97	29	0	0
10	Ikura	4	8	12 - 200 ml jars	31	31	0	0
11	Queso Cabrales	5	4	1 kg pkg.	21	22	30	30
12	Queso Manchego La Pastora	5	4	10 - 500 g pkgs.	38	86	0	0
13	Konbu	6	8	2 kg box	6	24	0	5

SupplierID	CompanyName	ContactName
1	Exotic Liquids	Charlotte Cooper
2	New Orleans Cajun Delights	Shelley Burke
3	Grandma Kelly's Homestead	Regina Murphy
4	Tokyo Traders	Yoshi Nagase
5	Cooperativa de Quesos 'Las Cabras'	Antonio del Valle Saavedra
6	Mayumi's	Mayumi Ohno
7	Pavlova, Ltd.	Ian Devling
8	Specialty Biscuits, Ltd.	Peter Wilson
9	PB Knäckebröd AB	Lars Peterson

CATEGORIES TABLE

In addition to having a supplier, each product belongs to a category. Categories are not stored with product names, but in a separate table, the **Categories** table, whose structure is shown in Figure 2.4. Again, each category is identified by a numeric value and has a name (the **CategoryID** and **Category-Name** fields, respectively). In addition, the **Categories** table has two more columns: **Description**, which contains text, and **Picture**, which stores a bitmap in the form of an image data type.

The **Products** table (back in Figure 2.2) has a **CategoryID** column as well, which links each product to its category. By storing the categories in a separate table, you don't have to enter the actual name of the category (or its bitmap) along with each product. The **CategoryID** field of the **Products** table points to the product's category, and you can locate each product's category very quickly in the **Categories** table. You will learn how to do that in the "Database Objects" section later in this chapter.

FIGURE 2.4

The structure of the
Categories table
(top) and the
rows of the table
(bottom)

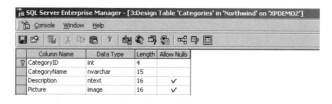

CUSTOMERS TABLE

The **Customers** table stores information about the company's customers. Before you can accept an order, you must create a new row in the **Customers** table with the customer's data (name, phone number, address, and so on), if one doesn't exist already. Each row in the **Customers** table represents a different customer and is identified by the **CustomerID** field. This field has a unique value for each row, similar to the **ProductID** field of the **Products** table. However, the **CustomerID** field is a five-character-long string, and not an integer (refer to Figure 2.1). As you can see, a primary key does not have to be a numeric value.

ORDERS TABLE

The **Orders** table stores information (customer, shipping address, date of order, and so on) about the orders placed by Northwind's customers. The **OrderID** field, which is an integer value, identifies each order. Orders are numbered sequentially, so this field is also the order's number. As you will see in the "Database Objects" section later in this chapter, each time you append a new row to the **Orders** table, the value of the new **OrderID** field is generated automatically by the database. Moreover, you can set this feature on only one column set in the table. A *column set* can consist of one or more columns. When you define multiple columns as a primary key, you create a *composite key*. If you have already declared a primary key, you won't get any warning if you try to declare another primary key column set; SQL Server automatically reverts the previous primary key to a non-key column.

The **Orders** table is linked to the **Customers** table through the **CustomerID** field. By matching rows with identical values in their **CustomerID** fields in the two tables, you can combine a customer with their orders as shown in Figure 2.1.

ORDER DETAILS TABLE

You probably have noticed that the Northwind database's **Orders** table doesn't store any details about the items ordered. This information is stored in the **Order Details** table. Each order is made up of one or more items, and each item has a price, a quantity, and a discount. In addition to these fields, the `Order Details` table contains an `OrderID` column, which holds the order number to which the detail line belongs. In other words, the details of all invoices are thrown into this table and are organized according to the order to which they belong.

The reason details aren't stored along with the order's header is that the `Orders` and `Order Details` tables store different entities. The order's header, which contains information about the customer who placed the order, the date of the order, and so on, is quite different from the information you must store for each item ordered. Try to come up with a different design that stores all order-related information in a single table, and you'll soon realize that you end up duplicating information. Figure 2.5 shows how three of the tables in the Northwind database, `Customers`, `Orders`, and `Order Details`, are linked to one another.

We should probably explain why the order's total doesn't appear in any table. To calculate an order's total, you must multiply the quantity by the price, taking into consideration the discount. If the order's total were stored in the `Orders` table, you'd be duplicating information. The order's total is already available for you. Because you can derive the total from existing columns, and those column values may change, there's no guarantee that the total values will always be correct. A good rule of thumb is to avoid storing calculated information in your database, because you can dynamically generate it.

FIGURE 2.5

Linking customers to orders and orders to their details

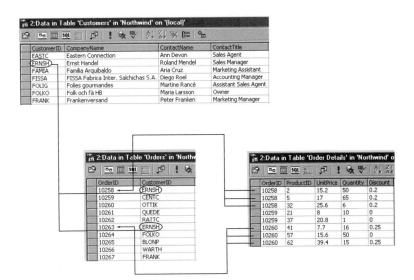

EMPLOYEES TABLE

This table holds employee information. The employees of the Northwind Corporation work on commission. When a sale is made, the ID of the employee who made the sale is recorded in the `Orders` table.

SHIPPERS TABLE

Northwind Corporation uses three shippers. The Shippers table holds information about the shippers, and each shipper's ID appears in the Orders table, along with the order date, shipment date, address, and so on.

TERRITORIES TABLE

Northwind uses the Territories table to capture the regions and cities that are associated with sales people. A separate *association table* called EmployeeTerritories enforces this relationship. We explain association tables in the "Database Objects" section later in this chapter.

Exploring the Pubs Database

The Pubs database is a sample database that comes with SQL Server, and it is used almost exclusively in the examples of SQL Server's online help. The tables of the Pubs database contain very few rows, but they were designed to demonstrate many of the operations you perform on databases. We use this database in many of the examples in this book.

As you did with the Northwind database, in this section you'll examine the tables of the Pubs database and the relationships between them. This will give you a prelude to the next section, where you'll examine relationships in more detail.

TITLES TABLE

This table holds book information. Each book is identified by the title_id field, which is neither its ISBN nor an Identity field, but a made-up key. This table also contains a column named ytd_sales (year-to-date sales), which is the number of copies sold in the current year. Because there's no information about the total sales, you can assume that this column contains the running total of sales for each title.

AUTHORS TABLE

This table contains author information. Each author is identified by the au_id field (which is the author's social security number), as well as contact information (phone number, address). The last column in the authors table is the contract column, which indicates whether the author has a contract.

TITLEAUTHOR TABLE

This table connects titles to authors. Its rows contain pairs of title IDs and author IDs. In addition, it contains each author's order in a title, along with the author's royalty split per title. The title ID BU1032 appears twice in this table, which means that this title has two authors. The first one is the author with ID 409-56-7008, and his share of the royalties is 60 percent. The second author has the ID 213-46-8915, and his share of the royalties is 40 percent. The same person is the single author of another title (ID BU2075) and gets 100 percent of the royalties generated by this title.

ROYSCHED TABLE

This table stores the information needed to calculate the royalties generated by each title. Books earn royalties according to a royalty schedule; the royalty escalates as sales increase. The title with ID BU1032 has a breakpoint at 5,000 copies. For the first 5,000 copies, it will make a royalty of 10 percent. After that, this percentage increases to 12 percent. The title with ID BU2075 has many breakpoints (10 percent for the first 1,000 copies, 12 percent for the next 2,000 copies, 14 percent for the next 2,000 copies, 16 percent for the next 3,000 copies, and so on). Figure 2.6 shows the relationships between the tables of the Pubs database that are used in calculating royalties. The royalty breakpoints are shown in Figure 2.7.

FIGURE 2.6

Linking titles, authors, and royalties in the Pubs database

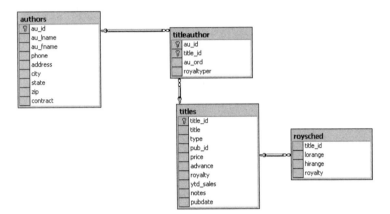

FIGURE 2.7

Applying the relationships of Figure 2.6 to some actual data

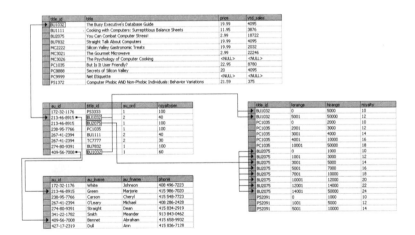

***PUB_INFO* TABLE**

This table holds information about the publishers. Each publisher is identified in the `pub_id` field, and the same value is repeated in the `titles` table.

STORES TABLE

This table stores the names and addresses of a number of bookstores to which sales are made. Each store is identified by a store ID (stor_id field). This table is linked to the sales table.

SALES TABLE

This table contains sales information. The stor_id field holds information about the store to which the sale was made, the ord_num field is the order's number, and title_id and qty are the title and quantity sold. Unfortunately, this table doesn't contain all the sales, and you can't find out how many copies of each title were sold by adding quantities in this table.

DISCOUNTS TABLE

This table holds the initial, usual, and volume discounts for each store. Each discount range is determined by a low and high quantity. The initial discount is 10.5 percent. For a volume discount, a store must order 100 or more copies. In addition, you can store specific discounts for each store in this table.

The remaining tables of the Pubs database have to do with employees and jobs and are not used in this book's examples. The employees table holds personnel information, and the jobs table holds job descriptions.

Understanding Relations

In a database, each table has a field with a unique value for every row. This field is marked with a key icon in front of its name, as you can see back in Figure 2.4, and it's the table's primary key.

The primary key does not have to be a meaningful entity, because in most cases there's no single field that's unique for each row. The primary key need not resemble the entity it identifies. The only requirement is that primary keys are unique in the entire table. You can even have more than one column serving as a primary key, which is referred to as a *composite key*. Keep in mind that the combined values of a composite key must be unique.

In most designs, you use an integer as the primary key. To make sure they're unique, you can even let the DBMS generate a new integer for each row added to the table. Each table can have one primary key only, and this field can't be Null.

The references to primary keys in other tables are called *foreign keys*. Foreign keys need not be unique (in fact, they aren't), and any field can serve as a foreign key. What makes a field a foreign key is that it matches the primary key of another table. The CategoryID field is the primary key of the Categories table, because it identifies each category. The CategoryID field in the Products table is the foreign key, because it references the primary key in the Categories table. The same CategoryID might appear in many rows in the Products table, because many products can belong to the same category. When you relate the Products and Categories tables, for example, you must also make sure of the following:

◆ Every product added to the foreign table must point to a valid entry in the primary table. If you are not sure which category the product belongs to, you can leave the CategoryID field of the Products table empty. The primary keys, however, can't be Null.

◆ No rows in the Categories table should be removed if there are rows in the Products table pointing to the specific category. This will make the corresponding rows of the Products table point to an invalid category.

These two restrictions would be quite a burden on the programmer if the DBMS didn't protect the database against actions that could impair its integrity. The integrity of your database depends on the validity of the relations. Fortunately, all DBMSs can enforce rules to maintain their integrity. You'll learn how to enforce rules that guarantee the integrity of your database in the "Database Integrity" section later in this chapter.

Querying Relational Databases

Now let's consider the most common operations you'd like to be able to perform on the Northwind database's tables. The process of retrieving data from tables is known as *querying*, and the statements you execute against a database to retrieve selected rows are called *queries*. These statements are written in Structured Query Language (SQL), which is discussed in detail in Chapter 4, "Structured Query Language." In this section, you'll look at a few simple queries and how the DBMS combines rows from multiple tables to return the data you're interested in.

RETRIEVING A CUSTOMER'S ORDERS

This is probably the most common operation you would perform on a database such as Northwind. To retrieve a customer's orders, start with the customer's ID and locate all the lines in the Orders table whose CustomerID field matches the CustomerID field of the selected row in the Customers table. To retrieve the customer's orders, the DBMS must search the Orders table with its foreign key. To help the DBMS with this operation, you should index the Orders table by using the CustomerID field. Both versions of the Northwind database define an index on this field. We discuss indexes in the "Database Objects" section later in this chapter.

RETRIEVING THE PRODUCTS FOR A CATEGORY

This example is a great way to understand how relationships work. The CategoryID field in the Categories table is the primary key, because it identifies each row in the table. Each category has a unique CategoryID, which can be repeated many times in the Products table. The CategoryID field in the Products table is the foreign key.

When you look up products, you want to be able to quickly locate the category to which they belong. You read the value of the CategoryID field in the Products table, locate the row in the Categories table with the same value in the CategoryID column, and voila!—you have matched the two tables. You can also search the Products table for products that belong to a specific category. You start with the ID of a category and then locate all the rows in the Products table with a CategoryID field that matches the selected ID. The relationship between the two tables links each row of the first table to one or more rows of the second table.

Here is a simple T-SQL statement that retrieves a list of products for the "Seafood" category:

```
SELECT Products.ProductName from Products, Categories
    WHERE Categories.CategoryName = 'Seafood' AND
    Products.CategoryID =  Categories.CategoryID
```

NOTE *The operation of matching rows in two (or more) tables based on their primary and foreign keys is called a join. Joins are basic operations in manipulating tables, and they are discussed in detail in Chapter 4.*

CALCULATING THE TOTAL FOR EACH ORDER

The Orders table doesn't contain the total for each order—and it shouldn't. The totals must be calculated directly from the details. As mentioned earlier, databases shouldn't duplicate information, and storing the totals in the Orders table would be a form of duplication; you'd duplicate the information that's already present in another table. Had you stored the totals along with each order, then every time you changed a detail line, you'd have to change a row in the Orders table as well.

To calculate an order's total, the DBMS must search the Order Details table with its foreign key (OrderID), multiply quantities by prices, and add the results for all rows that belong to the specific order (it must also take into consideration the discount). To help the DBMS with this operation, you should index the Order Details table on its OrderID field. The Northwind database defines an index on the OrderID field to allow fast retrieval of orders based on the OrderID.

CALCULATING THE TOTAL FOR EACH CUSTOMER

This operation is similar to totaling an order, but it uses three tables. Start with the customer's ID and select all the rows in the Orders table whose CustomerID field matches the ID of the specific customer. This is a list with the IDs of the orders placed by the selected customer. Then scan all the rows of the Order Details table whose OrderID field is in this list, multiply quantities by prices, and then add those results.

Database Objects

Now that you've been introduced to the basic concepts (and objects) of a relational database by means of examples, you should have a good idea of what a relational database is. You understand how data is stored in separate tables in the database and how the tables are linked to one another through relationships. You also know how relationships are used to execute complicated queries that retrieve data from multiple tables. You might have questions about specific attributes and techniques, which are addressed in the following sections of this chapter. Let's begin our detailed discussion of the objects of a relational database with the most basic objects, tables.

Tables

A *table* is a collection of rows with the same structure that stores information about an entity such as a person, an invoice, a product, and so on. Each row contains the same number of columns, and each column can store data of the same data type. You can think of a table as a grid that stores records, much like a spreadsheet.

A DBMS such as SQL Server doesn't store tables in separate files. All the data resides in a single file, along with auxiliary information required by the DBMS to access the data quickly. In reality, the DBMS uses more space to store the auxiliary information than for the data itself. The tables in a database are an abstraction; they form a conceptual model of the data. This is how we, humans, view the database. Tables don't reflect the actual structure of the data in the database. Instead, they reflect the logical entities in the database, and the relations between tables reflect actions (products are *purchased*, customers *place* orders, and so on).

Internally, every DBMS stores information in a proprietary format, and you need not know anything about this format. In effect, this is one of the requirements of the relational database model: *The physical structure might change, but these changes shouldn't affect how you see the database.* For example, SQL Server databases are physically stored with an `.mdf` (Master Data File) extension. Microsoft might change the physical structure of the data in an MDF file, but SQL Server will still see tables and indexes, it will still be able to relate tables to each other by using common field values (the primary and foreign keys), and your applications will keep working. You will see the same tables, the same SQL statements will retrieve the same data, and you won't even notice the difference (there will be new features, of course, but existing applications will continue to work without any modifications).

CUSTOMERS AND SUPPLIERS: SAME ENTITIES, DIFFERENT FUNCTION

You will notice that the Northwind database's `Customers` and `Suppliers` tables have the exact same structure. As far as the operations of an application are concerned, customers and suppliers are two separate entities, and there's no overlap between the two. This is a rather unusual situation, where two different entities have the same (or nearly the same) structure.

Keep in mind that Northwind is a sample database. In a real-world situation, the two tables might not be totally isolated, because the same company might act both as a supplier and as a customer. In other words, it might not only sell to your company, but buy from it as well. In some instances, using a single table for customers and suppliers might make sense. This approach can complicate the programming a little, but it simplifies operations from a user's point of view. If you don't know that a supplier is also a customer, you might end up paying for the items you purchase regularly and never know that the other party is not keeping up with their obligations. There are other practical reasons for treating both customers and suppliers as a single entity, such as preferring a supplier who is also a good customer of yours.

Although this approach makes logical sense and might improve the performance of ad hoc reporting, you should always keep scalability in mind. If you expect to have another entity, such as Distributors, it might make sense to keep the tables separate. Keeping the tables separate will allow for looser coupling of your entities, thereby increasing your scalability. Many articles on the Web can give you data design patterns that can help you map your object relationships back to your database.

CREATING TABLES

To create a table, you must specify its structure by declaring its columns: specify how many columns the table has, their names, and their types. Generally, no matter what DBMS you're using, here's how tables are created:

1. Make up a name for the table. Table names can be quite long (128 characters, maximum), so you should name them after the entity they represent. Table names, as well as column names, can include spaces as long as you enclose them in a pair of square brackets (`[Order Details]`, `[Sales in Europe]`, and so on) in your code. SQL Server Enterprise Manager will automatically add the brackets for you behind the scenes.

SHOULD YOU USE NAMING CONVENTIONS?

Naming standards make it easier for other developers to work with your database. Many corporations will provide development guidelines to follow. Although Northwind doesn't follow a strict naming convention, you should stick with a consistent naming convention when designing your database. Here are some sample naming conventions that you might find effective when you create your table structure:

Naming tables   You should name your table as a singular, lowercase noun. Although Northwind doesn't follow this convention, it is a generally accepted practice. Keep in mind that a SQL Server database can be case sensitive, depending on installation settings. So two tables called ORDERS and Orders can exist in the same database.

Intersection tables (also known as *crossover, linking,* or *association tables*) are used to store many-to-many relationships. You should name an intersection table after the two tables that they connect. For example, if you have an intersection table for Order and Item, your table should be named OrderItem. You will learn more about many-to-many relationships later, in the "Establishing Relationships" subsection.

Naming columns   Although SQL Server supports the use of spaces in a name (enclosed in square brackets), try to avoid them. If your column is a primary or foreign key, distinguish it with an *ID* suffix for easier readability. If possible, use the same name for the foreign key as the primary key. If you are pointing to more than one table that has the same primary key name, then use the referenced table name as a prefix for the foreign key.

Casing   The .NET Framework embraces the support of *camel casing* to separate words. Camel casing keeps the first word as lowercase, uppercasing the rest (for example, orderItem). However, in database structures, *Pascal casing* is the generally accepted practice. This involves title casing your entities (for example, OrderItem). If you need to increase readability due to long names or duplication, underscores can be used. For example, if you have an intersection table for Order and OrderItem, you would name your table Order_OrderItem. It really doesn't matter which standard you choose, as long as your development team is using the same standard consistently.

2. Make up a name for each column of the table. Columns are the attributes of the entity represented by the table. Think of the items that uniquely describe your table when you determine your columns. For example, the columns of a table that stores customers should probably contain a customer's name, address, phone numbers, electronic address, and so on. Each column must have a name with a maximum length of 128 characters (for SQL Server databases). You can have up to 1024 columns in a table.

TIP   If you can, limit your column names to 30 characters or fewer. Some SQL Server utilities, such as the isql utility, will truncate the name of a column to 30 characters. The same thing will happen if you are using ODBC drivers from SQL Server 6.5 or earlier.

3. Decide the data type for each column. Because different columns store different types of information, the value should match the column type. A column that stores quantities should be defined as Integer, whereas a column that stores prices should be defined as Currency. Likewise, a column that stores dates should be defined accordingly. By default, SQL Server 2000 will use the data type *char*. You will learn more about data types later in this section.

That's all it takes to design a simple table. If later you decide that you need an additional column, you can always add one without affecting the structure, or the content, of the existing ones. You will see the tools for creating new databases from scratch, or editing existing databases, in the following chapter. You'll also learn about more advanced table design options, such as triggers and constraints.

TIP   Deleting a column is also referred to as dropping a column. Be careful when dropping columns from a database that's already in production. Although SQL Server 2000 now supports robust features for replicated data, such as maintaining data schema in the subscriber databases, you have to do it in a very specific way. Moreover, you can't drop columns if there is full-text indexing enabled on that column.

When you create a new table, a grid with the names and the attributes of the fields is displayed. Figure 2.8 shows the table design grid for SQL Server 2000. Each row in the grid corresponds to a table column.

FIGURE 2.8

Designing a table in SQL Server's Enterprise Manager

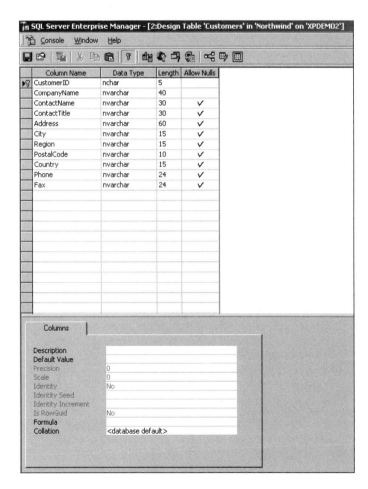

DETERMINING COLUMN DATA TYPES

Different DBMSs use different names for the data types they support, yet they support all the basic data types according to standards published by the American National Standards Institute (ANSI) and the International Organization for Standardization (ISO). In SQL Server, you select the column's data type—one of the values shown in the first column of Table 2.1—from a drop-down list. When you program against your database by using ADO.NET, the SQL Server data types equate to .NET Framework types, rather than the constants you once used with ADO 2.x. The .NET Framework types don't apply only to SQL Server; they are independent of their data source. For those of you who have worked with ADO 2.x, we have included the list of ADO constants for comparison. This table will help you understand the conversion between ADO 2.x, and ADO.NET and will help you understand how they relate back to OLE DB provider types, such as SQL Server.

TABLE 2.1: SQL SERVER DATA TYPES, .NET FRAMEWORK TYPES, AND ADO CONSTANTS

SQL SERVER	.NET FRAMEWORK TYPES	ADO 2.x CONSTANT
bigint	Int64	adBigInt
binary	Byte[]	adBinary
bit	Boolean	adBoolean
char	String	adChar
	Char[]	
datetime	DateTime	adDBTimeStamp
decimal	Decimal	adNumeric
float	Double	adDouble
image	Byte[]	adVarbinary
int	Int32	adInteger
money, smallmoney	Decimal	adCurrency
nchar, nvarchar, ntext	String	adWChar
	Char[]	
numeric	Decimal	adNumeric
real	Single	adSingle
smalldatetime	DateTime	adTimeStamp
smallint	Int16	adSmallInt
sql_variant	Object	adVariant
text	String	adChar
	Char[]	

Continued on next page

TABLE 2.1: SQL SERVER DATA TYPES, .NET FRAMEWORK TYPES, AND ADO CONSTANTS *(continued)*

SQL SERVER	.NET FRAMEWORK TYPES	ADO 2.X CONSTANT
timestamp	Byte[]	adBinary
tinyint	Byte[]	adVarbinary
uniqueidentifier	Guid	adGUID
varbinary	Byte[]	adVarBinary
varchar	String	adChar
	Char[]	

NEW SQL SERVER 2000 DATA TYPES

New!

SQL Server 2000 has introduced several new data types, most of which have serious advantages if you are considering making the move from SQL Server 7 code to SQL Server 2000. Here are a few pointers:

◆ The *bigint* data type is a 64-bit integer that you can use when your integers exceed the traditional maximum integer size. Note an important caveat: SQL Server will not convert the other integer types to bigint, so if you want to get a row count, you'll have to use the new SQL function ROWCOUNT_BIG, which returns a data type of bigint. Use the bigint judiciously, because it takes up 8 bytes of storage capacity, versus the 4 bytes used by the int data type.

◆ You should use the *nchar, nvarchar,* and *ntext* data types only when your application needs to support Unicode. (Unicode format is often used for non-English data storage.) Using Unicode support increases the size of your traditional char, varchar, and ntext values, so use these data types sparingly.

◆ The *sql_variant* data type converts to an Object type in the .NET Framework. It works almost like the Variant data type in VB6, except that it doesn't support all the SQL data types, such as text or image. It is useful with the new SQL Server 2000 feature, user-defined functions, which we explain in Chapter 5, "Transact-SQL." As with the bigint, be careful when using the sql_variant data type because it adversely affects performance. Another caveat is that sql_variant cannot be part of any keys or computed columns.

New!

Another new feature of SQL Server 2000 is the *table* data type. The table data type works as a local variable for storing rows and can be used in lieu of temporary tables. It cannot be used for column data types. Unlike temporary tables, the table data type is not written to the *tempdb* database and is instead stored in memory. Temporary tables cause performance degradation, which can be avoided by judicious use of the table data type. We talk more about this data type in Chapter 10, "The Role of XML."

You can also define *user-defined data types.* You can use the SQL Server 2000 data types as the base type for your own user-defined data types. For example, you could create a special zip code data type based on the char data type and name it accordingly. In the Pubs database, a user-defined data type is used to represent the employee ID as a `char` data type with a length of nine characters. You can see this user-defined data type, `empid`, from the SQL Server Enterprise Manager in the `User Defined Data Types` folder.

As you can see, there are many types to choose from. Here are some tips that can help you decide the best data type to use:

◆ Always choose the smallest data type to hold your data. For example, choose the `tinyint` instead of the `int` if you are storing only numbers 0 through 255. This not only reduces the amount of data you pass across the network, but also gives you more room in your data pages to store data rows and indexes. *Data pages* are 8KB units of storage in SQL Server.

◆ If you have a large string that has fewer than 8000 characters, use the `varchar` data type instead of the `text` data type because you will have better performance, with less overhead.

◆ Only use the *n*-prefixed data types (for example, `nvarchar`, `nchar`, `ntext`) if you need to support Unicode, because they take up more space and will slow down your server performance.

◆ Use `varchar` instead of `char` if you expect considerable changes in the length of your values. Although the `varchar` data type has more overhead, it can ultimately save more space, which will increase your performance. However, if you don't have much variation in the length, use the `char` data type because it will speed up processing.

New!

NOTE   *Prior to SQL Server 2000, larger data types were stored outside the row, on a separate data page. SQL Server would store a pointer in the row, rather than the actual data. Now, you can specify the new "text in row" property so that your `image`, `ntext`, and `text` data types are stored with the data row. If you expect your data to be small for these data types, definitely choose this option, because you will get faster performance and use less storage space.*

Data types are much richer in ADO.NET, providing greater interoperability, because they inherently support XML text streams rather than proprietary and binary COM data types. ADO.NET data types also improve performance because they eliminate the overhead of COM marshalling when transmitting data across the network. We discuss what goes on "under the covers" in detail in Chapter 6, "A First Look at ADO.NET."

ENTERING DATA INTO TABLES

There are many ways to enter data into a database's tables. You can use SQL statements; the `INSERT` statement appends a new row to a table and sets its fields to the value specified with the command. You can also open the actual table and edit it. Just right-click the name of a SQL server and choose Open Table ➢ Return All Rows from the shortcut menu. Of course, you can write applications that enable users to edit tables through a custom interface, such as Windows Forms or Web Forms. Obviously, this is the recommended method, because it enables you to validate the data and protect the database against user mistakes. You'll find a lot of information in this book on building practical, functional user interfaces with Visual Basic .NET and ASP.NET.

Null Values

If you're not familiar with database programming, you probably haven't used Null values yet, and you'll be surprised how important Null values are to databases. A *Null value* means that the actual field value is unknown. A numeric field with a zero value is not Null. Likewise, a blank string is not a Null value either. Nulls were introduced to deal with incomplete or exceptional data, and they should be handled in a special manner. A field that has not been assigned a value is considered incomplete. If this field is involved in an operation, the result of the operation is considered exceptional, because it's neither zero nor a blank string. When a new row is created, all of its nullable columns are set to Null, and unless you specify a value, they remain Null. You can modify this default behavior by requesting that certain columns can't be Null. If you attempt to add a new row with a Null value in a column that's not allowed to accept Nulls, the database will reject the insertion. The same will happen if you edit a row and set to Null the value of a column that's not allowed to accept Nulls. Another option is to set a *default definition* on that column. Default definitions enable you to pre-populate the column value for a new row.

Primary key fields (the fields that link tables to one another), for example, can never be Null. To specify that any other field cannot accept the Null value, you must set the `Allow Nulls` property in SQL Server to `False`.

If your tables contain Null values, you should be aware of how the DBMS handles them. When you total the values of a column with the `SUM()` function, Null values are ignored. If you count the rows with the `COUNT()` function, the Null fields are also ignored. The same is true for the `AVG()` function, which calculates the average value. If it treated the Null values as zeros, then the average would be wrong. The `AVG()` function returns the average of the fields that are not Null. If you want to include the Null values in the average, you must first replace them with the zero numeric value.

TIP   Where it is possible, limit the use of Nulls. Nulls can increase the complexity of your queries and adversely affect the performance of your database. The use of Nulls forces you to check for Nulls in your SQL statements so you don't perform operations on invalid data. In addition, comparison of Null values can result in an UNKNOWN *return, which adds a third element of logic to a* TRUE/FALSE *evaluation. Moreover, SQL Server 2000 will use more processing power and storage to store and process Nulls. This is because Nulls are treated as fixed-length data types. For example, if you would like to have a nullable* char *data type, opt to use the* varchar *data type instead, especially if you have large variations in the length of your data.*

Null values are so important in working with databases that SQL recognizes the keywords `IS NULL` and `IS NOT NULL`. (SQL statements are not case sensitive, but this book uses uppercase so that you can quickly spot the SQL keywords in the examples.) To exclude the Null values in an SQL statement, use the following clause:

```
WHERE column_name IS NOT NULL
```

You'll learn just about everything you need to know about SQL statements in Chapter 4, but here's a simple example of an SQL statement that retrieves the customers who have a postal code, ignoring those who don't:

```
SELECT CompanyName, Phone
FROM Customers
WHERE PostalCode IS NOT NULL
```

To retrieve the customers without a postal code, use a statement similar to this:

```
SELECT CompanyName, Phone
FROM Customers
WHERE PostalCode IS NULL
```

Indexes

OK, so you've created a few tables and have entered some data into them. Now the most important thing you can do with a database is extract data from it (or else, why store the information in the first place?). And we don't mean view all the customers or all the products. You'll rarely browse the rows of a single table. Instead, you should be interested in summary information that will help you make business decisions. You'll need answers to questions like "What's the most popular product in California?" or "What's the month with the largest sales for a specific product?" and so on. To retrieve this type of information, you must combine multiple tables. To answer the first question, you must locate all the customers in California, retrieve their orders, total the quantities of the items they have purchased, and then select the product with the largest sum of quantities. As you can guess, a DBMS must be able to scan the tables and locate the desired rows quickly. An index is nothing more than a mechanism for speeding up searches.

SQL Server uses a special technique, called *indexing*, to locate information very quickly. This technique requires that the data or data references be maintained in some order. This works just like the index at the back of this book, which uses page numbers as references. As you will see, the indexed rows in a database need not be in a specific physical order, as long as you can retrieve the references in a specific order. If you want to retrieve the name of the category of a specific product, the references to the rows of the Categories table must be ordered according to the CategoryID field. CategoryID links each row in the Products table to the corresponding row in the Categories table.

To search for a value in an ordered list, the DBMS compares the middle element of the list with the value you're looking for. If the value is larger than the middle element, you know that you need not search in the first (upper) half of the list. The same process is repeated with the bottom half of the list. Again, it compares the value with the middle element in the remaining list, and rejects one half of the list again. This process repeats until you're left with a single element. This element must be the one you're looking for.

This searching scheme is called a *binary search* and it's the basic idea behind indexing. To get an idea of the efficiency of this method, consider a list with 1024 elements. After the first comparison, the list is reduced to 512 elements. After the second search, the list is reduced to 256 elements. After the tenth comparison, the list is reduced to a single element. It takes only 10 comparisons to locate an element in a list with 1024 elements. If the list had a million elements, it would take just 20 comparisons.

Fortunately, you don't have to maintain the rows of the tables in any order yourself. The DBMS does it for you. You simply specify that a table maintains the rows in a specific order according to a column's value, and the DBMS will take over. SQL Server supports two types of indexing schemas: *clustered index* and *non-clustered indexes*. A clustered index maintains the actual data in order, whereas a non-clustered index does not maintain a specific order on the data. The DBMS can maintain multiple indexes for the same table. You might wish to search the products by name and supplier. It's customary to search for a customer by name, city, zip code, country, and so on. To speed up the searches, you maintain an index for each field you want to search.

TIP   *The best way to come up with an index is to examine the* WHERE *clause of your SQL statement. Generally, the items that appear in a* WHERE *clause are good candidates for indexing because they are used as search criteria. Foreign keys are often a good candidate for indexes, because they are often referenced to extract related data. In addition, the SQL Profiler and Index Tuning Wizard can help you identify areas that need indexing. SQL Server 2000 Query Analyzer introduces a new tool that uses a graphical interface to manage indexes. We discuss these tools in Chapter 3. You will learn more about the* WHERE *clause in Chapter 4.*

The binary search algorithm just described is a simplified description of how a DBMS locates items in an ordered list. As you have probably guessed, searching an ordered list is the easy part. The difficult part is to make sure that each time a new row is added (or edited), it's inserted in the proper place so that the table's rows are always ordered. The details of maintaining ordered lists are far more complicated. SQL Server uses a data structure known as *Balanced Trees (B-Trees)* to maintain the rows of a table in order at all times and search them. You need not understand what B-Trees are, because this is exactly what a DBMS does for you: it frees you from low-level details and enables you to focus on data, rather than the actual organization of the data on the disk.

The DBMS doesn't actually sort the rows of a table. It keeps a list of numbers, which reflects the order of the elements sorted according to a field. This list is the *index*. After a table has been indexed, every time you add a new row to the table, the table's indexes are updated accordingly. If you need to search a table in many ways, you can maintain multiple indexes on the same table. Keep in mind, you can have only one clustered index and up to 249 non-clustered indexes on a table. Indexes take additional storage room, so use them judiciously.

Indexes are manipulated by the DBMS, and all you have to do is define them. Every time a new row is added, or an existing row is deleted or edited, the table's indexes are automatically updated. You can use the index at any time to locate rows very quickly. Practically, indexes enable you to instantly select a row based on an indexed field. When searching for specific rows, the DBMS will automatically take into consideration any index that can speed the search.

EFFICIENCY ISSUES

Tables are not static objects. Most tables in a database change constantly: new rows are added, and existing rows are deleted or edited. This also means that the DBMS must constantly update the table indexes. This process can become quite a burden, so you shouldn't create too many indexes. On the other hand, indexes speed up lookup operations enormously. So, where do you draw the line?

One of the many tools that comes with SQL Server 7 and SQL Server 2000 is the Index Tuning Wizard, which helps you decide which indexes to keep and which ones to drop. The Index Tuning Wizard monitors the performance of the database, logs the necessary statistics, and tells you which indexes are responsible for most of the performance. These are the indexes you need in your database; the rest can be dropped at the price of slowing down some queries that are not used as frequently. The wizard can also create a script with the changes it suggests and implement them immediately. Keep in mind that indexes that worked well for previous versions of SQL Server might not be efficient for SQL Server 2000. Use the wizard to help resolve such issues. Chapter 14 covers the Index Tuning Wizard in more detail.

Views

In addition to tables, SQL Server 2000 supports views. A *view* is a virtual table: it looks and behaves just like a table (and in some cases, it can be updated too), but standard views do not exist as an object in the database. Views derive from *base tables.* Views come to life when you request them, and they're released when they're no longer needed. Any operations you perform on a view automatically translate into operations on the base table(s) from which the view is derived.

New!

NOTE SQL Server 2000 (Developer and Enterprise editions) enhances views by now allowing you to create indexed views. Indexed views work similarly to the table indexing we talked about in the previous section. Unlike standard views, which store only the source code, indexed views are stored as objects in the database. SQL Server treats these indexed views the same way it treats the base tables. A good time to use indexed views is when you are working with large data sets or multiple tables. You can improve performance by creating an index on the view to speed up processing, because now the view doesn't have to generate on the fly. Indexed views offer a fantastic benefit that you might not have considered. Even if you don't explicitly reference a view, when you pull data from a base table, SQL Server 2000 will determine and choose the fastest index—whether it comes from the base table or any derived views. To really take advantage of this new feature, try to select indexed views that can be used by many of your queries.

Views enhance the security of the database. Consider a personnel table, which stores information about employees, including their salaries and other sensitive information. Although most of the information is public (names, telephone extensions, departments, the projects each employee is involved with, and so on), some fields should be restricted to authorized users only. While you could split the table into smaller ones, SQL Server enables you to create unique views and assign access rights to those views to selected user groups.

You can also use views to hide the complexity introduced by the normalization process and the relationships between tables. Users don't really care about normalization rules or relationships. They would rather see a list of customer names, their orders, and the actual product names. This information exists in the database, but it could be scattered in four tables: `Customers`, `Orders`, `Order Details`, and `Products`. By defining a view on the database, you can maintain a structure that eases your development, yet gives the users the "table" they would rather see.

UPDATING TABLES AND VIEWS

Changes in the data of a view are reflected immediately to the underlying table(s). When the underlying tables change, however, these changes are not reflected immediately in the views based on them. Views are based on the data in the tables the moment the query was executed. You can think of them as a snapshot of time. A view that hides a few of its base table rows (or columns) can be updated, as long as it contains the primary key of the base table. (As we mentioned already, the primary key uniquely identifies a table's row. Without this piece of information, SQL Server wouldn't know which row to update.)

Some views cannot be updated. Views based on SQL statements that combine multiple tables and views that contain aggregate functions can't be updated. *Aggregate functions* such as `AVG()`, `COUNT()`, and `MAX()` are based on many rows, and SQL Server doesn't know which specific data row it must change.

Figure 2.9 shows a section of the Invoices view. (We hid many of the columns by setting their width to zero.) Start SQL Server's Enterprise Manager, open the `Northwind` database folder in the left pane, and click Views under the Northwind database name. The names of all the views defined for the database will be displayed in the right pane. To open a view, right-click on its name and select Open View ➢ Return All Rows from the shortcut menu.

FIGURE 2.9

The Invoices view displays the order details along with customer names and product names.

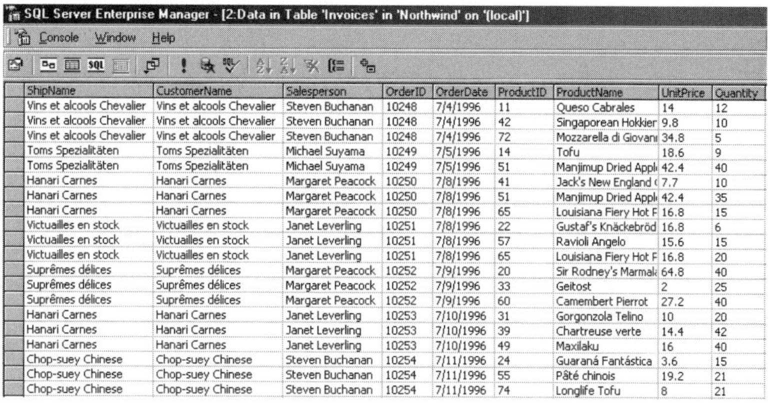

ShipName	CustomerName	Salesperson	OrderID	OrderDate	ProductID	ProductName	UnitPrice	Quantity
Vins et alcools Chevalier	Vins et alcools Chevalier	Steven Buchanan	10248	7/4/1996	11	Queso Cabrales	14	12
Vins et alcools Chevalier	Vins et alcools Chevalier	Steven Buchanan	10248	7/4/1996	42	Singaporean Hokkier	9.8	10
Vins et alcools Chevalier	Vins et alcools Chevalier	Steven Buchanan	10248	7/4/1996	72	Mozzarella di Giovani	34.8	5
Toms Spezialitäten	Toms Spezialitäten	Michael Suyama	10249	7/5/1996	14	Tofu	18.6	9
Toms Spezialitäten	Toms Spezialitäten	Michael Suyama	10249	7/5/1996	51	Manjimup Dried Appl	42.4	40
Hanari Carnes	Hanari Carnes	Margaret Peacock	10250	7/8/1996	41	Jack's New England (	7.7	10
Hanari Carnes	Hanari Carnes	Margaret Peacock	10250	7/8/1996	51	Manjimup Dried Appl	42.4	35
Hanari Carnes	Hanari Carnes	Margaret Peacock	10250	7/8/1996	65	Louisiana Fiery Hot F	16.8	15
Victuailles en stock	Victuailles en stock	Janet Leverling	10251	7/8/1996	22	Gustaf's Knäckebröd	16.8	6
Victuailles en stock	Victuailles en stock	Janet Leverling	10251	7/8/1996	57	Ravioli Angelo	15.6	15
Victuailles en stock	Victuailles en stock	Janet Leverling	10251	7/8/1996	65	Louisiana Fiery Hot F	16.8	20
Suprêmes délices	Suprêmes délices	Margaret Peacock	10252	7/9/1996	20	Sir Rodney's Marmal	64.8	40
Suprêmes délices	Suprêmes délices	Margaret Peacock	10252	7/9/1996	33	Geitost	2	25
Suprêmes délices	Suprêmes délices	Margaret Peacock	10252	7/9/1996	60	Camembert Pierrot	27.2	40
Hanari Carnes	Hanari Carnes	Janet Leverling	10253	7/10/1996	31	Gorgonzola Telino	10	20
Hanari Carnes	Hanari Carnes	Janet Leverling	10253	7/10/1996	39	Chartreuse verte	14.4	42
Hanari Carnes	Hanari Carnes	Janet Leverling	10253	7/10/1996	49	Maxilaku	16	40
Chop-suey Chinese	Chop-suey Chinese	Steven Buchanan	10254	7/11/1996	24	Guaraná Fantástica	3.6	15
Chop-suey Chinese	Chop-suey Chinese	Steven Buchanan	10254	7/11/1996	55	Pâté chinois	19.2	21
Chop-suey Chinese	Chop-suey Chinese	Steven Buchanan	10254	7/11/1996	74	Longlife Tofu	8	21

Try editing the data in the Invoices view to see how it behaves. Bring the `CustomerName` column into view, change the name *Hanari Carnes* into uppercase, and then move to another cell. The customer's name changes, not only in the open view, but in the base table as well. If you opened the `Customers` table, you would see that the changes have already been committed to the database. Yet, the remaining instances of the same name on the view didn't change. That's because the view isn't refreshed constantly. Because SQL Server doesn't maintain a "live" link to the database, it can't update the view every time.

Things can get even worse. Locate another instance of the same customer in the view and change the name to *Hanny Carnes.* As soon as you move to another cell, the following message will pop up:

```
Data has changed since the Results pane was last updated. Do you
want to save your changes now?
Click Yes to save your changes and update the database
Click No to discard your changes and refresh the Results pane
Click Cancel to continue editing
```

What's happened here? The name of the customer you read from the database was Hanari Carnes, and you changed it to uppercase. This change was committed to the `Customers` table. Then you attempted to change the name Hanari Carnes into something else again, and SQL Server attempted to update the Customers table for a second time. This time, SQL Server didn't find the name Hanari Carnes there; it had already been changed (to HANARI CARNES). And that's exactly what the message tells you. You have attempted to change a field, but its original value is no longer the same as when it was read.

Of course it isn't. You just changed it, right? But SQL Server doesn't keep track of who's changing what in the database. For all it knows, the changes could have been made by another user, so it simply tells you that the record you're about to change is no longer the same. Imagine if this was a seat reservation application. You'd assign the same seat to two different customers. When you change a row in a table, you must be sure that the row hasn't changed since you last read it.

Confusing? Welcome to the world of database programming! As you can understand, this behavior is not unique to views. It's a major issue in database programming known as *concurrency control*. In a multiuser environment, there's always a risk of two or more people attempting to update the same information at once. The behavior you just witnessed is actually a feature of the database: it lets you know that someone else has already changed the row you read. Otherwise, you'd have to implement the same logic from within your application. We've introduced you to one of the most troublesome aspects of database programming. You'll find more information on the topic of concurrency control and how to handle simultaneous updates in Chapter 11, "More ADO.NET Programming."

Establishing Relationships

After the information has been broken up logically into separate tables, you must establish relationships between the tables, which is the essence of the relational database model. To relate tables to each other, you use fields with common values.

PRIMARY AND FOREIGN KEYS

Primary and foreign keys are one way of ensuring data integrity. The `Categories` table has a `CategoryID` field, which holds a value that identifies each category. This value must be unique for each row of the `Categories` table, and it's the table's primary key. The `Products` table also has a `CategoryID` field, which is set to the ID of the product's category. The two fields have the same name, but this is not a requirement. It's just a convenience. The mere existence of the two fields doesn't mean that the two tables are related to each other. You must specify how the tables will be related, as well as which field is the primary key and which field is the foreign key. As we already discussed, the primary key is unique to each row, while the foreign key may appear in more than one row. This relationship is called one-to-many, because a single row of the `Categories` table is usually pointed to by multiple rows of the `Products` table.

BE CAREFUL WHEN APPLYING FOREIGN KEYS

Be judicious in your use of foreign keys. Too many foreign keys can cause *deadlocking* because they not only lock the table that they reference, but they also make it hard for data to resolve itself. Deadlocking occurs when units of processing, or *threads*, hold onto resources, causing bottlenecks for the other threads waiting to use those same resources. SQL Server 2000 can identify and terminate deadlocks. Even so, you might not accomplish what you originally wanted to do. For example, if your DELETE query has to go through more than 16 foreign key validations, it will end up timing out, and you won't be able to delete the desired entry. You would end up with a deadlock on not only the table containing the foreign key, but also the table containing the primary key referenced by the foreign key. You might think that you could get around this by disabling the foreign key constraints, but unfortunately, you can do this only on INSERT and UPDATE statements.

Continued on next page

BE CAREFUL WHEN APPLYING FOREIGN KEYS *(continued)*

Consider another caveat. If you would like to track who created your customer records, you could create a column in your `Customers` table called `CreateUserID`. This column stores the foreign key reference to `UserID` in the `Users` table. However, what if you also wanted to track who updates your customer data? It would be nice to add another foreign key column, `UpdateUserID`, that points to the `UserID` in the `Users` table. Unfortunately, SQL Server doesn't allow you to have more than one foreign key relationship between two tables. You could add some validation code to your INSERT statement, but that would really hinder performance. The other alternative is to make sure your application logic outside the database ensures that invalid IDs are not added.

Figure 2.10 shows how SQL Server depicts relationships between tables. To view the relationships between the tables of a database, start the Enterprise Manager and open the Northwind database in the left pane. Right-click the Diagrams icon under the database's name and select New Diagram. The Database Diagram Wizard pops up. Select the `Orders` and `Customers` tables from the available table list and finish the wizard. The Relationships diagram will appear in a new window. Each table is represented by a list box with the table's field names, and the relationships between tables are represented by arrows. On one end of the arrow is the key icon, which indicates the primary key. On the other end of the arrow is the infinity symbol, which indicates the table with the foreign key. The infinity symbol means that there can be many rows pointing to the row with the primary key.

FIGURE 2.10

The `CustomerID` field in the `Orders` table is the foreign key, which points to the primary key in the `Customers` table.

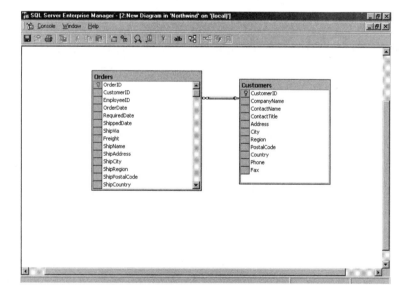

Here's a simple SQL statement that retrieves the orders placed by the customer Alfreds Futterkiste:

```
SELECT * FROM Orders, Customers
WHERE Customers.CompanyName = 'Alfreds Futterkiste' AND
    Orders.CustomerID = Customers.CustomerID
```

This statement tells the DBMS to retrieve the rows of the Orders and Customers tables that match the following criteria:

◆ The customer's CompanyName field is the customer's name.

and

◆ The foreign key in the Orders table matches the primary key in the Customers table.

This query will return all the rows of the Orders and Customers tables whose CustomerID field is the same as the CustomerID field of the specified customer's row. Primary and foreign keys are used to match rows in two tables. (The asterisk is a special character that means "all the fields." You could have specified a comma-separated list of the desired fields in the place of the asterisk.)

You can use foreign keys to prevent deletions if there are related records, as already explained. Foreign keys are also useful to prevent inserts or updates to records if there is no parent record. For example, if you tried to insert an order detail to an order that didn't exist, foreign key constraints would prevent this from happening.

VIEWING AND EDITING RELATIONSHIPS

You can modify the relationship from this same Relationships diagram. To delete a relationship, right-click the line that joins the two tables and select Delete Relationship From Database. To view or edit the properties of the relationship, again, right-click the line that joins the tables and select the Properties option. The Properties window specifies the primary and foreign keys, the relationship name, and some other options.

IDENTITY AND IDENTITY INCREMENT

SQL Server can automatically increment the value of the primary key, every time you add a new row. SQL Server uses the term *Identity* for this data type. You can specify the initial value of an Identity field and its increment amount by using the *Identity seed* and the *Identity Increment* properties respectively. To use the Identity data type, your column needs to be a numeric value such as bigint, decimal, int, numeric, smallint, or tinyint. Refer to the earlier section, "Database Objects," for an explanation of these data types.

To create the new value for an Identity field, the DBMS adds a value (usually 1, which is the default value) to the last value of this field in the same table. This operation is simple in principle, but it would be quite a task if you had to implement it on your own. With many users adding rows to the same table, you'd have to lock the table, read the last row's Identity value, add the proper increment, and then commit the newly added row.

GUIDs

As you can see in the Northwind example, the `CustomerID` is a string, created from the company name. Keep in mind that it is much easier to have an integer represent a primary key, because keeping an integer unique by incrementing the number is easier than ensuring that your algorithm for generating keys stays unique. Numeric IDs provide a unique identifier for a single record, making it much easier to merge disparate sources of data with minimal conflicts. However, they are certainly not globally unique.

Integers as primary keys are easy to use and very useful; however, they have limits, especially if you are dealing with heterogeneous data sources. An integer primary key is unique only to the table from which it was generated. Globally Unique Identifiers (GUIDs) should be used when you need an identifier across a database or multiple databases. A good example for using GUIDs is when you need to combine data from multiple databases into a single reporting system.

Lately, GUIDs have become popular as primary key data types. Microsoft has embraced the concept of GUIDs as primary keys in its release of Active Directory. This triggered an evolution from using numeric identity columns to using GUIDs.

In SQL Server, the `uniqueidentifier` data type designates GUIDs. Keep in mind that SQL Server doesn't automatically generate these values for you. An easy way to program this is to designate a *default* on the column that uses the `NEWID()` function to generate a value for you.

MORE COMPLICATED RELATIONS

Not all relations can be resolved with a pair of primary and foreign keys. Let's say you're designing a database for storing book titles. The structure of the table with the titles is rather obvious. The relationship between titles and publishers is also obvious: each title has a single publisher, and the same publisher might appear in multiple titles. The relationship between publishers and titles is called one-to-many. Conversely, the relationship between titles and publishers is called many-to-one, because multiple titles might point to the same publisher. One-to-many and many-to-one relationships interpret relationships in a similar fashion—both follow the order of the related tables when asserting the type of relationship.

But how about the relationship between titles and authors? Each book has a varying number of authors: some books have no author, and others might have six authors. Likewise, the same author might have written more than one title. The relationship between titles and authors is called many-to-many. To establish a direct relationship between the `titles` and `authors` tables, some rows in the `titles` table should point to many rows in the `authors` table. Likewise, some rows in the `authors` table should point to many rows in the `titles` table. To avoid this type of relationship in your design, introduce a new table, which is linked with a one-to-many relationship to the `titles` table and a many-to-one relationship to the `authors` table.

This example introduces an intermediate table between the `titles` and `authors` tables: the `titleauthor` table, which contains one row per title-author pair, as shown in Figure 2.11. This table has a simple structure (you could say that it doesn't even contain any original information). It simply maps books to authors. If a book has three authors, you add three rows to the `titleauthor` table. All rows have the same ISBN (the title's key) and the authors' ID keys.

Intermediate tables such as the `titleauthor` table are common in database design. Practically, there's no other method of implementing many-to-many relations between tables.

FIGURE 2.11

Connecting the
titles table
to the authors
table with an
intermediate table,
the titleauthor
table

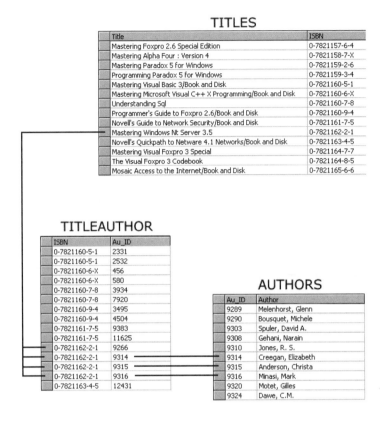

TITLES

Title	ISBN
Mastering Foxpro 2.6 Special Edition	0-7821157-6-4
Mastering Alpha Four : Version 4	0-7821158-7-X
Mastering Paradox 5 for Windows	0-7821159-2-6
Programming Paradox 5 for Windows	0-7821159-3-4
Mastering Visual Basic 3/Book and Disk	0-7821160-5-1
Mastering Microsoft Visual C++ X Programming/Book and Disk	0-7821160-6-X
Understanding Sql	0-7821160-7-8
Programmer's Guide to Foxpro 2.6/Book and Disk	0-7821160-9-4
Novell's Guide to Network Security/Book and Disk	0-7821161-7-5
Mastering Windows Nt Server 3.5	0-7821162-2-1
Novell's Quickpath to Netware 4.1 Networks/Book and Disk	0-7821163-4-5
Mastering Visual Foxpro 3 Special	0-7821164-7-7
The Visual Foxpro 3 Codebook	0-7821164-8-5
Mosaic Access to the Internet/Book and Disk	0-7821165-6-6

TITLEAUTHOR

ISBN	Au_ID
0-7821160-5-1	2331
0-7821160-5-1	2532
0-7821160-6-X	456
0-7821160-6-X	580
0-7821160-7-8	3934
0-7821160-7-8	7920
0-7821160-9-4	3495
0-7821160-9-4	4504
0-7821161-7-5	9383
0-7821161-7-5	11625
0-7821162-2-1	9266
0-7821162-2-1	9314
0-7821162-2-1	9315
0-7821162-2-1	9316
0-7821163-4-5	12431

AUTHORS

Au_ID	Author
9289	Melenhorst, Glenn
9290	Bousquet, Michele
9303	Spuler, David A.
9308	Gehani, Narain
9310	Jones, R. S.
9314	Creegan, Elizabeth
9315	Anderson, Christa
9316	Minasi, Mark
9320	Motet, Gilles
9324	Dawe, C.M.

Normalization Rules

By now you have a good idea as to how relational databases are designed, and you could easily design
a simple relational database yourself by using the information discussed earlier and your common
sense. Most important, you should be able to understand how information is stored in a database by
looking at its relational diagram.

However, there are a few rules in relational database design, known as the *normalization rules*. These
rules will help you design a normalized database, or at least verify your design. A database is *normalized* if it doesn't repeat information and doesn't exhibit update and delete anomalies. Although the
number of these rules varies, the basic normalization rules are just three: the first, second, and third
normalization rules. Don't be surprised, however, if you find as many as half a dozen normalization
rules listed within a particular database standard.

A table normalized according to the first rule is said to be in *first normal form (1NF)*. A table normalized according to the second rule is said to be in *second normal form (2NF)*. Notice that a table must
be in 1NF before you can apply the second normalization rule. Finally, a table that's in 2NF can be
normalized according to the third rule, in which case it's said to be in *third normal form (3NF)*. Higher

normal forms are often used with very specific and rare situations, which most programmers handle on an individual basis.

TIP   *Normalization applies to OLTP rather than OLAP systems. However, even in an OLTP system, there is a trade-off between normalization and performance. You might sometimes want to de-normalize some of your tables if you find that the tables are accessed for read-only purposes and the performance isn't satisfactory.*

Database Design Errors

To help you understand the need for database normalization, this section illustrates a few common mistakes in database design. These mistakes are so obvious that it doesn't take a degree in computer science to understand why and how to avoid them. Yet the same mistakes are repeated over and over. You'll find it easy to spot the mistakes in the example designs, which are small in size. In larger databases, even ones with a few dozen tables, it's not as simple to spot the same mistakes.

Let's start with the following simple table for storing information about books:

```
Table Title
ISBN   Title   Pages   Topic
```

This table seems perfectly good, until you decide to add a second topic to a title. A book about HTML could be classified under the category "programming," but also under the category "Internet." To add multiple topics, you'd have to repeat each title's data for each category:

```
0144489890   Total .NET   850   programming
0144489890   Total .NET   850   Internet
```

The problem with this table is that certain information is repeated (actually, most of the information is repeated). The primary objective in designing OLTP databases is to avoid duplication of information. To avoid this unnecessary duplication, you must move the topics to another table. Some of you might consider adding columns for multiple topics, but then you must make an (arbitrary) assumption as to the maximum number of topics per title and come up with a table like the following one:

```
Table Title
ISBN   Title   Pages   Topic1   Topic2   Topic3
```

This table is even worse. In trying to avoid duplicating the table's data, you've introduced duplication of information in the structure of the table itself. As you will see, the first rule in database design is to avoid groups of columns with information of the same type. If you decide to change the name of the "programming" category to something else, for example, "computer languages," you'd have to change too many rows, in too many places. Some titles might have "programming" under Topic1, others under Topic2, and so on.

Another common mistake people make is to create a Boolean flag. Often, as a database matures, more types are added. A lazy approach is to create a bunch of columns rather than a whole new table as seen in the next example.

Table Title
ISBN Title Pages ProgrammingTopic InternetTopic

You end up with data that looks like the following:

```
0144489890   Total .NET   850   0 1
0144489890   Total .NET   850   1 0
```

But as you can already deduce, this isn't a very scalable design. As more topics are added, the actual design of the database will have to change.

To solve the problem of multiple columns of the same type, you introduce two new tables, as shown here:

Table Title
ISBN   Title   Pages
Table TitleTopic
ISBN   TopicID
Table Topic
TopicID   TopicName

This design uses a table that stores topics only. To change the description of a topic, you must change a single row in the Topic table. Topics are related to titles through the TitleTopic table, the link table. If a title must be classified under multiple topics, you insert multiple lines in the TitleTopic table. To find out the topics of a specific title, use its ISBN to search the TitleTopic table and extract the rows whose ISBN matches the ISBN of the book. You'll end up with none, one, or a few rows of the TitleTopic table. Use the TopicID of these lines to locate the topic(s) of the title. Sounds complicated? It's simpler than it sounds, because all tables are appropriately indexed, and the DBMS will perform the necessary searches for you.

UPDATE AND DELETE ANOMALIES

Now drop the Topic column from your original table design and add some publication information. Here's the structure of another table that holds information about books:

Table Title
ISBN   Title   Pages   PubYear   Publisher   PubAddress

Notice that the publisher's address doesn't belong to the Title table. This structure can lead to two highly undesirable situations:

◆ If a publisher relocates, then you must change the address in not one, but hundreds, perhaps thousands, of records. This is known as an *update anomaly*. If you forget to change the publisher's address in a few records, the database will contain bad information. This situation can be avoided by moving the publishers to a different table.

◆ Even worse, if you delete the last book of a publisher, you will lose all the information about the specific publisher. This situation is known as a *delete anomaly*, and it can also be avoided by moving the publishers to a different table.

Here's a better structure for storing the same information:

Table Title
```
ISBN    Title    Pages    PubYear    PublisherID
```

Table Publisher
```
PublisherID    Publisher    PubAddress
```

The `PublisherID` field is a unique number that identifies a publisher, and it must have the same value in both tables. To find out a title's publisher, you retrieve the `PublisherID` field from the `Title` table and then locate the row in the `Publisher` table that has the same value in its `PublisherID` field. In effect, the `PublisherID` field in the `Publisher` table is the primary key (it cannot appear in more than one row), and the `PublisherID` fields in the `Title` table are the foreign keys (they can appear in many rows).

OK, this is pretty obvious, but why did you have to introduce a new field? Couldn't you use the publisher's name to relate the two tables? Had you used the publisher's name as a key, then you wouldn't be able to change the publisher's name in a single place. If Drennan Press is incorporated and changes its name to Drennan Press Inc., you should be able to change the publisher's name in a single place to avoid update anomalies.

Using a number to identify each row in a table is a common practice. Numeric IDs need not be changed, so they will not cause any update anomalies. Assuming names do not change is dangerous in database design. Companies merge, they incorporate, and you can't assume their names won't change. Even when such an assumption might appear reasonable, you shouldn't base the design of a database on an assumption.

First Normal Form

This rule is simple. It says that a table shouldn't contain repeating groups. Here's a table that contains all the mistakes of the previous (unacceptable) designs. Let's start with the repeating groups (the book's topics):

```
ISBN  Title  Pages  Publisher  PubAddress  Topic1  Topic2
```

To remove a group from a table, keep the first column of the group and repeat the additional topics in multiple rows of the table. A title with two topics will be stored in this table as follows:

```
ISBN          Title        Pages   Publisher   Topic
01254889391   SQL Server   850     Sybex       Programming
01254889391   SQL Server   850     Sybex       Databases
```

NOTE *The first row in the preceding code contains field names, and the following rows are data. We have omitted the* `PubAddress` *column to shorten the lines.*

The first normal form doesn't require that a table be broken into multiple tables. It turns some of the table's columns into additional rows. This structure has the following advantages:

No empty fields   If a title belongs to a single topic, then the fields `Topic2` and `Topic3` in the example would be empty.

No artificial limitations   If a specific title should be located under half a dozen categories, you can add as many lines as necessary to the table.

We've discussed the shortcomings of this design already. The table design is in first normalized form, and you must now apply the second normalization rule.

Second Normal Form

The second normalization rule says that any fields that do not depend fully on the primary key should be moved to another table. The Topic field in the last table structure is not functionally dependent on the ISBN (the primary key). *Functionally dependent* means that a field is fully determined by the key. A book's page count is functionally dependent on the book's ISBN. If you know the book's ISBN, you can determine the book's page count uniquely. The same is true for the book's publication year. But the topic is not dependent on the ISBN, because the same ISBN can lead to multiple topics.

The second normalization rule requires that the topics be moved to a different table:

```
Table Title
ISBN   Title   Pages   Publisher   PubAddress
Table TitleTopic
ISBN   Topic
```

Now, why is this better than the previous table structure? The same ISBN can lead to multiple topics. The TitleTopic table doesn't repeat information. Only the primary key is repeated, and you can't avoid it. A single title might have multiple topics. This is a one-to-many relationship, and you can't avoid the duplication of the primary key.

However, there's a problem with this table, too. Because a book's topic is described with a string, you haven't avoided the update anomaly. If you change the description of a category, you'd have to change many rows in the TitleTopic table. To avoid the update anomaly, you must create a separate table with the topics and assign a unique ID to each topic:

```
Table Topic
TopicID   Topic
```

To connect each title to one or more topics, you must change the TitleTopic table that connects the Title and Topic tables. The TitleTopic table must contain pairs of ISBNs and topic IDs:

```
Table TitleTopic
ISBN   TopicID
```

Third Normal Form

The third normalization rule says that there should be no dependency between non-key fields. In the preceding table design, you have such a dependency. The publisher's address depends on the publisher, not the book's ISBN. To remove this type of dependency, you must move the publisher information to another table. Because each book must have a publisher, you add the PubID field to the Title table and to the new table with the publishers. The PubID field of the Title table must have the same value as the PubID field in the Publisher table. Here's the original table in the third normal form:

```
Table Title
ISBN   Title   Pages   PubID
```

```
Table Publisher
PubID    PubAddress
Table Topic
TopicID    Topic
Table TitleTopic
ISBN    TopicID
```

Figure 2.12 shows the final tables and the relationships between them. As you can see, the normalization rules are simple and resemble the practical rules we derived earlier based on our intuition and common sense. The second and third rules are almost identical—some people combine them into a single rule. The difference is that the second rule removes the dependencies between the fields and the primary key: you test the dependency of each field against the key field. The third rule removes the dependencies between fields other than the key field.

To summarize, you must use your common sense to split your data into separate tables. Use a separate table for each entity. Then establish relationships between tables (if they can be related, of course). In the process, you might need to introduce additional tables to connect the basic tables of your design. Some tables can't be linked directly. At each stage, apply the three normalization rules to your tables to make sure your database is normalized.

FIGURE 2.12

A normalized database's relational diagram

NORMALIZATION AND JOINS

Let's return to the Northwind database for a moment and see how the DBMS uses relations. Each time you connect two tables with a common key, the DBMS must perform an operation known as *join*. It logically joins the two tables by using the primary and foreign keys. Joins are quite expensive operations, and you should try to minimize them. You must also see that the foreign keys used in the join operations are indexed, to help the DBMS with the lookup operations. Some databases might use as many as a few dozen joins to get the desired results out of the database—very slow operations.

As you might notice, a conflict exists between normalization and the performance of joins. In a very large database, you might end up with too many related tables, which also means a large number of joins. Many database administrators and programmers will de-normalize their databases a little to reduce the number of joins in the queries. Although this is a rather common practice, don't base the design of your databases on this premise. If you ever design a database with many tables, you might have to trade off some normalization for fewer joins.

Continued on next page

NORMALIZATION AND JOINS *(continued)*

When you do use joins, make sure that they are efficient. Here are a couple tips on making sure your joins work well:

◆ Try to join only numeric columns.

◆ It's better to join columns that are the same data type. This way, SQL Server can do the comparison more quickly.

◆ Try to limit your joins on columns that have unique values. SQL Server can ignore the index if most of your data is not unique.

◆ Keep your join column length as small as you can.

◆ Don't put indexes on data with a small number of rows, because it would be faster for SQL Server to scan the table rather than use the index.

Previous versions of SQL Server had a limit of 16 joins in a single SQL statement. SQL Server 2000 supports a larger number of joins, but even 16 joins are too many. If an operation requires too many joins, you could replace them with subqueries. *Subqueries* are queries that are nested within a query and in some cases might yield faster performance than a join. We discuss subqueries in more detail in Chapters 4 and 5. If some of your queries require excessive joins, you should probably revise the design of the database. For more information on joins, see the "Joining Tables" section in Chapter 4.

Database Integrity

The major challenge in database design is maintaining the integrity of the database. Designing a database is only the beginning; you must also make sure that you keep the database in good shape at all times. The burden of keeping a database in good shape is shared by the database administrator (DBA) and the programmers. As a programmer, you must make sure that all the data your code places into the database is valid. This is quite a task and would require an enormous amount of validation, but, as you'll learn in this section, the database itself can help.

Modern databases include tools that enable you to protect the integrity of the database from within. SQL Server, for example, by letting you incorporate rules that enforce database integrity. By specifying each column's type, you're actually telling the database not to accept any data that doesn't conform. If a user or an application attempts to assign a numeric value to a field that stores dates, the database will reject the value to protect data integrity.

The rules for enforcing the integrity of a database can be classified into three categories, which are described next.

Domain Integrity

The first, and simplest, type of integrity is *domain integrity*, a fancy term that means each column must have a specific data type. If a column holds dates, then users shouldn't be allowed to store integers or Boolean values in this column. As you already know, when you create a table, you must declare the data type for each column. If you attempt to assign a value of the wrong type to a column, the database will reject the operation and raise a trappable runtime error. As far as your application is concerned, you can either test the data type of a user-supplied value against the column's data type, or intercept the runtime error that will be raised and act accordingly.

Entity Integrity

The second type of integrity is *entity integrity*. This means that an entity (a customer, product, invoice, and so on) must have a unique column, such as a primary key, identifying the entity with a valid value. If a table's primary key is Null, then no rows in other tables can connect to this row. All DBMSs can enforce this type of integrity by not allowing the insertion of rows with Null keys, or by preventing changes that would result in a Null value for a primary key. All you have to do to enforce this type of integrity is to choose a column type (such as primary key or identity properties) that does not allow Nulls.

Referential Integrity

Referential integrity (RI) is one of the most important topics in database design. Designing the database is a rather straightforward process, once you understand the information that will be stored in the database, how you will retrieve it, and the relations among the various tables. Just as important, if not more important, is ensuring that the various relationships remain valid at all times.

Relationships are based on primary and foreign keys. What will happen if the primary key in a relationship is deleted? If you delete a row in the `Customers` table, for instance, then some orders will become orphaned; they will refer to a customer who doesn't exist. Your applications will keep working, but every now and then you'll get incorrect results. Nothing will go wrong in calculating the total for an existing customer, for example.

If you calculate the grand total for all customers, you'll get one value. If you calculate the grand total for all the detail lines, you'll get a different value. This inconsistency shouldn't exist in a database. After you realize that your database is in an inconsistent state, you must start examining every table to find out why and when it happened and what other reports are unusable. This is a major headache that you want to avoid. And it's simple to avoid such problems by enforcing the database's referential integrity.

Problems related to the referential integrity of the database can be intermittent, too. If the deleted customer hasn't placed an order in the last 12 months, all the totals you calculate for the last 12 months will be correct. If you receive a (very) late payment from this customer, however, you won't be able to enter it into the database. There's no customer to link the payment to!

Enforcing Referential Integrity

Primary and foreign keys are a form of *declarative referential integrity (DRI)*. This means that you can create this integrity by adding constraints to the table design. *Constraints* are exactly what you think they are—a way of preventing an action from occurring.

If you enforce the integrity of the relationship between `Customers` and `Orders`, for example, when an application attempts to delete a customer, the database will raise a runtime error and not allow the deletion of the record. If the customer has no orders in the `Orders` table, then the application will be allowed to delete the customer. This action will not impair the integrity of the database, because there are no related rows.

TIP *Enforcing referential integrity is expensive. High performance database systems often remove referential integrity on their production machines in order to increase speed. Of course, this is done only after the database has been fully tested to ensure that there is no chance for data corruption.*

The good news is that you don't need to write any code to enforce referential integrity. When you specify a relationship, you can also specify that the integrity of the relationship be enforced.

SQL Server enforces referential integrity by rejecting any changes in the primary key if this key is referenced by another table. Open the Properties window of a relationship by right-clicking the arrow that represents the relationship between two tables in the Relationships diagram and then selecting Properties from the shortcut menu. Click the Relationships tab, which is shown in Figure 2.13, and check Enforce Relationship For INSERTs And UPDATEs. The Check Existing Data On Creation option is valid when you create a new relationship between two tables that contain data already. It tells SQL Server to make sure that existing data does not violate the new relationship.

You can also use triggers to enforce referential integrity. Generally, using DRI is much more efficient than using triggers for RI. You would use triggers when you are trying to enforce cross-database referential integrity because DRI does not support it.

With SQL Server 2000, you now have the ability to create expanded programmatic referential integrity with cascading updates and deletes. This is a new feature of SQL Server 2000. You will explore both of these options next.

FIGURE 2.13

Specifying the properties of a relationship in a SQL Server database

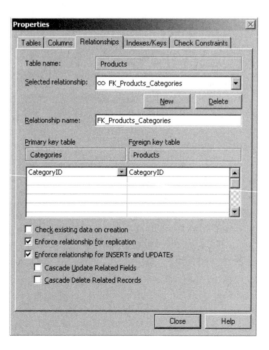

CASCADING REFERENTIAL INTEGRITY

Imagine you try to delete an order that has order details associated to it. The foreign keys in Northwind would prevent you from doing this. You would have to first delete the associated order details, then delete the order itself. With cascading deletes, you can opt to programmatically delete the order details with the order. Now you have a choice to *cascade updates* and *cascade deletes* from the referred table (for example, `Order Details`) to the table it refers to (for example, `Orders`).

New!

NOTE   *As you can see from Figure 2.13, SQL Server 2000 supports cascading referential integrity constraints for updates and deletes, based on ANSI specifications. If you have worked with Access, this feature might be familiar to you; but until now, it was not supported in SQL Server.*

When the Cascade Delete option is in effect and you delete an order, all related rows in every table in the database will also be deleted. If you use cascade deletes to enforce referential integrity, then all the orders placed by the specific customer in the `Orders` table will also be deleted. As each row in the `Orders` table is deleted, it must take with it all the related rows in the `Order Details` table as well.

Cascading updates are a less drastic method of enforcing referential integrity. When you change the value of a primary key, SQL Server 2000 changes the foreign keys in all tables related to the updated table. If you change a customer's ID, for example, SQL Server will change the `OrderID` field in the `Orders` table for all orders placed by that customer.

Cascading referential integrity offers greater performance value than using triggers. If you are upgrading a pre–SQL Server 2000 database, then you should consider migrating your referential integrity triggers to utilize cascading updates and deletes instead. Actually, this is one of the top reasons to migrate over to SQL Server 2000 from previous versions.

You will learn more about the syntax of how you would do this in Chapter 4.

TRIGGERS

A *trigger* is a special stored procedure that's invoked automatically, like an event. For example, you can write a trigger that runs every time a row is updated and takes the appropriate action. Triggers are commonly used to store information about the changes made to a table's rows, such as the name of the user and the time of the action. In the case of deletions, the trigger could save the original row into an auditing table.

Triggers are implemented in T-SQL, an extension of SQL (which is covered in detail in Chapter 5). T-SQL is a mix of SQL statements and more traditional programming statements such as control flow statements, loop structures, and so on. Chapter 5 discusses the `CascadeCustomerDelete` trigger, which is invoked automatically every time a row is deleted in the `Customers` table. This trigger deletes all the rows in the `Order Details` table that correspond to customer orders being deleted. After the detail lines have been deleted, the trigger deletes the rows of the `Orders` table that correspond to orders placed by the same customer. Because the details of these orders no longer exist, you can delete the order without violating the integrity of the database. Finally, the trigger deletes a row from the `Customers` table.

New!

NOTE   *SQL Server 2000 greatly enhances the power of triggers with the* INSTEAD OF *and* AFTER *triggers.* INSTEAD OF *triggers give you a new ability to update views, which never existed in SQL Server before. You will learn more about these new features in Chapter 5.*

Summary

This concludes the introduction to database design. You've learned about important database concepts such as normalization, database integrity, and data types. We discussed how these concepts can be implemented with the use of relationships, primary and foreign keys, and column data types. You will rely on these concepts throughout the book as you learn how to build your own database systems by using VS .NET.

In the following chapter, you will learn to use the visual database tools. Visual Studio .NET provides a fantastic unified IDE for working with both VB .NET code and your SQL databases. Now that you've reviewed the fundamentals, it's time to begin working with the tools that will enable you to design databases.

Chapter 3

The Visual Database Tools

- A first look at the visual database tools
- Data access strategies
- Using connection strings
- Connecting to databases
- Using the Server Explorer
- Using the Database Designer
- Using the Query Designer
- Using the SQL Editor
- Using the Component Designer
- Using the XML Designer

SO FAR, YOU'VE LEARNED about normalization, basic database objects, and the principles of relational databases. Before you start building database applications by using VB .NET to access a database, you should look at the visual database tools. Visual Studio .NET (VS .NET) makes a tremendous leap at unifying the integrated development environment (IDE) for all languages. In this chapter, you will learn about the shared development environment in VS .NET as well as explore traditional database tools, such as the Enterprise Manager and Query Analyzer in SQL Server 2000. You will learn how to connect to a database from VS .NET and use the VS .NET tools to generate VB .NET code that retrieves data from SQL Server.

Think of this chapter as a walk-through. Read it to understand what each tool does, follow the examples, and don't worry if it raises a few questions. The tools discussed here will help you follow the examples in the upcoming chapters and will ease your way into developing database applications. The SQL Query Designer, for example, is a tool that lets you generate SQL statements with point-and-click operations. If you're not familiar with SQL statements, the Query Designer is an excellent starting point. Use it to learn how to write complicated SQL statements by using visual design tools. After you have mastered query generation with the Query Designer, you should be able to type your SQL statements without a visual tool.

NOTE *To make this chapter more useful to the majority of you, we introduce many topics that are discussed in detail in following chapters. In addition, this chapter provides a great walk-through of the visual tools now available in VS .NET. For those of you already familiar with topics such as SQL statements, stored procedures, and so on, this chapter is both a review and a summary. If you haven't designed a database in the past, or if you don't know SQL, then follow along. You'll learn how to design with visual tools, and in the following chapters, you'll get into real programming.*

To build efficient, scalable applications with SQL Server, you must master the various tools offered by Visual Studio .NET and SQL Server. We focus mostly on the new VS .NET tools, because Microsoft makes great advancements in this area. The Data Adapter Configuration Wizard is a prime candidate for demonstrating how ADO.NET works. No other tool is as intuitive and easy for generating DataAdapter and Command objects, exponentially reducing your development time.

Our focus is mostly on working with SQL Server as a back-end. Not only does the .NET Framework embrace SQL Server data access in its base classes, Microsoft also markets SQL Server 2000 as one of the .NET Servers. These tools are friendly, easy to use, and extremely powerful. After you learn T-SQL, you'll be ready to write your own stored procedures and triggers. In the meantime, you'll be able to do just about everything with the visual database tools.

You'll start with an overview of the various data access tools in VS .NET. We briefly touch on the tools offered by SQL Server 2000, focusing mainly on the newer technologies. Next, you'll learn how to connect to an existing SQL Server database from VB .NET by using these tools. Finally, you'll see an exciting example of how you can work with ADO.NET objects to retrieve data from SQL Server.

NOTE *Although this chapter focuses primarily on the VS .NET visual database tools, you will see that most of the VS .NET tools derive from the ones in SQL Server 2000. Microsoft doesn't reinvent the wheel, enabling you to spend more time mastering a unified toolset, rather than learning a new one for each IDE.*

A First Look at the Visual Database Tools

The *visual database tools* of VS .NET and SQL Server simplify operations such as database design and the extraction of data from a database. Using drag-and-drop operations, you can quickly connect to a database and retrieve data. The VS .NET visual database tools fully support the new features of SQL Server 2000, such as indexed views and user-defined functions. So now you have the power of SQL Server 2000, right from the Visual Studio .NET IDE. In addition, the VS .NET tools abstract the ADO.NET and XML model into an easy-to-understand visual representation. This makes it much easier for you to learn the `System.Data` and `System.Xml` namespaces if you are new to the .NET Framework.

The more you do with these tools, the less code you'll have to write later. It's not unlike building regular applications with VB .NET, if you think about it. Have you ever considered how much functionality you bring into your applications when you drop a control from the toolbox on a form and then set the properties of the control in the Properties window?

This chapter focuses on the visual tools for data access; however, keep in mind that just about everything we show you can be done programmatically. The beauty of VS .NET is that it exposes all the source code generated by these visual drag-and-drop operations. This makes it useful for you to learn by exploring the code generated by VS .NET, especially if you are just learning the new language syntaxes offered with VB .NET and C#.

NOTE   *For those of you who have worked with previous editions of SQL Server, this chapter draws your attention to the new visual tools offered in SQL Server 2000 and makes comparisons between the VS .NET and SQL Server 2000 tools. Those of you who have not worked with SQL Server will still be able to follow the detailed examples given throughout the book.*

TIP   *This chapter is very interactive. You might want to launch the VS .NET IDE now, so that you can follow along. If this is your first time launching VS .NET, you will have to use a wizard to configure your My Profile page. After you configure your settings, subsequent launches will take you directly to the Start page.*

Visual Studio .NET Tools

Microsoft's release of Visual Basic 6 made great progress at unifying the development environment for application and database code. The Data Environment Designer and T-SQL Debugger enabled you to access your database objects and code right from your VB IDE. VS .NET matures this unification by using the shared development environment, which unites all the code development tools into a single IDE. This enables you to use the same code designer with multiple languages, such as VB .NET, C#, XML, and SQL. A unified code designer sets the stage for cross-language debugging.

In addition, VS .NET coordinates closely with the SQL Server visual tools. In fact, you will see many of the same interfaces in VS .NET that you've used in SQL Server. This saves you time because you can focus more on your code, and less on learning new tools.

Although there are many new tools that come with VS .NET, we are focusing on the ones that you can use for data access. After all, this is a book about database programming. We begin with the Solution Explorer.

SOLUTION EXPLORER

New!   The Solution Explorer replaces the Project Explorer window in Visual Basic 6. Through the Solution Explorer window, you can browse the different files belonging to your project, including XML data and schema files. Your project's metadata is stored in a solution file, which has an `.sln` extension. These solution files are analogous to VB6 project group files, which had the `.vbg` extension.

Although you can work with databases from this window, it is somewhat limiting because you can work only with *database references*, rather than the actual database. Database references do not expose the entire database object hierarchy, limiting you to only pointing to connections, rather than actually being able to drill down and manipulate the database objects within that connection. However, the Server Explorer, which we review next, provides this drill-down capability.

NOTE   The Solution Explorer is fairly intuitive to use, even if you are new to VS .NET. Those of you who have worked with the Project Explorer in previous versions of Visual Studio should find it familiar. We are not going to spend much time reviewing the Solution Explorer in this chapter.

SERVER EXPLORER

New!

One of the most powerful tools that VS .NET provides is the Server Explorer. The Server Explorer window is a container for any services that you have running on your local or remote machines. To bring up this window, click the Server Explorer tab on the left side of the VS .NET IDE. This pops up the Server Explorer window, which works like the Windows Start menu's Auto-hide feature. Click the little thumbtack icon to keep it in place.

The Server Explorer extends the concept of the Data View you had in VB6. VS .NET expands the ability to manipulate database objects into a full-fledged power to manipulate all kinds of services. And you can do this all from one console! If you look at this window, you will see all your services, such as Database Services, and Message Queue Services, as indicated in Figure 3.1. The Server Explorer also gives you the ability to drag and drop database objects into your component designer to simplify your programming tasks. Imagine being able to generate an ADO.NET DataSet from a database table with a single drag-and-drop motion.

You can perform many significant database tasks from the Server Explorer. You can add and edit connections to databases. You can even create a new database from scratch!

FIGURE 3.1

A typical Server Explorer window

TOOLBOX

You access the Toolbox the same way you brought up the Server Explorer. Just click the Toolbox tab on the left side of the VS .NET IDE. Alternately, you can select it from the View menu. The Toolbox will look familiar to those of you who have worked with Visual Studio 6 products.

NOTE   The Toolbox is simple to use, even if you are new to VS .NET. Those of you who have worked with the Toolbox in previous versions of Visual Studio should find it familiar. We are not going to spend much time reviewing the Toolbox in this chapter.

New! As you can see in Figure 3.2, the Toolbox has a new Data tab that contains the various .NET data access components, such as the SqlDataAdapter and DataSet. You will be working with these controls at the end of this chapter.

FIGURE 3.2

The Toolbox
Data tab

COMPONENT DESIGNER

The Component Designer provides a visual interface for manipulating the .NET Framework objects, such as the ADO.NET components. To work with the Component Designer, drag and drop components from the Toolbox to the design workspace. This functionality for nonvisual controls did not exist in previous editions of Visual Studio, because the Component Designer acts as a storage tray rather than an actual user interface. Only nonvisual components, such as the Timer object, are stored here. Traditional visual controls are displayed on the actual form, as in previous versions of VS .NET. Figure 3.3 shows you what the SqlDataAdapter looks like when it sits in the Component Designer tray. When you use DataAdapter objects with the Component Designer, Visual Studio .NET will automatically generate a data schema for you. If you wish, you can also use the Component Designer to generate DataSets without writing a line of code.

FIGURE 3.3

The Component Designer

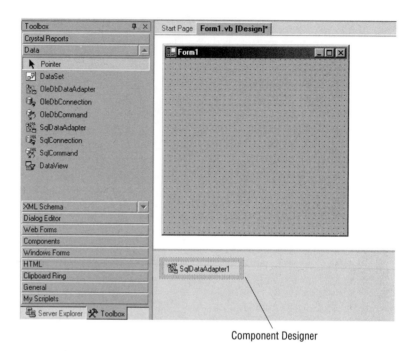

Component Designer

THE DATABASE DESIGNER

As the name indicates, the Database Designer is the tool for designing existing databases. It works in conjunction with the Server Explorer, which enables you to create new databases, as well as tables, stored procedures, and diagrams. After you create a database, you can use the Database Designer to build the database (define its tables, relationships, and so on).

Let's experiment with creating a new database from VS .NET. First, expand the Servers node in the Server Explorer. Drill down into SQL Servers and expand your SQL Server name and choose New Database, as you can see in Figure 3.4. Specify a name, such as TestDb, and click OK. The Database Designer hooks right into SQL Server, creating a SQL Server database for you. You will be prompted to specify authentication information. You can opt to use SQL Server native authentication, specifying a login name and password. Alternately, you can opt to use Windows NT integrated security.

WARNING *Beware of the limitations of the Server Explorer. Although you can create new databases from the SQL Server node, you are not able to delete them. You will have to use the SQL Server Enterprise Manager to drop any databases.*

FIGURE 3.4

Creating a new SQL
Server Database
from the Server
Explorer

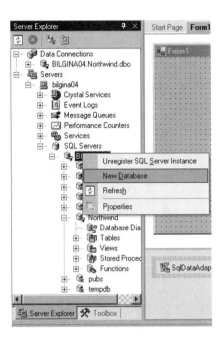

Table Designer

In addition to creating a new database, you can work with the database objects within a database, such as tables, stored procedures, and user-defined functions. Expand the node for the Northwind database. You will see the various objects under the database node. Expand the Tables node to view the Northwind tables. Double-click the `Customers` table, which brings back all the records in that table. This is a handy way to make edits to existing records or to add new rows to the table. This works just like the SQL Server 2000 Enterprise Manager.

Again, as with SQL Server, you can right-click the `Customers` table and chose from many table actions, as shown in Figure 3.5.

As you can see in the pop-up menu, you can add new tables or triggers, or export data, right from Visual Studio .NET. Choose Design Table from the pop-up menu to launch the Table Designer. The changes you make here are saved into the associated database.

Microsoft made some improvements to the Table Designer in VS .NET. For those of you who have worked with it in Visual Studio 6 (VS6), the first thing you will notice is an enhanced user interface, which is consistent with the properties interface you will find throughout the VS .NET IDE. Microsoft supplements the grid interface with a property window that you can use to view all the details of a column (see Figure 3.6). The grid saves real-estate by showing only the most commonly used properties of a column.

FIGURE 3.5

Table design options from the Server Explorer

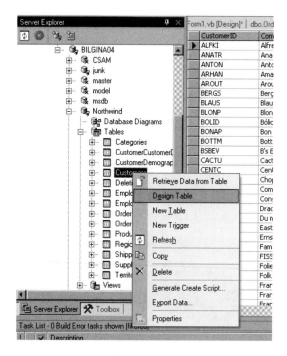

FIGURE 3.6

The enhanced VS .NET Table Designer

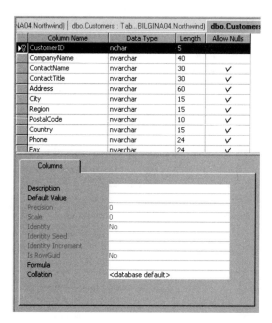

In previous versions, you were limited to a grid-like view of the table attributes. The interface was very cumbersome, as it required a good amount of horizontal scrolling to view the column properties. The developers of VS .NET took their inspiration from no better tool for SQL Server management: the SQL Server Enterprise Manager. As you can see, the VS .NET Table Designer works much like the table design tool in SQL Server Enterprise Manager, and even uses a similar interface. The designer presents the columns in a grid at the top. By clicking on a column, the associated detail displays below it (as depicted later in Figure 3.16).

Database Diagram Designer

The Database Diagram Designer has replaced the concept of the relationship designer; however, you can see it hasn't changed much from Visual Studio 6. You can access this designer by expanding the Database Diagrams node in the Server Explorer.

WARNING *If you don't have any diagrams in the database, you will be unable to work with the Diagram Designer. You will need to create a new diagram, by right-clicking the Database Diagrams node in the Server Explorer and selecting New Diagram.*

Like the Table Designer, the Diagram Designer mimics the functionality of the Enterprise Manager and looks identical to the Diagram Designer you find in the SQL Server 2000 Enterprise Manager, as you can see in Figure 3.7. By clicking on a relationship, you are able to edit its properties. As you can see, you can also take advantage of the new relationship features of SQL Server 2000, such as cascading updates and deletes.

FIGURE 3.7

Use the Database Designer to view the structure of the tables and to establish relationships between them.

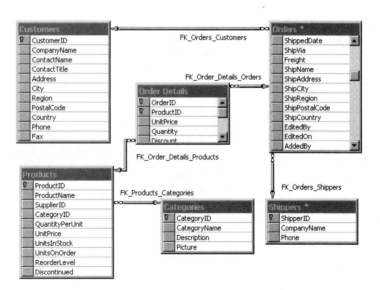

THE QUERY DESIGNER AND VIEW DESIGNER

The Query Designer is based on a fairly old technology, known as query by example (QBE). It was included in Office 95, and many of you might have used it already.

Regardless of its antediluvian nature, this is still a great visual tool, especially for people who are not familiar with SQL. The Query Designer, shown in Figure 3.8, enables you to build SQL statements with point-and-click operations. You just drop the tables you want to include in the query on a pane of the Query Designer, select the fields you want to use in the query, and, finally, specify the constraints. The Query Designer is an "intelligent" and flexible tool, and you'll probably use it more than any other visual database tool. Even programmers familiar with SQL statements use the Query Designer to design queries, especially if they use many field names from multiple tables, to minimize typing mistakes.

Because views and queries share so much in common, the Query Designer interface can also be used to work with views as well.

NOTE   The View Designer uses the Query Designer to design views, which you can see by right-clicking on a view from the Server Explorer and then selecting the Design View option.

FIGURE 3.8

A typical Query and View Designer window

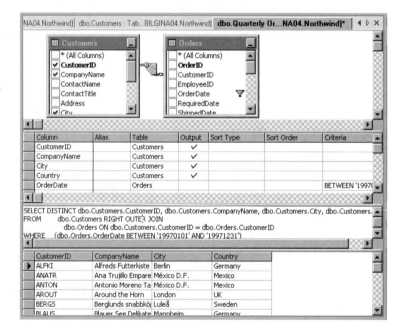

XML DESIGNER

As you might have already guessed, XML plays a big part in Visual Studio .NET and the .NET Framework. To support this notion, VS .NET provides visual tools for working with XML and XML schema. One of the most important tools in this area is the XML Designer. Because

ADO.NET DataSets are actually stored as XML, you will be able to manipulate DataSets, XML Schema Definitions (XSDs), and XML data files by using the XML Designer. The XML Designer enables you to perform functions that you cannot do by using another tool, such as visually adding DataRelation objects between different DataTables.

The XML Designer provides a powerful tool for combining data from heterogeneous data sources into an ADO.NET DataSet without typing a line of code. Using the XML Designer, you can view a representation of your data schema, as well as edit the XSD file in which the schema is stored.

The XML Designer provides three views of your DataSet: a grid-like, visual representation of your data, raw XML, and a schema view. We don't talk about the XML Designer too much in this chapter. We do go into detail about the XML code in Chapter 7, "ADO.NET Programming," where you'll work with XML schema files, and also in Chapter 8, "Data Aware Controls," where we show you how to add DataRelations from the XML Designer by following our Shopping Cart example. In addition, we review the XML Designer again in Chapter 10, "The Role of XML," a chapter completely dedicated to XML.

SQL EDITOR

The code editor in VS .NET not only supports the .NET languages, such as VB .NET and C#, but it also is capable of handling SQL code as well. The SQL Editor enables you to create new stored procedures and triggers, or edit existing ones. You can also execute and debug stored procedures from within the Visual Basic environment. The SQL Editor doesn't really qualify as a visual tool, but because it tightly integrates with the Query Designer, we include it in this chapter.

NOTE   VS .NET integrates the development environment with an integrated code editor as well. The SQL Editor is more frequently referred to as the Code Editor, as it is a unified code and text editor across multiple languages. We call it the SQL Editor in this book to differentiate between editing SQL code versus VB .NET code. The code editor adjusts to the language you are using. Because of this, certain features, such as IntelliSense, do not work when editing SQL code.

VS .NET language unification doesn't stop at mere editing. You can also debug your mixed language code all from the same IDE. Cross-language debugging not only enables you to debug code between VB .NET and SQL, but also any of the other VS .NET languages, such as C#. Visual Studio 6 didn't support this widely requested feature.

The debugging tools are the same between languages, enabling you to debug your SQL stored procedures, triggers, and functions as if they were regular VB .NET code. If you want to debug a stored procedure, expand the Stored Procedure node from the Server Explorer. Right-click on the stored procedure you wish to debug, and choose the Step Into Stored Procedure option from the pop-up menu, as shown in Figure 3.9. If you have any input parameters, a dialog box will pop up, prompting you for their values. Then, the VS .NET debugger will walk you through the stored procedures. The integrated VS .NET debugger replaces the T-SQL Debugger you had used in the past.

WARNING   If you are unable to edit and debug your stored procedures, you might be using the Professional edition of Visual Studio. The Enterprise Architect version must be installed in order to edit and debug stored procedures. You might want to consider upgrading to the Enterprise Architect edition, after examining its features, which are listed in MSDN.

FIGURE 3.9

The VS .NET
Debugger lets
you debug your
stored procedures
interactively.

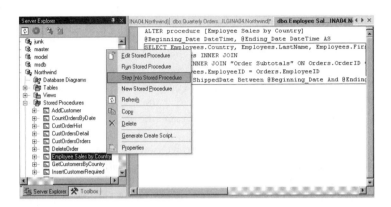

SQL Server 2000 Tools

This section provides a high-level overview of the more important tools that you can work with in SQL Server 2000. We don't cover all the tools that are available, just the ones that you need to know to work with the examples in this book. Later chapters introduce other visual tools and wizards, as you delve into more advanced topics.

ENTERPRISE MANAGER

If you have worked with SQL Server before, you are most likely familiar with the Enterprise Manager. Similar to the SQL Server node in the Server Explorer in VS .NET, the Enterprise Manager gives you a visual interface for applying declarative settings on your database objects. Almost everything you do in the Enterprise Manager can be written with SQL code, so you can imagine how the Enterprise Manager reduces the amount of time you spend coding.

QUERY ANALYZER

New! SQL Server 2000's Query Analyzer is much more robust than previous versions. The biggest change that you will notice is the Object Browser. Those of you who program with VB .NET might find this a refreshing feature, as it gives you an object-oriented drill-down of your database objects. You no longer need to use Alt+Tab to switch between writing your query code and referencing an object name in the Enterprise Manager. It even saves you time coding because all the database objects you see in this window can be dragged and dropped into your code. In addition, the Query Analyzer provides a robust stored procedure debugger, which integrates nicely with the VS .NET debugging environment.

We mention these SQL Server 2000 tools here so that you can understand how they compare to the VS .NET visual database tools. We aren't going to spend much time on the SQL Server IDE in this chapter, because the best way to understand the SQL Server 2000 tools is to work with them, which you will do as you explore the T-SQL syntax in Chapter 4, "Structured Query Language," and Chapter 5, "Transact-SQL."

In the following sections, you will explore each of the VS .NET tools. First, you'll review the different strategies for establishing connections to databases. Next, you'll learn how to connect to a database from VS .NET. After all, no matter what you're going to do with a database, you must connect to it first.

Data Access Strategies

Before you actually connect to a database, you need to first review the data access options that you have with the .NET Framework. Your data access strategy plays a vital role if you want to design a quality solution. By choosing the appropriate data access strategy, your application will have better performance and scalability. By understanding these concepts, you can ensure your application efficiency.

This section covers the strategies you can use when accessing data by using .NET. We show how the architecture has changed from the WinDNA architecture and explain the benefits of using .NET.

Data access dramatically changes with the advent of the .NET Framework. Microsoft doesn't expect that you will change your data access technologies overnight, so they have designed the .NET Framework to be backward-compatible with existing technologies. However, if you want your application to scale gracefully, you should seriously consider migrating to one of the newer data access technologies. Figure 3.10 shows the evolution of Microsoft's data access strategy.

FIGURE 3.10

Evolution of data access

Evolution of Data Access

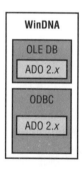 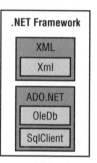

You can choose to use existing data providers or the new .NET Framework data access technologies. The more common choices for data access are the following:

◆ ODBC

◆ OLE DB

◆ ADO 2.*x*

◆ ADO.NET

ODBC

ODBC is a data access technology created to work with relational databases. ODBC is an older driver, and many legacy applications use it today. It's a well-established driver, and there are ODBC drivers for most databases. However, for your new applications, you should use OLE DB because OLE DB is much more independent of its data source than ODBC. In addition, while ODBC architecture focuses more on relational databases, OLE DB can be used for both relational and non-relational data sources, such as message, XML, and file-based data stores.

NOTE   *The advent of the .NET platform does not make all data access technologies obsolete. As new .NET data providers become available, they will be available for download on Microsoft's website. For example, ODBC.NET is the .NET data provider you can use to connect to legacy ODBC systems.*

OLE DB

Unlike ODBC, OLE DB supports a wide variety of data stores—relational or non-relational. This makes it a great choice for bringing together heterogeneous data sources. OLE DB still exists with the .NET Framework; however, it still uses the old COM OLE DB data provider. This means that you will have slower performance because the .NET data providers must translate the calls by using COM marshaling. You should use OLE DB when you are accessing versions of SQL Server prior to SQL Server 7, or other data sources. Regardless of whether you use the OleDb or SqlClient namespace, ADO.NET gives you a common model for generating DataSets and DataReaders.

ADO 2.x

Classic ADO provides an object-oriented interface for working with OLE DB. Because ADO can support client-side disconnected RecordSets, it is useful for Internet applications. Although ADO was originally designed for relational data, you can still do hierarchical representations of the data by using OLE DB data shaping, or you can convert the ADO RecordSets into XML structures.

However, compared to ADO.NET, ADO 2.x is quite limiting. For example, ADO RecordSets make it awkward to work with multiple tables. You can either bring back multiple tables into a single RecordSet, or you have to use multiple RecordSets for each table. Moreover, ADO RecordSets do not support the concept of relationships between RecordSets, which you get when you use ADO.NET DataSets.

In addition, classic ADO does not integrate tightly with XML. ADO 2.x treats XML as just another file format mechanism, rather than using XML natively. Because XML has become the *lingua franca* for data exchange between business, it is important to have a data access mechanism that supports it natively.

ADO 2.x RecordSets are a bit bloated, because they are built to do so many things: work both disconnected and connected, work with both relational and hierarchical data, and work with XML or without it. This makes ADO RecordSets flexible, yet heavy. As Internet applications mushroomed, there was a need for a data access layer that's more lightweight, inherently disconnected, and tightly integrated with XML. This naturally led to the evolution of ADO.NET within the .NET Framework.

ADO.NET

New!

ADO.NET truly takes data abstraction a step further than ADO, by providing a distinct separation between the data access engine (DataAdapter) and the data (DataSet, DataReader). In addition, ADO.NET clearly disassociates the data storage from the data schema, much like XML. ADO 2.*x*, on the other hand, focuses on a database-centric model, rather than viewing the data independently of its data source.

ADO.NET introduces the concept of managed providers. Managed providers in .NET replace unmanaged OLE DB providers. Right now, the current release of the .NET Framework supports two managed providers—one for SQL Server and one for OLE DB to use with any other kind of data source.

ADO.NET uses XML for data persistence, which makes it easier for applications to share data. Because of this, ADO.NET simultaneously stores data in both a relational and hierarchical format.

TIP *If you are debating whether to upgrade your ADO 2.x components to ADO.NET, a good reason to do so is to enable your data to cross a firewall. Although DCOM provides tunneling TCP/IP, which uses Port 80, firewalls can still filter any non-HTTP traffic, such as proprietary COM marshaling. ADO.NET uses HTTP as its transfer protocol, which is a widely accepted and ubiquitous protocol. In addition, consider the receiving application. Almost all applications can support XML data, rather than a binary COM-based RecordSet.*

There are two managed providers under the umbrella of ADO.NET: the `SqlClient` and `OleDb` namespaces, both of which fall under the `System.Data` namespace.

SQLCLIENT NAMESPACE

If you know for sure that your data source is SQL Server, definitely use this namespace over the `OleDb` namespace. You will get a lot more speed when accessing your data because it goes straight to the SQL Server file system, rather than the OLE DB layer to retrieve your data.

OLEDB NAMESPACE

Use the `OleDb` managed provider for all other data sources, including a non-relational database such as message stores and text files.

TIP *The `OleDb` managed provider isn't as efficient as the SQL managed provider because it still has to go through the COM interoperability layer to talk to OLE DB by using COM. Managed providers offer better performance as they generally avoid COM and talk directly to the data source using native API calls. Unfortunately, the `OleDb` managed provider that comes with .NET doesn't really do this because OLE DB providers are COM-based. This makes it slower because it has to translate the COM code and data types into .NET-compatible objects. At this time, SQL Server is the only native data provider that ships with .NET; however, Microsoft expects this number to grow.*

Both the `OleDb` and `SqlClient` namespaces use the same mechanism for data storage—a DataSet or a DataReader. You don't have to worry about the details of ADO.NET in this chapter. The VS .NET visual database tools handle much of the work for you. You will go "under the hood" with the different ADO.NET objects, such as the DataAdapter, in Chapter 7.

Using Connection Strings

In ADO.NET, the Connection object enables you to communicate with your data source. In order for the Connection object to know how to connect to your data source, you need to specify a connection string, which contains the various connection parameters. You have several ways to create your connection string. You can do it visually or programmatically by using the Data Link Properties dialog box:

◆ Specify the name of an external file that stores information about the connection. This file is known as a *data link file* and has an extension .udl. The problem with this approach is that you must prepare a different link file for each user on the network.

◆ Use the *Data Link Properties* dialog box from VS .NET to visually create or edit your connection string. Later in this chapter, you will bring up this box by adding a connection via the Server Explorer. Keep in mind, if you create a connection by using this dialog box, it will not create the .udl file for you, instead dynamically concatenating the attributes into a connection string, which can be seen in the connection's properties window in VS .NET.

◆ Programmatically specify a *connection string*, which passes all the information needed by the driver to establish a connection to a database. This information includes the name of the machine on which SQL Server is running, authentication information, and the name of the database. The problem with this approach is that you must hard-code all the information needed to connect to the database. However, you can place your connection string in a place that makes it easier to edit, such as the `web.config` file. You will work with these options later in Part IV, "Data Access for the Web," when you'll build Web Applications.

Using Data Link Files

Data link files are text files that you can create from Windows Explorer. To create a data link file in Windows 2000, open the folder where you want to create the file and right-click on an empty area. In the shortcut menu, choose New ➤ Text Document. Rename the file with a .udl extension. The file's icon automatically changes to a Microsoft Data Link icon. Then right-click the data link file to open the shortcut menu. Select the file `Properties`. This opens the Data Link Properties dialog box, explained next.

Using the Data Link Properties Dialog Box

Aside from using a data link file, you can also access this dialog box from the Server Explorer in VS .NET. The Data Link Properties dialog box contains four tabs:

Provider This is where you specify the provider that will be used to connect to the database. The other tabs will dynamically reflect properties that apply to the provider you choose in this tab.

Connection This is where you specify the data source of the connection (the database to which you want to connect).

Advanced This tab enables you to specify some advanced connection options.

All This tab contains all the attributes of the connection (most of them have been specified on the other three tabs), and you can edit their values.

Programmatically Declaring Connection Strings

The visual tools will create a connection string for you. Alternately, you can pass this connection string directly to your ADO.NET Connection object. For example, if you would like to connect to the Northwind database, you would type the following:

```
Dim nwindConn As SqlConnection = New SqlConnection
    ("Integrated Security=SSPI; Initial Catalog=Northwind;Data Source=SAM")
```

NOTE *The* `Data Source` *property represents the database server name, so replace that parameter with your own SQL Server name.*

As you can see, the attributes of the connection string correlate to the fields that you saw in the Data Link Properties dialog box. To visually create a connection string, you must open the Server Explorer window, right-click the Data Connections icon, and from the shortcut menu select Add Connection. You will see the Data Link Properties window, which has the same four tabs discussed earlier.

Connecting to Databases

Now that you've reviewed the tools and data access strategies, you're ready to dig in and start generating some code. You'll start from the most logical place to begin coding your database access applications—Visual Studio .NET. In this section, you will learn a visual way of coding your applications first. Then, you will look at the code generated behind the scenes and learn the purpose of each object.

Later, in Chapter 7, you'll learn more powerful code for manipulating your database objects. All the examples in this section use preexisting T-SQL code from the Northwind database. In the next couple of chapters, you'll learn how to write your own custom T-SQL code.

Connecting to the Northwind Database by Using a Windows Project

Let's connect to the Northwind database from VB .NET and begin working with the new tools. Start by launching the VS .NET IDE (if you haven't already) and creating a new project from the Start page.

After you select the New Project button, you will see a list of project choices. You are going to use the Windows Application and Database Project types in this chapter, but if you are curious about the other project types, Table 3.1 helps you compare them to Visual Basic 6 project types.

TABLE 3.1: VB .NET VERSUS VB 6 PROJECT TYPES

.NET PROJECT TYPE	VB6 COMPARISON
Windows Application	Similar to VB6 standard executable
Class Library	Similar to ActiveX DLLs and ActiveX EXEs
Windows Control Library	Similar to ActiveX control
ASP.NET Web Application	Similar to InterDev web projects
ASP.NET WebService	No direct comparison (analogous to a remote COM component that uses HTTP and SOAP, rather than DCOM)

Continued on next page

TABLE 3.1: VB .NET VERSUS VB 6 PROJECT TYPES *(continued)*

Web Control Library	No direct comparison (analogous to ActiveX controls, but for a web page, rather than a Windows application)
Console Application	No VB6 comparison (similar to a C++ command-line application)
Windows Service	No VB6 comparison
Empty Project	No VB6 comparison
Empty Web Project	No VB6 comparison
New Project In Existing Folder	No VB6 comparison

Select a name and file path for your Windows application. We chose `NWProject` as our project name. The Solution Explorer will show you all the default files that were created with your new project. As we said earlier, the Solution Explorer is similar to the Project Explorer in VB6. One of the files created with your project is a standard Windows form, which you can see in the form designer window.

NOTE   *Those of you who have worked with previous versions of Visual Basic might be startled to see that Visual Studio .NET automatically saves your project to disk on creation. In the past, you were able to build a throw-away application by creating a new project and closing it without saving it. Those of you who have worked with Visual InterDev will find this feature familiar.*

Before you can see the visual database tools in action, you must connect to a database and create a few commands that retrieve information from the database. Follow the steps below to establish a connection to the SQL Server Northwind database, to make sure you can follow the examples in this chapter. Following similar steps, you can connect to an Oracle or Access database.

1. Open your Server Explorer window and right-click the Data Connections node. Choose Add Connection from the menu.

2. This pops up a window where you can set the Data Link properties. This is similar to the Data Link window that you've seen in previous editions.

3. By default, the active tab will be the Connection tab, as you can see in Figure 3.11. (This is the only tab we focus on in this example; we reviewed the other tabs earlier in this chapter.) Specify the name of your database server, your authentication method, and the database you wish to use. In this case, use the Northwind database on your local machine. Notice that no database names will appear in the initial database drop-down list until you specify a user ID and a password—unless, of course, you choose the Windows NT integrated security option.

NOTE   *VS .NET automatically configures the data provider for you. On the Provider tab of the Data Link Properties dialog box, you can see that the provider uses Microsoft OLE DB provider for SQL Server.*

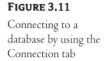

FIGURE 3.11

Connecting to a database by using the Connection tab

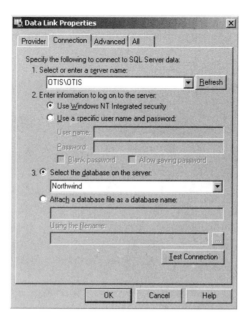

4. Click the Test Connection button at the bottom of the window to make sure everything works, and then click OK to close the dialog box.

That's it! That's all you have to do to connect to the Northwind database. If you look at the Server Explorer, you will see your new connection in the tree view. If you expand the folder, you will see the associated database objects, such as tables, views, and stored procedures.

WARNING *You can't edit an existing connection by selecting Properties from its shortcut menu. The Properties dialog box will display the properties of the connection, but they will be grayed out and read-only. To change the properties of a data link, you must remove the existing data link and establish a new one.*

Connecting to the Northwind Database by Using a Data Project

Another way to create database connections from VS .NET is by leveraging an existing project type called the *Database Project*. The Database Project serves as a template, which contains the various objects you need to connect to a database and program it from within your VB .NET code. Follow these steps:

1. Create a new project by selecting File ➢ New Project from your menu. In the project types tree view, navigate to the `Other Projects` folder and select the `Database Projects` folder.

2. Select a project name and path for your file. Make sure you leave the Close Solution option checked. Click the Database Project template, as shown in Figure 3.12.

FIGURE 3.12

Selecting a new
Database Project

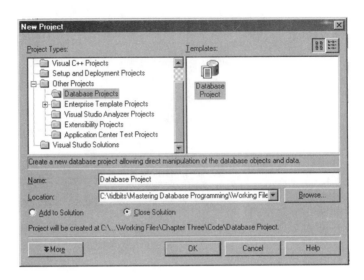

3. The next thing that you will see is a dialog box that asks whether you want to use an existing database reference or create a new one. Because you already created a connection to Northwind in the previous example, you will see it listed in this box. Highlight this and click OK. (If you didn't have any connections created in the Server Explorer, you would see the Data Link Properties dialog box that you worked with earlier.)

NOTE *Keep in mind that a database reference works differently from the connections in the Server Explorer. The database reference is a pointer to the connection in the Server Explorer. Also, the database references are stored with the database project. When you reopen the project, you will see the database references. If the data connection is no longer valid, VS .NET will automatically re-create the connection for you.*

Unlike the Windows application sample above, you will not see a visual designer, such as a form. You will also notice a difference in your Solution Explorer window, as shown in Figure 3.13. In this window, you will see several folders: `Change Scripts`, `Create Scripts`, `Queries`, and `Database References`. The `Change Scripts` folder gives you the power to create and modify existing database objects. It enables you to store a modification script for changing database objects. You would create a change script when you are not quite ready to implement the changes directly on the database. The `Create Scripts` folder provides a place to store your database object definition scripts. This option was not available in previous versions of Visual Studio. The `Queries` folder provides you with the ability to access the Query Designer, as we explained earlier. This way, you can create data manipulation statements to access your data.

If you expand the `Database References` folder, you will see that VS .NET automatically created a reference to the Northwind database for you. It looks like the Connection object you added in the Server Explorer earlier. However, unlike the Server Explorer, this is only a pointer to the connection, so you can't drill down to the objects within a database connection from the database reference.

FIGURE 3.13

The components of a new Database Project template

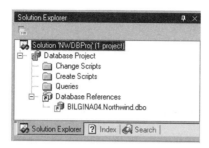

You will find the Database Projects a useful place to centralize your database references, as well as a great place to run SQL code. You will learn how to run queries and scripts later in this chapter. Save this project as **Database Project**, because you will use it again in "The Query Designer Window" section.

Using the Server Explorer

Regardless of whether you used the Windows Application or the Database Project to create your connection, after you have established a connection to a database, the objects of the specified database will automatically appear in the Server Explorer. The database objects are stored in folders, according to their type. For SQL Server and Oracle databases, you will see the following folders beneath your database Connection object.

◆ Database Diagrams

◆ Tables

◆ Views

◆ Stored Procedures

◆ Functions

NOTE   *All the objects under a Data Connection in the Server Explorer are stored in the database and are not specific to the project. Even if you remove a Data Connection from this window, all the changes you made to the database through that link will not be lost.*

Database Diagrams

This folder holds the relational diagrams of the database. As you know, a relational diagram specifies how the various tables relate to each other. To specify new relationships, right-click the Database Diagrams icon and choose New Diagram. You can add whatever tables you would like to your diagram. To edit an existing diagram, just double-click it.

The reason you can have multiple database diagrams is to group tables and their relationships. If the database contains many tables, you can create a different diagram for each group of interconnected tables. Individual tables can belong to multiple diagrams, as long as the relationships in all diagrams are consistent.

If you expand the node for your diagram, you will see sub-nodes for all the tables represented in the diagram. You continue expanding to see the table columns, or choose to design the table by selecting the Design Table option from the pop-up menu.

WARNING   *You must use VS .NET Enterprise Architect edition to use these database editing functions.*

Tables

This folder contains all the tables of the database, except it is filtered behind the scenes so that system tables are not visible, unlike what you see with the Enterprise Manager. You will see in the next section how you can add new tables to the database, or edit existing ones. If you have connected to a database that has just been created but not yet designed, you can add all the tables and their relationships from within the Server Explorer. To design a new table, right-click the Tables icon and choose New Table. To edit an existing one, right-click its name and choose Design Table. You can also double-click a table and see its data rows on a grid. You can even edit the rows of the table on this grid, right from within the VB .NET environment.

You also use the `Tables` folder to access the triggers of the database. Triggers are specific to tables, and they are listed under the table they belong to, as shown in Figure 3.14. If you expand a table in the Server Explorer window, you will see its columns. If the table contains triggers, their names will also appear after the list of the table's fields. To design a new trigger, right-click the Tables icon and choose New Trigger. To edit an existing trigger, right-click the desired trigger and choose the Edit Trigger option, also shown in Figure 3.14.

FIGURE 3.14

Working with tables and triggers in the Server Explorer

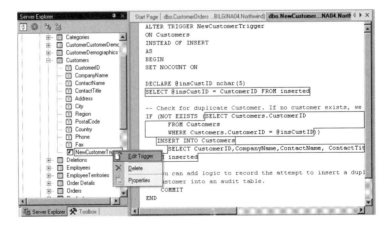

Views

This folder contains the views already attached to the database. If you expand a view, you will see its columns. To design a new view, right-click the Views icon and choose New View. To edit an existing one, right-click its name and choose Design View. This launches the Query Designer interface, which we discuss in detail later in this chapter, in the "Using the Query Designer" section. You can also open a view by double-clicking its name; you will see its rows on a grid. If the view is updateable, you can edit its rows (or the ones you're allowed to edit) right from within the VB .NET environment.

Stored Procedures

This folder contains the stored procedures already attached to the database. If you click the plus sign in front of a stored procedure's name, the item will expand to show the input and output parameters of the stored procedure.

Functions

This folder shows you the user-defined functions that exist in the database, as you can see in Figure 3.15. If you expand the node for a particular function, you will see its input and output parameters.

FIGURE 3.15

Working with functions in the Server Explorer

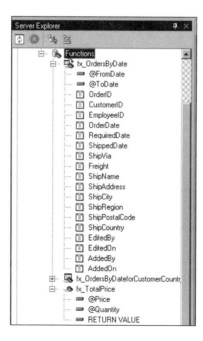

WHAT DO ALL THOSE FUNNY LITTLE ICONS MEAN?

You'll explore the types of user-defined functions in greater detail in Chapter 5. However, this is a good place to explain why some of the function icons appear different from others, as you can see in Figure 3.15.

There are three types of user-defined functions: scalar, inline table-valued, and multi-statement table-valued. *Scalar functions* perform operations on multiple input parameters, but can return only a single value. They are represented by a small green rectangle, as you can see for the fx_TotalPrice function in Figure 3.15. *Inline table-valued functions* use the new SQL Server 2000 table data type as their return values. These display a small red arrow next to the function name, as you can see for the fx_OrdersByDate function in Figure 3.15. *Multi-statement table-valued* functions are the most complex. These functions use multiple statements to generate the table return value and are represented by an icon that shows a small green rectangle alongside a table image. You can see the fx_OrdersByDateforCustomerCountry table-valued function in Figure 3.15.

Using the Database Designer

This section discusses the Database Designer and uses the Northwind database for the examples. Instead of designing new tables, you'll edit the tables of the Northwind database, examine the existing constraints and relationships, and add new ones. You will use the connection you established earlier to Northwind.

Through the windows of the Database Designer, you can design SQL Server and Oracle databases. There is no Database Designer window per se among the visual database tools. There are five tools for designing database objects:

♦ The Design Table window, where you can edit the attributes of the table

♦ The Table Property Pages dialog box, where you can view and edit table properties such as indexes, constraints, and relationships

♦ The Database Diagram window, where you can view and edit the relationships between the tables of the database

♦ The Query Designer window, which lets you visually create SQL statements for views and stored procedures

♦ The SQL Editor window, where you can edit the raw SQL code, much like you would VB .NET code

The Design Table Window

Open the Server Explorer window, create the Northwind Data Connection (if you haven't done so already), and then expand the Data Connection and the folders under it. To open the Products table in design mode, locate it in the Tables folder, right-click its icon and choose Design Table. Figure 3.16 shows the Products table in design mode.

FIGURE 3.16

The **Products** table in design mode

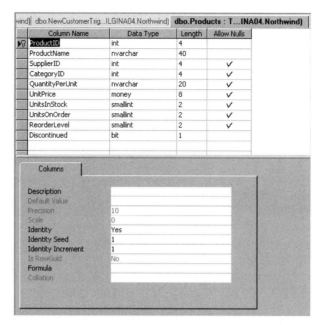

Column Name	Data Type	Length	Allow Nulls
ProductID	int	4	
ProductName	nvarchar	40	
SupplierID	int	4	✓
CategoryID	int	4	✓
QuantityPerUnit	nvarchar	20	✓
UnitPrice	money	8	✓
UnitsInStock	smallint	2	✓
UnitsOnOrder	smallint	2	✓
ReorderLevel	smallint	2	✓
Discontinued	bit	1	

Columns

Description	
Default Value	
Precision	10
Scale	0
Identity	Yes
Identity Seed	1
Identity Increment	1
Is RowGuid	No
Formula	
Collation	

Each table column has a name and a data type, and every data type has a length. The length of most data types is fixed, and you can't change it. Integers are stored in 4 bytes, datetime columns are stored in 8 bytes, and so on. The varchar and nvarchar data types are variable length strings, and you specify their maximum length in the Length column. The same is true for binary columns. Some numeric types have Precision and Scale attributes. The Precision attribute is the number of digits used to represent a numeric data type—the total number of digits in the number. The Scale attribute is the number of fractional digits of a numeric data type (the number of digits to the right of the decimal point).

NOTE *Data types were discussed in Chapter 2, "Basic Concepts of Relational Databases," with special attention paid to the new SQL Server 2000 data types.*

The Allow Nulls column must be cleared for fields that can't be Null. Primary key fields, for example, can't be Null. Before you specify the table's primary key, you must clear its Allow Nulls attribute. Depending on the data you intend to store in the table, other non-key fields might not be allowed to accept Null values. An order's date, for example, is usually not allowed to be Null.

To set the table's primary key field (if any), right-click the gray box in front of the column name and choose Set Primary Key from the shortcut menu. The table's primary key field is identified by a key icon.

Below the table, you will see the details for a particular column you have selected. There are many different attributes that you can select for a column. In the Default Value field, you can specify a default value for the column, which is assigned automatically to each new row if no other value is specified. The default value could be a value of the same type as the column, or a function returning the same data type. The default value for the OrderDate field in the Orders table could be the following expression, which returns the current date and time:

```
GetDate()
```

Other fields in the Columns tab include Identity, Identity Seed, Identity Increment, and Is-RowGuid. Primary key fields are often set to integer values, and you let the database assign a unique integer value to the key field of each row added to the table. To specify that SQL Server should automatically assign values to a field, specify Yes in the drop-down list for the Identity field. When you indicate an Identity field, you can additionally specify the initial value (Identity Seed) as well as the increment (Identity Increment). The next box, Is RowGuid, should be set to Yes if the corresponding column is a global identifier, a value that's unique not only in the context of the table, but in the entire database.

This is how you design tables. So far, it's quite simple, almost intuitive. Tables, however, are more than collections of columns. To ensure the integrity of the database, you should be able to impose restrictions on the values of the various columns, specify indexes and key fields, and, finally, create relationships between primary and foreign key fields. You can do this by using the Property Pages dialog box for a table.

The Table Property Pages Dialog Box

To view the properties of a table, right-click somewhere on the table's design window and choose Property Pages from the shortcut menu. The Property Pages dialog box has four tabs, which are explained next.

TIP   To view the Properties Pages of a table, you must first open the table in design mode and then right-click the table's design window. If you right-click the table's name in Server Explorer and select Properties, you will see a dialog box with the table's name and its owner name, not the Table Properties window.

THE TABLES TAB

The Tables tab, shown in Figure 3.17, enables you to modify the attributes of a selected table and change its name by typing the name in the Table Name box. You can specify the owner of a table by using a drop-down box. The primary key of the table often appears in the Table Identity Column drop-down field. If a table has a global unique identifier, it will be listed in the Table ROWGUID Column field. The next two boxes will display the value PRIMARY, unless the database administrator has split the database into multiple files. Leave these boxes to the DBA. (In short, a SQL Server database can be stored in multiple files, but this will not affect your code. The conceptual view of the database remains the same, whether its tables are stored in one or more tables.) Finally, you can specify a description for the table in the last field.

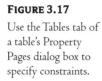

FIGURE 3.17

Use the Tables tab of a table's Property Pages dialog box to specify constraints.

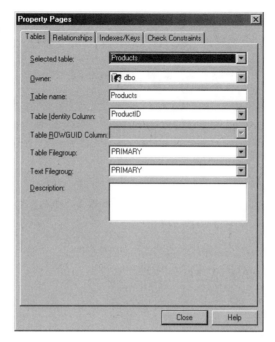

THE RELATIONSHIPS TAB

Relationships are the most important aspect in the design of a relational database. Not only must you specify the correct relationships for the joins you'll execute later in your queries, but you must also establish rules for the integrity of the references between tables. This tab is further explained in the section "Using the Database Diagram," later in this chapter.

THE INDEXES/KEYS TAB

Use the Indexes/Keys tab, shown in Figure 3.18, to manipulate the indexes and keys of your tables. Each table is indexed on one or more columns and usually has one primary key. From the Selected Index box, you can select one of the selected table's indexes. To create a new index, click the New button. You can delete an existing index by clicking the Delete button.

Each index has a name, a definition, and a few attributes, which are specified in the lower section of the tab. The definition of the index is the name of one or more columns. If you anticipate that your applications will be searching for products by their last name, index the `Customers` table on the `LastName` field. When you index a table on a field, you designate an order for the field(s) involved in the index. The rows of the table are not necessarily rearranged, but they are retrieved in the order specified by the index. You can also index a table on two or more fields. If the field you're indexing on isn't unique, for example, the last name, you can specify additional keys. It is possible to index a table on the last name and first name fields, so that rows with the same last name are clustered together and ordered according to first name.

FIGURE 3.18

Use the Indexes/ Keys tab of a table's Property Pages dialog box to specify new indexes and key fields.

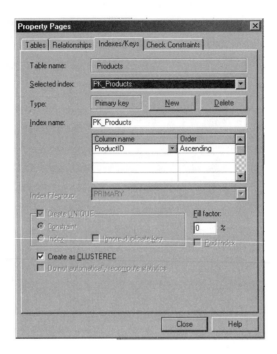

The Create UNIQUE check box lets you specify that an index is unique. The index on the `LastName` field, for example, can't be unique. It's quite possible for two or more contacts in the `Customers` table to have the same last name. An index based on a field such as a product's ID or a book's ISBN is unique. This field is used as a primary key, and primary keys are by definition unique. There are situations, however, when a field can't be used as a primary key, yet it must be unique. Let's say you're maintaining a table with teacher IDs and room numbers. Because a teacher can't be in two rooms at the same time, you can specify that the combination `TeacherID + RoomNumber` is unique. If you don't want to create an index on these two columns, check the Constraint option. If you want to be able to search the table with the field combination `TeacherID + RoomNumber` (or with the field `TeacherID` only), then create a new index by checking the Index option.

The Create As CLUSTERED check box lets you specify that an index will be created as a clustered index. Each table can have only one clustered index, and this index must be based on the field that's used most often for searching. Clustered indexes are very efficient, because SQL Server stores rows in the same order as dictated by the clustered index. In other words, the physical order of the rows is the same as the logical order of the key values. As a result, when SQL Server searches the B-Tree structure of the index, it locates the actual data, not a pointer to the data. To maintain a clustered index, SQL Server works a little harder every time a new row is added, but operations that involve the clustered index are performed very efficiently.

THE CHECK CONSTRAINTS TAB

In the lower half of the Check Constraints tab, you can specify any number of constraints for the selected table. Each constraint is identified by a name (so that you can lift the constraint and reimpose it later) and a definition. To add a new constraint, click the New button, type a name for the constraint, and type its definition in the appropriate text boxes. The definition of the constraint is an expression. Most constraints are often comparisons, for example:

```
Discount > 0 And Discount < 1
```

This expression, which uses relational and logical operators, tells SQL Server that the discount should have a value between 0 and 1. To specify that the Unit Price field should be positive, use the following constraint:

```
[Unit Price] >= 0
```

The Employees table contains a slightly more complex constraint, which requests that the employee's birth date is less than (earlier than) the current date:

```
([BirthDate] < getdate())
```

NOTE *This is a textbook example. A constraint like this one doesn't really protect your data at all.*

You might not have noticed it, but the Employees table is a bit unusual: it references itself. It contains a field named ReportsTo, which is the ID of another employee. In most corporations, employees do not report to themselves, so a more meaningful constraint for the Employees table would be one that prevents the ReportsTo field from being the same as the EmployeeID field. Can you imagine what would happen if you created a hierarchy of employees based on who reports to whom, and one of the employees referred to themselves? To remedy this unlikely situation, you can add a new constraint with the following definition (also shown in Figure 3.19):

```
(ReportsTo <> EmployeeID)
```

FIGURE 3.19

Adding a new constraint

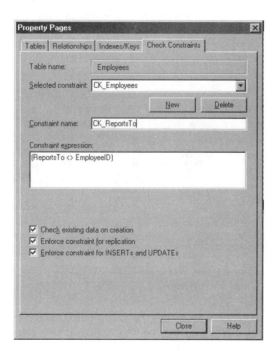

Name this constraint CK_ReportsTo and test it. First, you must close the Employee design grid and agree to save your changes at the prompt. Then open the same table for editing by double-clicking its name. If you attempt to make the ReportsTo field equal to the EmployeeID of the same row, the update will be rejected, as shown in Figure 3.20.

FIGURE 3.20

This error message will appear if you enter a value that violates the CK_ReportsTo constraint.

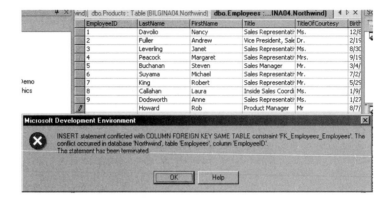

Using the Database Diagram Window

To view and edit the relationships in a database, switch to the Server Explorer and expand the Database Diagrams folder. To view the relationships in a database, you must have an existing diagram. If there's no relational diagram for the database, right-click the Database Diagrams icon and choose New Diagram.

The Database Diagram window appears on the screen. Now drop the tables you want to include in the diagram from the Data View window onto the Database Diagram window. Tables are represented by boxes, which contain each table's field names. Primary key fields are marked with a key icon in front of their name, as shown in Figure 3.21.

FIGURE 3.21

The Customer-Order relational database diagram of the Northwind database

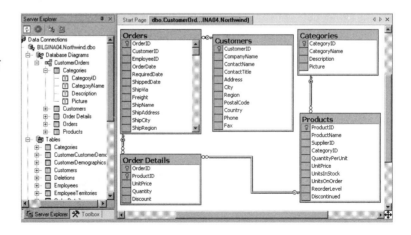

Each relationship is represented by an arrow connecting the two linked tables. A normalized database has two types of relationships:

◆ One-to-many (or many-to-one)

◆ One-to-one

NOTE   *Many-to-many relationships also exist, but are usually specified with the use of an additional link table.*

On the unique side of the relationship, there's a key icon, because you have a key field. On the other side you have, usually, the symbol of infinity. The "many" side of a relationship is a foreign key. The relationship between `Customers` and `Orders` is a typical one-to-many relationship: each customer might appear in multiple orders. One-to-one relationships are not as common.

If you rest the pointer on a relationship, you'll see its name and the names of the two tables it links. To view the labels of the relationships, right-click somewhere on the pane and choose the Show Relationship Labels command from the shortcut menu.

To view more information about a relationship, right-click its line and choose Property Pages. You will see the Table Property Pages dialog box with the Tables, Relationships, Check Constraints, and Indexes/Keys tabs, which we discussed already. The Relationships tab is shown in Figure 3.22 (it depicts the relationship between the tables `Orders` and `Order Details`).

FIGURE 3.22

The Relationships tab of the Properties dialog box

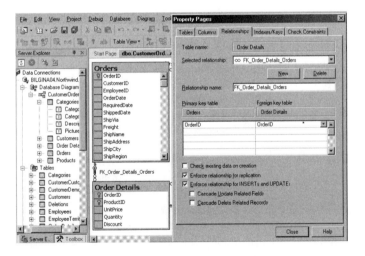

On the Relationships tab, you'll see the name of the selected relationship, the two fields involved in the relationship (the primary and foreign key), and three options for enforcing the integrity of the relationship at the bottom. The options are as follows:

◆ The Check Existing Data On Creation check box tells SQL Server to make sure that the existing rows don't violate the relationship. If a pair of primary/foreign keys violates the relationship (the foreign key in a row points to a nonexisting primary key), a warning will be displayed and the relationship will not be added to the database. You must manually correct the offending row(s) and then attempt to establish the relationship again.

- ◆ The Enforce Relationship For Replication check box tells SQL Server to apply the constraint when the foreign table is replicated to a different database.

- ◆ The third check box, Enforce Relationship For INSERTs And UPDATEs, tells SQL Server to abort any insert or update operation that violates the integrity of the relationship. If you check this box, two additional options will be enabled: the Cascade Update Related Fields and Cascade Delete Related Records options. These enable you to enforce cascading updates and deletes to related tables, should any of the base columns change.

New!   *NOTE*   *The cascading deletes and updates feature is new to SQL Server 2000.*

To establish a new relationship between two tables, drag one of the two fields involved in the relationship and drop it on the other field from the Database Diagram window. As soon as you drop the field, the Create Relationship window appears. The Database Designer is "intelligent" enough to figure out which is the primary field and which is the foreign one. In most cases, all you need to change is the name of the relationship.

TIP   *When you make changes within the Database Diagram design window, an asterisk appears beside the table names whose attributes have been altered. When you close the Database Diagram window, you are prompted to save the changes to these tables. If you choose to save these changes, the asterisks will no longer appear when you reopen the diagram.*

Using the Query Designer

The most important, and most common, operation you'll perform on a database is querying it. To query a database, you must write commands in a special language, the Structured Query Language (SQL), and execute them against the database. In this section, you'll build SQL statements by using another visual tool, the Query Designer. The Query Designer is an excellent tool, but as a programmer you probably will not want to rely on visual tools only; eventually, you will master SQL so that you can simply type in your queries.

With the Query Designer, you can use a visual query diagram to drag tables into the query and specify which fields will appear in the query's output by pointing and clicking. In addition, you can limit the number of rows returned by the query by specifying search criteria on a grid. The Query Designer will generate the SQL statement that implements your query and display it in a separate pane. Finally, you can execute the query to find out whether it works as intended. The query will be executed against the database, so be sure you don't execute *action queries* (queries that modify the database) against a production database. Keep in mind that if you change any of the sample databases by executing action queries against them, you might not get the same results as in the examples in the following chapters. It's quite safe, however, to execute *selection queries,* which retrieve rows and display them in the lower pane of the Query Designer's window. Many programmers simply enter the SQL statements in the Query Designer's middle pane and execute them; you don't have to specify the statements visually. An interesting feature of the Query Designer is that it can build the visual representation of an SQL statement, and you can tweak the query with the visual tools.

The Query Designer Window

To start the Query Designer, reopen the Database Project that you created earlier. In the Solution Explorer, right-click the Queries folder and choose Add Query. This pops up the Add New Item dialog box that you see in Figure 3.23. This dialog box enables you to select from a variety of different Database Project items, such as scripts, stored procedures, and queries. Select the Database Query Item.

DIFFERENT WAYS TO LAUNCH THE QUERY DESIGNER

There are many different ways to launch the Query Designer. In the end, you end up with the same functionality. In this chapter, we show you how to use it from a Database Project. Alternately, you can launch it by editing a view's design. To do so, you expand the Views node from the Server Explorer and right-click an existing view. Select the Design View option from the pop-up menu, which will then launch the Query Designer. Choosing the New View option will also launch the Query Designer.

Another way to load the Query Designer interface is by working with *SQL blocks*. These are specified regions of SQL code that can be edited by using the visual Query Designer. You'll learn more about this in the section "The SQL Editor" later in this chapter.

You can also launch the Query Designer from a preconfigured DataAdapter control. Launch the properties window for the DataAdapter control if it isn't displayed already and expand the SelectCommand property. Below the SelectCommand, you will see a CommandText property that shows the SQL statement associated with the Command object. If you click the ellipse next to the SQL statement, you will launch the Query Designer window. The same goes for the other Command objects, such as the InsertCommand, DeleteCommand, and UpdateCommand. We discuss DataAdapter controls in Chapter 6, "A First Look At ADO.NET."

FIGURE 3.23

The Add New Item dialog box

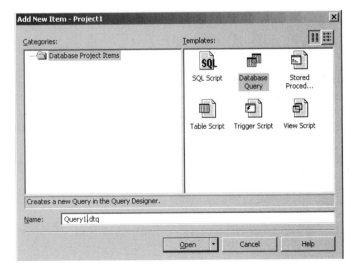

The next dialog box prompts you with some tables, views, or functions to choose. We selected the Customers table. Click the Add button to display the tables in the Diagram pane. The Query Designer window that opens has four panes, shown in Figure 3.24.

FIGURE 3.24

The panes of the Query Designer's window

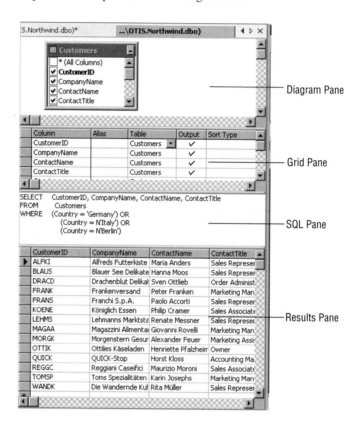

Diagram Pane

Grid Pane

SQL Pane

Results Pane

THE DIAGRAM PANE

In the Diagram pane, you display the tables involved in the query. Tables are represented by boxes, which list the table's columns. If you'd like to add more tables, right-click on this pane and select Add Table. As soon as you add a new table, it is linked automatically to its related tables in the diagram. By default, the Query Designer creates inner joins. (Types of joins are explained in Chapter 4, but this is an important detail.) You will see the various types of joins and how to change the default join type shortly.

THE GRID PANE

The Grid pane contains a spreadsheet-like grid in which you specify criteria for limiting the number of rows and the columns to be included in the query (for example, orders placed in a specified interval, books published by a specific publisher, and so on). If you want to calculate totals (sums, counts, averages), you specify them on the Grid pane.

THE SQL PANE

The SQL pane displays the SQL statement for the current query. The SQL statement implements the query you've specified visually on the Diagram pane. You can edit the SQL statement or you can enter your own SQL statement from scratch. When you do so, the Query Designer places the tables involved in the query on the Diagram pane and fills the selection criteria for you automatically.

If you're new to SQL, you'll probably use the Diagram pane to create queries visually and then see the SQL statements generated automatically by the Query Designer. If you're familiar with SQL, you'll probably enter the SQL statements manually (or you might use the Diagram pane to avoid entering long lists of field names and then edit the initial statement).

THE RESULTS PANE

After you have specified the SQL statement, either in the Diagram pane or in the SQL pane, you can execute the query and view the rows it returns. To execute a query, use the Run command from the Query menu (or press Ctrl+R). You can also right-click the SQL or Diagram pane and choose Run from the shortcut menu. In addition, you can ensure the validity of your SQL statement, by right-clicking the SQL pane and choosing Verify SQL Syntax from the shortcut menu. This doesn't guarantee the validity of your data results, but you can verify your SQL statements, especially the action queries.

You can drag columns from the Diagram pane into the Grid pane. This automatically refreshes the SQL pane. The Query Designer generates the appropriate SQL statement and displays it on the SQL pane. This works both ways. If you have entered the SQL statement, the Query Designer will update the Diagram pane accordingly. When you run the query, it will display the qualifying rows in the Results pane at the bottom of the window.

WARNING *If the query changes one or more rows of a table (an action query), it will not return any rows, and nothing will be displayed on the Results grid. The database, however, will be updated. If needed, test your action queries with temporary tables, or even a copy of the database. Most queries are selection queries, and they can be safely tested. But many of us are so used to testing selection queries in the Query Designer that we might invoke the Run command without realizing we're running an action query.*

Building Simple Queries

If you're not familiar with SQL, you must build a few queries with the Query Designer to see what it can do for you. This will help you get started, and you might choose to use this tool on a regular basis.

The simplest type of query is one that retrieves a number of fields from selected rows in a single table. To retrieve the names of the companies in Germany and their contacts from the Northwind database, follow these steps:

1. Arrange the Server Explorer and Query Designer windows on your screen so that they're both visible. Then drag the table(s) you need in your query from the Server Explorer window and drop them on the Query Designer's Diagram pane. For this example, you'll need the Customers table only.

2. Check the names of the fields you want to appear in the query's output. Check the fields CustomerID, CompanyName, ContactName, and ContactTitle. The names of the fields will appear in the Grid pane, where you must specify the restrictions of the query—namely, that you want to select only the rows in which the Country field is "Germany."

3. Click the first blank line in the Grid pane and select the Country field in the drop-down list of all fields that will appear. Then move to the Criteria column and enter this expression:

```
= 'Germany'
```

This is the only criterion you will apply to the query. Because all customers will be from Germany, you don't want to include the Country field in the output. To exclude a field from the query's output, clear the corresponding box in the Output column.

As soon as you move the cursor to another cell, the SQL pane will be updated. The SQL statement that implements the query you specified with the visual tools is as follows:

```
SELECT CompanyName, ContactName, ContactTitle
FROM Customers
WHERE (Country = 'Germany')
```

4. Open the Query menu and choose Run to execute the query. The qualifying rows of the Customers table will appear on the Results pane, as shown earlier in Figure 3.24.

If you want to specify multiple criteria for the same field, enter them in the columns with the Or ... heading. All the criteria will be combined with the OR operator. To select all customers from Germany and Italy, for example, enter the following expression in the column to the right of the Criteria column:

```
= 'Italy'
```

If you want to specify criteria with different columns, repeat step 3 with a different field name. To select customers from Germany and Berlin, you can select the City field in the next available row of the Grid pane, and enter the following expression in the Criteria column:

```
= 'Berlin'
```

Don't forget to clear the Output box for the City field, because you don't want to include the city name in the output.

To retrieve all customers from Berlin, you need not specify the country restriction. In general, city names are not unique, so you should specify the country as well.

NOTE *You might notice that the Grid pane prefixes your search criteria with an N before the value, such as:* = N'Italy'*. This occurs because the Grid pane converts your values to Unicode. This won't happen if you directly type your criteria into the SQL pane.*

Building Queries with Aggregate Functions

In this section, you'll include aggregate functions in SQL statements by using the visual tools of the Query Designer. First, however, let's quickly review aggregate functions.

SQL can calculate aggregates on selected fields. An *aggregate* is a function that counts rows, calculates sums and averages, and performs a few more common math operations used to summarize data. SQL supports the following aggregate functions:

AVG( )   Returns the average of the values in a column

COUNT( )   Returns the count of the values in a column

MAX( )   Returns the highest value in a column

MIN( )   Returns the lowest value in a column

SUM( )   Returns the sum of all values in a column

NOTE   *Chapter 4 shows how these functions are used in SQL statements.*

SIMPLE AGGREGATES

Simple aggregate queries commonly present calculated information, such as sums and averages. They do not involve any conditional evaluation or complex calculations. Let's create a simple aggregate query to perform counting operations.

Now, revise your first query, so that instead of all customers in a specific country, it will return the number of customers in each country.

To replace the CompanyName field with the count of customers in each country, reset your query by using the following steps:

1. Start a new query, drag and drop the Customers table on the Diagram pane, and check the CompanyName and Country fields. This query will return all the customers along with their country.

2. Right-click the Diagram pane to open the pop-up Query menu and check the Group By option. A new column with the heading Group By is inserted between the Sort Order and Criteria columns in the Grid pane. All cells in this column are assigned the value Group By.

3. In the CompanyName row, and under the Group By column, select the Count option (click this cell with the mouse and select Count from the drop-down list). If you look at the Diagram pane, you will see a summation symbol appear next to the CompanyName field, and the grouping symbol appear next to the Country field.

After you're finished, you see the corresponding SQL statement in the SQL pane:

```
SELECT COUNT(CompanyName) AS Expr1, Country
FROM Northwind.dbo.Customers
GROUP BY Country
```

This statement tells SQL Server to group all rows of the Customers table according to the Country field, so that customers from the same country are grouped together. Then, it must count the rows in each group. The result of the query is a list of country names and customer counts, as shown on the next page (only the first few countries are included in the list).

```
3    Argentina
2    Austria
2    Belgium
8    Brazil
3    Canada
```

The clause AS Expr1 is an alias for the first column of the result. To display a more meaningful column name, rename it to use an alias such as "Customers" or "Number of Customers."

Other aggregate functions are just as easy to use. If the CompanyName field were a numeric one, you could calculate the average with the AVG() function, or the total for all rows in the group with the SUM() function.

AGGREGATES ON MULTIPLE TABLES

Let's build one more query with an aggregate, this time a query involving two tables. This query will retrieve the category names and the count of products in each category. Right-click the Queries folder in your Solution Explorer and choose Add Query, selecting the Database Query item. To build this statement, you need the Categories and Products tables. Add these two tables from the Add Table dialog or drag them from the Server Explorer window onto the Diagram pane of the Query Designer. (You can launch the Add Table dialog by right-clicking on the Diagram Pane and selecting Add Table.) You want a list of category names and the number of products in each category, so check the field CategoryName in the Categories table. You don't want to include the ID of the categories in the output list, and you aren't going to include any fields of the second table—you'll count only the products.

Open the Query menu in the VS .NET IDE and check the Group By option. This command will group the results according to the selected field in the Categories table. As soon as you check the Group By option, the grouping symbol appears next to the name of the CategoryName field in the Categories table. Select the drop-down list from the first cell in the second row of the grid pane. You will see the items Count and Count_Big in addition to the field names. These functions return the number of items in the current group. Select the Count option. You will need to re-select the CategoryName field. Whether you count a single field or all the fields doesn't make any difference. Open the Query menu again, select Run, and observe the results of the query in the lower pane of the Query Designer. The corresponding SQL statement appears in the SQL pane of the window, as shown here:

```
SELECT    Categories.CategoryName, COUNT(*) AS Expr1
FROM      Categories
INNER JOIN Products
ON Categories.CategoryID = Products.CategoryID
GROUP BY Categories.CategoryName
```

The INNER JOIN statement combines rows from two tables based on a common field value (the CategoryID field in this example) and it's discussed in the next section. Here are a few lines of the output produced by this statement:

```
Beverages      12
Condiments     12
Confections    13
```

Building Multi-Table Queries

Queries are rarely that simple. Most queries involve multiple tables linked to one another and restrictions that apply to fields or more than one table. Let's build a query that retrieves all the customers, along with their orders and the products they have purchased. This query uses four tables: Customers, Orders, Order Details, and Products, because the Order Details table contains product IDs, not their actual names. The specification of this query sounds complicated, but building the query is not difficult when using the visual database tools. In this example, you will see how quickly you can generate a multi-table query, avoiding tedious typing.

Right-click the Queries folder in your Solution Explorer and choose Add Query from the shortcut menu. Select the Database Query item and add the four tables listed above to your diagram. The Query Designer automatically links them together based on the existing relationships, as shown in Figure 3.25. It also prepares the core of the SQL statement and displays it on the SQL pane. Notice that the selection list is empty. Start checking the names of the fields you want to include in the output and watch the selection list of the SQL statement grow. Table 3.2 indicates the field names you need to select.

TABLE 3.2: SELECTED FIELDS FOR YOUR QUERY

TABLE	SELECTED FIELDS
Customers	CompanyName
Orders	OrderID, OrderDate
Order Details	UnitPrice, Quantity, Discount
Products	ProductName

FIGURE 3.25

The Query Designer can link tables to one another based on the primary/foreign key definitions in the database.

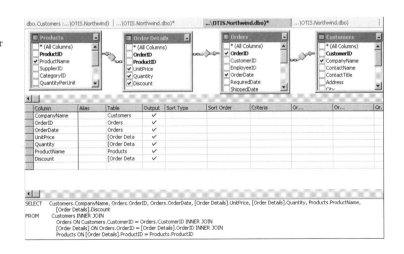

The Query Designer generates a long selection list:

```
SELECT     Customers.CompanyName, Orders.OrderID, Orders.OrderDate,
    [Order Details].UnitPrice, [Order Details].Quantity, [Order Details].Discount,
    Products.ProductName
```

All field names are prefixed by the name of the table they belong to, with a period between the table and field name. The FROM clause of the SQL statement is a long list of inner joins. Joins are discussed in detail in Chapter 4, but here's a brief explanation of the join operation: a join combines rows from two tables based on the values of a field that's common to both tables (usually, a primary and foreign key combination). The rows of the Customers and Orders tables are joined as follows: SQL Server scans all the rows of the Customers table. Each row of the Customers table links to one or more rows of the Orders table, whose CustomerID field has the same value as the CustomerID field of the current row in the Customers table. If the customer with ID of "BLAUS" has five matching rows in the Orders table, five new rows will be appended to the output. These five rows will have the same CustomerID, but a different OrderID. Tables are linked automatically to each other in the Diagram pane based on the relationships between the tables.

The Query Designer also populates the Grid pane with the fields you have checked, as shown in Figure 3.25. Now right-click somewhere on the Diagram pane and choose Run from the shortcut menu to see the output of the query.

The query's specification might sound complicated, and the SQL statement that implements it is quite lengthy, but you were able to build it by simply dropping four tables on the Diagram pane and selecting the names of the fields to be included in the output.

Using the SQL Editor

The last of the visual database tools isn't really visual. The SQL Editor is a text editor customized for entering Transact-SQL statements, and it's the tool you'll be using to write your own stored procedures and triggers. You'll learn how to debug your stored procedures with the T-SQL Debugger.

Stored procedures and triggers are not trivial topics, and although they're introduced in this section, they're discussed in detail in Chapter 5. This section uses simple examples to show you what T-SQL can do for your application.

Working with Stored Procedures

A *stored procedure* is a program in T-SQL that queries or updates the database. In its simplest form, a stored procedure is a query, which is stored in the database itself. If you call your queries often, or if they contain complicated logic, it definitely pays to implement those as stored procedures and save them to the database. SQL Server optimizes the stored procedure, which enables it to execute faster than the equivalent ad hoc SQL statement.

To demonstrate how to use the unified VS .NET debugging tools to debug your custom stored procedures, you'll use a sample stored procedure that comes with the Northwind database. Open the Stored Procedures folder on the Server Explorer and double-click the icon of the SalesByCategory stored procedure. You will see a Design window for stored procedures, as shown in Figure 3.26.

WARNING *Again, certain versions of VS .NET do not support stored procedure editing from the Server Explorer.*

FIGURE 3.26

Editing stored procedures in Visual Basic's development environment

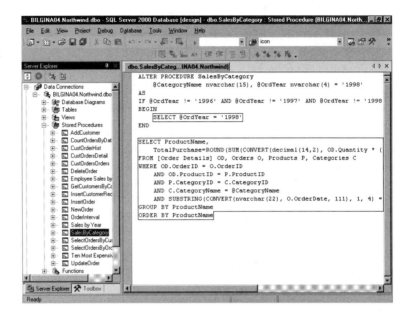

Stored procedures are written in T-SQL, which is a mix of SQL and more traditional programming structures, such as IF statements, loops, and so on. As a VB .NET programmer, you'll have no problem learning and using T-SQL.

WARNING *If you are debugging against a remote SQL Server, you will have to set up remote SQL debugging, which uses DCOM, shockingly enough. Configuring remote SQL debugging by using DCOM is beyond the scope of this book. You can find information on this topic in the MSDN documentation that ships with VS .NET.*

The SalesByCategory stored procedure accepts two input parameters, the @CategoryName and the @OrdYear parameters. They are the names of a category and the year in which the total is calculated. The two variables are declared right after the declaration of the procedure. Notice that the @OrdYear parameter has a default value of 1998, which is used if you call the stored procedure without supplying a value for this argument.

The first three lines examine the value of the @OrdYear parameter. If it's not in the range 1996 through 1998, the procedure ignores the original value (which is in error) and calculates the total of the specified category for 1998:

```
IF @OrdYear != '1996' AND @OrdYear != '1997' AND @OrdYear != '1998'
BEGIN
     SELECT @OrdYear = '1998'
END
```

Although you have yet to explore T-SQL syntax, all you need to know for the purposes of this exercise is that all T-SQL variable names begin with the @ sign.

The rest of the code is an SQL statement that combines the Products, Categories, Orders, and Order Details tables to calculate the total sales for a specific category in a year's period.

NOTE   You might notice blue boxes around certain segments of the SQL code. These are called SQL Blocks. *By right-clicking anywhere within the SQL Block and choosing Design Sql Block, you can launch the Query Designer to visually modify the SQL code.*

EXECUTING AND DEBUGGING A STORED PROCEDURE

Now you're ready to test the SQL statement with the Query Designer. Right-click the stored procedure code anywhere within the Designer window and choose the Step Into Stored Procedure option to execute the SalesByCategory stored procedure. Before the stored procedure is executed, you'll be prompted to enter the values of the expected parameters in the Run Stored Procedure dialog box shown in Figure 3.27. Enter the desired values in the last column and click OK to continue.

After clicking the OK button on the Run Stored Procedure window, you will see a small yellow arrow at the first line of executable code. This is just like what you would see if it were VB .NET code! You can even use the same keyboard shortcuts: F5 to run, and F11 to step through the code. The VS .NET debugger enables you to define breakpoints, step through a procedure, and monitor the values of the variables in the code. You can see all the available options in Figure 3.28.

LIMITATIONS WITH VS .NET DEBUGGING

By default, VS .NET doesn't allow you to edit your source code while you are in debug mode. You can change this behavior by editing the debug settings. Choose the Tools ➤ Options menu and open the Debugging folder. Choose the Edit And Continue option under the Debugging folder. Check the box for Allow Me To Edit VB Files While Debugging.

Even if you set this option, editing source code in debug mode is still cumbersome. In past versions of Visual Studio, you might have enjoyed the feature which allowed you to modify lines of code as you were debugging. This was useful when you wanted to experiment with a change in code logic while the application was running. This way, you didn't have to stop and restart the application to execute new logic. Unfortunately, the Edit And Continue option in VS .NET doesn't work the same way. If you turn on the option to Allow Me To Edit VB Files While Debugging, this doesn't mean that your new code will execute. In fact, it will not. Edits, additions, or deletions to your code while you are in debug mode will not dynamically compile into the rest of your source code. This is because the VS .NET compiler no longer interprets code at design time. When you run your application at design time, your code is fully compiled. You can debug the code because the VS .NET debugger hooks into the source code so that you can pause execution and test values in the Immediate window. However, the actual source code itself does not recompile when you make changes in debug mode. This is why the Allow Me To Edit VB Files While Debugging is turned off by default. What this really means is: Allow me to edit VB files while debugging, but continue with the originally compiled source code.

FIGURE 3.27

Supply the parameters of a stored procedure in the Parameters window.

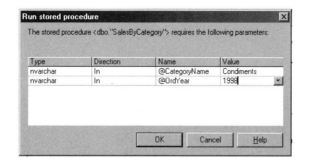

FIGURE 3.28

Debugging a stored procedure with the unified VS .NET debugger

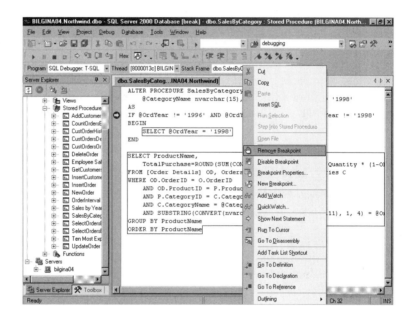

MIXED-LANGUAGE DEBUGGING

Previous versions of Visual Studio used the T-SQL Debugger to debug SQL code. The T-SQL Debugger isn't much help with mixed-language code.

With VS .NET, you can set up mixed-language debugging from your VB .NET and ADO.NET code. You can do this by right-clicking on your VB .NET project and choosing the Properties option. From here, choose Debugging from the `Configuration Properties` folder. Check the SQL Server Debugging check box and choose Apply. Now when you debug your VB .NET and ADO.NET code, you will automatically step into the relevant SQL code within the stored procedures you reference.

The VS .NET debugging commands are the same across all languages. You can step through the statements of a stored procedure, set breakpoints, and examine the values of the local variables during execution.

You've learned a lot in the last few sections. To summarize, the Database Designer is a collection of tools that enables you to:

◆ Create new tables and edit existing ones

◆ View and edit the rows of an existing table

◆ Establish constraints for the individual columns

◆ Create new indexes and edit existing ones

◆ Establish new relationships between tables and edit existing relationships

◆ Debug SQL code within a mixed-language environment

These are all the operations you need to design a new database or refine the design of an existing one. Even the simplest DBMS provides these capabilities, and you can design databases for various DBMSs from within the Visual Studio .NET environment. The Database Designer can handle Access, SQL, and Oracle databases—you have a common tool for all these different types of databases and across different types of languages.

Using the Component Designer

You've covered a lot of ground in this chapter, but not a single line of VB .NET code. The visual database tools are integrated into Visual Studio's environment, but how do they help the VB .NET developer? As we mentioned earlier, the more you do with the database tools, the less code you'll have to write later. Set up your constraints and relationships properly now, and you won't have to worry about maintaining referential integrity from within your code. Write stored procedures for the most common tasks, for example, adding customers, products, invoices, and so on, and you can call these procedures like methods of the database. Finally, by testing and debugging your queries ahead of time, you can simply copy the SQL statements from the Query Designer and paste them into your code.

To get an idea of how the visual database tools can help you develop database applications, you will go through some examples in this section. These are topics you'll explore in depth in the following chapters, but we'd like to end this chapter with some tangible proof of the usefulness of the tools we've discussed. You won't write any code; you'll continue with the visual approach to database programming. The goal is to end up creating a DataSet by using the visual tools and wizards.

Configuring DataAdapter Objects

As you recall, you created a Data Connection by using a standard Windows application in the section "Connecting to Databases" earlier in this chapter. Let's review how you can extend that Connection object and visually work with the ADO.NET objects. We are going to show you how you can visually configure your DataAdapter objects by using a wizard. This wizard will automatically generate your ADO.NET Connection and Command objects for you.

NOTE   *An ADO.NET Command object is any database object that returns one or more rows from the database. It can be a stored procedure, a table, or an SQL statement. If you've worked with ADO 2.x before, Command objects should be familiar to you.*

First, establish your Data Connection (if you haven't done so already) to the Northwind database. The process of establishing a connection to a database with a Connection object is the same as the one outlined in the section "Connecting to Databases," earlier in this chapter.

If you don't have a project with a Data Connection to the Northwind database, create one now:

1. Start a new Windows application, open its Server Explorer window, and add a Data Connection to the Northwind database.

2. Open the Toolbox window. From the Data tab, drag and drop a SqlDataAdapter to your form. This will launch the Data Adapter Configuration Wizard. Select Next to navigate from the introduction screen.

3. The first screen in the wizard prompts you for a data connection to use. You can use an existing one or create a new one. Select the Northwind connection that you created earlier.

4. The next screen gives you three options you can use for generating your Command object. In later chapters, you will work with all the options, but for now, let's keep it simple, and choose the option Use Existing Stored Procedures.

TIP   *It's always a good idea to stick with stored procedures, rather than SQL statements, because stored procedures are pre-optimized and will run faster.*

5. After you click the Next button, you will see a screen prompting you for stored procedure mappings. In the Select drop-down list, select the stored procedure titled *Ten Most Expensive Products*. After you do this, you will see the parameters automatically populate, as you can see in Figure 3.29.

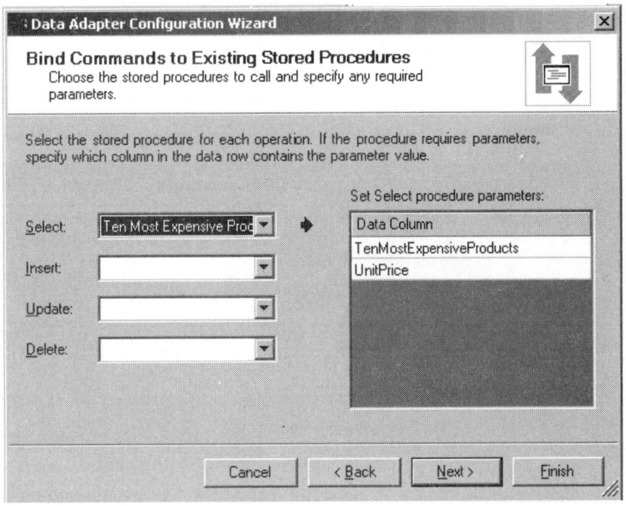

FIGURE 3.29

Mapping stored procedures by using the Data Adapter Configuration Wizard

NOTE *This screen might be quite different from what you've seen before in earlier versions of Visual Studio, as it presents you with the capability to not only choose one stored procedure, but to map multiple stored procedures to different actions. We cover this in more detail in Chapter 6.*

6. Select Next and then Finish to exit the wizard. If you look at the Component Designer tray, you should see two new controls: `SqlDataAdapter1` and `SqlConnection1`.

Because there's no ADO.NET Connection for the `Customers` table, VS .NET added a new SqlConnection control into the Component Designer. You can see that VS .NET automatically selected the most expedient Connection type based on the provider that you had selected. In this case, it uses the SqlClientConnection object. This `SqlClientConnection1` is based on the original connection of the `Customers` table in the Server Explorer (only there, it's a Data Connection that's named based on your machine and database name). If you click on this control, you will see the connection string properties listed in the Properties window.

TIP *VS .NET enables you to edit the connection string right from this window. This is great for prototyping because you can let the wizard generate the connection string for you, then copy/paste it into your actual code.*

Now let's harness the power of the Component Designer and step through the visual ADO.NET controls. In the next section, we show you how to get the best use out of the Component Designer for data access by using point-and-click operations to dynamically create an XML schema and ADO.NET DataSet. You will also get to see the XML Designer in action.

Using the XML Designer

Now that you have your SqlClientConnection and SqlDataAdapter controls in your Component Designer, you can go ahead and generate a DataSet. You will populate the DataSet based on the stored procedure you selected in the DataAdapter.

1. Click the `SqlDataAdapter1` control to bring up its properties window. Below the Properties pane, you should see a small gray box, as seen in Figure 3.30, which contains several hyperlinks: Configure Data Adapter, Generate Dataset, Preview Data.

2. Because you've already configured your DataAdapter, select the second option, Generate DataSet. This launches a dialog box prompting you for some options.

NOTE *The third option, Preview Data, brings up a visual interface for you to examine the data returned by your DataSet. You can experiment with that now, if you would like, but don't worry, we cover that in detail in Chapter 7.*

3. Choose the New option and type in the name `dsExpensive` for your DataSet. Leave the Ten Most Expensive Products stored procedure as your selection criteria, as shown in Figure 3.31. You'll also want to leave the Add This DataSet To The Designer option checked so that you can work with it.

FIGURE 3.30

Working with the Data Adapter options

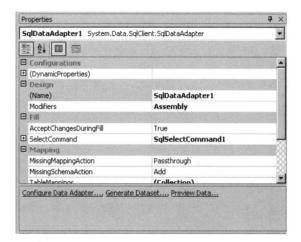

FIGURE 3.31

Configuring the DataSet

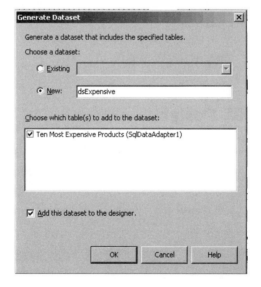

4. After you click OK, VS .NET automatically creates your ADO.NET DataSet for you. If you look in your Component Designer, you will see a new control called **dsExpensive** (or the name that you chose).

5. Click on this **dsExpensive** DataSet control to bring up the properties.

6. Below the Properties pane, you will see some hyperlinks. Select the View Schema option.

Selecting the View Schema option launches the XML Designer that we mentioned earlier. This enables you to see a visual representation of your DataSets in a grid format, as shown in Figure 3.32, or in XML format (by clicking the XML tab at the bottom of the screen), as shown in Figure 3.33. Not only can you view the data in XML format, but VS .NET also automatically creates an XML schema file with an `.xsd` extension, appropriately named after your DataSet. You can view this file in your Solution Explorer.

FIGURE 3.32

Viewing DataSets in a visual grid

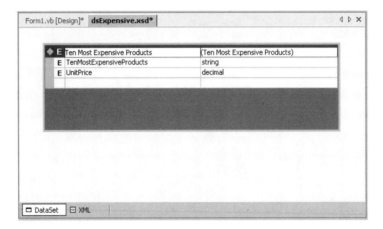

FIGURE 3.33

Viewing DataSets in XML format

As you can see, the Component Designer provides a powerful way to generate DataSets on the fly. You can even combine data from multiple tables and heterogeneous data sources by using the Data Adapter Configuration Wizard. In addition, these tools enable you to easily generate XML schema files that you can distribute to external applications in a universally accepted format.

WARNING *The XML Designer provides an indirect way of working with your DataSet schema. If you change the properties of your DataAdapter, you will have to regenerate your DataSet or manually edit the XSD file.*

Summary

This ends our discussion of the visual database tools, which you'll use frequently in the following chapters. Whether you want to design a new database, tune an existing database, or create queries or stored procedures, you'll find these tools indispensable. The new visual database tools give you a powerful way to work with the ADO.NET framework without typing a line of code.

In the next chapter, you'll switch gears and explore the language for manipulating databases, the Structured Query Language (SQL). SQL is a universal language for manipulating databases (both their contents and their structure) and it's a "must" for a database developer. The Query Designer is a great tool, but it can't substitute for a thorough understanding of SQL statements and their syntax.

Chapter 4

Structured Query Language

- ◆ Selection and action queries
- ◆ Executing SQL statements
- ◆ Joining tables
- ◆ Action queries

YOU HAVE USED QUITE a few SQL statements in the previous chapters, without a formal discussion of the statements and keywords of SQL. It's about time to look at this language and see what it can do for your application. Even though this chapter doesn't deal directly with VB .NET statements, it covers the language behind every database management system (DBMS), and you should spare the time and effort to learn it. You can generate SQL statements with point-and-click operations (as in the Query Designer, as you saw in Chapter 3, "The Visual Database Tools"), but they are no substitute for writing your own SQL statements.

Before we proceed, a few words on how SQL is used. Every database comes with a tool for executing SQL statements and displaying the results. Using VS .NET, you can execute SQL statements against a database from within your VB .NET applications. The rows returned by the statement are intercepted by the .NET Framework, and you can write the code to display them graphically, process them, or place them in a web application and send them to a browser.

Structured Query Language (SQL) is a non-procedural language. SQL doesn't provide traditional programming structures. Instead, it's a language for specifying the operation you want to perform at an unusually high level. The details of the implementation are left to the DBMS. This is good news for non-programmers, but many programmers new to SQL wish it had the structure of a more traditional language. You will get used to SQL and soon be able to combine the best of both worlds: the programming model of VB and the simplicity of SQL.

To retrieve all the company names from the Customers table of the Northwind database, you issue a statement like this one:

```
USE Northwind
SELECT CompanyName
FROM Customers
```

To select customers from a specific country, you issue the following statement:

```
USE Northwind
SELECT CompanyName
FROM Customers
WHERE Country = 'Germany'
```

The DBMS will retrieve and return the rows you requested. With SQL, you don't have to specify how the selection operation will take place. You simply specify *what* you want the database to do for you—not *how* to do it.

SQL statements are categorized into two major categories, which are actually considered separate languages: the statements for manipulating the data, which form the Data Manipulation Language (DML), and the statements for defining database objects, such as tables or their indexes, which form the Data Definition Language (DDL). Almost all the examples in this book work with existing database structures, and we do not cover the Data Definition Language in detail. The Data Manipulation Language is covered in depth because you'll use these statements to retrieve data, insert new data to the database, and edit or delete existing data. Toward the end of this chapter, we discuss how SQL Server automatically generates the statements that reproduce the structure of an existing database so that you can create a fresh database during installation.

NOTE *VS .NET is a powerful tool for working with DDL actions. You can create new databases and tables and modify existing schemas with point-and-click operations. Although you will work with stored procedure creation scripts, you might find it useful to examine some of the DDL statements, such as creating and altering database schema, in the SQL Server Books Online (which comes with your SQL Server installation). You can access the SQL Server Books Online from the Start menu. Select Programs ➤ Microsoft SQL Server ➤ Books Online.*

Selection and Action Queries

The statements of the DML part of the SQL language are also known as *queries*. As we have mentioned earlier, there are two types of queries: selection queries and action queries. *Selection queries* retrieve information from the database and don't modify the database in any way. All selection queries start with the SELECT statement. *Action queries* modify the data in the database's tables and start with one of three keywords: INSERT, DELETE, or UPDATE.

The majority of this chapter covers selection queries. Action queries can be simpler, but the principles of selection queries apply to action queries as well. After all, you rarely modify an entire table unconditionally. You first specify the rows to be modified and then act on them. As you see, you won't go far without mastering selection queries.

Executing SQL Statements

If you are not familiar with SQL, we suggest that you follow the examples in this chapter and modify them to perform similar operations. To follow these examples, you have two options—the Visual Studio .NET Query Designer or the SQL Server Query Analyzer—which are described here. Note that the screenshots for the examples alternate between the tools, so that you can see examples of each. We touched upon these tools in Chapter 3, and in this section we show you how to use them to generate result sets by using SQL.

VS .NET Query Designer

One way to execute queries is to use the Query Designer, which ships with Visual Studio .NET. In order to work with SQL statements by using the Query Designer, create a new Database Project. After the project is loaded, right-click the Queries node in the Solution Explorer and choose Add Query. This opens the Query Designer, where you can type your SQL statement in the SQL pane. We used the Query Designer for some of the SQL code in this chapter, and you can find the solution files and source code on the companion CD.

NOTE The Database Project isn't the only way to bring up the Query Designer. Alternate ways to launch the Query Designer interface are listed in the sidebar in Chapter 3, "Different Ways to Launch the Query Designer.".

The Query Analyzer

Besides the Query Designer's SQL pane, you can also use SQL Server's Query Analyzer to follow the examples. The Query Analyzer is much more robust than the SQL pane in VS .NET's Query Designer, and we recommend using the Query Analyzer tool to execute your SQL statements.

Start the Query Analyzer (select Start ➤ Programs ➤ Microsoft SQL Server ➤ Query Analyzer), and you will see a Query window. (You can also launch the Query Analyzer from the Enterprise Manager's Tools menu.) Initially, the Query window will be empty. Enter the SQL statement you want to execute and then select the desired database's name in the DB drop-down list in order to execute the SQL statement against the selected database. Alternately, you can add the USE statement before the SQL statement to specify the database against which the statement will be executed. To retrieve all the Northwind customers located in Germany, enter this statement:

```
USE Northwind
SELECT CompanyName FROM Customers
WHERE Country = 'Germany'
```

Then select the Execute command from the Query menu, or press F5 to execute the statement. The results appear in the lower pane, as shown in Figure 4.1. For a selection query, such as the previous one, you will see the rows selected and their count at the bottom of the Results pane. If the query updates the database, you will see only the number of rows affected.

NOTE Pressing the Ctrl+E key combination will also execute your query; however, SQL Server 2000 maintains this shortcut only for backward compatibility for users of previous versions of SQL Server. The F5 shortcut is more consistent with the VS .NET keyboard shortcuts.

To execute another query, enter another statement in the upper pane, or edit the previous statement, and press F5 again. You can also save SQL statements into files so that you won't have to type them again. To do so, open the File menu, choose Save As or Save, and enter the name of the file where the contents of the Query pane will be stored. Optionally, select the Save All Queries option to simultaneously save all the queries that you are working with. The statement will be stored in a text file with the extension .sql.

NOTE *The examples of this chapter, and other chapters, can be found in SQL files on the companion CD. Instead of entering the statements yourself, you can load the corresponding .sqlfile from the CD and execute it.*

FIGURE 4.1

The result of executing queries with the Query Analyzer

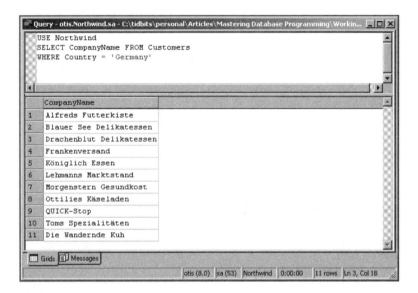

Data Manipulation Language

SQL contains three main types of commands, Data Definition Language (DDL), Data Manipulation Language (DML), and Data Control Language (DCL) statements. DDL is used to create and modify database objects and schema. DML is used to work with the data within these structures. DCL is used to specify permissions on the various database objects. The focus of this book is to work with DML statements that enable you to manipulate SQL Server databases within the .NET Framework. The Data Manipulation Language enables you to work with the data in a SQL Server database by using the four fundamental statements, described in Table 4.1.

NOTE *DDL is an invaluable language for learning how to construct and design database systems. However, the focus of this book is working with existing systems and learning how to master programming against them by using DML.*

TABLE 4.1: THE DATA MANIPULATION STATEMENTS

STATEMENT	ACTION
SELECT	Retrieves records from the database
UPDATE	Updates records in the database
DELETE	Deletes records in the database
INSERT	Inserts records in the database

These statements can get quite complex, because you must also define which records will be selected and acted upon. The selection criteria you specify can apply to multiple tables, and SQL provides many operators and functions that let you specify the desired records. The mechanisms for specifying the desired rows are the same, regardless of whether you simply retrieve them from the database, update them, or delete them. The INSERT statement is the simplest one: it appends rows to a table in the database.

We'll start our discussion of SQL with the SELECT statement. After you learn how to express the criteria for selecting the desired rows with the SELECT statement, you'll be able to apply this information to other DML statements.

Here is the simplest form of the SELECT statement:

```
SELECT fields
FROM tables
```

The keywords *fields* and *tables* represent comma-separated lists of the fields you want to retrieve from the database and the tables they belong to. To select the contact information from all the companies in the Customers table, use this statement:

```
USE Northwind
SELECT CompanyName, ContactName, ContactTitle
FROM Customers
```

To retrieve all the fields, use the asterisk (*) or the ALL keyword. The statement

```
USE Northwind
SELECT * FROM Customers
```

will select all the fields from the Customers table.

Alternately, you can specify the name of the database in the FROM clause by using fully qualified names:

```
SELECT * FROM Northwind.dbo.Customers
```

This alleviates you from having to type the USE statement to set the database reference. The syntax follows the *DatabaseName.Owner.ObjectName* naming convention.

THE *WHERE* CLAUSE

The unconditional form of the SELECT statement used in last few examples is simplistic. You rarely retrieve selected columns of all rows in a table. Usually you specify criteria, such as "all companies in Germany," or "all customers who have placed three or more orders in the last six months," or even more complicated expressions. To restrict the rows returned by the query, use the WHERE clause of the SELECT statement.

The syntax of the WHERE clause can get quite complicated, so we'll start with the simpler forms of the selection criteria. Here's an example of the most common form of a SELECT statement:

```
SELECT fields
FROM tables
WHERE condition
```

The *condition* argument can be a relational expression, like the ones you use in VB. To select all the customers from Germany, use this statement:

```
WHERE Country = 'Germany'
```

To select customers from German-speaking countries, use a condition like this:

```
WHERE Country = 'Germany' OR
      Country = 'Austria' OR
      Country = 'Switzerland'
```

Long lines can break anywhere—you can't break words, of course.

USING MULTIPLE TABLES

When you combine multiple tables in a query, you should always include the WHERE clause to specify some criteria. Let's say you want a list of all product names, along with their categories. The information you need is not contained in a single table. You must extract the product name from the Products table and the category name from the Categories table and specify that the ProductID field in two tables must match. The statement

```
USE NORTHWIND
SELECT ProductName, CategoryName
FROM Products, Categories
WHERE Products.CategoryID = Categories.CategoryID
```

will retrieve the names of all products, along with their category names. Here's how this statement is executed: For each row in the Products table, the SQL engine locates the matching row in the Categories table and then appends the ProductName and CategoryName fields to the result. The rows are matched with the CategoryID field (both rows must have the same CategoryID value). If a product has no category, then it will not be included in the result.

NOTE *Note that when fields in two tables have the same names, you must add the table name as a prefix to remove the ambiguity. In this book, we have tried to use table names as prefixes for all field names. Doing so makes the statements lengthier, but they are easier to read, especially if the user is not familiar with the database. Also note that some field names might contain spaces. These field names must appear in square brackets. The* publishers *table of the Pubs sample database contains a field named* Publisher Name. *To use this field in a query, enclose it in brackets:* publishers.[Publisher Name]. *The table prefix is optional (if no other table contains a column by that name), but the brackets are mandatory.*

This type of restriction is used in nearly every SELECT statement that combines two or more tables. Here's another statement that uses a similar restriction to retrieve data from the Pubs database. It retrieves all the titles from the titles table, along with the matching publisher:

```
USE Pubs
SELECT Title, Pub_name
FROM Titles, Publishers
WHERE Titles.pub_id = Publishers.pub_id
```

(Actually, this statement doesn't retrieve all the titles, because some titles might not have a publisher. This topic is discussed in detail in "Joining Tables," later in this chapter).

You can also combine multiple restrictions with logical operators. To retrieve all the titles published by a specific publisher, use the publisher's ID in the WHERE clause, as in the following statement:

```
USE Pubs
SELECT Titles.Title
FROM Titles
WHERE Titles.pub_id=0736
```

This statement assumes that you know the publisher's ID—or you look it up in the publishers table first and then plug it into the statement. A more flexible coding of the same statement would be the following:

```
USE Pubs
SELECT Titles.Title
FROM Titles, Publishers
WHERE Titles.pub_id=Publishers.pub_id AND
      Publishers.pub_name='New Moon Books'
```

This statement combines two tables and selects the titles of a publisher specified by name. To match titles and publisher, it requests that:

- The publisher's name in the publishers table is *New Moon Books.*

- The PubID field in the titles table matches the PubID field in the publishers table.

Notice that we did not specify the publisher's name in the SELECT list; all the desired books have the same publisher, so we used the PubID field in the WHERE clause, but did not include any information about the publisher in the result.

If you specify multiple tables without the WHERE clause, the SQL statement will return an enormous result set. If you issue the statement

```
USE Northwind
SELECT ProductName, CategoryName FROM Categories, Products
```

you will not get a line for each product name followed by its category. You will get a result set with 616 rows, which are all possible combinations of product names and category names. This is known as a *Cartesian product* (or *cross-product*) of the two tables and contains all possible combinations of the rows of the two tables. In this example, the Categories table has 8 rows, and the Products table has 77 rows, so their cross-product contains 616 rows ($8 \times 77 = 616$). If you create the cross-product of two tables with a few thousand records, you will retrieve a result set so large it's practically useless.

THE *AS* KEYWORD

By default, each column of a query is labeled after the actual field name in the output. If a table contains two fields named CustLName and CustFName, you can display them with different labels by using the AS keyword. The SELECT statement

```
SELECT CustLName, CustFName
```

will produce two columns labeled CustLName and CustFName. The query's output will look much better if you change the labels of these two columns with a statement like the following one:

```
SELECT CustLName AS [Last Name], CustFName AS [First Name]
```

It is also possible to concatenate two fields in the SELECT list with the concatenation operator. Concatenated fields are not automatically labeled, so you must supply your own header for the combined field. This statement creates a single column for the customer's name and labels it Customer Name:

```
SELECT CustFname + ',' + CustLName AS [Customer Name]
```

SQL Server automatically labels the combined columns in your result set. SQL Server recognizes a single concatenation operator (the + symbol). If the two values are numeric, they will be added. If they are both text, they will be concatenated. If one of them is numeric, SQL Server will not perform any conversion automatically. You must convert the numeric value to text with the CONVERT() function before you can concatenate the two with the + operator. The CONVERT() function is covered in Chapter 5, "Transact-SQL."

THE *TOP* KEYWORD

Some queries might retrieve a large number of rows, but you're interested in only the top few rows. The TOP *n* keyword enables you to select the first *n* rows and ignore the remaining ones. Let's say you want to see the list of the 10 most wanted products. Without the TOP keyword, you'd have to calculate how many items from each product have been sold, sort them according to items sold, and examine the first 10 rows returned by the query.

The TOP keyword is used only when the rows are ordered according to some meaningful criteria. Limiting a query's output to the alphabetically top *n* rows isn't very practical. When the rows are sorted according to items sold, revenue generated, and so on, it makes sense to limit the query's output to *n* rows. You will also find it useful for prototyping your SQL statements quickly. You'll see many examples of the TOP keyword later in this chapter, after you learn how to order a query's rows.

THE *LIKE* OPERATOR

Quite often you won't be interested in an exact match, especially when you receive search criteria from a user. Most search engines enable you to search within a value. The LIKE operator enables you to do this. A publisher's name might be followed by several initials, such as Inc., SA, and so on. Or you might be interested in retrieving books with specific words in their titles. To handle similar searches, which use patterns rather than exact matches, SQL provides the LIKE operator, which is a very general pattern-matching operator.

The LIKE operator uses pattern-matching characters, like the ones you use to select multiple files in DOS. The expression Sales% stands for "all files that begin with the string Sales," and %.xls stands for "all files with the extension .xls." The LIKE operator recognizes a number of pattern-matching characters (or wildcard characters) to match one or more characters, numeric digits, ranges of letters, and so on.

If you are not sure about a book's title, but know it starts with the word *Cooking*, use an expression such as the following one:

```
USE Pubs
SELECT * FROM titles
WHERE title LIKE 'cooking%'
```

This expression will locate all rows in the titles table that start with the string "Cooking" and are followed by any other character(s) (or no characters at all). The search is not case sensitive, so you need not capitalize the arguments. This will return one record whose title begins with *Cooking*.

You can use the LIKE operator to retrieve all titles about cooking with a statement like this one:

```
USE Pubs
SELECT * FROM titles
WHERE title LIKE '%cooking%'
```

The two percent symbols mean that any characters can appear in front of or after the word *cooking* in the title. This is how you code the expression "The title should contain the word *cooking*."

This statement will retrieve three titles, including titles ranging from *Cooking with Computers: Surreptitious Balance Sheets* to *The Psychology of Computer Cooking*. To limit the selection to books about Mediterranean cooking, use this statement:

```
USE Pubs
SELECT * FROM titles
WHERE title LIKE '%cooking%' AND
title LIKE '%mediterranean%'
```

The AND keyword enables you to specify multiple search criteria by using the LIKE operator. In this case, you will retrieve only those books that contain *cooking* and *Mediterranean* somewhere in the title.

The LIKE operator recognizes many wildcard characters, but the syntax is not uniform across all databases. Even Microsoft Access and SQL Server use different wildcard characters. If you're using a single product, you'll get used to the notation quickly. If you're consulting for various companies, the syntax of the LIKE operator can be a real problem. The wildcard characters for SQL Server are listed in Table 4.2.

TABLE 4.2: SQL SERVER 2000 WILDCARD CHARACTERS

WILDCARD CHARACTER	FUNCTION
%	Matches any number of characters. The pattern program% will find *program*, *programming*, *programmer*, and so on. Notice that the percent symbol can be used as the first or last character in the character string, or as both the first and last character. The pattern %program% will locate strings that contain the words *program, programming, nonprogrammer*, and so on.
_	Matches any single character. The pattern b_y will find *boy* and *bay*, but not *boysenberry*.
[ ]	Matches any single character within the brackets. The pattern Santa [IY]nez will find both *Santa Inez* and *Santa Ynez*. This pattern is quite useful in locating possibly misspelled words in a single pass.
[-]	Matches any one of a range of alphanumeric characters. The characters must be consecutive in the alphabet and specified in ascending order (A to Z). The pattern [a-c]% will find all words that begin with *a, b,* or *c* (in lowercase or uppercase).
[^]	Matches any character not in the brackets. The pattern %q[^u]% will find words that contain the character *q* not followed by *u* (they are likely to be misspelled words in English). You can also use the hyphen to specify a range, such as %t[^h-o]%, when you are looking for names that are not Thomas or a variation, such as Tom or Tommy.

To use the special symbols of Table 4.2 as literal, you must enclose them in a pair of square brackets. To search for the value *50%*, you would need to use the pattern 50[%], so that the LIKE operator doesn't interpret the percent sign as a wildcard. This way, you can search for the opening bracket, question mark, number sign, and asterisk as literal in your search argument by enclosing them in square brackets. The closing bracket can't appear inside a pair of brackets (it will close the opening bracket prematurely), but you can use it as a literal on its own. The closing bracket in the argument abc] has no special meaning, because there's no opening bracket.

When performing string comparisons with LIKE, all characters in the pattern string are significant, including leading and/or trailing spaces. To ignore the spaces in the search arguments, use the LTRIM() and RTRIM() functions with SQL Server. LTRIM() and RTRIM() remove leading and trailing spaces, respectively. Another tricky situation occurs when a value is shorter than the column length. Trailing spaces will be inserted until the value matches the length of the column. Fields declared as char(20) will contain trailing spaces if the value stored is fewer than 20 characters long. To avoid this, store variable-length strings as varchar.

NOTE *If you want to search for values that do not match your specified pattern, use the* NOT LIKE *operator. If you want to search for all the titles that do not begin with s, you would use the pattern* NOT LIKE 's%'.

Some search arguments might include one or more of the special wildcard characters themselves. A column that stores discounts might contain numeric values followed by the percent sign (%), and the underscore character (_) is not uncommon in product codes. In addition to containing the wildcard with square brackets, you can also use a method called *escaping*, which means that you can opt to escape certain characters. To include a wildcard character in the search argument as a regular character, you must repeat the special character. To search for the string, "up to 50% off the list price," use the following WHERE clause:

```
WHERE Comments LIKE "%up to 50%% off the list price%"
```

What if you want to search for the string "50%"? You want to locate a string that ends with the percent sign, followed by any character. This time you must use the ESCAPE clause. This clause specifies an escape character, which cancels the effect of a special character when placed in front of it. To locate strings that contain the string "50," you use a WHERE clause such as the following:

```
WHERE Comments LIKE '%50%'
```

If you want to locate the string "50%", however, you must first select an escape character, which doesn't appear in the search argument (the exclamation mark is used commonly as an escape character). The condition must change to '%50!%%' and be followed by the ESCAPE clause:

```
WHERE Comments LIKE '%50!%%' ESCAPE '!'
```

The first and last percent signs in the search argument have the usual meaning (any characters in front or after the string). The exclamation mark tells SQL Server to treat the following percent sign as part of the string and not as a special string. The last SQL statement will retrieve all rows with the string "50%" in their Comments column.

Locating Null Values

A common operation in manipulating and maintaining databases is to locate Null values in fields. The expressions IS NULL and IS NOT NULL find field values that are (or are not) Null. A string comparison such as this one will not return Null values:

```
WHERE CompanyName = " "
```

Actually, this statement will return rows in which the CompanyName column was set to an empty string, but not the rows in which it was never assigned a value. They could be rows that were assigned values in the CompanyName field, but these values were deleted later. Perhaps there's a reason to set certain fields to an empty string. To locate the rows that have a Null value in their CompanyName column, use the following WHERE clause:

```
WHERE CompanyName IS NULL
```

A Null price in the Products table means that the product's price was not available at the time of the data entry. You can easily locate the products without prices and edit them. This statement locates products without prices:

```
WHERE Price IS NULL
```

If you compare the Price field to the numeric value 0, you'll retrieve the products with zero price (they could be discontinued products, freebies, but certainly not the products that have never had a price).

Here's a more practical example. While you're entering titles in the Pubs database, you might not know a book's royalty and leave this field blank. At a later stage, you can locate all the titles without a price and edit them. This statement retrieves all the rows without a price:

```
USE Pubs
SELECT Titles.Title
FROM Titles
WHERE Titles.price IS NULL
```

A more useful SQL statement would locate not only titles without prices, but also titles that point to nonexisting publishers. For example, you might have deleted rows in the publishers table without removing the corresponding references in the titles table. This situation should never arise in a well-designed database, but most databases in use today are far from perfect, and consultants face similar problems when they take over someone else's projects. After you develop a basic understanding of the database, you should examine the rules for establishing referential integrity.

NOTE   *For a detailed discussion of referential integrity and the rules for enforcing referential integrity among the tables of the database, see the "Database Integrity" section in Chapter 2, "Basic Concepts of Relational Databases."*

If you suspect that some titles refer to invalid publishers, use the following statements to retrieve all the titles that have no publisher or refer to nonexistent publishers. This statement retrieves titles without a publisher:

```
USE Pubs
SELECT Titles.Title
```

```
FROM Titles
WHERE (Titles.pub_id IS NULL)
```

This statement retrieves titles with an invalid publisher:

```
USE Pubs
SELECT Titles.Title
FROM Titles, Publishers
WHERE Titles.pub_id =[Publishers].[pub_id] AND
      Publishers.pub_name IS NULL
```

If you want to, you can edit the titles table in the Pubs database to add a few rows with NULL pub_id values to test the IS NULL statement. The pub_id column permits Null values, so you will have no problem adding these records.

How about combining the two WHERE clauses with the OR operator so that you can retrieve all the titles with a single statement? The following statement seems valid, but it's not:

```
USE Pubs
SELECT Titles.Title
FROM Titles, Publishers
WHERE ((Titles.pub_id IS NULL) OR
      (Titles.pub_id =[Publishers].[pub_id] AND
       Publishers.pub_name IS NULL))
```

This statement will return an enormous result set that contains all combinations of titles and publishers. We come back to queries that generate large result sets later in this chapter and discuss them in detail. There's a simple method to combine the results of two or more queries with the UNION operator that combines the unique rows from two result sets.

The *UNION* Operator

The UNION operator enables you to combine the results of two separate queries into a single result set. The final result set is the union of the result set returned by the individual queries, and it doesn't contain duplicate rows. Here's how you can use the UNION operator to combine the rows retrieved by the two previous examples:

```
USE Pubs
(SELECT Titles.Title
    FROM Titles, Publishers
    WHERE Titles.pub_id IS NULL)
UNION
    (SELECT Titles.Title
        FROM Titles, Publishers
        WHERE Titles.pub_id=Publishers.pub_id AND
        Publishers.pub_name IS NULL)
```

In short, this statement will find all titles with a problem in their publisher entry. The IS NULL and IS NOT NULL expressions are used quite frequently in establishing the integrity of a database; a simple SQL statement can locate the Null values in a table. Later in this chapter, in "The UPDATE Statement," you will learn how to use SQL statements to edit these fields in a table.

When you use the UNION keyword, you should ensure that each query has the same number of columns. The order of the columns must match. Additionally, the data types for the matching columns must be compatible with one another.

How about the records that have an invalid publisher ID (a publisher ID that points to a nonexistent record in the publishers table)? To find the rows of the Title table that point to nonexistent publishers, you must use the IN (and NOT IN) keyword, which is described later in this chapter.

The *DISTINCT* Keyword

The DISTINCT keyword eliminates any duplicates from the result set retrieved by the SELECT statement. Let's say you want to find out which regions have Northwind customers. If you retrieve all regions from the Customers table, you'll end up with many duplicates. To eliminate them, use the DISTINCT keyword as shown in this statement:

```
USE Northwind
SELECT DISTINCT Region
FROM Customers
```

The result set returned by this statement is shown in Figure 4.2. The NULL entry means that one or more rows in the Customers table have no value in the Region column.

FIGURE 4.2

Selecting unique country names from the Northwind Customers table

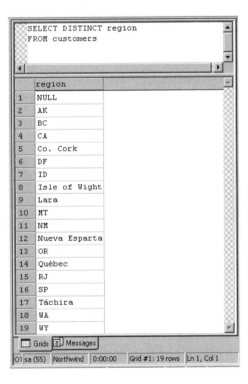

NOTE   *According to our discussion of database normalization, the database should have a separate table for storing region names and force each row in the* Customers *table to point to a region name in this new table. You could have done so, but the designers of the Northwind database decided not to go too far with the normalization.*

The DISTINCT keyword can also be used with multiple fields. The statement

```
USE Northwind
SELECT DISTINCT Country, City
FROM Customers
```

will retrieve values where the combination of the country and city values are unique. The preceding statement retrieves 69 rows. If you omit the DISTINCT keyword, you'll get 91 rows. There are three customers in Buenos Aires, Argentina, but this city-country combination appears only once if the DISTINCT statement is used.

Sorting Rows with the *ORDER BY* Clause

The rows of a query rarely return in the order you want them. They are ordered according to the order in which the column names were specified in the SELECT statement and the order in which the rows were entered in each table. To request that the rows be returned in a specific order, use the ORDER BY clause. The syntax of ORDER BY is as follows:

```
ORDER BY col1, col2, . . .
```

You can specify any number of columns in the order list. The output of the query is ordered according to the values of the first column (col1). If two rows have identical values in this column, then they are sorted according to the second column, and so on. Let's say you want a list of all customers in the Customers table ordered by country. Because you have multiple customers in each country, you must also define how each group of customers from the same country will be ordered. The statement

```
USE Northwind
SELECT CompanyName, ContactName, Country, City
FROM Customers
ORDER BY Country, City
```

will display the customers ordered by country and by city within each country's section. If you want to order the rows by company name within each country group, use this statement:

```
USE Northwind
SELECT CompanyName, ContactName, Country, City
FROM Customers
ORDER BY Country, CompanyName
```

Or you can use the following statement to order them by country, by city within each country, and by company name within each city:

```
USE Northwind
SELECT CompanyName, ContactName, Country, City
FROM Customers
ORDER BY Country, City, CompanyName
```

Figure 4.3 shows the output produced by two SELECT statements, one without the ORDER BY clause, and the other with the ORDER BY clause.

FIGURE 4.3

The Northwind companies as retrieved from the Customers table (a), and the same companies ordered by country and city within each country (b)

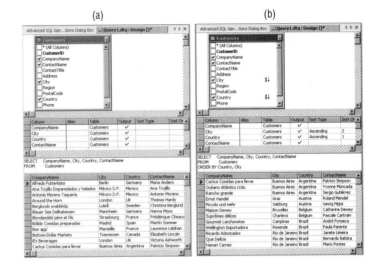

You can also specify how you want the columns to be ordered by using the ASC and DESC keywords. ASC lists the values from lowest to highest, and DESC does the reverse. The statement

```
USE Northwind
SELECT CompanyName, ContactName, Country, City
FROM Customers
ORDER BY CompanyName DESC
```

returns customer information, listing the records in reverse alphabetical order according to CompanyName.

Calculated Fields

In addition to column names, you can specify calculated fields in the SELECT statement. The Order Details table contains a row for each invoice line. Invoice 10248, for instance, contains three lines (three items sold), and each detail line appears in a separate row in the Order Details table. Each row holds the number of items sold, the item's price, and the corresponding discount. To display the line's subtotal, you must multiply the quantity by the price minus the discount, as shown in the following statement:

```
USE Northwind
SELECT Orders.OrderID, ProductID,
    [Order Details].UnitPrice *
    [Order Details].Quantity *(1 - [Order Details].Discount) AS SubTotal
FROM Orders, [Order Details]
WHERE Orders.OrderID = [Order Details].OrderID
```

This statement will calculate the subtotal for each line in the invoices issued to all Northwind customers and display them along with the order number, as shown in Figure 4.4. The order numbers are repeated as many times as there are products in the order (or lines in the invoice). In the following section, "Totaling and Counting," you will find out how to calculate totals, too.

FIGURE 4.4

Calculating the subtotals for each item sold

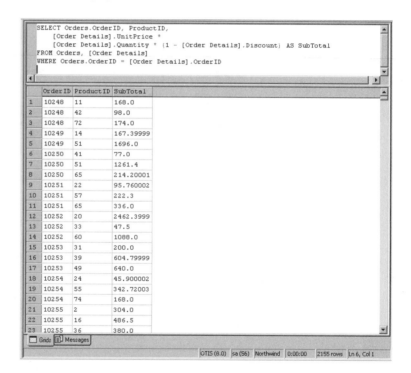

WORKING WITH ALIASES

The preceding SQL statement is quite lengthy. You can shorten it by omitting the table name qualifier for the Quantity and UnitPrice fields, because their names do not appear in any other table. You can't omit the table qualifier from the OrderID field's name, because it appears in both tables involved in the query.

Continued on next page

WORKING WITH ALIASES *(continued)*

You can also specify a short alias for the Order Details table name with the AS keyword (which is optional) and then use the alias in the place of the actual table name:

```
USE Northwind
SELECT Orders.OrderID, ProductID, UnitPrice * Quantity *(1 - Discount) AS SubTotal
FROM Orders, [Order Details] as details
WHERE Orders.OrderID = details.OrderID
```

While we are on the subject of aliases, this could be expanded on slightly. For example:

```
USE Northwind
SELECT o.OrderID, ProductID, UnitPrice * Quantity *(1 - Discount) AS SubTotal
FROM Orders o, [Order Details] od
WHERE o.OrderID = od.OrderID
```

Notice that the AS keyword is optional and you can specify the alias without it for brevity.

TOTALING AND COUNTING

SQL supports a number of aggregate functions, which act on selected fields of all the rows returned by the query. The aggregate functions, listed in Table 4.3, perform basic calculations such as summing, counting, and averaging numeric values. Aggregate functions accept field names (or calculated fields) as arguments, and they return a single value, which is the sum (or average) of all values.

TABLE 4.3: SQL'S AGGREGATE FUNCTIONS

FUNCTION	ACTION
AVG()	Returns the average of the values in a specified column
COUNT()	Returns the number (count) of values in a specified column
MAX()	Returns the largest value in a specified column
MIN()	Returns the smallest value in a specified column
SUM()	Returns the sum of values in a specified column

These functions operate on a single column (which could be a calculated column) and they return a single value. The rows used in the calculations are specified with the proper WHERE clause. The SUM() and AVG() functions can process only numeric values. The other three functions can process both numeric and text values.

WARNING   *The MAX() and MIN() functions cannot process bit data types.*

These functions summarize data from one or more tables. Let's say you want to know how many of the Northwind database customers are located in Germany. The following SQL statement will return the desired value:

```
USE Northwind
SELECT     COUNT(CustomerID) AS GermanyCount
FROM       Customers
WHERE      (Country = 'Germany')
```

This is a simple demonstration of the COUNT() function. If you want to count unique values, you must use the DISTINCT keyword along with the name of the field to count. If you want to find out the number of countries that have Northwind customers, use the following SQL statement:

```
USE Northwind
SELECT     COUNT(DISTINCT Country) AS DistinctCustomerCount
FROM       Customers
```

This returns 21 records, which don't include any Null values. If you omit the DISTINCT keyword, the statement will return the number of rows that have a Country field. The COUNT() statement ignores the Null values, unless you specify the * argument. The asterisk indicates that you want to include the Null values. The following statement will return the count of all rows in the Customers table, even if some of them have a Null value in the Country column:

```
USE Northwind
SELECT  COUNT(*) AS CountWithNulls
FROM    Customers
```

This returns 91 records, which indicates that 70 records contained Null values.

The SUM() function is used to total the values of a specific field in the specified rows. To find out how many units of the product with ID = 11 (Queso Cabrales) have been sold, use the following statement:

```
USE Northwind
SELECT     SUM(Quantity) AS UnitsSold
FROM       [Order Details]
WHERE      (ProductID = 11)
```

The SQL statement that returns the total revenue generated by a single product is a bit more complicated. This time you must add the products of quantities multiplied by prices, taking into consideration each invoice's discount:

```
USE Northwind
SELECT SUM(Quantity) AS UnitsSold, Sum((Quantity * UnitPrice) * (1-Discount)) AS
Revenue
FROM [Order Details]
WHERE (ProductID = 11)
```

You will find out that Queso Cabrales sold 706 units, which generated a total revenue of $12,901.77, as shown in Figure 4.5.

FIGURE 4.5

Using the COUNT()
function to calculate
sums on numeric
fields

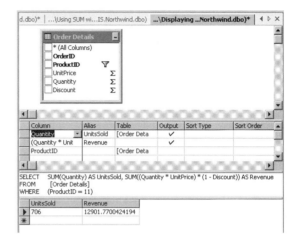

Here's a SELECT statement that returns all product IDs along with the number of invoices that contain them and the minimum, maximum, and average quantity ordered, the results of which are shown in Figure 4.6:

```
USE Northwind
SELECT ProductID AS PRODUCT,
    COUNT(ProductID) AS [INVOICES],
    MIN(Quantity) AS [MIN],
    MAX(Quantity) AS [MAX],
    AVG(Quantity) AS [AVERAGE]
FROM [Order Details]
GROUP BY ProductID
ORDER BY ProductID
```

GROUPING ROWS

The aggregate functions operate on all the rows selected by the query. Sometimes you need to group the results of a query, so that you can calculate subtotals. Let's say you need not only the total revenues generated by a single product, but a list of all products and the revenues they generated. The last example in the previous section calculates the total revenue generated by a single product. If you omit the WHERE clause, it will calculate the total revenue generated by all products. It is possible to use the SUM() function to break the calculations at each new product ID, as demonstrated in Listing 4.1. To do so, you must group the product IDs together with the GROUP BY clause.

LISTING 4.1: THE *PRODUCTREVENUES* QUERY

```
USE NORTHWIND
SELECT ProductID, SUM(Quantity * UnitPrice *(1 - Discount))
    AS [Total Revenues]
FROM [Order Details]
GROUP BY ProductID
ORDER BY ProductID
```

FIGURE 4.6

Using the multiple aggregate functions

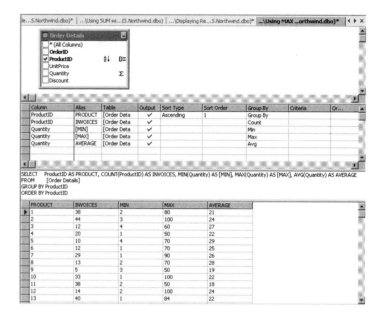

The preceding statement will produce an output like this one:

```
ProductID    Total Revenues
_____    _____

1            12788.100059509277
2            16355.96004486084
3            3044.0
4            8567.8999938964844
5            5347.2000045776367
6            7137.0
7            22044.299987792969
8            12772.0
9            7226.5
10           20867.340026855469
11           12901.770042419434
12           12257.660041809082
```

NOTE   *You will see all 77 product IDs, but we omit most of them for brevity.*

As you can see, the SUM() function works in tandem with the GROUP BY clause (when there is one) to produce subtotals. The GROUP BY clause is not another ordering mechanism, like the ORDER BY clause. It groups all the rows with the same values in the specified column and forces the aggregate functions to act on each group separately. SQL Server will sort the rows according to the column specified in the GROUP BY clause and start calculating the aggregate functions. Every time it runs into a new group, it prints the result and resets the aggregate function(s).

If you use the GROUP BY clause in a SQL statement, you must be aware of this rule: *All the fields included in the* SELECT *list must be either part of an aggregate function or part of the* GROUP BY *clause.* Let's say you want to change the previous statement to display the names of the products, rather than their IDs. The following statement in Listing 4.2 will display product names, instead of product IDs. Notice that the ProductName field doesn't appear as an argument to an aggregate function, so it must be part of the GROUP BY clause.

LISTING 4.2: THE *PRODUCTREVENUES1* QUERY

```
USE NORTHWIND
SELECT ProductName,
       SUM(Quantity * [Order Details].UnitPrice *
       (1 - Discount)) AS [Total Revenues]
FROM [Order Details], Products
WHERE Products.ProductID = [Order Details].ProductID
GROUP BY ProductName
ORDER BY ProductName
```

These are the first few lines of the output produced by this statement:

```
ProductName              Total Revenues
-------------------      -------------------
Alice Mutton             32698.379981994629
Aniseed Syrup            3044.0
Boston Crab Meat         17910.629892349243
Camembert Pierrot        46825.480133056641
Carnarvon Tigers         29171.875
Chai                     12788.100059509277
Chang                    16355.96004486084
Chartreuse verte         12294.539949417114
```

If you omit the GROUP BY clause, the query will return the total revenue generated by all the products in the database. If you remove the GROUP BY clause, you must also remove the ProductName field from the SELECT list, as well as the ORDER BY clause. For more information on using aggregate functions, see the following sidebar, "How to Use Aggregate Functions."

You can also combine multiple aggregate functions in the SELECT field. The following statement will calculate the units of products sold, along with the revenue they generated and the number of invoices that contain the specific product:

```
USE Northwind
SELECT ProductID AS PRODUCT,
    COUNT(ProductID) AS [INVOICES],
    SUM(Quantity) AS [UNITS SOLD],
    SUM(Quantity * UnitPrice *(1 - Discount)) AS REVENUE
FROM [Order Details]
GROUP BY ProductID
ORDER BY ProductID
```

The COUNT() function counts how many times each product ID appears in the Order Details table. This value is the number of invoices that contain a line with the specific product. The following SUM() functions calculate the total number of items sold and the total revenue they generated. The SQL statement and the output it generated in the Query Analyzer are shown in Figure 4.7.

FIGURE 4.7

Combining multiple aggregate functions in the same SELECT list

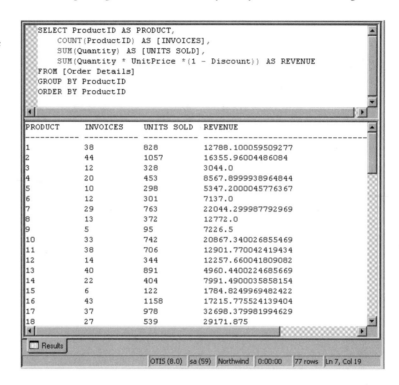

HOW TO USE AGGREGATE FUNCTIONS

Aggregate functions can be used only in the list of fields following a SELECT statement, in a COMPUTE or COMPUTE BY clause (discussed in the following chapter), or in a HAVING clause (discussed next in this chapter). They can't be used in a FROM or a WHERE clause. Moreover, if a SELECT list includes an aggregate function, then you can't include other fields in the same list, unless they are part of an aggregate function or part of a GROUP BY clause. The statement

```
USE Northwind
SELECT ProductID,
    SUM(Quantity * UnitPrice *(1-Discount))
    AS REVENUE
FROM [Order Details]
WHERE ProductID=11
```

Continued on next page

will not display the product ID along with the revenues generated by the specified product. Instead, it will generate the following error message:

```
Column 'Order Details.ProductID' is invalid in the select list because it is not
    contained in an aggregate function and there is no GROUP BY clause.
```

To avoid this error message and display both the product ID and the revenues it generated, use the GROUP BY clause, as in the following statement. It doesn't make much sense to group a single product, but it will do the trick and you'll get the desired output.

```
USE Northwind
SELECT ProductID,
    SUM(Quantity * UnitPrice *(1 - Discount))
    AS REVENUE
FROM [Order Details]
WHERE ProductID=11
GROUP BY ProductID
```

Limiting Groups with *HAVING*

The HAVING clause limits the groups that will appear in the result set. In a way, it is similar to the WHERE clause, which limits the number of rows that will appear in the result cursor. However, the HAVING clause can be used only in a GROUP BY clause, and any fields used in the HAVING clause must also appear in the GROUP BY list, or as arguments in an aggregate function.

The following statement will return the IDs of the products whose sales exceed 1000 units:

```
USE Northwind
SELECT ProductID, SUM(Quantity) as TotalSold
FROM [Order Details]
GROUP BY ProductID
HAVING SUM(Quantity)>1000
```

If you want to see product names instead of IDs, you must add a slightly longer statement that includes the Products table and maps them to the ProductIDs in the Order Details table with a WHERE clause:

```
USE Northwind
SELECT Products.ProductName, [Order Details].ProductID,
        SUM(Quantity) AS [Items Sold]
FROM Products, [Order Details]
WHERE [Order Details].ProductID = Products.ProductID
GROUP BY [Order Details].ProductID, Products.ProductName
HAVING SUM(Quantity)>1000
ORDER BY Products.ProductName
```

Use the WHERE clause to include additional restrictions. To retrieve all the "expensive" products with large sales volume, replace the WHERE clause in the preceding example with the following one:

```
WHERE [Order Details].ProductID = Products.ProductID AND
      Products.UnitPrice >= 50
```

(Products that cost $50 or more are considered expensive.) A more reasonable method to isolate the expensive products would be to calculate the average price and then use it to select products whose regular price exceeds the average product price.

IN and *NOT IN* Keywords

The IN and NOT IN keywords are used in a WHERE clause to specify a list of values that a column must match (or not match). They are more of a shorthand notation for multiple OR operators. The following is a simple statement that retrieves the names of the customers in Germany, Austria, and Italy (16 rows in all):

```
USE Northwind
SELECT CompanyName
FROM Customers
WHERE Country='Germany' OR
      Country='Austria' OR
      Country='Italy'
```

This statement is verbose as is. Imagine that you want to select orders that contain one of many products, or customers from all European countries. The same statement could be rewritten with the help of the IN keyword as follows:

```
USE Northwind
SELECT CompanyName
FROM Customers
WHERE Country IN ('Germany', ''Austria', 'Italy')
```

The second statement is shorter, and therefore easier to read and edit.

Subqueries

The IN and NOT IN keywords can also be used with subqueries. A *subquery* is a regular query whose result set is used as part of another query. Let's say you want to find the products that have never been ordered by Austrians. The first step is to create a list of products that have been ordered by companies in Austria. Here's the statement that returns the IDs of these products:

```
USE Northwind
SELECT DISTINCT ProductID
FROM [Order Details], Customers, Orders
WHERE [Order Details].OrderID = Orders.OrderID AND
      Orders.CustomerID = Customers.CustomerID AND
      Customers.Country = 'Austria'
```

You want the product IDs that do not appear in this list. You can get these rows with another statement that uses the NOT IN operator to locate IDs that do not belong to the list returned by the preceding query. This query will become a subquery for the statement in Listing 4.3.

LISTING 4.3: THE *SALESOUTSIDEAUSTRIA* QUERY

```
USE Northwind
SELECT ProductID, ProductName
FROM Products
WHERE ProductID NOT IN
    (SELECT DISTINCT ProductID
     FROM [Order Details], Customers, Orders
     WHERE [Order Details].OrderID = Orders.OrderID AND
           Orders.CustomerID = Customers.CustomerID AND
           Customers.Country = 'Austria')
```

The entire SQL statement that retrieves the products sold in Austria was enclosed in a pair of parentheses and became the list for the NOT IN operator.

You might think there's a simpler method. If you change the equal sign in the subquery to not equal, you will get the products that have never been sold to Austria when you run the subquery on its own. If you change

```
Customers.Country = 'Austria'
```

to

```
Customers.Country <> 'Austria'
```

you will get the products that have been sold everywhere but Austria. This is a different set than the set of products not sold in Austria. Chances are that every single product in the database has been sold to at least another country, regardless of whether it's been sold to an Austrian customer.

Here's another example that uses subqueries. This time you'll construct three lists: one with countries that are unique to customers (countries you sell to but never buy from), another one with countries that are unique to suppliers (customers that you buy from but never sell to), and a third list with countries that are common to both customers and suppliers (countries you buy from and sell to). The results of the three queries are shown in Table 4.4. The blank cells are not part of the result set; we left them blank to simplify comparisons between rows.

TABLE 4.4: COUNTRIES UNIQUE TO THE *CUSTOMERS* AND *SUPPLIERS* TABLES

UNIQUE CUSTOMER COUNTRIES	UNIQUE SUPPLIER COUNTRIES	COMMON CUSTOMER/SUPPLIER COUNTRIES
Argentina		
	Australia	
Austria		

Continued on next page

TABLE 4.4: COUNTRIES UNIQUE TO THE *CUSTOMERS* AND *SUPPLIERS* TABLES *(continued)*

UNIQUE CUSTOMER COUNTRIES	UNIQUE SUPPLIER COUNTRIES	COMMON CUSTOMER/SUPPLIER COUNTRIES
Belgium		
		Brazil
		Canada
		Denmark
		Finland
		France
		Germany
Ireland		
		Italy
	Japan	
Mexico		
	Netherlands	
		Norway
Poland		
Portugal		
	Singapore	
		Spain
		Sweden
Switzerland		
		UK
		USA
Venezuela		

The columns of Table 4.5 were filled with three separate SQL statements, which are quite similar. The first two queries that display unique countries use a subquery to locate the countries that appear in the other table and then exclude them from the final cursor. The third query, which generates the list of common countries, uses a subquery to locate customers in the Suppliers table and then uses them to select the same countries in the Customers table. Here are the three SQL statements:

Unique Customer Countries:

```
USE Northwind
```

```
SELECT DISTINCT Country FROM Customers
WHERE Country NOT IN (SELECT Country FROM Suppliers)
```

Unique Supplier Countries:

```
USE Northwind
SELECT DISTINCT Country FROM Suppliers
WHERE Country NOT IN (SELECT Country FROM Customers)
```

Common Customer/Supplier Countries:

```
USE Northwind
SELECT DISTINCT Country FROM Customers
WHERE Country IN (SELECT Country FROM Suppliers)
```

Listing 4.4 is another example of the HAVING clause. This statement retrieves the total items sold of the products that are more expensive than the average price. This statement uses a subquery in the HAVING clause to calculate the average price and limit the qualifying groups to those that contain expensive products.

LISTING 4.4: THE *PRODUCTSABOVEAVERAGE* QUERY

```
USE Northwind
SELECT Products.ProductName, Products.UnitPrice,
        SUM(Quantity) AS [Items Sold]
FROM Products, [Order Details]
WHERE [Order Details].ProductID = Products.ProductID
GROUP BY [Order Details].ProductID, Products.UnitPrice, Products.ProductName
HAVING Products.UnitPrice >
            (SELECT AVG(Products.UnitPrice) FROM Products)
ORDER BY Products.ProductName
```

The output of the ProductsAboveAverage query is shown in Figure 4.8.

The *BETWEEN* Keyword

The BETWEEN keyword lets you specify a range of values and limit the selection to the rows that have a specific column in this range. The BETWEEN keyword is a shorthand notation for an expression such as the following:

```
column >= minValue AND column <= maxValue
```

To retrieve the orders placed in the first quarter of 1997, use the following statement:

```
USE Northwind
SELECT OrderID, OrderDate, CompanyName
FROM Orders, Customers
WHERE Orders.CustomerID = Customers.CustomerID AND
      (OrderDate BETWEEN '1/1/1997' AND '3/31/1997')
```

FIGURE 4.8

Sales for products with prices above average

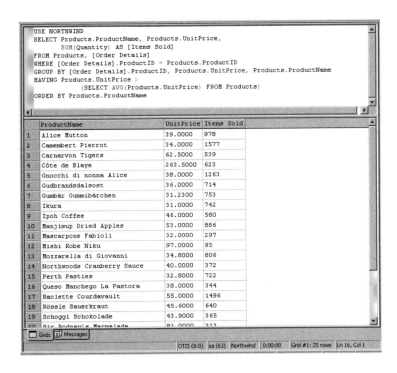

```
USE NORTHWIND
SELECT Products.ProductName, Products.UnitPrice,
       SUM(Quantity) AS [Items Sold]
FROM Products, [Order Details]
WHERE [Order Details].ProductID = Products.ProductID
GROUP BY [Order Details].ProductID, Products.UnitPrice, Products.ProductName
HAVING Products.UnitPrice >
             (SELECT AVG(Products.UnitPrice) FROM Products)
ORDER BY Products.ProductName
```

	ProductName	UnitPrice	Items Sold
1	Alice Mutton	39.0000	978
2	Camembert Pierrot	34.0000	1577
3	Carnarvon Tigers	62.5000	539
4	Côte de Blaye	263.5000	623
5	Gnocchi di nonna Alice	38.0000	1263
6	Gudbrandsdalsost	36.0000	714
7	Gumbär Gummibärchen	31.2300	753
8	Ikura	31.0000	742
9	Ipoh Coffee	46.0000	580
10	Manjimup Dried Apples	53.0000	886
11	Mascarpone Fabioli	32.0000	297
12	Mishi Kobe Niku	97.0000	95
13	Mozzarella di Giovanni	34.8000	806
14	Northwoods Cranberry Sauce	40.0000	372
15	Perth Pasties	32.8000	722
16	Queso Manchego La Pastora	38.0000	344
17	Raclette Courdavault	55.0000	1496
18	Rössle Sauerkraut	45.6000	640
19	Schoggi Schokolade	43.9000	365
20	Sir Rodney's Marmalade	81.0000	313

Grids Messages

OTIS (8.0) sa (63) Northwind 0:00:00 Grid #1: 25 rows Ln 16, Col 1

The list of orders includes the ones placed on the first and last date of the specified interval.

You can use the BETWEEN operator to specify a range of numeric values (such as prices) and strings (from *A* through *E*, for example). The statement

```
USE Northwind
SELECT CompanyName
FROM Customers
WHERE CompanyName BETWEEN 'A' AND 'E'
```

will retrieve all customers with a company name that begins with *A*, *B*, *C*, or *D* and a company named E (if such a company exists). A company name such as Eastern Connection is alphabetically larger than *E* and it will not be included in the cursor. To include companies whose name starts with *E*, use a statement such as this one:

```
USE Northwind
SELECT CompanyName
FROM Customers
WHERE CompanyName BETWEEN 'A' AND 'EZZZ'
```

The last statement can be rewritten with the LIKE operator:

```
USE Northwind
SELECT CompanyName
```

```
FROM Customers
WHERE CompanyName LIKE '[A-E]%'
```

Examples

This is a good point to present a few practical SQL statements that combine several of the keywords discussed so far. The following examples are useful to people who maintain databases and are responsible for the integrity of their data.

Specifying constraints during the design of the database is never adequate. Bad data will inevitably creep into the database. If you're in charge of the database, you must search for bad data from time to time to catch mistakes early enough so that you can fix them. For example, a program that imports titles from text files into the Pubs database might assign a few hundred authors to a given title, or assign the same author to every book that doesn't have an author. You can retrieve the titles with more than three authors, or the titles of the most productive authors. If you are familiar with the information stored in the database, you will be able to spot many common mistakes. An author with two dozen or more titles isn't just another name to a bookseller. Likewise, a large number of titles with more than half a dozen authors is a good indication that the data-entry mechanism might not be working perfectly.

BOOKS WITH MULTIPLE AUTHORS

This example uses the Pubs database. You are going to locate books that have multiple authors by using the COUNT() function to count the number of authors for each book. How do you convert the English statement "for each book" into an SQL statement? Simply by grouping the results according to the title_id (you can't use title names, because multiple books could have the same title). Because you don't care about the author names, just their count, you are not going to use the authors table. The author count can be extracted from the titleauthor table.

You start with the SELECT statement:

```
USE Pubs
SELECT Titles.Title, COUNT(TitleAuthor.Au_ID)
FROM   TitleAuthor,Titles
WHERE  Titles.title_id = TitleAuthor.title_id
```

This statement can't be executed because the first two fields in the SELECT list do not appear in an aggregate function or a GROUP BY clause. To make a valid SQL statement, you must add a GROUP BY clause, as shown in Listing 4.5.

LISTING 4.5: THE *MULTIPLEAUTHORS* QUERY

```
USE Pubs
SELECT Titles.Title, COUNT(TitleAuthor.Au_ID) AS AuthorCount
FROM   TitleAuthor,Titles
WHERE  Titles.title_id = TitleAuthor.title_id
GROUP BY Titles.Title, TitleAuthor.title_id
```

If you execute this query against the Pubs database, you'll get the list of titles in the `titles` table along with the number of authors per book, as shown in Figure 4.9. To display only the titles with multiple authors, append the following HANG clause to the previous statement:

```
HAVING COUNT(TitleAuthor.au_id) > 1
```

FIGURE 4.9

The output of the `MultipleAuthors` query

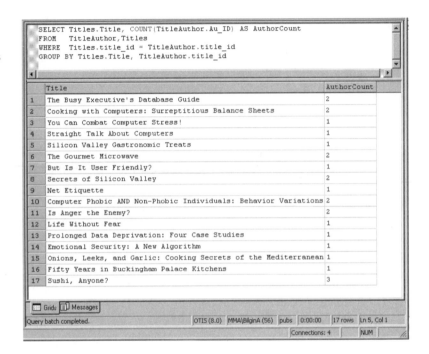

```
SELECT Titles.Title, COUNT(TitleAuthor.Au_ID) AS AuthorCount
FROM    TitleAuthor,Titles
WHERE   Titles.title_id = TitleAuthor.title_id
GROUP BY Titles.Title, TitleAuthor.title_id
```

	Title	AuthorCount
1	The Busy Executive's Database Guide	2
2	Cooking with Computers: Surreptitious Balance Sheets	2
3	You Can Combat Computer Stress!	1
4	Straight Talk About Computers	1
5	Silicon Valley Gastronomic Treats	1
6	The Gourmet Microwave	2
7	But Is It User Friendly?	1
8	Secrets of Silicon Valley	2
9	Net Etiquette	1
10	Computer Phobic AND Non-Phobic Individuals: Behavior Variations	2
11	Is Anger the Enemy?	2
12	Life Without Fear	1
13	Prolonged Data Deprivation: Four Case Studies	1
14	Emotional Security: A New Algorithm	1
15	Onions, Leeks, and Garlic: Cooking Secrets of the Mediterranean	1
16	Fifty Years in Buckingham Palace Kitchens	1
17	Sushi, Anyone?	3

Grid Messages

Query batch completed. | OTIS (8.0) | MMA\BilginA (56) | pubs | 0:00:00 | 17 rows | Ln 5, Col 1
Connections: 4 | NUM

AUTHORS WITH MULTIPLE BOOKS

The next example is not too different from the previous one. This time you'll locate the authors who have written more than one book. You want to display author names and the number of books they have authored (or coauthored). You are not interested in the actual titles they have written, so you are not going to use the `titles` table in your query. The SELECT statement includes a field name and a count:

```
USE Pubs
SELECT Authors.au_lname, Count(TitleAuthor.title_id) AS Books
FROM TitleAuthor, Authors
```

The rows of the two tables must have a matching field, which is the book's `title_id`. In addition, the author's last name (`authors.au_lname` field) must appear in a GROUP BY clause. Listing 4.6 shows the complete SQL statement.

LISTING 4.6: THE *BOOKSBYAUTHOR* QUERY

```
USE Pubs
SELECT Authors.Au_lname, Count(TitleAuthor.title_id) AS Books
FROM TitleAuthor, Authors
WHERE Authors.Au_ID=TitleAuthor.Au_ID
GROUP BY Authors.au_lname
```

Again, if you want to limit the authors displayed to those who have authored more than a single book, use a HAVING clause:

```
HAVING COUNT(TitleAuthor.title_id) > 1
```

CUSTOMERS, ORDERS, DETAILS

The next example uses four tables in the Northwind database. You are going to write a statement that retrieves all customers, their orders, and each order's details in a single report. The desired output is shown next. Notice that customer and product names have been abbreviated, so that all the information fits on a single line on the page. The actual result set contains many more lines than the ones shown here:

Company	OrderID	Product	Price	Qty	Disc	ExtPrice
Alfreds	10643	Rössle	45.60	15	25	513.00
Alfreds	10643	Chartreuse	18.00	21	25	283.50
Alfreds	10643	Spegesild	12.00	2	25	18.00
Alfreds	10692	Vegie	43.90	20	0	878.00
Alfreds	10702	Aniseed	10.00	6	0	60.00
Alfreds	10702	Lakkalikööri	18.00	15	0	270.00
Alfreds	10835	Raclette	55.00	15	0	825.00
Alfreds	10835	Original	13.00	2	20	20.80
Alfreds	10952	Grandma's	25.00	16	5	380.00
Alfreds	10952	Rössle	45.60	2	0	91.20
Alfreds	11011	Escargots	13.25	40	5	503.50
Alfreds	11011	Flotemysost	21.50	20	0	430.00
Ana	10308	Gudbrandsdal	28.80	1	0	28.80
Ana	10308	Outback Lager	12.00	5	0	60.00
Ana	10625	Tofu	23.25	3	0	69.75
Ana	10625	Singaporean	14.00	5	0	70.00
Ana	10625	Camembert	34.00	10	0	340.00
Ana	10759	Mascarpone	32.00	10	0	320.00
Ana	10926	Queso	21.00	2	0	42.00
Ana	10926	Konbu	6.00	10	0	60.00
Ana	10926	Teatime	9.20	7	0	64.40
Ana	10926	Mozzarella	34.80	10	0	348.00

As usual, you start with the list of the desired columns:

```
USE Northwind
SELECT CompanyName, Orders.OrderID, ProductName,
    [Order Details].UnitPrice AS Price,
    Quantity, Discount * 100 AS Discount,
    Quantity * (1 - Discount) *
    [Order Details].UnitPrice AS SubTotal
FROM Products, [Order Details], Customers, Orders
```

The desired fields are the company name (CompanyName), the invoice's ID (OrderID), and each invoice's details: product name, price, quantity, discount, and extended price. The extended price is a calculated field, which is computed as follows:

```
Quantity * Price * (1 - Discount)
```

Next, you must provide the restrictions to match selected fields in all four tables. If not, the Cartesian product generated by this query will be enormous. The restrictions are as follows:

◆ Each product ID in the Order Details table must match a row in the Products table:

```
[Order Details].ProductID = Products.ProductID
```

◆ Each order ID in the Order Details table must match a row in the Orders table:

```
[Order Details].OrderID = Orders.OrderID
```

◆ Each customer ID in the Orders table must match a row in the Customers table:

```
Orders.CustomerID = Customers.CustomerID
```

Finally, you must sort the rows of the cursor by CompanyName and OrderID, so that each customer's invoices appear together within the customer's section. Listing 4.7 shows the complete SQL statement that retrieves customer, order, and detail information from the Northwind database.

LISTING 4.7: THE ALLORDERS QUERY

```
USE Northwind
SELECT CompanyName, Orders.OrderID, ProductName,
    [Order Details].UnitPrice AS Price,
    Quantity, Discount * 100 AS Discount,
    Quantity * (1 - Discount) *
    [Order Details].UnitPrice AS [Ext. Price]
FROM Products, [Order Details], Customers, Orders
WHERE [Order Details].ProductID = Products.ProductID AND
    [Order Details].OrderID = Orders.OrderID AND
    Orders.CustomerID=Customers.CustomerID
ORDER BY Customers.CompanyName, Orders.OrderID
```

NOTE   *You have seen SQL statements that calculate all kinds of subtotals, but how about totals? You would probably want to see the total for each invoice, customer totals, and the grand total in the report of this example. It is possible to build subtotals and grand totals, and you'll see how this is done in the section "The* COMPUTE BY *Clause" in Chapter 5.*

PUBLISHERS, BOOKS, AUTHORS

Let's end this section with a similar SQL statement that retrieves all the titles in the Pubs database and orders them by publisher. Within each publisher category, the books will be sorted by title and author. Here's the desired output format:

```
Title                Publisher Name        Author Last Name
But Is It User...    Algodata...           Carson
Computer Phobic...   Binnet & Hardley      MacFeather
Computer Phobic...   Binnet & Hardley      Karsen
Cooking with...      Algodata              O'Leary
Cooking with...      Algodata              MacFeather
Emotional...         New Moon Books        Locksley
Fifty Years in...    Binnet & Hardley      Blotchet...
Is Anger the...      New Moon Books        Ringer
```

It would be nice to display all the authors of any given book under its title, without repeating the book's title, title ID, and publisher. This is not possible with straight SQL, but you will find out how to format a result set in Chapter 5. In Chapter 7, "ADO.NET Programming," you will learn how to work with multiple DataTables, which enable you represent your data in a hierarchical fashion.

Let's return to the example and generate the preceding list by using the statements and keywords you have learned so far. The statement should select the following fields:

```
USE Pubs
SELECT Titles.Title, Publishers.pub_name, Authors.au_lname
FROM Titles, TitleAuthor, Authors, Publishers
```

This is the simpler part of the desired statement. Now you must construct the WHERE clause to relate the titles to their publishers and authors. The clause for combining titles and publishers is quite simple:

```
Titles.pub_id = Publishers.pub_id
```

To connect titles and authors, you must take into consideration the titleauthor table, which sits between the titles and authors tables:

```
Titles.title_id = TitleAuthor.title_id AND
     TitleAuthor.Au_ID = Authors.Au_ID
```

The complete statement that combines the three restrictions is shown in Listing 4.8. We added an ORDER BY clause to order the titles alphabetically. The output of the AllBooks query is shown in Figure 4.10.

LISTING 4.8: THE *ALLBOOKS* QUERY

```
USE Pubs
SELECT Titles.Title, Publishers.pub_name, Authors.au_lname
FROM Titles, TitleAuthor, Authors, Publishers
WHERE Titles.pub_id = Publishers.pub_id AND
      Titles.title_id = TitleAuthor.title_id AND
      TitleAuthor.Au_ID = Authors.Au_ID
ORDER BY Titles.Title
```

FIGURE 4.10

Executing the
AllBooks query
with the Query
Designer

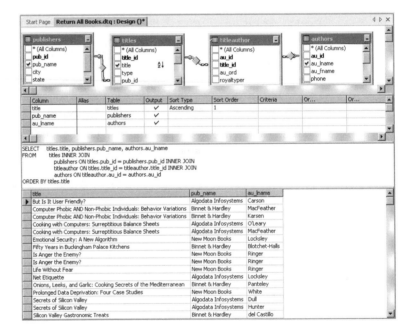

Joining Tables

The WHERE clause enables you to connect two or more tables, based on the values of two columns in the two tables. The WHERE clause, however, should be used to express constraints involving one or more tables, and not for connecting tables—although many programmers use the WHERE clause almost exclusively. The proper method of linking tables is the JOIN operation. Before you look at the JOIN operation, let's discuss the shortcomings of the WHERE clause that lead to the need for a more elaborate mechanism for connecting multiple tables.

The two columns involved in the WHERE clause are usually the primary key in one table and a foreign key in the other table. When you connect the titles to the publishers table, for example, you request that the publishers table's primary key (publishers.pub_id) is equal to a foreign key in the titles table (the titles.pub_id field):

```
USE Pubs
SELECT * FROM Titles, Publishers
WHERE Titles.pub_id = Publishers.pub_id
```

The columns you use to combine the two tables need not be indexed, but it helps if they are. If you omit the WHERE clause, the query will return the cross-product of the rows in the two tables (that is, all possible combinations of the rows in the two tables).

Combining multiple tables with the WHERE clause, though, will not work if one of the two columns contains Null values. The titles with a Null value in the pub_id column won't match any row in the publishers table, and they will be left out.

The question now is how to retrieve all the titles, regardless of whether they have Nulls. You can do this with the JOIN operation. The operation of combining multiple tables is known as a *join*, and it can be coded with the JOIN operation. The JOIN operation was designed specifically to combine multiple tables. The WHERE clause does the trick in simple situations, but it doesn't always work, as the previous example demonstrates.

NOTE   Many tables can be joined by the WHERE clause because of their nature. The Orders *and* Order Details *tables can be joined by the WHERE clause, because you can't have an order without details (an order without details would indicate a serious flaw in the design of the database). Sometimes, programmers take this convenient circumstance for granted and abuse the WHERE clause. You should try to implement all your joins with the JOIN operation and use the WHERE clause to limit the number of qualifying rows. It's not coincidental that JOIN is an operation, whereas WHERE is a simple keyword.*

The JOIN operation combines columns of two tables where the rows have a matching field. Its syntax is as follows:

```
FROM Table1 INNER JOIN Table2 ON Table1.col = Table2.col
```

NOTE   You can ignore the INNER keyword for now; you will see shortly that there are various types of joins, and you must specify the type of join you want to perform with another keyword.

The two columns need not be matched with the equal operator (=), although this is the most common method of matching multiple tables. You can use any of the relational operators (>, >=, <, <=, and <>). The JOIN operator might appear only in a SELECT statement's FROM clause, which is why we've included the FROM keyword in the statement's syntax. In addition, you can combine multiple restrictions with the logical operators. For example, you might require that a pair of columns match exactly and another pair are different:

```
FROM Table1 INNER JOIN Table2 ON Table1.col1 = Table2.col1 AND
     Table1.col2 <> Table2.col2
```

This statement retrieves all the rows whose *col1* column in *Table1* matches *col2* in *Table2*, and excludes from this set the rows with different *col2* values.

Types of Joins

SQL supports two types of joins:

Inner join   This join returns all matching pairs of rows in the two tables and discards unmatched rows from both tables. This is the default if no join type is specified.

Full (or outer) join   This join returns all rows usually returned by the INNER JOIN operation plus rows from either the left or right table that do not meet the join condition. A full join would return all titles with their publishers, as well as the titles without a publisher. Rows with unmatched columns in either table are set to NULL. In the titles/publishers example, titles without a publisher would appear with a Null value in the publisher's column.

Both inner and full (or outer) joins can be modified by specifying which table to be used as the basis for the join. For example, you might want to retrieve all rows of one table and the matching rows of the other table. Therefore, outer joins can be further classified according to the order in which they look up the tables involved in the operation:

Left join   This inner join returns all the records from the first (left) of two tables, even if there are no matching values for records in the second (right) table.

Right join   This inner join returns all the records from the second (right) of two tables, even if there are no matching values for records in the first (left) table.

To demonstrate the types of joins, we constructed a trivial database with two tables: a table with city names (Cities) and a table with country names (Countries).

NOTE   *You can create this database by restoring the CitiesDB, which is located on the CD that accompanies this book. You can do this from SQL Server Enterprise Manager. Right-click on the Databases node, select AllTasks ➤ Restore Database. From the Restore Database dialog, type the name **CitiesDB** and select the From Device option. Use the Select Devices button to browse for the CitiesDB.dat file on the CD. Chapter 14, "Advanced SQL Server 2000 Features," contains information on the backup and restore activities, should you need further assistance with this restoration.*

Each country has a unique ID, which is used by the Cities table to indicate the country to which a city belongs. The CountryID field is a primary key in the Countries table and a foreign key in the Cities table. Here's the structure of the two tables and their contents:

Cities Table

CityName	varchar(50)
CountryID	Int

Countries Table

CountryName	varchar(50)
CountryID	Int

Table 4.6 shows all the entries in the two tables of the database and their mapping. If a city isn't mapped to a country, then the second column has a Null value in that city's row. If a country isn't mapped to a city, then the first column has a Null value in that country's row.

TABLE 4.6: CITIES AND COUNTRIES IN THE *CITIESDB* DATABASE

CityName	CountryName
NULL	Argentina
NULL	China
NULL	France
NULL	Japan
Alexandria	Egypt
Atlanta	USA
Barcelona	NULL
Berlin	Germany
Cairo	Egypt
Chicago	USA
Frankfurt	Germany
Hamburg	Germany
Istanbul	NULL
London	UK
Madrid	NULL
Manchester	UK
New York	USA
Rome	Italy
San Francisco	USA
Venice	Italy
Zurich	NULL

As you can see, the `Cities` table contains cities that don't reference any country (Barcelona, Istanbul, Madrid, and Zurich), and the `Countries` table contains countries that are not referenced by any row in the `Cities` table (Argentina, China, France, and Japan). Let's join the two tables by using all the variations of the `JOIN` keyword.

INNER JOIN

This first query uses an `INNER JOIN` keyword, which retrieves matching rows only:

```
USE CitiesDB
SELECT Cities.CityName, Countries.CountryName
```

```
FROM Cities INNER JOIN Countries
        ON Cities.CountryID = Countries.CountryID
ORDER BY Countries.CountryName, Cities.CityName
```

The result of the query is shown here—13 rows of cities that are mapped to a country. Cities that don't belong to any country are not included in the result.

```
CityName                    CountryName
---------------------------------------
Alexandria                  Egypt
Cairo                       Egypt
Berlin                      Germany
Frankfurt                   Germany
Hamburg                     Germany
Rome                        Italy
Venice                      Italy
London                      UK
Manchester                  UK
Atlanta                     USA
Chicago                     USA
New York                    USA
San Francisco               USA
```

LEFT JOIN

If you replace INNER JOIN with LEFT JOIN in the previous statement, the query will retrieve all the cities, regardless of whether they map to a country. If a city isn't mapped to a country, then the corresponding row in the second column will contain a Null value. This query will return 17 rows in all (the number of rows in the left table). The statement that retrieves all cities is as follows:

```
USE CitiesDB
SELECT Cities.CityName, Countries.CountryName
FROM Cities LEFT JOIN Countries
    ON Cities.CountryID = Countries.CountryID
ORDER BY Countries.CountryName, Cities.CityName
```

Here's the result of the query:

```
CityName                    CountryName
---------------------------------------
Barcelona                   NULL
Istanbul                    NULL
Madrid                      NULL
Zurich                      NULL
Alexandria                  Egypt
Cairo                       Egypt
Berlin                      Germany
Frankfurt                   Germany
Hamburg                     Germany
Rome                        Italy
```

Venice	Italy
London	UK
Manchester	UK
Atlanta	USA
Chicago	USA
New York	USA
San Francisco	USA

RIGHT JOIN

If you use RIGHT JOIN, the query will retrieve all the countries, regardless of whether they map to a city. If a country isn't mapped to a city, then the corresponding row in the second column will contain a Null value. This query will return 18 rows in all (the number of rows in the right table). Here is the statement that retrieves all countries:

```
USE CitiesDB
SELECT Cities.CityName, Countries.CountryName
FROM Cities RIGHT JOIN Countries
     ON Cities.CountryID = Countries.CountryID
ORDER BY Countries.CountryName, Cities.CityName
```

Here's the result of the query:

CityName	CountryName
NULL	NULL
NULL	Argentina
NULL	China
Alexandria	Egypt
Cairo	Egypt
NULL	France
Berlin	Germany
Frankfurt	Germany
Hamburg	Germany
Rome	Italy
Venice	Italy
NULL	Japan
London	UK
Manchester	UK
Atlanta	USA
Chicago	USA
New York	USA
San Francisco	USA

FULL JOIN

The FULL JOIN keyword returns all the rows of both tables. All cities have a country value (even if it's a Null value), and every country has a city value (even if it's a Null value). Country names are repeated as needed. The result doesn't contain duplicate city names, because a city can't belong to more than one country.

```
USE CitiesDB
SELECT Cities.CityName, Countries.CountryName
FROM Cities FULL JOIN Countries
    ON Cities.CountryID = Countries.CountryID
ORDER BY Cities.CityName, Countries.CountryName
```

The result of this query contains 22 rows, shown here:

CityName	CountryName
NULL	NULL
NULL	Argentina
NULL	China
NULL	France
NULL	Japan
Alexandria	Egypt
Atlanta	USA
Barcelona	NULL
Berlin	Germany
Cairo	Egypt
Chicago	USA
Frankfurt	Germany
Hamburg	Germany
Istanbul	NULL
London	UK
Madrid	NULL
Manchester	UK
New York	USA
Rome	Italy
San Francisco	USA
Venice	Italy
Zurich	NULL

As you might guess, full joins are not used frequently because they can generate quite large result sets.

We hope that this simple database has helped you clarify the concept of inner and outer joins. Now you can use these keywords to write a few advanced queries that combine multiple tables with the JOIN operator.

JOINING TITLES AND AUTHORS

Let's return to the AllBooks example (Listing 4.8) and implement it with a JOIN. Because you want all the titles along with their authors, you must use two left joins, one after the other. First, you must join the titleauthor and authors tables with a LEFT JOIN operation. The result will be a virtual table with all the title IDs on the left and the corresponding author names on the right. Even `title_id` values that appear in the `titleauthor` table but have no matching authors in the `authors` table will appear in the result. This virtual table must then be joined with the `titles` table, with another LEFT JOIN operation. The `titles` table will be on the left side of the first join, so that the titles with no entry in the `titleauthor` table will be included in the result. Listing 4.9 shows the query that retrieves all titles and their authors with the JOIN operation.

LISTING 4.9: THE *TITLESAUTHORS* QUERY

```
USE Pubs
SELECT Titles.Title, Authors.au_lname
FROM Titles
    LEFT JOIN (TitleAuthor
        LEFT JOIN Authors
        ON TitleAuthor.Au_ID = Authors.Au_ID)
            ON Titles.title_id = TitleAuthor.title_id
ORDER BY Titles.Title
```

This statement is processed as follows: The SQL Server starts by evaluating the innermost join, which combines the rows of the `titleauthor` and `authors` tables. This join selects all the rows of the `titleauthor` table and the columns of the `authors` table that have the same `au_id` value. If a row in the left table has no matching row in the right table, it is included in the query's result anyway. If a row in the right table has no matching row in the left table, then it is ignored. (This would be an author name referring to a title that was removed from the `titles` table, but the corresponding entries in the `titleauthor` and `authors` tables were not removed.) Here's the first join that will be executed by the DBMS:

```
(TitleAuthor LEFT JOIN Authors
ON TitleAuthor.Au_ID = Authors.Au_ID)
```

The result of this join is another table—it exists only during the execution of the query. Let's call this table `matchingauthors`. If you replace the expression of the innermost join with `matchingauthors`, the original query becomes the following:

```
USE Pubs
SELECT Titles.Title, Authors.Author
FROM Titles
    LEFT JOIN MatchingAuthors
            ON Titles.title_id = TitleAuthor.title_id
ORDER BY Titles.Title
```

After the creation of the innermost join, the DBMS will execute another join. This time it will join the `titles` table with the result of the previous join, and it will combine the rows of the `titles` table with the rows returned by the join already executed by matching their `title_id` values. The rows retrieved by the `TitlesAuthors` query are shown in Figure 4.11.

FIGURE 4.11

Displaying all titles in the Pubs database and their authors

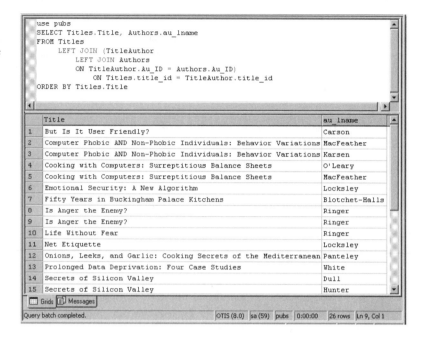

PUBLISHERS, BOOKS, AUTHORS

Listing 4.10 extends the previous example by including the `publishers` table. This time you'll add a third join to connect titles and publishers. This intermediate table will then become the first (left) table of another join that returns titles, publishers, and authors.

LISTING 4.10: THE *ALLTITLESJOIN* QUERY

```
USE Pubs
SELECT Publishers.pub_name, Titles.Title, Authors.au_lname
FROM (Titles LEFT JOIN Publishers
     ON Titles.Pub_ID = Publishers.Pub_ID)
     LEFT JOIN (TitleAuthor LEFT JOIN Authors
         ON TitleAuthor.Au_ID = Authors.Au_ID) ON
     Titles.title_id = TitleAuthor.title_id
ORDER BY Publishers.pub_name, Titles.Title
```

CUSTOMERS, ORDERS, DETAILS

This example will retrieve sales-related information from the Northwind database. You want to retrieve all customers, invoices, and invoice details in a query with the following structure:

CustomerName	OrderID	ProdName	QTY	Price	Disc	SubTot
Alfreds Futt.	10643	Rössle	15	45.60	0.25	513.0
Alfreds Futt.	10643	Chartreuse	21	18.00	0.25	283.5
Alfreds Futt.	10643	Spegesild	2	12.00	0.25	18.0
Alfreds Futt.	10692	Vegie	20	43.90	0.0	878.0
Alfreds Futt.	10702	Aniseed	6	10.00	0.0	60.0
Alfreds Futt.	10702	Lakkalik	15	18.00	0.0	270.0

NOTE *We shortened the names of the customers and products for brevity. You can execute the query in the Query Analyzer to see the actual rows returned.*

Let's build the SELECT statement that retrieves this information. First, you must select all customers. Within each customer's section, you must list all the orders (their ID and the date they were placed). Finally, within each order's section, you want to list all the details of the specific order. The fields will come from the Customers, Orders, and Order Details tables. Notice that the Order Details table contains product IDs and not actual product names, so you must include the Products table. For each product ID in the Order Details table, you must retrieve the product name from the matching row in the Products table.

Let's start with the Customers table and specify the CompanyName as the first field in the SELECT list. The Customers table must be joined with the Orders table on the CustomerID field. This join will repeat each customer name as many times as there are orders for that customer. The output of the first join will begin something like this:

```
Alfreds Futterkiste                       10643
Alfreds Futterkiste                       10692
Alfreds Futterkiste                       10702
Alfreds Futterkiste                       10835
Alfreds Futterkiste                       10952
Alfreds Futterkiste                       11011
Ana Trujillo Emparedados y helados        10308
Ana Trujillo Emparedados y helados        10625
Ana Trujillo Emparedados y helados        10759
Ana Trujillo Emparedados y helados        10926
```

(The first customer has six orders, the second customer has four orders, and so on.) Here's the join that produced the preceding list:

```
USE Northwind
SELECT Customers.CompanyName, Orders.OrderID
FROM   Customers INNER JOIN Orders
       ON Customers.CustomerID = Orders.CustomerID
ORDER BY Customers.CompanyName
```

Now you must bring in the `Order Details` table and join it with the `Orders` table on the `OrderID` field. If the first order has three items, the line

```
Alfreds Futterkiste 10643
```

must be repeated three times. Let's expand the last statement to include the `Order Details` table. For the purposes of this example, use the `UnitPrice`, `Quantity`, and `Discount` columns of the `Order Details` table:

```
USE Northwind
SELECT Customers.CompanyName, Orders.OrderID,
       [Order Details].ProductID, [Order Details].Quantity,
       [Order Details].UnitPrice
FROM   (Customers INNER JOIN Orders
       ON Customers.CustomerID = Orders.CustomerID)
          INNER JOIN [Order Details]
          ON [Order Details].OrderID=Orders.OrderID
ORDER BY Customers.CompanyName
```

Notice the placement of the parentheses in the `FROM` clause of the statement. They are not required, but we want to emphasize that the first join (the one we designed in the first step) is, in effect, another table. It's called a *virtual table*, because it might not exist in the database, but SQL server must create it in order to join its rows with the `Order Details` table.

You're almost there. You must now match the `Order Details.ProductID` field to the `ProductID` field of the `Products` table, so that instead of a product ID, you'll display the actual product name. Here's the final SQL statement:

```
USE Northwind
SELECT Customers.CompanyName, Orders.OrderID,
       Products.ProductName, [Order Details].Quantity,
       [Order Details].UnitPrice, [Order Details].Discount,
       [Order Details].Quantity * [Order Details].UnitPrice *
          (1 - [Order Details].Discount) AS SubTotal
FROM   Customers INNER JOIN Orders
       ON Customers.CustomerID = Orders.CustomerID
       INNER JOIN [Order Details] ON
          [Order Details].OrderID = Orders.OrderID
       INNER JOIN Products ON
          [Order Details].ProductID = Products.ProductID
ORDER BY Customers.CompanyName
```

We dropped the `ProductID` field from the `SELECT` list and replaced it with the `Products.ProductName` field. In addition, we added a calculated field, which is the line's subtotal (`quantity * (price - discount)`).

Action Queries

In addition to selection queries, SQL supports a few statements for action queries. You use action queries to manipulate the contents of the database. You can perform three types of actions: insertions, updates, and deletions. SQL provides three action statements, one for each action: the INSERT, UPDATE, and DELETE statements. Their syntax is simple, so you don't have to learn any additional keywords. As you can guess, you wouldn't want to perform actions unconditionally on all rows of a table. The rows that will be affected by an action query are specified by the appropriate WHERE clause. Most of the information covered in the previous sections applies to action queries as well.

A substantial difference between selection and action queries is that action queries do not return any data rows. When you execute an action query with the Query Analyzer, you will see the number of rows affected in the Results pane.

The *DELETE* Statement

Let's start with the simplest action query, which is the deletion of one or more rows of a table. The DELETE statement deletes entire rows, and you need not specify a field list. The syntax of the DELETE statement is as follows:

```
DELETE FROM table_name
WHERE condition
```

where *table_name* is the name of the table from which the qualifying rows will be removed. The rows that meet the *condition* specified by the WHERE clause will be deleted. The statement

```
USE Northwind
DELETE FROM Customers
WHERE Country = 'Germany'
```

will remove all German customers from the Northwind database. The WHERE clause of the DELETE statement (as well as of the other action statements) can get as complicated as you make it. You can also omit it entirely, in which case all the rows will be removed from the table. In this case, you don't even have to use the FROM keyword. Just specify the table's name with a statement like the following one:

```
DELETE Categories
```

This statement should delete all the rows of the Categories table. However, the DELETE statement is subject to the referential integrity rules incorporated into the database. The rows of the Categories table are referenced by the rows of the Products table, and the DBMS will refuse to delete them. If a category is not referenced by any product, then it will be deleted.

An unconditional statement will delete all rows of a table that are not referenced as foreign keys in another table. If you're using SQL Server, there's a more elegant alternative, namely the TRUNCATE TABLE statement, which removes the same rows, only faster. To remove all categories that are not used as foreign keys in the Products table, use this statement:

```
TRUNCATE TABLE Categories
```

WARNING *Although the* TRUNCATE TABLE *option is useful for removing unnecessary data, do so with caution. Because truncate activities are not recorded into the transaction log, you cannot recover from them if you should change your mind.*

The *INSERT* Statement

The INSERT statement inserts a new row into a table. Here is the complete syntax of the INSERT statement:

```
INSERT table_name (column list) VALUES (value list)
```

This statement will add a row to the table *table_name* and assign the specified values to the row's fields. The two lists must be enclosed in parentheses, as shown above. The first value in the *value list* is assigned to the first column in the *column list*, the second value in the *value list* is assigned to the second column in the *column list*, and so on. Obviously, the two lists must match each other: They must have the same number of items, and the values' types must match the types of the columns. Identity fields cannot be specified in the *column list*. The DBMS will assign values to these fields automatically.

To insert a new customer in the Customers table, use the following statement:

```
USE Northwind
INSERT (CustomerID, CompanyName, ContactName)
    VALUES ("SYBEX", "Sybex, Inc.", "Nesli Aybeniz")
```

This statement doesn't assign values to all the columns of the new row. Only three of them will have a value. You can always update a table row with the UPDATE statement, which is discussed next. The columns that are not listed in the *column list* will take their default value (if they have one) or the Null value. If a column does not have a default value and it's not nullable, then you must explicitly assign a value to it.

If you are going to supply a value for each field in the new row, then you can omit the *column list*, as long as you supply them in the proper order.

Another mechanism for passing column values to the INSERT statement is to SELECT them from another table. Let's say you want to insert the contacts from the Customers table into the PhoneBook table. The first step is to retrieve the required information from the Customers table:

```
USE Northwind
SELECT ContactName, Phone, Fax
FROM Customers
```

This list can then become the *value list* of an INSERT statement:

```
USE Northwind
INSERT PhoneBook
SELECT ContactName, Phone, Fax
FROM Customers
```

This form of the INSERT statement enables you to insert multiple rows at once.

The *UPDATE* Statement

The last action statement is the UPDATE statement, which can update columns in selected rows. The UPDATE statement can affect multiple rows, but it still acts on a single table, and its syntax is as follows:

```
UPDATE table_name
    SET column1 = value1, column2 = value2, . . .
WHERE condition
```

The following statement will change the Country column of the rows in the Customers table that correspond to German customers:

```
USE Northwind
UPDATE Customers
    SET Country = 'Germany'
WHERE Country = 'W. Germany' OR Country = 'E. Germany'
```

Here's a more complicated statement that updates the price of specific products. Let's say a supplier has increased the discount by 5 percent and you want to pass half of the savings to your customers. The following statement will adjust the prices of the products you buy from the supplier with ID = 4 by 2.5 percent. Here's the UPDATE statement (the result of the execution of the statement is shown in Figure 4.12):

```
USE Northwind
UPDATE Products
SET UnitPrice = UnitPrice * 0.025
WHERE SupplierID = 3
```

FIGURE 4.12

When updating rows through the Query Analyzer, the number of updated rows is displayed in the Results pane.

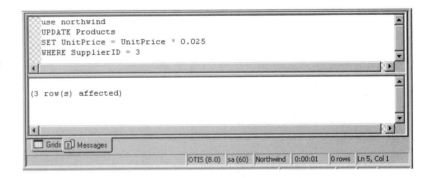

Summary

The SQL statements you have learned so far are not specific to any particular DBMS. You'll delve deeper into SQL in the next chapter, where you'll explore SQL Server's extensions to standard SQL. In that chapter, you'll learn SQL Server's built-in programming language, Transact-SQL (T-SQL), which combines the power of a nonprocedural language, SQL, with the flexibility of traditional programming languages.

This concludes the first part of this book, "Database Concepts." By now, you should have a firm understanding of the fundamental concepts of database programming, such as the SQL language, normalization, and DML commands. Additionally, we presented an overview of the visual database tools, which gives you a taste of the different ways you can work with databases structures and data. In the next part, we dive deeper into working with databases, by showing you how you can build code by using T-SQL, ADO.NET, and VB .NET to create applications. Toward the end of the second part, we seriously examine how XML fits into the database programming picture. Let's begin at the database server and review the T-SQL commands that you can use to design stored procedures and SQL statements.

Part 2

Database Programming

In this section:
- Chapter 5: Transact-SQL
- Chapter 6: A First Look at ADO.NET
- Chapter 7: ADO.NET Programming
- Chapter 8: Data-Aware Controls
- Chapter 9: Working with DataSets
- Chapter 10: The Role of XML

Chapter 5

Transact-SQL

- ◆ The COMPUTE BY clause
- ◆ Stored procedures
- ◆ T-SQL: the language
- ◆ User-defined functions
- ◆ Triggers
- ◆ Implementing business rules with stored procedures

IN CHAPTER 4, "STRUCTURED Query Language," you built SQL statements to retrieve and update rows in a database. You also learned all the variations of the SELECT statement. Some restrictions, however, can't be expressed with basic SQL statements. Most database management systems include extensions, which enhance SQL and make it behave more like a programming language. SQL Server provides a set of statements known as Transact-SQL (T-SQL). T-SQL recognizes statements that fetch rows from one or more tables, flow-control statements such as IF...ELSE and WHILE, and numerous functions that manipulate strings, numeric values, and dates (similar to VB .NET functions). With T-SQL, you can do everything that can be done with SQL, as well as program these operations. At the very least, you can attach lengthy SQL statements to a database as stored procedures, so that you can call them by name. In addition, you can use parameters, so that the same procedure can act on different data.

In this chapter, you'll explore T-SQL and build stored procedures to perform complicated tasks on the server. You'll start with the COMPUTE BY statement, which enables you to calculate totals on groups of rows retrieved from the database. This statement looks and feels much like the straight SQL statements discussed in Chapter 4. Yet it's not part of standard SQL—and as such it can't be used with Access queries. It's one of the most important extensions to SQL, and you will use it even if you do not plan to write stored procedures with T-SQL.

Then you'll look at T-SQL in depth. Even if you're not new to T-SQL, you should read this material, because there is a good amount of functionality introduced with SQL Server 2000, such as user-defined functions and enhanced triggers. This chapter might also refresh your memory regarding features you haven't used in a while. In addition, you'll develop a deeper understanding of database programming with VB .NET. By understanding the flexibility that T-SQL offers, you will not only gain a deeper understanding of database programming, but will also be able to optimize your database code for the maximum performance.

The *COMPUTE BY* Clause

As discussed in Chapter 4, an SQL statement can return either details or totals, but not both. For example, you can calculate the order totals for all customers with a GROUP BY clause, but this clause displays totals only. Let's say you want a list of all customers in the Northwind database, their orders, and the total for each customer. Listing 5.1 provides an SQL SELECT statement that retrieves the desired information from the database.

LISTING 5.1: THE *ORDERTOTALS.SQL* QUERY

```
USE NORTHWIND
SELECT CompanyName, Orders.OrderID,
    SUM([Order Details].UnitPrice *
        Quantity * (1 - Discount))
FROM Products, [Order Details], Customers, Orders
WHERE [Order Details].ProductID = Products.ProductID AND
      [Order Details].OrderID = Orders.OrderID AND
      Orders.CustomerID=Customers.CustomerID
GROUP BY CompanyName, Orders.OrderID
ORDER BY CompanyName, Orders.OrderID
```

This statement calculates the totals for each order. (The Orders.OrderID field is included in the GROUP BY clause because it's part of the SELECT list, but it doesn't appear in an aggregate function's arguments. See the sidebar "How to Use Aggregate Functions" in Chapter 4). This statement will display the totals for all customer orders, grouped by the company name.

If you want to see the totals per customer, you must modify Listing 5.1 as shown in Listing 5.2.

LISTING 5.2: *ORDERTOTALS BY CUSTOMER.SQL* QUERY

```
USE NORTHWIND
SELECT CompanyName,
    SUM([Order Details].UnitPrice *
        Quantity * (1 - Discount))
FROM Products, [Order Details], Customers, Orders
WHERE [Order Details].ProductID = Products.ProductID AND
      [Order Details].OrderID = Orders.OrderID AND
      Orders.CustomerID=Customers.CustomerID
GROUP BY CompanyName
ORDER BY CompanyName
```

This time you omit the `Orders.OrderID` field from the `SELECT` list and the `GROUP BY` clause. This statement will display the total for each customer, because you are not grouping by `OrderID`:

```
Alfreds Futterkiste                      4272.9999980926514
Ana Trujillo Emparedados y helados  1402.9500007629395
Antonio Moreno Taquería              7023.9775543212891
. . .
```

What you need is a statement that can produce a report of the details with total breaks after each order and each customer, as shown here. (We have shortened the company and product names to fit the lines on the printed page without breaks.)

Company	OrderID	Product	UnitPrice	Quantity	Discount	ExtendedPrice
Alfreds...	10643	Rössle...	45.6000	15	25	513.0000
Alfreds...	10643	Chartreuse	18.0000	21	25	283.5000
Alfreds...	10643	Spegesild	12.0000	2	25	18.0000
						sum
						====================
						814.5000

T-SQL provides an elegant solution to this problem with the `COMPUTE BY` clause. The `COMPUTE BY` clause calculates aggregate functions (sums, counts, and so on) while a field doesn't change value. This field is specified with the `BY` keyword. When the field value changes, the total calculated so far is displayed and the aggregate function is reset. To produce the list shown here, you must calculate the sum of line totals (multiply quantity by price and then subtract the discount) and group the calculations according to `OrderID` and `CustomerID`. Listing 5.3 shows the complete statement that produced the list shown earlier.

LISTING 5.3: *THE ORDERSGROUPED.SQL* QUERY

```
USE NORTHWIND
SELECT CompanyName, Orders.OrderID, ProductName,
    UnitPrice=ROUND([Order Details].UnitPrice, 2),
    Quantity,
    Discount=CONVERT(int, Discount * 100),
    ExtendedPrice=ROUND(CONVERT(money,
                   Quantity * (1 - Discount) *
                   [Order Details].UnitPrice), 2)
FROM Products, [Order Details], Customers, Orders
WHERE [Order Details].ProductID = Products.ProductID And
      [Order Details].OrderID = Orders.OrderID And
      Orders.CustomerID=Customers.CustomerID
ORDER BY Customers.CustomerID, Orders.OrderID
COMPUTE SUM(ROUND(CONVERT(money, Quantity * (1 - Discount) *
            [Order Details].UnitPrice), 2))
            BY Customers.CustomerID, Orders.OrderID
```

```
COMPUTE SUM(ROUND(CONVERT(money, Quantity * (1 - Discount) *
           [Order Details].UnitPrice), 2))
       BY Customers.CustomerID
```

The first COMPUTE BY clause groups the invoice line totals by order ID within each customer. The second COMPUTE BY clause groups the same totals by customer, as shown in Figure 5.1. The CONVERT() function converts data types similar to the Format() function of VB .NET, and the ROUND() function rounds a floating-point number. Both functions are discussed later in this chapter.

The COMPUTE BY clause can be used with any of the aggregate functions you have seen so far. Listing 5.4 displays the order IDs by customer and calculates the total number of invoices issued to each customer.

FIGURE 5.1

Using the COMPUTE BY clause to calculate totals on groups

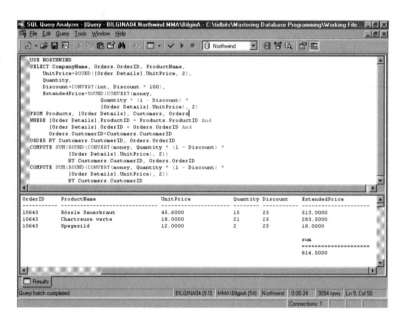

LISTING 5.4: *THE COUNTINVOICES.SQL* QUERY

```
USE NORTHWIND
SELECT Customers.CompanyName, Orders.OrderID
FROM Customers, Orders
WHERE Customers.CustomerID=Orders.CustomerID
ORDER BY Customers.CustomerID
COMPUTE COUNT(Orders.OrderID) BY Customers.CustomerID
```

The SQL engine will count the number of orders while the `CustomerID` field doesn't change. When it runs into a new customer, the current total is displayed and the counter is reset to zero in anticipation of the next customer. Here's the output produced by the preceding statement:

```
CompanyName                      OrderID
------------------------------   ----------
Alfreds Futterkiste              10643
Alfreds Futterkiste              10692
Alfreds Futterkiste              10702
Alfreds Futterkiste              10835
Alfreds Futterkiste              10952
Alfreds Futterkiste              11011

                                 cnt
                                 ===========
                                 6


CompanyName                      OrderID
------------------------------   ----------
Ana Trujillo Emparedados y hel   10308
Ana Trujillo Emparedados y hel   10625
Ana Trujillo Emparedados y hel   10759
Ana Trujillo Emparedados y hel   10926

                                 cnt
                                 ===========
                                 4
```

In addition to combining multiple COMPUTE BY clauses in the same statement (as in Listing 5.2), you can add another COMPUTE statement without the BY keyword to display a grand total—as shown in Listing 5.5.

LISTING 5.5: *COUNT INVOICES GRAND TOTAL.SQL*

```
USE NORTHWIND
SELECT Customers.CompanyName, Orders.OrderID
FROM Customers, Orders
WHERE Customers.CustomerID=Orders.CustomerID
ORDER BY Customers.CustomerID
COMPUTE COUNT(Orders.OrderID) BY Customers.CustomerID
COMPUTE COUNT(Orders.OrderID)
```

The COMPUTE BY clause requires the rows to be listed in the proper order, so all the fields following the BY keyword must also appear in an ORDER BY clause. The COMPUTE BY clause will not change the order of the rows to facilitate its calculations. Actually, the SQL engine will refuse to execute a statement that contains a COMPUTE BY clause but not the equivalent ORDER BY clause; it will abort the statement's execution and display the following error message:

```
A COMPUTE BY item was not found in the order by list.
All expressions in the compute by list must also be
present in the order by list.
```

Stored Procedures

A *stored procedure* is a routine written in T-SQL by using the DML, which acts on a database's rows. All SQL statements you have seen so far act on selected rows (they select, update, or delete rows), but SQL alone doesn't provide the means to alter the course of action depending on the values of the fields. SQL has no support for IF statements and no functions to manipulate strings, formatting functions, and so on. Every DBMS manufacturer extends standard SQL with statements that add the functionality of a programming language. For example, T-SQL recognizes the SUBSTRING() function, which is similar to the VB .NET Mid() function by the same name. It extracts part of a string field and uses it as another field. In the rest of this chapter, you'll look at the statements and functions of T-SQL.

Stored procedures are stored in SQL Server databases. The simplest application of stored procedures is to save complicated queries to the database and call them by name, so that users won't have to enter the SQL statements more than once. As you will see, stored procedures have many more applications, and you can even use them to build business rules into the database (but more on that in the next chapter).

After a stored procedure has been stored to the database, users and applications can call it as if it were another SQL statement or a built-in T-SQL function. Let's say you have written a stored procedure to add a new order to the database. You supply the input parameters, such as the customer ID and the ordered products' IDs, quantities, and discounts, and the stored procedure does the rest: it creates a new entry in the Orders table, adds the detail lines, and connects them to the appropriate order. The stored procedure verifies that the customer exists, extracts the product prices from the Products table, thus eliminating any chances for errors. Users and applications can call this stored procedure to add a new order and never have to worry about the structure of the tables. If you do change the underlying table structure, you must modify this procedure accordingly, and the dependent applications will not even be aware of the changes.

Writing T-SQL Stored Procedures

The main advantage of using stored procedures is performance. Stored procedures execute on the database server, close to the data. Your data manipulation code executes faster than passing in ad hoc SQL statements from ASP.NET or VB .NET. A stored procedure can scan thousands of records, perform calculations, and return a single number to your application. Finally, stored procedures execute faster than the equivalent ad hoc SQL statements because they don't have to move data across the network; all the calculations can occur on the database server.

Another good reason for using stored procedures is that after they're defined, they become part of the database and appear as database objects, like tables or views. This makes it easy to find and manipulate the stored procedures directly from the DBMS, rather than having to dig through VB source code to find them. Additionally, modifying stored procedures by using the DBMS is easier than recompiling VB DLLs and their dependencies, just to make a minor change to a SQL statement. Finally, most DBMSs come with native security permissions that you can set on various database objects, such as stored procedures. This enables you to declaratively manage your security, without having to write custom access checks.

Stored procedures also provide tighter security. Earlier we described a stored procedure that adds new orders to a database. This stored procedure is part of the database, and you can set up the database so that users and applications can't modify the Orders table directly. By forcing them to go through a stored procedure, you can be sure that all orders record properly. In addition, you can set security on the stored procedure so that only callers with appropriate permissions can execute the logic.

Stored procedures help encapsulate your business logic, hiding database structure changes from your Application layer. If you change the structure of the underlying tables, you can modify the stored procedure without affecting applications that use the stored procedure. You can implement business rules in the stored procedure (decrease the stock, update a list of best-sellers, and so on). If you provide a procedure for editing the Orders table, no one can tamper with the integrity of your data. By incorporating all this functionality into the stored procedure, you simplify the coding of the client application.

Creating and Executing Stored Procedures

To write, debug, and execute stored procedures against an SQL Server database, you can use the SQL Server Query Analyzer, VS .NET, or the Enterprise Manager. This chapter focuses on the Query Analyzer.

To create a stored procedure, enter the definition of the procedure in the Query pane and then press F5 to execute that definition. This action attaches the procedure to the database, but it does not actually execute it. To execute a procedure that's already been stored to the database, you must use the EXECUTE statement, which is discussed shortly.

To create a new stored procedure and attach it to the current database, use the CREATE PROCEDURE statement. The basic syntax of the statement is

```
CREATE PROCEDURE procedure_name
AS
{procedure definition}
```

where *procedure_name* is the name of the new stored procedure, and the block following the AS keyword is the body of the procedure.

TIP A shortcut for the CREATE PROCEDURE statement is CREATE PROC.

In its simplest form, a stored procedure is an SQL statement, like the ones we discussed in the previous chapter. If you think you'll be frequently executing the AllInvoices query (shown in Figure 5.2), you should create a stored procedure containing the SQL statement that retrieves customers, orders, and order details. Every time you need this report, you can call this procedure by name. To create the AllInvoices stored procedure, enter the following lines in the Query pane of the Query Analyzer:

```
CREATE PROCEDURE AllInvoices
AS
```

Then enter the SQL DDL statement shown in Figure 5.2. Because this is not the DML SQL statement, the first time you execute it, it will not return the list of invoices. DDL statements create system objects, whereas DML statements actually work with the data in a system. Instead, it will add the AllInvoices procedure to the current database—so be sure to select the Northwind database in the DB drop-down list, or use the USE keyword to make Northwind the active database:

```
USE NORTHWIND
CREATE PROCEDURE AllInvoices
AS
… procedure statements …
```

If the procedure exists already, you can't create it again. You must either drop it from the database with the DROP PROCEDURE statement, or modify it with the ALTER PROCEDURE statement. The syntax of the ALTER PROCEDURE statement is identical to that of the CREATE PROCEDURE statement. By replacing the CREATE keyword with the ALTER keyword, you can replace the definition of an existing procedure.

A common approach is to test for the existence of a stored procedure and drop it if it exists. Then you can add a new procedure with the CREATE PROCEDURE statement. For example, if you are not sure the myProcedure procedure exists, use the following statements to find and modify it:

```
USE DataBase
IF EXISTS (SELECT name FROM sysobjects
        WHERE name = 'myProcedure')
    DROP PROCEDURE myProcedure
GO

CREATE PROCEDURE myProcedure
AS
    . . .
```

The SELECT statement retrieves the name of the desired procedure from the objects database (again, be sure to execute it against the desired database). If a procedure by the name of *myProcedure* exists already, EXISTS returns True and drops the procedure definition from the database. Then it proceeds to add the revised definition.

In the preceding chapter, you saw the SQL statement that retrieves all the orders from the Northwind database. To implement it as a stored procedure, you must insert a few lines that declare a new stored procedure and then append the SQL statement that implements the procedure as is. Figure 5.2 shows the code for the implementation of the AllInvoices batch as a stored procedure.

FIGURE 5.2

The AllInvoices query stored procedure

```
USE NORTHWIND
IF EXISTS (SELECT name FROM sysobjects
        WHERE name = 'AllInvoices')
    DROP PROCEDURE AllInvoices
GO

CREATE PROCEDURE AllInvoices
AS
SELECT CompanyName, Orders.OrderID, ProductName,
    UnitPrice=ROUND([Order Details].UnitPrice, 2),
    Quantity,
    Discount=CONVERT(int, Discount * 100),
    ExtendedPrice=ROUND(CONVERT(money, Quantity * (1 - Discount) *
                    [Order Details].UnitPrice), 2)
FROM Products, [Order Details], Customers, Orders
WHERE [Order Details].ProductID = Products.ProductID And
    [Order Details].OrderID = Orders.OrderID And
    Orders.CustomerID=Customers.CustomerID
ORDER BY Customers.CustomerID, Orders.OrderID
COMPUTE SUM(ROUND(CONVERT(money, Quantity * (1 - Discount) *
            [Order Details].UnitPrice), 2))
            BY Customers.CustomerID, Orders.OrderID
COMPUTE SUM(ROUND(CONVERT(money, Quantity * (1 - Discount) *
            [Order Details].UnitPrice), 2))
            BY Customers.CustomerID
```

Press F5 to execute the procedure's declaration. If you haven't misspelled any keywords, the message The command(s) completed successfully will appear in the lower pane of the Query Analyzer's window, as shown in Figure 5.3. You can find the creating the AllInvoices stored procedure.sql file in this chapter's folder on the CD. Load it in the Query Analyzer with the File ➢ Open command and then execute it.

FIGURE 5.3

When you execute a stored procedure's definition, you add it to the database, but the procedure's statements are not executed.

```
USE NORTHWIND
IF EXISTS (SELECT name FROM sysobjects
        WHERE name = 'AllInvoices')
    DROP PROCEDURE AllInvoices
GO

CREATE PROCEDURE AllInvoices
AS
SELECT CompanyName, Orders.OrderID, ProductName,
    UnitPrice=ROUND([Order Details].UnitPrice, 2),
    Quantity,
    Discount=CONVERT(int, Discount * 100),
    ExtendedPrice=ROUND(CONVERT(money, Quantity * (1 - Discount) *
                    [Order Details].UnitPrice), 2)
FROM Products, [Order Details], Customers, Orders
WHERE [Order Details].ProductID = Products.ProductID And
    [Order Details].OrderID = Orders.OrderID And
    Orders.CustomerID=Customers.CustomerID
ORDER BY Customers.CustomerID, Orders.OrderID
COMPUTE SUM(ROUND(CONVERT(money, Quantity * (1 - Discount) *
            [Order Details].UnitPrice), 2))
            BY Customers.CustomerID, Orders.OrderID
COMPUTE SUM(ROUND(CONVERT(money, Quantity * (1 - Discount) *
            [Order Details].UnitPrice), 2))
            BY Customers.CustomerID
```

```
The command(s) completed successfully.
```

To execute a stored procedure, you must use the EXECUTE statement (or its abbreviation, EXEC) followed by the name of the procedure. Assuming that you have created the AllInvoices procedure, here's how to execute it:

1. First, clear the Query pane of the Query Analyzer or open a new window in the Query Analyzer.

2. In the fresh Query pane, type

```
USE Northwind
EXECUTE AllInvoices
```

and press F5. The result of the query appears in the Results pane of the Query Analyzer, as shown in Figure 5.4.

FIGURE 5.4

Executing the AllInvoices stored procedure with the Query Analyzer

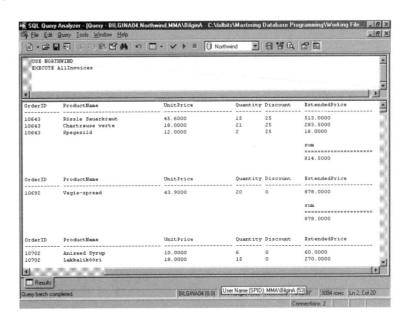

NOTE *For those of you working with the source code on the CD, you can load and execute the file* Executing the AllInvoices stored procedure.sql.

The first time you execute the procedure, SQL Server will put together an execution plan, so the processing will take a few seconds. An *execution plan* works like a compiler, translating the statements in a stored procedure or SQL statement for native execution directly against the database. After they've been compiled, the execution plan is saved in a cache. This enables SQL Server to reuse execution plans, even for SQL statements.

After the execution plan is generated, the procedure's execution will start immediately, and the rows will start appearing on the Results pane as soon as they become available.

TIP *If a procedure takes too long to execute or returns too many rows, you can interrupt it by pressing the Stop button (a red rectangular button on SQL Server's toolbar). If you execute an unconditional join by mistake, for example, you can stop the execution of the query and not have to wait until all rows arrive.*

Using Parameters with Stored Procedures

Stored procedures can benefit you the most when you use them with parameters. Parameters not only enable you to customize your result sets based on specified criteria, but also can help improve performance, by enabling SQL Server to optimize the execution plan based on expected input data types.

TIP *To improve performance, replace your constants with parameters. This will enable SQL Server to build an optimized execution plan.*

Let's now explore how you can use both input and output parameters with your stored procedures to maximize your application's efficiency.

USING INPUT PARAMETERS

In this section, we show you how to use input parameters with stored procedures. Input parameters give you flexibility: instead of simply hard-coding values in your T-SQL statements, you can pass input parameters from your application's front end to the appropriate stored procedure. The stored procedure will execute with the supplied input parameters, producing results based on specific criteria. If you want to view the customers from specific countries, for example, you don't have to write a different query for each country. You can write a single query that prompts the user for the country name and then uses that name in its WHERE clause to select rows that match the criteria.

SQL stored procedure parameters must be declared with the @ symbol before the SQL statement that uses them. Each parameter has a name and a type. The syntax to declare input parameters is as follows:

```
CREATE PROCEDURE StoredProcedureName
@ParameterName datatype[(length)],
@ParameterName2 datatype[(length)],
...
@ParameterNameN dataype[(length)]
```

You can specify up to 2100 parameters for a stored procedure.

The stored procedure (`Creating the GetCustomersByCountry stored procedure.sql`) that selects customers from a specific country can be written as follows:

```
CREATE PROCEDURE GetCustomersByCountry
    @CountryName varchar(15)
AS
    SELECT * FROM Customers
    WHERE Country = @CountryName
```

After you create this stored procedure, you can retrieve all the customers for Brazil, by executing it with the appropriate input value (retrieving customers in brazil using the GetCustomers-ByCountry stored procedure.sql):

```
EXEC GetCustomersByCountry "Brazil"
```

To declare multiple parameters, use commas to separate them. Listing 5.6 shows the code for the OrdersByDate stored procedure, which will select the orders placed during a user-supplied interval.

LISTING 5.6: *OrdersByDate Stored Procedure.sql*

```
CREATE PROCEDURE OrdersByDate
    @FromDate datetime,
    @ToDate datetime
AS
    SELECT *
    FROM Orders
    WHERE OrderDate BETWEEN @FromDate AND @ToDate
```

As we explained in Chapter 3, "The Visual Database Tools," Visual Studio .NET provides an intuitive interface for executing stored procedures. Let's execute the OrdersByDate stored procedure from VS .NET.

To run this stored procedure, expand the Northwind connection in the Server Explorer. Below the Stored Procedures node, you should find the OrdersByDate stored procedure. Select the Run Stored Procedure option from the shortcut menu.

This pops up a dialog box prompting you for the values of the two input parameters that you created, as illustrated in Figure 5.5.

FIGURE 5.5

Using input parameters with stored procedures in VS .NET

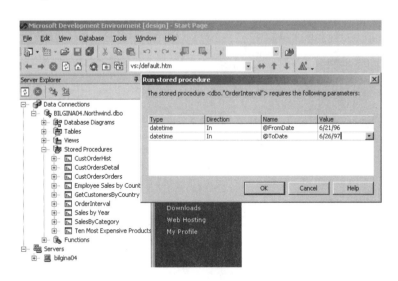

When you run this stored procedure, it prompts you for two dates. After you supply the dates in the dialog box, the stored procedure retrieves all the rows from the Orders table whose OrderDate lies between the two supplied dates, including the end dates. The results are displayed in the output window.

NOTE *You aren't required to supply input parameters if your stored procedure specifies default values for its input parameters. By not providing a value, the stored procedure uses its default values.*

USING OUTPUT PARAMETERS

Stored procedures wouldn't be nearly as useful without the capacity to pass output parameters. Stored procedures are implemented as functions: they accept one or more arguments and return one or more values to the caller. Stored procedures also return one or more result sets, which display in the Results pane of the Query Analyzer's window when you execute a SELECT statement.

Notice that you don't have to use the DECLARE statement. Other variables declared in the procedure's body must be prefixed with the DECLARE keyword. Let's build on the OrdersByDate procedure created earlier, in Listing 5.6.

As you can see, it is a simple stored procedure that accepts two datetime arguments and returns the orders placed in the specified interval. To test this procedure, you must first attach it to the Northwind database. If you haven't already created this stored procedure, do so now. Select Northwind in the DB box and then execute the preceding lines by pressing F5.

To test this stored procedure, open a new query window and execute the following lines:

```
DECLARE @date1 datetime
DECLARE @date2 datetime
SET @date1='6/21/1996'
SET @date2='6/26/1997'
EXECUTE OrdersByDate @date1, @date2
```

The orders placed between the specified dates will appear in the Results pane. Notice that you didn't have to specify the output result set as an argument; the rows retrieved are returned automatically to the caller. Let's add an output parameter to this stored procedure. This time you'll request the number of orders placed in the same interval. Here's the Creating CountOrdersByDate.sql stored procedure:

```
CREATE PROCEDURE CountOrdersByDate
@StartDate datetime, @EndDate datetime,
@CountOrders int OUTPUT
AS
SELECT @CountOrders = COUNT(OrderID) FROM Orders
WHERE OrderDate BETWEEN @StartDate AND @EndDate
```

The argument that will be returned to the procedure is marked with the OUTPUT keyword. Notice also that it must be assigned a value from within the stored procedure's code. The SELECT statement assigns the values returned by the SELECT query to the @CountOrders variable.

To test the new procedure, execute the following lines. The output they'll produce is shown in Figure 5.6.

```
DECLARE @date1 datetime
DECLARE @date2 datetime
SET @date1='6/21/1996'
SET @date2='3/31/1997'
DECLARE @orderCount int
EXECUTE CountOrdersByDate @date1, @date2, @orderCount OUTPUT
PRINT 'There were ' + CONVERT(varchar(5), @orderCount) +
        ' orders placed in the chosen interval'
```

This batch is similar to the batch you used to test the OrdersByDate procedure, with the exception of the new argument. In addition to declaring the argument, you must specify the OUTPUT keyword to indicate that this argument will be passed back to the caller. You can specify input/output arguments, which pass information to the procedure when it's called and return information back to the caller. The INPUT keyword is the default, so you don't have to specify it explicitly.

There's nothing complicated about parameters. In the next chapter you'll learn how to pass arguments to stored procedures from within your VB .NET code.

FIGURE 5.6

Testing the CountOrders-ByDate with a T-SQL batch

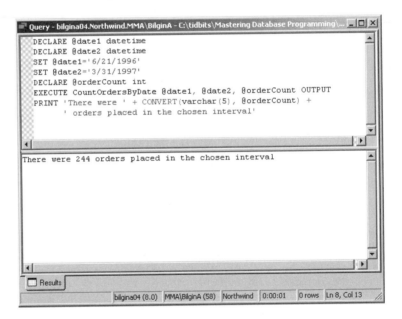

Executing Command Strings

In addition to executing stored procedures, you can use the EXECUTE statement to execute strings with valid T-SQL statements. If the variable @TSQLcmd (all T-SQL variables must begin with the

@ symbol) contains a valid SQL statement, you can execute it by passing it as an argument to the EXECUTE procedure:

```
EXECUTE (@TSQLcmd)
```

The parentheses are required. If you omit them, SQL Server will attempt to locate the `@TSQLcmd` stored procedure. Here's a simple example of storing SQL statements into variables and executing them with the EXECUTE method:

```
DECLARE @Country varchar(20)
DECLARE @TSQLcmd varchar(100)
SET @Country='Germany'
SET @TSQLcmd = 'SELECT City FROM Customers
                WHERE Country=''' + @Country + ''''
EXECUTE (@TSQLcmd)
```

All T-SQL variables must be declared with the DECLARE statement, have a valid data type, and should be set with the SET statement. You will find more information on the use of variables in the following sections of this chapter.

Why Use Stored Procedures?

Stored procedures are far more than a programming convenience. When an SQL statement, especially a complicated one, is stored in the database, the database management system can execute it efficiently. When the SQL statement is stored in the database as a procedure, its execution plan is designed once, cached, and is ready to be used again. Moreover, stored procedures can be designed once, tested, and used by many users and applications. If the same stored procedure is used by more than one user, the DBMS keeps only one copy of the procedure in memory, and all users share the same instance of the procedure. This means more efficient memory utilization. Finally, you can limit user access to the database's tables and force users to access the database through stored procedures. This is a simple method of enforcing business rules.

New! | **STORED PROCEDURES ARE NOT PARTIALLY PRECOMPILED**

To execute an SQL statement, the Query Engine must analyze it and put together an execution plan. The execution plan is analogous to the compilation of a traditional application. The DBMS translates the statements in the procedure into statements it can execute directly against the database.

A common misconception is that stored procedures execute faster because they are partially precompiled. This was the case with previous versions of SQL Server; however, SQL Server 7 and SQL Server 2000 no longer precompile the stored procedure. Both SQL statements and stored procedures are compiled upon execution. After they've been compiled, the execution plan is saved in a cache. This enables SQL Server to reuse execution plans, even for SQL statements. Thus, stored procedures don't have an advantage over SQL statements for these reasons.

Stored procedures do give you better performance, but for other reasons. By storing all your statements in one stored procedure, SQL Server can analyze and optimize all your logic into a single execution plan. A series of SQL statements doesn't take advantage of the single execution plan, because a separate plan would be generated for each statement. Each individual plan might not be the most efficient for the sequential series as a whole.

Let's say you designed a database like Northwind, and you want to update each product's stock, and perhaps customer balances, every time a new invoice is issued. You could write the applications yourself and hope you won't leave out any of these operations, and then explain the structure of the database to the programmers and hope they'll follow your instructions. Or you could implement a stored procedure that accepts the customer's ID and the IDs and quantities of the items ordered, and then updates all the tables used in the transaction. Application programmers can call this stored procedure and never have to worry about remembering to update some of the tables. At a later point, you might add a table to the database for storing the best-selling products. You can change the stored procedure, and the client applications that record new orders through this stored procedure need not be changed. Later in this chapter you will see examples of stored procedures that implement business rules.

T-SQL: The Language

The basic elements of T-SQL are the same as those of any other programming language: variables, control-of-flow statements, and functions. In this section, we quickly present the elements of T-SQL. Because this book is addressed to VB .NET programmers, we don't waste any time explaining what variables are and why they must have a type. We do discuss T-SQL by comparing its elements to the equivalent .NET Framework objects and stress the differences in the statements and functions of the two systems.

T-SQL Variables

Unlike VB .NET or ASP.NET, T-SQL is a typed language. Every variable must be declared before it is used, which you should do regardless of the language you are using. Variables are local to the scope to which they are declared. If you need to pass a variable between batches or stored procedures, you should use a function.

NOTE   Global variables were phased out with SQL Server 7 and have been replaced with functions.

Variables are declared with the DECLARE statement, and their names must begin with the @ character. The following are valid variable names: @CustomerTotal, @Avg_Discount, @i, @counter. To use them, declare them with the DECLARE statement, which has the syntax

```
DECLARE @var_name var_type
```

where *var_name* is the variable's name and *var_type* is the name of a data type supported by SQL Server.

Control-of-Flow Statements

T-SQL supports the basic control-of-flow statements that enable you to selectively execute blocks of statements based on the outcome of a comparison. In addition, they enable you to circumvent the traditional linear T-SQL language by executing your logic in a nonsequential fashion. They are similar to the equivalent VB .NET statements and, even though there aren't as many, they are adequate for the purposes of processing rows.

IF...ELSE

The IF...ELSE statement executes a block of statements conditionally, and its syntax is as follows:

```
IF condition
    {statement}
ELSE
    {statement}
```

Notice that there's no THEN keyword and that a T-SQL IF block is not delimited with an END IF keyword. To execute more than a single statement in the IF or the ELSE clause, you must use the BEGIN and END keywords to enclose the block of statements:

```
IF condition
    BEGIN
    {multiple statements}
    END
ELSE
    BEGIN
    {multiple statements}
    END
```

Depending on the *condition*, one of the two blocks of statements between the BEGIN and END keywords are executed. Here's an example of the IF statement with statement blocks:

```
IF (SELECT COUNT(*) FROM Customers WHERE Country = 'Germany') > 0
    BEGIN
    SELECT* FROM customers
    END
ELSE
    BEGIN
    PRINT 'The database contains no customers from Germany.'
    END
```

Notice the second pair of BEGIN/END keywords are optional because the ELSE clause is followed by a single statement. However, it is a good practice to use the BEGIN/END pair for easier readability.

CASE

The CASE statement is similar to the VB .NET Select Case statement. SELECT is a reserved T-SQL keyword and shouldn't be used with the CASE statement. The CASE statement compares a variable (or field) value against several values and executes a block of statement for the comparison that returns a True result.

Consider this example: A car rental company might need to calculate insurance premiums based on a car's category. Instead of multiple IF statements, you can use a CASE structure like the following:

```
CASE @CarCategory
    WHEN 'COMPACT' THEN 25.5
    WHEN 'ECONOMY' THEN 37.5
    WHEN 'LUXURY'  THEN 45.0
END
```

The CASE statement will return a single value: the one that corresponds to the first WHEN clause that's true. If the variable @CarCategory is ECONOMY, then the value 37.5 is printed in the Results pane of the Query Analyzer's window.

To include the value returned by the CASE statement to the result set, you must combine the SELECT and CASE statements as shown here:

```
SELECT @premium=
    CASE @CarCategory
        WHEN 'COMPACT' THEN 25.5
        WHEN 'ECONOMY' THEN 37.5
        WHEN 'LUXURY'  THEN 45.0
    END
```

THE T-SQL *CASE* STATEMENT VERSUS THE VB .NET *SELECT CASE* STATEMENT

T-SQL CASE statements have one important difference as compared to the equivalent VB .NET Select Case statements: how they assign variables based on the case conditions. As a VB programmer, you might accidentally code this T-SQL logic by using a Select Case. The result will not be an error message. The statement will simply select the result of the CASE statement (SELECT is a T-SQL keyword that assigns a value to a variable).

Let's clarify this with an example. The following statements will return the value 7.5. This value will be printed in the Results pane of the Query Analyzer, but you won't be able to use it in the statements following the CASE statement.

```
DECLARE @state char(2)
SET @state = 'CA'
SELECT CASE @state
    WHEN 'AZ' THEN 5.5
    WHEN 'CA' THEN 7.5
    WHEN 'NY' THEN 8.5
END
```

If you want to store the result to a variable, use the following syntax:

```
DECLARE @state char(2)
DECLARE @stateTAX real
SET @state = 'CA'
SET @stateTAX =
    CASE @state
        WHEN 'AZ' THEN 5.5
        WHEN 'CA' THEN 7.5
        WHEN 'NY' THEN 8.5
    END
PRINT @stateTAX
```

This syntax has no counterpart in Visual Basic .NET. Note that the entire CASE statement is, in effect, embedded into the assignment. The @stateTAX variable is set to the value selected by the CASE statement.

WHILE

The WHILE statement repeatedly executes a single statement or a block of T-SQL statements until a specified condition is reached. If you want to repeat multiple statements, enclose them in a pair of BEGIN/END keywords, as explained in the description of the IF…ELSE statement. The most common use of the WHILE statement is to scan the rows of a cursor, as shown in the following example:

```
FETCH NEXT INTO variable_list
WHILE @@FETCH_STATUS = 0
    BEGIN
    {statements to process the fields of the current row}
    FETCH NEXT INTO variable_list
    END
```

The FETCH NEXT statement reads the next row of a cursor set and stores its fields' values into the variables specified in the *variable_list*, which is a comma-separated list of variables. The FETCH statement is discussed in the following chapter. For the purposes of this example, you can think of a cursor as a table and FETCH NEXT as the equivalent of the MoveNext() method of the ADO 2.*x* RecordSet object. Finally, @@FETCH_STATUS is a global variable that returns 0 while there are more records to be fetched. When you reach the end of the cursor, @@FETCH_STATUS returns -1.

NOTE *We discuss cursors in the context of T-SQL procedures in Chapter 6.*

CONTINUE AND BREAK

These two keywords are used with the WHILE statement to alter the flow of execution. The CONTINUE keyword ends the current iteration and forces another one. In other words, the WHILE statement's condition is evaluated and the loop is re-entered. If the condition is False, then the WHILE loop is skipped and execution continues with the line following the END keyword that delimits the loop's body of statements.

The BREAK keyword terminates the loop immediately and branches to the line following the loop's END keyword. The following code segment shows how the two keywords are used in a WHILE loop:

```
WHILE condition
    BEGIN
        {read column values into variables}
        IF @balance < 0
            CONTINUE
        IF @balance > 999999
            BREAK
        {process @balance variable and/or other variables}
    END
```

This loop reads the rows of a table or cursor and processes only the ones with a positive balance, less than 1,000,000. If a row with a negative balance is found, the code doesn't process it and continues with the next row. If a row with a balance of 1,000,000 or more is found, the code stops processing the rows by breaking out of the loop.

WAITFOR

The WAITFOR statement is analogous to a timer in VB .NET. This statement enables you to specify an interval of time before executing a statement. This command is most useful for off-peak scheduling, such as running nightly batches, so that you don't affect performance when there is high demand for the data. The syntax is simple: just pass in the interval of time you wish to wait, or the exact time that you want the statement to execute. If you want to run a statement at midnight, you would code WAITFOR TIME '24:00' or if you wanted to wait an hour before executing a query. As you do with other control-of-flow statements, you should specify BEGIN and END statements around your WAITFOR statement.

GOTO **AND** *RETURN*

These last two control-of-flow statements enable you to alter the flow of execution by branching to another location in the procedure. The GOTO statement branches to a line identified by a label. Here's a simple example of the GOTO statement (in effect, it's a less elegant method of implementing a WHILE loop):

```
RepeatLoop:
    FETCH NEXT INTO variable_list
    IF @@FETCH_STATUS = 0
        BEGIN
        {process variables}
        GOTO RepeatLoop
    END
```

While more records are in the result set, the GOTO statement branches to the FETCH NEXT statement. The identifier RepeatLoop is a label (a name identifying the line to which you want to branch), and it must be followed by a colon. If there are no more records to be fetched and processed, the procedure continues with the statement following the END keyword.

TIP *Try to avoid using the GOTO statement because it makes code difficult to follow. If you design your stored procedures properly, you should be able to minimize its use.*

The RETURN statement ends a procedure unconditionally and, optionally, returns a result. To return a value from within a stored procedure, use a statement such as the following:

```
RETURN @error_value
```

@error_value is a local variable, which can be set by the procedure's code. The calling application, which could be another stored procedure, should be aware of the possible values returned by the procedure.

If you don't specify your own error code, SQL Server returns its error code, which can be one of over 20,000 nonzero values. You can look up the different error codes in the SQL Server Books Online (from the Start menu, choose Programs ➤ Microsoft SQL Server ➤ Books Online).

Debugging Statements

There are a couple additional SQL statements—PRINT and RAISERROR—that you might find useful for debugging your stored procedures.

PRINT

The `PRINT` statement is similar to VB .NET's Console.WriteLine method: it prints its return value to the Results pane and is used for debugging purposes. The output of the `PRINT` statement doesn't become part of the result set returned by the procedure or T-SQL statement, which you have already seen demonstrated in this chapter. The syntax of the `PRINT` statement is as follows:

```
PRINT output_list
```

The *output_list* can be any combination of literals, variables, and functions. To display a message, use a statement like the following one:

```
PRINT "No rows matching your criteria were found in the table."
```

You can also display variable values along with literals, but this requires some conversions. Unlike VB .NET's Console.WriteLine statement, the T-SQL `PRINT` statement can't print multiple arguments separated with commas. You must format all the information you want to print as strings, concatenate them with the + operator, and then print them. If you want to print a customer name (field `CustName`) and a total (field `CustTotal`), you can't use a statement such as the following:

```
PRINT CustName, CustTotal    - WRONG!
```

Instead, you must concatenate the two values and print them as a single string. Because T-SQL is a typed language, you must first convert the numeric field to a string value and concatenate the two:

```
PRINT CustName + CONVERT(char(12), CustTotal)
```

The `CONVERT()` function converts (casts) a data type to another data type, and it's discussed in the next section of this chapter.

NOTE   *Typically, all the output produced by the T-SQL statements forms the result set. This output is usually the data retrieved from the database. To include titles or any other type of information in the result set, use the* `PRINT` *statement. When you use the* `PRINT` *statement with the Query Analyzer, its output appears in the lower pane of the window. You can't use the* `PRINT` *statement to insert additional lines into a result set.*

RAISERROR

Although `PRINT` is useful for returning error values, the `RAISERROR` statement gives you more control. You can write detailed error information to the SQL Server, to the Windows Server 2000 application log, or to your own custom user interface. Raising errors follows the .NET Framework error handling strategy, and we highly recommend using this technique.

Usually, when an error occurs during the execution of a stored procedure, SQL Server displays an error message in the lower pane of the Query Analyzer and aborts the execution. It is possible to raise your own error messages from within your stored procedures with the `RAISERROR` statement. The basic syntax of the statement is as follows:

```
RAISERROR errorNum | errorDescription, severity, state
```

The first argument is the error's number or message. The error number must be a value in the range 50,001 to 2,147,483,648. The first 50,000 error codes are reserved for SQL Server. The error message should not exceed 400 characters; otherwise, SQL Server will truncate it. The second argument indicates the severity of the error and should be a value from 0 to 18 (18 being the most severe custom error). The last argument is an integer in the range 1 to 127, and you can use it to return additional information about the error.

NOTE *The severity of an error can be higher than 18; however, such errors are extremely severe and require that you set extra logging options. Lower errors are less serious. When they are under 10, they most often indicate errors in the data rather than the system.*

SQL Server comes with a special `sysmessages` table, where you can store your custom error numbers and description. To associate a description with your custom errors, use the `sp_addmessage` system stored procedure, whose basic syntax is shown here:

```
sp_addmessage errorNum, severity, errorDescription
```

This statement adds new error messages to a database and associates them to error numbers. To add a custom error, use a statement such as the following one:

```
sp_addmessage 60000, 15, 'Can't accept IOU from this customer'
```

Then, every time you run into customers you can't accept IOUs from, raise this error with the `RAISERROR` statement. Your error message will be handled just like any native SQL Server error message, as shown in Figure 5.7.

FIGURE 5.7

Raising custom errors from within your stored procedures

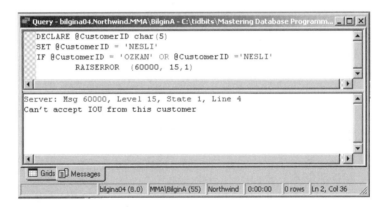

TIP *If you'd like, you can add the optional* **WITH LOG** *clause to the end of the* **RAISERROR** *statement. This records errors into the NT Event log.*

T-SQL Functions

T-SQL supports a number of functions that simplify the processing of the various data types, interacting with the server and implementing the operations you take for granted in application development. This section covers the T-SQL functions by comparing them to the equivalent VB .NET functions. Some T-SQL functions have no equivalent in VB .NET, and these functions are discussed in more detail. Notice that the following functions are part of T-SQL, but they can be used outside T-SQL procedures. You can use them in the Query Analyzer's window to process or format the output of plain SQL statements.

SQL Server 2000 supports three types of functions: scalar, aggregate, and rowset functions. *Scalar functions* are the simplest; they operate on a single value and return a single value. *Aggregate functions* operate on multiple values, but still return a single value. As you might guess, *rowset functions* work with sets of data such as native tables or XML. We review some of the more commonly used functions in this section.

CURSOR FUNCTIONS

Cursors enable you to work with a subset of data on a row-by-row basis. All cursor functions are nondeterministic because the results might not always be consistent. A user might delete a row while you are working with your cursor. Here are a few functions that work with cursors (note that these were called global variables in previous versions of SQL):

@@FETCH_STATUS   The @@FETCH_STATUS function is a scalar function that works with cursors. It enables you to track your progress as you fetch data from your cursors. @@FETCH_STATUS, for example, is zero if the FETCH statement successfully retrieved a row, nonzero otherwise. This variable is set after the execution of a FETCH statement and is commonly used to terminate a WHILE loop that scans a cursor.

@@CURSOR_ROWS   The @@CURSOR_ROWS scalar function returns the number of rows in the most recently opened cursor.

SYSTEM FUNCTIONS

System functions are scalar functions that can be either nondeterministic or deterministic. Many system functions are available in SQL Server. Here are some tips about working with some of the more commonly used functions:

@@ROWCOUNT   Similar to the @@CURSOR_ROWS function, the @@ROWCOUNT variable returns the number of rows affected by a retrieve or action query. The @@ROWCOUNT variable is commonly used with UPDATE and DELETE statements to find out how many rows were affected by the SQL statement. To find out how many rows were affected by an UPDATE statement, print the @@ROWCOUNT global variable after executing the SQL statement, as shown here:

```
UPDATE Customers
   SET Phone = '030' + Phone
   WHERE Country = 'Germany'
PRINT @@ROWCOUNT
```

@@ERROR   The @@ERROR scalar function returns an error number for the last T-SQL statement that was executed. If this variable is zero, then the statement was executed successfully. The error values are stored in the sysmessages table, which we mentioned earlier in our discussion of the RAISERROR statement.

@@IDENTITY   The @@IDENTITY scalar function returns the most recently used value for an Identity column. As you recall from Chapter 2, "Basic Concepts of Relational Databases," Identity columns can't be set; they are assigned a value automatically by the system, each time a new row is added to the table. Applications usually need this information because Identity fields are referenced by foreign keys in other tables. Let's say you're adding a new order to the Northwind database. First, you must add a row to the Orders table. You can specify any field's value, but not the OrderID field's value. When the new row is added to the Orders table, you must add rows with the invoice details to the Order Details table. To do so, you need the value of the OrderID field, which can be retrieved by the @@IDENTITY global variable. If you need local identity values, use the IDENT_CURRENT or SCOPE_IDENTITY functions. In the section "Implementing Business Rules with Stored Procedures" later in this chapter, you'll find examples on how to use the @@IDENTITY variable.

TIP   Never use the MAX() function to return the highest value of an Identity column. This forces a table scan, hindering your performance.

New!   *NOTE   In versions prior to SQL Server 7, global variables were differentiated from local variables by using an extra @ symbol in the declaration. @@ERROR would be a global function, whereas @MyError would be a local variable. As of SQL Server 7, global variables are considered functions. This is why you will see some functions that have @@ prefixes and others that don't.*

SUSER_SID()   This function accepts the user's login name as an argument and returns the user's security identification number (SID).

SUSER_SNAME()   This function does the opposite. It accepts the user's SID and returns the user's login name.

WARNING   Don't use the SUSER_ID() function. The SUSER_ID() function degrades performance because it is not part of SQL Server's security model. It has been deprecated in SQL Server 2000 and will always return a Null value. For the same reasons, don't use the SUSER_NAME() function. This also has been deprecated in SQL Server 2000 and will always return a Null value.

USER_ID() and USER_NAME()   These functions are similar to SUSER_SID() and SUSER_SNAME(), only instead of the login name, they work with the database username and database ID.

USER, CURRENT_USER   These functions accept no arguments and must be called without the parentheses; they return the current user's database username. If you have logged in as "sa," your database username will most likely be "dbo." They work just like the USER_NAME function.

COALESCE(*expression, expression, …*)   This function returns the first non-Null expression in its argument list. The function COALESCE(CompanyName, ContactName) returns the company's name, or the customer's name, should the CompanyName be NULL. Use this function to retrieve alternate information for Null columns in your SELECT statements:

```
SELECT CustomerID, COALESCE(CompanyName, ContactName)as ContactOrCompany
FROM Customers
```

You can also use a literal as the last argument, in case all the values retrieved from the database are Null:

```
SELECT CustomerID, COALESCE(CompanyName, ContactName, 'MISSING!')
FROM Customers
```

ISNULL(*expression, replacement value*)   The ISNULL() function differs from the IsDBNull() method of VB .NET. The T-SQL ISNULL() function accepts two arguments: a field or variable name, and a replacement value. If the first argument is not Null, then the function returns its value. If the first argument is Null, then the *replacement value* argument is returned. If certain products haven't been assigned a value, you can still include them in a price list with a zero value:

```
SELECT ProductName, ISNULL(UnitPrice, 0.0) AS UnitPrice
FROM Products
```

This statement will select all the rows in the Products table along with their prices. Products without prices will appear with a zero value (instead of the "Null" literal).

On the other hand, in VB.NET, Null values from a database are handled with the DBNull object. This class differentiates between a Null value that is not set versus one that is purposely set to Null. In VB.NET, uninitialized fields from a database have the DBNull value.

TIP   *In VB6, you used the* IsNull() *function to determine whether a database value was Null. This is no longer the case with VB .NET. You should replace the* IsNull() *function with* IsDBNull() *when you migrate your code from VB6 to VB .NET. In VB .NET, Null values from SQL Server should be handled with the* System.DBNull *class.*

NULLIF(*expression, expression2*)   The NULLIF() function accepts two arguments and returns NULL if they are equal. If not, the first argument is returned. The NULLIF() function is equivalent to the following CASE statement:

```
CASE
    WHEN expression1 = expression2 THEN NULL
    ELSE expression1
END
```

STRING MANIPULATION

T-SQL supports a number of functions for the manipulation of strings that are similar to the equivalent string functions of VB .NET, but many of them have different names. The following list summarizes these functions and their arguments.

WARNING *SQL Server 7 introduced several changes in how strings are treated. For example, SQL Server 7 and SQL Server 2000 treat empty strings differently than previous versions. Previous versions interpreted empty strings as a single space, whereas SQL Server 7 and SQL Server 2000 handle them as empty strings. This will cause most of these string manipulation functions to act differently depending on the version of SQL Server you work with.*

CHARINDEX(*expression1, expression2*) Similar to the `InStr()` function of VB .NET, the CHARINDEX() function returns the position of the first occurrence of the first argument in the second argument.

LEFT(*string, integer*), RIGHT(*string, integer*) These are the same as the `Left()` and `Right()` functions of VB .NET, respectively. The first argument specifies the string to examine, and the second argument refers to the length of the characters to return, starting from the left or right, respectively.

LEN(*string*) Similar to the `Len()` function of VB .NET, it returns the length of a string. The LEN() function will return the length of the string stored in the variable, even if the variable was declared as char.

TIP *In VB .NET, you are not limited to only string data types; you can use other types such as Booleans, doubles, or objects. Keep in mind that if you check the length of objects, VB .NET will treat the object as a string, counting the number of characters in the converted object.*

DATALENGTH(*expression*) This function returns the declared length of an expression, usually a variable length column, unlike the LEN() function, which returns the length of the value stored in the column.

LOWER(*string*), UPPER(*string or character expression*) Same as the `LCase()` and `UCase()` functions or the `String.ToLower()` and `String.ToUpper()` methods of VB .NET, respectively, which convert the argument to lowercase or uppercase characters.

LTRIM(*string*), RTRIM(*string*) These are the same as the `LTrim()` and `RTrim()` functions of VB .NET; they remove the leading leftmost or rightmost spaces from the string argument, respectively.

STR(*float, length, decimal*) This function converts a float expression to a string by using *length* digits in all and *decimal* digits for the fractional part of the expression. If the numeric value has more fractional digits than specified with the *decimal* argument, the STR() function will round, not simply truncate, the numeric value. The function PRINT STR(3.14159, 4, 2) will return the value 3.14, whereas the expression PRINT STR(3.14159, 5, 3) will return 3.142.

REPLACE(*Expression, FindString, ReplacementString*) Same as the `Replace()` function of VB .NET. It replaces all occurrences of the *FindString* in the *Expression* with *ReplacementString*.

REVERSE(*string*)   Same as the StrReverse() function of VB .NET. It reverses the order of the characters in the specified string.

SUBSTRING(*string, start, length*)   Similar to the Mid() function of VB .NET. It returns a segment of a text or binary value; *string* is the variable on which the SUBSTRING() function will act, and *start* and *length* are the starting position and length of the desired segment of the string. The function

```
SUBSTRING('February 21, 1999',10,2)
```

returns the string 21 (the two characters at the 10th position in the specified string).

PATINDEX(*pattern, expression*)   Similar to the InStr() function of VB .NET and the CHARINDEX() function of T-SQL. It returns the location of the first occurrence of the *pattern* string in the *expression* string.

STUFF(*string1, start, length, string2*)   This function replaces part of *string1* with *string2*. The part of the first string to be replaced is determined by the position of the first character (*start*) and the *length* to be replaced. If you execute the following lines

```
DECLARE @a char(30)
SET @a='Free range chicken cooking'
SET @a= STUFF(@a, 1, 26, 'Farm raised chicken cooking')
PRINT @a
```

the string "Free range chicken cooking" will be printed. The STUFF () function supplies the string to replace, beginning with the 1st character and ending with the 26th character of the initial string.

CONVERSION FUNCTIONS

The internal representation of the various columns is not always the most appropriate for reports. T-SQL provides two functions for converting between data types—CONVERT() and CAST():

CONVERT(*data_type, expression, style*)   The CONVERT() function converts an expression to the specified data type. The *data_type* argument can be any valid SQL Server data type. If the data type is nchar, nvarchar, char, varchar, binary, or varbinary, you can specify its length as a numeric value in parentheses.

WARNING   You can't use the CONVERT() function to convert an expression to a user-defined data type.

The *style* argument specifies the desired date format when you convert datetime and smalldatetime variables to character data. You can look up the appropriate values for the style argument in the SQL Server Books Online.

Use the CONVERT() function to convert data types before displaying them in the Query Analyzer's window, or to concatenate character and numeric values before passing them to the PRINT statement.

The CompanyName and ContactName columns in the Customers table of the Northwind database have a maximum length of 40 and 30 characters, respectively. You can display them in shorter columns with a statement such as the following:

```
USE NORTHWIND
```

```
SELECT CONVERT(nchar(30), CompanyName),
       CONVERT(nchar(15), ContactName)
FROM Customers
```

TIP   Alternately, you can shorten the column values returned in the Query Analyzer, by selecting the Results tab from the Tools ➤ Options menu and specifying the maximum characters to return per column.

The following statement retrieves the total for all companies and displays it along with the company's name:

```
USE NORTHWIND
SELECT CONVERT(char(25), CompanyName),
       CONVERT(char(10),
               SUM(Quantity * UnitPrice * (1 - Discount)))
FROM [Order Details], Orders, Customers
WHERE [Order Details].OrderID = Orders.OrderID AND
      Orders.CustomerID = Customers.CustomerID
GROUP BY CompanyName
ORDER BY CompanyName
```

A section of output produced by the preceding statement is shown here:

```
Around the Horn           13390.7
Berglunds snabbköp        24927.6
Blauer See Delikatessen   3239.8
```

If you omit the CONVERT() functions, the company name will be displayed in 40 spaces and the totals will be displayed with too many fractional digits:

```
Around the Horn                  13390.650009155273
Berglunds snabbköp               24927.57746887207
Blauer See Delikatessen          3239.8000030517578
```

CAST(*variable* AS *data_type*)   The CAST() function converts a variable or column value to the specified data type. This function doesn't do anything more than the CONVERT() function, but it's included for compatibility with the SQL-92 standard.

DATE AND TIME FUNCTIONS

Like VB .NET, T-SQL recognizes the following date and time manipulation functions:

GETDATE()   Returns the current date and time on the machine that runs SQL Server.

DATEADD(*interval, number, date*)   Increments its *date* argument by the specified number of intervals. The *interval* argument indicates which part of the date to increment, such as the day, hour, or seconds of the *date*.

DATEDIFF(*interval, startdate, enddate*)   Returns the difference between two date arguments in a number of *intervals*, which can be days, hours, months, years, and so on.

DATEPART(*interval, date*) Returns an integer that represents the specified *interval* of a given *date*, such as number of seconds or hours.

DATENAME(*interval, date*) This is a nondeterministic function that returns the name of a part of a date argument. The function DATENAME(month, varDate) returns the name of the month in the varDate argument (January, February, and so on), and DATENAME(weekday, varDate) returns the name of the weekday in the varDate argument (Monday, Tuesday, and so on).

DAY(), MONTH(), YEAR() These deterministic functions return the weekday, month, and year part of their argument, which must be a date value.

User-Defined Functions

New! In addition to the built-in functions, SQL Server 2000 introduces user-defined functions (UDFs), which work like stored procedures. SQL Server 2000 creates execution plans for both stored procedures and user-defined functions. These plans can later be reused when the stored procedure or UDF is called again.

The main difference between stored procedures and UDFs is that UDFs are a bit limited in the type of data that they can return. UDFs provide a powerful way to reuse your code and easily execute powerful logic that would be complicated if you used stored procedures, views, or temporary tables.

WARNING *Don't go overboard creating UDFs. Depending on the code you use in them, UDFs can adversely affect performance. You should always run benchmarking tests to ensure that it makes sense to encapsulate your code in a function.*

There are three types of UDFs: scalar, inline table-valued, and multi-statement table-valued.

Scalar Functions

Scalar functions are the least complicated UDF type. They perform operations on multiple input parameters, but can return only a single value.

Here is a simple, but useful, scalar UDF that calculates a total price based on price and quantity (UDF TotalPrice.sql):

```
CREATE FUNCTION fx_TotalPrice (@Price money, @Quantity smallint)
RETURNS  money
AS
BEGIN
   RETURN (ROUND(@Price,2) * @Quantity)
END
```

If you want to call this function, all you have to type is the following:

```
select dbo.fx_TotalPrice(4.00,10)
```

Calling this function with these parameters returns a total price of 40.0000. Notice that the dbo qualifier was used to call the function. Scalar functions must be called with the *owner.function_name* syntax. You don't have to do this for the other two UDF types.

WARNING *Scalar UDFs are not limited to only a single return type. They are also limited in the data type that they return. They cannot return* text, ntext, image, *or* timestamp *data types. You also cannot return user-defined data types. Non-scalar types, such as the table or cursor type, are also not supported.*

You can also nest functions within each other. If you want to apply a discount to the total price, you could create a fx_CalculateDiscount function that accepts price, quantity, and discount as input parameters. You can then call the fx_TotalPrice function from within your new function, passing the Price and Quantity parameters.

Inline Table-Valued

In Chapter 2, we mentioned that the SQL Server 2000 table type was useful with user-defined functions. Both inline table-valued and multi-statement table-valued UDFs use the table data type as their return values.

Let's take your OrdersByDate stored procedure logic and convert it to an inline table-valued UDF. To create this function, you would execute the following code (UDF OrdersByDate.sql), after selecting the Northwind database:

```
CREATE FUNCTION fx_OrdersByDate(@FromDate datetime,
    @ToDate datetime)
RETURNS table
AS
RETURN(
    SELECT *
    FROM Orders
    WHERE OrderDate BETWEEN @FromDate AND @ToDate)
```

To execute this function, you would use the following statement (Call UDF OrdersByDate.sql):

```
SELECT * FROM fx_OrdersByDate('6/21/1996','6/26/1997')
```

Does this look familiar? The FROM clause is used with tables, which is exactly what this UDF returns. Thus, you can go ahead and run table commands to return the rows returned by this function. The results will look like the ones you saw returned for the OrdersByDate stored procedure.

WARNING *Earlier in this chapter, we explained the difference between nondeterministic and deterministic functions, mentioning that it would be important for UDFs. You cannot call a built-in nondeterministic function from your user-defined function. You couldn't use the* GetDate() *function in your* fx_OrdersByDate *function.*

Multi-Statement Table-Valued

Multi-statement table-valued functions are a bit more complex because they use multiple statements to generate the table return value. Because you will need to manipulate the table variable from within your function, you must explicitly declare the table variable, which you didn't have to do in the preceding example. After you create the table structure, you can manipulate it as you would a temporary table, inserting and updating values into it.

Table-valued functions are a powerful alternative to using temporary tables or views. You can use complicated logic to determine the rows returned, as well as use input parameters, which you can't do with a single view. After you've created a table-valued function, you can further manipulate it in the FROM clause of your T-SQL statements, which you can't do with stored procedures.

Let's build on your previous OrdersByDate logic, adding another variable, Country, which will show us the orders by date, for customers from a specific country. You will create a special CountryStatus column that will show you the orders from customers that match your specified country. Listing 5.7 shows the complete listing for this function.

LISTING 5.7: THE *ORDERSBYDATEFORCUSTOMERCOUNTRY* FUNCTION
(*UDF ORDERSBYDATEFORCUSTOMERCOUNTRY.SQL*)

```
CREATE FUNCTION fx_OrdersByDateforCustomerCountry (@FromDate datetime,
    @ToDate datetime,@Country nvarchar(15))
RETURNS @OrdersByDateCountry table
(  OrderID int,
   OrderDate datetime,
   Country nvarchar(15),
   CountryStatus nvarchar(40))
AS
BEGIN
   - Part 1
   - We will leave CountryStatus as Country for now
INSERT @OrdersByDateCountry
SELECT Orders.OrderID,
       Orders.OrderDate,
    Customers.Country,
       Customers.Country
FROM Orders, Customers
   WHERE Orders.OrderDate BETWEEN @FromDate AND @ToDate AND
   Customers.CustomerID = Orders.CustomerID

   - Part 2
   - Update the CountryStatus field
   UPDATE @OrdersByDateCountry
   SET CountryStatus = 'Your chosen country'
   WHERE Country = @Country

RETURN
END
```

You can see the results of this function (Call UDF OrdersByDateforCustomerCountry.sql) in Figure 5.8.

FIGURE 5.8

Executing your
custom multi-
statement table-
valued UDF

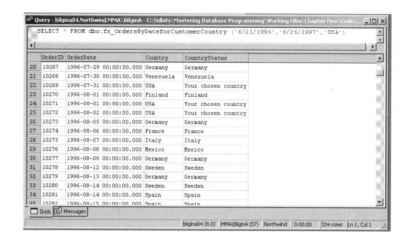

Triggers

Triggers are special types of stored procedures. Although they are used mostly for administrative tasks, triggers play an important role in SQL Server programming.

A trigger is a procedure that SQL Server invokes automatically when certain actions take place. These actions are inserting, deleting, and updating a row. You can think of triggers as VB .NET event handlers for onUpdate, onInsert, and onDelete events.

Triggers are commonly used for auditing purposes. If you want to know who's doing what with the company's sensitive data, you can add a few fields in the Orders table and record the user and time information every time a record is added, deleted, or updated. Without triggers, you'd have to implement this feature into every routine that accesses the Orders table for updates. To ensure that every action on the Orders table is recorded, you can create a trigger that's invoked automatically and updates these fields in a special auditing table.

Creating a trigger is similar to creating a stored procedure. You use the CREATE TRIGGER statement, whose core syntax is as follows:

```
CREATE TRIGGER trigger_name
ON table
{FOR | AFTER | INSTEAD OF} [DELETE] [,] [INSERT] [,] [UPDATE]
AS
Block of T-SQL Statements
```

Each trigger has a name and is defined for a specific table and for one or more specific actions (DELETE, INSERT, UPDATE).

New!   *NOTE*   INSTEAD OF *and* AFTER *keywords are new to SQL Server 2000. In previous versions, all triggers were treated as* AFTER *triggers.*

The FOR, AFTER, and INSTEAD OF keywords are used to indicate when you want to fire the trigger. For example, you could fire them FOR INSERT, INSTEAD OF INSERT, or AFTER INSERT. The FOR indicates that you want the trigger to fire for a particular insert, update, or delete action. INSTEAD OF triggers fire in lieu of the insert, update, and delete actions. AFTER triggers fire after the insert, update, or delete action completes. You can have multiple AFTER triggers, but only one INSTEAD OF trigger per insert, update, or delete action.

TIP   *If you have multiple* AFTER *triggers, use the* `sp_settriggerorder` *stored procedure to set the order. You can find more details on this stored procedure in the SQL Server Books Online, which comes with your SQL Server installation.*

Following the AS keyword comes a block of statements that defines the trigger's actions. As you can see, the same trigger might apply to multiple actions. To distinguish between them, use the statement

```
IF UPDATE(column)
```

where *column* is a column name. The IF statement will return True if the specified column was inserted or updated. To keep the triggers short, write a separate one for each action.

The CREATE TRIGGER statement is similar to the CREATE PROCEDURE statement. It is followed by the name of the trigger and the keyword ON, which specifies the table on which the trigger will act. The FOR keyword must be followed by the name of an action that invokes the trigger: UPDATE, INSERT, and DELETE. Following the AS keyword, you specify the T-SQL code to be executed every time the Customers table is updated.

New!   **TIP**   *Prior to SQL Server 2000, many developers used triggers to support cascading updates and deletes. As we indicated in Chapter 2, you should replace these triggers with declarative referential integrity (DRI) for cascading updates and deletes. DRI will give you better performance than triggers.*

Implementing Triggers

Let's add a trigger for each action (insert/update/delete) to the Orders table. The EditOrder and NewOrder triggers will update the fields EditedBy/EditedOn and AddedBy/AddedOn, respectively. EditedBy and EditedOn fields hold the name of the user that edited the order and the date and time; the AddedBy and AddedOn fields hold the same information but apply to additions of new rows. When a row is deleted, you'll save the same data (the user's name and the date of the action), as well as the order's ID, the customer's ID, and the order's date in a new table. This information will be stored in the Deletions table, which holds information about deleted orders.

Before adding the triggers to the Northwind database, you must add four new fields to the Orders table:

EditedBy	Varchar(20)
EditedOn	Datetime(10)
AddedBy	Varchar(20)
AddedOn	Datetime(10)

You must also add a new table to the database. Here's the structure of the table, called Deletions:

DeletedBy	Varchar(20)
DeletedOn	Datetime(10)
DelOrderID	Int(4)
DelCustomerID	Char(5)
DelOrderDate	Datetime(10)

EditOrderTrigger, shown in Listing 5.8, updates the EditedOn and EditedBy fields of the updated row. The GETDATE() function returns the current date, and the USER function returns the name of the current user. Notice how the WHERE statement selects the updated row: it extracts the order's ID from the inserted row. This is a variable maintained by the system, and it contains the columns of the most recently updated or inserted row.

TIP *Use* SET NOCOUNT ON *to improve the performance of your SQL statements when you don't care about how many rows were affected by your statement. This turns off the message in the Results pane that shows the number of rows affected.*

LISTING 5.8: THE *EDITORDER* TRIGGER

```
CREATE TRIGGER EditOrderTrigger ON [Orders]
FOR UPDATE
AS
SET NOCOUNT ON

DECLARE @OrderID char(5)
SELECT @OrderID = OrderID FROM inserted
UPDATE Orders SET EditedOn=GETDATE(), EditedBy=USER
WHERE Orders.OrderID=@OrderID
```

Notice the inserted item. This is not a variable, but a temporary row that holds the values of the columns. The inserted row contains the values you're about to insert into the table. In Listing 5.10, you see a similar use with the deleted row, which contains the original values. You can retrieve any column's value by specifying its name with the FROM keyword, as shown in the example. The NewOrder trigger, shown in Listing 5.9, is identical to the EditOrder trigger.

LISTING 5.9: *NEWORDERTRIGGER.SQL*

```
CREATE TRIGGER NewOrderTrigger ON [Orders]
FOR INSERT
AS
SET NOCOUNT ON
```

```
DECLARE @newOrderID char(5)
SELECT @newOrderID = OrderID FROM inserted
UPDATE Orders SET AddedOn=GETDATE(), AddedBy=USER
WHERE Orders.OrderID=@newOrderID
```

The DeleteOrderTrigger, shown in Listing 5.10, extracts more fields from the deleted variable and inserts their values in a new row of the Deletions table—by the time the DeleteOrderTrigger is invoked, the row has already been removed from the table.

LISTING 5.10: *DELETEORDERTRIGGER.SQL*

```
CREATE TRIGGER DeleteOrderTrigger ON [Orders]
FOR DELETE
AS
SET NOCOUNT ON

DECLARE @delOrderID int
DECLARE @delCustID char(5)
DECLARE @delOrderDate datetime

SELECT @delOrderID = OrderID FROM deleted
SELECT @delCustID = CustomerID FROM deleted
SELECT @delOrderDate = OrderDate FROM deleted

INSERT DELETIONS (DeletedOn, DeletedBy,
                  DelOrderID, DelCustomerID, DelOrderDate)
       VALUES (GETDATE(), USER,  @delOrderID,
              @delCustID,  @delOrderDate)
```

To test the triggers, add, update, and delete rows in the Orders table. Notice that you can't delete a row from the Orders table unless the related rows in the Order Details table have already been deleted. You can add a fake row to the Orders table, and then edit it and finally delete it. Then open the Orders and Deletions tables to see the rows added by the triggers (a few sample rows are shown in Figure 5.9).

The three triggers shown so far can also be used to keep track of changes in one or more tables for synchronization purposes. If you need to maintain some degree of synchronization with a different database (it could be a products database in another company that doesn't use SQL Server, for instance), you can keep track of the inserted/updated/deleted rows in a table and then transmit these rows only.

FIGURE 5.9

Use special fields in your audit tables to monitor who's doing what in the database.

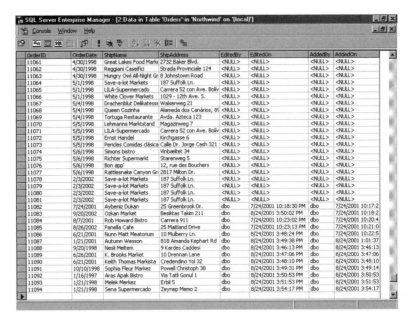

Before leaving the topic of triggers, let's use the INSTEAD OF keyword to check whether a customer ID exists before you add a new customer to the database. This will prevent a new customer ID from being added if it already exists. The code for this trigger is depicted in Listing 5.11.

LISTING 5.11: *NEWCUSTOMERTRIGGER.SQL*

```
CREATE TRIGGER NewCustomerTrigger ON [Customers]
INSTEAD OF INSERT
AS
BEGIN
SET NOCOUNT ON

DECLARE @insCustID nchar(5)
SELECT @insCustID = CustomerID
FROM inserted

-- Check for duplicate Customer.
-- If no customer exists,
-- we can safely add the record
IF (NOT EXISTS (SELECT Customers.CustomerID
    FROM Customers
    WHERE Customers.CustomerID = @insCustID))
  INSERT INTO Customers
    SELECT CustomerID,CompanyName,ContactName,
```

```
                ContactTitle, Address,City,
                Region,PostalCode, Country,
                Phone, Fax
   FROM inserted
ELSE
-- You can add logic to record the attempt to insert a
-- duplicate customer into an audit table.
   COMMIT
END
```

If you examine this trigger closely, you will see that there are some new T-SQL commands listed within the code, such as the BEGIN and COMMIT keywords. These keywords are used to manage transactions, which enable you to commit or roll back a sequence of activity, such a trigger.

Transactions

A *transaction* is a series of database operations that must succeed or fail as a whole. If all operations complete successfully, then the entire transaction succeeds and the changes are committed to the database. If a single operation fails, then the entire transaction fails and no changes are written to the database. If the transaction fails, the changes are removed from the tables and replaced with their original values.

SQL implements transactions with three statements: BEGIN TRANSACTION, COMMIT TRANSACTION, and ROLLBACK TRANSACTION.

BEGIN TRANSACTION   This statement marks the beginning of a transaction. If the transaction fails, the tables will be restored to the state they were in at the moment the BEGIN TRANSACTION statement was issued. It is implied here that the database is restored to a previous state with regard to the changes made by your application. Changes made to the database by others are not affected.

COMMIT TRANSACTION   This statement marks the successful end of a transaction. When this statement is executed, all the changes made to the database by your application since the execution of the BEGIN TRANSACTION statement are committed finally and irrevocably to the database. You can undo any of the changes later on, but not as part of the transaction.

ROLLBACK TRANSACTION   This statement marks the end of an unsuccessful transaction. When this statement is executed, the database is restored to the state it was in when the BEGIN TRANSACTION statement was executed. It's as if the statements between the BEGIN TRANSACTION and ROLLBACK TRANSACTION statement were never executed.

Here's how the transaction-related statements are used in a batch:

```
BEGIN TRANSACTION
{T-SQL statement}
IF @@ERROR <> 0
BEGIN
    ROLLBACK TRANSACTION
    RETURN -100
END
```

```
{T-SQL statement}
IF @@ERROR <> 0
BEGIN
    ROLLBACK TRANSACTION
    RETURN -101
END
COMMIT TRANSACTION
{more T-SQL statements}
```

The error codes -100 and -101 identify error conditions. After each operation, you must examine the @@ERROR variable. If it's not zero, then an error occurred, and you must roll back the transaction. If all operations succeed, you can commit the transaction.

In the next section, under "Adding Orders," you'll learn how to handle transactions with T-SQL.

Implementing Business Rules with Stored Procedures

In Chapter 1, "Database Access: Architectures and Technologies," we discussed practical reasons for determining where you should place your business logic. Business rules can be implemented as stored procedures. You can implement stored procedures for all the actions to be performed against the database, embed the business rules in the code, and ask or force application programmers to act on the database through your procedures.

In this section, you'll build a couple of stored procedures for some of the most common tasks you will perform with a database such as Northwind. The first one adds new customers to the Customers table—a straightforward procedure. The second one adds orders and is a fairly complicated stored procedure, because it must update two tables in a transaction.

Adding Customers

We'll start with a simpler example of a stored procedure that implements a business rule: writing a stored procedure to add customers. The stored procedure accepts as arguments all the columns of the Customers table and inserts them into a new row. The addition of the new row is implemented with the INSERT statement. If the insertion completes successfully, the error code 0 is returned. If the insertion fails, the procedure returns the error code generated by the INSERT statement. This action could fail if the ID of the customer you attempt to add exists in the Customers table already.

The AddCustomer stored procedure doesn't even examine whether a customer with the same ID exists already. If the customer exists already, the INSERT statement will fail. Besides, there's always a (very slim) chance that, between the test and the actual insertion, another user might add a customer with the same ID (this condition can be prevented with the use of GUIDs). For the purposes of this example, let's detect the error after the fact and notify the user.

The AddCustomer stored procedure is shown in Listing 5.12. At the beginning, it declares all the input arguments. Then it uses these arguments as values in an INSERT statement, which adds a new row to the Customers table. If the INSERT statement encounters an error, the procedure doesn't crash. It examines the value of the @@ERROR global variable. If the @@ERROR variable is not zero, then an error occurred. If the operation completed successfully, the @ERROR variable is zero.

Notice that @@ERROR is stored in a local variable, which is used later in the code. The @@ERROR variable is updated after each line's execution. If you attempt to return the value @@ERROR with the RETURN statement, the calling application will receive an error code that's always zero. That's why you must store the value of @@ERROR after an operation if you want to use it later in your code.

LISTING 5.12: THE *ADDCUSTOMER.SQL* STORED PROCEDURE

```
USE NORTHWIND
IF EXISTS (SELECT name FROM sysobjects
        WHERE name = 'AddCustomer')
    DROP PROCEDURE AddCustomer
GO
CREATE PROCEDURE AddCusto
mer
      @custID nchar(5), @custName nvarchar(40),
      @custContact nvarchar(30), @custTitle nvarchar(30),
      @custAddress nvarchar(60), @custcity nvarchar(15),
      @custRegion nvarchar(15), @custPostalCode nvarchar(10),
      @custCountry nvarchar(15),
      @custPhone nvarchar(24), @custFax nvarchar(24)
AS
DECLARE @ErrorCode int
INSERT Customers (CustomerID, CompanyName, ContactName,
                  ContactTitle, Address, City, Region,
                  PostalCode, Country, Phone, Fax)
VALUES (@custID, @custName, @custContact,
        @custTitle, @custAddress,
        @custCity, @custRegion, @custPostalCode, @custCountry,
        @custPhone, @custFax)
SET @ErrorCode=@@ERROR
IF (@ErrorCode = 0)
   RETURN (0)
ELSE
   RETURN (@ErrorCode)
```

To test the AddCustomer stored procedure, open the AddCustomer.sql file with the Query Analyzer and execute it by pressing F5. This will attach the stored procedure to your database. Now you can test it by calling it with the appropriate arguments. The AddACustomer.sql batch adds a new customer with the ID SYBEX. Figure 5.10 shows the code for the AddACustomer.sql batch.

The AddACustomer batch will add a new customer only the first time it's executed. If you execute it again without changing the customer's ID, the error code 2627 will be returned, along with the following error message:

```
Violation of PRIMARY KEY constraint 'PK_Customers'.
Cannot insert duplicate key in object 'Customers'.
The statement has been terminated.
```

You can either change the values passed to the stored procedure, or switch to the Enterprise Manager, open the `Customers` table, and delete the newly added line.

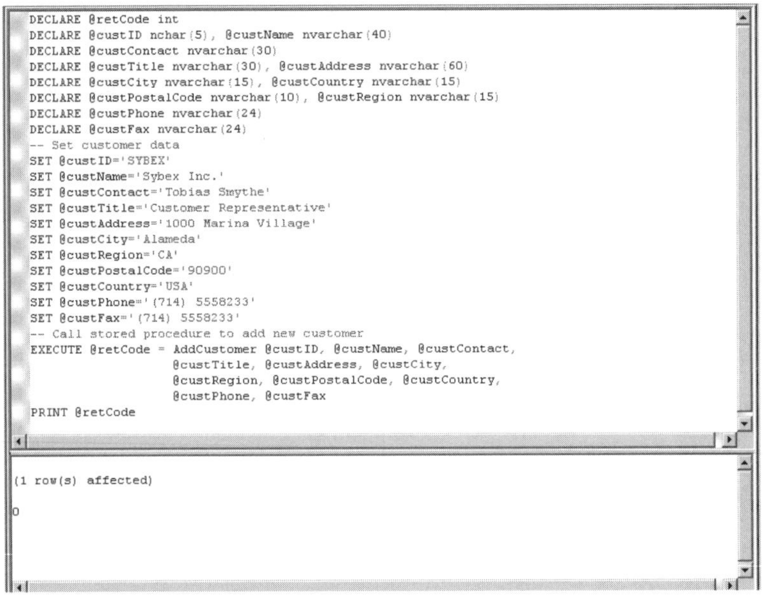

FIGURE 5.10

Adding a new customer with the `AddACustomer` procedure

```
DECLARE @retCode int
DECLARE @custID nchar(5), @custName nvarchar(40)
DECLARE @custContact nvarchar(30)
DECLARE @custTitle nvarchar(30), @custAddress nvarchar(60)
DECLARE @custCity nvarchar(15), @custCountry nvarchar(15)
DECLARE @custPostalCode nvarchar(10), @custRegion nvarchar(15)
DECLARE @custPhone nvarchar(24)
DECLARE @custFax nvarchar(24)
-- Set customer data
SET @custID='SYBEX'
SET @custName='Sybex Inc.'
SET @custContact='Tobias Smythe'
SET @custTitle='Customer Representative'
SET @custAddress='1000 Marina Village'
SET @custCity='Alameda'
SET @custRegion='CA'
SET @custPostalCode='90900'
SET @custCountry='USA'
SET @custPhone='(714) 5558233'
SET @custFax='(714) 5558233'
-- Call stored procedure to add new customer
EXECUTE @retCode = AddCustomer @custID, @custName, @custContact,
                   @custTitle, @custAddress, @custCity,
                   @custRegion, @custPostalCode, @custCountry,
                   @custPhone, @custFax
PRINT @retCode
```

```
(1 row(s) affected)

0
```

Adding Orders

The next example is substantially more complicated. This time you'll write a procedure to add a new order. By its nature, this stored procedure must perform many tests, and it might abort the entire operation at various stages of its execution. The `NewOrder` stored procedure must accept the customer's ID, the employee's ID, the shipper's ID, the shipping address, and the order's details. If the specified customer, employee, or shipper does not exist, the procedure must abort its execution and return an error code to the caller. If any of these tests fail, then the stored procedure exits and returns the appropriate custom error code (`-100` if the customer doesn't exist, `-101` if the employee doesn't exist, and `-102` if the shipper doesn't exist).

If these tests don't fail, you can safely add the new order to the `Orders` table. The following operations are implemented as a transaction. If one of them fails, then neither an order nor details will be added to the corresponding tables. The stored procedure must add a new row to the `Orders` table, insert the current date in the `OrderDate` field, and then use the `OrderID` field's value to add the order's lines in the `Order Details` table. The `OrderID` field is assigned a value automatically by SQL Server when a row is added to the `Orders` table. You can find out the ID of the new order by examining the `@@IDENTITY` variable, which holds the value of the most recently added Identity value for the current connection. This value will be used to add detail rows in the `Order Details` table.

Then the order's details are added to the `Order Details` table, one row at a time. Again, if one of them fails, the entire transaction will fail. The most common reason for failure is the submission of a non-existing product ID. If you force your application's users to select product IDs from a list and validate the quantity and discount for each product, then none of the operations will fail.

The order details are passed to the `AddOrder` procedure as a long string, and this part deserves some explanation. In this example, we've decided to store the ID, quantity, and discount of each product into a string variable. Each field has a fixed length in this string, so that it can be easily parsed. The product ID is stored as an integer in the first six characters of the string, the quantity as another integer in the next six characters, and the discount in the last six characters. Each order, therefore, takes up 18 characters. If you divide the length of this string by 18, you'll get the number of detail lines. Then, you can call the `SUBSTRING()` function repeatedly to extract each detail's values and insert them into the `Order Details` table.

After the product ID has been extracted from the string variable, you can use it to retrieve the product's price from the `Products` table. Here are T-SQL statements that retrieve the first product's price and insert it along with the quantity and discount fields into the `Order Details` table:

```
SET @ProdID = SUBSTRING(@Details, 1, 6)
SET @Qty = SUBSTRING(@Details, 7, 6)
SET @Dscnt = SUBSTRING(@Details, 13, 6)
SELECT @Price=UnitPrice FROM Products
        WHERE ProductID=@ProdID
INSERT [Order Details] (OrderID, ProductID, Quantity,
        UnitPrice, Discount)
        VALUES (@OrderID, @ProdID, @Qty, @Price, @Dscnt)
```

If a product with the specific ID doesn't exist in the `Products` table, the procedure doesn't take any special action. The `INSERT` statement will fail to add the detail line because it will violate the COL- UMN FOREIGN KEY constraint FK_Order_Details_Products, and the procedure will roll back the transaction and return the error code 547.

Listing 5.13 shows the complete listing of the `NewOrder` stored procedure. Apart from syntactical differences, it's equivalent to the VB .NET code you would use to add an order to the database. You can find this code in the `NewOrder.sql` file on this book's companion CD.

LISTING 5.13: *NEWORDER.SQL* STORED PROCEDURE

```
USE NORTHWIND
IF EXISTS (SELECT name FROM sysobjects
        WHERE name = 'NewOrder')
    DROP PROCEDURE NewOrder
GO


CREATE PROCEDURE NewOrder
@custID nchar(5), @empID int, @orderDate datetime,
@shipperID int, @Details varchar(1000)
AS
```

```
DECLARE @ErrorCode int
DECLARE @OrderID int
- Add new row to the Orders table
DECLARE @shipcompany nvarchar(40)
DECLARE @shipAddress nvarchar(60), @shipCity nvarchar(15)
DECLARE @shipRegion nvarchar(15), @shipPCode nvarchar(10)
DECLARE @shipCountry nvarchar(15)
SELECT @shipCompany=CompanyName,
       @shipAddress=Address,
       @shipCity=City,
       @shipRegion=Region,
       @shipPCode=PostalCode,
       @shipCountry=Country
       FROM Customers
       WHERE CustomerID = @custID
IF @@ROWCOUNT = 0
    RETURN(-100)    -Invalid Customer!
SELECT * FROM Employees WHERE EmployeeID = @empID
IF @@ROWCOUNT = 0
    RETURN(-101)    - Invalid Employee!
SELECT * FROM Shippers
       WHERE ShipperID = @shipperID
IF @@ROWCOUNT = 0
    RETURN(-102)    - Invalid Shipper!
BEGIN TRANSACTION
INSERT Orders (CustomerID, EmployeeID, OrderDate, ShipVia,
               ShipName, ShipAddress, ShipCity, ShipRegion,
               ShipPostalCode, ShipCountry)
VALUES (@custID, @empID, @orderDate, @ShipperID,
        @shipCompany, @shipAddress, @ShipCity, @ShipRegion,
        @shipPCode, @shipCountry)
SET @ErrorCode=@@ERROR
IF (@ErrorCode <> 0)
   BEGIN
   ROLLBACK TRANSACTION
   RETURN (-@ErrorCode)
   END
SET @OrderID = @@IDENTITY
- Now add rows to the Order Details table
- All new rows will have the same OrderID
DECLARE @TotLines int
DECLARE @currLine int
SET @currLine = 0
- Use the CEILING function because the length of the
- @Details variable may be less than 18 characters long !!!
SET @TotLines = Ceiling(Len(@Details)/18)
DECLARE @Qty smallint, @Dscnt real, @Price money
DECLARE @ProdID int
```

```
WHILE @currLine <= @TotLines
   BEGIN
   SET @ProdID = SUBSTRING(@Details, @currLine*18 + 1, 6)
   SET @Qty = SUBSTRING(@Details, @currLine*18 + 7, 6)
   SET @Dscnt = SUBSTRING(@Details, @currLine*18 + 13,6)
   SET @currLine = @currLine + 1
   SELECT @Price=UnitPrice FROM Products WHERE ProductID=@ProdID
   INSERT [Order Details] (OrderID, ProductID, Quantity,
         UnitPrice, Discount)
         VALUES (@OrderID, @ProdID, @Qty, @Price, @Dscnt)
   SET @ErrorCode = @@ERROR
   IF (@ErrorCode <> 0) GOTO DetailError
   END
   COMMIT TRANSACTION
   RETURN (0)
DetailError:
   ROLLBACK TRANSACTION
   RETURN(@ErrorCode)
```

NOTE   Here's the most important reason for using the NewOrder *stored procedure: If you allow users and applications to add rows to the* Order Details *table, it's possible that someone might modify an existing order. This is a highly undesirable situation, and you should make sure it never happens. With the* NewOrder *procedure, users can't touch existing orders. Each order takes a new ID and all details inherit this ID, eliminating the possibility of altering (even by a programming mistake) an existing order.*

Testing the *NewOrder* Procedure

To test the NewOrder stored procedure, you must declare a number of local variables, assign the desired values to them, and then execute the stored procedure with the EXECUTE statement, passing the variables as arguments. Most arguments represent simple fields, like the ID of the shipper, the customer ID, and so on. The last argument, however, is a long string, with 18 characters per detail line. In each 18-character segment of the string, you must store three fields: the product's ID, the quantity, and the discount. The AddAnOrder batch that exercises the NewOrder procedure is shown in Listing 5.14, and its output is shown in Figure 5.11.

LISTING 5.14: THE *ADDANORDER.SQL* SCRIPT

```
USE Northwind
DECLARE @retCode int
DECLARE @custID nchar(5), @empID int
DECLARE @orderDate datetime, @shipperID int
DECLARE @Details varchar(1000)
SET @shipperID=2
SET @custID='SAVEA'
```

```
SET @empID=4
SET @orderDate = '2/3/2002'
SET @Details='32     10     0.25  47     8      0.20'
SET @Details=@Details + '    75     5     0.05  76     15     0.10'
EXECUTE @retCode = NewOrder @custID, @empID, @orderDate,
                            @shipperID, @Details
PRINT @retCode
```

FIGURE 5.11

Testing the
NewOrder stored
procedure with a
T-SQL batch

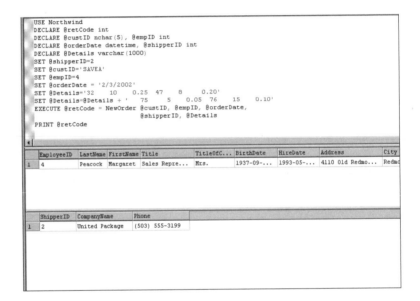

Summary

By now you should have a good understanding of SQL and Transact-SQL and what stored procedures, user-defined functions, and triggers can do for you. The next step is to see how stored procedures can be accessed from within your VB .NET code. In the next chapter, you will work with
the .NET data providers and explore the ADO.NET object model. Using this knowledge you will
be able to see the advantages of using ADO.NET over classic ADO. You'll also see how XML fits
into the ADO.NET architecture within the DataSet object. Additionally, you'll learn the architectural differences between streamed and cached data, which will enable you to make the best choice
in your data access strategy.

Chapter 6

A First Look at ADO.NET

- ◆ How does ADO.NET work?
- ◆ Using the ADO.NET object model
- ◆ The Connection object
- ◆ The Command object
- ◆ The DataAdapter object
- ◆ The DataReader object
- ◆ The DataSet object
- ◆ Navigating through DataSets
- ◆ Updating Your Database by using DataSets
- ◆ Managing concurrency

IT'S TIME NOW TO get into some real database programming with the .NET Framework components. In this chapter, you'll explore the Active Data Objects (ADO).NET base classes. ADO.NET, along with the XML namespace, is a core part of Microsoft's standard for data access and storage. As you recall from Chapter 1, "Database Access: Architectures and Technologies," ADO.NET components can access a variety of data sources, including Access and SQL Server databases, as well as non-Microsoft databases such as Oracle. Although ADO.NET is a lot different from classic ADO, you should be able to readily transfer your knowledge to the new .NET platform. Throughout this chapter, we make comparisons to ADO 2.x objects to help you make the distinction between the two technologies.

For those of you who have programmed with ADO 2.x, the ADO.NET interfaces will not seem all that unfamiliar. Granted, a few mechanisms, such as navigation and storage, have changed, but you will quickly learn how to take advantage of these new elements. ADO.NET opens up a whole new world of data access, giving you the power to control the changes you make to your data. Although native OLE DB/ADO provides a common interface for universal storage, a lot of the data activity is hidden from you. With client-side disconnected RecordSets, you can't control how your updates occur. They just happen "magically." ADO.NET opens that black box, giving you more granularity with your data manipulations. ADO 2.*x* is about common data access. ADO.NET extends this model and factors out data storage from common data access. Factoring out functionality makes it easier for you to understand how ADO.NET components work. Each ADO.NET component has its own specialty, unlike the RecordSet, which is a jack-of-all-trades. The RecordSet could be disconnected or stateful; it could be read-only or updateable; it could be stored on the client or on the server—it is multifaceted. Not only do all these mechanisms bloat the RecordSet with functionality you might never use, it also forces you to write code to anticipate every possible chameleon-like metamorphosis of the RecordSet. In ADO.NET, you always know what to expect from your data access objects, and this lets you streamline your code with specific functionality and greater control.

Although a separate chapter is dedicated to XML (Chapter 10, "The Role of XML"), we must touch upon XML in our discussion of ADO.NET. In the .NET Framework, there is a strong synergy between ADO.NET and XML. Although the XML stack doesn't technically fall under ADO.NET, XML and ADO.NET belong to the same architecture. ADO.NET persists data as XML. There is no other native persistence mechanism for data and schema. ADO.NET stores data as XML files. Schema is stored as XSD files.

There are many advantages to using XML. XML is optimized for disconnected data access. ADO.NET leverages these optimizations and provides more scalability. To scale well, you can't maintain state and hold resources on your database server. The disconnected nature of ADO.NET and XML provide for high scalability.

In addition, because XML is a text-based standard, it's simple to pass it over HTTP and through firewalls. Classic ADO uses a binary format to pass data. Because ADO.NET uses XML, a ubiquitous standard, more platforms and applications will be able to consume your data. By using the XML model, ADO.NET provides a complete separation between the data and the data presentation. ADO.NET takes advantage of the way XML splits the data into an XML document, and the schema into an XSD file.

By the end of this chapter, you should be able to answer the following questions:

◆ What are .NET data providers?

◆ What are the ADO.NET classes?

◆ What are the appropriate conditions for using a DataReader versus a DataSet?

◆ How does OLE DB fit into the picture?

◆ What are the advantages of using ADO.NET over classic ADO?

◆ How do you retrieve and update databases from ADO.NET?

◆ How does XML integration go beyond the simple representation of data as XML?

Let's begin by looking "under the hood" and examining the components of the ADO.NET stack.

How Does ADO.NET Work?

ADO.NET base classes enable you to manipulate data from many data sources, such as SQL Server, Exchange, and Active Directory. ADO.NET leverages .NET data providers to connect to a database, execute commands, and retrieve results.

The ADO.NET object model exposes very flexible components, which in turn expose their own properties and methods, and recognize events. In this chapter, you'll explore the objects of the ADO.NET object model and the role of each object in establishing a connection to a database and manipulating its tables.

Is OLE DB Dead?

Not quite. Although you can still use OLE DB data providers with ADO.NET, you should try to use the managed .NET data providers whenever possible. If you use native OLE DB, your .NET code will suffer because it's forced to go through the COM interoperability layer in order to get to OLE DB. This leads to performance degradation. Native .NET providers, such as the System.Data.SqlClient library, skip the OLE DB layer entirely, making their calls directly to the native API of the database server.

However, this doesn't mean that you should avoid the OLE DB .NET data providers completely. If you are using anything other than SQL Server 7 or 2000, you might not have another choice. Although you will experience performance gains with the SQL Server .NET data provider, the OLE DB .NET data provider compares favorably against the traditional ADO/OLE DB providers that you used with ADO 2.*x*. So don't hold back from migrating your non-managed applications to the .NET Framework for performance concerns. In addition, there are other compelling reasons for using the OLE DB .NET providers. Many OLE DB providers are very mature and support a great deal more functionality than you would get from the newer SQL Server .NET data provider, which exposes only a subset of this full functionality. In addition, OLE DB is still the way to go for universal data access across disparate data sources. In fact, the SQL Server distributed process relies on OLE DB to manage joins across heterogeneous data sources.

Another caveat to the SQL Server .NET data provider is that it is tightly coupled to its data source. Although this enhances performance, it is somewhat limiting in terms of portability to other data sources. When you use the OLE DB providers, you can change the connection string on the fly, using declarative code such as COM+ constructor strings. This loose coupling enables you to easily port your application from an SQL Server back-end to an Oracle back-end without recompiling any of your code, just by swapping out the connection string in your COM+ catalog.

Keep in mind, the only native OLE DB provider types that are supported with ADO.NET are SQLOLEDB for SQL Server, MSDAORA for Oracle, and Microsoft.Jet.OLEDB.4 for the Microsoft Jet engine. If you are so inclined, you can write your own .NET data providers for any data source by inheriting from the System.Data namespace.

At this time, the .NET Framework ships with only the SQL Server .NET data provider for data access within the .NET runtime. Microsoft expects the support for .NET data providers and the number of .NET data providers to increase significantly. (In fact, the ODBC.NET data provider is available for download on Microsoft's website.) A major design goal of ADO.NET is to synergize the native and managed interfaces, advancing both models in tandem.

You can find the ADO.NET objects within the `System.Data` namespace. When you create a new VB .NET project, a reference to the `System.Data` namespace will be automatically added for you, as you can see in Figure 6.1.

FIGURE 6.1

To use ADO.NET, reference the `System.Data` namespace.

To comfortably use the ADO.NET objects in an application, you should use the `Imports` statement. By doing so, you can declare ADO.NET variables without having to fully qualify them. You could type the following `Imports` statement at the top of your solution:

```
Imports System.Data.SqlClient
```

After this, you can work with the SqlClient ADO.NET objects without having to fully qualify the class names. If you want to dimension the SqlClientDataAdapter, you would type the following short declaration:

```
Dim dsMyAdapter as New SqlDataAdapter
```

Otherwise, you would have to type the full namespace, as in:

```
Dim dsMyAdapter as New System.Data.SqlClient.SqlDataAdapter
```

Alternately, you can use the visual database tools to automatically generate your ADO.NET code for you. As you saw in Chapter 3, "The Visual Database Tools," the various wizards that come with VS .NET provide the easiest way to work with the ADO.NET objects. Nevertheless, before you use these tools to build production systems, you should understand how ADO.NET works programmatically. In this chapter, we don't focus too much on the visual database tools, but instead concentrate on the code behind the tools. By understanding how to program against the ADO.NET object model, you will have more power and flexibility with your data access code.

Using the ADO.NET Object Model

You can think of ADO.NET as being composed of two major parts: .NET data providers and data storage. Respectively, these fall under the connected and disconnected models for data access and presentation. *.NET data providers*, or *managed providers*, interact natively with the database. Managed providers are quite similar to the OLE DB providers or ODBC drivers that you most likely have worked with in the past.

The .NET data provider classes are optimized for fast, read-only, and forward-only retrieval of data. The managed providers talk to the database by using a fast data stream (similar to a file stream). This is the quickest way to pull read-only data off the wire, because you minimize buffering and memory overhead.

If you need to work with connections, transactions, or locks, you would use the managed providers, not the DataSet. The DataSet is completely disconnected from the database and has no knowledge of transactions, locks, or anything else that interacts with the database.

Five core objects form the foundation of the ADO.NET object model, as you see listed in Table 6.1. Microsoft moves as much of the provider model as possible into the managed space. The Connection, Command, DataReader, and DataAdapter belong to the .NET data provider, whereas the DataSet is part of the disconnected data storage mechanism.

TABLE 6.1: ADO.NET CORE COMPONENTS

OBJECT	DESCRIPTION
Connection	Creates a connection to your data source
Command	Provides access to commands to execute against your data source
DataReader	Provides a read-only, forward-only stream containing your data
DataSet	Provides an in-memory representation of your data source(s)
DataAdapter	Serves as an ambassador between your DataSet and data source, proving the mapping instructions between the two

Figure 6.2 summarizes the ADO.NET object model. If you're familiar with classic ADO, you'll see that ADO.NET completely factors out the data source from the actual data. Each object exposes a large number of properties and methods, which are discussed in this and following chapters.

FIGURE 6.2

The ADO Framework

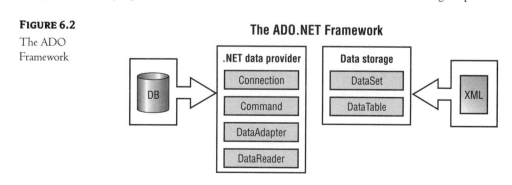

The ADO.NET Framework

NOTE *If you have worked with collection objects, this experience will be a bonus to programming with ADO.NET. ADO.NET contains a collection-centric object model, which makes programming easy if you already know how to work with collections.*

Four core objects belong to .NET data providers, within the ADO.NET managed provider architecture: the Connection, Command, DataReader, and DataAdapter objects. The *Connection object* is the simplest one, because its role is to establish a connection to the database. The *Command object* exposes a Parameters collection, which contains information about the parameters of the command to be executed. If you've worked with ADO 2.x, the Connection and Command objects should seem familiar to you. The *DataReader object* provides fast access to read-only, forward-only data, which is reminiscent of a read-only, forward-only ADO RecordSet. The *DataAdapter object* contains Command objects that enable you to map specific actions to your data source. The DataAdapter is a mechanism for bridging the managed providers with the disconnected DataSets.

The *DataSet object* is not part of the ADO.NET managed provider architecture. The DataSet exposes a collection of DataTables, which in turn contain both DataColumn and DataRow collections. The DataTables collection can be used in conjunction with the DataRelation collection to create relational data structures.

First, you will learn about the connected layer by using the .NET data provider objects and touching briefly on the DataSet object. Next, you will explore the disconnected layer and examine the DataSet object in detail.

NOTE *Although there are two different namespaces, one for* OleDb *and the other for the* SqlClient, *they are quite similar in terms of their classes and syntax. As we explain the object model, we use generic terms, such as Connection, rather than SqlConnection. Because this book focuses on SQL Server development, we gear our examples toward SQL Server data access and manipulation.*

In the following sections, you'll look at the five major objects of ADO.NET in detail. You'll examine the basic properties and methods you'll need to manipulate databases, and you'll find examples of how to use each object. ADO.NET objects also recognize events, which we discuss in Chapter 12, "More ADO.NET Programming."

The Connection Object

Both the `SqlConnection` and `OleDbConnection` namespaces inherit from the `IDbConnection` object. The Connection object establishes a connection to a database, which is then used to execute commands against the database or retrieve a DataReader. You use the `SqlConnection` object when you are working with SQL Server, and the `OleDbConnection` for all other data sources. The `ConnectionString` property is the most important property of the Connection object. This string uses name-value pairs to specify the database you want to connect to. To establish a connection through a Connection object, call its `Open()` method. When you no longer need the connection, call the `Close()` method to close it. To find out whether a Connection object is open, use its `State` property.

WHAT HAPPENED TO YOUR ADO CURSORS?

One big difference between classic ADO and ADO.NET is the way they handle cursors. In ADO 2.x, you have the option to create client- or server-side cursors, which you can set by using the `CursorLocation` property of the Connection object. ADO.NET no longer explicitly assigns cursors. This is a good thing.

Under classic ADO, many times programmers accidentally specify expensive server-side cursors, when they really mean to use the client-side cursors. These mistakes occur because the cursors, which sit in the COM+ server, are also considered client-side cursors. Using server-side cursors is something you should never do under the disconnected, *n*-tier design. You see, ADO 2.x wasn't originally designed for disconnected and remote data access. The `CursorLocation` property is used to handle disconnected and connected access within the same architecture. ADO.NET advances this concept by completely separating the connected and disconnected mechanisms into managed providers and DataSets, respectively.

In classic ADO, after you specify your cursor location, you have several choices in the type of cursor to create. You could create a static cursor, which is a disconnected, in-memory representation of your database. In addition, you could extend this static cursor into a forward-only, read-only cursor for quick database retrieval.

Under the ADO.NET architecture, there are no updateable server-side cursors. This prevents you from maintaining state for too long on your database server. Even though the DataReader does maintain state on the server, it retrieves the data rapidly as a stream. The ADO.NET DataReader works much like an ADO read-only, server-side cursor. You can think of an ADO.NET DataSet as analogous to an ADO client-side, static cursor. As you can see, you don't lose any of the ADO disconnected cursor functionality with ADO.NET; it's just architected differently.

Connecting to a Database

The first step to using ADO.NET is to connect to a data source, such as a database. Using the Connection object, you tell ADO.NET which database you want to contact, supply your username and password (so that the DBMS can grant you access to the database and set the appropriate privileges), and, possibly, set more options. The Connection object is your gateway to the database, and all the operations you perform against the database must go through this gateway. The Connection object encapsulates all the functionality of a data link and has the same properties. Unlike data links, however, Connection objects can be accessed from within your VB .NET code. They expose a number of properties and methods that enable you to manipulate your connection from within your code.

NOTE *You don't have to type this code by hand. The code for all the examples in this chapter is located on the companion CD that comes with this book. You can find many of this chapter's code examples in the solution file* **Working with ADO.NET.sln**. *Code related to the ADO.NET Connection object is listed behind the Connect To Northwind button on the startup form.*

Let's experiment with creating a connection to the Northwind database. Create a new Windows Application solution and place a command button on the Form; name it **Connect to Northwind**. Add the `Imports` statement for the `System.Data.SqlClient` name at the top of the form module. Now you can declare a Connection object with the following statement:

```
Dim connNorthwind As New SqlClient.SqlConnection()
```

As soon as you type the period after SqlClient, you will see a list with all the objects exposed by the SqlClient component, and you can select the one you want with the arrow keys. Declare the connNorthwind object in the button's click event.

NOTE   *All projects on the companion CD use the setting (local) for the data source. In other words, we're assuming you have SQL Server installed on the local machine. Alternately, you could use localhost for the data source value.*

The *ConnectionString* Property

The ConnectionString property is a long string with several attributes separated by semicolons. Add the following line to your button's click event to set the connection:

```
connNorthwind.ConnectionString="data source=(local);"& _
   "initial catalog=Northwind;integrated security=SSPI;"
```

Replace the data source value with the name of your SQL Server, or keep the local setting if you are running SQL Server on the same machine. If you aren't using Windows NT integrated security, then set your user ID and password like so:

```
connNorthwind.ConnectionString="data source=(local);"& _
    "initial catalog=Northwind; user ID=sa;password=xxx"
```

TIP   *Some of the names in the connection string also go by aliases. You can use Server instead of data source to specify your SQL Server. Instead of initial catalog, you can specify database.*

Those of you who have worked with ADO 2.x might notice something missing from the connection string: the provider value. Because you are using the SqlClient namespace and the .NET Framework, you do not need to specify an OLE DB provider. If you were using the OleDb namespace, then you would specify your provider name-value pair, such as Provider=SQLOLEDB.1.

OVERLOADING THE CONNECTION OBJECT CONSTRUCTOR

One of the nice things about the .NET Framework is that it supports constructor arguments by using overloaded constructors. You might find this useful for creating your ADO.NET objects, such as your database Connection. As a shortcut, instead of using the ConnectionString property, you can pass the string right into the constructor, as such:

```
Dim connNorthwind as New SqlConnection _
   ("data source=localhost; initial catalog=Northwind; user ID=sa;password=xxx")
```

Or you could overload the constructor of the connection string by using the following:

```
Dim myConnectString As String = "data source=localhost; initial
    catalog=Northwind; user ID=sa;password=xxx"
```

You have just established a connection to the SQL Server Northwind database. As you remember from Chapter 3, you can also do this visually from the Server Explorer. The `ConnectionString` property of the Connection object contains all the information required by the provider to establish a connection to the database. As you can see, it contains all the information that you see in the Connection properties tab when you use the visual tools.

Keep in mind that you can also create connections implicitly by using the DataAdapter object. You will learn how to do this when we discuss the DataAdapter later in this section.

In practice, you'll never have to build connection strings from scratch. You can use the Server Explorer to add a new connection, or use the appropriate ADO.NET data component wizards, as you did in Chapter 3. These visual tools will automatically build this string for you, which you can see in the properties window of your Connection component.

TIP   The connection pertains more to the database server rather than the actual database itself. You can change the database for an open SqlConnection, by passing the name of the new database to the `ChangeDatabase()` method.

The *Open ( )* Method

After you have specified the `ConnectionString` property of the Connection object, you must call the `Open()` method to establish a connection to the database. You must first specify the `ConnectionString` property and then call the `Open()` method without any arguments, as shown here (`connNorthwind` is the name of a Connection object):

```
connNorthwind.Open()
```

NOTE   Unlike ADO 2.x, the `Open()` method doesn't take any optional parameters. You can't change this feature because the `Open()` method is not overridable.

The *Close ( )* Method

Use the Connection object's `Close()` method to close an open connection. Connection pooling provides the ability to improve your performance by reusing a connection from the pool if an appropriate one is available. The OleDbConnection object will automatically pool your connections for you. If you have connection pooling enabled, the connection is not actually released, but remains alive in memory and can be used again later. Any pending transactions are rolled back.

NOTE   Alternately, you could call the `Dispose()` method, which also closes the connection: `connNorthwind.Dispose()`

You must call the `Close()` or `Dispose()` method, or else the connection will not be released back to the connection pool. The .NET garbage collector will periodically remove memory references for expired or invalid connections within a pool. This type of lifetime management improves the performance of your applications because you don't have to incur expensive shutdown costs. However, this mentality is dangerous with objects that tie down server resources. Generational garbage collection polls for objects that have been recently created, only periodically checking for those objects that have been around longer. Connections hold resources on your server, and because you don't get deterministic cleanup by the garbage collector, you must make sure you explicitly close the connections that you open. The same goes for the DataReader, which also holds resources on the database server.

The Command Object

After you instantiate your connection, you can use the Command object to execute commands that retrieve data from your data source. The Command object carries information about the command to be executed. This command is specified with the control's `CommandText` property. The `CommandText` property can specify a table name, an SQL statement, or the name of an SQL Server stored procedure. To specify how ADO will interpret the command specified with the `CommandText` property, you must assign the proper constant to the `CommandType` property. The `CommandType` property recognizes the enumerated values in the `CommandType` structure, as shown in Table 6.2.

TABLE 6.2: SETTINGS OF THE CommandType PROPERTY

CONSTANT	DESCRIPTION
Text	The command is an SQL statement. This is the default CommandType.
StoredProcedure	The command is the name of a stored procedure.
TableDirect	The command is a table's name. The Command object passes the name of the table to the server.

When you choose `StoredProcedure` as the `CommandType`, you can use the `Parameters` property to specify parameter values if the stored procedure requires one or more input parameters, or it returns one or more output parameters. The `Parameters` property works as a collection, storing the various attributes of your input and output parameters. For more information on specifying parameters with the Command object, see Chapter 8, "Data-Aware Controls."

Executing a Command

After you have connected to the database, you must specify one or more commands to execute against the database. A command could be as simple as a table's name, an SQL statement, or the name of a stored procedure. You can think of a Command object as a way of returning streams of data results to a DataReader object or caching them into a DataSet object.

Command execution has been seriously refined since ADO 2.x., now supporting optimized execution based on the data you return. You can get many different results from executing a command:

- If you specify the name of a table, the DBMS will return all the rows of the table.

- If you specify an SQL statement, the DBMS will execute the statement and return a set of rows from one or more tables.

- If the SQL statement is an action query, some rows will be updated, and the DBMS will report the number of rows that were updated but will not return any data rows. The same is true for stored procedures:

  - If the stored procedure selects rows, these rows will be returned to the application.

  - If the stored procedure updates the database, it might not return any values.

TIP   As we have mentioned, you should prepare the commands you want to execute against the database ahead of time and, if possible, in the form of stored procedures. With all the commands in place, you can focus on your VB .NET code. In addition, if you are performing action queries and do not want results being returned, specify the NOCOUNT ON *option in your stored procedure to turn off the "rows affected" result count.*

You specify the command to execute against the database with the Command object. The Command objects have several methods for execution: the ExecuteReader() method returns a forward-only, read-only DataReader, the ExecuteScalar() method retrieves a single result value, and the ExecuteNonQuery() method doesn't return any results. We discuss the ExecuteXmlReader() method, which returns the XML version of a DataReader, in Chapter 7, "ADO.NET Programming."

NOTE   ADO.NET simplifies and streamlines the data access object model. You no longer have to choose whether to execute a query through a Connection, Command, or RecordSet object. In ADO.NET, you will always use the Command object to perform action queries.

You can also use the Command object to specify any parameter values that must be passed to the DBMS (as in the case of a stored procedure), as well as specify the transaction in which the command executes. One of the basic properties of the Command object is the Connection property, which specifies the Connection object through which the command will be submitted to the DBMS for execution. It is possible to have multiple connections to different databases and issue different commands to each one. You can even swap connections on the fly at runtime, using the same Command object with different connections. Depending on the database to which you want to submit a command, you must use the appropriate Connection object. Connection objects are a significant load on the server, so try to avoid using multiple connections to the same database in your code.

WHY ARE THERE SO MANY METHODS TO EXECUTE A COMMAND?

Executing commands can return different types of data, or even no data at all. The reason why there are separate methods for executing commands is to optimize them for different types of return values. This way, you can get better performance if you can anticipate what your return data will look like. If you have an AddNewCustomer stored procedure that returns the primary key of the newly added record, you would use the ExecuteScalar() method. If you don't care about returning a primary key or an error code, you would use the ExecuteNonQuery(). In fact, now that error raising, rather than return codes, has become the de facto standard for error handling, you should find yourself using the ExecuteNonQuery() method quite often.

Why not use a single overloaded Execute() method for all these different flavors of command execution? Initially, Microsoft wanted to overload the Execute() method with all the different versions, by using the DataReader as an optional output parameter. If you passed the DataReader in, then you would get data populated into your DataReader output parameter. If you didn't pass a DataReader in, you would get no results, just as the ExecuteNonQuery() works now. However, the overloaded Execute() method with the DataReader output parameter was a bit complicated to understand. In the end, Microsoft resorted to using completely separate methods and using the method names for clarification.

Selection queries return a set of rows from the database. The following SQL statement will return the company names for all customers in the Northwind database:

```
SELECT CompanyName FROM Customers
```

As you recall from Chapter 4, "Structured Query Language," SQL is a universal language for manipulating databases. The same statement will work on any database (as long as the database contains a table called `Customers` and this table has a `CompanyName` column). Therefore, it is possible to execute this command against the SQL Server Northwind database to retrieve the company names.

NOTE *For more information on the various versions of the sample databases used throughout this book, see the sections "Exploring the Northwind Database," and "Exploring the Pubs Database" in Chapter 2, "Basic Concepts of Relational Databases."*

Let's execute a command against the database by using the `connNorthwind` object you've just created to retrieve all rows of the `Customers` table. The first step is to declare a Command object variable and set its properties accordingly. Use the following statement to declare the variable:

```
Dim cmdCustomers As New SqlCommand
```

NOTE *If you do not want to type these code samples from scratch as you follow along, you can take a shortcut and load the code from the companion CD. The code in this walk-through is listed in the click event of the Create DataReader button located on the startup form for the Working with ADO.NET solution.*

Alternately, you can use the `CreateCommand()` method of the Connection object.

```
cmdCustomers = connNorthwind.CreateCommand()
```

OVERLOADING THE COMMAND OBJECT CONSTRUCTOR

Like the Connection object, the constructor for the Command object can also be overloaded. By overloading the constructor, you can pass in the SQL statement and connection, while instantiating the Command object—all at the same time. To retrieve data from the `Customers` table, you could type the following:

```
Dim cmdCustomers As OleDbCommand = New OleDbCommand _
("Customers", connNorthwind)
```

Then set its `CommandText` property to the name of the `Customers` table:

```
cmdCustomers.CommandType = CommandType.TableDirect
```

The `TableDirect` property is supported only by the OLE DB .NET data provider. The `TableDirect` is equivalent to using a `SELECT * FROM` *tablename* SQL statement. Why doesn't the SqlCommand object support this? Microsoft feels that when using specific .NET data providers, programmers should have better knowledge and control of what their Command objects are doing. You can cater to your Command objects more efficiently when you explicitly return all the records in a table by using an SQL statement or stored procedure, rather than depending on the `TableDirect` property to do so for you. When you explicitly specify SQL, you have tighter reign on how the data is returned, especially considering that the `TableDirect` property might not choose the most efficient execution plan.

The `CommandText` property tells ADO.NET how to interpret the command. In this example, the command is the name of a table. You could have used an SQL statement to retrieve selected rows from the `Customers` table, such as the customers from Germany:

```
strCmdText = "SELECT ALL FROM Customers"
strCmdText = strCmdText & "WHERE Country = 'Germany'"
cmdCustomers.CommandText = strCmdText
cmdCustomers.CommandType = CommandType.Text
```

By setting the `CommandType` property to a different value, you can execute different types of commands against the database.

NOTE   *In previous versions of ADO, you are able to set the command to execute asynchronously and use the* `State` *property to poll for the current fetch status. In VB .NET, you now have full support of the threading model and can execute your commands on a separate thread with full control, by using the* `Threading` *namespace. We touch on threading and asynchronous operations in Chapter 11, "More ADO.NET Programming."*

Regardless of what type of data you are retuning with your specific `Execute()` method, the Command object exposes a `ParameterCollection` that you can use to access input and output parameters for a stored procedure or SQL statement. If you are using the `ExecuteReader()` method, you must first close your DataReader object before you are able to query the parameters collection.

WARNING   *For those of you who have experience working with parameters with OLE DB, keep in mind that you must use named parameters with the* `SqlClient` *namespace. You can no longer use the question mark character (?) as an indicator for dynamic parameters, as you had to do with OLE DB.*

The DataAdapter Object

The DataAdapter represents a completely new concept within Microsoft's data access architecture. The DataAdapter gives you the full reign to coordinate between your in-memory data representation and your permanent data storage source. In the OLE DB/ADO architecture, all this happened behind the scenes, preventing you from specifying how you wanted your synchronization to occur.

The DataAdapter object works as the ambassador between your data and data-access mechanism. Its methods give you a way to retrieve and store data from the data source and the DataSet object. This way, the DataSet object can be completely agnostic of its data source.

The DataAdapter also understands how to translate *deltagrams*, which are the DataSet changes made by a user, back to the data source. It does this by using different Command objects to reconcile the changes, as shown in Figure 6.3. We show how to work with these Command objects shortly.

The DataAdapter implicitly works with Connection objects as well, via the Command object's interface. Besides explicitly working with a Connection object, this is the only other way you can work with the Connection object.

The DataAdapter object is very "polite," always cleaning up after itself. When you create the Connection object implicitly through the DataAdapter, the DataAdapter will check the status of the connection. If it's already open, it will go ahead and use the existing open connection. However, if it's closed, it will quickly open and close the connection when it's done with it, courteously restoring the connection back to the way the DataAdapter found it.

FIGURE 6.3

The ADO.NET
`SqlClient`
DataAdapter
object model

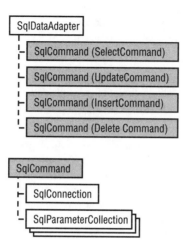

The DataAdapter works with ADO.NET Command objects, mapping them to specific database update logic that you provide. Because all this logic is stored outside of the DataSet, your DataSet becomes much more liberated. The DataSet is free to collect data from many different data sources, relying on the DataAdapter to propagate any changes back to its appropriate source.

Populating a DataSet

Although we discuss the DataSet object in more detail later in this chapter, it is difficult to express the power of the DataAdapter without referring to the DataSet object.

The DataAdapter contains one of the most important methods in ADO.NET: the `Fill()` method. The `Fill()` method populates a DataSet and is the only time that the DataSet touches a live database connection. Functionally, the `Fill()` method's mechanism for populating a DataSet works much like creating a static, client-side cursor in classic ADO. In the end, you end up with a disconnected representation of your data.

The `Fill()` method comes with many overloaded implementations. A notable version is the one that enables you to populate an ADO.NET DataSet from a classic ADO RecordSet. This makes interoperability between your existing native ADO/OLE DB code and ADO.NET a breeze. If you wanted to populate a DataSet from an existing ADO 2.*x* RecordSet called **adoRS**, the relevant segment of your code would read:

```
Dim daFromRS As OleDbDataAdapter = New OleDbDataAdapter
Dim dsFromRS As DataSet = New DataSet
daFromRS.Fill(dsFromRS, adoRS)
```

WARNING   *You must use the* `OleDb` *implementation of the DataAdapter to populate your DataSet from a classic ADO RecordSet. Accordingly, you would need to import the* `System.Data.OleDb` *namespace.*

Updating a Data Source from a DataSet by Using the DataAdapter

The DataAdapter uses the `Update()` method to perform the relevant SQL action commands against the data source from the deltagram in the DataSet.

TIP   *The DataAdapter maps commands to the DataSet via the DataTable. Although the DataAdapter maps only one DataTable at a time, you can use multiple DataAdapters to fill your DataSet by using multiple DataTables.*

USING SQLCOMMAND AND SQLPARAMETER OBJECTS TO UPDATE THE NORTHWIND DATABASE

NOTE   *The code for the walkthrough in this section can be found in the* Updating Data Using ADO.NET.sln *solution file. Listing 6.1 is contained within the click event of the Inserting Data Using DataAdapters With Mapped Insert Commands button.*

The DataAdapter gives you a simple way to map the commands by using its SelectCommand, UpdateCommand, DeleteCommand, and InsertCommand properties. When you call the Update() method, the DataAdapter maps the appropriate update, add, and delete SQL statements or stored procedures to their appropriate Command object. (Alternately, if you use the SelectCommand property, this command would execute with the Fill() method.) If you want to perform an insert into the Customers table of the Northwind database, you could type the code in Listing 6.1.

LISTING 6.1: INSERT COMMANDS BY USING THE DATAADAPTER OBJECT WITH PARAMETERS

```
Dim strSelectCustomers As String = "SELECT * FROM Customers ORDER BY CustomerID"
Dim strConnString As String = "data source=(local);" & _
  "initial catalog=Northwind;integrated security=SSPI;"
' We can't use the implicit connection created by the
' DataSet since our update command requires a
' connection object in its constructor, rather than a
' connection string
Dim connNorthwind As New SqlConnection(strConnString)
' String to update the customer record - it helps to
' specify this in advance so the CommandBuilder doesn't
' affect our performance at runtime
Dim strInsertCommand As String = _
  "INSERT INTO Customers(CustomerID,CompanyName) VALUES (@CustomerID,
@CompanyName)"
Dim daCustomers As New SqlDataAdapter()
Dim dsCustomers As New DataSet()
Dim cmdSelectCustomer As SqlCommand = New SqlCommand _
              (strSelectCustomers, connNorthwind)
Dim cmdInsertCustomer As New SqlCommand(strInsertCommand, connNorthwind)
daCustomers.SelectCommand = cmdSelectCustomer
daCustomers.InsertCommand = cmdInsertCustomer
connNorthwind.Open()
daCustomers.Fill(dsCustomers, "dtCustomerTable")
cmdInsertCustomer.Parameters.Add _
 (New SqlParameter _
 ("@CustomerID", SqlDbType.NChar, 5)).Value = "ARHAN"
cmdInsertCustomer.Parameters.Add _
 (New SqlParameter _
```

```
    ("@CompanyName", SqlDbType.VarChar, 40)).Value = "Amanda Aman Apak Merkez Inc."
cmdInsertCustomer.ExecuteNonQuery()
connNorthwind.Close()
```

This code sets up both the `SelectCommand` and `InsertCommand` for the DataAdapter and executes the insert query with no results. To map the insert command with the values you are inserting, you use the `Parameters` property of the appropriate SqlCommand objects. This example adds parameters to the `InsertCommand` of the DataAdapter. As you can see from the DataAdapter object model in Figure 6.3, each of the SqlCommand objects supports a `ParameterCollection`.

As you can see, the `Insert` statement need not contain all the fields in the parameters—and it usually doesn't. However, you must specify all the fields that can't accept Null values. If you don't, the DBMS will reject the operation with a trappable runtime error. In this example, only two of the new row's fields are set: the `CustomerID` and the `CompanyName` fields, because neither can be Null.

WARNING   *In this code, notice that you can't use the implicit connection created by the DataSet. This is because the* `InsertCommand` *object requires a Connection object in its constructor rather than a connection string. If you don't have an explicitly created Connection object, you won't have any variable to pass to the constructor.*

TIP   *Because you create the connection explicitly, you must make sure to close your connection when you are finished with it. Although implicitly creating your connection takes care of cleanup for you, it's not a bad idea to explicitly open the connection, because you might want to leave it open so you can execute multiple fills and updates.*

Each of the DataSet's Command objects have their own `CommandType` and `Connection` properties, which make them very powerful. Consider how you can use them to combine different types of command types, such as stored procedures and SQL statements. In addition, you can combine commands from multiple data sources, by using one database for retrievals and another for updates.

As you can see, the DataAdapter with its Command objects is an extremely powerful feature of ADO.NET. In classic ADO, you don't have any control of how your selects, inserts, updates, and deletes are handled. What if you wanted to add some specific business logic to these actions? You would have to write custom stored procedures or SQL statements, which you would call separately from your VB code. You couldn't take advantage of the native ADO RecordSet updates, because ADO hides the logic from you.

In summary, you work with a DataAdapter by using the following steps:

1. Instantiate your DataAdapter object.

2. Specify the SQL statement or stored procedure for the `SelectCommand` object. This is the only Command object that the DataAdapter requires.

3. Specify the appropriate connection string for the `SelectCommand`'s Connection object.

4. Specify the SQL statements or stored procedures for the `InsertCommand`, `UpdateCommand`, and `DeleteCommand` objects. Alternately, you could use the `CommandBuilder` to dynamically map your actions at runtime. This step is not required.

5. Call the `Fill()` method to populate the DataSet with the results from the `SelectCommand` object.

6. If you used step 4, call the appropriate `Execute()` method to execute your command objects against your data source.

WARNING   *Use the `CommandBuilder` sparingly, because it imposes a heavy performance overhead at runtime. You'll find out why in Chapter 9, "Working with DataSets."*

The DataReader Object

The DataReader object is a fast mechanism for retrieving forward-only, read-only streams of data. The SQL Server .NET provider have completely optimized this mechanism, so use it as often as you can for fast performance of read-only data. Unlike ADO RecordSets, which force you to load more in memory than you actually need, the DataReader is a toned-down, slender data stream, using only the necessary parts of the ADO.NET Framework. You can think of it as analogous to the server-side, read-only, forward-only cursor that you used in native OLE DB/ADO. Because of this server-side connection, you should use the DataReader cautiously, closing it as soon as you are finished with it. Otherwise, you will tie up your Connection object, allowing no other operations to execute against it (except for the `Close()` method, of course).

As we mentioned earlier, you can create a DataReader object by using the `ExecuteReader()` method of the Command object. You would use DataReader objects when you need fast retrieval of read-only data, such as populating combo-box lists.

Listing 6.2 depicts an example of how you create the DataReader object, assuming you've already created the Connection object `connNorthwind`.

LISTING 6.2: CREATING THE DATAREADER OBJECT

```
Dim strCustomerSelect as String = "SELECT * from Customers"
Dim cmdCustomers as New SqlCommand(strCustomerSelect, connNorthwind)
Dim drCustomers as SqlDataReader
connNorthwind.Open()
drCustomers = cmdCustomers.ExecuteReader()
```

NOTE   *The code in Listing 6.2 can be found in the click event of the Create DataReader button on the startup form for the `Working with ADO.NET` solution on the companion CD.*

Notice that you can't directly instantiate the DataReader object, but must go through the Command object interface.

WARNING   *You cannot update data by using the DataReader object.*

The DataReader absolves you from writing tedious `MoveFirst()` and `MoveNext()` navigation. The `Read()` method of the DataReader simplifies your coding tasks by automatically navigating to a position prior to the first record of your stream and moving forward without any calls to navigation methods, such as the `MoveNext()` method. To continue our example from Listing 6.2, you could retrieve the first column from all the rows in your DataReader by typing in the following code:

```
While(drCustomers.Read())
    Console.WriteLine(drCustomers.GetString(0))
End While
```

NOTE   *The* `Console.WriteLine` *statement is similar to the* `Debug.Print()` *method you used in VB6.*

Because the DataReader stores only one record at a time in memory, your memory resource load is considerably lighter. Now if you wanted to scroll backward or make updates to this data, you would have to use the DataSet object, which we discuss in the next section. Alternately, you can move the data out of the DataReader and into a structure that is updateable, such as the DataTable or DataRow objects.

WARNING   *By default, the DataReader navigates to a point prior to the first record. Thus, you must always call the* `Read()` *method before you can retrieve any data from the DataReader object.*

The DataSet Object

There will come a time when the DataReader is not sufficient for your data manipulation needs. If you ever need to update your data, or store relational or hierarchical data, look no further than the DataSet object. Because the DataReader navigation mechanism is linear, you have no way of traversing between relational or hierarchical data structures. The DataSet provides a liberated way of navigating through both relational and hierarchical data, by using array-like indexing and tree walking, respectively.

Unlike the managed provider objects, the DataSet object and friends do not diverge between the `OleDb` and `SqlClient` .NET namespaces. You declare a DataSet object the same way regardless of which .NET data provider you are using:

```
Dim dsCustomer as DataSet
```

Realize that DataSets stand alone. A DataSet is not a part of the managed data providers and knows nothing of its data source. The DataSet has no clue about transactions, connections, or even a database. Because the DataSet is data source agnostic, it needs something to get the data to it. This is where the DataAdapter comes into play. Although the DataAdapter is not a part of the DataSet, it understands how to communicate with the DataSet in order to populate the DataSet with data.

DataSets and XML

The DataSet object is the nexus where ADO.NET and XML meet. The DataSet is persisted as XML, and only XML. You have several ways of populating a DataSet: You can traditionally load from a database or reverse engineer your XML files back into DataSets. You can even create your own customized application data without using XML or a database, by creating custom DataTables and DataRows. We show you how to create DataSets on the fly in this chapter in the section "Creating Custom DataSets."

DataSets are perfect for working with data transfer across Internet applications, especially when working with WebServices. Unlike native OLE DB/ADO, which uses a proprietary COM protocol, DataSets transfer data by using native XML serialization, which is a ubiquitous data format. This makes it easy to move data through firewalls over HTTP. Remoting becomes much simpler with XML over the wire, rather than the heavier binary formats you have with ADO RecordSets. We demonstrate how you do this in Chapter 16, "Working with WebServices."

As we mentioned earlier, DataSet objects take advantage of the XML model by separating the data storage from the data presentation. In addition, DataSet objects separate navigational data access from the traditional set-based data access. We show you how DataSet navigation differs from RecordSet navigation later in this chapter in Table 6.4.

DataSets versus RecordSets

As you can see in Figure 6.4, DataSets are much different from tabular RecordSets. You can see that they contain many types of nested collections, such as relations and tables, which you will explore throughout the examples in this chapter.

FIGURE 6.4

The ADO.NET DataSet object model

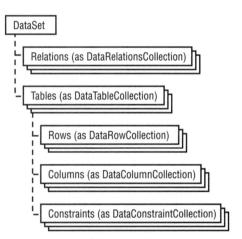

What's so great about DataSets? You're happy with the ADO 2.x RecordSets. You want to know why you should migrate over to using ADO.NET DataSets. There are many compelling reasons. First, DataSet objects separate all the disconnected logic from the connected logic. This makes them easier to work with. For example, you could use a DataSet to store a web user's order information for their online shopping cart, sending deltagrams to the server as they update their order information. In fact, almost any scenario where you collect application data based on user interaction is a good candidate for using DataSets. Using DataSets to manage your application data is much easier than working with arrays, and safer than working with connection-aware RecordSets.

Another motivation for using DataSets lies in their capability to be safely cached with web applications. Caching on the web server helps alleviate the processing burden on your database servers. ASP caching is something you really can't do safely with a RecordSet, because of the chance that the RecordSet might hold a connection and state. Because DataSets independently maintain their own state, you never have to worry about tying up resources on your servers. You can even safely store the DataSet object in your ASP.NET Session object, which you are warned never to do with RecordSets. RecordSets are dangerous in a Session object; they can crash in some versions of ADO because of issues with marshalling, especially when you use open client-side cursors that aren't streamed. In addition, you can run into threading issues with ADO RecordSets, because they are apartment threaded, which causes your web server to run in the same thread

DataSets are great for remoting because they are easily understandable by both .NET and non-.NET applications. DataSets use XML as their storage and transfer mechanism. .NET applications don't even have to deserialize the XML data, because you can pass the DataSet much like you would a RecordSet object. Non-.NET applications can also interpret the DataSet as XML, make modifications using XML, and return the final XML back to the .NET application. The .NET application takes the XML and automatically interprets it as a DataSet, once again.

Last, DataSets work well with systems that require tight user interaction. DataSets integrate tightly with bound controls. You can easily display the data with DataViews, which enable scrolling, searching, editing, and filtering with nominal effort. You will have a better understanding of how this works when you read Chapter 8.

Now that we've explained how the DataSet gives you more flexibility and power than using the ADO RecordSet, examine Table 6.3, which summarizes the differences between ADO and ADO.NET.

TABLE 6.3: WHY ADO.NET IS A BETTER DATA TRANSFER MECHANISM THAN ADO

FEATURE SET	ADO	ADO.NET	ADO.NET'S ADVANTAGE
Data persistence format	RecordSet	Uses XML	With ADO.NET, you don't have data type restrictions.
Data transfer format	COM marshalling	Uses XML	ADO.NET uses a ubiquitous format that is easily transferable and that multiple platforms and sites can readily translate. In addition, XML strings are much more manageable than binary COM objects.
Web transfer protocol	You would need to use DCOM to tunnel through Port 80 and pass proprietary COM data, which firewalls could filter out.	Uses HTTP	ADO.NET data is more readily transferable though firewalls.

Let's explore how to work with the various members of the DataSet object to retrieve and manipulate data from your data source. Although the DataSet is designed for data access with any data source, in this chapter we focus on SQL Server as our data source.

Working with DataSets

Often you will work with the DataReader object when retrieving data, because it offers you the best performance. As we have explained, in some cases the DataSet's powerful interface for data manipulation will be more practical for your needs. In this section, we discuss techniques you can use for working with data in your DataSet.

The DataSet is an efficient storage mechanism. The DataSet object hosts multiple result sets stored in one or more DataTables. These DataTables are returned by the DBMS in response to the execution of a command. The DataTable object uses rows and columns to contain the structure of a result set. You use the properties and methods of the DataTable object to access the records of a table. Table 6.4 demonstrates the power and flexibility you get with ADO.NET when retrieving data versus classic ADO.

TABLE 6.4: WHY ADO.NET IS A BETTER DATA STORAGE MECHANISM THAN ADO

FEATURE SET	ADO	ADO.NET	ADO.NET'S ADVANTAGE
Disconnected data cache	Uses disconnected RecordSets, which store data into a single table.	Uses DataSets that store one or many DataTables.	Storing multiple result sets is simple in ADO.NET. The result sets can come from a variety of data sources. Navigating between these result sets is intuitive, using the standard collection navigation.
			DataSets never maintain state, unlike RecordSets, making them safer to use with *n*-tier, disconnected designs.
Relationship management	Uses JOINs, which pull data into a single result table. Alternately, you can use the SHAPE syntax with the shaping OLE DB service provider.	Uses the DataRelation object to associate multiple DataTables to one another.	ADO.NET's DataTable collection sets the stage for more robust relationship management. With ADO, JOINs bring back only a single result table from multiple tables. You end up with redundant data. The SHAPE syntax is cumbersome and awkward. With ADO.NET, DataRelations provide an object-oriented, relational way to manage relations such as constraints and cascading referential integrity, all within the constructs of ADO.NET. The ADO shaping commands are in an SQL-like format, rather than being native to ADO objects.

Continued on next page

TABLE 6.4: WHY ADO.NET IS A BETTER DATA STORAGE MECHANISM THAN ADO *(continued)*

FEATURE SET	ADO	ADO.NET	ADO.NET'S ADVANTAGE
Navigation mechanism	RecordSets give you the option to only view data sequentially.	DataSets have a nonlinear navigation model.	DataSets enable you to traverse the data among multiple DataTables, using the relevant DataRelations to skip from one table to another. In addition, you can view your relational data in a hierarchical fashion by using the tree-like structure of XML.

There are three main ways to populate a DataSet:

◆ After establishing a connection to the database, you prepare the DataAdapter object, which will retrieve your results from your database as XML. You can use the DataAdapter to fill your DataSet.

◆ You can read an XML document into your DataSet. The .NET Framework provides an `XMLDataDocument` namespace, which is modeled parallel to the ADO.NET Framework. You will explore this namespace in Chapter 7.

◆ You can use DataTables to build your DataSet in memory without the use of XML files or a data source of any kind. You will explore this option in the section "Updating Your Database by Using DataSets" later in this chapter.

Let's work with retrieving data from the Northwind database. First, you must prepare the DataSet object, which can be instantiated with the following statement:

```
Dim dsCustomers As New DataSet()
```

Assuming you've prepared your DataAdapter object, all you would have to call is the `Fill()` method. Listing 6.3 shows you the code to populate your DataSet object with customer information.

LISTING 6.3: CREATING THE DATASET OBJECT

```
Dim strSelectCustomers As String = "SELECT * FROM Customers ORDER BY CustomerID"
Dim strConnString As String = "data source=(local);" & _
   "initial catalog=Northwind;integrated security=SSPI;"
Dim daCustomers As New SqlDataAdapter(strSelectCustomers, strConnString)
Dim dsCustomers As New DataSet()
Dim connNorthwind As New SqlConnection(strConnString)

daCustomers.Fill(dsCustomers, "dtCustomerTable")
MsgBox(dsCustomers.GetXml, , "Results of Customer DataSet in XML")
```

NOTE   The code in Listing 6.3 can be found in the click event of the Create Single Table DataSet button on the startup form for the `Working with ADO.NET` *solution on the companion CD.*

This code uses the `GetXml()` method to return the results of your DataSet as XML. The rows of the `Customers` table are retrieved through the `dsCustomers` object variable. The DataTable object within the DataSet exposes a number of properties and methods for manipulating the data by using the DataRow and DataColumn collections. You will explore how to navigate through the DataSet in the upcoming section, "Navigating Through DataSets." However, first you must understand the main collections that comprise a DataSet, the DataTable, and DataRelation collections.

The *DataTableCollection*

Unlike the ADO RecordSet, which contained only a single table object, the ADO.NET DataSet contains one or more tables, stored as a `DataTableCollection`. The `DataTableCollection` is what makes DataSets stand out from disconnected ADO RecordSets. You never could do something like this in classic ADO. The only choice you have with ADO is to nest RecordSets within RecordSets and use cumbersome navigation logic to move between parent and child RecordSets. The ADO.NET navigation model provides a user-friendly navigation model for moving between DataTables.

In ADO.NET, DataTables factor out different result sets that can come from different data sources. You can even dynamically relate these DataTables to one another by using DataRelations, which we discuss in the next section.

NOTE   If you want, you can think of a DataTable as analogous to a disconnected RecordSet, and the DataSet as a collection of those disconnected RecordSets.

Let's go ahead and add another table to the DataSet created earlier in Listing 6.3. Adding tables is easy with ADO.NET, and navigating between the multiple DataTables in your DataSet is simple and straightforward. In the section "Creating Custom DataSets," we show you how to build DataSets on the fly by using multiple DataTables. The code in Listing 6.4 shows how to add another DataTable to the DataSet that you created in Listing 6.3.

NOTE   The code in Listing 6.4 can be found in the click event of the Create DataSet With Two Tables button on the startup form for the `Working with ADO.NET` *solution on the companion CD.*

LISTING 6.4: ADDING ANOTHER DATATABLE TO A DATASET

```
Dim strSelectCustomers As String = "SELECT * FROM Customers ORDER BY CustomerID"
Dim strSelectOrders As String = "SELECT * FROM Orders"
Dim strConnString As String = "data source=(local);" & _
    "initial catalog=Northwind;integrated security=SSPI;"
Dim daCustomers As New SqlDataAdapter(strSelectCustomers, strConnString)
Dim dsCustomers As New DataSet()
Dim daOrders As New SqlDataAdapter(strSelectOrders, strConnString)
daCustomers.Fill(dsCustomers, "dtCustomerTable")
daOrders.Fill(dsCustomers, "dtOrderTable")
Console.WriteLine(dsCustomers.GetXml)
```

> **WARNING**   *DataTables are conditionally case sensitive. In Listing 6.4, the DataTable is called* `dtCustomerTable`*. This would cause no conflicts when used alone, whether you referred to it as* `dtCustomerTable` *or* `dtCUSTOMERTABLE`*. However, if you had another DataTable called* `dtCUSTOMERTABLE`*, it would be treated as an object separate from* `dtCustomerTable`*.*

As you can see, all you had to do was create a new DataAdapter to map to your `Orders` table, which you then filled into the DataSet object you had created earlier. This creates a collection of two DataTable objects within your DataSet. Now let's explore how to relate these DataTables together.

The DataRelation Collection

The DataSet object eliminates the cumbersome shaping syntax you had to use with ADO RecordSets, replacing it with a more robust relationship engine in the form of DataRelation objects. The DataSet contains a collection of DataRelation objects within its `Relations` property. Each DataRelation object links disparate DataTables by using referential integrity such as primary keys, foreign keys, and constraints. The DataRelation doesn't have to use any joins or nested DataTables to do this, as you had to do with ADO RecordSets.

In classic ADO, you create relationships by nesting your RecordSets into a single tabular Record-Set. Aside from being clumsy to use, this mechanism also made it awkward to dynamically link disparate sets of data.

With ADO.NET, you can take advantage of new features such as cascading referential integrity. You can do this by adding a `ForeignKeyConstraint` object to the `ConstraintCollection` within a DataTable. The `ForeignKeyConstraint` object enforces referential integrity between a set of columns in multiple DataTables. As we explained in Chapter 2, in the "Database Integrity" section, this will prevent orphaned records. In addition, you can cascade your updates and deletes from the parent table down to the child table.

Listing 6.5 shows you how to link the `CustomerID` column of your `Customer` and `Orders` DataTables. Using the code from Listing 6.3, all you have to do is add a new declaration for your DataRelation.

LISTING 6.5: USING A SIMPLE DATARELATION

```
Dim drCustomerOrders As DataRelation = New DataRelation("CustomerOrderRelation",
    dsCustomers.Tables("Customers").Columns("CustomerID"),
    dsCustomers.Tables("Orders").Columns("CustomerID"))
    dsCustomers.Relations.Add(drCustomerOrders)
```

> **NOTE**   *The code in Listing 6.5 can be found in the click event of the Using Simple DataRelations button on the startup form for the* `Working with ADO.NET` *solution on the companion CD.*

As you can with other ADO.NET objects, you can overload the DataRelation constructor. In this example, you pass in three parameters. The first parameter indicates the name of the relation. This is similar to how you would name a relationship within SQL Server. The next two parameters indicate the two columns that you wish to relate. After creating the DataRelation object, you add it to the `Relations` collection of the DataSet object.

WARNING *The data type of the two columns you wish to relate must be identical.*

Listing 6.6 shows you how to use DataRelations between the `Customers` and `Orders` tables of the Northwind database to ensure that when a customer ID is deleted or updated, it is reflected within the `Orders` table.

LISTING 6.6: USING CASCADING UPDATES

```
Dim fkCustomerID As ForeignKeyConstraint
fkCustomerID = New ForeignKeyConstraint
  ("CustomerOrderConstraint", dsCustomers.Tables
  ("Customers").Columns("CustomerID"),
dsCustomers.Tables("Orders").Columns("CustomerID"))
fkCustomerID.UpdateRule = Rule.Cascade
fkCustomerID.AcceptRejectRule = AcceptRejectRule.Cascade
dsCustomers.Tables("CustomerOrder").Constraints.Add
(fkCustomerID)
dsCustomers.EnforceConstraints = True
```

NOTE *The code in Listing 6.6 can be found in the click event of the Using Cascading Updates button on the startup form for the* `Working with ADO.NET` *solution on the companion CD.*

In this example, you create a foreign key constraint with cascading updates and add it to the `ConstraintCollection` of your DataSet. First, you declare and instantiate a `ForeignKeyConstraint` object, as you did earlier when creating the DataRelation object. Afterward, you set the properties of the `ForeignKeyConstraint`, such as the `UpdateRule` and `AcceptRejectRule`, finally adding it to your `ConstraintCollection`. You have to ensure that your constraints activate by setting the `EnforceConstraints` property to `True`.

Navigating through DataSets

We already discussed navigation through a DataReader. To sum it up, as long as the DataReader's `Read()` method returns `True`, then you have successfully positioned yourself in the DataReader. Now let's discuss how you would navigate through a DataSet.

In classic ADO, to navigate through the rows of an ADO RecordSet, you use the `Move()` method and its variations. The `MoveFirst()`, `MovePrevious()`, `MoveLast()`, and `MoveNext()` methods take you to the first, previous, last, and next rows in the RecordSet, respectively. This forces you to deal with cursoring and absolute positioning. This makes navigation cumbersome because you have to first position yourself within a RecordSet and then read the data that you need.

In ADO 2.x, a fundamental concept in programming for RecordSets is that of the *current row*: to read the fields of a row, you must first move to the desired row. The RecordSet object supports a number of navigational methods, which enable you to locate the desired row, and the `Fields` property, which enables you to access (read or modify) the current row's fields. With ADO.NET, you no longer have to use fixed positioning to locate your records; instead, you can use array-like navigation.

Unlike ADO RecordSets, the concept of the current row no longer matters with DataSets. DataSets work like other in-memory data representations, such as arrays and collections, and use familiar navigational behaviors. DataSets provide an explicit in-memory representation of data in the form of a collection-based model. This enables you to get rid of the infamous `Do While Not rs.EOF() And Not rs.BOF()` loop. With ADO.NET, you can use the friendly `For Each` loop to iterate through the DataTables of your DataSet. If you want to iterate through the rows and columns within an existing DataTable named `tblCustomers`, stored in a `dsCustomers` DataSet, you could use the following loop in Listing 6.7.

LISTING 6.7: NAVIGATING THROUGH A DATASET

```
For Each tblCustomer In dsCustomers.Tables
        Dim rowCustomer As DataRow
        For Each rowCustomer In  tblCustomer.Rows
            Dim colCustomer As DataColumn
            For Each colCustomer In  thisTable.Columns
                Console.WriteLine (rowCustomer (colCustomer))
            Next colCustomer
        Next rowCustomer
    Next tblCustomer
```

This will print out the values in each column of the customers DataSet created in Listing 6.3. As you can see, the `For Each` logic saves you from having to monitor antiquated properties such as `EOF` and `BOF` of the ADO RecordSet.

DataTables contain collections of DataRows and DataColumns, which also simplify your navigation mechanism. Instead of worrying about the `RecordCount` property of RecordSets, you can use the traditional `UBound()` property to collect the number of rows within a DataTable. For the example in Listing 6.7, you can calculate the row count for the customer records by using the following statement:

```
UBound(rowCustomer)
```

DataTable Capacities

In classic ADO, you could specify *paged RecordSets*—the type of RecordSets displayed on web pages when the results of a query are too many to be displayed on a single page. The web server displays 20 or so records and a number of buttons at the bottom of the page that enable you to move quickly to another group of 20 records. This technique is common in web applications, and ADO supports a few properties that simplify the creation of paged RecordSets, such as the `AbsolutePage`, `PageSize`, and `PageCount` properties.

With ADO.NET, you can use the `MinimumCapacity` property to specify the number of rows you wish to bring back for a DataTable. The default setting is 25 rows. This setting is especially useful if you want to improve performance on your web pages in ASP.NET. If you want to ensure that only 50 customer records display for the `Customers` DataTable, you would specify the following:

```
dtCustomers.MinimumCapacity = 50
```

If you have worked with paged RecordSets, you will realize that this performance technique is much less involved than the convoluted paging logic you had to use in ADO 2.*x*.

Navigating a Relationship between Tables

ADO.NET provides a navigation model for navigating through DataTables by using the relationships that connect them. Keep in mind that relations work as separate objects. When you create the relationship between the `Customers` and `Orders` tables, you can't directly jump from a customer DataRow to the related order DataRows. You must open the DataRelation separately and then pull the related rows. This is fine with one-to-many relationships; however, if you are using one-to-one relationships, you should stick with SQL `JOIN` statements.

You will explore the many techniques you can do with your retrieved data later in this chapter. First, let's review basic ways of updating your data sources by using DataSets.

Updating Your Database by Using DataSets

The two connected and disconnected models of ADO.NET work very differently when updating the database. Connected, or managed, providers communicate with the database by using command-based updates. As we showed you in "The DataSet Object" section earlier, disconnected DataSets update the database by using a cached, batch-optimistic method. DataSets work independently from a connection, working with the deltagram of data on the disconnected DataSet and committing the changes only after you call the `Update()` method from the DataAdapter. The separation between the command-based model used with managed providers and the optimistic model carried out by the DataSet objects enables the programmer to make a distinction between server-side execution and cached execution.

WARNING   *In ADO 2.x, there was a good amount of confusion regarding client-side cursors. Some implementations mistakenly used server-side cursors when they meant to use client-cursors on the application server. Don't confuse disconnected, cached DataSets as user-side data. The DataSets can also be stored on your middle tier, which you should consider as a client-side cache, even though it is stored on your application server. You'll explore how to use DataSets within your ASP.NET code in Part IV, "Data Access from the Web."*

To update data, you make changes to your DataSet and pass them up to the server. Obviously, you can't use the DataReader, because its forward-only, read-only nature can't be updated. There are many ways that you can make updates to a DataSet:

♦   Make changes to an existing DataSet which was retrieved from a query executed on your database server(s). Pass the changes to the data source via the Data Adapter.

◆ Load data from an XML file by using the `ReadXml()` method. Map the resulting DataSet to your data source by using the DataAdapter.

◆ Merge multiple DataSets by using the `Merge()` method, passing the results to the data source via the DataAdapter.

◆ Create a new DataSet with new schema and data on the fly, mapping it to a data source by using the DataAdapter.

As you can see, all these options have one thing in common: your changes are not committed back to the server until the DataAdapter intervenes. DataSets are completely unaware of where their data comes from and how their changes relate back to the appropriate data source. The DataAdapter takes care of all this.

Realize that updating a record is not always a straightforward process. What happens if a user changes the record after you have read it? And what will happen if the record you're about to update has already been deleted by another user? In this chapter, you will learn the basics of updating databases through the ADO.NET DataSet, assuming no concurrency is involved. However, we discuss the implications of concurrency at the end of this chapter. In the meantime, let's set up your ADO.NET objects to insert a customer row into the Northwind database.

Updating Your DataSet by Using the DataTable and DataRow Objects

Earlier in this chapter, we showed you how to update your database by using parameterized stored procedures. Although this is efficient for making single row changes, it isn't quite useful when you have a significant number of changes to pass to the server. What happens when you want to apply changes in bulk? Consider an e-commerce application that uses an online shopping cart. The shopping cart could have multiple rows of data that would be inserted and updated as the user browsed through the site. When it comes time to push these changes to the server, it would be much easier to pass them in one single batch, rather than call the stored procedure multiple times for each row that's modified.

In ADO 2.*x*, you use disconnected RecordSets along with the `UpdateBatch()` method to pass your changes on to the server. In ADO.NET, you pass the disconnected deltagram from the DataSet object to the DataAdapter `Update()` method. Once again, ADO.NET clearly draws the line between your data and your data source. The DataSet object doesn't directly contact the data source.

First, let's see how you can manage changes within a DataSet. As the user edits the in-memory cache, the changes are stored into a buffer and not yet committed to the DataSet. You can commit modifications to a DataSet by using the `AcceptChanges()` method of the DataSet, DataTable, or DataRow objects. If you execute this method on the parent object, it will propagate down onto the children. For example, if you call `AcceptChanges()` on the DataSet object, it will cascade down onto the DataTables within the DataSet's `Table` collection (likewise for a DataTable to its relevant DataRow collection).

When you insert a row into a DataTable, you can monitor the "dirtiness" of a row by examining the `RowState` property. Let's go ahead and add a new row to your `dsCustomers` DataSet. In Figure 6.5, we continue the logic that we used in Listing 6.3 to populate your `dsCustomers` DataSet.

NOTE *Until you call the `Update()` method, your DataSet changes will not be committed to your data source.*

First, let's look at the code that pulls down the data that you want to work with from your database into a DataSet. Using the existing DataSet, you will add a new row directly to the DataSet by using the DataTable and DataRow collections of the DataSet.

NOTE   The code depicted in Figure 6.5 can be found in the `Updating Data using ADO.NET.sln` *solution file, within the click event of the Inserting Data With DataSets and DataTables button.*

As you see in Figure 6.5, DataSet updates are very straightforward. All you have to do is fill your DataSet, as we've shown you earlier in the chapter. Then you set up a new DataRow object with the DataTable's `NewRow()` method. The `Add()` collection of the `Rows` collection will add your new row to the collection. Finally, you call the `AcceptChanges()` method of the DataSet, which will automatically cascade all changes down to its inner DataTables and DataRows. Alternately, you could call the `AcceptChanges()` method specifically on the inner object you wish to update because the DataTable and DataRow also support the `AcceptChanges()` method.

As the note indicates, the source code for this example is available on the accompanying CD. Go ahead and load the code into Visual Studio .NET and place a breakpoint on the `Add()` method. Execute the code by pressing F5. When you get to your breakpoint, type the following in the Command window:

```
?dtcustomer.rows.count
```

FIGURE 6.5

Updating your
DataSet object

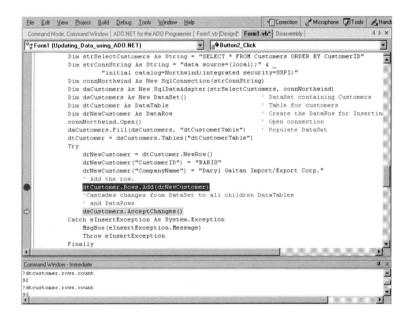

WARNING   If you have difficulty working with the Command window, it might be because you are not in Immediate mode. If you see a > prompt, then this is most likely the case. Toggle the mode from Command mode to Immediate mode by typing **immed** *at the prompt and pressing Enter. Now you should be able to debug your code.*

You will see the number of rows in your Customers table, within your DataSet, prior to making changes. Hit F11 to step into the Add() method. This will update your DataSet with the newly added row. Go back to the Command window and hit the Up arrow key and Enter to re-execute the row count statement. The results will show that the Add() method increments your row count in your DataRow by one record. However, if you compare the result to the data in the database, you will see that your data still has the same number of original rows. This is an important point. None of your changes will be committed to the data source until you call the Update() method of the DataAdapter object. Finish the execution of the code to commit the changes in your DataSet.

In summary, all you have to do is execute the following steps to commit updates to your DataSet:

1. Instantiate your DataSet and DataAdapter objects.

2. Fill your DataSet object from the DataAdapter object.

3. Manipulate your DataSet by using the DataRow objects.

4. Call the AcceptChanges() method of the DataSet, DataTable, or DataRow object to commit your changes to your DataSet.

Updating Your Data Source by Using the DataSet and DataAdapter

In this section, we show you how to insert a new row into your DataSet with the DataRow and DataTable objects. After you've updated your DataSet, we show you how you can commit those changes to the DataSet. Committing changes to a DataSet doesn't mean that they are committed to the database. To commit your changes to the database, you use the Update() method, which is similar to the Fill() method, only it works in reverse, updating your data source with the deltagram from the DataSet. Listing 6.8 contains the code that enables you to update a database with changes from a DataSet object.

NOTE *The code in Listing 6.8 can be found in the* Updating Data Using ADO.NET *solution on the companion CD, within the click event of the Committing Changes From Your DataSet To Your Database button.*

Although the Update() method is the only method you need to call to commit your changes back to the database, you must do some preparation work in advance. You must set up the appropriate action-based Command objects before you call the DataAdapter's Update() method. These Command objects map to the relevant insert, update, and delete stored procedures or SQL statements. Alternately, you can use the CommandBuilder object to dynamically generate the appropriate SQL statements for you.

LISTING 6.8: COMMITTING DATASET CHANGES TO A DATABASE

```
Dim strSelectCustomers As String = "SELECT * FROM Customers ORDER BY CustomerID"
Dim strConnString As String = "data source=(local);" & _
   "initial catalog=Northwind;integrated security=SSPI;"
Dim connNorthwind As New SqlConnection(strConnString)
Dim daCustomers As New SqlDataAdapter(strSelectCustomers, connNorthwind)
```

```
Dim dsCustomers As New DataSet()
Dim dtCustomer As DataTable
Dim drNewCustomer As DataRow
Dim custCB As SqlCommandBuilder = New SqlCommandBuilder(daCustomers)
connNorthwind.Open()
daCustomers.Fill(dsCustomers, "dtCustomerTable")
connNorthwind.Close()
dtCustomer = dsCustomers.Tables("dtCustomerTable")
Try
  drNewCustomer = dtCustomer.NewRow()
  drNewCustomer(0) = "OTISP"
  drNewCustomer(1) = "Otis P. Wilson Spaghetti House."
  dtCustomer.Rows.Add(drNewCustomer)
Dim drModified As
  DataRow() = dsCustomers.Tables("dtCustomerTable").Select(Nothing,Nothing,_
  DataViewRowState.Added)
  connNorthwind.Open()
  daCustomers.Update(drModified)
Catch eInsertException As Exception
  MsgBox(eInsertException.Message)
  Throw eInsertException
Finally
  connNorthwind.Close()
End Try
```

In summary, all you have to do is execute the following steps to update your data source from your DataSet, after you've made your changes to the DataSet:

1. Create a new row object that contains all the modified rows. You can use the DataViewRowState property to extract the appropriate rows. In our case, we used the DataViewRowState.Added value.

2. Call the Update() method of the DataAdapter object to send your changes back to the appropriate data source(s). Pass a copy of the DataRow containing your changes.

That's it. As you see, it's quite simple to add new rows to your database. Updates and deletes work the same way.

Managing DataSet Changes

Because the DataSet is inherently disconnected from the data source, it must manage its changes by itself. The DataSet supports several "dirty" flags that indicate whether changes have occurred. These flags come in the form of the GetChanges() and HasChanges() methods, which enable it to reconcile changes back to its data source via the DataAdapter object. These methods are used in conjunction with the RowState property, which we discuss next.

THE *ROWSTATE* PROPERTY

The RowState property enables you to track the condition of your rows. It works hand in hand with the AcceptChanges() method, which we discuss next. Until the AcceptChanges() method is called, the row state will be dirty. After AcceptChanges() has been called on the row, the row state will reflect a committed record that is no longer in flux. The RowState depends on what type of modification was made on the row, such as an insert, update, or delete. Table 6.5 shows you the possible values that the RowState might contain and why.

TABLE 6.5: VALUES OF THE *ROWSTATE* PROPERTY

CONSTANT	DESCRIPTION
Added	Occurs when a new row is first added to the DataRowCollection
Deleted	Indicates that the row was marked for deletion
Detached	Indicates that the row is "floating" and not yet attached to a DataRowCollection
Modified	Indicates that the row is "dirty"
Unchanged	Indicates that either the row was never touched in the first place, or the AcceptChanges() method was called, committing the changes to the row

If you want advanced information on how the RowState property works, please refer to Chapter 11, where we show you its importance with event-based programming.

THE *ACCEPTCHANGES ()* METHOD

Until you call this method, all the modified rows in your DataSet will remain in edit mode. The AcceptChanges() commits your modifications to a DataSet. The DataTable and DataRow objects also support this method. Keep in mind that this will not update your database, just your DataSet and friends. AcceptChanges() works incrementally, updating the DataSet with the modifications since the last time you called it. As we noted earlier, you can cascade your changes down to children objects. If you wanted to automatically accept changes for all the DataRows within a DataTable, you would need to call only the AcceptChanges() method on the DataTable, which automatically commits the changes for all its member DataRows.

THE *REJECTCHANGES ()* METHOD

If you decide not to commit the new row to the DataSet, call the RejectChanges() method. This method doesn't require any arguments. It simply deletes the newly added row or reverses the changes you made to an existing row.

THE *HASCHANGES ()* METHOD

The HasChanges() method queries whether a DataSet contains "dirty" rows. Generally, you would call this method before you called the GetChanges() method, so you don't unnecessarily retrieve changes that might not exist. This method can be overloaded by passing in the RowState as a parameter. By doing this, you can filter out specific change types. If you only wanted to query if the DataSet had any deletions, you would type:

```
If dsCustomers.HasChanges(DataRowState.Deleted)Then
   ' Do some logic to get the changes
End If
```

THE *GETCHANGES ( )* METHOD

The GetChanges() method creates a DataSet containing the changes made to it since the last time you called the AcceptChanges() method. If you haven't called AcceptChanges(), then it will retrieve a copy of the DataSet with all your changes. You can optionally use the overloaded version of this method, which accepts the DataRowState as a parameter. This way, you can get only the changes based on a certain state. If you wanted to get only the deletions for a DataSet, you would first call the HasChanges() method to see if any deletions occurred and then retrieve the changes:

```
dsCustomers = dsCustomers.GetChanges(DataRowState.Deleted)
```

Merging

Another technique for working with DataSets uses the ability to merge results from multiple DataTables or DataSets. The merge operation can also combine multiple schemas together. The Merge() method enables you to extend one schema to support additional columns from the other, and vice versa. In the end, you end up with a union of both schemas and data. This is useful when you want to bring together data from heterogeneous data sources, or to add a subset of data to an existing DataSet. The merge operation is quite simple:

```
dsCustomers.Merge (dsIncomingCustomers)
```

Typed DataSets

There are many data typing differences between ADO and ADO.NET. In classic ADO, you have more memory overhead than ADO because the fields in a RecordSet are late-bound, returning data as the Variant data type. ADO.NET supports stricter data typing. ADO.NET uses the Object, rather than the Variant data type for your data. Although Objects are more lightweight than Variants, your code will be even more efficient if you know the type ahead of time. You could use the GetString() method to convert your column values to strings. This way, you avoid boxing your variables to the generic Object type. You can use similar syntax for the other data types, such as GetBoolean() or GetGuid(). Try to convert your values to the native format to reduce your memory overhead.

When you work with classic ADO, you experience performance degradation when you refer to your fields by name. You would type the following:

```
strName = rsCustomers.Fields("CustomerName").Value
```

Now, with ADO.NET, you can use strong typing to reference the fields of a DataSet directly by name, like so:

```
strName = dsCustomers.CustomerName
```

Because the values are strictly typed in ADO.NET, you don't have to write type-checking code. ADO.NET will generate a compile-time error if your have a type mismatch, unlike the ADO runtime errors you get much too late. With ADO.NET, if you try to pass a string to an integer field, you will raise an error when you compile the code.

Creating Custom DataSets

You don't need a database to create a DataSet. In fact, you can create your own DataSet without any data at all. The ADO.NET DataSet enables you to create new tables, rows, and columns from scratch. You can use these objects to build relationships and constraints, ending up with a minidatabase into which you can load your data.

Listing 6.9 contains code that enables you to build a simple three-column online shopping cart DataSet on the fly. First, let's create a `BuildShoppingCart()` method that will create your table schema.

LISTING 6.9: CREATING A DATASET ON THE FLY

```
Public Function BuildShoppingCart() As DataTable
  Dim tblCart As DataTable = New DataTable("tblOrders")
  Dim dcOrderID As DataColumn = New
   DataColumn("OrderID", Type.GetType("System.Int32"))
  Dim dcQty As DataColumn = New
   DataColumn("Quantity",Type.GetType("System.Int32"))
  Dim dcCustomerName As DataColumn = New _
   DataColumn("CustomerName",
   Type.GetType("System.String"))
  tblCart.Columns.Add(dcOrderID)
  tblCart.Columns.Add(dcQty)
  tblCart.Columns.Add(dcCustomerName)
  Return tblCart
End Function
```

Now, all you have to do is set a DataTable variable to the results of your method and populate it. If you load the code from the companion CD, place a breakpoint on the `Add()` method of the DataRow collection, as shown in Figure 6.6. This way, you can use the Immediate mode of the Command window to see if your custom DataSet was successfully updated. With ADO.NET, it's easy to use array-like navigation to return the exact value you are looking for. In this example, you query the value of the customer name in the first row by using the `tblCart.Rows(0).Item(2)` statement. Figure 6.6 shows you the results.

TIP   *Again, you can see the power of constructors. In this sample, you see how you can set your constructor to a method result.*

FIGURE 6.6

Populating your custom DataSet object

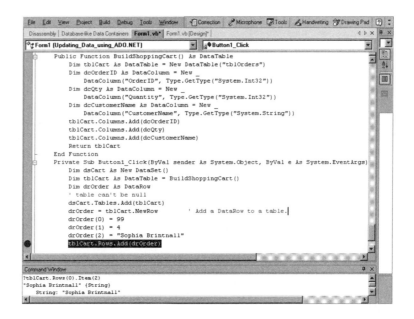

Being able to create your own DataSet from within your code enables you to apply many of the techniques discussed in this book. You can use these custom DataSets to store application data, without incurring the cost of crossing your network until you need to commit your changes.

Managing Concurrency

When you set up your DataSet, you should consider the type of locking, or concurrency control, that you will use. Concurrency control determines what will happen when two users attempt to update the same row.

ADO.NET uses an optimistic architecture, rather than a pessimistic model. *Pessimistic locking* locks the database when a record is retrieved for editing. Be careful when you consider pessimistic locking. Pessimistic locking extremely limits your scalability. You really can't use pessimistic locking in a system with a large number of users. Only certain types of designs can support this type of locking.

Consider an airline booking system. A passenger (let's call her Sam) makes a request to book a seat and retrieves a list of the available seats from the database. Sam selects a seat and updates the information in the database. Under optimistic locking, if someone else took her seat, she would see a message on her screen asking her to select a new one. Now let's consider what happens under pessimistic locking. After Sam makes a request for the list of available seats, she decides to go to lunch. Because pessimistic locking prevents other users from making changes when Sam is making edits, everyone else would be unable to book their seats. Of course, you could add some logic for lock timeouts, but the point is still the same. Pessimistic locking doesn't scale very well. In addition, disconnected architecture cannot support pessimistic locking because connections attach to the database only long enough to read or update a row, not long enough to maintain an indefinite lock. In classic ADO, you could choose between different flavors of optimistic and pessimistic locks. This is no longer the case. The .NET Framework supports only an optimistic lock type.

An *optimistic lock* type assumes that the data source is locked only at the time the data update commitment occurs. This means changes could have occurred while you were updating the disconnected data cache. A user could have updated the same CompanyName while you were making changes to the disconnected DataSet. Under optimistic locking, when you try to commit your CompanyName changes to the data source, you will override the changes made by the last user. The changes made by the last user could have been made after you had retrieved your disconnected DataSet. You could have updated the CompanyName for a customer, after someone else had updated the Address. When you push your update to the server, the updated address information would be lost. If you expect concurrency conflicts of this nature, you must make sure that your logic detects and rejects conflicting updates.

If you have worked with ADO 2.*x*, you can think of the Update() method of the DataAdapter object as analogous to the UpdateBatch() method you used with the RecordSet object. Both models follow the concept of committing your deltagram to the data source by using an optimistic lock type.

Understanding how locking works in ADO.NET is an essential part of building a solid architecture. ADO.NET makes great strides by advancing the locking mechanism. Let's take a look at how it changes from classic ADO in order to get an idea of how much power ADO.NET gives you.

In ADO 2.*x*, when you make changes to a disconnected RecordSet, you call the UpdateBatch() method to push your updates to the server. You really don't know what goes on under the covers and you hope that your inserts, updates, and deletes will take. You can't control the SQL statements that modify the database.

When you use optimistic concurrency, you still need some way to determine whether your server data has been changed since the last read. You have three choices with managing concurrency: time-date stamps, version numbers, and storing the original values.

Time-date stamps are a commonly used approach to tracking updates. The comparison logic checks to see if the time-date of the updated data matches the time-date stamp of original data in the database. It's a simple yet effective technique. Your logic would sit in your SQL statements or stored procedures, such as:

```
UPDATE Customers SET CustomerID = "SHAMSI",
 CustomerName = "Irish Twinkle SuperMart"
WHERE DateTimeStamp = olddatetimestamp
```

The second approach is to use version numbers, which is similar to using the time-date stamp, but this approach labels the row with version numbers, which you can then compare.

The last approach is to store the original values so that when you go back to the database with your updates, you can compare the stored values with what's in the database. If they match, you can safely update your data because no one else has touched it since your last retrieval. ADO.NET does data reconciliation natively by using the HasVersion() method of your DataRow object. The HasVersion() method indicates the condition of the updated DataRow object. Possible values for this property are Current, Default, Original, or Proposed. These values fall under the DataRowVersion enumeration. If you wanted to see whether the DataRow changes still contained original values, you could check to see if the DataRow has changed by using the HasVersion() method:

```
If r.HasVersion(datarowversion.Proposed) Then
' Add logic
End if
```

Summary

This concludes our discussion of the basic properties of the ADO.NET objects. After reading this chapter, you should be able to answer the questions that we asked you in the beginning:

- What are .NET data providers?

- What are the ADO.NET classes?

- What are the appropriate conditions for using a DataReader versus a DataSet?

- How does OLE DB fit into the picture?

- What are the advantages of using ADO.NET over classic ADO?

- How do you retrieve and update databases from ADO.NET?

- How does XML integration go beyond the simple representation of data as XML?

Although you covered a lot of ground in this chapter, there is still a good amount of ADO.NET functionality we haven't discussed. We use this chapter as a building block for the next few chapters. In the next chapter, we show you how to search and filter ADO.NET DataSets. You will learn about such things as data binding and data-aware controls in Chapter 8.

Chapter 7

ADO.NET Programming

- ◆ Building an ADO.NET application by using VB .NET
- ◆ Searching and filtering rows
- ◆ Calling stored procedures from ADO.NET
- ◆ ADO.NET and XML

IN THIS CHAPTER, WE show you more advanced data retrieval functionalities, such as searches, filters, and sorts. We show you how to populate form controls by using both cached DataSets and streamed DataReaders. You'll examine two ways to pull data from a DataSet: by cycling through the DataSet or by binding to the DataSet. This introduction to data binding serves as a prelude for the next chapter, where you'll explore data binding in detail.

Of course, no discussion of ADO.NET would be complete without reference to XML, whose functionality is assembled in the `System.Xml` base class. Although the chapter title indicates that we will be discussing ADO.NET functionality, we focus on the XML framework classes in the second half of this chapter. This is because ADO.NET is virtually indistinguishable from XML. Specifically, we discuss the ADO.NET DataSet's `ReadXml()` and `WriteXml()` methods, as well as review some of the `System.Xml` objects, such as the XmlDataDocument. We show you how to stream XML data by using the XmlReader and XmlWriter objects.

By the end of this chapter you should be able to answer the following questions:

- ◆ How does the `System.Data` namespace, used with ADO.NET, coordinate with the `System.Xml` namespace?
- ◆ What's the best way to search and filter data by using ADO.NET?
- ◆ How do Windows Forms work with ADO.NET?
- ◆ How can you load ADO.NET DataSets to and from XML?
- ◆ How does ADO.NET data streaming work?
- ◆ How does XML data streaming work?

After you have finished going through the examples in this chapter, you should be able to readily answer all these questions—and especially to understand the role of ADO.NET and XML in the .NET Framework. First, let's begin by creating a rudimentary ADO.NET application, which takes advantage of the full XML integration that you have with the .NET Framework.

Building an ADO.NET Application by Using VB .NET

The best way to absorb the functionality that you learned in the preceding chapter is to use it to build an application. Using your sample application, which works with the customers of the North-wind database, you will step through the various advanced feature-sets available in ADO.NET, XML, and the .NET Framework. As you go through each sample, you will supplement your main application one feature at a time. Although you are not going to end up with a production-capable system, you will be able to mix and match the logic from these examples and use them in your own production system.

.NET Base Classes

Before you begin following our examples, you should have a solid idea of how base classes work in the .NET Framework, because you will be working with many of these classes within the System.Data and System.Xml namespaces. As you know from Chapter 6, "A First Look at ADO.NET," the System.Data namespace houses the ADO.NET object model. You will work with the System.Data objects, such as the DataReader and DataSet, in this chapter. However, those aren't the only base classes that you will work with. You can't neglect the tight relationship between the System.Data namespace and the System .Xml namespace. Almost every ADO.NET object has an XML counterpart that mimics the functionality of the other. Because the ADO.NET and XML objects work in a similar fashion, it makes it easy to cross over from one object model to the other. Figure 7.1 illustrates how the ADO.NET and XML libraries work in harmony.

As you can see, DataSets work in conjunction with the XmlDataDocument. Any changes to either store are synchronized in real time. The DataReader object in the System.Data namespace has a corresponding XmlReader object from the System.Xml namespace. The DataReader and XmlReader work in a similar fashion: both read and write data streams. Figure 7.1 also illustrates that your data store can be accessed with a double-sided interface, by using both ADO.NET and XML interchangeably.

Let's begin working with these base classes by creating a new Windows Form application called Northwind System, which you will use in all the examples in this chapter. To make programming easier, first import the base classes that you will use in this chapter. This way, you don't have to use the fully qualified namespaces to refer to the data access objects. In the Form Declarations section of your new Windows application, type the following:

```
Imports System.Data
Imports System.Data.SqlClient
Imports System.Xml
```

NOTE   *Alternately, you can use the* System.Data.OleDb *library to access your database.*

FIGURE 7.1

Commonalities between ADO.NET and XML

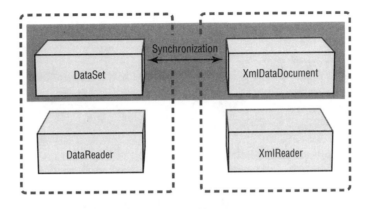

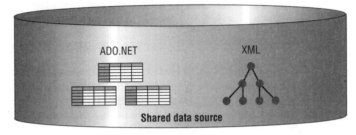

Before you can create your project, you need to configure your ADO.NET objects to work with the Northwind database. This is easy to do, and you've done this already in Chapter 3, "The Visual Database Tools." Add a connection to the Northwind database in your Server Explorer, if you haven't already done so from Chapter 3. Then, drag over a SqlDataAdapter control from the Data tab of your Toolbox onto your Windows Form and name it **SqlDataAdapterCustomers**. Next, launch the Data Adapter Configuration Wizard by clicking on the the Configure Data Adapter option in the properties window of the Data Adapter you have just created. Choose the Northwind connection you set up earlier.

NOTE   *If you are following along with these exercises, building code from scratch, realize that many of these examples auto-generate controls by using VS .NET. Although the auto-generated code creates a system-specified name for your control, you can safely rename each control from the Properties window. If you use the same names as we do, it makes the examples much easier to follow. Alternately, you can load the finished application code (*Northwind System.sln*) from the accompanying CD.*

Configuring Your Query

After the Data Adapter Configuration Wizard launches, select the Use SQL Statements option for the query type and click the Next button. The next screen asks how you wish to populate your Data Adapter. As you can see in Figure 7.2, you can enter a SQL statement directly into the wizard, or you can click the Query Builder button to pop up the Query Builder interface, as shown in Figure 7.3. The Query Builder should be familiar to you from Chapter 3.

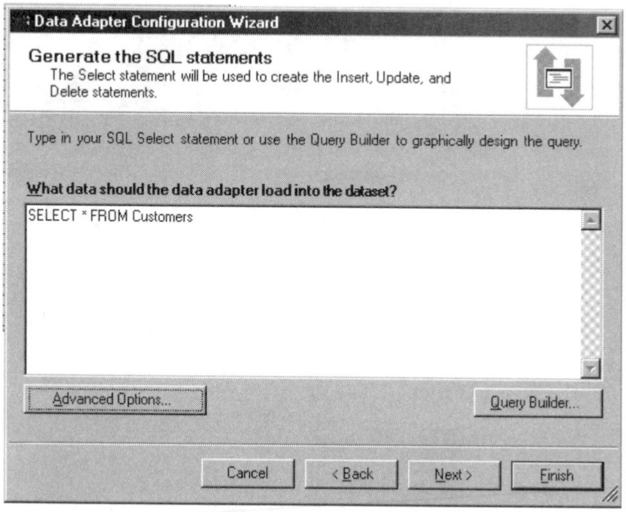

FIGURE 7.2

You can type SQL statements directly into the Data Adapter Configuration Wizard.

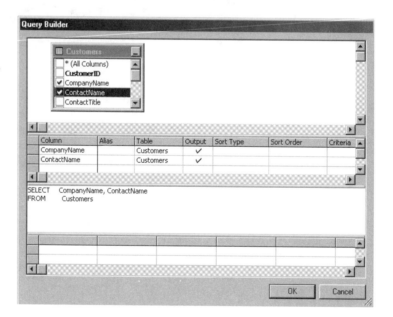

FIGURE 7.3

Alternately, you can use the Query Builder dialog box to create your queries.

Let's stick with the query shown in Figure 7.2, where you list all the information from your Customers table. Keep in mind, most application functionality requires only a few of the table's columns, so you should be sure to limit your results to only the data you need. Short of data-entry applications, you'll rarely have to download column values in their entirety to the client. We do so here only for simplicity's sake.

TIP   For demonstration purposes, we show you how to build an ad hoc SQL statement by using the Data Adapter Configuration Wizard. Ideally, you would use a stored procedure to bring back a subset of the data you need. It's not a good idea to bring back all the data from a table, because it slows down performance and bloats your DataSet. Stored procedures should always be used when you can predict the query in advance. We discuss stored procedures in the "Calling Stored Procedures from ADO.NET" section later in this chapter

After you click OK, your SQL statement will be listed in the Data Configuration dialog box. Now click the Advanced Options button. As you can see in Figure 7.4, the first option will automatically generate the INSERT, UPDATE, and DELETE statements for you. Because you don't plan to update your data, you don't need to select this option. If you had checked this option, VS .NET would custom map your action queries to stored procedures or SQL statements. We recommend using stored procedures for all your action commands, so that you can take advantage of optimization as well as implement custom business rules. However, the automatic SQL statement generation used by this feature is great for quickly prototyping data updates in your application.

FIGURE 7.4

Advanced SQL generation options

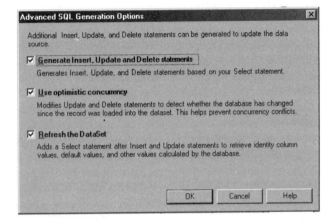

Let's take a look what happens when you choose to auto-generate your action queries. When you want VS .NET to automatically generate your action queries, it will create Command objects for each of the INSERT, UPDATE, and DELETEstatements behind the scenes. The InsertCommand object mapping for your query is shown in Listing 7.1.

LISTING 7.1: VS .NET CAN AUTO-GENERATE YOUR ACTION QUERIES (WINDOWS FORM DESIGNER GENERATED CODE)

```
Me.SqlInsertCommand1 = New System.Data.SqlClient.SqlCommand()
Me.SqlDataAdapter1.InsertCommand = Me.SqlInsertCommand1
Me.SqlInsertCommand1.CommandText = "INSERT INTO Customers" & _
    "(CustomerID, CompanyName, ContactName, ContactTitle, Address" & _
    ", City, Region, PostalCode, Country, Phone, Fax) " & _
    " VALUES (@CustomerID, @CompanyName, " & _
    " @ContactName, @ContactTitle, @Address, @City, " & _
```

```
    "@Region, @PostalCode, @Country" & _
    ", @Phone, @Fax); SELECT CustomerID, " & _
    "CompanyName, ContactName, ContactTitle, Address, " & _
    " City, Region, PostalCode, Country, " & _
    "Phone, Fax FROM Customers WHERE (CustomerID = @Select_CustomerID)"
Me.SqlInsertCommand1.Connection = Me.SqlConnection1
```

In addition to creating the appropriate Command objects, VS .NET will also specify the appropriate SQL statement along with appropriate input parameters. The Parameters collection is used to map each of the parameters, such as the `CustomerID`, as shown in Listing 7.2.

LISTING 7.2: VS .NET CAN AUTO-POPULATE YOUR PARAMETERS COLLECTION (WINDOWS FORM DESIGNER GENERATED CODE)

```
Me.SqlInsertCommand1.Parameters.Add(New _
System.Data.SqlClient.SqlParameter _
"@CustomerID", System.Data.SqlDbType.NChar, _
5, System.Data.ParameterDirection.Input, False, _
CType(0, Byte), CType(0, Byte), "CustomerID", _
System.Data.DataRowVersion.Current, Nothing))
```

This is only one parameter out of the dozen that VS .NET automatically codes for you. This auto-generation is a compelling reason to make the switch to VS .NET. You can imagine just how much coding effort and time this saves you, giving you the ability to rapidly prototype your applications. We talk more about the Parameters collection in the "Calling Stored Procedures from ADO .NET" section of this chapter.

In our first example, you are going to create a simple read-only navigation system for your Northwind customers. When you deselect the Generate Insert, Update And Delete Statements option, VS .NET will automatically disable the latter two options. This should come as no surprise, because if you aren't updating your data, you won't need to worry about concurrency or refreshing your results a second time.

The second option in the Advanced Options specifies whether you'd like VS .NET to automatically add the appropriate SQL statements for optimistic locking. As you remember from the preceding chapter, optimistic concurrency locks the record upon update, not retrieve. This way, you can prevent the blocking you might get from pessimistic concurrency. This option adds special code to your UPDATE statement. You can compare the code in Listings 7.3 and 7.4.

LISTING 7.3: THE AUTO-GENERATED UPDATE STATEMENT WITHOUT OPTIMISTIC CONCURRENCY (WINDOWS FORM DESIGNER GENERATED CODE)

```
Me.SqlUpdateCommand1.CommandText = "UPDATE Customers SET CustomerID =
    @CustomerID, " & _
    " CompanyName = @CompanyName,  ContactName = @ContactName, " & _
    "ContactTitle = @ContactTitle, Address = @Address, City = @" & _
```

```
"City, Region = @Region, PostalCode = @PostalCode, " & _
"Country = @Country, Phone = @Phone, " & _
"Fax = @Fax WHERE (CustomerID = @Original_CustomerID); " & _
"SELECT CustomerID, CompanyName, " & _
" ContactName, ContactTitle, Address, " & _
"City, Region, PostalCode, Country, " & _
"Phone, Fax FROM Customers " & _
"WHERE (CustomerID = @Select_CustomerID)"
```

LISTING 7.4: THE AUTO-GENERATED UPDATE STATEMENT WITH OPTIMISTIC CONCURRENCY (WINDOWS FORM DESIGNER GENERATED CODE)

```
Me.SqlUpdateCommand1.CommandText = _
    "UPDATE Customers SET CustomerID = @CustomerID, " & _
    "CompanyName = @CompanyName, ContactName " & _
    " = @ContactName, ContactTitle = @ContactTitle, " & _
    " Address = @Address, City = @City, Region = @Region, " & _
    "PostalCode = @PostalCode, Country = @Country, Phone = @Phone, " & _
    " Fax = @Fax WHERE (CustomerID = @Original_CustomerID) AND " & _
    " (Address = @Original_Address OR @Original_Address1 IS NULL " & _
    "AND Address IS NULL) " & _
    " AND (City = @Original_City OR @Original_City1 IS NULL " & _
    "AND City IS NULL) " & _
    " AND (CompanyName = @Original_CompanyName) AND " & _
    " (ContactName = @Original_ContactName OR " & _
    "@Original_ContactName1 IS NULL AND ContactName IS NULL) " & _
    " AND (ContactTitle = @Original_ContactTitle " & _
    "OR @Original_ContactTitle1 IS NULL AND ContactTitle IS NULL) " & _
    "AND (Country = @Original_Country OR @Original_Country1 IS NULL " & _
    "AND Country IS NULL) AND " & _
    "(Fax = @Original_Fax OR @Original_Fax1 IS NULL AND Fax IS NULL)" & _
    "AND (Phone = @Original_Phone OR @Original_Phone1 IS NULL " & _
    "AND Phone IS NULL)" & _
    "AND (PostalCode = @Original_PostalCode " & _
    "OR @Original_PostalCode1 IS NULL AND PostalCode IS NULL)" & _
    "AND (Region = @Original_Region OR @Original_Region1 IS NULL" & _
    "AND Region IS NULL);" & _
    " SELECT CustomerID, CompanyName, ContactName," & _
    " ContactTitle, Address, City, Region, PostalCode, " & _
    "Country, Phone, Fax FROM Customers WHERE (CustomerID = @Select_CustomerID)"
```

As you can see in Listing 7.4, comparison logic is added to compare the original values in the parameters with the newly updated values. If your system consists of read-only data, you would leave this option unchecked, because you have little chance for concurrency conflicts. However, when you use updatable data, it's a good idea to have concurrency controls in place.

The last option, Refresh The DataSet, pulls the newly updated data from the DataSet, after changes are made by your action commands. A handy use for this option would be in lieu of the @@IDENTITY statement, in order to retrieve the primary key of a newly added record. Keep in mind that the Refresh The DataSet option does a full SELECT and might bring back data that you might not need. It's always best to spend the time designing your system so you bring back only the data you need. The bottom line is that client-side DataSets should be small in both length and width. Don't retrieve unnecessary rows or columns. Because you aren't going to be updating the data, this option will be unchecked.

Using Windows Forms for Data Access

Now let's set up your Windows Form to display the Northwind data. First, you'll need to populate a DataSet. Select the Generate DataSet option from the Properties window for the DataAdapter control or from the Data menu. Name your DataSet whatever you would like. In our case, we called it dsCustomers, as shown in Figure 7.5. The DataSet gives you a data cache for your Windows controls to hook into, in order to display data.

FIGURE 7.5

Creating your DataSet

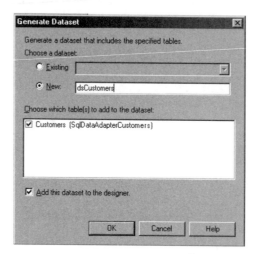

Next, you'll need a combo box. Feel free to name your combo box whatever you would like. We left it with the default name ComboBox1. Now you need to hook up the data returned from the DataSet to your control. There are many different methods for linking your data to your combo box:

◆ You could use the IBindingList interface of the DataSet object to bind your data to the combo box.

◆ You could manually write code to cycle through the DataSet's tables and rows and load them into your combo box.

◆ Alternately, you could completely forgo the DataSet and load the data into the combo box with a data stream by using the DataReader object.

Let's explore all three options. If you want to walk through existing code while you read, just load the solution from the companion CD that accompanies this book. Otherwise, you can continue building the application from scratch as you step through these examples. By the end of this chapter, you will have an application that demonstrates the many ways to access data by using ADO.NET and XML. By having them all within one application, you can easily compare performance and functionality between different methodologies.

CYCLING THROUGH A DATASET

Our first example uses the DataSet to populate the combo box. To retrieve data from the DataSet, you cycle through the DataTable and DataRow collections of the DataSet by using a `For Each` loop. Create a new button and navigate to its click event by double-clicking the button. In this example, you're going to use only one DataTable, which you populate with the following line of code:

```
SqlDataAdapterCustomers.Fill(DsCustomers1, "Customers")
```

This code creates and fills a new DataTable called `Customers`, adding the DataTable into the DataSet specified in the first parameter.

WARNING   *As you build more examples in your application, you might want to compare the different functions to one another. This might mean that you end up filling your DataSet repeatedly. Use the* `dscustomers1.Clear()` *method to clear the previous DataSet. If you don't, newly retrieved records will be added to the end of the DataSet every time you execute the* `Fill()` *method.*

Now that you have a DataTable named `Customers`, you can use it as a reference to loop through the rows. Declare a new DataRow object by using the following dimension statement:

```
Dim dsRow As DataRow
```

Now you can code your `For Each` loop like so:

```
For Each dsRow In DsCustomers1.Tables("Customers").Rows
    Me.ComboBox1.Items.Add(dsRow("CustomerID"))
Next
```

When you execute this code by hitting F5, you should end up with a form similar to the one in Figure 7.6.

FIGURE 7.6

Cycling through a DataSet to populate a combo box

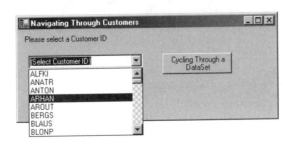

USING THE *IBINDINGLIST* INTERFACE OF THE DATASET

The .NET Framework has greatly improved data binding functionality. The IBindingList interface gives control over how you bind to different types of objects: web controls, Windows controls, custom classes, and WebServices. Because we dedicate nearly an entire chapter (Chapter 8, "Data-Aware Controls") to data binding, we don't get into too much detail in this chapter. However, a brief overview of Windows control binding provides a useful comparison between the different ways to populate controls.

Let's add some code to the click event of a new button. As in the previous example, you want to first fill the DataSet. To properly bind to the combo box, you need to specify the binding property of the control, the data source, and the member of the data source to which you wish to bind. You can do this by using the following code:

```
ComboBox1.DataSource = DsCustomers1.Customers
ComboBox1.DisplayMember = "CustomerID"
```

TIP   As you can see, you can take advantage of the typed DataSet to call the DataTable directly as an attribute of the DataSet, rather than using ordinals. This enables you to do a direct lookup for that DataTable, rather than the indirect lookup you get with using string values for the name. At every turn, ADO.NET significantly improves the efficiency of your data access code.

This code sets values for the DataSource and DisplayMember properties of the combo box. The former indicates your data source, which is the Customers table of the DataSet. The DisplayMember property indicates the binding column within that DataTable. When you run this code, the data from this column will be displayed in the combo box. The results will be the same as you saw in Figure 7.6.

CONTROL INHERITANCE

Many of the VS .NET controls inherit from base controls, which provide them with supplementary attributes. These supplementary attributes serve as a common denominator between different control implementations.

Our combo box binding example uses the DisplayMember property. This is not a native property of the combo box control. Instead, it is inherited from the ListControl class. In turn, the ListControl inherits from the IList interface, which provides a common functionality for manipulating arrays and collections. This way, other controls, such as the ListBox control, can consistently share the same interface, and most often, the same implementation. This makes programming much easier, because the DisplayMember property is consistent between different controls.

STREAMING DATA FROM A DATAREADER

Another way to populate a combo box is by using the DataReader object. In fact, DataReaders are the best way to go for one-time, read-only calls, which often happen in an application, especially when populating combo boxes (as in this example). The DataReader is a fast implementation for reading data off the wire, because it uses a rapid non-buffered format. Truth be told, did you know that behind the scenes, the DataAdapter actually uses a DataReader to populate a DataSet? It's true.

Under the hood, the DataAdapter uses a DataReader when you pass in a DataSet to the `Fill()` method. After you call the `Fill()` method, the ADO.NET objects perform the following operations:

1. The DataAdapter implicitly opens a connection, if an explicit connection is not given.

2. The DataAdapter uses the `SelectCommand` to execute via this connection based on the `CommandText` supplied.

3. The DataAdapter creates a DataTable by using the DataSet you've supplied.

4. The Command object returns the requested data in a DataReader object.

5. The DataAdapter populates the newly created DataTable by using the DataReader. Your DataSet now contains the newly retrieved data.

6. The DataAdapter closes the DataReader.

7. The DataAdapter returns the Connection object to its original state, based on how it found the Connection in step 1.

WARNING   If you plan on reusing the data in your combo box to select multiple customers over and over again, you would be better off using the cached DataSet. This saves you from making unnecessary network trips to retrieve a new DataReader data stream.

You can see that you save time not only by using a streamed object, but also by eliminating most of the steps performed by the DataAdapter. In addition, the DataReader is a slenderized mechanism for storing data, much slimmer than a server-side `ADO.RecordSet`, giving you yet another reason to make the move to .NET if you haven't already. So how do you populate the combo box with a DataReader? First, you must create a DataReader object, as you see in Listing 7.5.

LISTING 7.5: POPULATING A COMBOBOX FROM A DATAREADER (BUTTON3_CLICK_1)

```
Dim drCustomer As SqlDataReader
SqlConnection1.Open()
drCustomer = Me.SqlSelectCommand1.ExecuteReader(CommandBehavior.CloseConnection)
While drCustomer.Read
  ComboBox1.Items.Add(drCustomer.Item("CustomerID"))
End While
drCustomer.Close()
```

You set the DataReader to the results of your `ExecuteReader()` method, using the Select-Command object that was automatically created by the Data Adapter Configuration Wizard. The `CommandBehavior.CloseConnection` parameter closes the connection that's associated with the DataReader. You created the Connection object on a separate line, but you don't have to type a separate line to close it. You see how the clever design of the ADO.NET library intends to save lines of code at every angle. The `Read()` method of the DataReader enables you to cycle through the elements in the DataReader until there are no more records left. As you can see, the code is more elegant than the cumbersome `MoveNext()` statements of classic ADO.

TIP   *The default position of a newly populated DataReader points before the first row. The* `Read()` *method automatically points you to the first record.*

Now that you've seen three ways to populate a combo box, you might find it useful to compare their behaviors and performance in order to find the solution that best meets your needs. Feel free to experiment with the examples so far, to see how the performance varies from one to the other. Here's a summary of the three methods:

♦   You use the `IBindingList` interface of the DataSet object when you want a tightly coupled user interface that uses data binding.

♦   You cycle through the DataSet's tables and rows to load them into your user interface control. This technique is useful when you want to manipulate the data locally to avoid network trips back to the data source.

♦   You can stream the data to the control by using the DataReader object. This is best for fast data access off the wire.

After you have finished comparing the different techniques, you are going to expand your application to populate customer detail based on the `CustomerID` selected from your combo box. You will retrieve the data you need by using more advanced ADO.NET functionality such as filtering and searching within your DataTable.

Searching and Filtering Rows

To locate a desired record quickly in ADO 2.x, you can use the `Find()` method, or apply a filter to the cursor to further limit the rows. After you locate the desired row, you must access the desired fields through the Fields collection. ADO 2.x also uses a `Filter` property and a `Seek()` method, which can locate one or more rows based on any criteria you specify.

ADO.NET is not much different conceptually, but you'll find that the implementation is a bit different. You directly access your desired row by using the `Find()` method of the DataRow collection. This method returns your desired DataRow by using a primary key, unlike the ADO 2.x `Find()` implementation. Additionally, ADO.NET replaces the slew of search and filtering mechanisms—`Find()`, `Seek()`, `Filter`—with a single, elegant, and permutable `Search()` method.

Besides working with ADO.NET by searching directly, you can leverage the back-end database to run your searches for you. Especially if you are working with complicated searches, this is often the better alternative. ADO.NET provides an object-oriented way to do this as well, by using the Parameters collection of a stored procedure Command object to locate your desired rows. In this section, you will explore all these ways of searching and filtering through your DataSets to find DataRows based on specific criteria.

The *Find ( )* Method

The `Find()` method returns a DataRow object based on the primary key that you specify. Let's add two new text boxes to your form for the company name and address for a given customer. Next, in your combo box's `SelectedIndexChanged` event, you can call a subroutine to retrieve a customer record based on the primary key you specified. Listing 7.6 shows the subroutine that you use to retrieve this data and populate your text boxes.

LISTING 7.6: RETRIEVING A CUSTOMER RECORD BY USING THE FIND METHOD (FINDBYCUSTOMERID)

```
Public Sub FindByCustomerID(ByVal dtCustomers As DataTable, ByVal
    strCustID As String)
Dim drFoundCustomer As DataRow = dtCustomers.Rows.Find(strCustID)
  If IsNothing(ComboBox1.Text) = False Then
    TextBox1.Text = drFoundCustomer.Item("CompanyName")
    TextBox2.Text = drFoundCustomer.Item("Address")
  End If
End Sub
```

This subroutine accepts a DataTable object containing the records that you want to use for your search, as well as the primary key for the customer that you want to retrieve. As you can see, you can use your DataRow constructor to return the DataRow returned from the Find() method. Add this subroutine to your form and call it from the SelectedIndexChanged event of the combo box by using this line:

```
FindByCustomerID(DsCustomers1.Customers, ComboBox1.Text)
```

WARNING   *Do not confuse the* Find() *method of the* RowCollection *with the* Find() *method of the* ADO.RecordSet *object. They are two entirely different animals. In ADO.NET, the* Find() *method is used to retrieve rows based on their primary key, whereas in ADO 2.x, the* Find() *method retrieves rows based on expressions containing your search criteria.*

Locating Column Values in a Strongly Typed DataSet

Up until this point, you haven't really explored strongly typed DataSets in detail. Of course, the best way to do this is by example, while learning background information along the way. Because typed DataSets greatly improve your searching programmability for column values, it's appropriate to discuss them in this section.

ADO.NET simplifies your searching by enabling you to search for values within a strongly typed DataSet. Let's experiment searching with a strongly typed DataSet by adding one to your project.

Typed DataSets derive from a DataSet object, and you can have VS .NET do all the work for you to generate a typed DataSet. In your form's design mode, drag over a DataSet control from your Toolbox. This will launch the Add DataSet dialog box. Choose the option to create a typed DataSet and select the existing DataSet that you had created earlier. From the Properties window of this new DataSet, rename the DataSet to **dsCustomersTyped**.

Now let's add a new button to your form to populate your combo box from a typed DataSet. By now, your form should look like Figure 7.7.

FIGURE 7.7

The Northwind
system project's
main form

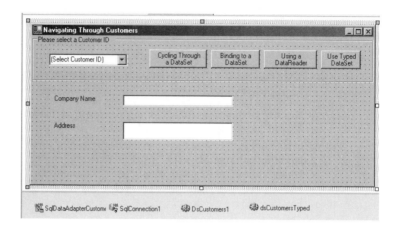

FIGURE 7.7

The Northwind
system project's
main form

You will need to add some code to your button's click event in order to populate the combo box from the typed DataSet. Populating a typed DataSet is no different from an untyped DataSet: you use the `Fill()` method as usual.

Strongly typed DataSets come with one main advantage: IntelliSense. Look at Figure 7.8, where we show you how the `Customers` DataRow attributes pop up in your IntelliSense code. You can easily refer to your `CustomerID` column as if it were a property of DataRow. Right above that line, you can see the commented code that you would have to use with an untyped DataSet. You don't have this option in classic ADO. ADO 2.x just didn't treat your data objects in an object-oriented fashion. You would have to drill down through the Fields collection, using the string index to access the desired field, as in: `rsCustomer.Fields("Country")`. This prevented the compiler from being able to check the validity of the column name. Not only do typed DataSets simplify your coding and readability, but they also enable you to take advantage of compile-type error checking to ensure that you don't run into type mismatch errors.

FIGURE 7.8

Using typed
DataSets

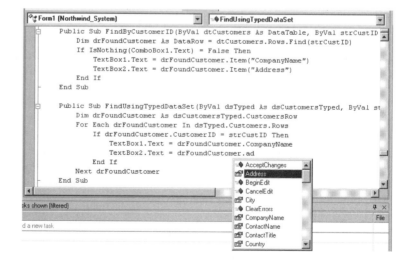

The listing for your button's click event is shown in Listing 7.7. Some lines have been removed for brevity.

```
Dim dsTyped As New dsCustomersTyped()
Dim drCustomer As dsCustomersTyped.CustomersRow

dsTyped.Clear()          ' Clear the typed DataSet
SqlDataAdapterCustomers.Fill(dsTyped, "Customers")

For Each drCustomer In dsTyped.Customers.Rows
    ComboBox1.Items.Add(drCustomer.CustomerID)
Next
```

Notice that you declare the DataRow a bit differently. Instead of declaring it by using a generic DataRow object, you use the dsCustomersTyped.CustomersRow, which enables you to iterate through your columns of the typed DataSet. This DataRow represents a class containing properties that enable you to access the column values in the row.

Next, you can directly find the row based on your DataRow properties. In the changed event for the combo box, you can add the code from Figure 7.9, which retrieves the desired row directly by using the properties of the DataRow object. Figure 7.9 illustrates the advantages of using strongly typed DataSets.

FIGURE 7.9

Locating a row by using strongly typed DataSets

```
Private Sub Button4_Click(ByVal sender As System.Object, ByVal e As System.E
    Dim dsTyped As New dsCustomersTyped()
    Dim drCustomer As dsCustomersTyped.CustomersRow
    Button1.Enabled = False ' Disable the Cycling button
    Button2.Enabled = False ' Disable the Binding button
    Button3.Enabled = False ' Disable the DataReader button
    ClearCombo()                  ' Clear combo box
    EnableDetail()                ' Enable the Details
    dsTyped.Clear()               ' Clear the typed DataSet

    SqlDataAdapterCustomers.Fill(dsTyped, "Customers")

    'Untyped:    For Each drCustomer In dsTyped.Tables("Customers").Rows
    For Each drCustomer In dsTyped.Customers.Rows
        'Untyped: ComboBox1.Items.Add(drCustomer("CustomerID"))
        ComboBox1.Items.Add(drCustomer.CustomerID)
    Next
```

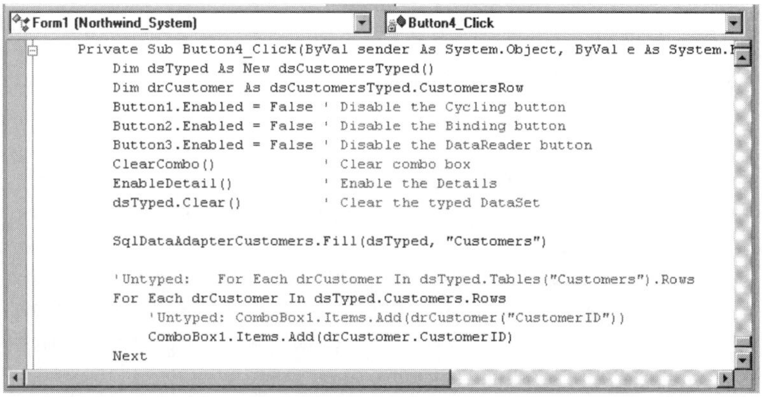

Let's take the code a little bit further and iterate through the typed DataSet by using user-supplied criteria, rather than a mere lookup. Using comparison logic, you will retrieve the relevant rows that match your search criteria. You will have to add a couple more controls to your form to perform this search. First, add a TextBox control, which you will use to capture the search criteria for the country field. Next, add a ListBox control to show the results of your search, as well as a Search button that includes the code in Listing 7.8.

LISTING 7.8: LOOPING THROUGH A TYPED DATASET TO SEARCH FOR ROWS (BUTTON5_CLICK)

```
' Search based on country
Dim dsTyped As New dsCustomersTyped()
Dim drCustomer As dsCustomersTyped.CustomersRow
dsTyped.Clear()        ' Clear the typed DataSet
SqlDataAdapterCustomers.Fill(dsTyped, "Customers")
For Each drCustomer In dsTyped.Customers.Rows
    If drCustomer.IsCountryNull = False Then
      If drCustomer.Country = TextBox3.Text Then
          ListBox1.Items.Add(drCustomer.CompanyName &
            " (" & drCustomer.Country & ")")
      End If
    End If
Next
```

When the button is clicked, the program reads the selected country from the TextBox control and finds the first record from this country. This code uses the typed DataSet's column values to loop through the RowsCollection, pulling out matches and storing them in the list box. It continues scanning the records until it researches the end of the RowCollection. Later in this chapter, you will expand this search to use stored procedures, which you can use to search for non-exact matches.

TIP   You might notice something a bit unusual in Listing 7.8: the IsCountryNull() *method. We didn't add a special method to check for Nulls. In fact, VS .NET automatically generates Null-checking methods for all the columns of the typed DataSet. You can use these methods, rather than the* IsNull() *method, to check for Null values.*

The *Select ( )* Method

ADO.NET replaces the Seek() and Find() methods with a single method: the Select() method. The Select() method can be overloaded to do both sorts and filters. In classic ADO, you had several ways to search for data in your retrieved records: the Find(), Seek(), and Filter methods and properties. As we discussed earlier, the Find() method enables you to retrieve values based on specific search criteria. The Seek() method works like the Find() method, except it enables you to use an index to locate the desired row, which is much faster than the Find() method in ADO 2.x. You specify the seek index by using the Index property. The Filter property enables you to select certain records in the current RecordSet, either for viewing purposes, or to operate on them as a group (to delete or update them as a group, for example). The Filter property recognizes more complicated criteria than the Find() method, as you can combine multiple comparisons with logical operators. In ADO.NET, the plethora of searching functions have been supplanted by a single, customizable Select() method.

FILTERING

To filter your data, ADO.NET enables you to use one of the overloaded versions of the Select() method to locate a specific row. This multipurpose method lets you perform a variety of data manipulations functionalities, such as filtering and sorting based on specific row states.

Let's use your application to filter out rows from a specified country. The overloaded version that you will use for our filtering example uses the following syntax:

```
Select(ByVal FilterExpression as String) As DataRow()
```

Add another button to your form and call the code in Listing 7.9 from its click event.

LISTING 7.9: FILTERING BY USING THE SELECT METHOD (SEEKUSINGCOUNTRY)

```
Dim dsTyped As New dsCustomersTyped()
Dim dtCustomer As DataTable
' Array of typed rows
Dim drCustomer() As dsCustomersTyped.CustomersRow
Dim strFilterCriteria As String
Dim intRowCount As Integer
Dim intCounter As Integer = 0

dsTyped.Clear()          ' Clear the typed DataSet
SqlDataAdapterCustomers.Fill(dsTyped, "Customers")
dtCustomer = dsTyped.Tables("Customers")
' Set our filter criteria
strFilterCriteria = "Country = '" & _
 strCountryName & "'"
' Use the Select method to populate row array
' based on filtering criteria
drCustomer = dtCustomer.Select(strFilterCriteria)
' Get upper bound of CustomerID column
intRowCount = drCustomer.GetUpperBound(0)
For intCounter = 0 To intRowCount
 ListBox1.Items.Add _
    (drCustomer(intCounter).CompanyName _
        & " (" & drCustomer(intCounter).Country & ")")
Next intCounter
```

After you click the button, all rows that match your filtering criteria will be returned in a DataRow array. When you call the `Select()` method, you pass in your filter criteria; in this case, it looks for country names matching the value in the text box. You specify the filter criteria in the form of a simple expression. This example uses the equals expression, but you can choose other types of evaluations, including greater than, less than, or arithmetic operations such as multiplication. In addition, you can link multiple expression components by using the Boolean concatenations such as AND, OR, and NOT. If you don't specify a sort parameter, the rows return in order of the primary key.

A useful expression is the LIKE keyword. This works like the SQL LIKE keyword, enabling you to pull substrings within a column's values. You could replace your filter criteria in Listing 7.9 with the following LIKE expression:

```
strFilterCriteria =
 "Country LIKE '%" & strCountryName & "%'"
```

Now when you search for "US," you will retrieve all companies that come from countries containing "US" in their name.

TIPS FOR FILTER EXPRESSIONS

Here are a few tips to remember when building your expression string:

◆ Make sure you escape out special characters, such as * or % in your string.

◆ When you are filtering based on string values, make sure you enclose the string in single quotes, as shown in the example.

◆ When you are filtering by using the LIKE keyword, you can use the % or * symbol to specify a wildcard, but only at the start or the end of the string.

The filter expression uses one or more field names and/or constants combined with relational operators. In simpler terms, it's an expression similar to the ones you would use with an If statement. The following filter expression will isolate the rows whose OrderDate field's value falls in the first quarter of 1997:

```
strFilterCriteria = "OrderDate >= '1/1/1997' And OrderDate <= '3/31/1997'"
```

As you saw in the Country filter, you can also combine VB .NET variables to build the filter expression, because it's parsed at runtime and passed to ADO.NET. The following statement will select the orders placed in a user-supplied interval:

```
strFilterCriteria = "OrderDate >= '" & dtmstartDate & _
        "' And OrderDate <= '" & dtmendDate & "'"
```

If the variables dtmstartDate and dtmendDate are assigned the values 1/1/1997 and 3/31/1997 respectively, the last two examples are identical.

NOTE   To remove a filter, you can either supply an empty string as the filter criteria or call the Select() method with no parameters.

If the original DataSet is very large, ADO.NET will take some time to filter out the unwanted rows, especially if the expression is complicated and involves many columns. You should avoid downloading large DataSets to the client or middle tier and filtering them there. Instead, build the corresponding SQL statement and retrieve only the subset of rows you want from the database.

SORTING

The Search() method can be overloaded by specifying a second sorting parameter. The same expression rules apply for the sorting direction as they do for the filter expression. Let's use the previous example to return your company names in descending alphabetical order, by using the company name as your sorting column. To do this, add an additional input parameter value to your Search() method call, like so:

```
strSortCriteria = "CompanyName DESC"
drCustomer =
dtCustomer.Select(strFilterCriteria, strSortCriteria)
```

This works differently than the Sort property in classic ADO, where you pass in a field list of comma-separated field names. Using ADO 2.x, when you supply a value to this property, the records of the current RecordSet sorts according to the field(s) you have specified.

NOTE *If you don't specify the* ASC *or* DESC *flag, passing just a column name, you will receive the rows ordered by their primary key.*

Sorting a large DataTable will take some time, so you must avoid sorting rows on the client or middle tier. You should try to download the desired rows in the desired order (use the ORDER BY clause in your SQL statements). If the rows must be sorted differently once on the client or application server, then use the Search() method.

The DataView Object

Another way to sort, search, or filter through your DataSets is by using the DataView object. The DataView object enables you to create a customized view of a DataTable within your DataSet by using methods inherited from a whole slew of interfaces, such as IBindingList, IList, ICollection, IEnumerable, and ITypedList. Because ADO.NET abstracts the representation of your data (DataView) from the data source (DataTable), you can reuse the same data source over and over again by using different representations of the data. You can do this by binding your DataView objects to controls, much as you would a DataTable. This way, you don't have to make many network trips to the data server to bring back different subsets of data.

You can use the DataView to perform sorting and filtering operations by using the Sort and Rowfilter properties, respectively. In addition, DataViews enable you to modify the rows in the DataTable by using the AddNew() and Delete() methods.

Let's try it now. On your form, create a new button and list box. You're going to use the DataView object to return the list of customer cities from your existing DataSet. You will use the Sort property of the DataView to return your cities in descending order.

In the click event of the button you just created, add the code in Listing 7.10.

LISTING 7.10: WORKING WITH THE DATAVIEW OBJECT (BUTTON11_CLICK)

```
Dim dvcityView As DataView = New DataView(DsCustomers1.Customers)
Dim intCount As Integer
Dim intCounter As Integer = 0
SqlDataAdapterCustomers.Fill(DsCustomers1, "Customers")
dvcityView.Sort = "City DESC" ' Sort DataView
intCount = dvcityView.Count
For intCounter = intCounter To intCount - 1
    'Retrieve the City column for the DataRowView
ListBox2.Items.Add(dvcityView.Item(intCounter).Item("City"))
Next
```

As you can see in the code, you create a new DataView by using the overloaded constructor to pass in the DataTable that will serve as its source. After filling the DataTable, you apply a sort to the DataView object. In this case, you sort the cities in descending order. Then, you loop through the DataRowView objects nested within the DataView, retrieving the value of each city column into your list box. This way, you can use the same DataTable with different controls. This enables you to present the data in a manner unique to each control, without affecting the original DataTable.

In addition to sorting, you can also apply filters to your DataView objects. You can specify the filter you wish to apply by using the `RowFilter` property. Go ahead and add another line after the sort code to set a filter based on the country name:

```
dvcityView.RowFilter = "Country = 'France'"
```

Now your code will bring back your cities in descending order, for those cities located in France.

You have reviewed different ways to perform searches, sorts, and filters by using the native ADO .NET objects without going back to the database. Now you're ready to see how ADO.NET works with searches performed on the back-end, by using stored procedures and parameters.

Calling Stored Procedures from ADO.NET

As we indicated earlier, when you are working with large DataSets to filter or search for criteria, you should limit the data that you bring back to the client or middle tier. As we've already demonstrated, you can apply your filters on the data returned to the middle tier or client. However, if you are working with complicated filters, it's better to apply the specific filters and searches on the back-end database server, where it will process more expediently. We showed you how to filter by using SQL statements in Chapter 4, "Structured Query Language" (by using the `WHERE` clause). In this section, we show you how to write filters, passing user-defined parameter values into the `WHERE` clause of the stored procedure.

ADO.NET uses the `ParameterCollection` of the DataAdapter object to store the input and output parameters of a stored procedure. You learned how to use this collection in Chapter 6, when we discussed the ADO.NET object model. We are going to build upon that knowledge, giving you yet another means of comparison for performing searches.

First, you'll need to create a stored procedure that accepts the country name as an input parameter. Then, you can call this stored procedure from ADO.NET. If you haven't already created the stored procedure in Chapter 5, "Transact-SQL," use the code in Listing 7.11 to create your `GetCustomersByCountry` stored procedure.

LISTING 7.11: THE *GETCUSTOMERSBYCOUNTRY* STORED PROCEDURE

```
CREATE PROCEDURE GetCustomersByCountry
    @CountryName varchar(15)
AS
    SELECT * FROM Customers
    WHERE Country = @CountryName
```

This stored procedure performs an exact match based on the country name value you pass in, returning all the customers for that country. If you want, you can modify the stored procedure to use the LIKE clause, so you don't have to use exact matches.

TIP   You can use the Server Explorer to create the stored procedure without leaving VS .NET. Right-click on the stored procedure node and select New Stored Procedure.

Now you can use ADO.NET to call this stored procedure. Earlier, we showed you how to filter and search by using ADO.NET methods with the country name as your parameter. Let's expand this example so you can see how much faster your searches work when you use optimized stored procedures. Add another button to your solution by calling the code in Listing 7.12 in its click event.

LISTING 7.12: USING THE *GETCUSTOMERSBYCOUNTRY* SQL STORED PROCEDURE PARAMETERS FOR SEARCHES (BUTTON7_CLICK)

```
Dim cmdCustomers As New SqlCommand()
Dim drCustomer As SqlDataReader
SqlConnection1.Open()
cmdCustomers = SqlConnection1.CreateCommand
cmdCustomers.CommandType = CommandType.StoredProcedure
cmdCustomers.CommandText = "GetCustomersByCountry"
cmdCustomers.Parameters.Add(New SqlParameter("@CountryName", TextBox3.Text))
drCustomer = cmdCustomers.ExecuteReader(CommandBehavior.CloseConnection)
While drCustomer.Read
    ListBox1.Items.Add(drCustomer.Item("CompanyName") & " (" &
drCustomer.Item("Country") & ")")
End While
drCustomer.Close()
SqlConnection1.Close()
```

As you can see in the code, you use a DataReader object to stream the results from your stored procedure into the list box. You create a new Command object, specifying the type as a stored procedure, and pass in the name of the stored procedure. Then you add a new parameter to the Parameters collection of the Command object: the country name with the value provided by your text box. If you run this code and type **USA** into the text box, you will get a list of all customers in the United States. As you can see, it's simple to use stored procedures and their parameters from ADO.NET.

ADO.NET and XML

As you read in the beginning of this chapter, ADO.NET and XML work hand in hand, and really cannot be distinguished from each other. They are both part of the core .NET building blocks for data access. Almost every object in the System.Data namespace works in conjunction with an object from the System.Xml namespace, as shown earlier in Figure 7.1. In addition, DataSets are stored as XML, both for the data and schema. The XmlDataDocument serves as a bridge between XML and ADO.NET, providing relational access to your data from XML content.

There are many advantages of using XML as a data storage format. In classic ADO, you are limited to tight navigation using tabular RecordSets. This makes it awkward to navigate between related RecordSets or through hierarchical data. With ADO.NET and XML, you can move beyond the traditional up/down navigation of relational data by moving in all directions, in a relational or tree-like fashion. The tight integration between ADO.NET and XML makes it easy to switch from ADO.NET objects, such as the DataSet, to XML strings, and vice versa. ADO has come a long way, with XML integration not just another format for writing data to a file.

Another advantage of using XML data storage lies in its capability to be readily transported. Because XML strings are not proprietary binary objects, they are more viable for transport through firewalls via HTTP. Not only is XML a great network transport, but it's also easily understood by any browser-enabled device. All these reasons make XML a fantastic choice for businesses to transfer their data, not only within applications, but also between applications.

In this section, we talk about the visual tools for working with XML, specifically the XML Designer. We show you how DataSets work with XML by using the `ReadXml()` and `WriteXml()` methods. In addition, we discuss the objects within the `System.Xml` namespace, and show you how to read and write XML by using the two core XML objects of the .NET Framework: XmlReader and XmlWriter. These enable you to load data from and write data to XML, respectively. We focus mostly on XML's interaction with ADO.NET in this chapter. We reserve Chapter 10, "The Role of XML," for discussing XML in depth, including SQL Server 2000's support for XML functionality.

Note   This section is not meant to be a tutorial on how to work with XML. We assume that you have some familiarity with XML and understand the basic concepts and vocabulary. For further information on this topic, check out Mastering XML: Premium Edition by Chuck White, Liam Quin, and Linda Burman (Sybex 2001).

XML Schemas

Let's continue our example and show you how to work with XML schema files. Earlier, you created two DataSets whose schema files you see in the Solution Explorer. Double-click the `dsCustomers.xsd` file to view your XML schema. At the bottom of your design window, you will see two tabs: DataSet and XML, as shown in Figure 7.10.

FIGURE 7.10

XML schemas within VS .NET

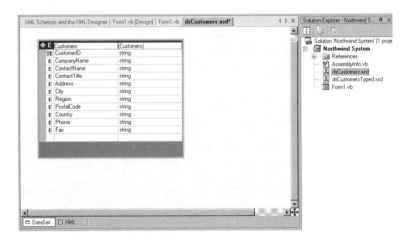

By default, you will see the DataSet view of the XSD file, which presents a structured grid showing the different columns and data types of your schema file. You can think of this as the Schema view. Click on the XML tab to view the XML schema code that VS .NET automatically generates for you. If you examine the XML source, you will see that the name of the DataTable is represented as an element:

```
<xsd:element name="Customers">
```

Below this, you will see the sub-elements, which represent the column names within the complex data type. The complex data type enables you to specify the column names as sub-elements within your table element, which you cannot do with simple data types.

XML schema files consist of two core components: elements and attributes. *Elements* provide a format for describing your data, enabling you to use names and types to represent your field. In the dsCustomers.xsd file, you will see the CustomerID column represented as such:

```
<xsd:element name="CustomerID" type="xsd:string" />
```

Attributes enable you to provide additional information regarding your element by using simple types. (This means that you cannot store sub-elements within the attribute). You could use attributes to specify a range of valid values for an element, marking required elements, or for deriving from base data types to impose specific business rules.

TIP   *To determine when elements or attributes should be used, you should think of elements as tags that enclose your data items, and attributes as tags that further describe the data item that is encapsulated in your element tag.*

If you manipulate any of these elements within the XML code, your changes will automatically synchronize with the DataSet schema in the DataSet view. The same synchronization will occur back to the XML source when you manipulate the DataSet grid view.

All relational database elements are represented within the XML schema, as well. You can see that your primary key constraint also translates back to XML at the end of the listing, using the unique XML schema tag:

```
<xsd:unique name="Constraint1" msdata:PrimaryKey="true">
        <xsd:selector xpath=".//Customers" />
        <xsd:field xpath="CustomerID" />
</xsd:unique>
```

NOTE   *The .NET Framework relies on the XML Schema Definition (XSD) standard for representing your data schema, rather than the Document Type Definition (DTD) format. You should convert your DTD schemas to XSD formats when you migrate your applications to .NET.*

XML Designer

VS .NET makes working with XML DataSets easy, by providing yet another visual data tool: the XML Designer. The XML Designer enables you to manipulate XML schema and data files. Although it's not as tightly integrated into VS .NET as the other code editors, you can still take advantage of such features as IntelliSense and color-coding that you have when working with VB .NET source code.

You used the XML Designer in the previous section when viewing the XSD file. Because you were viewing only schema, you saw only the DataSet and XML tabs. If you were working with raw XML data, you would see the Data view, which enables you to peruse the actual data (as shown later in Figure 7.11). You'll further explore the XML Designer a bit later.

The XML Designer gives you more refined control to tweak your XML source code when auto-generation doesn't meet your needs. You can directly modify the XML data file or the XSD schema as you see fit. In addition, you can work with the XML in a visual manner. You can modify existing XSD files by dragging database objects from the Server Explorer into the XML Designer. You don't even need a database to generate XSD files. You can also create XSD files from scratch when you use the XML Designer in conjunction with the XML controls in the XML Schema tab of your Toolbox.

WARNING   *Be judicious when making edits in the XML Designer because you don't have any Undo functionality to roll back to the previous code base. As a workaround, you should save your file before making any risky changes.*

WARNING   *If you make changes to the XSD schema file, remember that they will not be reflected back to the underlying DataAdapter. Any changes you make to the schema do not validate against the original data source.*

The second DataSet in our solution is a strongly typed DataSet. Working with a typed DataSet's XML source code works a bit differently. As you know, when you create a typed DataSet, VS .NET creates a class file containing the properties that map to column attributes. When you make edits to the XML source code, the class file and properties adjust accordingly. This synchronization slows performance in the design environment, because the class file regenerates in response to changes in the schema file.

Generating an XML File from an Existing DataSet

ADO.NET DataSets come with a `WriteXml()` method that enables you to persist your DataSet as an XML file. Let's go ahead and turn your `Customers` DataSet into an XML file. Then, later in this chapter, you can use this XML file to work with the various classes of the `System.Xml` namespace. To do this, create a new button on your form and in its click event, type the following:

```
SqlDataAdapterCustomers.Fill(DsCustomers1)
DsCustomers1.WriteXml("Customers.xml", XmlWriteMode.WriteSchema)
```

The `WriteXml()` method will create a new XML file called `Customers.xml` in the bin directory of your solution directory. We had to first fill the DataSet in order to create the XML data; otherwise, you would see only the inline schema within the `Customers.xml` file.

NOTE   *You won't see the XML file in the* bin *directory within your Solution Explorer unless you select the Show All Files option.*

The `XmlWriteMode` parameter enables you to specify how you want the XML file generated. This example uses the default `WriteSchema` enumerator, which indicates that you want your XML schema written inline.

Open the XML file within VS .NET to examine the results of the `WriteXml()` method. You can do this by double-clicking the XML file, which will launch the XML Designer. Listing 7.13 shows an excerpt of the well-formed XML encapsulating one of the customer records.

LISTING 7.13: AN XML EXCERPT GENERATED BY THE WRITEXML METHOD OF THE DATASET

```
<Customers>
    <CustomerID>ALFKI</CustomerID>
    <CompanyName>Alfreds Futterkiste</CompanyName>
    <ContactName>Maria Anders</ContactName>
    <ContactTitle>Sales Representative</ContactTitle>
    <Address>Obere Str. 57</Address>
    <City>Berlin</City>
    <PostalCode>12209</PostalCode>
    <Country>Germany</Country>
    <Phone>030-0074321</Phone>
    <Fax>030-0076545</Fax>
</Customers>
```

As we mentioned earlier, the XML Designer provides a visual representation of your data, as you can see in Figure 7.11. You can see this view by clicking the Data tab of the XML Designer.

FIGURE 7.11

The Data view of the XML Designer

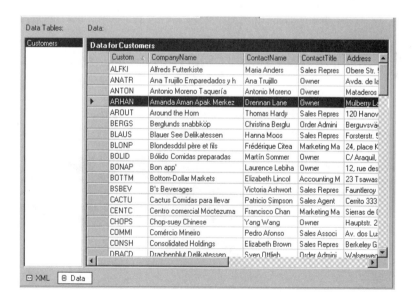

You have only one DataTable, the `Customers` table. If you had more tables, you would see them in the list box on the left, and you could iterate through data items in each one. You can also directly edit the data in the Data view, and your changes immediately synchronize with the underlying XML source file.

Loading DataSets from XML by Using the *ReadXml ( )* Method

The `ReadXml()` method of a DataSet enables you to load data from XML. As a parameter, one of its overloaded versions expects the XML filename that you wish to load. This method is useful for working with previously generated XML files that come from a legacy data source.

If a schema is provided, it is used for the relational structure of the DataSet. If no schema is specified, schema interference is used. *Schema inference* means that the schema is determined on-the-fly. To do this, the existing XML data file is examined to identify nested elements, which can be used to map tables and columns to form a relational representation of your data. Any non-scalar elements are mapped to tables, and attributes and scalar elements are mapped to columns. The inference process is not perfect, and can adversely affect performance and memory. The adverse effects to performance occur because multiple passes of your XML source are required to first load to the Document Object Model (DOM) and then again read the schema. It is much better to load the schema up front if you know it.

TIP   The full details behind XML schema inference are beyond the scope of this book. Just remember that if you know the schema ahead of time, use it, because XML inference comes with a lot of tricky drawbacks, such as improper inference and performance slowdowns. If you really need to infer the schema, do it the first time and save the schema file for subsequent use, rather than creating ad hoc schemas each time.

When you load data from an XML file, it's known as *shredding*, because your XML is parsed to identify significant elements and attributes that can be mapped to relational items. Any items that it can't map are disregarded, hence the name *shredding*, because you might end up losing vital information. Now that you have an XML file to work with, you can examine some of the `System.Xml` classes.

The XmlDocument Objects of the *System.Xml* Namespace

In this section, you will explore the fundamental objects within the `System.Xml` namespace that are used in conjunction with the ADO.NET objects. In addition to using visual tools to work with XML, you can also use the `System.Xml` namespace to programmatically design XML schema and data. Figure 7.12 provides a layout of the XmlDocument `System.Xml` objects that we discuss in this section.

FIGURE 7.12

The XmlDocument object model

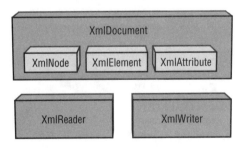

THE XMLDATADOCUMENT

As we indicated earlier, the XmlDataDocument object serves as a bridge between relational data format (ADO.NET) and hierarchical data format (XML). This object understands how to read both relational and XML data, and manipulate it. The XmlDataDocument inherits from the `XmlDocument` class, which uses the DOM representation of data as nodes. The XmlDataDocument is useful when you want to do XML transforms by using XSLT, or when you need to query the XML file by using the XPath specification. We discuss both XSLT transforms and XPath functionality in more detail in Chapter 12.

As we showed you in the preceding section, you could use the `WriteXml()` method of the DataSet to push the schema and data into an XML file. Then, you could use the `ReadXml()` method to retrieve the XML file back into the DataSet. However, this has one major disadvantage: it doesn't preserve the fidelity of your XML file. The order of your elements could be changed, white space could be added or removed, or certain elements and attributes could be lost. The `WriteXml()` and `ReadXml()` methods don't guarantee that your DataSet and XML file are synchronized. This is where the XmlDataDocument comes into play.

As you saw in Figure 7.1, the XmlDataDocument works in conjunction with the DataSet object, synchronizing changes from one to the other in real time. If you make changes to the XmlDataDocument, they will be reflected in the associated DataSet. The synchronization works both ways.

Instead of using the `WriteXml()` and `ReadXml()` methods, you can create a new XmlDataDocument to synchronize your XML file with your DataSet. You can construct the XmlDataDocument by using the following line:

```
Dim xmlDoc As XmlDataDocument = New XmlDataDocument(DsCustomers1)
```

Now you can display subsets of your DataSet and manipulate the data or schema without affecting the original XML source. If you used the `WriteXml()` method to pump the modified DataSet into XML, you would lose the formatting and structure of your original XML file.

NOTE   *To declare the XmlDataDocument without the full namespace, make sure you import the* System.Xml *class in your form declarations area.*

Why are XmlDataDocument objects useful? Imagine that you have a shipping and billing process that order information has to go through, and you need to hide certain elements of your DataSet as it evolves through the process. Imagine that the orders contain credit card information as well as shipping information. You might want only certain users to view that credit card information. Using an XmlDataDocument, you could display only a subset of that DataSet containing shipping information to a shipping department. You can do this by loading the appropriate schema mappings to the full document, which show only the data you want. You can view the relational subset of the data by using the DataSet's `ReadXmlSchema()` method to load a separate XML schema, which would provide you with the partial view of the full data.

After the shipping department handles the order, making necessary changes to the shipping status, you would like the data passed to the invoicing department. You could then display the credit card information to the invoicing department, without losing the changes made by the shipping department. The XmlDataDocument makes round-trip data transfers a reality—whether you are using relational or hierarchical data structures. The XmlDataDocument object not only enables you to preserve the fidelity of your original XML file, but also provides the ability to add customized views for security purposes.

Now let's explore how you can work with streams of XML data, much like you would with the ADO.NET DataReader object.

THE XMLREADER OBJECT

The XmlReader class enables you to read data from XML files. You can use the XmlReader to load data into the XmlDataDocument or a DataSet. Either way, your changes will be synchronized between the XmlDataDocument and its relevant DataSet.

The XmlReader works much like the ADO.NET DataReader object, providing fast, stream-based access to XML content. Like the DataReader, the non-cached XmlReader is a read-only, forward-only stream of data. The XmlReader works similarly to the Simple API for XML (SAX) model, using a stream-based approach that is more streamlined than the DOM standard. However, the XmlReader differs from the SAX model, because it doesn't use event-based parsing. The SAX model notifies the client for each XML item it reads, whereas the XmlReader can skip elements that you don't need to scan. This makes your XML parsing much more efficient. The XmlReader is useful for parsing through large XML files to find small subsets of data. In addition, the stream-based approach manages memory more efficiently, especially when working with large files. You should use the XmlReader implementation when you don't need to focus on a specific node of your XML file, and your requirements need to read your content nodes very quickly, off the wire.

NOTE *This section is not intended to be a full tutorial on the different XML models. We discuss the differences between the SAX and DOM models in Chapter 10, "The Role of XML."*

WARNING *The XML data read by the XmlReader must be well formed; otherwise, an exception will generate.*

Keep in mind, the XmlReader class is an abstract base class with interface definitions that you can extend by using other objects. One of the objects that implements this interface is the XmlTextReader, which you will use in your example to read the XML file containing your customer data. Alternately, you can use the XmlNodeReader object that enables you to navigate to a subtree of a specific node. Figure 7.13 illustrates how the various XML streaming objects work.

FIGURE 7.13

Reading and writing XML streams

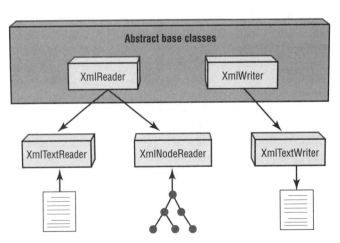

Let's use the XmlTextReader class to pull data from your Customers XML file to bring back a list of company names from your data. Add another combo box to the form. You will populate this combo box with company names by using the XmlTextReader object. In addition, create a new button on your form and add the code in Listing 7.14 to its click event.

LISTING 7.14: USING THE XMLTEXTREADER TO POPULATE A COMBO BOX FROM AN XML FILE (BUTTON9_CLICK)

```
Dim xmlTextReaderCustomer As New XmlTextReader("Customers.xml")

While xmlTextReaderCustomer.Read
    xmlTextReaderCustomer.MoveToContent()
xmlTextReaderCustomer.WhitespaceHandling() = WhitespaceHandling.None
  If xmlTextReaderCustomer.NodeType = XmlNodeType.Element Then
    If xmlTextReaderCustomer.Name = "CompanyName" Then
       ComboBox2.Items.Add
       (xmlTextReaderCustomer.ReadInnerXml())
     End If
   End If
End While
xmlTextReaderCustomer.Close()
```

First, you declare your XmlTextReader object, specifying the filename of your XML file. Like the DataReader, the XmlReader base class supplies a Read() method that you can use to loop through the XML data stream. The Read() method advances the internal pointer to the next node, returning True if a node exists.

The extremely useful MoveToContent()method enables you to quickly navigate to your data and schema nodes, skipping over unnecessary nodes such as comments or processing instructions. The WhitespaceHandling attribute is set to None so that you don't have to parse through insignificant white space. Otherwise, you would unnecessarily return blank spaces in the Name property of the XmlTextReader. By setting this, you speed up your processing. The two conditionals check whether the node type is an element; if so, you examine its Name property to see if it is a company name. After you find the company names, you add them to your combo box, by using the ReadInnerXml() method, which retrieves your data. And again, as with the DataReader object, you must close your XML stream by using the Close() method.

As you can see, much thought has gone into the .NET Framework to ensure that both ADO.NET objects and XML objects work in a similar fashion, reducing your learning curve when moving from one to the other.

THE XMLWRITER OBJECT

The XmlWriter object does the reverse of the XmlReader and writes well-formed XML streams from a specified data source. Like the XmlReader, the data is not cached. You could use the Xml-Writer to pull data from legacy data formats, such as EDI, into the more universal XML format.

Like the XmlReader, the XmlWriter is an abstract base class, and you can see how such implementations as the XmlTextWriter extend the XmlWriter class, as shown in Figure 7.13.

You can use the XmlWriter implementations to create your own custom schemas from scratch or to modify existing schemas programmatically. The best thing about the XmlWriter is that it provides a no-brainer method for creating syntactically valid XML documents that comply with the World Wide Web Consortium (W3C) standards.

WRITING DATASETS TO XML BY USING THE *EXECUTEXMLREADER ( )* METHOD

You stepped through the different Command execution methods in the preceding chapter, but we haven't really discussed the `ExecuteXmlReader()` method. You can generate XML data files by using the `ExecuteXmlReader()` method of the ADO.NET Command object. This method creates an Xml-Reader object, which is analogous to the DataReader object that you use with ADO.NET. We discussed the XmlReader object previously, so you should be familiar with working with its results.

The SQL statement or stored procedure used with the `CommandText` property should return results in XML format. You can do this by using the `FOR XML` clause in your SQL statement. We review how SQL Server 2000 works with XML in Chapter 10. We mention this method here because it often works hand in hand with the `ReadXml()` method we discussed earlier. For example, if you wanted to process the XML results of the `ExecuteXmlReader()`method, you could use the following statement:

```
dsCustomers1.ReadXml(cmdCustomer.ExecuteXmlReader(), XmlReadMode.Fragment)
```

This code will generate XML results of using the `ExecuteXmlReader()`method. It then loads these results into the DataSet with the `ReadXml()` method.

Summary

So far, you've learned how to manipulate databases through the ADO interface and to develop database applications. You should have a robust understanding of the various data access namespaces, such as `System.Data` and `System.Xml`. In addition, you should have a firm grasp of how to work with data sources, such as SQL Server, by using the advanced filtering, sorting, and searching techniques using either ADO.NET cached data or streamed data.

You'll continue exploring ADO.NET in the next chapter, where we discuss data-aware controls. You will expand the Northwind application to include data manipulation and updates through data binding techniques. In later chapters, you will evolve your interaction with the Northwind database by using the usual suspects for data manipulation: update, add, and delete data actions. After you understand the fundamentals of how the .NET Framework interacts with the database, you will be able to design efficient systems by using both Windows- and web-based functionality.

By now, you should understand how ADO.NET and XML tightly interlace to form applications that are readily consumable by other systems. This book contains two chapters entirely dedicated to XML and its related technologies. Chapter 10 discusses how SQL Server integrates with XML and how you can take advantage of this integration from ADO.NET. In Chapter 12, "Integration with XML," we again focus only on XML, teaching you more advanced technologies such as XPath navigation and XSLT transformations.

Chapter 8

Data-Aware Controls

- ◆ Data binding
- ◆ Data-aware controls
- ◆ Building data-bound controls by using a custom user control
- ◆ Using binding with a hierarchical DataGrid
- ◆ Updating the data-bound controls

A MAJOR ASPECT OF client applications is how they present data to and interact with the user. To simplify this aspect of client applications, the .NET Framework provides a number of data-bound and data-aware controls. In fact, data binding is one of the most powerful improvements in the .NET Framework, especially with server-side ASP.NET controls. Previous versions did not support disconnected data-binding by using web applications.

NOTE *Although this chapter focuses on Windows applications, we make comparisons to the web version of these controls wherever necessary. We discuss web-based data-bound controls in more detail in Chapter 17, "Working with WebServices."*

In this chapter, you'll learn how to build data-bound *user controls*, which are customized controls that contain nested constituent controls. *Constituent controls* are members of their parent container—a user control. User controls promote reuse and can shorten development time. Just as you can build custom, reusable classes for a specific database, you can build custom controls to simplify the user interface of the client application. The custom user controls you'll design can be used in multiple applications, giving each interface a consistent look. Custom user controls simplify the programming by embedding much of the functionality you need on the Presentation layer into custom components. If you're familiar with building custom user controls, you'll see how to turn different Windows Form controls into a data-bound control.

This chapter contains a bonus. Not only will you be learning about data binding, but you will also become familiar with the .NET implementation of shaping, by using the ADO.NET replacement for shaped RecordSets: the DataSet object. So far, all our discussions have centered around a single DataTable in a DataSet. You haven't worked with parent/child DataSets in this book. In this chapter, you'll learn how to combine data from multiple DataTables into a single data-bound control. Additionally, you'll understand how to work with DataRelations by using the XML Designer.

The best way to understand how something works is to see it in action. The applications of this chapter work with the Northwind database, which should be very familiar to you by now, as well as the Pubs database.

In our first example, you will create a customer user control that serves as a shopping cart for viewing customer orders. The shopping cart control uses two DataGrid controls to display master and detail records. Our second application demonstrates the features of the DataGrid control by using it to display data hierarchically. Last, we show you how to update, add, and delete data from your data-bound controls and commit them to your data source.

By the end of this chapter, you should be able to answer the following questions:

- How can you build a .NET user control?

- How does data binding work in .NET Windows Applications?

- How does Windows Form–based binding work differently from Web Form–based binding?

- How do .NET data-aware controls work?

- How can you work with multiple DataTables and DataRelations by using data-bound controls?

- How can you bind a data source to a DataGrid control?

- How do data controls commit updates, deletions, and additions back to the data source?

Data Binding

Data binding was quite powerful in both web-based and Windows-based systems prior to the release of .NET. The capability of data-aware controls to pull data asynchronously is especially handy for web-based applications, where performance is key. Because you can load the data in the background, your application can be more responsive, and your page load doesn't have to wait until all the data is retrieved. In addition, data binding reduces the number of trips that are made to the database server, because processing can be done on the client or Application layer.

Contrary to popular thought, data binding is not something of the past, nor relegated to only prototyping purposes. Depending on your requirements, data-aware controls might be the most optimal solution for your production application.

You have two ways to bind your controls: you can bind either a value or a list. The former is called *simple data binding*, which means that the control will show only a single value. You could use simple data binding to map the Text property of a TextBox control to the CustomerName column of a Customers DataTable. You aren't limited to only the Text or Value property of a control. A powerful feature of VB .NET is the capability to bind data to any property of a control.

The second type of data binding involves more than one value from a data source. This type of binding is called *complex data binding* because it works with lists of data rather than single values. We use the DataGrid control to show you how to implement complex data binding.

Data-Aware Controls

Data-aware controls are controls that are capable of being bound to a data source. When they are bound, they become (obviously) *data-bound controls,* which enable you to retrieve data from a data source asynchronously. You can use data-aware controls from both Windows- and web-based applications. Data-bound controls provide a programmatic way to load-balance data processing, so your database server isn't overly tasked. They do this by bringing the data to the client or middle tier, away from the web server. You perform actions on the data, locally, without making any network trips to the database server, nor asking the database server to do the processing.

Just as binding can be grouped into two categories (simple and complex), data-aware controls also can be differentiated as either *property-binding* or *list-binding* control types. The former involves simple binding a single attribute of a control to one value. Text boxes and combo boxes use property-based binding. The latter uses lists or a table interface to represent multiple data elements. Examples of this type of control are the DataGrid, ListBox, and ComboBox controls.

In the following examples, you will explore the data-related controls by using the `System.Data` namespace in ADO.NET. We show you how to quickly prototype your application by using the various wizards and data-bound controls. Web-based data-aware controls have come a long way in the .NET Framework.

You explored data binding briefly in the preceding chapter, getting a small taste of data-bound controls by binding a data source to a combo box. Now we expand that topic by showing you how to create your own custom user control that uses an advanced control such as the DataGrid

NOTE   *You will find all the source code for the examples in this chapter on the accompanying CD.*

Building Data-Bound Controls by Using a Custom User Control

Building data-bound controls is as easy as setting a few properties of a control. As we mentioned earlier, data-bound controls come in two flavors: text controls and list controls. Text controls are quite simple to use, and we don't spend much time on them in this chapter. Instead, you should be able to understand how to use the simple text controls after understanding how the advanced list controls work. You'll begin working with the list controls by creating a user control that contains some DataGrid controls.

A *user control* gives you the ability to create a custom visual interface that you can reuse from multiple projects. The UserControl class is part of the .NET Framework, and can be found in two namespaces: the `System.Web.UI` and the `System.Windows.Forms.UserControl` namespaces. To work with these controls, you use the `Inherits System.Windows.Forms.UserControl` or `Inherits System.Web.UI.UserControl` statement. To build a data-bound control, just put together a UserControl object with one or more *constituent controls,* which are the controls that make up your custom control's visible interface, and many of the properties of the custom control are delegated to the constituent controls.

What are you going to build in this chapter? First, you will build a shopping cart display control by using two DataGrid controls. A common metaphor for applications is that of the master/detail display. In this scenario, a user selects a single record from a DataGrid, and the details for that record are automatically displayed in the `Order Details` DataGrid control below the `Orders` DataGrid. The

Shopping Cart project uses the Northwind database to present order information for a specific customer. The shopping cart can be used not only to track orders, but also to track order fulfillments as well. Additionally, the shopping cart can be updated by the user to reflect additional orders or modifications. Now that you understand the business purpose of this application, let's go ahead and build it.

The Shopping Cart Project

Earlier, in Chapter 6, "A First Look at ADO.NET," we briefly mentioned that DataSets could be used to create a shopping cart data cache for an ordering system. You could use a DataSet to store a user's order information in a locally cached shopping cart, sending deltagrams to the database server when they update their order information. Now we'll show you how to do it. Let's start building a DataSet-based shopping cart by using a custom user control.

Begin by creating a new Windows Control Library project and typing **NWShoppingCart** in the name box. This project will contain your user control, which inherits from the System.Windows.Forms .UserControl class, as you can see from the code generated by VS .NET.

NOTE *Alternately, you could have selected the Web Control Library, which would create a web-based user control. We show you how to work with web controls in Chapter 17.*

Designing a custom user control has much in common with designing a Form. The first thing you see will be the User Control Designer, which works just like the Form Designer. You can drag and drop controls from the Toolbox, write custom code in the control events, and store nonvisual elements in the component tray. Rename the user control **NWShoppingCartControl** from the Solution Explorer or the properties window. Additionally, modify the class declaration for the user control to reflect this new name: **Public Class NWShoppingCartControl**.

User controls can't exist on their own; they must reside on a Form. Therefore, you need a Form on which to place the control before you can test it. It's a good idea to add the test project as early as possible, so add a new Windows Application project to the current project with the File ➤ Add Project command. Name the new project **TestProject**, and then name its Form **TestForm**. Alter the class declaration for the form as well, to **Public Class TestForm**.

Now, let's open the UserControl object in design mode. You are going to build a custom control, which displays the results of a one-to-many relationship between Orders and Order Details. You can do this by using a record/details-type interface, where you see the master record in the top half of the user control. As you select records in the top half, the respective details display on the lower half of the user control. Figure 8.1 shows the shopping cart for a particular Northwind customer; the orders for the customer are displayed in the top half of the user control.

Let's begin to build your user control. First, drag and drop a DataGrid control onto the user control. This will serve to display your master records in the top half of the screen. Name this grid **OrderGrid**. Drag another DataGrid control from your Toolbox and place it below the first DataGrid. Name this grid **OrderDetailsGrid**. The second DataGrid control displays the associated order details by referencing the OrderID for the selected order. Place the controls on the UserControl object, as shown in Figure 8.1. You can rearrange them on the user control as you like. The UserControl object, which is the "Form" of the custom control, should be large enough to hold the controls. Your final user control will look something like Figure 8.1.

FIGURE 8.1

Completed shopping cart user control

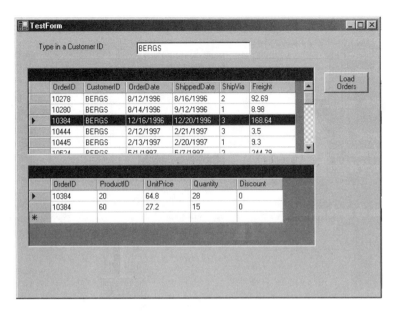

At the top of the form, add a TextBox control, which you will use to input the CustomerID. Clear out the Text property so that nothing displays in the text box. Next to the top DataGrid, add a button and set its Text property to Load Orders. You will use this button to programmatically bind your Orders DataGrid at runtime.

As you build your shopping cart user control, you are going to bind your Orders and OrderDetails DataGrid controls one at a time. You will use the Text value from your TextBox to retrieve data based on the customer ID. Finally, you will bind a ComboBox to the Customers table and use its CustomerID property secretly, behind the scenes, while you display the company name to the user. However, first you'll have to configure your data source controls.

CONFIGURING DATA ACCESS

To bind your controls to your data source, you need to configure your user control for data access. You should be able to do this with your eyes closed by now. You're going to use the Northwind connection, created in earlier chapters, to create a DataSet that can be used to persist your order information.

You are going to first build your DataSet with a single DataTable for the customer orders. Later, you will attach additional DataTables by using DataRelation objects to store your hierarchy. This way, you don't have to use joins, nested RecordSets, or shaping language to depict the hierarchical relationship between Orders and Order Details. ADO.NET's XML heritage enables you to store and display hierarchies naturally, without any forced joins or awkward shaping. Instead, you use the DataRelation and DataTable objects to enforce your relationships.

First, let's create your Orders DataSet. From the Data tab of the Toolbox, drag over a SqlDataAdapter control. Launch the Data Adapter Configuration wizard by choosing the Configure Data Adapter link in the properties box for the Data Adapter. After the wizard launches, select the Northwind connection and choose Next. The next screen presents the three options for your data access mechanism. This time, you are going to do something different from what you've done in previous chapters. Choose the Create New Stored Procedures option.

Why are you creating a new stored procedure? You use a stored procedure for your shopping cart so you don't pass unnecessary data across the network. Your shopping cart is customer-specific, so there is no need to bring back all the orders for every customer. Also, you improve your performance by placing your processing on the database server.

So now you'll create a stored procedure that retrieves order information for a particular customer. You want to use an input parameter for `CustomerID` in your stored procedure. You will then pass the appropriate `CustomerID` to your stored procedure by using the ADO.NET Parameter collection. Click the Next button and select the Query Builder button from the next screen to launch the Query Builder.

From the Add Table dialog box, choose the `Orders` table. Select the `CustomerID`, `OrderID`, `OrderDate`, `ShippedDate`, `ShipVia`, and `Freight` columns from the Query Builder.

In the grid window below the SQL statement, navigate to the criteria column for the `CustomerID` column. In this cell, type **@CustomerID**, which you'll use as a parameter. This way, you can set the value of the `CustomerID` from a VB .NET method in your application by using the `Parameters.Value` property of the SelectCommand object. For a web application, you could set the `CustomerID` from a Session variable or a cookie by using the same property.

Click OK to close the Query Builder. Click the Advanced Options button and then deselect the option to Generate Insert, Update And Delete Statements. In this example, you are not going to be updating your data. If you had chosen this option, VS .NET would automatically generate both the retrieval and action stored procedures for you in the database.

WARNING   *If you were displaying columns from multiple tables, you couldn't use the Generate Insert, Update And Delete Statements option, because VS .NET is not capable of generating action stored procedures with columns from multiple tables.*

Click the Next button from the wizard. A screen prompts you for information regarding the configuration of your stored procedures, as shown in Figure 8.2. VS .NET can automatically create stored procedures for you based on your `SELECT` statement. Additionally, you can view the stored procedure creation script and make modifications.

FIGURE 8.2

Creating new stored procedures from VS .NET

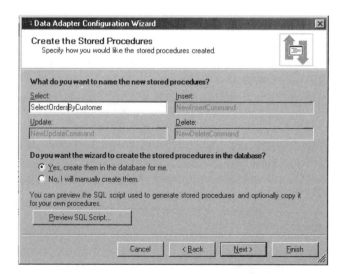

Rename the `Select` stored procedure to **SelectOrdersByCustomer**, leaving the other option with its default value. This saves the stored procedure to the database where you are going to modify it later. Click the Next button and finish the wizard.

The stored procedure code should be similar to the code in Listing 8.1.

LISTING 8.1: ORDER RETRIEVAL BY CUSTOMER STORED PROCEDURE (SELECTORDERSBYCUSTOMER.SQL)

```
CREATE PROCEDURE dbo.SelectOrdersByCustomer
(@CustomerID nchar(5))
AS
    SET NOCOUNT ON;
SELECT OrderID, CustomerID, OrderDate, ShippedDate, ShipVia, Freight FROM Orders
WHERE (CustomerID = @CustomerID)
GO
```

Now let's create a DataSet to work with. Click the DataAdapter control in the component tray and select the Generate DataSet command from its properties window. Create a new DataSet, naming it **dsOrders**.

Data Binding the *Orders* DataGrid

In this section, you are going use the newly created DataSet and bind it to a DataGrid by using the `DataSource` and `DataMember` properties. You might remember the `DataSource` and `DataMember` properties from VB6.

The `DataSource` property is used to bind a control to a specific collection or list, such as a DataTable, DataView, or single-dimension array. In fact, any object that implements the `IList` interface is a potential `DataSource`. Unlike classic ADO, in which you were limited to binding only to a RecordSet data type, ADO.NET allows you to bind to any type of data source, such as a list or array.

The `DataMember` property enables you to specify a subitem within the `DataSource` to which you bind your control. The `DataMember` property enables you to bind to nested subdata sources within the `DataSource` property. If you select a DataSet as your `DataSource`, then you might have multiple DataTables within that DataSet.

TIP   *In this section, you will set the properties individually for your DataGrid. You do this so that you can learn what each property does. However, a faster way to set these properties at runtime is to use the* `SetDataBinding()` *method of the DataGrid control. This method can set the* `DataSource` *and* `DataMembers` *by using input parameters. We discuss the* `SetDataBinding()` *method later in this chapter.*

THE POWER OF DATA BINDING

Although you might think data binding is a feature of ADO.NET, this is not the case. Almost any data structure can be bound to a control. You don't have to use only ADO.NET data sources. You can use anything that uses the `IList` interface, such as an in-memory array. As you know, XML plays a huge role with .NET, and you can use an XML data file as the data source, without ever referencing any of the ADO.NET objects in the `System.Data` namespace. You can imagine the flexibility that this gives you, because any type of data can be portrayed as XML. Data binding is truly a powerful mechanism, enabling you to treat any memory or file structure as a potential data-binding source.

You are going to use the `DataSource` property to bind your `Orders` DataGrid to the `Orders` DataTable. In the Declarations section of the user control, add a new method called `LoadOrder-Grid()`, as shown in Listing 8.2.

LISTING 8.2: BINDING THE ORDERS DATAGRID (LOADORDERGRID ( ))

```
Private Sub LoadOrderGrid()
    SqlSelectCommand1.Parameters("@CustomerID").Value = TextBox1.Text
    SqlDataAdapter1.Fill(DsOrders1, "Orders")
    OrderGrid.DataSource =
    DsOrders1.Tables("Orders").DefaultView
End Sub
```

Now, double-click the Load Order button created earlier and add the following code into its click event: **LoadOrderGrid()**. This method first populates your `CustomerID` parameter by using a value specified from your CustomerID text box. Then, you fill your DataSet, creating an `Orders` table containing your data. Then, you set your `DataSource` to the `Orders` DataTable by using its default view.

NOTE   *Alternately, you could set the `DataSource` property from the properties window of your DataGrid. Our examples focus on programmatic implementation at runtime, rather than at design time.*

WORKING WITH THE PARAMETERS COLLECTION

Don't try skipping ahead to test your user control quite yet. You won't be able to use the control until you supply the required `CustomerID`. You can do this by using the `CustomerID` property created earlier, passing its value along to the Parameters collection of the SelectCommand object.

Change the default value of the parameter added to the SelectCommand's Parameters collection by editing the code generated by VS .NET. Expand the Windows Form Designer–generated code region and change the last parameter of the `SqlParameter` property from `Nothing` to **CustomerID**. We've used bold text in Listing 8.3 to mark the relevant change for you.

LISTING 8.3: USING THE PARAMETER COLLECTION TO PASS A DEFAULT VALUE (WINDOWS FORM DESIGNER–GENERATED CODE)

```
Me.SqlSelectCommand1.Parameters.Add(New
    System.Data.SqlClient.SqlParameter("@CustomerID",
    System.Data.SqlDbType.NChar, 5,
    System.Data.ParameterDirection.Input, True, CType(0, Byte), CType(0,
    Byte), "", System.Data.DataRowVersion.Current, CustomerID))
```

This way, your CustomerID property will be passed to the SelectOrdersByCustomer stored procedure you created earlier. Again, you wouldn't normally hard-code this when your control is part of a full-fledged application that can supply this value for you. That's it! As you can see, binding to a DataGrid control is quite simple, requiring only a few lines of hand-typed code.

Now, if you want, you can skip ahead to the "Testing the Shopping Cart User Control" section to test your first binding attempt. For those of you who would like to see the complete application, keep on coding. Next, you are going to bind the OrderDetails DataGrid. However, first you must relate the OrderDetails DataTable to your Orders DataTable.

Binding the *OrderDetails* DataGrid

Now that you have created the Orders DataSet, you need to relate it to your previous dsOrders DataSet by using the DataRelation object. There is an easy way to do this. In the Server Explorer, navigate to the Northwind database and select the Order Details table. Drag the table onto the user control. This will automatically create a DataAdapter and Connection control in the component tray. Generally, when you want to work with more than one table from a database, you add another DataAdapter. You did this by dragging the Order Details table onto the design interface.

DIFFERENCES IN DATA BINDING BETWEEN WINDOWS AND WEB APPLICATIONS

Data-bound controls used by Web Forms work differently than those used in Windows Forms. The DataBindings property is used for Windows Forms, whereas DataBind() is used for Web Forms. The DataBind() method can be called from either the data-bound control or the Page object itself.

There is no explicit binding with Windows applications. In web applications, when you set the DataSource property, the control is not actually bound to the data source yet. In ASP.NET, you have to explicitly bind your objects by using the DataBind() method.

Whether you are working with web data-bound controls, you have to use the DataBind() method to actually bind the control to the data source. Before .NET, the data binding would occur automatically, giving you less control over your application. Although you could use server-side binding with ASP, it was COM based and built for traditional connected GUIs. In fact, the DataBind() method didn't even exist, and you would just work with the DataSource and DataField properties that served as binding mappings.

Continued on next page

DIFFERENCES IN DATA BINDING BETWEEN WINDOWS AND WEB APPLICATIONS *(continued)*

This automatic binding caused a lot of headaches. Because you couldn't determine exactly when the binding would occur, you couldn't manage state very efficiently, which is very important with web applications. By giving you power over when the binding is executed, you can manage state much more efficiently and add custom logic to determine exactly when you want to execute the binding.

Another difference comes from the fact that ASP.NET doesn't generate updateable data-bound controls. You have to write the custom update code yourself. This limitation arises from the need to ensure that a developer fully understands the ramifications of the update from the web application. By ensuring that you manually set up the update, you can ensure that the timing of the update meets your needs.

GENERATING THE *ORDERDETAIL* DATASET

Instead of using the properties dialog box for the Data Adapter to create your OrderDetail DataSet, let's try something new. Select the Generate DataSet command from the Data menu, as shown in Figure 8.3.

FIGURE 8.3

Using the
Data menu

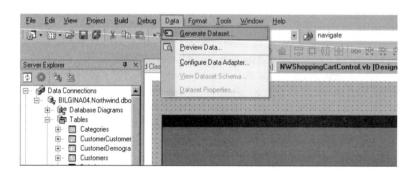

From the Generate DataSet dialog box, create a new DataSet named **dsOrderDetail**. You will see both the Orders and Order Details tables from the two DataAdapters in the dialog box. Select both of them, as shown in Figure 8.4; then click OK to add the DataSet to the user control.

ADDING A DATARELATION

Next, you need to configure your DataRelation object. To do so, double-click the dsOrderDetail .xsd file to launch the XML Designer. As you remember, you worked with the XML Designer in Chapter 7, "ADO.NET Programming." From the Schema view, right-click on the Order Details table, and select Add ➢ New Relation, as shown in Figure 8.5.

FIGURE 8.4

Working with multiple DataAdapters

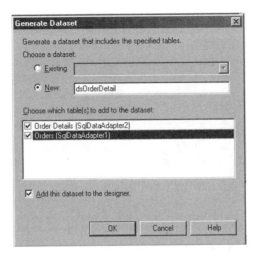

FIGURE 8.5

Adding DataRelations by using the XML Designer

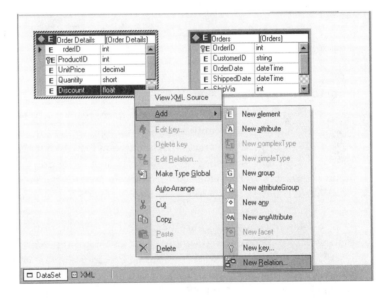

This launches the Edit Relation dialog box. You can rename the new relation anything you like. Next, set the Parent Element to the Orders table, and the Child Element to the Order Details table. The foreign key constraints should automatically map for you, based on the existence of the two identically named columns in both tables. If they don't map automatically, set the OrderID as the foreign key field. From the bottom of the dialog box, you can configure cascading updates or deletes, should you need to. The final configuration is shown in Figure 8.6. Click OK to accept the changes.

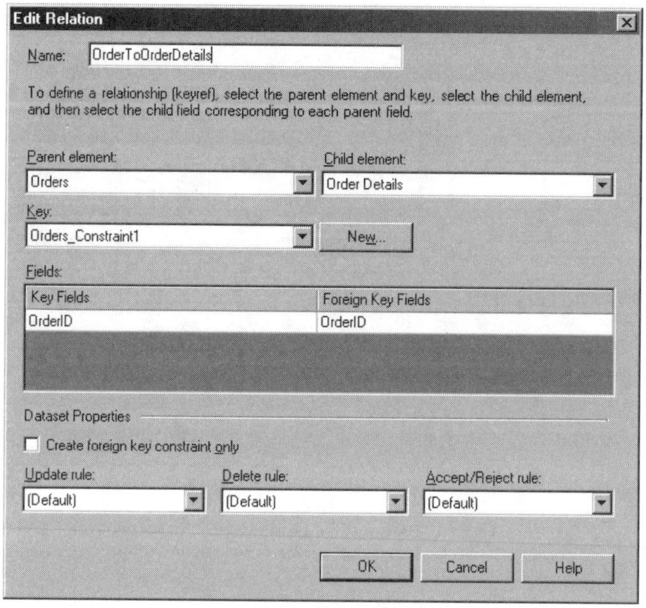

FIGURE 8.6

Configuring a
DataRelation object

ADDING AN INPUT PARAMETER

Your work is not through yet. Now you have to configure the OrderDetail DataSet to take into account the appropriate OrderID for which you want to show the details. To do so, you need to add an OrderID input parameter: right-click the second DataAdapter control (sqlDataAdapter2) from the component tray. From the pop-up menu, choose the option Configure DataAdapter. You need to adjust your DataAdapter to take into account the OrderID parameter. The Data Adapter Configuration Wizard launches. Skip through the introduction screen and connection screens to get to the Query Type.

By default, when you first create the DataAdapter, it automatically generates the appropriate SQL statement for you. Instead, you want to create a new stored procedure, as you did before for the Order DataAdapter. Choose the Create New Stored Procedures option and click Next. You will see the SQL statement that had been automatically created for you. Click the Query Builder button. In the criteria column for OrderID, add @OrderID as the value. This creates an OrderID input parameter, which you can later use to populate the appropriate OrderDetail records in your DataGrid. Click OK to accept these changes. Click the Advanced Options button to deselect the Generate Insert, Update And Delete Statements option, and click OK. Continue through the wizard by clicking the Next button.

On the next screen, you will be prompted for a name for your stored procedure. Use the name **SelectOrderDetailsByOrderID**.

You will see the resulting SQL statement displayed; it looks like Listing 8.4.

LISTING 8.4: THE SELECTORDERDETAILSBYORDERID STORED PROCEDURE (SELECTORDERDETAILSBYORDERID.SQL)

```
CREATE PROCEDURE dbo.SelectOrdersByOrderID
(@OrderID int)
AS
    SET NOCOUNT ON;
SELECT OrderID, ProductID, UnitPrice, Quantity, Discount FROM [Order
    Details] WHERE (OrderID = @OrderID)
GO
```

DATAGRID EVENTS

The next thing you need to do is hook into the events of the main Order Grid. You need to capture the CurrentCellChanged event as your user selects different rows in the Order DataGrid. This way, you can update your OrderDetail DataGrid based on the selected order record. Although we focus mostly on the CurrentCellChanged event, other events you might find interesting are the Load, Init, and Unload events, which are shared by all objects that implement the Control interface.

DATAGRID WEB FORM CONTROL VERSUS DATAGRID WINDOWS FORM CONTROL

Do not confuse the Windows Form DataGrid control that you use here with the one used for a Web Forms application. They are two different animals.

The DataGrid for Windows Forms inherits from the System.Windows.Forms namespace, whereas the web-based version derives from the System.Web.UI.WebControls namespace. Thus, the DataGrid controls in each type of application implement their own unique properties and methods. Although a full discussion of their differences is beyond the scope of this chapter, a brief overview of some of the main differences between the two implementations is warranted. We do this to avoid confusion if you ever try to reuse code from a Windows-based DataGrid for a web-based DataGrid, and vice versa.

The main difference is the way that the two controls handle the current column/row ordinals. In the web-based version, you can use the SelectedIndexChanged event to determine whether a user has navigated to a different item in the DataGrid list. The Windows Form version of the DataGrid control does not have such an event. In our examples, we determined the row and column ordinal based on the Current-CellChanged event, obtaining our RowNumber and ColumnNumber by using the CurrentCell property. The CurrentCell property is not supported with the web-based DataGrid.

Another difference comes from the way paging is handled between the two DataGrid classes. Unlike the Windows Form DataGrid, the web-based DataGrid supports a PageIndexChanged event. If you wanted to take advantage of the paging capabilities of the DataGrid, you should use the PageIndexChanged event to track when a user moves through pages of data records. Paging can heighten your response time when working with browser-based interfaces by limiting the amount of data that you bring back.

We discuss web applications in detail in Chapter 17.

Let's add some code to the CurrentCellChanged event in your OrderDataGrid. When you click on an order, you want to show the details in the DataGrid below. Let's set up a method that you will call from this event. In the user control Declarations area, add the method by using the code in Listing 8.5.

LISTING 8.5: BINDING THE ORDERDETAIL DATAGRID (LOADORDERDETAILS ( ))

```
Private Sub LoadOrderDetails()
    Dim intOrderID As Integer
    Dim intOrderOrdinalColumn As Integer
    Dim intOrderOrdinalRow As Integer
    Dim cellOrder As DataGridCell
    cellOrder = OrderGrid.CurrentCell ' Current order cell
    ' clear the OrderDetail DataSet
    DsOrderDetail1.Clear()
    'Clear OrderDetail DataGrid
    OrderDetailsGrid.Refresh()
    ' determine column - 0 indicates the order ID column
    intOrderOrdinalColumn = 0
    ' determine row
    intOrderOrdinalRow = cellOrder.RowNumber.ToString()
    ' get value of order id column for that row
    intOrderID = (OrderGrid(intOrderOrdinalRow, intOrderOrdinalColumn))
    ' use the order id value for the parameter
    SqlSelectCommand2.Parameters("@OrderID").Value = intOrderID
    SqlDataAdapter2.Fill(DsOrderDetail1, "OrderDetails")
    OrderDetailsGrid.DataSource = DsOrderDetail1.Tables("OrderDetails").DefaultView
End Sub
```

Next, you'll need to add some code to call this event from the CurrentCellChanged event of the Order DataGrid, as shown in Listing 8.6.

LISTING 8.6: USING THE CURRENTCELLCHANGED EVENT
(ORDERGRID_CURRENTCELLCHANGED)

```
Private Sub OrderGrid_CurrentCellChanged(ByVal sender As Object, ByVal
    ➥e As System.EventArgs) Handles OrderGrid.CurrentCellChanged
Dim intRowNumber As Integer = m_intRowNumber
m_intRowNumber = (OrderGrid.CurrentCell.RowNumber())
If m_intRowNumber <> intRowNumber Then
LoadOrderDetails()
End If
End Sub
```

Let's walk through this code. In the `CurrentCellChanged` event of the `Order` DataGrid, you first set a subroutine-scoped variable to capture the latest row ordinal value. The value is obtained from another variable, which is declared at the user control class scope. You can declare the `m_intRowNumber` variable by adding the following line within the Declarations section of the user control class:

```
Private m_intRowNumber as Integer
```

You then compare the two variables in order to determine whether the user has navigated to a different row. If so, you call your `LoadOrderDetailGrid()` method. So far, it's pretty simple. Now let's explore what you do in the `LoadOrderDetails()` method, as shown in Listing 8.5.

After declaring your variables, you first need to clear your DataSet and DataGrid controls to eliminate any residual data from previous runs. Next, you determine the current row by using the `RowNumber` property of the `CurrentCell` from the `Order` DataGrid. You hard-code your `ColumnNumber` to zero, because you know that represents the `OrderID` value. (In production code, you would determine this dynamically.) Then, you set the value of the `intOrderID` variable to the ordinals for the column and row that you set earlier. You pass in this `intOrderID` variable to your Parameters collection's `@OrderID` input parameter value. As you did for the `Order` DataGrid earlier, you then fill your DataSet, which brings back only the data you need from the `SelectOrderDetailsByOrderID` stored procedure, based on the supplied `OrderID` value.

BINDING FORM AND CONTROL ATTRIBUTES

A great use for data binding is retrieving application data for your user interface. You could store interface attributes, such as the height of a column, back color, or font size, in your database. Then you can bind control properties directly to this data and change your runtime user interface in real time. Data binding in the .NET Framework works with a binding collection. To specify the mapping, use the `DataBindings` collection, and add a new mapping between the data source and the control. If you wanted to map the Backcolor for a form to a column value in the database, you could use the `Add()` method of the `DataBindings` collection, like so:

```
frmMyForm.DataBindings.Add("frmMyForm.BackColor", DtAppData, "ColorNumber")
```

In this code, the first parameter of the `Add()` method specifies the fully qualified name of the property to which you wish to map. The second parameter specifies a filled DataTable. The last parameter specifies a string representing the column number that you wish to apply to the control property. In this example, we set the `BackColor` of a form at runtime based on dynamic data.

Instead of using the `Add()` method, you can opt to overload the constructor of the binding class and pass in the three input parameters to configure the mapping: the name of the control attribute, the data source, and the data source property. This way, you can take advantage of the ability to overload the constructor and create and configure the binding object with one line of code. After you create the binding object, add it to the Bindings collection of the appropriate control.

Your binding code for the DataGrid sets the data source property to your `OrderDetails` DataSet. After this is done, you can test this code to see what happens.

Testing the Shopping Cart User Control

To test the new control, switch to the test project and open its Form. Make sure that all the windows of the custom control (its design and code windows) are closed. From the Build menu of the user control project, choose Build.

In the Solution Explorer, expand the References node for the TestProject. As you can see, there is no reference to your user control. Right-click and choose the Add Reference option to launch the Add Reference dialog box. Select the Projects tab and click the Select button. After you do this, the Shopping Cart project appears in the Selected Components pane, as shown in Figure 8.7.

FIGURE 8.7

Adding a reference to a user control

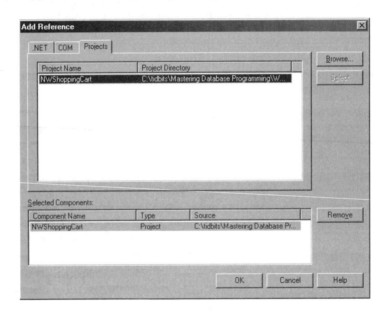

Because your references point to the project for the shopping cart user control, your changes to the user control will automatically be reflected within your TestProject. Click OK to close the Add Reference dialog box. Now the control will show up in the Windows Form tab within the Toolbox. There you see a new icon, which represents the control you just designed.

HOW TO CHANGE THE ICON OF A USER CONTROL

For those of you who aren't happy with the default icon for the user control, there is a way to change the image. The method differs from previous versions of Visual Studio. In the previous version of Visual Studio, you could change the control's default icon by setting its ToolboxBitmap property to a file with an icon—a .bmp file). In VS .NET, in order to change the icon for any control, add the desired bitmap file to the project. Ensure that the file is named the same as the control. In our example, the shopping cart user control is called NWShoppingCartControl, so you would call your image bitmap NWShoppingCartControl.bmp. The image must be 16 × 16, using 256 colors. Click the bitmap file in the Solution Explorer. From its properties window, change the Build Action attribute to Embedded Resource.

Place an instance of the new control on the Form and size it accordingly. To use real estate intelligently, open the Properties window for the newly added user control and set the docking and anchor properties. By doing so, you allow VS. NET to manage constituent control resizing when you resize the Windows Form container. Docking a control keeps it flush along the side of its container. Anchoring ensures that the controls stay proportional in size, respective to their container. Based on the type of anchoring you specify, an anchored control will stretch as the container is resized. You no longer have to write ugly resizing code to make your application look nice. Automatic resizing works superbly in Windows Forms. See for yourself by running the application and resizing your form.

Your solution contains two projects: a user control project and a Windows application project. You must set the `TestProject` as the project group's Startup Object. Right-click the test project's name in the Project window and select Set As Startup Project. Set the Startup Object to be `TestForm`. Then, press F5 to run the test project.

Now you can test your user control. After you load the orders into the top DataGrid, click on a different row. The bottom details DataGrid will change as you cycle through the different orders.

Using Lookups with a Data-Bound Combo Box

Data binding also is handy for lookup lists. In fact, you can even bind your control to show one data item, yet store a different value behind the scenes. You specify this by using the `ValueMember` property of your control. In our example, let's display the `CompanyName`, storing the `CustomerID` to use for your `Orders` DataGrid binding.

Let's improve your application by getting rid of the hand-typed `CustomerID` and instead use a ComboBox to bind to your `CustomerID` from the `Customers` table. You'll present a drop-down list of `CompanyNames`, and then store the `CustomerID` for the relevant company.

First, you need to create a DataSet for your customer data. Drag the `Customers` table from your Server Explorer window and drop it onto your user control, leaving the default name `SqlDataAdapter3`. This creates a new DataAdapter. From the properties window of this DataAdapter, generate a new DataSet and name it **dsCustomers**.

Hide or remove the TextBox from your form and add a new ComboBox, named **cboCustomers**, to the top of your form. Clear out the default text value of the ComboBox. In the user control's load event, add the code in Listing 8.7.

LISTING 8.7: POPULATING A LOOKUP COMBO BOX WITH DATA-BOUND VALUES (NWSHOPPINGCARTCONTROL_LOAD)

```
SqlDataAdapter3.Fill(DsCustomers1, "Customers")
cboCustomers.DataSource = DsCustomers1.Tables("Customers")
cboCustomers.DisplayMember = "CompanyName"
cboCustomers.ValueMember = "CustomerID"
```

Because you are no longer using the TextBox to retrieve the `CustomerID`, replace your TextBox code with the information you get from the new ComboBox. In the `LoadOrderGrid()` method, replace this line of code:

```
SqlSelectCommand1.Parameters("@CustomerID").Value = TextBox1.Text
```

with this line:

```
SqlSelectCommand1.Parameters("@CustomerID").Value = cboCustomers.SelectedValue
```

The `SelectedValue` property of the ComboBox will retrieve the `CustomerID` based on the item displayed in the ComboBox. Do not use the `Text` property of the ComboBox, because that retrieves the data that is displayed—in this case, the `CompanyName`. Experiment with this new code by pressing F5 to run your project. When you select a name from the ComboBox, the `Order` DataGrid should populate as soon as you click the Load Orders button.

Using Binding with a Hierarchical DataGrid

The previous Shopping Cart example is a good example of how to display parent and child records in sync by using two DataGrid controls. Alternately, you can take advantage of the hierarchical capabilities of the DataGrid control.

Next, you will build an application that works with a DataSet composed of multiple DataTables. You will bind the DataSet to a DataGrid and display the parent records and child records by using a hierarchical display. This lets you expand parent rows to access their related children. In addition, we'll show you how you can add, update, and delete the rows in the DataGrid.

Let's create a new solution by using a Windows Application. This time you will use a user control and a single DataGrid. You will use two DataAdapters to retrieve your data from the `Customers` and `Orders` tables. Then, you will set up a DataRelation between the two by using the XML Designer interface. When you set up your application, we aren't going to spend much time on the steps you've already run through. If you get confused about any of the steps, refer to the Shopping Cart application that you built earlier in this chapter. Don't worry, we'll take time to explain any functionality that you haven't worked with yet. In the end, you want your final product to look like Figure 8.8.

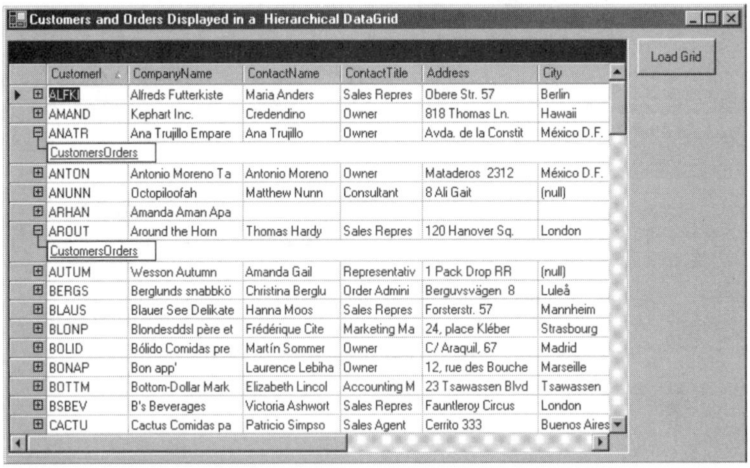

FIGURE 8.8

Customers and orders in a hierarchical DataGrid

Designing the Hierarchical DataGrid Application

Create a new DataGrid and Button on the form. Then, open the Northwind database node from the Server Explorer and drag the Customers table onto the form. This will create a new Connection and Customers DataAdapter control. Name this control **SqlDataAdapter1**. Do the same with the Orders table to create the Orders DataAdapter and name it **SqlDataAdapter2**. This time, only a DataAdapter control will appear in the Component Designer.

Now you need to create your DataSet objects. Click on the first DataAdapter control, and from its properties window select Generate DataSet. From the Generate DataSet dialog box, select both the Customers and Orders tables from each of the DataAdapter controls. Name your DataSet **dsCustOrders**.

From the Solution Explorer window, double-click the newly created dsCustOrders.xsd file. This launches the XML Designer, which you will use to relate your Customers DataTable with your Orders DataTable, much like you did before.

From the Data tab in the XML Designer, right-click on the Customers DataTable and select the Add ➤ New Relation option from the shortcut menu. Using the Edit Relation Dialog box, select Customers as the Parent Element, and Orders as the Child Element. Click OK to create the new DataRelation.

Next, you'll need to bind your DataSet to the DataGrid control. Previously, you used the DataSource property to create the binding. This time you'll try something new and use the SetDataBinding() method. This method enables you to reset the DataSource and DataMember at runtime. This function is useful if you want to display a different DataTable in a DataGrid based on specific runtime criteria. Listing 8.8 shows the code that you need to place in the button's click event.

WARNING   Keep in mind, the DataGrid is capable of displaying only one DataTable at a time. When you expand a parent row to display its children, instead of seeing the child rows, you will see a hyperlink with the name of the child table. When you click the link, the DataGrid will refresh to show the child rows independently of their parent table.

LISTING 8.8: WORKING WITH A HIERARCHICAL DATAGRID (LOADGRID_CLICK)

```
Private Sub LoadGrid_Click(ByVal sender As System.Object, ByVale As
    ➥System.EventArgs) Handles LoadGrid.Click
DsCustOrders1.Clear()
SqlDataAdapter1.Fill(DsCustOrders1, "Customers")
SqlDataAdapter2.Fill(DsCustOrders1, "Orders")
With CustOrdersGrid()
      .AllowNavigation = True
  .AllowSorting = True
  .SetDataBinding(DsCustOrders1, "Customers")
End With
End Sub
```

In our example, you first clear your DataSet to ensure that you don't populate it with redundant data on each button click. Next, you fill your DataSet by using both DataTables from each of the DataAdapter objects. To have the DataGrid display your records hierarchically, you must enable the `AllowNavigation` property. Additionally, you set the `AllowSorting` property to `True` so that you can click the different column headers to sort your data rows. Figure 8.8 shows the `CustomerID` sorted in ascending order, as indicated by the small gray arrow. Most important, you call the `SetDataBinding()` method to set your `DataSource` to a DataSet and the `DataMember` to a DataTable.

TIP   *For those of you who are VB fans, it is interesting to note that the* `With...End With` *construct is one of the unique VB .NET language nuances that C# doesn't support.*

Testing the Hierarchical DataGrid Application

Now that you have your code in place, press F5 to run the application. After you click the Load Grid button, your customer records will be displayed in the DataGrid with a small expander icon next to each one. When you expand an `Order` row, the children will not display within the same DataGrid. Instead, the DataGrid will be refreshed to display only the children rows. Again, a DataGrid is capable of displaying only one set of rows at a time. If you need to navigate back, use the Back button on the top right of the DataGrid.

Updating the Data-Bound Controls

What happens if you want to update your data-bound control? Updating DataGrid controls is quite easy when they are bound to a data source. Let's elaborate the previous application and allow updates to the hierarchical DataGrid.

When you edit the rows in the DataGrid, your changes are automatically committed back to the DataSet, but are not yet sent to the data source. You'll need to add some code that sends your changes back to the database. It's quite simple to send your deltagram back to the database. All you need to do is call the `Update()` method of the two DataAdapter objects. When you dragged your `Customers` and `Orders` tables to the form, all the action queries were automatically generated for you. The `Update()` method compares the deltagram with the database and updates the dirty rows by using the appropriate SqlCommand object. It's that easy!

Let's add another button, called Update, that will call this method of your `DsCustOrders1` DataSet. In it's click event, type the following two lines of code:

```
SqlDataAdapter1.Update(DsCustOrders1)
SqlDataAdapter2.Update(DsCustOrders1)
```

If you want to add rows to and from the DataGrid, just scroll to the end of the DataGrid until you see an empty row with an asterisk before it. (This works much like the Enterprise Manager in SQL Server 2000.) Add your data to the empty row and click the Update button to save your changes to the database.

DON'T YOU HATE USING YOUR MOUSE?

Sometimes using the mouse can be awkward when you are working with controls. Scrolling to the bottom of a large DataTable in a DataGrid can be time-consuming. For those of you who want to use shortcut keystrokes to work with the DataGrid, here is a quick list of common keyboard shortcuts that you can use instead of your mouse:

◆ The Delete key removes the selected row from the DataGrid.

◆ Ctrl+Home navigates to the top of the DataGrid.

◆ Ctrl+End navigates to the end of the DataGrid, where you can add new rows.

◆ Ctrl+ expands your parent row to expose its child DataTable.

◆ Ctrl- does the reverse and collapses the child DataTable.

Summary

This chapter concludes our discussion of data-bound objects. By now, you should feel comfortable working with the basic features of the ADO.NET objects, both programmatically and visually.

In the next chapter, we further elaborate on the DataSet object, explaining what happens "under the covers" when you work with DataSets in your applications. At the start of the next chapter, we segue nicely into a discussion about the Data Form Wizard, which also uses bound controls.

Chapter 9

Working with DataSets

- ◆ The Data Form Wizard
- ◆ The CommandBuilder object
- ◆ The TableMapping object

IN THIS CHAPTER, YOU are going to examine tools and technologies that revolve around the DataSet object. You might sigh exasperatedly: what else is there to learn? The answer is: a lot. We still haven't talked about the `Merge()` method, the CommandBuilder object, the TableMapping object, or the `EnforceConstraints` property. In addition, we haven't discussed other tools that you can use with DataSets, such as the Data Form Wizard or the Command Builder engine.

First, we review the Data Form Wizard, which uses advanced data binding, segueing nicely from the discussions of the preceding chapter. This section builds upon your binding knowledge as you examine the code generated from this wizard. In addition, you'll learn how to automatically generate the associated Command objects, which update your DataSet by using the Command Builder engine. Finally, we discuss how to use the TableMapping property, which separates the physical source from the logical representation of your data.

The Data Form Wizard

Those of you who have worked with Visual InterDev 6 (VI6) might find the Data Form Wizard familiar. The .NET version of this wizard conceptually advances the same tool from VI6; however, its features tightly integrate with ADO.NET and data-bound controls, saving you a lot of programming time and energy.

Using the Data Form Wizard to Create a Navigational Form

Like any other wizard, the Data Form Wizard has its pros and cons. The advantages stem from its automatic generation of so much code. The disadvantages stem from the same fact—that so much code is automatically generated for you. Never assume that you won't have to change some of the code generated by any wizard; however, by examining the working auto-generated code, you will better understand how all the objects of ADO.NET come together.

In this section, you will focus on the more advanced ADO.NET techniques, such as the `Merge()` method of the DataSet object, as well as the BindingContext objects that also generate from the wizard. Because you've already reviewed many of the fundamental DataSet methods and properties, we don't discuss them in this chapter. You can always review the previous chapters should you need a refresher. In Chapter 6, "A First Look at ADO.NET," we reviewed the object model of the DataSet, and in Chapter 7, "ADO.NET Programming," we reviewed how you can call stored procedures by using the DataSet object.

The Data Form Wizard enables you to quickly generate Connection, DataAdapter, and DataSet objects from your data source onto your Windows Application Form. The wizard engine automatically creates controls on the form that match the attributes of your data source and binds them to that data source. It will even type the controls to match the data types of the underlying data. As you can imagine, it's a quick and easy way to increase your productivity—and an excellent tool for getting started and prototyping applications. You can guess why we saved it for after the introductory ADO.NET material; otherwise you wouldn't have bothered to learn all that manual programming!

In this section, we create a working application that uses the Data Form Wizard to bind controls to the Pubs `titles` and `publishers` tables.

TIP   *The Data Form Wizard can be used with any application that supports forms, such as ASP.NET Web Applications.*

Let's begin examining this wizard by creating a new Windows Application project. Name the project **Using the DataForm Wizard**. This project is going to serve as a way to show the different attributes of a single publisher, with the titles belonging to that publishing house in a grid below.

After your new Windows Application is loaded, browse to the Solution Explorer and right-click the project name, **Using the DataForm Wizard**. Select Add ➢ Add New Item from the pop-up menu. This launches the Add New Item dialog box that you might remember from Chapter 3, "The Visual Database Tools;" you used this dialog to add new query files.

Select the Data Form Wizard icon from the dialog box and name the newly added form **PubTitles .vb**, as shown in Figure 9.1.

FIGURE 9.1

Using the Add New Item dialog box to launch the Data Form Wizard

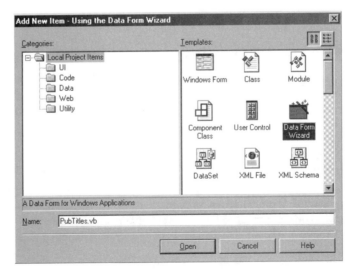

Click Open, which first creates a new form named, appropriately, after the name you typed in the Add New Item dialog box. Second, the Data Form Wizard launches with an introductory screen that you can skip by clicking Next. The following screen, as shown in Figure 9.2, prompts you for an existing DataSet or a new one. Because this is a new project, you don't have any preconfigured DataSets, so choose the Create A New DataSet option, naming the DataSet **dsTitles**, as in Figure 9.2.

FIGURE 9.2

Creating a new DataSet from the Data Form Wizard

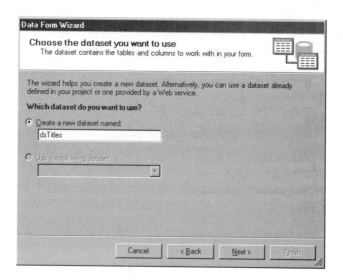

The next screen should be a familiar one; here you choose the appropriate connection for your ADO.NET Connection object. If you have been following along the examples throughout this book, you'll realize that you've created only a Northwind connection. (Those of you who have created a Pubs connection in a previous lifetime can skip this next step.) If you don't see the Pubs connection in the drop-down list, click the New Connection button. This launches the Data Link Properties window that you used in Chapter 3. Select the server name, authentication method, and the Pubs database, and click OK. You should now see the Pubs connection listed in the Data Form Wizard dialog box. Click Next to continue through the wizard.

The next screen prompts you for the database objects that you wish to add, as shown in Figure 9.3. You are going to choose two tables so that we can demonstrate how to add relationships between the two. For this example, use the `titles` and `publishers` tables. Double-click on each of these tables to move them to the Selected Item(s) box. Alternately, you can single-click them to select them and use the arrow keys to move them. Behind the scenes, this creates two DataTables: `titles` and `publishers`. Soon you will specify a DataRelation to associate the two DataTables to each other.

We'd like to point out an interesting fact regarding the Data Form Wizard. The forms and controls created by the wizard can be displayed in two ways: simple and complex. A *simple form* uses property-based bindings, such as TextBox controls, to map a single DataTable to a control. A *complex form* uses list-based bindings, such as a DataGrid control, to link multiple DataTables to list-based controls.

In this chapter, you will use multiple DataTables to generate a form with both property- and list-based controls. When you choose more than one table, the Data Form Wizard will generate a master and detail form much like the one you created in your Shopping Cart user control in the preceding chapter. You can opt to display the master data by using list-based controls or property-based controls. First, you will examine the property-based data-bound controls.

TIP *The Data Form Wizard can help you create relationships between DataTables without any code.*

FIGURE 9.3

Selecting database objects by using the Data Form Wizard

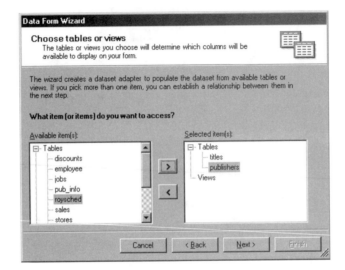

Click Next to navigate to the next screen in the wizard. Now you should see the Create A Relationship Between Tables screen, which Figure 9.4 displays. Don't be intimidated by the amount of information on this screen. Although it looks like a lot for a wizard, it's not much different from the Relationships tab that you used in the Table Property Pages dialog box in Chapter 3.

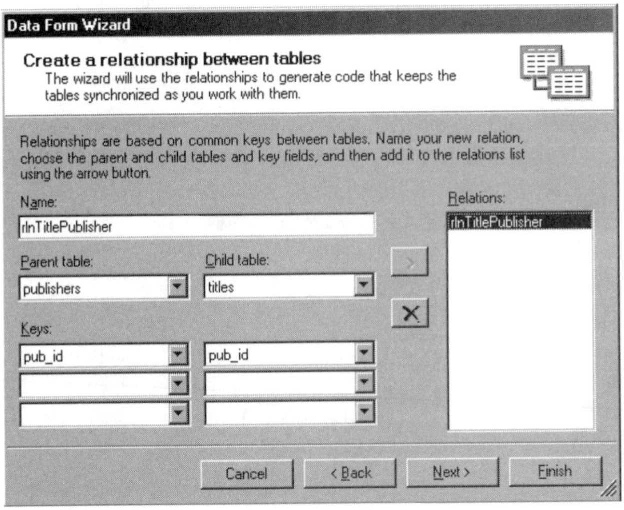

FIGURE 9.4

Creating relationships by using the Data Form Wizard

Specify a name for your relationship. We chose `rlnTitlePublisher`, but you can use any name you'd like. You want to link the `titles` and `publishers` tables together by using the `PubID` that they both share. For the parent table, specify the `publishers` table, because that's where the primary key for `PubID` is located. Use the `titles` table as the child table, because it contains the foreign key for `PubID`. This will automatically populate the list of columns for each table in the Keys drop-down list. Choose the `PubID` column for each table.

WARNING *Unlike the Table Property Pages dialog box, the Data Form Wizard does not automatically populate the primary and foreign keys based on column matches between your parent and child tables. You have to manually specify the columns you wish to relate.*

Click the arrow button to add the relationship to the list on the right-hand side. That's all you need to do to create a DataRelation. Your relationship will be stored, clearing the fields so that you can add a new relationship should you so desire. If you click on any existing relationship in the right-hand column, its attributes automatically display in the fields on the left. Additionally, you can delete existing relationships from the list. Later, you can examine this DataRelation from the XML Designer, via the XML schema file. Click the Next button to continue through the wizard.

WARNING *Don't click Next without hitting the arrow button. If you leave the Create A Relationship Between Tables screen without clicking the arrow button to save your relationship, your relationship will be lost and you will have to re-create it.*

Because you've chosen more than one table as your data source, the wizard prompts you to select columns from both the master and detail tables. This screen also gives you a chance to change your mind if you want to swap master and detail DataTables. Leave the defaults, using the `publishers` table as your master table, and the `titles` table as the detail table. Below the drop-down boxes for the table choices, you will see a series of check boxes that enable you to specify the columns you wish to display on the final form, shown in Figure 9.5.

FIGURE 9.5

Selecting the columns to display from the master and detail tables

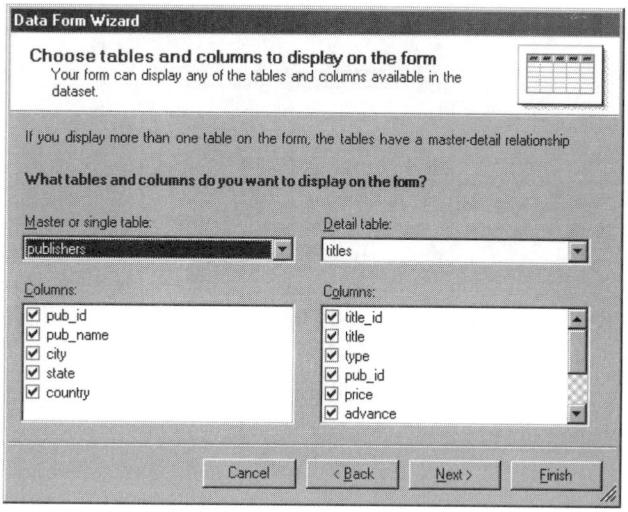

To keep things simple, just leave all the columns selected and click Next. The final screen prompts you for display information. You can choose to display the master and detail records in a grid or as a series of controls. The first option will display your master and detail tables by using two DataGrid controls. Alternately, you can select the second option, which enables you to scroll through your individual master records by using traditional navigation: Back, Next, Move First, and Move Previous.

Because you've already experimented with using two DataGrid controls in our Shopping Cart example from the previous chapter, let's spend more time with property-based controls. Choose the second option: Single Record In Individual Controls. After you select this option, the dialog box enables the bottom check boxes concerning navigation. These options let you specify which buttons you wish to see on the form. Because you want to see all the buttons, keep the default settings and click Finish.

After the wizard completes, you should see a fairly robust form containing the attributes of the `publishers` table, represented with various data-bound controls. Figure 9.6 illustrates the resulting form within the Form Designer.

FIGURE 9.6

Navigational form created by the Data Form Wizard

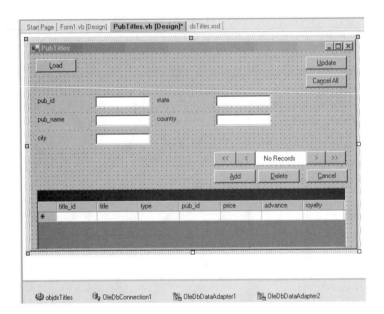

Each of the data-bound TextBox controls links to a column in the `publishers` table. You can investigate these bindings at design time by examining the Properties window for each control. In the Properties window, expand the `DataBindings` attribute, as illustrated in Figure 9.7.

The `DataBindings` property enables you to specify simple binding for the various properties of a control. Each binding maps a column value from the database to a property of the control. Altogether, these bindings comprise a DataBindings collection, which you can also access programmatically by using the `Control.DataBindings` class, which inherits from the `System.Windows.Forms` namespace.

FIGURE 9.7

Using the
`DataBindings`
collection at
design time

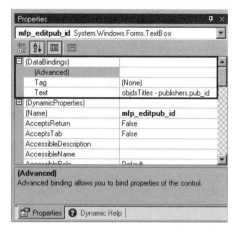

Click the ellipse next to the `Advanced` attribute, below the `DataBindings` property. This launches the Advanced Data Binding dialog box, as shown in Figure 9.8.

FIGURE 9.8

The Advanced Data
Binding dialog box

In this dialog box, you can set up simple-binding to the listed attributes for a control. This property-based binding enables you to dynamically retrieve control attribute values at runtime. In our example, the Data Form Wizard binds only the `Text` property for the `pub_id` TextBox control to the `publishers.pub_id` column value.

Below the data-bound controls, you will see traditional navigation buttons, which will maneuver you through the DataSet. In addition, you will see Add and Delete buttons that enable you to modify the DataSet. Keep in mind that any modifications you make will not be reflected in the database until you select the Update button.

Beneath these fields and buttons, you will see a DataGrid that contains the information in the publishers table. Unlike our Shopping Cart DataGrid, the publishers DataGrid is pre-populated at design time with the appropriate headers for the column names in the publishers table.

Take a look at the component tray and examine the nonvisual data controls that the Data Form Wizard generated for you. You will see a DataSet control that contains both the titles and publishers DataTables. (If you look in the Solution Explorer, you will see the dsTitles.xsd file, which represents the XML schema for this DataSet.) The component tray also contains two DataAdapters and a Connection control.

Why are there two DataAdapters? Each DataAdapter contains a TableMapping to each database table: titles and publishers. You can fill your DataSet respectively from each DataAdapter, ultimately combining the rows from each table by using the relationship you specified earlier.

As you might have already surmised, the Data Form Wizard is a powerful feature of VS .NET, saving you time spent on configuring the ADO.NET objects one by one. Instead, not only are they all created for you in one fell swoop, but you also get a tightly bound data form that lets you navigate through the data. Now you're ready to execute the application.

Testing the Data Form Wizard

Before discussing the code behind the form, let's execute the application and examine its behavior at runtime. Before you press F5, make sure you set your newly generated form as the startup form. You can do so by right-clicking your project in the Solution Explorer and selecting Properties. This displays the Properties Pages window for this project, as shown in Figure 9.9.

FIGURE 9.9

Specifying the startup form from the project Properties window

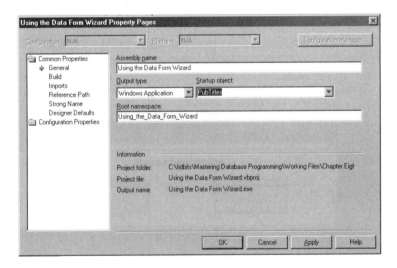

From the Properties window, click the Startup Object drop-down list and select the PubTitles form. Click the Apply button and then click OK. You might want to resize your form and DataGrid so you can see your data a bit better. Feel free to delete the unused form, Form1, from your project.

After you configure the controls to display the way you would like, press F5 to run the application. After the application is loaded, click the Load button at the top of the form to load your `titles` DataTable. Behind the scenes, the Load button calls the `Fill()` method of your DataAdapter objects, populating the DataSet with data from both tables. The populated form should look like Figure 9.10.

FIGURE 9.10

Using a navigational form generated by the Data Form Wizard

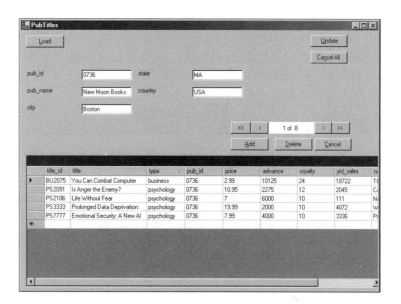

After the data loads into the form, you can use the navigation buttons to scroll through the data. As you scroll from title to title, you will see the relevant publisher information in the detail DataGrid. You can even edit the data in either the `titles` or `publishers` table. If you want to add a new title to the `titles` table, all you have to do is click the Add button, which will clear all the data-bound fields at the top. Feel free to add a new title and click the Update button to save the information to the Pubs database. As you might have already guessed, the Data Form Wizard not only binds your controls to your database, but also automatically creates methods that cycle through, add, and delete data records. Additionally, after you create a new title, you can add the related publisher information into the DataGrid, by using the methods we showed you in the previous chapter for our hierarchical DataGrid application.

WARNING *The Data Form Wizard creates editable data for Windows form-based applications. When you work with Web Applications, many of the auto-generated functionalities for database updates will not be available.*

Experiment with the runtime navigational form that results from the Data Form Wizard. When you're through, you can examine some of the methods that were generated.

Examining the Code Generated by the Data Form Wizard

In this section, we present the auto-generated code, pausing only to explain new concepts to you. By now, you should recognize a lot of the traditional ADO.NET methods, such as Fill() and Update(). The best way to understand new methods and properties is to see them in context, which you can do by examining the code generated by the Data Form Wizard.

LOADING A DATASET

Open the code behind the PubTitles.vb form and navigate to the LoadDataSet() method. This method is called when you click the Load button. Listing 9.1 shows you the code from this method.

LISTING 9.1: THE *LOADDATASET ()* METHOD

```
Public Sub LoadDataSet()
  Dim objDataSetTemp As Using_the_DataForm_Wizard.dsTitles
  objDataSetTemp = New Using_the_DataForm_Wizard.dsTitles()

  Try
     'Execute the SelectCommand on the
     DatasetCommmand and fill the dataset
    Me.FillDataSet(objDataSetTemp)
  Catch eFillDataSet As System.Exception
     'Add exception handling code here.
  Throw eFillDataSet
  End Try

  Try
     'Merge the records that were just pulled
      from the data store into the main dataset
     objdsTitles.Merge(objDataSetTemp)
  Catch eLoadMerge As System.Exception
     'Add exception handling code here
     Throw eLoadMerge
  End Try
End Sub
```

The first Try/Catch block calls the FillDataSet() method, passing the temporary DataSet object. You'll explore the FillDataSet()code shortly. The temporary DataSet is used to retrieve current data from the database by using the Fill() methods of the DataAdapters. Then, you combine the refreshed DataSet with the main DataSet by using the Merge() method.

The Merge() *Method*

The Merge()method combines two DataSets with similar schema. The temporary, source DataSet containing all current data is merged into the local, target DataSet so that you end up with a fully reconciled DataSet. This way, you won't lose any of your local DataSet additions, yet ensure that you are working with current database data.

There is an important caveat to note here: only additions will be preserved. You can see this for yourself by running the code and adding a new title to the first publisher. Don't click the Update button to send your changes back to the database. Instead, click the Load button. You will see that your rows are preserved because the `Merge()` method combines them back into the original, target DataSet.

However, this is not the case for updates. If you update or delete an existing publisher or title record, when you click the Load button, your changes will be overridden by the database data.

The Data Form Wizard uses one implementation of the `Merge()` method, which accepts only the source DataSet as a parameter. Optionally, you can use another implementation of the `Merge()` method, which accepts a Boolean flag, `PreserveChanges`; this indicates whether you want to keep your changes to your target DataSet.

Change the line containing the merge call to the following:

```
objdsTitles.Merge(objDataSetTemp, True)
```

Now run the code and update a publisher or title record. Click the Load button. You will see that your modifications are not lost.

Let's go back to the first `Try/Catch` block, where you populate your DataSet. The code behind the `FillDataSet()` method is shown in Listing 9.2.

LISTING 9.2: THE *FILLDATASET* () METHOD

```
Public Sub FillDataSet(ByVal dataSet As Using_the_DataForm_Wizard.dsTitles)
  Me.OleDbConnection1.Open()
  dataSet.EnforceConstraints = False
  Try
    Me.OleDbDataAdapter1.Fill(dataSet)
    Me.OleDbDataAdapter2.Fill(dataSet)
  Catch fillException As System.Exception
  Throw fillException
  Finally
    dataSet.EnforceConstraints = True
    Me.OleDbConnection1.Close()
  End Try
End Sub
```

As you can see, the `FillDataSet()` method populates a temporary DataSet with data from both the `titles` and `publishers` tables, by using each of the two DataAdapters. Based on our explanations from the previous chapter, this code should be pretty familiar to you. The only property new to you is the `EnforceConstraints` property.

The EnforceConstraints *Property*

The default value for this property is `True`. By setting `EnforceConstraints` to `False` prior to filling your DataSet, the code turns off any rules for that table. This prevents any `ConstraintExceptions` from being generated. You must set this to `False` when you combine your two tables into a single DataSet.

UPDATING THE DATASET

The code generated for the DataSet update is inherently more complex. If you look at the code behind the Update button's click event, you will see that the `UpdateDataSet()` method is called. Let's see what happens there by walking through the code shown in Listing 9.3.

LISTING 9.3: THE *UPDATEDATASET ()* METHOD

```
Public Sub UpdateDataSet()
  'Get a new dataset that holds only the changes that have been made to the main
dataset
  Dim objDataSetChanges As
    Using_the_DataForm_Wizard.dsTitles = New
    Using_the_DataForm_Wizard.dsTitles()
  Dim objDataSetUpdated As System.Data.DataSet = New
    Using_the_DataForm_Wizard.dsTitles()
  'Clear out the current edits
  Me.BindingContext(objdsTitles, "publishers").EndCurrentEdit()
  Me.BindingContext(objdsTitles, "titles").EndCurrentEdit()
  'Get a new dataset that holds only the changes that have
   been made to the main dataset
  objDataSetChanges = CType(objdsTitles.GetChanges,
   Using_the_DataForm_Wizard.dsTitles)
  'Check to see if the objCustomersDatasetChanges holds any
   records
  If (Not (objDataSetChanges) Is Nothing) Then
    Try
      'Call the update method passing in the dataset and any
       parameters
      Me.UpdateDataSource(objDataSetChanges)
    Catch eUpdate As System.Exception
    Throw eUpdate
    End Try

    'Merge the returned changes back into the main dataset
    Try
      objdsTitles.Merge(objDataSetUpdated)
    Catch eUpdateMerge As System.Exception
      'Add exception handling code here
```

```
    Throw eUpdateMerge
    End Try

  'Commit the changes that were just merged
  'This moves any rows marked as updated, inserted or
   changed to being marked as original values
  objdsTitles.AcceptChanges()
  End If
End Sub
```

Don't be intimidated by the lengthy listing. In summary, only four basic steps occur throughout this code:

◆ Current edits are finalized by using the `BindingContext` property.

◆ The changes to the in-memory DataSet are stored into a temporary DataSet, which contains only the changed DataTables and DataRows.

◆ If changes exist, they are sent to the database, committing the DataTable deltagram by using the `GetChanges()` method.

◆ The newly updated DataSet from the database is merged with the in-memory changes from the local DataSet

When you break the code down like this, it is much easier to digest. Let's go through each of these steps, paying close attention to any new concepts.

Finalizing Edits by Using the BindingContext *Property*

Before you begin your update process, you must first ensure that you don't leave the user in the middle of an edit. Otherwise, the edit will be lost and the user will be confused. To commit the edit to memory, you must call the `EndCurrentEdit()`method. This method belongs to the BindingManagerBase object, whose collection is managed via the `BindingContext` property.

The `BindingContext` property belongs to the Control class. Your form inherits from the Control class, and you use its `BindingContext` to manage all the data-bound controls contained within the form. The `BindingContext` property "understands" how each control maps back to your `titles` and `publishers` DataTables.

By using the `EndCurrentEdit()`method of your `BindingContext` property, you can manage the state of the data-bound controls. You call this method for both the `titles` and `publishers` DataTables, as such:

```
Me.BindingContext(objdsTitles, "publishers").EndCurrentEdit()
Me.BindingContext(objdsTitles, "titles").EndCurrentEdit()
```

The `BindingContext` property provides a single point of reference for your form, enabling you to manage all the data-bound controls at once. Additionally, you can use the `Position` property of the `BindingContext` to determine the user's navigation point within each DataTable. You use this property when you navigate through your DataTable by using your navigation buttons. For example, the

Next button uses the `BindingContext.Position` property to move to the next record in your DataSet by using the following code:

```
Me.BindingContext(objdsTitles, "publishers").Position =
(Me.BindingContext(objdsTitles, "publishers").Position + 1)
```

Committing the DataTable Deltagram by Using the GetChanges ( ) Method

After finalizing your edits, you now update the database. The code in Listing 9.3 calls the `UpdateDataSource()` method, passing in a deltagram contained within a DataSet object. In Listing 9.4, we display the code within the `UpdateDataSource()` method.

LISTING 9.4: THE *UPDATEDATASOURCE ( )* METHOD

```
Public Function UpdateDataSource(ByVal dataSet As
Using_the_DataForm_Wizard.dsTitles) As System.Int32
  Me.OleDbConnection1.Open()

  Dim UpdatedRows As System.Data.DataSet
  Dim InsertedRows As System.Data.DataSet
  Dim DeletedRows As System.Data.DataSet
  Dim AffectedRows As Integer = 0

  UpdatedRows =
     dataSet.GetChanges
     (System.Data.DataRowState.Modified)
  InsertedRows =
    dataSet.GetChanges
    (System.Data.DataRowState.Added)
  DeletedRows =
    dataSet.GetChanges
    (System.Data.DataRowState.Deleted)
  Try
     If (Not (UpdatedRows) Is Nothing) Then
       AffectedRows =
        OleDbDataAdapter1.Update(UpdatedRows)
       AffectedRows =
       (AffectedRows +
        OleDbDataAdapter2.Update(UpdatedRows))
     End If

     If (Not (InsertedRows) Is Nothing) Then
       AffectedRows =
       (AffectedRows +
         OleDbDataAdapter1.Update
           (InsertedRows))
       AffectedRows =
       (AffectedRows +
```

```
        OleDbDataAdapter2.Update
        (InsertedRows))
    End If

    If (Not (DeletedRows) Is Nothing) Then
      AffectedRows =
      (AffectedRows +
       OleDbDataAdapter1.Update
        (DeletedRows))
      AffectedRows =
      (AffectedRows +
       OleDbDataAdapter2.Update
        (DeletedRows))
    End If
  Catch updateException As System.Exception
  Throw updateException
  Finally
    Me.OleDbConnection1.Close()
  End Try
End Function
```

As for the previous listing, you can break this code into a few simple steps:

◆ The `GetChanges()` method is used to store updated DataRows into a new DataSet object.

◆ The `GetChanges()` method is used to add inserted DataRows into a new DataSet object.

◆ The `GetChanges()` method is used to remove deleted DataRows from the new DataSet object.

◆ If any of these DataSets contain data, the `Update()` method of each DataAdapter object sends each deltagram to the database.

You can combine these three steps into one explanation, because they all use the same `GetChanges()` method along with the `DataRowState` property. Basically, they just poll the DataSet for any modifications, submitting the deltagram to the new DataSet.

TIP   The ability to divide your deltagram into additions, deletions, and updates gives you granular control for updating your database. You can change the sequence for each of these modifications. For example, you might want your updates committed after all row additions occur, when your business rules require that updates to existing rows depend upon newly added rows.

As you remember from Chapter 6, the `DataRowState` property enables you to identify DataRows with specific states (Modified, Added, and Deleted). You can then use the `GetChanges()` method to capture these rows into a DataSet.

This type of processing is very efficient, because it reduces the amount of memory used by your application server, by working only with changed data rather than the full DataSet. By using only a subset of the DataSet, you also minimize your network traffic to your database, by sending only modified data back to the database.

By splitting the deltagram into Modified, Added, and Deleted records, you can add specific business logic that is applicable to each function. You might want to ensure that the publication date for a new title meets a certain date range. By encapsulating only the additions into a separate DataSet, you can focus your business logic on only the relevant deltagram. If you find a record that conflicts with your business rules, you can skip the call to the Update() method for the appropriate DataAdapter. Again, this saves you from unnecessary network traffic and lightens the processing load on the database server.

The code in Listing 9.4 checks whether data exists for each DataRow state. If the DataSet contains data, the Update() methods are called.

Merging Changes Back to the In-Memory DataSet

After your changes are committed to the database, you merge the updated DataSet back into the local DataSet. Because we already explained the Merge() method earlier, we won't rehash the functionality.

Using the Data Form Wizard to Create a List-Based Form

In this section, you'll explore the code that the Data Form Wizard generates if you choose the other display option, which displays the data in two DataGrid controls. The Data Form Wizard automatically generates a similar interface to the Shopping Cart project that you had to manually program in the previous chapter.

Let's use the same DataSet from our previous example to create a new form by using the Data Form Wizard. As before, right-click your project file and select Add New Item. Select the Data Form Wizard to create a new form and name it **PubTitlesGrid.vb**. Again, this launches the wizard. After the introduction screen, you will be prompted to choose a DataSet. Because you already have an existing DataSet, you will see it listed in this screen, as shown in Figure 9.11. (Note that the DataSet name is prefixed with the name of the project.)

FIGURE 9.11

Selecting an existing DataSet from the Data Form Wizard

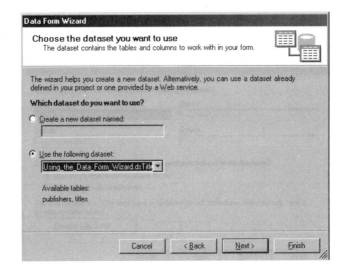

If you take a close look at this screen, you will notice that not only is the DataSet displayed, but also the DataTables that make up the DataSet; in our case, this would be the `titles` and `publishers` tables. Because this is the DataSet you wish to use, click the Next button to continue through the wizard.

The next screen prompts you for the methods you wish to use to fill and update the DataSet, as illustrated in Figure 9.12. You see this screen because the first iteration of the Data Form Wizard has already created methods that contain the `Fill()` and `Update()` methods to manipulate your DataSet. Respectively, these are called the `FillDataSet()` and `UpdateDataSource()` methods. By selecting the appropriate methods, as shown in Figure 9.12, you can leverage your existing code base. You want to be able to update your data, so select the check box to Include An Update Button, and select the `UpdateDataSource()` method from the drop-down list. Click the Next button to continue to the next screen.

FIGURE 9.12

Selecting methods to fill and update an existing DataSet

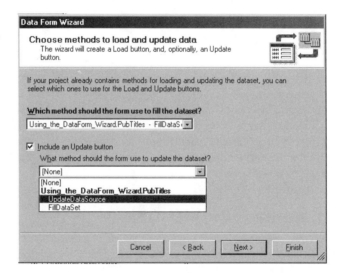

The following screen is identical to the one you saw previously in Figure 9.5, where you specify the master and child table, as well as the columns you wish to display. Use the `publishers` table as the parent table, and the `titles` table as the detail table.

After you click the Next button, you will see another familiar screen, shown in Figure 9.6, which enables you to specify how you wish to display your form. This time, you want to use the All Records In A Grid option. After you click the Finish button, a new Windows Form will be created, containing two DataGrid objects, which encapsulate both the parent table and the detail table. Additionally, you will see a new DataSet object in your component tray. Because VS .NET can reuse data objects from other forms, there is no need to create the DataAdapter objects or the Connection object.

As you might remember from the previous chapter, you manually created this code programmatically. You had to write code to set up your data access, bind your controls, and hook your control events. You can see how much time the Data Form Wizard saves you by auto-generating all that code.

Because we spent the last chapter reviewing how two DataGrid objects work in conjunction to display master and detail records, we will leave it up to you to execute the code and experiment with the behavior of this form. Make sure you set your startup form to this new form before running the project. The final execution should look like Figure 9.13.

FIGURE 9.13

Binding two DataGrid objects by using the Data Form Wizard

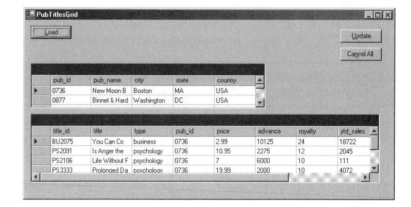

Using wizards not only saves development time, but also provides a way to learn new concepts by using functional code. After you understand the concepts behind the code, you can leverage this knowledge to build highly customized and sophisticated applications. There are a few more DataSet-related topics that warrant discussion—let's switch gears and discuss the CommandBuilder and TableMapping objects.

The CommandBuilder Object

Although the CommandBuilder object works with DataAdapter objects, we discuss it in this chapter because it affects how your DataSet updates data. The CommandBuilder uses inference to determine UPDATE, DELETE, and INSERT SQL commands that are not defined at design time. Additionally, the CommandBuilder can be used as the ADO.NET replacement for the batch updates you used with classic ADO RecordSets.

The CommandBuilder object enables ADO.NET to generate ad hoc Command objects at run-time. It relies on the SQL code from a SelectCommand object, using it to create the appropriate update, delete, and add methods to send your changes back to the database.

WARNING *The SelectCommand object is mandatory when using the CommandBuilder. VS .NET cannot use inference to create the appropriate SQL SELECT statement. Additionally, the results from the SelectCommand must return the primary key of the underlying table. The primary key is used for the WHERE clause of the DELETE and UPDATE statements. Otherwise, the CommandBuilder wouldn't be able to uniquely identify the specific rows you wish to update or delete.*

NOTE *If a primary key does not exist for the underlying table, you can use a unique column. As you remember from Chapter 2, "Basic Concepts of Relational Databases," it's generally a good practice to use a primary key.*

You can think of the CommandBuilder as a way to perform batch updates on your data source. Behind the scenes, the CommandBuilder queries the database by using the SelectCommand in order to retrieve the schema of the underlying table. Additionally, the CommandBuilder prepares the table for a batch update by creating hidden timestamp columns and specifying optimistic concurrency with the `SET NO_BROWSETABLE ON` command.

The CommandBuilder should be used sparingly because it requires an additional network call to the database server in order to retrieve the database schema. The database structure is then reconciled with the SelectCommand SQL statement to determine the appropriate ad hoc action queries.

The CommandBuilder object comes in handy when you want to quickly prototype your data manipulation without having to write the SQL statements by hand. Additionally, you can use the CommandBuilder object when you don't know the database structure at design time. This could happen if you are dynamically setting your data source at runtime, or if you expect your database structure to change over time and you don't want to change your VB .NET code.

There are performance penalties for using the CommandBuilder because additional processing is required to derive the appropriate Command object queries. You also give up a degree of control within your SQL statements, because you can't add the custom business logic to the action queries, as you could with stored procedures.

In this section, you will use the CommandBuilder object programmatically by using a preexisting DataSet. First, you will need to create a new Windows Application. In the Form Declaration section, import the `SqlClient` namespace, by adding this line of code:

```
Imports System.Data.SqlClient
```

NOTE *The code for this example is found in the solution file* `Using the Command Builder Object.sln` *on the accompanying CD.*

The CommandBuilder works with a single table within a DataTable. You want to ensure that only a SelectCommand is created for your DataAdapter. The easiest way to do this is to drag and drop a SqlDataAdapter control from the Toolbox onto your form. Navigate through the Data Adapter Configuration Wizard, choosing the Pubs connection as your Connection object. When you reach the Choose A Query Type screen, select the Use SQL Statement option and click Next. Type the following SQL statement into the next screen:

```
SELECT * FROM Authors
```

WARNING *You cannot use the CommandBuilder objects when you are using multiple tables, which include* `JOIN` *clauses.*

From the Advanced Options button, deselect the Generate Update, Insert and Delete Statements option. This way, you will have only a single SelectCommand object generated. After you complete the wizard, you will see a new SqlDataAdapter and SqlConnection object in your component tray.

Now you have to create a DataSet by using your DataAdapter. From the Properties window of the SqlDataAdapter, click the Generate DataSet option and name your DataSet **dsAuthors**.

Now you need an interface to update your DataSet. Create a DataGrid object on your form and set its DataSource property from the Properties window to **DsAuthors1.authors**. Your DataGrid column headers should automatically populate with the schema for each column from the underlying DataTable.

Create a new button on your form, setting its Text property to **Load DataGrid** and type the code in Listing 9.5 in its click event.

LISTING 9.5: USING THE COMMANDBUILDER OBJECT

```
Dim cbAuthors As SqlCommandBuilder = New
  SqlCommandBuilder(SqlDataAdapter1)
SqlConnection1.Open()
SqlDataAdapter1.Fill(DsAuthors1, "Authors")
SqlConnection1.Close()
```

This code creates a new SqlCommandBuilder object, passing in the DataAdapter as a parameter. When the CommandBuilder object is instantiated, it will use the SelectCommand object of the DataAdapter to automatically create the appropriate data manipulation Command objects in memory at runtime.

Create an Update button on the form and type the following code in its click event:

```
SqlDataAdapter1.Update(DsAuthors1, "Authors")
```

If you didn't create the CommandBuilder object, you would never be able to update your DataSet because there are no InsertCommand, UpdateCommand, or DeleteCommand objects created at design time.

Run the code by pressing F5, which creates a form similar to Figure 9.14. As you can see, you have a fully functional mechanism to update your data source by using a DataSet, with only a few lines of code. Go ahead and modify the data in the DataGrid by adding, updating, and deleting records. Click the Update button to commit your changes to the database. When you reload the DataGrid, you will see your modifications displayed in the DataGrid.

FIGURE 9.14

Updating a
DataGrid
by using the
CommandBuilder
object

As we noted earlier, the CommandBuilder is great for quickly prototyping your applications; however, you should seriously consider the drawbacks we mentioned before you use it for your production systems.

The TableMapping Object

The TableMapping object is analogous to a field's input mask for the field value. Input masks enable you to change the presentation structure of an underlying data item. TableMapping objects work the same way, providing a mask for a DataTable. Using DataTableMapping and DataColumnMapping objects, you can change the name of columns, set sorting order, or specify filtering. The TableMapping collection enables you to further abstract your ADO.NET objects from the data source, by enabling you to designate your own naming conventions for working with the data in your DataTable.

NOTE *The TableMapping object is unaware of the data source. It doesn't serve to map your DataTable to the underlying tables. Instead, it enables you to specify column names for your data that may be different from those of the data source. If the database has a column called* Name, *you can use the TableMapping object to rename that column to something that makes more sense, such as* CustomerName. *Once again, ADO.NET provides a distinct separation between your data presentation and the data source.*

Like most ADO.NET objects, the TableMapping object works as part of an item in a TableMappings collection. If you are working with more than one DataTable, you can add each TableMapping object to the TableMappings collection. The code

```
SqlDataAdapter1.TableMappings.Add ("Customers", "MyCustomers")
```

maps the DataTable Customers to the MyCustomers TableMapping specification in the TableMappings collection. This way, you can refer to the Customer DataTable as MyCustomer in your code. You can do the same for the columns in your DataTable, by using the DataColumnMapping object:

```
System.Data.Common.DataColumnMapping() {New System.Data.Common.DataColumnMapping
  ("CustomerID", "MyCustID")}
```

This way, you can specify a user-friendly MyCustID name for the CustomerID within your DataTable. As you can see, the DataColumnMapping property belongs to the System.Data.Common namespace, which is not mutually exclusive to any .NET data provider.

You don't necessarily have to manually create your TableMappings by hand. When you use the Data Adapter Configuration Wizard or the Data Form Wizard, VS .NET automatically sets your TableMapping properties for you.

The TableMapping name is almost a misnomer because it seems to indicate that the TableMapping object maps your ADO.NET DataTables to the tables in your data source. This is not the case. Instead, the TableMapping object maps your DataTables to a naming convention or display that you arbitrarily specify. When you fill or update your DataSet, the DataAdapter will look to the TableMapping object to match your code to the DataTable columns.

As you know, the DataAdapter provides several overloaded Fill() methods. One of these implementations accepts only a DataSet object as an input parameter:

```
SqlDataAdapter1.Fill(dsCustomer)
```

If you don't specify the DataTable in the second parameter, ADO.NET will use the default value for the DataTable. The default TableMapping object is called Table. If you do use a TableMapping, you can pass the name of that TableMapping to the DataAdapter's Fill() method, rather than the name of the DataTable itself:

```
SqlDataAdapter1.Fill(dsCustomer, "MyCustomers")
```

A DataAdapter might not always contain a TableMapping object. In fact, you don't have to use any TableMapping, which indicates that you want to use the actual names that were used by the data source. You should omit TableMappings only when you have a single DataTable that you are working with.

Use custom TableMappings when you want to abstract the names of DataTable and DataColumn objects from the names used by the underlying data source. This level of abstraction can come in handy should you ever need to reduce the dependency on your data source schema.

A good use for the TableMapping object is when you pull your schema from one source, such as an XML file, and your data from another source, such as a database. The two schemas might not coincide. For example, the Customer ID can be called `PK_Cust` in the database and `CustomerID` in the XML schema file. You can use the TableMapping object to bring the two sources together by matching the data source column names to the names used by your schema. You can then bind the user-friendly XML schema names to a data-bound control. This methodology further removes your data-bound control from the data source, by binding to the logical representation, rather than the physical representation, of the column name.

You can even use the TableMapping objects to map only the columns that you wish to use. This way, you can hide unnecessary columns that your DataAdapter retrieves. These are only a few of the clever ways you can leverage the TableMapping object to build a scalable database system.

Summary

In this chapter, you conquered yet another visual tool, the Data Form Wizard. The code generated by the wizard gave you the opportunity to discover new concepts behind data binding, as well as learn new methods and properties that work in conjunction with the DataSet object. Additionally, you learned how to leverage the CommandBuilder engine to create action queries on the fly, as well as logically represent your data by using the TableMapping property.

Our next chapter is dedicated entirely to XML, both in context of the .NET Framework, as well its integration with SQL Server 2000. XML is a fundamental technology for data access and presentation, and mastering this technology is crucial to building efficient database systems.

Chapter 10

The Role of XML

- ◆ What is XML?
- ◆ New XML features in SQL Server 2000
- ◆ Using XML with SQL Server 2000
- ◆ Using XML with the .NET Framework
- ◆ The role of XML with SOAP

BECAUSE EXTENSIBLE MARKUP LANGUAGE (XML) is often referred to as the *lingua franca* of the Internet, many people associate XML only with web-based development. This is not the case. In fact, XML plays a role in many technologies, most importantly in database systems such as SQL Server. After all, XML's primary purpose is to define and encapsulate data for universal data exchange.

XML's self-describing nature makes it easy for businesses to communicate with one another, without the help of any translation logic. XML is self-describing in the sense that it is able to describe its data schema along with the data, by using easy-to-read tags. This way, XML data can be readily consumed by multiple platforms and technologies for persistence in relational databases.

The shift to XML from COM-based data transfer significantly increases the scalability and interoperability of your applications. You extend the reach of your applications by using XML because almost any system is capable of encoding and decoding XML data. This interoperability enables organizations to communicate their business processes and information seamlessly. Because you can't guarantee that different businesses use the same technology, using platform-independent XML technology enables your applications to fully integrate with external systems.

XML has a visible role with the various Microsoft technologies, such as SQL Server, ADO.NET, and SOAP. Microsoft has made a serious effort not only to integrate, but to embrace XML as a core technology of both the .NET Framework and the .NET servers, some of which are listed in Table 10.1. Table 10.2 illustrates the degree of integration between XML and various Microsoft technologies.

TABLE 10.1: A FEW OF THE MICROSOFT .NET ENTERPRISE SERVERS

SERVER NAME
SQL Server 2000
Windows 2000 Server
Application Center 2000
Exchange Server 2000
SharePoint Portal Server
Commerce Server 2000

NOTE *Keep in mind that the concept of the .NET Enterprise Servers is a marketing term, rather than an indication that the servers rely on the .NET Framework (CLR, base classes, and so on).*

TABLE 10.2: ADOPTING XML IN MICROSOFT TECHNOLOGIES

TECHNOLOGY	ROLE OF XML
SQL Server 2000	SQL Server tightly integrates with XML, enabling you to read and write data to a database by using XML data and schema.
.NET Framework	XML is a native technology behind the .NET Framework and serves as the core of the .NET Framework.
WebServices	WebServices leverage XML to transfer data by using input and output parameters.
ADO.NET	DataSets persist as XML.
SOAP	SOAP replaces proprietary and binary DCOM by using XML and HTTP to make remote calls.

Remember, this is a book about database programming, so our main focus is on many of the native XML features of SQL Server 2000, such as reading and writing XML documents by using the FOR XML and OPENXML functions. SQL Server 2000 strongly integrates with XML, and we can't do justice to all these features in a single chapter. We expand upon the role XML plays with SQL Server in Chapter 12, "Integration with XML," where we talk about XPath expressions, XML templates, XML views, and XDR schema in detail.

Throughout this chapter, we first explain the various XML technologies conceptually, so that you can get a theoretical understanding of what they are and why they are important. We then expand this theory to practice by creating VB .NET applications, starting from the back end. Our first example creates an XML-based system that will display XML data from SQL Server via a TreeView interface. Additionally, we provide an example that uses the OPENXML function to pass an XML document from VB .NET to SQL Server for insertion.

By the end of this chapter, you should feel comfortable retrieving XML data from a relational database for presentation by using ADO.NET and VB .NET, as well as passing XML from the front end for storage into a relational database.

What Is XML?

XML provides a mechanism for structuring hierarchical data in a text-based format that is readily consumable by almost any technology, such as VB .NET methods, ADO.NET DataSets, SQL Server databases, or web browsers. Each discrete data item in an XML file is "tagged" with a definition of its content. All these tags make up a schema, which has both a business and a technical purpose.

XML schemas use a universal format that enables companies to describe their business process vocabulary to other organizations. In terms of technical application, the self-describing XML schemas provide a universally translatable format that database systems can "read" for processing. Examine this simple XML schema excerpt:

```
<Customer>
  <Name> </Name>
  <Telephone> </Telephone>
</Customer>
```

In this snippet, we define a `<Customer>` tag, which identifies a specific structure. This structure defines a specific Customer entity that can contain nested elements. The `<Customer>` tag indicates a root tag, which helps identify the overarching purpose of the XML document data.

The forward slash symbol (/) within a tag indicates the closing tag for each element. You must properly nest your elements within one another, specifying closing tags in the same order that they were created. You should never mix a start element tag within another element tag pair.

WARNING   *XML is case sensitive. If you specify a start tag of `<Customer>` and an end tag of `</CUSTOMER>`, you will generate a syntax error.*

The `<Name>` and `<Telephone>` tags work as elements within the Customer structure, encapsulating discrete bits of data that belong to a Customer entity. Multiple businesses share such schema in order to define their customer information. Diverse technologies consume this schema, perhaps to submit the schema to a back-end database for relational database storage.

As you remember from Chapter 1, "Database Access: Architectures and Technologies," XML is the technology that has enabled the Internet to evolve from an application-centric model to a highly consumable services-based model. Because XML is the *lingua franca* for all data communications, these global web services become agnostic programming languages. Using XML, web services become location-transparent and flow freely through firewalls.

Throughout this book, we have emphasized ADO.NET's tight relationship with XML, but we have never really discussed XML as a technology. You have viewed XML from the perspective of ADO.NET programming, rather than exploring it as its own entity, as you will do in this chapter.

Of course, by now almost everyone has heard of XML, and you have even used it as part of your solutions. For some of you, this section might be a refresher; if so, feel free to skip ahead to the next section. For those of you who haven't worked closely with XML, this section gives you an understanding of how you can leverage XML in your .NET solutions.

Parsing XML Documents

Prior to .NET, there were two traditional mechanisms for reading, writing, and updating XML data: the Simple API for XML (SAX) and the Document Object Model (DOM). The .NET Framework's System.Xml namespace uses neither of these technologies; however, it's vaguely similar to the SAX method because it uses a forward-only, noncached representation of the XML document. In this section, we discuss the three options for parsing through XML documents.

The SAX parser is the most efficient choice for working with large volumes of data. Like any streaming technology, the SAX method uses a fire-hose mechanism to read the data one element at a time in a flow. The Simple API for XML fires off events as it processes the XML document. You can write application logic to trap these events as the XML data is retrieved.

Unlike the DOM parser, the SAX is less memory-intensive. This is because the SAX processes XML documents in a serialized fashion, reading the document section by section, rather than in its entirety. You should opt to use SAX when you have XML data that is too large to store in memory.

The memory advantages of SAX come with a price. You can traverse the XML document in a forward-only basis, using a push model to render to XML data. The push model makes it a bit more challenging to receive multiple input streams, unlike the pull model used with the .NET Framework. Additionally, the SAX doesn't persist the XML document in-memory, leaving it up to you to create any persistent representation of the document or its elements. Depending on your requirements, this can be seen as either an advantage or a disadvantage. The advantage is that the SAX is more flexible, enabling you to use only the data you need. The disadvantage is that you have to write more code than you would if using a DOM tree, which automatically provides mechanisms to persist the XML document.

The DOM creates an in-memory representation of the XML tree by reading into memory the entire XML document as a text stream. This in-memory representation fully loads all the elements into nodes, keeping the entire document in memory. This is much more memory intensive than the SAX method.

However, the DOM offers more advanced features than the SAX parser, such as richer navigation. Because the entire document is loaded into memory, you can move from one part of the document tree to another. Additionally, you can attach new nodes to any portion of the tree. Unlike forward-only streams, you can walk the DOM both backward and forward, navigating to any section of the in-memory tree. Use the DOM approach if you plan on manipulating the content of your XML document.

The .NET Framework uses a completely different model, which is slightly similar to the streaming approach used by the SAX method—with one main difference. As we mentioned earlier, the SAX method uses a push model to dump out all the different items within an XML document: elements, attributes, comments, white space, or processing instructions. The base classes within System .Xml enable you to walk through an XML document, pulling only the data you need. This pull mechanism gives you better control over state, as you no longer have to rely on externally triggered events.

When you are working natively within SQL Server 2000, you don't have to worry about any of these parsers. SQL Server enables you to directly work with the XML data natively, without the use of a DOM or SAX parser.

Now that you have a rough idea how XML works, we can introduce the native XML features of SQL Server 2000. You will use these features to build some sample applications that read and write XML to a database.

New XML Features in SQL Server 2000

XML plays a strong role in SQL Server technology. XML packages data in a hierarchical format, increasing the need for relational database systems to be able to produce data in a hierarchical format. SQL Server 2000 greatly enhances T-SQL support for XML. You don't need to use the .NET Framework base classes to work with XML in SQL Server because SQL Server's support for the XML format is not dependent on the .NET Framework. You can use non-.NET technologies, such as COM, with SQL Server's OPENXML or FOR XML functions. On the .NET side of things, you can leverage the ADO.NET DataSet's ReadXml() and WriteXml() methods to process XML data and schema, sending the results back to SQL Server. We discussed the latter option in Chapter 7, "ADO.NET Programming." Additionally, you can leverage the XmlTextReader class to send and retrieve XML data to and from SQL Server.

In this section, we show you how to retrieve XML data by using the SELECT statement and the FOR XML clause. Additionally, we demonstrate how to leverage ADO.NET and the System.Xml classes to write XML data back to SQL Server by using the OPENXML rowset provider. You will learn how to stream XML data from SQL Server for presentation inside a VB .NET application. Let's begin by examining the different options that SQL Server 2000 provides for tight XML integration.

The *FOR XML* Statement

Traditionally, result sets from SQL Server are returned in a tabular format. SQL Server 2000 advances data integration with XML by supplying a FOR XML extension to the SELECT command. By specifying FOR XML in your SELECT statement, you can compose your results into an XML document. When you return your data as XML, the native relational structure is converted to a hierarchical format.

There are many advantages to representing your data hierarchically rather than relationally. Of course, the obvious advantage of the hierarchical display lies in the format itself: XML. We've already indicated the many business-to-business (B2B) advantages of using XML as your data format, such as platform independence and firewall-friendly text format.

Other advantages are internal to the application itself. Hierarchical controls, such as the TreeView control, can easily consume and display hierarchical XML data. Additionally, XML-based technologies such as ADO.NET can quickly grab the results with little or no conversion, especially when you return validated XML data that complies with the W3C requirements for well-formed XML structure.

The FOR XML statement is a great replacement for the classic ADO SHAPE command, which uses a proprietary format for displaying parent and child data.

The syntax for the T-SQL FOR XML statement is as follows:

```
FOR XML { RAW | AUTO | EXPLICIT }
        [ , XMLDATA ]
        [ , ELEMENTS ]
        [ , BINARY BASE64 ]
```

The RAW, AUTO, or EXPLICIT keywords specify the mode in which you wish your XML results to be displayed. The FOR XML clause cannot be used without specifying one of these modes. The latter three keywords are optional. The XMLDATA keyword returns both schema and data as your XML results. The ELEMENTS keyword is extremely useful for generating XML data that uses nested XML elements. Finally, the BINARY BASE64 option enables you to encode binary information, such as images, for text-based transport. You will explore all these options in this chapter.

THE *RAW* MODE

The RAW mode is the most generic, returning your data by using <ROW> tags rather than the actual column names. The <ROW> tags return your row data as elements. The column values are mapped to element attributes.

The XML data returned by the RAW mode is not well formed. *Well-formed* XML has both start and end tags that encapsulate data values. Additionally, well-formed XML data nests child elements within their parents, which the RAW clause does not support. XML's self-describing nature is truly one of the main advantages of the format. Unfortunately, the <ROW> tags aren't very descriptive.

WARNING *You can easily execute the examples of this section by using the Query Analyzer tool of SQL Server. When you use the Query Analyzer to execute this command, do not display the results in a grid. This truncates large result sets in an unintelligible fashion. Display the results as text. However, keep in mind that the Query Analyzer has serious limitations when displaying XML data as text. Instead of using an XML parser to read the data, it interprets the XML streams as textual rows, up to 2033 bytes long. This might end up truncating long XML results. You can increase the characters displayed by the Query Analyzer by selecting Tools ➢ Options from the menu and navigating to the Results tab. Adjust the Maximum Characters Per Column setting to a value larger than 2033, so that the examples of this chapter are not truncated. We use a value of 3000.*

The best way to compare each of the FOR XML modes is to examine the results of each SELECT statement. Take a peek at the results of the following SQL statement, which returns the Customer records from the Northwind database in RAW XML format:

```
USE Northwind
SELECT * from Customers
WHERE CustomerID = 'ALFKI'
FOR XML RAW
```

TIP *Instead of typing the statements from scratch, you can load the code from the CD that accompanies this book. In this case, the code is listed within the* Using FOR XML RAW.sql *file.*

As you can see from the excerpt of the results of this statement, there is a start <ROW> tag, but no end tag. Additionally, all the columns are stored in a single text block, as attributes of the element rather than as hierarchically nested sub-elements.

```
<row CustomerID="ALFKI" CompanyName="Alfreds Futterkiste"
   ContactName="Maria Anders"
   ContactTitle="Sales Representative"
   Address="Obere Str. 57" City="Berlin"
   PostalCode="12209" Country="Germany"
   Phone="030-0074321" Fax="030-0076545"
/>
```

Although the RAW mode is the quickest way to return XML data when using the FOR XML clause, it is not the most elegant way to display your XML data.

THE *AUTO* MODE

The AUTO mode improves the readability of your XML results by using the table name as the element tag name, rather than the generic <ROW> tag. Like the RAW mode, by default the AUTO mode will return the column data as attributes of the table element, unless you also use the ELEMENTS keyword.

Using the AUTO keyword alone, the following SQL statement will return the results in Listing 10.1, which can be found in the Using FOR XML AUTO.sql file on the CD:

```
USE Northwind
SELECT * from Customers
WHERE CustomerID = 'ALFKI'
FOR XML AUTO
```

LISTING 10.1: USING THE *AUTO* MODE WITH THE *FOR XML* CLAUSE

```
<Customers
  CustomerID="ALFKI"
  CompanyName="Alfreds Futterkiste"
  ContactName="Maria Anders"
  ContactTitle="Sales Representative"
  Address="Obere Str. 57"
  City="Berlin"
  PostalCode="12209"
  Country="Germany"
  Phone="030-0074321"
  Fax="030-0076545"
/>
```

The AUTO mode displays the data in a hierarchical way automatically. This enables applications to expand the Customer element hierarchy to examine the various attributes within this element.

Although it's nice to see the name of the Customers table in lieu of the <ROW> tag, this XML data does not use nested elements. You can fix that by adding the ELEMENTS keyword to the AUTO specification:

```
USE Northwind
SELECT * from Customers
WHERE CustomerID = 'ALFKI'
FOR XML AUTO, ELEMENTS
```

Listing 10.2 shows the results of this statement. This code can be found in the Using FOR XML AUTO ELEMENTS.sql file.

LISTING 10.2: USING THE *AUTO, ELEMENTS* MODE WITH THE *FOR XML* CLAUSE

```
<Customers>
  <CustomerID>ALFKI</CustomerID>
  <CompanyName>Alfreds Futterkiste</CompanyName>
  <ContactName>Maria Anders</ContactName>
```

```
    <ContactTitle>Sales Representative</ContactTitle>
    <Address>Obere Str. 57</Address>
    <City>Berlin</City>
    <PostalCode>12209</PostalCode>
    <Country>Germany</Country>
    <Phone>030-0074321</Phone>
    <Fax>030-0076545</Fax>
</Customers>
```

With the addition of the ELEMENTS tag, the XML data is returned in a nested hierarchy, using matching start and end tags for your elements. As you can see, the column values are no longer treated as attributes of the table element. Instead, they are treated as child elements within the parent, table element.

WARNING   Keep in mind that XML data from multiple tables as returned by the AUTO, ELEMENTS *mode is still not completely well formed in accordance with the W3C specifications. All well-formed XML documents must contain exactly one root element. You will see an example of this limitation later in this chapter, in the section "Retrieving XML-Formatted Data from a SQL Server Database."*

The AUTO mode provides another option, XMLDATA, which produces an XML schema as its output, as displayed in Listing 10.3. You can write the same query by using the XMLDATA option. (The code can be found in the Using FOR AUTO XMLDATA.sql file.)

```
USE Northwind
SELECT * from Customers
WHERE CustomerID = 'ALFKI'
FOR XML AUTO, XMLDATA
```

LISTING 10.3: USING THE *AUTO, XMLDATA* MODE WITH THE *FOR XML* CLAUSE

```
<Schema name="Schema2"
  xmlns="urn:schemas-microsoft-com:xml-data"
  xmlns:dt="urn:schemas-microsoft-com:datatypes">
  <ElementType name="Customers"
   content="empty" model="closed">
   <AttributeType name="CustomerID" dt:type="string"/>
   <AttributeType name="CompanyName" dt:type="string"/>
   <AttributeType name="ContactName" dt:type="string"/>
   <AttributeType name="ContactTitle" dt:type="string"/>
   <AttributeType name="Address" dt:type="string"/>
   <AttributeType name="City" dt:type="string"/>
   <AttributeType name="Region" dt:type="string"/>
   <AttributeType name="PostalCode" dt:type="string"/>
   <AttributeType name="Country" dt:type="string"/>
   <AttributeType name="Phone" dt:type="string"/>
   <AttributeType name="Fax" dt:type="string"/>
   <attribute type="CustomerID"/>
```

```
            <attribute type="CompanyName"/>
            <attribute type="ContactName"/>
            <attribute type="ContactTitle"/>
            <attribute type="Address"/>
            <attribute type="City"/>
            <attribute type="Region"/>
            <attribute type="PostalCode"/>
            <attribute type="Country"/>
            <attribute type="Phone"/>
            <attribute type="Fax"/>
        </ElementType>
    </Schema>

    <Customers
        xmlns="x-schema:#Schema2"
        CustomerID="ALFKI"
        CompanyName="Alfreds Futterkiste"
        ContactName="Maria Anders"
        ContactTitle="Sales Representative"
        Address="Obere Str. 57"
        City="Berlin"
        PostalCode="12209"
        Country="Germany"
        Phone="030-0074321"
        Fax="030-0076545"/>
```

As you can see from the results in Listing 10.3, the XMLDATA output is quite different from the output when using the AUTO mode alone. The results are constituted into two parts. The first part specifies the schema for each element, and the attribute along with its data type. The second part of the result set displays the data in a fashion similar to using the AUTO mode, with one main exception: the schema reference is specified at the beginning of the output.

WARNING   *The* XMLDATA *clause imposes a high performance overhead on your SQL Server and should be used only when you need to reference data types. This clause is far from perfect. It has trouble understanding table names that contain spaces and uses numeric encoding characters to represent the spaces. This encoding might misrepresent your element and attribute names. You are also not protected against naming collisions between elements or attributes that use the same name.*

You could opt to reuse this schema to create XML-Data Reduced (XDR) schema files, which can be used to generate an XML view of relational data.

THE *EXPLICIT* MODE

The EXPLICIT mode is the most complex of the three modes, requiring that you specify the parent/child relationship in advance. The query uses the parent/child relationship to create the appropriate nesting structure for the XML output. The relationship is temporarily stored in a universal table. The *universal table* contains the data grouped by the final XML elements, which encapsulate the data.

The EXPLICIT mode's main advantage is that you can create multiple SELECT statements and then relate them together by using Tag and Parent references. The Tag reference uses a number to uniquely identify an element. The Parent reference is used to point to the parent element of a child element. Together these fields enable you to track the node position and hierarchical relationships within the XML structure.

The SELECT statements used with the EXPLICIT mode use some funky specifications, such as requiring a tag number for all elements, as well as a reference to a tag number for child elements. By writing the SELECT statement in accordance with the specifications required by the universal table, you can supply directives that will shape the XML document to your requirements. This will make more sense after you construct the SQL statement.

The shaped results will be listed in the universal table. SQL references the universal table to create the multilevel hierarchy by using one or more UNION operators. Each SELECT statement provides rows that contain data for one type of node, such as Publishers or Employees.

Let's create a SELECT statement that uses the EXPLICIT mode to create a customized XML format. Before you construct this statement, it is useful to visually design the universal table, which represents the shaped XML document. You want to show the orders for Antonio Moreno Taquería, so an excerpt of the universal table structure you want would look like this:

Tag	Parent	Customers!1! CustomerID	Customers!1! CompanyName	Orders!2! OrderID! Element	Orders!2! ShippedDate! Element
1	NULL	ANTON	Antonio Moreno Taquería	NULL	NULL
2	1	ANTON	NULL	10365	12/2/1996
3	1	ANTON	NULL	10535	5/13/1997

The first thing you should notice is the addition of two new columns: Tag and Parent. Together, these column values specify the hierarchy in which you wish to build your XML document. By specifying a Parent value of Null, you indicate the root node. Because the Customer element appears first in the XML document, you specify a Null value for its parent. The Tag number for this row has a value of 1 because it is the first element tag within the XML document.

After the Tag and Parent columns, you have the actual data elements of your XML. These column names use the following naming convention:

ElementName!TagNumber!AttributeName!Directive

If you examine the OrderID column, which is the one of the more complicated specifications, you'll understand the purpose of this unusual column-naming convention.

As you can see, each column alias is delimited with exclamation points. The first variable indicates the element name; in this case, you want to call it Orders. The next variable indicates the tag number for your SELECT statement, which is "2" for the Orders element (generated from the Orders SELECT statement), as you will soon see in Listing 10.4. Do not confuse this tag number with the Tag specified for each row in the universal table.

The third variable, `AttributeName`, indicates the name of the attribute that you wish to use for the values in this column. You specify `OrderID` as your attribute name for this column. The `AttributeName` is required if you don't specify a directive. The fourth parameter, the directive, is optional. By default, if you don't specify a directive, the values in this column will display as attributes of the `Orders` element. However, in this case, you want nested sub-elements, so you choose to display both the `OrderID` and `ShippingDate` values as elements, using the Directive "element."

TIP   *Alternately, you could specify* `cdata`, `hide`, `xml`, *or* `xmltext` *as valid directives. Again, if you don't specify a directive, the data for this column will display as an attribute of the parent element.*

As you can see, your `Orders` elements specify a Null value for the `CompanyName`. These are place-holders that enable you to match both the `Customers` and `Orders` schema. The `UNION` operator requires that both schemas match, which will become clearer when you construct the `SELECT` statements in Listing 10.4.

Building a universal table design is similar to constructing a TreeView, where the root node would be Null. Keep in mind that SQL Server will automatically create the universal table for you. You're just constructing it here as a visual design aid. Each column in the preceding universal table represents an element or attribute in the resulting XML document. You can see this by executing your query and examining its results. The `SELECT` query is shown in Listing 10.4 and can be found on the CD within the `Using FOR XML EXPLICIT.sql` file. The results are displayed in Listing 10.5.

LISTING 10.4: USING THE *EXPLICIT* MODE OF THE *FOR XML* CLAUSE

```
USE Northwind
SELECT 1              as Tag,
       NULL           as Parent,
       Customers.CustomerID   as
         [Customer!1!CustomerID],
       Customers.CompanyName   as
         [Customer!1!CompanyName],
       NULL                as
         [Order!2!OrderID!element],
       NULL            as
         [Order!2!ShippedDate!element]
FROM Customers
WHERE (Customers.CustomerID = 'ANTON')


UNION ALL


SELECT 2 as Tag,
       1 as Parent,
       Customers.CustomerID,
       Customers.CompanyName ,
       Orders.OrderID,
       Orders.ShippedDate
FROM Customers, Orders
```

```
WHERE (Customers.CustomerID = 'ANTON') AND
      Customers.CustomerID = Orders.CustomerID
ORDER BY [Customer!1!CustomerID],
         [Order!2!OrderID!element]

FOR XML EXPLICIT
```

The SELECT statements must not only use the Tag and Parent values, but the result set must be ordered with the parents immediately preceding the relevant children result sets. The first SELECT expression supplies your Customer nodes, and the second SELECT expression provides your Orders nodes. For your Customer nodes, you look for a match for the CustomerID with the value ANTON. With the Order nodes, you use an inner join so that only Orders for the CustomerID with the value ANTON are returned. You then combine both result sets with the UNION ALL command. The UNION ALL command requires that all SELECT statements must have matching column types and the same number of columns. This is why you specify so many Null values in your first SELECT statement. The results for the query in Listing 10.4 are displayed in Listing 10.5, with some elements truncated for brevity.

LISTING 10.5: THE RESULTS OF THE *EXPLICIT* MODE OF THE *FOR XML* CLAUSE

```xml
<Customer
  CustomerID="ANTON"
  CompanyName="Antonio Moreno Taquería">

<Order>
    <OrderID>10365</OrderID>
    <ShippedDate>1996-12-02</ShippedDate>
  </Order>

  <Order>
   <OrderID>10507</OrderID>
   <ShippedDate>1997-04-22</ShippedDate>
  </Order>

  <Order>
   <OrderID>10535</OrderID>
   <ShippedDate>1997-05-21</ShippedDate>
  </Order>

</Customer>
```

Although you have to do a lot of grunt work when using the EXPLICIT mode, it does give you the greatest control over how you want your XML data displayed. You can choose to display your data as any valid XML item—such as elements, attributes, or even cdata (which works great with Content Management systems such as Interwoven)—to create a schema that meets your business needs.

CAVEATS AND LIMITATIONS

Recursive schema references within the FOR XML clause are not supported by SQL Server 2000. *Recursive schema* is schema containing a foreign key that points back to itself, usually the primary key of the same table. Therefore, you can't use the employee table to show a hierarchy of employees and their managers because the ReportsTo column in the employee table points back the same employee table.

There are some limitations with the FOR XML clause. You can't use the FOR XML clause in a subquery or nested SELECT statement. Additionally, you cannot return XML data with the FOR XML statement if your SELECT statement uses aggregation such as COMPUTE BY, GROUP BY, MIN(), MAX(), or AVG(). (We discussed these functions in Chapter 4, "Structured Query Language," and Chapter 5, "Transact-SQL.") You cannot use this clause within a view creation statement or with cursors. After you return the XML data by using the FOR XML clause, you cannot execute further processing on the results. You can work around this option by temporarily storing the data into a table data type variable, using that variable to process your data. We discuss this later in the chapter.

TRANSPORTING BINARY DATA VIA XML

It is possible to transport binary data via XML from SQL Server. You can encode the binary file into a Base-64 text format, which can then be passed to other applications or services. The recipient application or service decodes the text-based format back into a binary format. E-mail attachments work this way. When you send a binary e-mail attachment to someone, it is encoded into a Base-64 text format, which is then decoded by the e-mail system used by your recipient. The FOR XML statement translates binary data the same way.

If your table contains column data types of binary and varbinary, you will have to add the BINARY BASE64 clause after the RAW specification. You will have to do the same for the EXPLICIT mode. For the AUTO mode, you can optionally specify the BINARY BASE64 clause. If you don't specify it, your data will contain relative URLs that point to the path of the actual data for the binary and varbinary columns.

The pub_info table in the Pubs database contains an image column that stores the logo for each publishing house. Let's retrieve the data by using the AUTO statement alone, without Base-64 encoding:

```
USE Pubs
SELECT pub_id, logo
FROM pub_info
FOR XML AUTO
```

The code for this SELECT statement can be found in the Using BINARY BASE64 encoding with XML.sql file. The results for this statement are shown in Listing 10.6.

LISTING 10.6: RETURNING BINARY DATA WITHOUT *BASE-64* ENCODING

```
<pub_info pub_id="0736" logo="dbobject/pub_info[@pub_id='0736']/@logo"/>
<pub_info pub_id="0877" logo="dbobject/pub_info[@pub_id='0877']/@logo"/>
<pub_info pub_id="1389" logo="dbobject/pub_info[@pub_id='1389']/@logo"/>
<pub_info pub_id="1622" logo="dbobject/pub_info[@pub_id='1622']/@logo"/>
<pub_info pub_id="1756" logo="dbobject/pub_info[@pub_id='1756']/@logo"/>
```

```
<pub_info pub_id="9901" logo="dbobject/pub_info[@pub_id='9901']/@logo"/>
<pub_info pub_id="9952" logo="dbobject/pub_info[@pub_id='9952']/@logo"/>
<pub_info pub_id="9999" logo="dbobject/pub_info[@pub_id='9999']/@logo"/>
```

When you reference binary columns with the AUTO mode, you must specify the primary key of the table in the SELECT clause. If you do not specify the primary key, SQL Server generates the following error:

```
FOR XML AUTO requires primary keys to create references for
'logo'. Select primary keys, or use BINARY BASE64 to obtain
binary data in encoded form if no primary keys exist.
```

When encoding is not specified, the primary key is used to designate where the logo is stored. Change the stored procedure to use Base-64 encoding and examine the results in your SQL Query Analyzer.

```
USE Pubs
SELECT pub_id, logo
FROM pub_info
FOR XML AUTO, BINARY BASE64
```

The results are too cryptic and lengthy to list here, but basically you end up with the encoded source for the binary file. You can then pass the binary data as text through networks and firewalls.

The *OPENXML* Function

The OPENXML function enables you to insert XML documents into a SQL Server database. This function is new to SQL Server 2000, as part of its strategy for tighter XML integration. You use the OPENXML function to convert an XML document into a relational format that can be consumed by SQL Server.

Behind the scenes, the OPENXML function overlays a relational mask over the XML document, enabling you to access XML content as if were a relational database. You can choose to store the relational representation in a database.

To fully understand this function, you should have a complete understanding of XPath queries, which we discuss in Chapter 12. For the purposes of this chapter, we'll stick with using a simple XPath expression. Suffice it to say that XPath expressions enable you to navigate the nodes within an XML document to point to a specific row. An XPath expression is passed as a parameter into the OPENXML function.

The syntax for the OPENXML function is as follows:

```
OPENXML
  (intXMLDocumentHandle int        [in],
   rowpattern             nvarchar  [in],
   [flags                 byte      [in]])
[WITH (SchemaDeclaration | TableName)]
```

The first parameter expects a handle to an XML document, which you can obtain from the sp_xml_preparedocument stored procedure. We explain this stored procedure later in this section.

The second parameter indicates the XPath (XML Path Language) expression that defines the XML nodes that you wish to use as relational rows. XPath expressions enable you to hone in on a specific area within an XML document. Both the first and second parameters are required.

The third parameter, flags, is an optional parameter that you can use to specify different types of mapping levels, such as attribute, element or mixed. The mapping is used to relate the relational representation to the XML data. By default, the mapping will be attribute-centric, which means that XML attributes are mapped to columns that use the same name.

Finally, the last clause, WITH, indicates whether you desire to use an existing schema. This schema could be dynamic, by using the SchemaDeclaration keyword, or fixed, by basing the schema on an existing table with the TableName argument.

After you execute the OPENXML function, you can use the results as you would a standard relational result set. You can use it in lieu of a table or table parameter with the FROM clause of a SELECT or SELECT INTO statement. Additionally, you can perform traditional SELECT clause operations on the OPENXML function, such as using the WHERE or ORDER BY clause.

SQL SERVER 2000 SYSTEM XML STORED PROCEDURES

SQL Server 2000 comes with several new XML stored procedures that you can use to process XML data to and from a database. One of these functions is called sp_xml_preparedocument, which must be called against an XML document before you can use the OPENXML function against it. The sp_xml_preparedocument stored procedure parses the XML data into an in-memory format that is consumable by SQL Server.

The following is the syntax for this system stored procedure:

```
sp_xml_preparedocument
( intXMLDocumentHandle int [out]
[, txtXML {char, nchar, varchar, nvarchar, text, or ntext }[in],]
[, txtXPathExpression {char, nchar, varchar, nvarchar, text, or ntext }[in]])
```

The intXMLDocumentHandle is an output parameter that produces the handle to the in-memory XML document. When you call the sp_xml_preparedocument stored procedure, the first input parameter you pass in is an XML hierarchy in a text format. Later, in our OPENXML example, we will show you how you pass in the XML text for a new database record into the sp_xml_preparedocument stored procedure. The next, and last, parameter is the XPath expression, which points to a position inside the XML document. As we have said, you will learn more about XPath expressions in Chapter 12.

Keep in mind that in order to remove the in-memory representation of the XML document, you must call the sp_xml_removedocument stored procedure. Later in this chapter, we provide an example of using OPENXML. We'll show you how to read an XML document that you create from an ADO.NET XmlTextReader object, passing it to the OPENXML function.

XML with the *table* Data Type

Although we introduced the table data type in Chapter 2, "Basic Concepts of Relational Databases," discussing it again in this chapter makes sense because there is a clever way to use the table type with the OPENXML function.

Using the `table` data type is not much different from using the `OPENXML` function, in the sense that it can also be used in lieu of a table name in the `FROM` clause. In fact, the table type is very convenient as a container for the relational results generated by the `OPENXML` function. You can store the relational mask in a `table` data type and pass schema around just like any other variable.

Using XML with SQL Server 2000

In this section, you will combine the concepts you learned in the preceding section and pragmatically build the back-end logic for your XML. You will work with the `FOR XML` clause to retrieve XML data from a relational database. You will pass this information over to a VB .NET application to populate a TreeView control.

Retrieving XML-Formatted Data from a SQL Server Database

Let's apply the knowledge of the previous pages and create a stored procedure that pulls results from the SQL Server Pubs database and persists it as an XML document via the `FOR XML` clause.

This example will enable you to apply an additional concept. Not only will you apply your understanding of the `FOR XML` statement, but you will also see how to pass an XML document from a stored procedure. You will use the `FOR XML` statement to create a hierarchical representation of your relational data.

As a refresher, a quick summary of the `FOR XML` modes is shown in Table 10.3. This reference table will come in handy in a short while, when we show you which mode is used in the example.

TABLE 10.3: COMPARING MODES OF THE *FOR XML* CLAUSE

MODE	XML DISPLAY RESULTS
RAW	Uses <ROW> tag to display all row data within a single element. Column values are displayed as attributes. XML is not well formed.
AUTO	Uses table name as element tag, with column values listed as attributes of table element. XML is not well formed.
AUTO, ELEMENTS	Uses table name as element tag. Column values are listed as sub-elements below the table element. Although XML uses both nesting and matching start and end tags, it is not well-formed because it doesn't contain a single root node.
EXPLICIT	Enables you to create your custom XML schema. It is up to you to ensure that your XML is well formed.

CREATING A STORED PROCEDURE THAT RETURNS XML

Let's begin creating our XML application, by creating a stored procedure that will return hierarchical data in XML format. You will use two tables, `publishers` and `employee` from the Pubs database. Your business requirements are to extract the employees for each publishing house to send to an external system, Human Resources, for processing. The Human Resources system uses a different platform than your application, so you want to send your results in XML format.

In this example, you will opt to use the FOR XML EXPLICIT clause rather than the AUTO, ELEMENTS. Although the latter option is much simpler to program, it doesn't give you the well-formed XML data you need. Specifically, the results generated by the AUTO, ELEMENTS clause lack a root node, which your .NET objects will need to process the XML document. Without a root node, the XML document would be only a fragment, unable to be displayed by XML viewers, such as a web browser.

First, you will create a stored procedure to extract this information. You will use the FOR XML clause to extract the data as XML. The order of the column names in your SELECT statement is important. If you place the employee attributes before the publishing elements, the publishers will be a child element of the employees. Instead, you want to display your publishers as the parent node, with the relevant employees below. To do so, you specify the columns from the publishers table first, as shown in Listing 10.7. The code for Listing 10.7 is in the Creating the GetPublisherEmployees stored procedure .sql file.

LISTING 10.7: CREATING A STORED PROCEDURE BY USING THE *FOR XML* CLAUSE

```
CREATE PROCEDURE dbo.GetPublisherEmployees
AS

SELECT 1 as Tag, NULL as Parent,
NULL as [PubEmp!1!RootNode!element],
NULL as  [Publisher!2!PublishingHouse!element],
NULL as [Publisher!2!PublisherID!element],
NULL as [Employee!3!EmployeeID!element],
NULL as [Employee!3!EmployeeName!element]
UNION ALL

SELECT 2 as Tag, 1 as Parent,
NULL as [PubEmp!1!RootNode!element],
p.pub_name + ' (' + p.city + ')' as [Publisher!2!PublishingHouse!element],
 p.pub_id as [Publisher!2!PublisherID!element],
NULL as [Employee!3!EmployeeID!element],
NULL as [Employee!3!EmployeeName!element]
FROM publishers p
UNION ALL

SELECT 3 as Tag,
   2 as Parent,
NULL as [PubEmp!1!RootNode!element],
 p.pub_name  + ' (' + p.city + ')' as PublishingHouse,
p.pub_id as PublisherID,
e.emp_id As EmployeeID,
e.fname + ' ' + e.lname as EmployeeName

FROM employee e, publishers p
WHERE e.pub_id = p.pub_id
```

```
ORDER BY [Publisher!2!PublishingHouse!element],
         [Employee!3!EmployeeID!element]

FOR XML EXPLICIT
```

Although the listing is quite lengthy, there's nothing really complex about this stored procedure. All you do is retrieve employee information along with the relevant publisher name and city. You might notice the use of the FOR XML EXPLICIT clause to generate your XML document. Why not use the FOR XML AUTO, ELEMENTS mode? Although the query would have been much shorter and simpler if you did so, you would lose control over your XML schema. (Remember, we have summarized the differences between the available nodes in Table 10.3.) If you used the AUTO, ELEMENTS mode, you would end up missing the root node. You could opt to add the root node from your VB .NET code; however, you are using the XmlReader class to receive your XML data. The XmlReader class insists upon well-formed XML data as an input parameter. Without creating a root node, as you do, your XML data would not be well formed and you would generate an error from VS .NET, complaining that a Null was found, when a value was expected.

Notice that this example uses aliases to produce a more user-friendly output for your XML element names. For example, it uses the EmployeeName alias to specify a concatenation between the first and last name of an employee. When you examine the final XML output, you will see these aliases used as element names within the XML hierarchy.

You might wonder why there is an additional SELECT statement at the start of the query, especially because it doesn't seem to do anything. That's not the case; it does serve a purpose. In fact, you need this SELECT statement to set up your root node, <PubEmp>. By specifying an empty root node, you can reference it from your children nodes: Publisher and Employee. This way, you build a well-formed hierarchy of XML data, as depicted in Listing 10.8. Keep in mind that we show only one partial record listing for brevity.

LISTING 10.8: GENERATING XML RESULTS BY USING A ROOT NODE

```
<PubEmp>
  <Publisher>
    <PublishingHouse>Algodata Infosystems
            (Berkeley)</PublishingHouse>

    <PublisherID>1389</PublisherID>

    <Employee>
      <EmployeeID>A-C71970F</EmployeeID>
      <EmployeeName>Carol Sue
            Mulberry</EmployeeName>
    </Employee>

    <Employee>
      <EmployeeID>CGS88322F</EmployeeID>
      <EmployeeName>Jason
            Punk</EmployeeName>
```

```
    </Employee>

    <Employee>
      <EmployeeID>DWR65030M</EmployeeID>
      <EmployeeName>Diego
            Roel</EmployeeName>
    </Employee>

    <Employee>
      <EmployeeID>M-L67958F</EmployeeID>
      <EmployeeName>Frank Johnson-
            Suglia</EmployeeName>
    </Employee>

  </Publisher>
</PubEmp>
```

As you can see, this listing creates a well-formed XML document that uses the `<PubEmp>` root node. Additionally, all your values are encapsulated within appropriately named elements. The entire structure is accurately nested to reflect your relational data structure. Note that unlike a regular stored procedure, which returns a result set, you return stream of XML text instead. You can then intercept this stream from VS .NET and persist it into an XML document by using the ADO.NET objects.

RESERVED XML CHARACTERS WILL BE AUTOMATICALLY ESCAPED

Certain characters are reserved in the XML format. SQL Server 2000 has a useful feature, which automatically escapes special characters when it encounters them in the database. When SQL Server runs into these characters in the data, it will automatically encode them for you. If you examine the results of the stored procedure you just created, you will see an example of how ampersands are treated within a field name. In the relational database, the publishing house Binnet & Hardley contains an ampersand. When you execute the SELECT statement with the FOR XML clause, the ampersand character will be encoded into the name: `Binnet &amp; Hardley`.

Additional reserved characters include:

```
      <
      >
      "
      '
```

Respectively, these characters will be encoded as the following:

```
      &gt;
      %lt;
      &quot;
      &apos;
```

You will need to add some parsing logic to remove these characters from your final presentation.

Run the statement to create the stored procedure. You will use it to send an XML document to a .NET application for processing. You will then walk through the XML document, parsing its contents into a TreeView control.

RETRIEVING XML RESULTS FROM A STORED PROCEDURE BY USING VB .NET

In this section, you are going to create a VB .NET application that uses the XmlTextReader object to parse the XML data stream. To process the XML data generated from your T-SQL stored procedure, you must perform these basic steps:

1. Create an XmlTextReader object to stream your XML document.

2. Create a SqlCommand object to hook into your stored procedure.

3. Use the `ExecuteXmlReader()` method of your Command object to store the results of your query into an XmlTextReader object.

4. Use the `Read()` method of the XmlTextReader object to walk through the XML stream.

5. Walk through the elements of the XML document, adding the elements to the appropriate TreeView Node collections, using the `ReadInnerXml()` method to capture the data

STREAMING VERSUS CACHING XML

You have two choices when intercepting XML data from your stored procedure: streaming or caching the data. You can stream the data, which reads XML off the wire in a read-only, forward-only format. This is useful when you want to retrieve the data as quickly as possible and you don't care if all the data is read before you display it. A great example of a need for streaming data is paging. If you had a large result set and you wanted to display your data in a series of paged DataGrid controls, an XmlReader implementation would be an excellent choice.

Alternately, if you needed to retrieve all your data at once, before you could display it, a cached representation would be ideal. You can do this by pulling your data into an ADO.NET DataSet, rather than streaming the data.

Because we've spent a lot of time on DataSets in the previous chapters, we have opted to have you use streaming XML data in our example. You use an XmlTextReader implementation of the XmlReader abstract base class in order to stream the XML data through to your VB .NET code. The XmlReader class enables you to walk through the XML data by using the element nodes to read the inner XML values. Unlike the DOM, which loads the entire XML document into memory, the XmlTextReader pulls only one node at a time. This way, only one node is in memory at any given time.

If you were populating a DataSet, you would still have to walk through the nodes of the XML document. If you tried to directly shove the XML into a DataSet, you would end up with multiple DataRows containing bits and pieces of the XML source. You would then have to concatenate these DataRows together to form one XML string.

You can see what the XML looks like when populated into a DataSet. Add a SqlDataAdapter to the form and select the `GetPublisherEmployees` stored procedure from the Data Adapter Configuration Wizard. Select the Preview Data option from the DataAdapter Properties window. If you examine the results in the DataSet, you'll see four illogically parsed rows of XML data within the DataSet, as shown in Figure 10.1.

WARNING *The XmlReader class expects a well-formed XML document. Again, if you used the* FOR XML, AUTO ELEMENT *clause in your stored procedure, you would see two nodes for Publisher and Employee, but no single root node that unites them at the document level.*

FIGURE 10.1

Viewing the results of the FOR XML clause directly from a DataSet

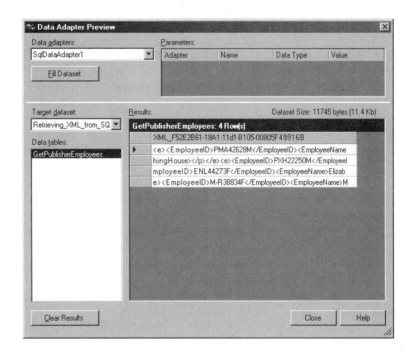

Create a new VS .NET Windows Application and call it **Retrieving XML from SQL Server 2000**. Correspondingly, this is what the source code solution file is called on the accompanying CD. From the Toolbox, drag a TreeView control onto the form, naming it **tvwEmployees**. Size the TreeView control accordingly and add a button next to the TreeView. You will use this button to store the code that will populate the TreeView from your SqlCommand object. Change the display text to read **Load TreeView**.

From the Server Explorer, expand the Data Connections node, and drag over the connection to the Pubs database onto your form. This will create a new SqlConnection control. You will create the appropriate Command object programmatically, as you will see later in Listing 10.9. You will have to import two namespaces from the .NET base classes. In the Declarations section of the Windows Form, add these import statements:

```
Imports System.Xml
Imports System.Data.SqlClient
```

Next, add the code in Listing 10.9 to the click event of the Load TreeView button.

LISTING 10.9: LOADING A TREEVIEW FROM SQL SERVER XML DATA

```vb
Private Sub Button1_Click( _
        ByVal sender As System.Object, _
        ByVal e As System.EventArgs) _
        Handles Button1.Click
    Dim xrEmployees As XmlTextReader
    Dim intOrdinal As Integer = 0
    Dim cmdPubEmp As SqlCommand = _
        New SqlCommand _
        ("dbo.GetPublisherEmployees", _
        SqlConnection1)
    SqlConnection1.Open()
    Try
        xrEmployees = _
            cmdPubEmp.ExecuteXmlReader()
    Catch errExecute As System.Exception
        Console.WriteLine _
        (errExecute.Message)
    End Try
    tvwEmployees.Nodes.Clear()
    xrEmployees.WhitespaceHandling() = _
        WhitespaceHandling.None
    While xrEmployees.Read()
        If xrEmployees.NodeType = _
          XmlNodeType.Element Then
            Select Case xrEmployees.Name
                Case "PubEmp"
                    tvwEmployees.Nodes. _
                        Add _
                        ("Root")
                Case "PublishingHouse"
                    ' add the publisher
                    ' name
                    tvwEmployees. _
                        Nodes(0).Nodes. _
                        Add _
                        (xrEmployees. _
                        ReadInnerXml)
                    If tvwEmployees. _
                        Nodes(0).Nodes. _
                        Count > 1 Then
                        intOrdinal = _
                            intOrdinal _
                            + 1
                    End If
```

```
                    Case "EmployeeName"
                         ' attach the
                         ' employees to each
                        'publisher
                        tvwEmployees. _
                          Nodes(0).Nodes _
                          (intOrdinal). _
                          Nodes.Add _
                          (xrEmployees. _
                          ReadInnerXml)
                End Select
            End If
        End While
        xrEmployees.Close()
        SqlConnection1.Close()
    End Sub
```

Because the only ADO.NET object you have created so far is a SqlConnection, you will have to programmatically create the SqlCommand object that uses this connection. You set the `CommandText` property of the SqlCommand object directly from an overloaded instance of the constructor. For the `CommandText` property, you specify the name of the stored procedure you just created: `dbo` `.GetPublisherEmployees`. You use the Pubs connection for the Connection parameter.

After you open the connection, you instantiate an instance of the XmlTextReader object by using the `ExecuteXmlReader()` method. The XmlReader class enables you to read data from XML files. You can use the XmlReader to load data into the XmlDataDocument or a DataSet. As you might remember from Chapter 7, the XmlReader class is an abstract base class with interface definitions that you can extend by using other objects. One of the objects that implements this interface is the XmlTextReader, which you will use in an upcoming example to read the XML file containing your employee and publisher data.

NOTE *You use the TreeView control to stream your data. In production, you wouldn't gain much advantage by stream-ing data into a TreeView, because it doesn't represent paged data. A great control for streamed content is the DataGrid with paging. However, because we've reviewed the DataGrid control many times in the previous chapters, we thought we would give you something new to work with.*

You use the `Read()` method of the XmlTextReader object to loop through the nodes in the XML document created by your stored procedure. For the `<PubEmp>` root, you add the main node for your TreeView, titling it **Root**. With a `Select Case` conditional, you iterate through the Publishing House nodes, adding them directly below your root node. Because the XmlReader base class reads XML as a forward-only stream, you must immediately add the children nodes as you come across them. Using an in-memory reference to your position within the Publishing House nodes, you add the children Employee nodes. The `ReadInnerXml()` method retrieves the XML data within your desired node. You use this information as your display text for your nodes. The resulting form at runtime should look similar to Figure 10.2.

FIGURE 10.2

Populating a
TreeView from an
XML-based stored
procedure

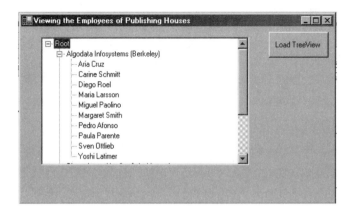

After you run the project, click the Load TreeView button. This will populate the TreeView control by using the XML stream. By default, the TreeView data will be collapsed under the Root node. If you expand this node, you will see a list of all the publishers within the Pubs database. Each of these Publishing House nodes can be expanded in turn, to show their respective employees.

TIP   Another way to write the code to populate the TreeView control would be with relative positioning, rather than fixed ordinals. Using positioning, you can track where you are in both the XML document and the TreeView, referencing the current node for relativity. Based on your location in the XML hierarchy, you can then add the appropriate data to the correct TreeView nodes collection.

Inserting XML-Formatted Data into a SQL Server Database

There are many ways to use XML for updating SQL Server without using .NET, such as using a stored procedure with the OPENXML function and INSERT FROM statement.

Additionally, you can take advantage of the XmlTextReader class to retrieve an XML stream from an XML document. You can then store the stream as an XML string, passing the XML string to a stored procedure that uses the OPENXML function. This is the example we show you later in this chapter.

USING A STORED PROCEDURE WITH THE *OPENXML* FUNCTION AND *INSERT FROM* STATEMENT

In this example, you are going to create an XML document from VS .NET and pass it to SQL Server via ADO.NET. The XML document will contain new data that will be added to the authors table of the Pubs database.

First, you will create a stored procedure in SQL Server that uses the OPENXML function, along with the INSERT FROM T-SQL statement. The OPENXML function provides a relational representation of an XML document. This way, you can pass an XML document to a stored procedure in order to update the relational back-end database.

The stored procedure you create next does just that. The INSERT FROM statement populates the database by using the handle to the in-memory XML document. The INSERT FROM statement treats the XML document handle as it would any other relational data source, such as a table or view.

Listing 10.10 displays the T-SQL code used to generate the dbo.InsertAuthorsXML stored procedure, which is contained in the Creating the InsertAuthorsXML stored procedure.sql file.

LISTING 10.10: CREATING A STORED PROCEDURE TO INSERT XML DATA BY USING THE
OPENXML FUNCTION

```
CREATE PROCEDURE dbo.InsertAuthorsXML
- XML Document representation
(@XmlAuthors NVARCHAR (4000))
AS
- handle to the XML document ID
DECLARE @XmlDocId int

- Create XML doc in memory
EXEC sp_xml_preparedocument @XmlDocId OUTPUT,  @XmlAuthors

INSERT Authors
SELECT *
- Use OPENXML to retrieve XML author data.
FROM OPENXML(@XmlDocId, N'/AuthRoot/Authors')
    WITH authors

- Remove XML Doc from memory
EXEC sp_xml_removedocument @XmlDocId
```

Let's step through the code in Listing 10.10. First, you create an input parameter, @XmlAuthors. This parameter receives the XML data for the new rows, storing it as a varchar with a length of 4000. This parameter will contain the data for insertion.

Next, you declare an integer data type variable that will store the handle to the in-memory XML document. The next statement executes the sp_xml_preparedocument system stored procedure, which receives an XML hierarchy as an input parameter and constructs an in-memory XML document. You will receive as an output parameter, an integer representing the handle to the in-memory XML structure. You can then store this handle into the parameter you declared earlier.

After you obtain a reference to the XML data handle, you can parse and manipulate the hierarchy, committing the changes back to the relational database. Because you keep all this manipulation on the data server, you reduce the amount of network trips you need to make between your database and your application server.

TIP   The OPENXML function works a lot like batch updates. Instead of doing multiple atomic inserts, by calling a traditional insert stored procedure for each row, you can pass in the entire batch with only one call by using a stored procedure similar to the one in Listing 10.10. Imagine the performance and scalability gains you get by passing in multiple rows with a single network trip!

The example in Listing 10.10 uses the OPENXML function to insert XML data into the database. You pass the handle to the XML document, as well as the XPath expression to identify the Authors node in the XML document. You will be adding your data to the Authors node.

As we mentioned earlier, the WITH clause formats the relational representation of your data by using a schema declaration, or by specifying the name of an existing table. In our example, we choose to have you leverage the schema from the authors table in the database. This way, you don't have to explicitly define your schema, saving some coding.

TIP   It is much faster to use a schema declaration up front when using the WITH clause because it doesn't have to query the database to retrieve the schema.

After the query is finished with the in-memory XML hierarchy, the sp_xml_removedocument stored procedure is called to remove the XML structure from memory. Create the stored procedure by executing the code in Listing 10.10. Later in this chapter, you are going to call it from your VB .NET project by using ADO.NET and XML objects.

Using XML with the .NET Framework

There is no question about XML's role in the .NET Framework. As you have learned throughout the course of this book, XML is the core of .NET data access technologies, such as ADO.NET. DataSets use XML to serialize their data. Back in Chapter 7, we discussed ADO.NET's integration with XML, in the section aptly titled "ADO.NET and XML." We reviewed some of the objects in the System.Xml namespace, such as the XmlDataDocument, and we also showed you how to persist both DataSets and DataReaders as XML. Additionally, we examined the visual tools in VS .NET for working with XML, such as the XML Designer. However, we never really went into detail about the XML side of things; we focused mainly on the ADO.NET angle.

Our focus in that chapter was to show how ADO.NET interacts with XML. In this section, you'll examine how XML fits into the .NET Framework, by using VB .NET to insert an XML document into a SQL Server database.

ADDING NEW DATABASE ROWS FROM VB .NET BY USING XML

In this example, you are going to use the OPENXML stored procedure you created earlier from VB .NET. You will use the System.Xml objects to pass an XML document to your stored procedure by using the ADO.NET objects, such as the SqlCommand and Parameter objects. This example demonstrates how you can leverage the OPENXML command to perform batch inserts.

Create a new Windows Application named **Inserting XML Data into a SQL Server Database**, which is also the name of the solution file on the accompanying CD. Navigate to the Solution Explorer. First, you will have to create an XML document containing the new data you wish to insert into the authors table. This example indicates that you should add two new records to the database, but you can add as many as you would like, taking advantage of the batch insert capabilities of the OPENXML statement.

Right-click on the project node in the Solution Explorer and select the Add ➤ Add New Item option from the pop-up menu. From the Add New Item dialog box, select the XML File icon, as shown in Figure 10.3. Name your XML file **NewAuthors.xml**. Move the newly added file to the bin directory of the Solution Explorer, by dragging it to the bin folder. By moving it to the bin directory, you can directly reference the relative path to the file from your code.

WARNING   If you don't see the bin folder, you will have to select the Show All Files option from the Solution Explorer.

FIGURE 10.3

Adding a new
XML file

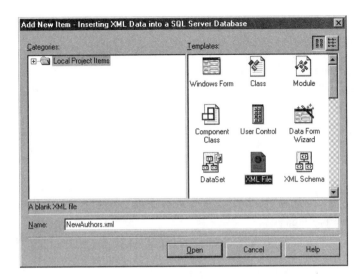

You will use the XML Designer to create the XML data that you wish to insert into the database. Double-click the newly created XML file to launch the XML Designer. By default, you should see the XML view. Add the code in Listing 10.11 to your XML document.

TIP   You should ensure that the XML data is well formed and contains only the data you wish to add. Additionally, you should add the necessary checkpoints to your VB .NET code to ensure that your data doesn't violate constraints, such as duplicate primary keys.

LISTING 10.11: CREATING NEW AUTHORS WITH AN XML DOCUMENT

```
<AuthRoot>
  <Authors
    au_id="111-51-1920"
    au_fname="Paul"
    au_lname="Cashion"
    contract="1"
    phone="2125551212">
  </Authors>
  <Authors
    au_id="121-72-0621"
    au_fname="Demi"
    au_lname="Poulathas"
    contract="1"
    phone="2125551212">
  </Authors>
</AuthRoot>
```

The XML document contains two new authors, which you will add to the Pubs database. Again, with a single network trip, you can send multiple data insertions. Also, notice that this example uses an attribute-centric representation for your XML data. As you might remember from Listing 10.10, you didn't supply the optional `flags` parameter for the `sp_xml_preparedocument` stored procedure, using the default attribute-centric mapping. The attributes of your Authors elements will be mapped to columns with the same names within the database.

TIP   Alternately, you could use the XmlTextWriter class to generate your XML document. For example, you could use the `WriteStartElement()` *and* `WriteAttribute()` *methods to construct your elements. For simplicity's sake, in this example you use the XML Designer to create your XML document. We discussed the XmlTextWriter class in Chapter 7.*

What VB .NET database project would be complete without ADO.NET? Now, you will have to set up your ADO.NET objects to call this stored procedure, passing in your XML document as an input parameter.

Now let's set up your VB .NET code. Expand the Server Explorer node for the Pubs connection and drag over the `dbo.InsertAuthorsXML` stored procedure onto the form displayed in the designer window. This automatically creates both a Connection and Command control in the component tray. Next, drag over a button and label control from the toolbar. You will use the click event of the button to call your stored procedure. You will use the `Text` property of the label control to display the results of your query.

After you import the `System.Xml` and `System.Data.SqlClient` namespaces from the Declarations section of the form, type the code in Listing 10.12 within the click event of the button.

LISTING 10.12: PASSING AN XML DOCUMENT TO A STORED PROCEDURE BY USING VB .NET

```
Dim xrNewAuthors As New _
            XmlTextReader("NewAuthors.xml")
Dim strXML As String
SqlConnection1.Open()
  Try
    While xrNewAuthors.Read()
      If xrNewAuthors.Name = _
                      "AuthRoot" Then
        strXML = _
            xrNewAuthors.ReadOuterXml
        SqlCommand1. _
            Parameters(1).Value = _
                strXML
      End If
    End While
  Catch errLoad As System.Exception
    Console.WriteLine _
          (errLoad.Message)
  End Try
    SqlCommand1.ExecuteScalar()
    If SqlCommand1.Parameters(0). _
```

```
            Value = 0 Then
      Label1.Text = _
            "Data was successfully added"
    Else
      Label1.Text = _
            "Data was not added"
    End If
```

The code in Listing 10.12 creates a new XmlTextReader class by using the constructor to specify the source XML filename. This is the file that you created earlier by using the XML Designer.

After opening the SqlConnection, you read the XML data stream until you get to the root node, AuthRoot. At that point, you use the `ReadOuterXml()` method to store the full XML string for the file into a string variable. The `ReadOuterXml()` method retrieves the content of the current node, the root node, as well as all its children. The `ReadInnerXml()` method would not be sufficient for our purposes, as it would not include the root tag, which the `OPENXML` function requires.

You set this string to the second parameter of your SqlCommand object, which represents the `@XmlAuthors` input parameter of the `dbo.InsertAuthorsXML` stored procedure. The first parameter is an output parameter that stores the results of your query. You will use this parameter later to examine your results.

Finally, you call the `ExecuteScalar()` method of the Command object. As you might remember from Chapter 6, "A First Look at ADO.NET," the `ExecuteScalar()`method retrieves a single result value from a stored procedure or SQL statement.

If you run this form and click the button, the contents of the XML document will be passed to the stored procedure in the Pubs database. Take a look at the data in the `authors` table after executing the VB .NET code. You will see the two new records in the database, as shown in Figure 10.4.

FIGURE 10.4

Viewing the results of the `OPENXML` stored procedure

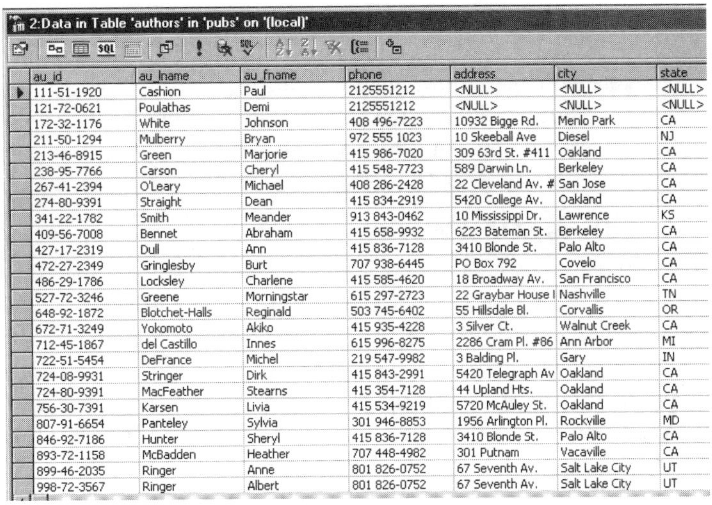

au_id	au_lname	au_fname	phone	address	city	state
111-51-1920	Cashion	Paul	2125551212	<NULL>	<NULL>	<NULL>
121-72-0621	Poulathas	Demi	2125551212	<NULL>	<NULL>	<NULL>
172-32-1176	White	Johnson	408 496-7223	10932 Bigge Rd.	Menlo Park	CA
211-50-1294	Mulberry	Bryan	972 555 1023	10 Skeeball Ave	Diesel	NJ
213-46-8915	Green	Marjorie	415 986-7020	309 63rd St. #411	Oakland	CA
238-95-7766	Carson	Cheryl	415 548-7723	589 Darwin Ln.	Berkeley	CA
267-41-2394	O'Leary	Michael	408 286-2428	22 Cleveland Av. #	San Jose	CA
274-80-9391	Straight	Dean	415 834-2919	5420 College Av.	Oakland	CA
341-22-1782	Smith	Meander	913 843-0462	10 Mississippi Dr.	Lawrence	KS
409-56-7008	Bennet	Abraham	415 658-9932	6223 Bateman St.	Berkeley	CA
427-17-2319	Dull	Ann	415 836-7128	3410 Blonde St.	Palo Alto	CA
472-27-2349	Gringlesby	Burt	707 938-6445	PO Box 792	Covelo	CA
486-29-1786	Locksley	Charlene	415 585-4620	18 Broadway Av.	San Francisco	CA
527-72-3246	Greene	Morningstar	615 297-2723	22 Graybar House I	Nashville	TN
648-92-1872	Blotchet-Halls	Reginald	503 745-6402	55 Hillsdale Bl.	Corvallis	OR
672-71-3249	Yokomoto	Akiko	415 935-4228	3 Silver Ct.	Walnut Creek	CA
712-45-1867	del Castillo	Innes	615 996-8275	2286 Cram Pl. #86	Ann Arbor	MI
722-51-5454	DeFrance	Michel	219 547-9982	3 Balding Pl.	Gary	IN
724-08-9931	Stringer	Dirk	415 843-2991	5420 Telegraph Av	Oakland	CA
724-80-9391	MacFeather	Stearns	415 354-7128	44 Upland Hts.	Oakland	CA
756-30-7391	Karsen	Livia	415 534-9219	5720 McAuley St.	Oakland	CA
807-91-6654	Panteley	Sylvia	301 946-8853	1956 Arlington Pl.	Rockville	MD
846-92-7186	Hunter	Sheryl	415 836-7128	3410 Blonde St.	Palo Alto	CA
893-72-1158	McBadden	Heather	707 448-4982	301 Putnam	Vacaville	CA
899-46-2035	Ringer	Anne	801 826-0752	67 Seventh Av.	Salt Lake City	UT
998-72-3567	Ringer	Albert	801 826-0752	67 Seventh Av.	Salt Lake City	UT

As you can see, the .NET `System.Xml` objects combined with the T-SQL `OPENXML` function provide a robust way to insert XML data into a relational database. This functionality is useful for processing XML data from legacy sources or from external applications.

The Role of XML in SOAP

XML plays a vital role in remoting technology standards, specifically with Simple Object Access Protocol (SOAP). SOAP is yet another technology that leverages XML at its core. Like XML, SOAP is not a platform-specific standard, but instead is an evolving W3C standard supported by many corporations, such as IBM, Sun Microsystems, and Microsoft.

In this section, we discuss the role XML plays in the SOAP specification. This section is not intended to be a tutorial on how to use SOAP with .NET remoting; instead, we focus on the XML technology underlying SOAP. Understanding the pervasive effect of XML on various technologies is fundamental to designing interoperable software.

NOTE *SOAP is not limited to the .NET Framework. You can leverage SOAP with Component Object Model (COM) services. Although exploring this topic is beyond the scope of this book, you can find information on this technology in the MSDN documentation that ships with VS .NET.*

The Need for SOAP

The need for a standard such as SOAP emerged with the advent of the Web as a serious application interface. Web browsers could transparently communicate with applications running on different platforms, without any regard to which programming language generated the code. This led to a strong demand for programmers to have that same platform transparency. Like web users, software developers wanted to take advantage of services running on remote machines, using them as if they were native components. Screen-scraping HTML results gave you the ability to reuse data, but that was no answer because this solution crippled scalability. There had to be a way for services to communicate with one another by using standard formats. XML and HTTP were an obvious choice. They both are widely accepted and ubiquitous technologies that could be leveraged to pass both data and instructions between remote servers.

How Does SOAP Work?

SOAP is used with Microsoft technologies as a replacement for the binary COM-based communications protocol, DCOM. SOAP leverages the industry-standard format and transport mechanism found with both XML and HTTP, providing a communications protocol for objects and services. All this is done in a platform-independent manner. SOAP clearly addresses the problem of interoperability between different applications and technologies. Because SOAP uses HTTP as its communication mechanism, using text-based XML for its message format, it is readily transportable across networks and firewalls. You didn't have this option with DCOM, which at best would use Port 80 to transfer binary information between systems, with TCP/IP tunneling. Firewalls can easily filter out any non-HTTP requests, making it difficult to use DCOM calls across companies' networks. You could leverage COM Internet Services (CIS) to pass DCOM calls across HTTP; however, this again is a proprietary solution that doesn't provide interoperability between different technologies.

PAYLOADS

SOAP transfers encapsulated XML data, called *payloads*, to methods on remote servers. SOAP doesn't use any new technology; instead it formalizes a contract for passing XML messages across remote services. Because ADO.NET is XML-based, you can easily pass DataSets by using SOAP. To pass your DataSet, you must properly package it by using the SOAP specifications. In the simplest SOAP format, the root of your XML document must use an `Envelope` tag, which contains the `Body` element. The `Body` element specifies the name of the method you wish to call, as well as any input or output parameters for the method. Let's review the structure in more detail.

STRUCTURE OF SOAP MESSAGES

All SOAP messages must adhere to a basic structure, which identifies the messages with XML namespaces. An *XML namespace* provides a mechanism to identify XML data types, as well as qualify both your element and attribute names. In fact, you used an XML namespace earlier in this chapter when you created an XML schema by using the `XMLDATA` operator with the `FOR XML` function. In that example, your query refers to two uniform resource namespaces for both the data structure and data type definitions for the XML schema:

```
<Schema name="Schema2"
  xmlns="urn:schemas-microsoft-com:xml-data"
  xmlns:dt="urn:schemas-microsoft-com:datatypes">
```

The XML namespace declarations are specified with the `xmlns` prefix. The next part specifies a Uniform Resource Identifier (URI), which maps to either a Uniform Resource Locator (URL) or a Uniform Resource Number (URN). A colon separates the URI from a local name, such as `dt` or `datatypes`. The combination of both the URI and the local name creates a unique namespace.

TIP *Refer to the W3C specifications for XML namespaces when creating your XML namespace. The specifications can be found at* `http://www.w3.org`.

XML namespaces enable you to distinguish between element names to avoid name collisions of elements that use the same name. At the start of your SOAP message, you should include a URL that references an XML schema that will define the structure of your message:

```
<SOAP-ENV:Envelope
xmlns:SOAP-ENV=
"http://schemas.xmlsoap.org/soap/envelope/">
</SOAP-ENV:Envelope>
```

Although you are not required to do so, you should point to a valid XML schema within your SOAP envelope. You can think of the `Envelope` tag as the root element of a SOAP message, specified with the `<SOAP-ENV:Envelope>` XML start and end tags.

As we indicated earlier, the envelope encapsulates the body of the SOAP message. You can specify the body by using the `<SOAP-ENV:Body>` start and end tags. It is a good practice to also specify a namespace, which defines the body of your SOAP document. By specifying an encoding style space, you indicate that the body of your SOAP message will follow the SOAP standards for data encoding:

```
SOAP-ENV:encodingStyle=
"http://schemas.xmlsoap.org/soap/encoding/"
```

The `Body` element contains the name of the method you wish to call, along with any related data, such as input parameters. You could call the `GetPublisherName()` method, which accepts the `PublisherID` as an input parameter by specifying the appropriate `Body` elements:

```
<SOAP-ENV:Body>
  <myMethod:GetPublisherName
     xmlns:myMethod="Your-URI">
   <PublisherID>0736</PublisherID>
  </myMethod:GetPublisherName>
 </SOAP-ENV:Body>
```

Optionally, the SOAP envelope can contain a `Header` tag, which can specify the `InterfaceName`, `MethodName`, and `MessageType`. The `InterfaceName` is optional and specifies the name of interface that contains the method you wish to call. The appropriately named `MethodName` identifies the name of the method you wish to call. The name of the method you use here should match the one listed in the `Body` element. This enables the SOAP server to understand the request, without having to delve into the XML payload. The `MessageType` indicates whether you expect the method you called to return a response. If you would like a response, you would use the value `CallResponse`; if not, use the value `Call`. In addition to these headers, you can create your own custom headers, which extend this functionality with logic specific to the SOAP server's application.

SOAP REQUESTS

To use SOAP, your program sends out a *SOAP request*, which consists of the XML payload. The payload contains data, which is serialized by using an XML-based structure. The SOAP request specifies the information you need to connect to a remote server and invoke a method by using the proper parameters. The receiving server, a SOAP server, receives that request and sends the appropriate response back to the calling server. The response indicates failure or success by using the appropriate output parameters. All this is again repackaged in the form of an XML document, which is sent back to the calling server.

COMMUNICATING BY USING SOAP

Both the SOAP client and the SOAP server understand the XML payload, which is packaged via SOAP. This is because SOAP specifies a base of acceptable data type definitions that serve as a contract between the SOAP client and SOAP server. These definitions are largely based on the W3C XML type system for schemas. SOAP augments these type definitions with specific behaviors. These behaviors are packaged in SOAP headers, which enable services to communicate supplementary invocation request information.

To create a SOAP service from .NET, you use the base classes listed in the `System.Web.Services` and `System.Web.Services.Protocols` namespaces. Keep in mind, SOAP is not limited to the .NET Framework by any means. You can create SOAP services by using COM and COM+ libraries or any other SOAP-compliant technology.

NOTE   *A full discussion of creating SOAP services with .NET is beyond the scope of this book. The documentation that installs with VS .NET provides detailed information on how to create your own SOAP services.*

XML and HTTP form the foundation for universal interoperability between platforms, technologies, and programming languages. Over time, SOAP will enable universal connectivity between web-enabled applications, so that the Internet becomes a single living entity rather than a myriad of independent, unrelated organs.

Summary

After reading this chapter, you should have a firm understanding of the pervasive role of XML in various technologies. You read about how SQL Server 2000 integrates with XML to retrieve and update relational data. The advantages of this tight integration with XML became apparent as you created sample VB .NET applications that receive, process, and send XML data by using the native XML technologies such as ADO.NET and the `System.Xml` objects. Additionally, you should have a conceptual understanding of XML's role with SOAP as a means for universal communication between remote services.

This chapter also compared the parsing technologies that are available for XML document processing, as well as provided an understanding of how XML documents are constructed with elements and attributes. You should now know the requirements for a well-formed XML document. Well-formed XML documents are vital to both SQL Server and .NET technologies, such as the `OPENXML` statement and XmlReader implementations. Using this knowledge, you should have no problem generating XML data and schema on the fly by using either SQL Server or Visual Studio .NET.

This concludes Part II of our book, "Database Programming." By this point, you should feel comfortable manipulating SQL Server data within the .NET Framework. In the next portion of this book, Part III, "Advanced Data Services," we immediately delve into data access by using VB .NET. Chapter 11, "More ADO.NET Programming," advances your understanding of the ADO.NET base classes. In Chapter 12, we continue many of the topics introduced in this chapter as we discuss XSL transforms and XPath expressions.

Part 3

Advanced Data Services

Chapter 11

More ADO.NET Programming

- ◆ Event handling
- ◆ Threading
- ◆ Exception handling

PROGRAMMING WITH ADO.NET IS a radical departure from programming with classic ADO. The .NET Framework provides many options for making your code more robust while at the same time keeping programming easy and efficient. In previous chapters, we focused primarily on the non-reactive components of ADO.NET, such as the data access objects, methods, and properties. In this chapter, we focus on the reactive elements of ADO.NET: events, exceptions, and threads.

Although some elements of event programming remain the same, VB .NET introduces new concepts, such as dynamic event wiring and multicasting. VB .NET's programmer-friendliness is apparent with the threading mechanism in VB .NET. It is now possible to create free-threaded applications without struggling with third-party solutions or other languages. Exception handling has greatly improved in VB .NET, supporting structured exception handling and enabling you to build highly specialized exception handlers.

By the end of this chapter, you should be able to answer the following questions:

- ◆ How do events work in ADO.NET?
- ◆ What is multicasting?
- ◆ What are delegates?
- ◆ How does threading work with ADO.NET?
- ◆ How are delegates used with threading?
- ◆ What advantages does structured exception handling provide over unstructured error handling?

Event Handling

Although this section focuses on the events raised by the ADO.NET objects, the concepts introduced here are not specific to ADO.NET. The entire .NET Framework uses a common event specification, which indicates that events must include the following components:

◆ A class containing the event data. This class should derive from the EventArgs base class.

◆ An event delegate, which works like a function pointer that holds a reference to a method containing the event-handling logic.

◆ The server class, which raises the event.

◆ The client class, which catches the event.

Classes that provide services to client code raise events to notify the calling code when specific activities occur. The client code captures the events in order to execute custom logic related to a change in the state of a server class.

Events are primarily used to perform validation when data is updated. Using events, your code could check that the data matches the appropriate data type and length requirements. You could also ensure that specific business rules are met, such as required fields or formatting rules. Events are most useful when used to notify calling code of the state of a particular activity. This becomes vital when working with free-threaded applications.

Event programming in ADO.NET is no giant leap from past versions of Visual Basic. If you have worked with events in classic ADO, the concepts in this section should be fairly easy to grasp. An important consideration when you work with ADO.NET events is the object-oriented nature of ADO.NET.

Many ADO.NET objects are a part of collections, which are nested within a parent object. For example, the DataSet is comprised of a collection of one or more DataTables. DataTables consist of one or more DataRows. Because of this, events can be raised from objects within the container object. Most of the update events that occur within a DataSet are actually raised by the DataTable object. Conversely, row change events that you might think would be handled by the DataRow object are actually raised by the DataTable container. Working with ADO.NET events is not difficult as long as you are aware of which objects trigger them. *Event bubbling* refers to the ability of events from a child object to spark up into their container objects.

A solid understanding of event programming is a vital precursor to understanding how to work with threaded applications, or exception handling. A good way to examine the behavior of events in the .NET Framework is to investigate those raised by the ADO.NET objects. By working with ADO.NET events, you will get an understanding of how .NET events work in general. In this section, we discuss how ADO.NET works with delegates, the EventArgs object, and event handling. All these concepts are fundamental to the .NET event architecture.

.NET Framework Event Concepts

Before we begin our discussion of event handling with ADO.NET, we must review some of the new features introduced with the .NET Framework. Event data is handled in a different way than in previous versions of Visual Basic, with the use of an EventArgs object. Additionally, the concept of delegates is a new one and is vital to understanding much of the information in this chapter.

As we mentioned in the beginning of this section, event programming in the .NET Framework consists of four components: the event data derived from the EventArgs base class, an event delegate, a server class, and a client class. The first two components follow a common architecture under the .NET realm. We discuss these next. Additionally, you should understand how event handling works in the .NET Framework, such as adding event handlers at runtime by using the `AddHandler` and `RemoveHandler` directives. When you examine the ADO.NET events in this section, you will see how the latter two components, client and server classes, work together to raise and handle system events.

UNDERSTANDING THE EVENTARGS OBJECT

The .NET Framework treats event data differently than did previous versions of Visual Basic, ADO, and COM. Instead of passing in a variety of parameters with multiple data types, all the event data and behavior is encapsulated into a single base class implementation derived from the EventArgs object.

The EventArgs object belongs directly to the `System` namespace. Events in the .NET Framework derive from this base class in order to provide event data for a specific event. Because ADO.NET events work like any other .NET event, you need to understand the basics of event programming in .NET before you focus on ADO.NET events.

As you might remember from classic ADO, events often expect a slew of arguments. These arguments are commonly listed within enumerations. The RecordSet's `ChangeComplete` event contains an `adReason` enumeration, which specifies the action that causes the RecordSet to be changed. This enumeration can have one of the following values: `adRsnRequery`, `adRsnResync`, `adRsnClose`, or `adRsnOpen`. Take a look at the method signature, and you can see it's a bit cumbersome to work with. Not only do you have many different input parameters, but also you have to deal with multiple enumerations, each containing its own values. That's a lot to remember!

```
RecordsetChangeComplete(adReason As EventReasonEnum, _
        pError As Error, adStatus As EventStatusEnum, _
        pRecordset As Recordset)
```

Most of the other events within classic ADO objects worked in a similar fashion, expecting multiple input parameters, with little similarity between each event signature. There wasn't much consistency between the number of arguments, nor their data types.

ADO.NET has changed the structure of event declarations with the concept of the EventArgs base class. The EventArgs base class provides consistency between the event definitions of .NET objects.

The EventArgs object is used for events throughout the .NET Framework. If you examine the signature of a button's click subroutine, you will see the following:

```
Private Sub Button1_Click _
(ByVal sender As System.Object, _
 ByVal e As System.EventArgs) Handles Button1.Click
```

This subroutine serves as an *event listener* for the `Button1.Click` event. When the event is fired, the listener is invoked to take appropriate actions based on the event that was fired. The `Handles` keyword glues the event to the event listener. You will learn more about the `Handles` keyword shortly.

In the `Button1_Click` event listener, the second argument is typed as `System.EventArgs`. When you pass in this parameter, you pass in all the data and behavior specific to each implementation of the EventArgs class. In this case, we directly used the EventArgs type rather than a derivation of this base class. This means that no custom event data will be passed to the `Button1_Click` event listener.

In cases when you do want to specify custom event data, you would create a class that would implement from the EventArgs base class. You can examine the properties of this class to determine the state of the event. Alternately, you could call the methods of the event to invoke interesting behaviors. Usually the properties of event data are customized for each implementation. You will see this is the case with most of the ADO.NET objects. Most often, the methods default to those inherited from the Object base class, on which the EventArgs class is based. You can examine the properties of the EventArgs implementation to perform custom logic based on each event invocation.

Later in this chapter, you will work with event programming by using the ADO.NET object model. You will use the `DataColumnChangeEventArgs` derivation, which contains specific event data when a column in a DataTable changes. Don't worry—this will all come together when you walk through code examples.

USING DELEGATES IN THE .NET FRAMEWORK

Previously, we reviewed the event listener for the `Button1.Click` event. The `Button1_Click` serves as the method that handles the `Button1.Click` event. We used the `Handles` keyword to set this reference. This process is referred to as *event wiring*. Delegates provide another means to wire your events to the appropriate methods that handle them.

A *delegate* is a class that references another method. For example, you can use a delegate to point to a method that serves as an event handler for a specific event. This event wiring is depicted in Figure 11.1.

FIGURE 11.1

Event wiring in .NET: simple delegate

A delegate acts as function pointer to the real method. This function pointer serves as a bridge between the object that invoked the method and the object that contains the method. These references work almost like a wrapper around the method, enabling you to indirectly call the method via the wrapper.

The concept of delegates should be familiar to you if you have worked with any type of callback functionality in VB6. Delegates work much like callbacks with one major difference: delegates are type-safe. Unlike callback methods, which pass only a reference to a memory address, delegates pass the entire signature of the method. The signature contains the method's return value, input parameters, and output parameters. Because delegates contain all this extra information, they can enforce strict type-safety. When you declare a delegate, you specify the signature of the method. Then, you can use the delegate object to wrap any methods that match this signature. Delegates don't care which object contains the method reference, as long as the signatures match. Any mappings that do not match this signature generate a type-safety violation.

A single delegate can be used to maintain a list of function pointers to several different methods. This concept is referred to as *multicasting*. Figure 11.2 illustrates how multicasting works with delegates.

FIGURE 11.2

Event wiring in .NET: multicast delegate

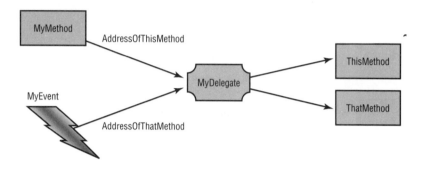

You can string multiple delegates together, pointing one to the other. The entire string of delegates is contained within a single delegate object. By triggering the first delegate in the string of delegates, you can ultimately broadcast a single message to the entire series of delegates at once.

WARNING *When you work with multicast delegates, all method signatures must match. Each function pointer contained by the delegate must reference methods that all share the same interface. What you do within those interfaces is up to you, as long as the external signatures are identical.*

Although delegates can be used in any circumstance when you need a function pointer, they really come in handy with event-based programming. When an object raises an event, it doesn't know which object will receive the event. Delegates serve as an ambassador between the event raiser and event receiver. As you are processing data in a method, you can use a delegate to send back status notifications to the calling code. Delegates enable the calling code to specify which method should be invoked when an event occurs. Delegates are a vital part of event-based programming using VB .NET and are used in the examples in this chapter.

Many of the ADO.NET events are handled via delegates. The RowChanged event corresponds to the OnRowChanged method, which serves as its delegate. Likewise, the OnColumnChanged delegate handles the ColumnChanged event. Delegates represent the method that contains the code to execute when a specific event has occurred. The delegate method contains the appropriate reaction code for a specific activity.

NOTE *There isn't necessarily a one-to-one relationship between an event and a delegate. You can designate a single delegate to handle multiple events.*

Later in this chapter, you will see how delegates function within the realms of .NET event programming. Additionally, you will learn more about delegates in the "Threading" section.

WORKING WITH EVENT HANDLERS

There are two ways to handle events when using VB .NET. One way is more traditional and uses the `WithEvents` and `Handles` keywords. You might be familiar with this approach if you have worked with previous versions of Visual Basic. Alternately, you can use a second option introduced with VB .NET, which uses `AddHandler` and `RemoveHandler`. This option enables you to dynamically add and remove event handlers.

Previously, we showed you an example of event handling using the click event of a Button. To handle this event, the `Handles` directive was supplied:

```
Handles Button1.Click
```

You append the `Handles` keyword to the end of a method that will be used to handle that event. After the `Handles` keyword, specify the name of the event you wish to reference. Figure 11.3 illustrates how a single event is wired to the appropriate subroutine.

You can even handle multiple events with a single event handler, as depicted in Figure 11.4.

FIGURE 11.3

Event wiring in .NET: single event wiring with the `Handles` keyword

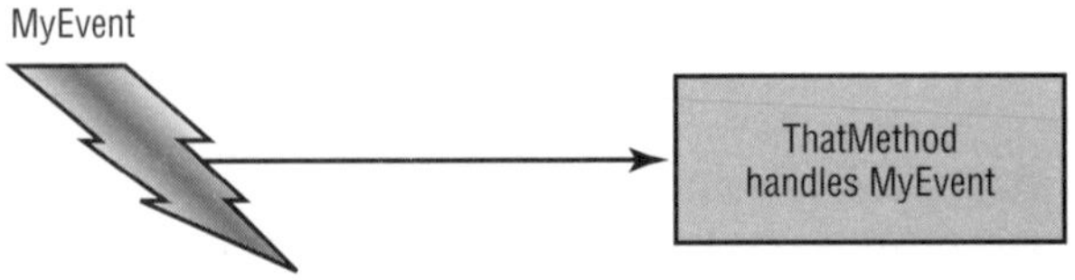

FIGURE 11.4

Event wiring in .NET: multiple event wiring with the `Handles` keyword

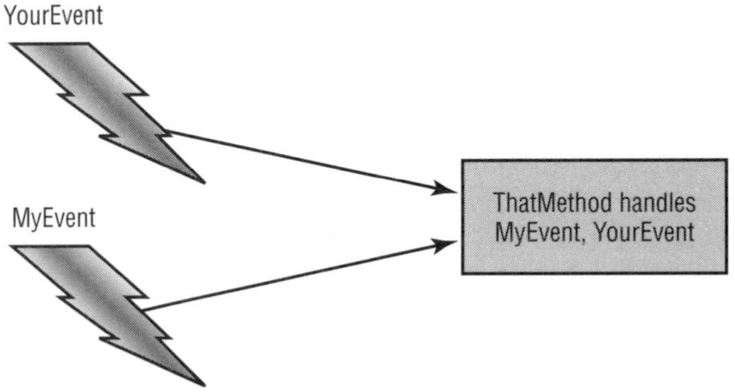

Handling multiple events with a single event handler is easy. If you want to write a single event handler for two different buttons, you just need to append the `Handles` keyword to the end of the event handler along with the names of the events you would like it to handle. Each event should be separated by a comma:

```
Handles Button1.Click, Button2.Click
```

In this example, the `Button1_Click` method is marked as an event handler:

```
Private Sub Button1_Click(ByVal sender As System.Object, ByVal e As
    System.EventArgs) Handles Button1.Click
```

The first argument, sender, provides a reference to the object from which the event was raised. The second parameter, e, provides the relevant event data for that event. This parameter is defined as the EventArgs base class, whose purpose we discussed earlier.

The Handles keyword doesn't work alone. It needs events to handle. To specify events for a class, you use the WithEvents statement to declare the variable that will handle the events of an object:

```
Friend WithEvents Button1 As System.Windows.Forms.Button
```

When you add a new button to your form, the Windows Form Generator will use the WithEvents statement to relate the Button1 class to the System.Windows.Forms.Button object's events. From there, you can map any of the events supported by the System.Windows.Forms.Button object to the Button1 variable.

The AddHandler directive works in a similar fashion, enabling you to map an event handler to an event. The AddHandler works in conjunction with its counterpart: RemoveHandler. The power of AddHandler comes from its ability to multicast a single event to multiple event handlers, unlike the Handles keyword. Although the Handles keyword enables you to map a single event handler to multiple events, as shown in Figure 11.4, it doesn't enable you to do the reverse: map multiple event handlers to a single event.

Figure 11.5 illustrates how the AddHandler keyword works with multicasting. Additionally, you can dynamically add and remove event handlers at runtime, which is not possible when using the Handles directive.

FIGURE 11.5

Multicasting with the AddHandler keyword

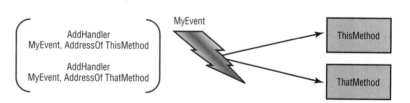

NOTE *Multicasting is the ability to broadcast a single message to multiple listeners. A multicast event could be distributed to multiple event handlers that receive the event. Imagine that you want to notify multiple applications that a central database log is full. You can use multicasting to notify all the applications at once.*

The AddHandler directive expects two parameters: the event you wish to handle and the method that will serve as a delegate for that event. Using a combination of the AddHandler and RemoveHandler operators, you can swap out event handlers at runtime based on specific business logic. You will be using the AddHandler keyword later in this chapter to bind an event to its delegate. Additionally, the AddHandler directive comes in handy when working with free-threaded applications. You will see some samples of event wiring in the "Threading" section of this chapter.

Understanding ADO.NET Events

This section provides a conceptual overview of the ADO.NET events that occur in the core ADO.NET objects: Connection, DataAdapter, DataSet, and DataTable. It also covers a few of the properties that manage the state of ADO.NET objects. Event programming and state management go hand in hand, and you must fully understand how each works in order to effectively build reactive and proactive applications.

NOTE *You might wonder why the DataRow object is not included in our overview of the ADO.NET events. This is because the DataRow object does not contain its own events. Activity within a DataRow is handled by its parent DataTable object. You should use the DataTable events to monitor the DataColumn object as well.*

After this overview, we provide an example of how these events are generated as you update DataRow objects within an existing DataSet. You will use the Northwind Shopping Cart application that you created in Chapter 8, "Data-Aware Controls." Later in this chapter, we continue to expand our practical implementation of the ADO.NET events within the "Exception Handling" section. Many of the ADO.NET events are caused by error conditions, which tie in nicely to our discussion of exception handling.

Let's begin with a detailed overview of the events raised by the main ADO.NET objects. After we are finished, you will have a solid foundation from which to build the data update and exception-handling examples later in this chapter. In our review of these events, we are going to focus on those specific to the ADO.NET objects, rather than those that inherit from base classes, such as the Component object. This way, we can keep our focus narrow and specific to data access.

CONNECTION EVENTS

When working with a data source, the most fundamental mechanism for establishing contact with the data is the Connection object. Many times, the data source exists on a remote server, requiring network trips to retrieve the data. These crossings are laden with the possibilities that your connection might not be established as planned. By using event handlers to hook into the `InfoMessage` or `StateChange` event of the Connection object, you can track the status of your connection, appropriately reacting to any conditions that might arise.

NOTE *Both the SqlConnection and OleDbConnection objects use the same events. There are some nuances between the two in terms of the event data that these events carry. We note the differences accordingly in our discussion.*

The `InfoMessage` *Event*

The `InfoMessage` event is triggered when any type of interesting activity occurs during the establishment of a connection. Think of interesting activity as any SQL Server event that has a severity of 10 or lower. Later in this chapter, you'll learn more about how SQL Server handles severity levels and about each of the properties within the `InfoMessage` EventArgs class. These properties contain event data regarding the `InfoMessage` event and are different based on the .NET data provider that you are using.

The* SqlInfoMessageEventArgs *Class When working with the SqlClient data provider, the `SqlInfo-MessageEventArgs` implementation contains the event data involving the `InfoMessage` event that was raised. This class exposes a single property:

◆ The `Errors` object contains the events raised from the database server. These events are stored in a collection as a `SqlErrorCollection` class. The SqlException class also works with this collection. You'll see how this works in the "Exception Handling" section later in this chapter.

The* OleDbInfoMessageEventArgs *Class The OleDb equivalent of the EventArgs object implementation is appropriately named `OleDbInfoMessageEventArgs`. The OleDb data provider actually contains different properties within its EventArgs implementation than the SqlClient's EventArgs implementation. These properties include the following:

◆ The `ErrorCode` property returns an integer containing the handle to the source of the error. This value is returned as an `HRESULT`.

◆ The `Errors` property is similar to the `Errors` property of the SQL .NET data provider, returning a collection of the events raised from the database server. Instead of working with a `SqlErrorCollection`, the `OleDbErrorCollection` class is used.

◆ The `Message` property contains information about the error. This is similar to the `Err` `.Description` property that you've probably used with previous versions of Visual Basic.

◆ The `Source` property lists the name of the object from which the error was generated. For example, this could contain the name of the .NET data provider, form, or class in which the error originated.

The StateChange *Event*

The `StateChange` event is triggered when the status of a connection changes. Like the `InfoMessage` event, this event also comes with event data in the form of a `StateChangeEventArgs` class.

The* StateChangeEventArgs *Class Both the OleDb and SqlClient data providers use this class to pass event data related to the `StateChange` event. This class contains two properties containing event data:

◆ The `CurrentState` property contains information regarding the current status of the connection.

◆ The `OriginalState` property contains information regarding the previous status of the connection.

When we discuss ADO.NET connection states later in this section, we will review the various enumeration values that these properties can contain.

DATAADAPTER EVENTS

As you know, the DataAdapter object is used by both the SqlClient and OleDb data provider. The SqlClient provider uses the SqlDataAdapter, whereas the OleDb provider uses the OleDbDataAdapter. Both these implementations inherit from the `DbDataAdapter` base class. Thus, they share some events in common, such as the `FillError` event. We note the discrepancies between the two data providers where relevant.

The `FillError` *Event*

The `FillError` event is thrown when there is an error with a `Fill()` operation. After this event is raised, you can examine its event data to take the appropriate action based on the error that was generated. If an error occurred at the back-end data source, the `FillError` event will not fire. The event handles only those errors that occurred within the ADO.NET data access layer.

FillErrorEventArgs   Both the OleDbDataAdapter and SqlDataAdapter use the same properties of the EventArgs implementation:

♦ The `Continue` property enables you to resume filling the DataSet if an error has occurred. This is a Boolean property that you can set to `True` should you wish to continue the operation.

♦ The `DataTable` property provides the DataTable object that the `Fill()` operation is working with.

♦ The `Errors` property provides an Exception object containing the errors that were generated by the `Fill()` method.

♦ The `Values` property retrieves the values in the DataRow in which the error occurred.

The `RowUpdating` *Event*

The `RowUpdating` event indicates that a modification, addition, or deletion to a DataRow is about to occur.

RowUpdatingEventArgs   The OleDbDataAdapter uses the `OleDbRowUpdatingEventArgs` object, and the SqlDataAdapter uses the `SqlRowUpdatingEventArgs` object. Both inherit from the generic `RowUpdatingEventArgs` base class.

NOTE   *For brevity, we have combined the properties of each into a single list. The two data providers share many properties in common and we note those that are supported only by either the SqlClient or OleDb data provider.*

♦ The `Command` property contains the Command object that is about to be used for that particular operation. The Command object is specific to the .NET data provider being used, such as `SqlCommand` or `OleDbCommand`.

♦ The `Row` property contains the DataRow object that is marked for modification, addition, or deletion.

♦ The `StatementType` property identifies the nature of the modification—whether it is an update, deletion, or insertion. It uses the `StatementType` enumeration to identify the operation. The possible enumeration values are `Insert`, `Update`, `Delete`, or `Select`.

◆ The `TableMapping` property contains the `DataTableMapping`, if one is being used. This mapping indicates the relationship between the DataTable object and the back-end table(s).

◆ The `Status` property is very useful because it provides information regarding the state of the operation. Possible values include `Continue`, `ErrorsOccurred`, `SkipAllRemainingRows`, and `SkipCurrentRow`. You can use this property to take appropriate action based on the status of the update.

◆ The `Errors` property contains a collection of any exceptions that the .NET data provider generates.

The RowUpdated *Event*

The `RowUpdated` event indicates that a modification, addition, or deletion to a DataRow has occurred.

RowUpdatedEventArgs   The event data for the `RowUpdated` event is the same as those for the `RowUpdating` event, with the addition of one more property:

◆ The `RecordsAffected` property contains the number of rows that were modified by the modification.

DATASET EVENTS

As you remember, the DataSet object belongs directly to the `System.Data` namespace. Thus, its events are not specific to any .NET data provider. The DataSet object can raise the `MergeFailed` event.

The MergeFailed *Event*

As you remember from Chapter 6, "A First Look at ADO.NET," the DataSet object provides the ability to merge data and/or schema from multiple DataTables or DataSets by using the `Merge()` method. If this merge operation should fail, the `MergeFailed` event is raised. This can occur when you attempt to merge DataSets containing DataRows that have the same primary key. To prevent this event from being raised, you need to turn off the `EnforceConstraints` property. However, there are not many cases where you would want to merge data that contains conflicting data items.

The MergeFailedEventArgs *Class*   When the `MergeFailed` event is raised, you can examine its properties to help determine what conditions raised the event:

◆ The `Conflict` property returns a string containing the description of the merge conflict.

◆ The `Table` property returns the name of the DataTable in which the conflict occurred.

Conflicts in a merge operation might occur due to constraint violations. As you know, DataSets are capable of processing constraint checks without querying the database server.

While you are in the process of updating data in a row, you might temporarily violate constraints. For example, if you are adding a new order, you might insert the `OrderID` before you update the

`CustomerID`. Because the `CustomerID` is required for referential integrity, your row would be in an error state until you added the appropriate `CustomerID`. There are several ways to resolve this situation.

You can opt to design your user interface so that a constraint-based field is populated first. However, this is not an optimal solution, especially if your back-end table(s) contain multiple constraints.

Alternately, you could supply default values for each constraint-based field so that your data is never left in an error state. This is also not ideal, because the user might accidentally commit the row without ensuring that the default values are indeed valid for that circumstance.

The most appropriate way to handle possible constraint violations is to address the cause rather than the symptom. You could handle this by suspending constraint checks while the data is in flux. When the user chooses to commit the data, you can re-enable constraint checking before the data is sent to the database server. Additionally, suspending constraint checks also suspends update events from firing.

DATATABLE EVENTS

When you fill a DataSet with data, certain events are triggered within the underlying DataTable objects. These events indicate the status of the update operation.

Like ADO, ADO.NET events are paired. One of the events in the pair fires right before an action takes place, and the other event fires when the action has completed. In classic ADO, the events that fire prior to the action begin with the prefix `Will`, and the events that fire upon completion end with the suffix `Complete`. The events `WillChangeRecord` and `RecordChangeComplete` are examples. In ADO.NET, DataTable events involving DataRow and DataColumn objects are paired by using the `Changing` and `Changed` suffixes. The events that occur when a DataTable is updated are straightforward, and you can pretty much infer what they do based on their names.

The RowChanging Event

The `RowChanging` event indicates that a piece of data is changing somewhere within the row. It doesn't indicate which column is undergoing the change. You would need to use the `ColumnChanging` event to capture that information. Keep in mind that the `RowChanging` event fires after the `ColumnChanging` event.

WARNING *Typed DataSets work with events differently than regular DataSets do. For example, the* `RowChanging` *event references a specific table within a typed DataSet. You wouldn't use the regular* `RowChanging` *event, but instead you would specify* `TableNameRowChanging`, *where* `TableName` *represents the name of your DataTable.*

If you want to suspend raising this event, you can invoke the `BeginEdit()` method of a DataRow. When you call the `BeginEdit()` method, you allow updates to each column without firing the `RowChanging` event. When you are ready to fire the `RowChanging` event, you can call the `EndEdit()` method of the DataRow object. That way, you can save execution time and performance, by firing the `RowChanging` logic only once rather than every time a column value changes. This way, you can execute multiple validation rules at once rather than on an individual basis.

The RowChanging event fires not only when a user updates a row, but also when the Fill() method of the DataAdapter is called. This way, you can validate the data that is returned from the data source as it is populated into a DataTable.

DataRowChangeEventArgs The DataColumnChangeEventArgs class inherits from the EventArgs base class. You can examine the properties contained by this class and execute specific logic based on the values of these properties.

◆ The Action property reveals the action taken on a DataRow. This property is a DataRowAction enumeration.

◆ The Row property refers to the newly changed DataRow object.

The Action property is very useful for analyzing the condition of a DataRow object. The DataRowAction enumeration is used by the RowChanging, RowChanged, RowDeleting, and RowDeleted events in order to describe the action that was performed on a DataRow. As you remember from Chapter 6, DataTable objects contain collections of DataRow and DataColumn objects. When you work with DataTables, you can examine the methods and attributes of its DataRow collection in order to determine the state of a DataRow.

The DataRowAction enumeration enables you to identify what sort of change occurred to a DataRow within your DataTable. Table 11.1 lists the possible values within the DataRowAction enumeration.

TABLE 11.1: DataRowAction ENUMERATION VALUES

ACTION	DESCRIPTION
Nothing	No modifications were performed on the DataRow.
Add	A new DataRow has been added.
Change	A DataRow is "dirty."
Delete	A DataRow has been marked for deletion.
Commit	Changes have been committed.
Rollback	Changes to a DataRow have been rolled back to their previous state.

NOTE *These values can be combined into a bitmask to record multiple actions at a single time. You must use the* FlagsAttribute *in order to treat an enumeration as a bitmask. For example, the* Commit *and* Delete *actions can occur at the same time, indicating that a deletion has been committed. Both these values can be retrieved by using bitwise operations.*

The **RowChanged** *Event*

The RowChanged event fires after row data is successfully updated. The EventArgs implementation contains the same properties as the RowChanging event: Row and Action.

> *NOTE* *You can refer to the* RowChanging *event for information regarding the event data. The consistency of event data between DataTable events lowers the learning curve of programming DataTable events.*

The RowDeleting *Event*

The RowDeleting event occurs when a DataRow is in the process of being deleted. The EventArgs implementation contains the same properties as the RowChanging event: Row and Action.

The RowDeleted *Event*

The RowDeleted event is raised after a row is deleted within a DataTable. The EventArgs implementation contains the same properties as the RowChanging event: Row and Action.

The ColumnChanging *Event*

The ColumnChanging event is raised each time a user changes data within a column. Unlike the Row-Changing event, this event enables you to hone in on the exact column that is being modified. You can add validation logic to confirm the changes as they occur. The ColumnChanging event fires before the RowChanging event.

DataColumnChangeEventArgs   The derived EventArgs class contains three properties that you can examine when the ColumnChanging event is fired:

◆ The ProposedValue property contains the new value for the column. This property comes in handy when you want to compare the new value with the old value.

◆ The Column property refers to the column object for which the change is occurring. This property is useful when you want to verify that a value confirms to the data type or length specified by a column.

◆ The Row property enables you to retrieve all the previous values for that row, before the change occurred. Of course, you would need an ordinal reference to point to the column that you wish to examine.

The ColumnChanged *Event*

The ColumnChanged event fires after new data is inserted or updated in a column. The EventArgs implementation uses the same properties as the ColumnChanging event: ProposedValue, Column, and Row.

> *NOTE* *You can refer to the* ColumnChanging *event for information regarding the event data.*

Working with ADO.NET Events

This section illustrates how events work within the ADO.NET programming model. As you step through the different ADO.NET objects, you will examine their events and programmatic examples of handling some of the events. Instead of creating a rudimentary project from scratch, you will expand the Northwind Shopping Cart user control and its relevant test project. You will focus on the events that are raised from non-error conditions, such as when column data changes. You will work with the events raised by error conditions in the "Exception Handling" section of this chapter.

NOTE *If you are following along with the examples in this book, you can migrate the code from the Northwind shopping cart example in Chapter 8. The source code for this project can be loaded from the solution file* NWShoppingCart.sln. *If not, the final application code can be found on the accompanying CD.*

CAPTURING DATA UPDATES

After you load the NWShoppingCart solution, open the NWShoppingCartControl user control within your design pane. At this point, your control should look similar to the one in Figure 11.6.

FIGURE 11.6

The NWShopping-CartControl user control in design mode

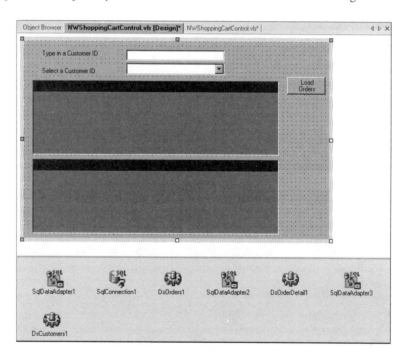

This contains all the ADO.NET code whose events you will explore in the following sections. Because the DataTable object is the most robust event-loaded object, we concentrate our examples on capturing the events raised by DataTable updates. Although our examples focus on the SQL Server .NET data provider, the same objects, properties, and methods can be applied to the OleDb data provider.

As you remember, our user control consisted of an Order grid and synchronized Order Detail grid, which showed you the detail items for each order you clicked in the main grid. You are going to add some event-handling code to capture the `ColumnChanging` event of the `Orders` DataTable. You will add some validation code to examine the modified data to ensure it complies with our business rules, which require a nonzero value for the freight data.

Specify the DataTable

The first thing you need to do is set your `Orders` DataTable in the user control to a variable. The original code had created the DataTable within the private `LoadOrderGrid()` method without setting it to a variable, as shown in Listing 11.1. Your event-handling code will be cleaner and more efficient if you use a variable for the DataTable.

LISTING 11.1: THE ORIGINAL LOADORDERGRID() METHOD

```
Private Sub LoadOrderGrid()
  OrderGrid.Refresh()
SqlSelectCommand1.Parameters("@CustomerID").Value = _
    cboCustomers.SelectedValue
  SqlDataAdapter1.Fill(DsOrders1, "Orders")
  OrderGrid.DataSource() _
    = DsOrders1.Tables("Orders").DefaultView()
End Sub
```

First, you need to declare a variable for the DataTable. Add this line to the beginning of the `LoadOrderGrid()` method:

```
Dim dtOrders As New DataTable()
```

You need to add a line to the end of the `LoadOrderGrid()` subroutine to set the `Orders` DataTable to the member variable you declared earlier:

```
dtOrders = DsOrders1.Tables("Orders")
```

Specify an Event Handler

Now you need to specify an event handler, which maps an event to its relevant delegate. Use the `AddHandler` keyword to specify your event handler for the `ColumnChanging` event. This directive should be added to the end of the `LoadOrderGrid()` method:

```
AddHandler dtOrders.ColumnChanging, _
    (New DataColumnChangeEventHandler _
    (AddressOf Me.NWColumnChanging))
```

As we indicated earlier, the `AddHandler` directive expects two parameters. The first one is the event that you wish to handle. IntelliSense will provide a list of available events for the object whose events you wish to handle, as you can see in Figure 11.7.

FIGURE 11.7

Choosing an event to handle

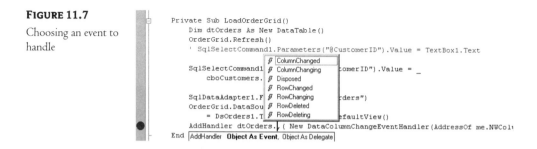

From this list of events, choose the ColumnChanging event.

Create an Event Delegate

Next, you specify the method that will handle the event, which is the second parameter for the AddHandler directive. Use the AddressOf keyword as a function pointer to the method that will be the delegate for the event. In this case, you specify the function pointer for the NWColumnChanging() method, whose code is depicted in Listing 11.2. Add the code in Listing 11.2 to create the method delegate.

LISTING 11.2: SPECIFYING AN EVENT DELEGATE

```
Private Sub NWColumnChanging _
      (ByVal NWSender As Object, _
           ByVal EventData As DataColumnChangeEventArgs)
   ' this code handles the ColumnChanging event
   ' raised by the Order DataGrid
   If EventData.Column.ColumnName = _
           "Freight" Then
     If EventData.ProposedValue = 0 Then
       Console.WriteLine _
         ("The freight cannot be zero")
       Throw _
         (New Exception("The freight cannot be
         zero"))
     End If
   End If
End Sub
```

When the ColumnChanging event is raised, the code within the NWColumnChanging() method will be invoked to handle the event. In our handler, you perform validation logic. You check whether the user modified the freight to a zero amount. If so, you will raise an exception, which will roll back the changes and prevent the modification from occurring. (We'll talk more about throwing exceptions later in this chapter.) Try running the code and changing the freight to zero. You will see that you are prevented from doing so by the logic within the event handler `NWColumnChanging`.

As you see, it is not difficult to write your own event handlers. In summary, you perform the following steps:

1. Identify the object whose events you wish to handle.

2. Specify an event handler.

3. Create an event delegate.

ADO.NET Object States

To handle events that are fired, you should understand the state of a particular object. The ADO.NET objects provide several properties that enable you to examine the state of a particular object so that you can take the appropriate action based on an event that has occurred.

THE *SQLCONNECTION* (AND *OLEDBCONNECTION*).*STATE* PROPERTY

The Connection object for both the SqlClient and OleDb data providers contain state information regarding the status of a connection. The same `ConnectionState` enumeration contains this information. Both the SqlClient and OleDb Connection objects can use this enumeration because it belongs directly to the `System.Data` namespace, rather than being specific to a single .NET data provider.

These values are stored as bits that can be combined into a bitmask. A *bitmask* contains a set of flags that can each contain values. You can examine the bitmask to determine multiple state conditions for a connection. By specifying an enumeration as a bitmask, you can combine multiple flag values into a single entity. Using bitwise operations, you can then parse out the different values contained within each flag. Table 11.2 contains the possible values for a connection state.

NOTE You must use the `FlagsAttribute` in order to treat an enumerated constant as a bitmask. The `FlagsAttribute` is a special class that inherits from the Attribute class.

TABLE 11.2: ConnectionState ENUMERATION VALUES

ACTION	DESCRIPTION
Open	The connection is open.
Closed	The connection is closed.
Connecting	The connection object is in the process of connecting to a data source.
Executing	A command is being executed for a specific connection.
Fetching	Data is being returned for a command belonging to a specific connection.
Broken	A connection is interrupted and disconnects from a data source after a connection has opened.

You can use the `StateChange` event to monitor the status of a Connection by querying the enumeration constants in Table 11.2. In classic ADO, you use events, which map to the possible connection states. For example, the `ConnectComplete` event would notify you after the connection starts. ADO.NET uses a centralized event to signal status changes. If you wanted to mimic the functionality that's found in classic ADO, you could write custom events that work with the `System.Threading` namespace. To raise events that capture the different status changes, you would need to block the calling thread until a particular status has occurred. This might not be desirable if you want your calling code to continue executing while the ADO.NET object continues operating. You can do this in classic ADO because it spins up a separate thread to handle the asynchronous operation. For example, if you choose to retrieve data asynchronously in classic ADO, you can take advantage of the `FetchComplete` event to notify the calling code when the data retrieval is complete. This way, the client code can continue executing while the data retrieval runs in the background. Native asynchronous operations are planned for a future release of ADO.NET.

THE *DATAROW.ROWSTATE* PROPERTY

The `RowState` property of the DataRow object is not specific to any .NET data provider and belongs directly to the `System.Data` namespace. You use this property to determine the condition that a row is in when changes are occurring to the data within the row. Generally, you wouldn't use this property alone. You should use the `HasChanges()` method to determine whether the parent DataSet is dirty. If so, you can use the `GetChanges()` method to retrieve a deltagram containing these changes.

The `RowState` property contains enumerated constants, much like the `State` property of the Connection object. You can query the values to determine the state of a DataRow object. We reviewed these enumerations in Table 6.5 of Chapter 6.

As we mentioned in Chapter 6, the RowState values aren't much use to you after the `AcceptChanges()` method has been called on the DataRow. This is because the `AcceptChanges()` method commits the changes to the DataRow, clearing the values in the `RowState` property.

Threading

The easiest way to understand threading is through a metaphor. Imagine that you are waiting in line at a fast-food restaurant. No matter what happens, you always end up in the line that takes the longest. Imagine your consternation when you realize that the couple in front of you is placing an order for themselves and a million of their best friends. And all you want to do is order a soda. You have to wait until they are done with their order, because they block your ability to order your item. You know that your order will take only a short time, and you wish that the cashier could prioritize their services based on the amount of time it takes to execute each order. That way, short orders could be taken care of immediately while longer orders queued up to take place in the background. Because all this can happen simultaneously, customers with shorter orders wouldn't have to wait for those with longer orders. This would definitely shorten the line in any fast-food chain.

Unfortunately, you don't have this option when you are ordering chicken nuggets; however, you can program your systems to take advantage of this order prioritization with the help of a concept called threading.

Introduction to Threading

Threading provides the ability to run multiple activities on separate threads of execution that appear to occur simultaneously to the user. (If you are using multiple processors, threads actually *can* execute simultaneously.) By threading out your application, you can distinguish priorities between different functionalities offered by your application. If you know a specific combo box will take a long time to load, you can run this long order in the background while the user continues working with the other functionalities offered by your application. Ultimately, this reduces the frustration and time that a user experiences with an application.

SHORT GLOSSARY OF THREADING TERMS

Although this section is certainly not a complete discussion of Windows and .NET threading concepts, here are some terms that are helpful to know as you work through the examples in this section:

◆ *Multitasking* refers to the ability of a system to run many programs at once.

◆ *Preemptive multitasking* pauses a process based on specified time intervals so that another process can run.

◆ *Cooperative multitasking* queues processes. One process is blocked until execution of another is completed.

◆ A *process* commits a slice of processor time and energy toward running a specific application or service. These independent slices prevent applications from interfering with one another.

◆ *Threads* run inside a process and enable you to track the execution point of your program.

◆ *Multithreading* refers to the ability to create more than one thread inside a process. These threads serve as multiple execution points that enable different segments of your application to run at the same time.

◆ An *application domain* is a concept introduced with the .NET Framework. Application domains, or App-Domains, enable multiple applications to run within a single process with the same security and process isolation that they would have if they ran in different processes. This level of isolation is provided by the CLR.

In the database access world, threading is useful when you want to populate a control with a large amount of data, without hindering the user's ability to work with other controls. Especially in web applications, a user might become impatient while waiting for a control to load its data. Instead, they could improve their efficiency by working with other application functionality while the control loads its data behind the scenes, on a separate execution thread.

The .NET Framework greatly enhances the programmability of running different threads of execution. If you have ever worked with asynchronous operations with ADO, you know asynchronous execution certainly isn't the easiest thing to program. Debugging is a nightmare because you have unexpected event behaviors. Because ADO hides so much of the functionality, you never really know what's going on "under the covers," nor do you have much control over it. How you implement asynchronous operations is quite different from how you program them with classic ADO.

WARNING   *Currently, ADO.NET does not natively support asynchronous events. You will have to roll your own events from inherited ADO.NET base classes if you want to use event handlers with asynchronous operations.*

The .NET Framework makes creating threads simple by using the `System.Threading` namespace. This is a beautiful yet dangerous thing. The beauty lies in the simplicity. All you need to do is to instantiate a thread, attach it to some method, and start running it. The danger is that thread creation becomes mindless and easy without requiring you to fully understand the implications of your application design.

Threading can lead to unexpected behavior that is difficult to troubleshoot. The errors could occur only one out of million times. How can you debug something that occurs so infrequently? It is truly difficult to debug threaded applications, yet debugging is crucial—especially when you are working with financial, mission-critical, or medical systems. Not only might you get unexpected results, but you might end up crashing your application and any application dependent upon yours. These dangers will be very apparent in the threading application that we write later in this section.

WARNING   *A full discussion of the dangers of poorly designed, threaded applications is beyond the scope of this chapter. Our purpose is to show you how threading works with ADO.NET objects. We hope that you fully understand threading concepts before you write threaded applications.*

Before you decide to use threading with your application, you need to ask yourself: what advantages does threading give my application? If the activities within your application do not take too long and the user is not left in limbo waiting for a thread to execute, you should avoid using threading. Because mismanaged threads can cause serious system failures, you must carefully review the design of your application to determine whether it merits threading.

The *System.Threading* Namespace

The `System.Threading` namespace houses the main components for building a multithreaded application. In this section, you are going to review some of the major characters within this namespace. The Thread object, for example, is the nucleus of the `System.Threading` namespace. You use the Thread object to create, manage, and control the threads of your multithreaded application. Many of the objects, properties, and methods introduced in this section are used in the threaded application example we provide later. By examining the threading objects on a conceptual level, you will have a better understanding of how threading works in a practical manner.

First, however, you need to understand the behavior of multi-threaded applications. You need to manage your threads carefully because threads within multithreaded applications actually share the same memory space. What does this mean? Consider a process. Each process within Windows has its own independent memory address. Within this memory space, a process stores its return values, temporary variables, and other information. No other process can invade the space of another. This concept is known as *process isolation*. A process must use a proxy to indirectly communicate with another process's memory space. This way, you avoid the accidental modification of memory addresses, causing unexpected behavior in a process.

Multithreaded applications work differently than multiple processes. When you run a thread, it serves as an independent flow of execution with its own variables and memory addresses. You can think of a thread as a set of execution instructions. These instructions run within the same memory address as its parent process. If you have more than one thread running in a process, it also shares that same memory address within its parent process. When you stop a thread, the variables and values are pulled out of memory and stored so that that another thread can use that same memory space. The risk is that this might not occur cleanly, and another thread can jump in, overriding important values from the last thread that was in that memory space. There is no concept of thread isolation, as you have with processes; this is a very important fact.

TIP   Threads share (compete for) the same memory space within a process.

The .NET Framework supplements physical process isolation by using AppDomains to provide logical isolation. The threads within your application run within the logical constraints of an AppDomain. Every application has a primary thread. Each AppDomain is started at runtime with a single thread. This primary thread serves as the main execution logic throughout the application process. You can spawn off additional threads from the main AppDomain thread.

WARNING   Keeping track of multiple threads is memory intensive because it forces the application to remember the state of each thread at all times.

Timing is crucial with threaded applications. You don't want to abruptly suspend or pause a thread right when it's in the middle of a long, conditional branch or loop. Again, this can cause unexpected behavior when you resume the thread, because values might have changed since the last run.

To help conquer the timing issues, you can use events. Although threads can be used alone, they are most effective when used with events. You can use events to notify the calling code with the status or results of a thread's activity.

Now you're ready to explore some of the main components within the `System.Threading` library.

THE *THREADSTART* DELEGATE

By using the `ThreadStart` thread delegate, you can specify the name of the method that you wish to execute when you create a thread. The `ThreadStart` delegate doesn't actually run the thread. That doesn't happen until the `Start()` method is invoked, at which time the thread begins executing by using the method you specified in the thread delegate. Think of the `ThreadStart` as the entry point into a thread.

When you create the `ThreadStart` object, you specify a pointer to the method that should run when the thread begins executing. You can specify this by using the overridden constructor:

```
Dim tsFill As System.Threading.ThreadStart = New System.Threading.ThreadStart _
        (AddressOf MyMethod)
```

NOTE   Notice that `ThreadStart` is a delegate, rather than a property or method. If you wish, review our previous discussion of delegates in the "Event Handling/NET Framework Event Concepts" section at the beginning this chapter.

Make sure you realize one important caveat: the method that you designate as the thread delegate cannot accept any parameters. When you attempt to do so, you will get a compilation error:

```
The operand to AddressOf must be the name of a method only,
no parens are needed
```

So what do you do when you want to specify specific input criteria? The best way to work around this issue is to move your method into a separate class. Then you set properties of that class at run-time, passing in the information that you would normally pass as method parameters. You will do this in the threading example provided later in this section.

Additionally, your method should be a subroutine rather than a function that returns a value. If your method delegate returns a value, you constrain yourself to synchronous operations rather than taking the advantages of threading asynchronously. Instead of a return value, raise an event when the subroutine finishes executing. That way, you can notify the calling code of any return information.

After you have your `ThreadStart` delegate set, you can pass it over to a new instance of a Thread object.

THE THREAD OBJECT

The `System.Threading.Thread` object serves as the base class from which you create a separate thread of execution within your application. You can create a thread by using the `System.Threading.Thread` object and pass the constructor a `ThreadStart` delegate.

```
Dim thdFill As System.Threading.Thread
thdFill = New Thread(tsFill)
```

In this code example, you pass an object, typed as a `ThreadStart` delegate, into the constructor of the Thread object.

Additionally, you can omit the creation of the `ThreadStart` object and directly pass the pointer to the method delegate:

```
Dim thdFill as New System.Threading.Thread (AddressOf MyMethod)
```

The constructor of the Thread object expects a single parameter, which is a thread delegate. Again, you can pass it by using the `ThreadStart` object or by using the `AddressOf` operator.

THE START ( ) METHOD

The `Start()` method is probably the most significant method within the `System.Threading` namespace. This method is responsible for actually spinning up the thread for you. It relies on the thread delegate you specified with the `ThreadStart()` object to pinpoint the exact method from which the thread execution should begin. The `Start()` method works with other thread manipulation methods, which we discuss later in this section.

WARNING   *A thread can be started only one time. If you attempt to call this method more than once, you will generate an exception.*

After you call this method, you can monitor the state of a thread by using the `ThreadState` property. We show you the various options for controlling and managing your threads by using such properties, in the "Managing Threads" subsection within this part of the chapter.

THE *CURRENTTHREAD* PROPERTY

When you are working with multiple threads, you might find it necessary to hone in on a specific thread that is being executed at any given time. The CurrentThread property gives you the ability to do this.

Using Threading with the .NET Framework

A great feature of the .NET Framework enables you to build multithreaded VB .NET applications with only a few lines of code. All you really need to do is pass a threading object the address of the method that you want to thread out, and a new thread is spun up for you. It's quite simple.

The System.Threading base class enables you to build VB .NET applications that can execute on multiple threads. Using the System.Threading objects, you can write ADO.NET code that processes in the background. This is much different from the asynchronous convention that you used with classic ADO. Figure 11.8 shows you how the Threading namespace fits into the .NET Framework within the System namespace.

FIGURE 11.8

The .NET Framework System classes

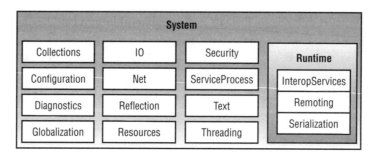

To perform asynchronous operations in classic ADO, you would use the native functions housed within the ADO library. In traditional ADO asynchronous programming, you would handle the events fired off by the appropriate ADO objects. ADO.NET does not contain methods for asynchronous operations in its first release; however, Microsoft intends to support native asynchronous operations in the next release of ADO.NET. Instead, you can roll your own events to respond to state changes in the data access objects.

DISADVANTAGES OF USING CLASSIC ADO'S EVENT-BASED ASYNCHRONOUS PROGRAMMING

As we mentioned earlier, working with the event-based asynchronous functionality of classic ADO is not simple. ADO 2.x has many quirky characters that you must account for.

First and foremost, debugging is challenging. Events might fire at unexpected times due to unusual event triggers. A potentially confusing situation occurs when an operation that you cancel might still fire events. If you decide to cancel an update from within the WillChangeField event handler, the Field-ChangeComplete event will still be fired to indicate that the operation has completed (unsuccessfully, but it has completed anyway).

Continued on next page

Sample Threading Application with ADO.NET

In this section, we show you how to program data access code to take advantage of background threading and improve the user experience. You are going to build an application that contains two search engines. You will spin off a separate thread for the first search, so the user can continue to use the application while the search continues executing. Let's begin by creating a new Windows application within VS .NET called **Threading**.

CREATE A DUAL SEARCH ENGINE

After you've created the application, construct your two search engines by dragging over two of each the following types of controls: TextBox, DataGrid, and Button onto `form1.vb`. Clear the text properties for both the search boxes. Line up the controls so that each search engine area has a TextBox control with a Button next to it and a DataGrid below the two. The control placement should look similar to Figure 11.9.

FIGURE 11.9

Creating a dual search engine

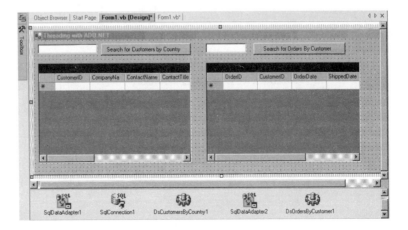

Configure the first search engine to search for customers based on the country that they live in. First, drag over a SqlDataAdapter and configure its SelectCommand to point to the GetCustomersByCountry stored procedure. Generate a DataSet by using this DataAdapter, saving it to your project. Name your DataSet **DsCustomersByCountry1**. Next, set the DataSource property of the first DataGrid to the newly created DsCustomersByCountry1 DataSet.

NOTE *If you haven't been following along with the examples of the preceding chapter, you might want to refer to Chapter 5, "Transact-SQL." The creation script for the* GetCustomersByCountry *stored procedure is part of the sample code in Chapter 5. You can also find this script on the accompanying CD, within the file* Creating the GetCustomersByCountry stored procedure.sql.

To configure the second search engine, drag over a SqlDataAdapter from the Data tab of the Toolbox. This search engine will retrieve orders based on a specific CustomerID. Configure the DataAdapter to retrieve data from the SelectOrdersByCustomer stored procedure. Generate a DataSet from the DataAdapter properties window. Name this DataSet **DsOrdersByCustomer1**. As with the previous search engine, map the DataSource property of the second DataGrid to the newly created DsOrdersByCustomer1 DataSet. The completed form in design mode should look similar to Figure 11.9.

NOTE *The code to create the* SelectOrdersByCustomer *stored procedure is available in Chapter 8 and on the CD that accompanies this book.*

The last thing you have to do to complete your dual search engine is to write some code to pass the search criteria from the TextBox control to the Value property of the Parameter object for each SelectCommand. Add the code in Listing 11.3 and Listing 11.4 to the click events of each button, respectively. Additionally, there are two subroutines, found in Listings 11.5 and 11.6, that encapsulate the fill logic for each DataSet. You might wonder why we encapsulate only a single line of code into a separate method; however, the reasons will soon become apparent as you work with thread delegates.

NOTE *The code in Listing 11.3 contains a good amount of exception-handling code, which we discuss in detail later in this chapter.*

LISTING 11.3: WIRING THE COUNTRY NAME SEARCH CRITERIA TO THE SELECTCOMMAND PARAMETERS COLLECTION

```
Private Sub Button1_Click _
    (ByVal sender As System.Object, _
    ByVal e As System.EventArgs) _
    Handles Button1.Click
    ' Populate customers by country name

    Try
      SqlSelectCommand1. _
      Parameters("@CountryName"). _
```

```
      Value() = TextBox1.Text
    Catch excParam As System.Exception
      Console.WriteLine _
      ("Error at populating parameter " _
      & excParam.Message)
    End Try

    Try
      FillCustomers()
    Catch excFill As SqlClient.SqlException
      Console.WriteLine(excFill.Message)
    Catch excGeneral As System.Exception
      Console.WriteLine(excGeneral.Message)
    End Try
End Sub
```

LISTING 11.4: WIRING THE CUSTOMERID SEARCH CRITERIA TO THE SELECTCOMMAND PARAMETERS COLLECTION

```
Private Sub Button2_Click _
    (ByVal sender As System.Object, _
    ByVal e As System.EventArgs) _
    Handles Button2.Click
  ' Populate orders by customer

  Try
    SqlSelectCommand2. _
    Parameters("@CustomerID").Value = _
    TextBox2.Text
  Catch excParam As System.Exception
    Console.WriteLine _
    ("Error at populating parameter " _
    & excParam.Message)
  End Try

  Try
    FillOrders()
  Catch excFill As SqlClient.SqlException
    Console.WriteLine(excFill.Message)
  Catch excGeneral As System.Exception
    Console.WriteLine(excGeneral.Message)
  End Try
End Sub
```

LISTING 11.5: THE FILLORDERS() SUBROUTINE

```
Private Sub FillOrders()
 Try
  dsordersbycustomer1.Clear
  Me.SqlDataAdapter2.Fill(DsOrdersByCustomer1)
 Catch excFill As SqlClient.SqlException
  Console.WriteLine(excFill.Message)
 Catch excGeneral As System.Exception
  Console.WriteLine(excGeneral.Message)
 End Try
End Sub
```

LISTING 11.6: THE FILLCUSTOMERS() SUBROUTINE

```
Private Sub FillCustomers()
  Try
    DsCustomersByCountry1.Clear()
    Me.SqlDataAdapter1.Fill( _
    DsCustomersByCountry1)
  Catch excFill As SqlClient.SqlException
    Console.WriteLine(excFill.Message)
  Catch excGeneral As System.Exception
    Console.WriteLine(excGeneral.Message)
  End Try
  End Sub
```

Feel free to run the project and experiment with each search engine. The first search engine accepts the name of a country as its search criteria. In return, it provides a list of customers who belong to the country you specified. The second search engine accepts a CustomerID as the criteria and returns the orders for the customer you specified. The main thing to notice is that you can't execute a new search until the last one has finished processing. Try it. You will see that you are unable to enter new search criteria while the DataGrid is still populating with search results. You can't even place your cursor in the TextBox until the search has completed. What if this wasn't satisfactory? Say you had a large amount of results returned and you wanted to resume working with the application while you were waiting. This is where threading comes into play.

To enable the form to remain responsive while the customer search DataGrid populates, you add some threading logic to your code. As we mentioned earlier, threading with .NET is relatively easy to implement:

1. Create the thread delegate method. You've already created this in advance with the Fill-Customers() method.

2. Pass the thread delegate to the ThreadStart object. As we mentioned earlier, the ThreadStart delegate receives the method that you wish to invoke upon the creation of your object's thread.

3. Create a new thread object.

4. Start the thread by calling the `Start()` method of the thread object.

CREATE A NEW THREAD DELEGATE

Let's work with the first search engine, which retrieves customers by country. First, you need to import the `System.Threading` namespace so that you can directly reference the members of the Threading class. Add the line `Imports System.Threading` to the Declarations section of your form. Next, you need to create a thread delegate that you will use in lieu of the direct method call to the `FillCustomers()` method.

Modify the logic within the `Try` block in the first button, replacing the call to the `FillCustomers()` method with the code in Listing 11.7.

LISTING 11.7: CREATE A THREADSTART OBJECT

```
'FillCustomers() ' We remove the direct method call
'  line and replace it with a thread delegate
Dim tsFill As ThreadStart = New ThreadStart(AddressOf FillCustomers)
```

This code creates a new `ThreadStart` object, passing the thread delegate to `FillCustomers()`as the constructor input parameter. As we explained previously, the `ThreadStart` object instantiation doesn't actually start the thread. It only points to a specific method that will serve as the initial execution point after the thread is activated.

CREATE A NEW THREAD

Next, you have to create a variable to actually store your thread. Dimension your thread object with this line:

```
Dim thdFill As Thread
```

You instantiate this thread with the following line:

```
thdFill = New Thread(tsFill)
```

This takes advantage of the overridden constructor, passing in the thread delegate as the jump point for the new thread. Finally, you start the thread execution by using the `Start()` method of the Thread object as such:

```
thdFill.Start()
```

BROADEN YOUR SCOPE

Although this is all the logic you need to spin up a new thread to fill the DataSet, your work is not done. When the thread is created, it runs external to the primary application thread. This means that objects, properties, and methods that are private to one thread cannot be accessed by another. We explained the logic behind this earlier. The .NET Framework provides thread isolation with the use of AppDomains. Otherwise, threads would compete for the same memory space within a process, causing potential harm should one thread override the values in another thread.

What does this mean to you? The `thdFill` thread kicks off with a call to the thread delegate for the `FillCustomers()` method. As you can see in the `FillCustomers()` method, local Form objects are manipulated, mainly the `SqlDataAdapter1` and `DsCustomersByCountry1` objects. These objects are hidden within the Form's AppDomain and cannot be accessed by the external `thdFill` thread.

The best way to do this is to create wrapper properties for each object within the thread. To create properties for your thread, you are going to have to move the thread logic into a separate class. Right-click on your solution in the Solution Explorer and select Add ➢ Add New Item. Select Class as the type of item you wish to add. Name the class **Filler.vb**. Move the `FillCustomers()` method into this class. Add the `Imports System.Data.SqlClient` line to the top of the code in the class. This enables you to readily work with the SqlClient .NET data provider objects.

TIP   *When your thread delegate works with parameters or wrapped properties, it's a good practice to encapsulate the target method, which serves as the thread delegate, into a separate class. You can use public properties or variables to receive the input parameters. This way, you can create a separate instance of the class for each thread you spin up.*

Next, you must add some public properties along with their corresponding member variables. These properties expose the DataAdapter and DataSet objects. Then you can set these values from the calling code that creates this thread.

You might be surprised to know that there is still one more object you need to wrap. Any ideas? It's the DataGrid object. Previously, you set the `DataSource` property of the DataGrid to the DataSet at design time. However, you cannot guarantee the safety of this data binding. Instead of allowing the original thread to control the DataGrid, create a new DataGrid data type property in the new thread and set the property from there.

TIP   *You can use properties in lieu of input parameters when you are working with threaded method calls. All the property* `Set` *statements must accept values* `ByVal` *rather than* `ByRef`. *Values passed by reference cannot be used across threads.*

It's a good idea to remove the design-time reference to the DataSet in the `DataSource` property of the first DataGrid. Instead, you will perform the data binding programmatically at runtime within the worker thread, in the Filler class. You want to set the DataSource property of the DataGrid to the DataSet from the newly created thread in the Filler class.

USING THE *INVOKE ( )* METHOD

The DataGrid object is part of `System.Windows.Forms`, which brings us to an important point. Objects within the `System.Windows.Forms` namespace can be properly controlled only from the thread in which they were created. This is because Windows Forms still use single-threaded apartments (STA), unlike other .NET objects, which are free-threaded.

Another way to do a cross-thread call to a `System.Windows.Form` object is to proxy your request via the `Invoke()` method of the Control object. You would use the `Invoke()` method when you directly access and manipulate the encapsulated windows handle to any of the Windows Form or control objects.

Continued on next page

The Invoke() method enables you to make synchronous requests, which is sufficient in this case to set the DataSource property. If you wanted to run this request asynchronously, you would use the BeginInvoke() method instead.

The final class code to create these new properties should look like Listing 11.8, placing the member variable dimension statements at the top of the class. Notice that the FillCustomers() method was modified to reflect the new properties.

LISTING 11.8: THE FILLER CLASS

```vb
Imports System.Data.SqlClient

Public Class Filler
    Private m_dsCustomer As DataSet
    Private m_daCustomer As SqlDataAdapter
    Private m_dgCustomer As DataGrid

    Public Sub FillCustomers()
        Try
            m_dsCustomer.Clear()
            m_dgCustomer.DataSource = m_dsCustomer
            m_daCustomer.Fill( _
            m_dsCustomer)
        Catch excFill As SqlClient.SqlException
            Console.WriteLine(excFill.Message)
        Catch excGeneral As System.Exception
            Console.WriteLine(excGeneral.Message)
        End Try
    End Sub

    Public Property CustDataSet() As DataSet
        Get
            CustDataSet = m_dsCustomer
        End Get
        Set(ByVal dsInput As DataSet)
            m_dsCustomer = dsInput
        End Set
    End Property

    Public Property CustDataAdapter() As SqlDataAdapter
        Get
            CustDataAdapter() = m_daCustomer
        End Get
        Set(ByVal daInput As SqlDataAdapter)
```

```
                m_daCustomer = daInput
            End Set
        End Property
        Public Property CustDataGrid() As DataGrid
            Get
                CustDataGrid = m_dgCustomer
            End Get
            Set(ByVal dgInput As DataGrid)
                m_dgCustomer = dgInput
            End Set
        End Property
    End Class
```

Now that you've moved the FillCustomers() method out of the original Form class, you must modify the Button1_Click event to reflect these changes. First, you will need to create a new variable to represent the Filler class:

```
Dim clsFiller As New Filler()
```

Now that you have your Filler object, you can set the DataAdapter and DataSet properties:

```
clsFiller.CustDataAdapter = Me.SqlDataAdapter1
clsFiller.CustDataSet = _
  Me.DsCustomersByCountry1
```

You will also have to point your thread delegate to the newly moved method:

```
Dim tsFill As ThreadStart = _
New ThreadStart _
 (AddressOf clsFiller.FillCustomers)
```

In the end, the final logic for the Button1_Click event should look like Listing 11.9.

LISTING 11.9: ADDING THREAD LOGIC TO POPULATE A DATASET

```
Private Sub Button1_Click _
    (ByVal sender As System.Object, _
    ByVal e As System.EventArgs) _
    Handles Button1.Click
        ' Populate customers by country name
        Dim thdFill As Thread
        Dim clsFiller As New Filler()
        DataGrid1.Refresh()
        Try
            SqlSelectCommand1. _
            Parameters("@CountryName"). _
            Value() = TextBox1.Text
        Catch excParam As System.Exception
            Console.WriteLine _
```

```
                    ("Error at populating parameter " _
                    & excParam.Message)
            End Try

            Try
                clsFiller.CustDataAdapter = Me.SqlDataAdapter1
                clsFiller.CustDataSet = _
                Me.DsCustomersByCountry1
                clsFiller.CustDataGrid = Me.DataGrid1
                'FillCustomers() ' We remove the direct method call
                '  line and replace it with a thread delegate
                Dim tsFill As ThreadStart = _
                New ThreadStart _
                (AddressOf clsFiller.FillCustomers)
                thdFill = New Thread(tsFill)
                thdFill.Start()
            Catch excFill As SqlClient.SqlException
                Console.WriteLine(excFill.Message)
            Catch excGeneral As System.Exception
                Console.WriteLine(excGeneral.Message)
            End Try
        End Sub
```

Execute the application by pressing F5. Unlike last time, when you begin executing the first search, you are able to continue working with the application. You can enter new data into the second search criteria box while the first search is still executing.

Please note that the threading code listed here is not production ready. What happens if you click the customer search button twice? Because there is no code to check the status of the thread to determine whether a search is already underway, you would end up calling the Start() method twice. As we mentioned earlier, this generates a runtime exception. Most likely, you will see an error that a Null value was found when an object was expected. This occurs because two threads are attempting to write to the same memory space at the same time within the Form object's thread. To prevent this from happening, you need to implement some event synchronization code, status checking, and event programming logic. Properly managing synchronization is one of the issues that makes writing solid multithreaded code very challenging.

Advanced Threading Concepts

In the simplest multithreaded application, all you really need to do is spin up the thread and let it run naturally. You don't need to pause it or to know what's going on when it's running. However, in certain scenarios you must have knowledge of a thread state so that you can manage the thread activity, for example, pausing or suspending the thread activity. You can monitor thread activity by using thread properties and events. Now you will see why event programming and threading are so closely related.

Additionally, at times multiple threads might need to access the same segment of code. Sudden switches between threads can lead to unexpected behavior within your shared code. To avoid this, you use a concept called *synchronization*, which ensures that your code is thread-safe by marking shared code segments with mutual exclusion locks, or *mutexes*. Synchronizing your threads in this way prevents memory access conflicts.

SYNCHRONIZATION

The previous example takes a casual approach to threading. The purpose of the exercise was to show you how easy it is to create and spin up threads. But as we warned earlier, although the .NET Framework makes it easy to create threads, the challenge is to effectively manage them.

When you attempt to execute simultaneous searches in the project you just built, you might encounter undesirable behavior. These issues are caused by a lack of proper thread management. If threads are not properly managed, one thread could invade the memory address of another, causing conflict. Additionally, one thread could read the memory of another thread, pulling values that are in flux and not stable. Unless you are using local thread storage, these situations might occur because threads share the same memory space.

Mismanaged threads can lead to serious application failures such as deadlocks and race conditions. *Deadlocks* occur when a vicious circle of dependency occurs between threads; each thread waits for the other to finish processing and nothing can execute. *Race conditions* occur when you rely on threads to execute in a certain order and an error occurs in the order of execution. This could lead a thread to use data from an incomplete thread, causing unexpected behavior in the dependent thread. The best way to avoid a race condition is to avoid relying on your threads to execute in a specific order.

Blocking

You have several options to prevent thread conflicts from occurring. One option is to block a thread from executing until all related threads have finished execution. This mechanism is known as *blocking*. When you block a thread, you place a thread in a dormant wait state. This means the thread will remain idle until some code signals it to resume executing. When a thread is in a wait state, the processor doesn't attend to the thread until the processor is signaled to resume processing the thread.

There are many ways to block a thread from accessing shared memory space. You could specify *critical sections* within your code, which mark a piece of logic as non-shared and accessible to only one thread at a time. However, if you think about it, there really isn't much advantage to marking critical sections of code. Why bother threading in the first place if you are going to end up with thread queues, or worse, bottlenecks, as threads wait until that critical section becomes available?

You can help prevent bottlenecks by specifying read-only critical sections. This mechanism enables other threads to access the information in the critical section, but does not allow them to modify the memory space. Depending on your requirements, this could be a viable option.

A third, more powerful option, is *on-demand blocking*, which enables you to tightly control thread activity. You control the thread activity by pausing and resuming threads, signaling other threads after one thread has finished processing. This way, you block threads until they are signaled to resume processing. Although this type of blocking is powerful, it can be dangerous if the manual synchronization isn't planned properly.

If you have any part of code that needs to be accessed by multiple threads (a shared variable, for instance), you need to secure the code section with a `SyncLock`. Then your code will be thread-safe. The `Threading` namespace provides a synchronization mechanism that you can use to coordinate memory access and resource sharing across multiple threads.

SYNCLOCK

The `SyncLock` construct enables you to mark a segment of code for restricted thread access, with the use of the `SyncLock…End SyncLock` block. This way, multiple threads will not step on one another's toes when working with shared memory. This code lockdown prevents other threads from executing the restricted code.

Let's experiment with synchronization by securing a segment of code. Add some dangerous non-thread-safe code. In the click event of your first Search button, add a line of code to some dangerous non-thread-safe code and add a line of code to change the DataGrid Text property:

```
DataGrid1.CaptionText = _
"Customers Grid - Thread 1"
```

This manipulates the DataGrid object from the primary thread of the application. Now add some code to modify the object from the other thread. In the Filler class, add a line to the start of the `FillCustomers()` method:

```
m_dgCustomer.CaptionText = _
"Customers Grid - Thread 2"
```

Without any locks, there could be a chance that the two threads attempt to access the DataGrid at the same time. To prevent memory access conflicts, lock down each line with a `SyncLock` block, as shown in Listing 11.10. (The code listing has been shortened for brevity.)

LISTING 11.10: WORKING WITH SYNCLOCK BLOCKS

```
Public Sub FillCustomers()
        SyncLock (m_dgCustomer)
            m_dgCustomer.CaptionText = _
            "Customers Grid - Thread 2"
        End SyncLock
...
End Sub

Private Sub Button1_Click _
    (ByVal sender As System.Object, _
    ByVal e As System.EventArgs) _
    Handles Button1.Click
...
        SyncLock (DataGrid1)
```

```
            DataGrid1.CaptionText = _
            "Customers Grid - Thread 1"
        End SyncLock
    ...
    End Sub
```

In these code segments, the SyncLock structure is used to prevent any thread from accessing the CaptionText changes to the DataGrid. This way, you can avoid any program error if an external thread attempted to modify the property at the same time you were.

USING EVENTS

Our next problem to solve is to prevent exceptions when you spawn multiple Filler threads rapid-fire. If you try to repeatedly click the Search button, you will eventually generate an exception. This happens because the Thread.Start method is being executed repeatedly, before existing resources are cleaned up. When you attempt to fill the DataSet while a DataReader is still populating the first thread's DataSet, you experience a memory-access conflict. By using events and monitoring thread state, you can prevent conflicts from occurring. You should give your Filler class a callback event, so that calling code can understand the condition that a thread is in before spinning up another thread. Then, you can add an event handler in the Windows Form class to monitor the Filler thread activity.

You might remember working with asynchronous events in classic ADO. You could use these to monitor threaded applications. For example, the FetchProgress event of the RecordSet object enabled you to monitor the status of data retrieval. With ADO.NET, you have to hand-roll your own events and handlers.

Events provide another way to synchronize your threads. Events enable threads to relay messages back to the calling code with information regarding the status of the thread. Then, the calling code can take the appropriate action based on the state of the thread.

As we mentioned earlier, events are a great way to provide return data from a threaded method, because free-threaded methods cannot be functions that have return values. Additionally, they do not support ByRef arguments, so you can never pass an original value back to the calling code. You can use events, instead, to notify the calling code of thread results.

You could use global variables to set the status of a thread, but that's cumbersome and you would have to write a lot of code to keep checking the value of that variable. Alternately, you could use the IsAlive and ThreadState properties of a Thread object to observe the thread. Again, this adds cumbersome code and unnecessary loop structures as you continuously monitor a thread for status changes. Events are the best way to examine the status of a thread, and this is what you will do in this example.

Instead of using the ADO.NET events we described earlier in this chapter, you are going to create a custom event to notify your calling code that the Fill() operation is complete. Add an event to your Filler class in the General Declarations area, after your class declaration:

```
Public Event FillComplete(ByVal intRecordsReturned as Integer)
```

Now you need to raise this event from the FillCustomers() method. Add this line of code after the call to the Fill() method of the DataAdapter:

```
RaiseEvent FillComplete (m_dsCustomer.Tables(0).Rows.Count)
```

After the Fill() method has executed, the FillComplete() event will fire as a callback event. The event returns the number of rows that fit the search criteria. By raising this event before the method completes its execution, you could immediately notify the calling code before the thread terminates and loses its current state.

The calling code must use an event handler to capture this event and take action accordingly. Earlier in this chapter, we discussed the AddHandler directive. You will use this directive to wire your calling code to the FillComplete event. As you remember, you first have to create a method delegate that will serve as your event handler. This method must have the same signature as your event. In this case, you have a single integer parameter to display the record count. In the Form class, create the method in Listing 11.11.

LISTING 11.11: CREATING A DELEGATE

```
Private Sub NotifyFill(ByVal intRecordsReturned As Integer)
      DataGrid1.CaptionText = _
      "Records returned " & intRecordsReturned
   End Sub
```

Next, use the AddressOf keyword as a function pointer to the method that will be the delegate for the event. Place this line of code right after you instantiate the Filler class in the Button1_Click event:

```
AddHandler clsFiller.FillComplete, AddressOf NotifyFill
```

Run your code and watch the event wiring in action. When the thread executes, the FillComplete event is raised and handled appropriately by the calling code.

Regardless of whether your thread needs to return data, you should always couple threaded logic with relevant events. When your code provides state information, calling systems can better manage the threads, greatly decreasing the chances for exceptions or failures.

MANAGING THREADS

At times spinning up a thread and letting it go like a top might not meet your needs. You might want to pause and resume thread execution based on some specific logic. Or you might want to use some thread safety controls to abort your thread execution if you think something has gone wrong. The Thread object comes with a series of methods that enable you to tightly control its behavior.

The Start ( ) Method

We discussed the Start() method earlier in this chapter. There's not much you can do with a thread without using this method. The Start() method of the Thread object does exactly what its name indicates: it executes the thread by calling the method passed into the thread delegate.

The Abort ( ) Method

The Abort() method of the Thread objects terminates the execution of a particular thread. This method is often used in conjunction with the ThreadState and IsAlive properties in order to determine the state of a particular thread.

TIP   When you call the Abort() method, an exception will be generated. Unfortunately, the Try...Catch block cannot catch this exception; however, the Finally block will execute. Be sure to place your logic there rather than relying on the exception handler.

When you call Abort(), the thread doesn't immediately die. You actually have to call the Join() method to finish the termination process. Even so, all Finally clauses of Try blocks are executed before the thread shuts down. When you call Abort() on a thread that has not been started, it will start and then stop. When you call Abort() on a thread that has been suspended, the thread will resume and then stop. If a thread is in a wait state, blocked or sleeping, calling the Abort() will first interrupt and then terminate the thread.

The Join ( ) Method

The Join() method waits for a thread to die or time out, by using the timeout parameter. The Join() method returns a Boolean value. If the thread has terminated, the method returns a True value. If a timeout occurs, the method returns a False.

The Sleep ( ) Method

The Sleep() method pauses a thread from any activity for a specific amount of time. Be careful when choosing which threads to put to sleep. You should avoid doing this for threads that work with external resources, such as a database connection, because you might cause unexpected locks on the resource. Additionally, you should avoid doing this with Windows Form objects, such as controls, because Windows Forms are still STA based.

The Suspend ( ) Method

The Suspend() method postpones a thread processing any activity. Processing continues if the Resume() method is called. Again, as with the Sleep() method, avoid suspending threads that work with database connections, Windows Forms, or controls. Ideally, rather than forcibly suspending and resuming threads, you should work with the thread state property to change thread behavior.

WARNING   Handling multiple threads is processor intensive. Like stopping and starting a car, pausing and resuming threads can choke up your processor. This process of pausing and resuming multiple threads is referred to as context switching. If you have many threads in a single process, the performance of external processes can be severely affected, because the processor is busy handling the thread requests within your process.

The Resume ( ) Method

The Resume() method continues processing for a suspended thread.

The Interrupt ( ) Method

You can think of the Interrupt() method as a knock on the door of the Thread object that is in a wait, sleep, or join state. Basically, the Interrupt() method asks for a thread to stop working after it leaves any of these states. If a thread is in none of these states, the Interrupt() method will wait until the next time the thread falls into one of these states and knock on its door at that time. The knock serves to interrupt the thread from its particular state. You would do this when you want to get the attention of a dormant thread. Using the Interrupt() method is not as invasive as calling the Abort() method, which generates an un-catchable ThreadAbortException.

Managing Thread State

Before you can even begin to control thread execution, you must have a firm grip on what state the thread is in at any given time. Earlier we mentioned that you could build event-driven programming to have the thread notify the calling code of its activity.

To raise the appropriate events, you must first determine the state of a thread. You have two options for checking the status of a thread.

First, you can use the ThreadState property of the Thread object and examine the ThreadState enumeration values. By default, a thread will be Unstarted. Table 11.3 lists the potential values of the ThreadStart enumeration.

TABLE 11.3: VALUES OF THE ThreadState ENUMERATION

VALUE	DESCRIPTION	BIT CONSTANT
Unstarted	A thread has not yet been started.	8
Running	A thread has been started, resumed, or interrupted from a wait or sleep state.	0
WaitSleepJoin	A thread has been set to a wait, sleep, or join status.	32
SuspendRequest	A thread is marked for suspension.	2
Suspended	A thread actually suspends activity.	64
AbortRequested	A thread has been marked for termination.	128
Aborted	A thread has terminated.	256
Background	A thread is running as a background thread.	4

The ThreadState enumeration works as a bitmask, enabling you to check for multiple states at a single moment in the lifetime of a thread.

Alternately, you can use the IsAlive Boolean property, which indicates whether a thread has been started by using the True or False return value, respectively. The IsAlive property is not nearly as robust as the ThreadState property in providing exact information regarding the state of a thread.

As you've seen already, the Start() method begins execution of the thread. You can choose to terminate the thread by using the Abort() method if you suspect it is misbehaving. If you want to pause the thread, you can opt to use the `Sleep()` or `Suspend()` method. When you are ready to continue processing, the `Resume()` method signals the thread to continue processing.

This section on threading can by no means provide a complete understanding of the ins and outs of threading within the .NET Framework. However, there's one thing that you should get out of this section: there's a lot more to threading than meets the eye. If anything, you should understand the importance of carefully managing your threads, especially when they work with external resources. When you design a multithreaded application, you should be judicious in the number of threads that you create. If you create too many threads, you will experience performance degradation because the system spends all its time switching between threads rather than performing normal system activity. Ultimately, your goal is to write *thread-safe* applications, which behave properly when more than one thread is running at a given time. To write thread-safe applications, your code should have full knowledge of system state, knowing the status of any thread at a given time. You can use various properties of the Thread object, such as `IsAlive` or `ThreadState`, to determine thread status. Alternately, custom event logic raised by your threads can also serve to help your application properly manage its threads.

There are many potential risks to writing multithreaded applications. In addition to writing solid, thread-safe code, proper use of exception handling can further ensure that your application code runs properly.

Exception Handling

Robust exception handling is essential in order to guarantee the quality and stability of your application. Error-handling code traps any errors that might be generated, handling them gracefully with the appropriate user-friendly notifications to the end user. Imagine a user's reaction if they were confronted with a hexadecimal jargon of error codes that they couldn't interpret. Experiences like that would surely shorten the life of your application, let alone your reputation as a respectable developer. Exception handling enables you to trap cryptic errors, shielding them from the end user.

NOTE   *What's the difference between error handling and exception handling? Exception handling isn't limited to error conditions only. At times you might want to notify the user that an exception event has occurred, even though it might not necessarily be an error. Although an error is always an exception, an exception might not always be an error. You might want to write custom handlers for non-error-producing exceptions.*

Exception handling is one of the most important topics of any language, and we're assuming you're familiar with the concepts of exception handling. .NET's structured exception-handling capabilities provide more power to the Visual Basic language. The structured exception handling uses cross-language `Try…Catch` exception trapping that you can use to handle any errors raised from ADO.NET. The focus of this section is on structured error handling, although unstructured error handling is still supported with .NET.

NOTE   *You can find more information on the concepts of exception handling in Mastering VB .NET by Evangelos Petroutsos, Sybex, 2002.*

ADO.NET reduces the chances of errors by using many new .NET features, such as side-by-side code execution. In classic ADO, one of the biggest obstacles stemmed from the ability to load a new version of the Microsoft Data Access Components (MDAC) over an existing version. If you wrote code that relied on the existence of a specific flavor of ADO, your application could blow up with errors that were difficult to eradicate. You would have to recompile DLLs or reload the proper version of MDAC. Although the .NET Framework absolves you of this problem by enabling you to run multiple versions of a component side by side, there will still be errors and exceptions that you will have to handle.

Regardless of how tightly you write your code, you are bound to run into runtime errors, or *exceptions*, due to circumstances that might be beyond your control. Most of the examples throughout this book depend on a back-end database server. If that server were not running due to reasons beyond your control, you would want to make sure you notified the user of the problem. Then they could take the appropriate actions to rectify the problem and continue working with your application.

An exception occurs at runtime. As we've said, an exception might not be an error, and even when a non-error-causing exception occurs, you might still want to deal with the exception. Imagine that a user wants to delete an order detail from an order. The order has not been shipped yet and is unfulfilled. There might be no technical reason why the user can't delete the order detail from the order. However, you might want to raise an exception to warn that the particular line item will not be shipped after the order is fulfilled.

Structured Exception Handling

Structured exception handling was introduced to Visual Basic with the .NET Framework. *Structured exception handling* provides the ability to capture specific pieces of execution logic within a specialized block of structured code. The structure is provided with three key operatives: `Try`, `Catch`, and `Finally`. You will examine what each of these operations do within the .NET Framework.

Previous versions of Visual Basic provided unstructured error handling with the use of the `On Error` statement. The .NET Framework increases the power of error handling by using `Try...Catch...Finally` blocks and the Exception object. In this section, we discuss the differences between structured and unstructured exception handling, providing tangible proof that structured exception handling is the way to go.

NOTE *Although unstructured error handling with the* `On Error` *statement is still supported in VB .NET, structured error handling is much more powerful. Therefore, we focus on the structured means of error handling. We point out reasons why structured error handling is preferable over unstructured error handling wherever it is applicable.*

The beauty of exception handling in .NET is that it is interoperable with any .NET-compliant language. You can throw an exception from a VB .NET method and gracefully handle it by using C# or C++ code. Structured error handling provides a consistent, cross-language infrastructure, with the `System.Exception` object at the heart of it all. All errors and exceptions derive from this object. The ability to inherit from this base class enables you to write highly specialized exception logic that can be explicitly trapped by the calling code. The .NET Framework comes with customized exception objects that contain unique exception data, properties, and methods.

The `Try...Catch...Finally` mechanism provides the foundation for error-handling code and is actually part of the Exception object. Additionally, structured error handling provides a consistent standard in returning exceptions to the calling code. This is because exceptions can be explicitly thrown back to the calling code. We show you how to do all of this in the remainder of this section.

Try...Catch...Finally Blocks

Structured exception handling is implemented within the .NET Framework through the use of a Try...Catch system. The essence of this system lies within the Try block, which turns on exception handling. Unlike the On Error statement, the Try block enables you to isolate certain sections within your procedure for exception testing. In the past, Visual Basic did not have native error handling of specific segments of code. The On Error statement would catch all errors within your procedure, regardless of which segment they came from. Additionally, the use of the antiquated Goto keyword would cause the execution point of your code to jump around throughout your procedure, adding unnecessary overhead and complications.

MIMICKING STRUCTURED ERROR HANDLING

There is a way to work around unstructured error handling in both VB .NET and previous versions of VB: using the On Error Resume Next statement.

When you use the On Error Goto statement, all error conditions are directed to a single, centralized section of your code, where all error-handling logic resides. Instead, you can use the On Error Resume Next statement to continue processing the code in the event of an error. When an error occurs, the line immediately following the error-causing code is executed. In this line, you can write some If...Then or Select...Case logic to trap specific errors. This is referred to as *inline error handling*. Technically, this is not structured error handling, but it enables you to isolate specific segments of your code to examine them for certain error conditions. If you can't anticipate every condition, you can add an Else condition to capture any unexpected errors.

Although this method mimics the functionality that you get with the Try...Catch block, the code is awkward and difficult to read. Structured error handling in .NET gives you the same ability, but in a much more robust and elegant manner.

Where's the best place to use a Try block? In essence, a Try block should be wrapped around any suspicious code that you think might be susceptible to errors. Additionally, you should wrap Try blocks around any code that you think might cause an exception to your business rules. For example, if you want to do some sort of data validation before setting a variable, you can use a Try block to generate an exception if a piece of data fails your validation logic. Additionally, you could use multiple Try blocks to check for different error conditions. Or, you could nest multiple Try blocks within each other. Let's experiment with using a simple Try...Catch block by using the Northwind Shopping Cart project that you worked with earlier in this chapter.

A SIMPLE *TRY...CATCH* BLOCK

After you have opened up the solution in your VS .NET IDE, navigate to the LoadOrderGrid() method. At this point, you don't have any exception-handling code to handle any errors with your data access code. You need to identify pieces of logic that are susceptible to errors. The most obvious item would be the Fill() method of the DataAdapter object. Many things could go wrong: the database connection could fail, the data could be corrupt, or a network connection could go down. Let's wrap this logic with a specialized Try...Catch block. Modify the code to look like Listing 11.12.

LISTING 11.12: WORKING WITH TRY...CATCH BLOCKS

```
Try
   SqlDataAdapter1.Fill(DsOrders1, "Orders")
Catch excFill As System.Exception
   ' Add exception handling code here.
         End Try
```

The code immediately following the `Try` statement contains the logic you want to test for exceptions. Any exceptions generated from within this guarded code will be caught. To capture any exceptions that might be thrown, you create a `Catch` wrapper. A `Catch` statement contains a variable of a specific exception type. The `excFill` variable designates a variable of type `System.Exception`, which will be used to store information regarding the error. Inside the `Catch` wrapper, you add logic to appropriately respond to the exception that was generated. You can determine the appropriate response by examining the attributes of the Exception object. You will examine the various properties of the Exception object shortly.

TIP   Always pair a `Try` statement with an `End Try`.

USING MULTIPLE CATCH HANDLERS

Additionally, you can specify multiple `Catch` handlers specific to different exceptions. `Catch` blocks act as filters, enabling you to search for specific conditions that might have occurred in the `Try` block. If you want to test your `Try` logic for multiple conditions, you can use multiple `Catch` statements.

After VB .NET examines the logic in a `Try` block, it will examine any `Catch` statements listed within the `Try...Catch` block until it finds a match. The order of your `Catch` blocks is very important. If an exception occurs at runtime, each `Catch` block is examined in the order it appears. You should place the most specific `Catch` conditions first. The more generic `Catch` conditions should appear last in your `Catch` block series. As you can see in Listing 11.13, the most specific Exception object was listed first in our `Catch` block series.

Another consideration would be to place the exception that you expect to occur more often toward the beginning of the `Catch` series. As VB .NET examines each `Catch` block, it examines each condition in the `Catch` block one at a time. Why bother checking a least suspect `Catch` block before one that is more likely to trap the exception? You should examine the likelihood of your `Catch` statements. This way, you can improve performance by not evaluating conditions that have a small chance of occurring.

Using Specific Exception Objects

In Listing 11.13, we supplement the exception-handling logic in the `LoadDataSet()` method with another `Catch` block. In this case, we use the SqlException object to trap any errors caused by SQL Server.

After you modify the exception-handling code to match Listing 11.10, place a breakpoint on the Try statement.

LISTING 11.13: USING MULTIPLE CATCH BLOCKS

```
Try
  SqlDataAdapter1.Fill(DsOrders1, "Orders")
Catch excSql As SqlClient.SqlException
  Console.WriteLine _
  ("Message is " & excSql.Message & _
   " Error number is " & excSql.Number)
Catch excFill As System.Exception
  ' Add exception handling code here.
  Throw excFill
End Try
```

Execute the project and load data into the grid by pressing the LoadOrders button. The execution should pause at the Try statement, where you are about to fill the DataSet. Now, manually create an error condition by stopping the SQL Server. You can stop the server from the Service Manager. From your Start button, select Programs ➤ Microsoft SQL Server ➤ Service Manager. Click the Stop button to halt the SQL Server. Continue executing your code by clicking F11. You will see that an exception will be generated and handled by your first Catch block. The exception will be stored in the excSql variable, which is typed as a SqlClient.SqlException. In this case, the error information was written to the output console, which, by default, is located at the bottom of the VS .NET IDE:

```
Message is SQL Server does not exist or access denied. Error number is 17
```

Because this is a SQL Server–generated exception, the SqlException was able to handle the exception. The purpose of this example is to illustrate multiple Catch blocks; we discuss SQL-specific errors later in this section. It is a good idea to try to plan for as many specific exceptions as possible and to add them in ordered Catch blocks. This way, you can write custom exception-handling code that's unique for each circumstance.

TIP   *It's always a good idea to have a generic Catch block at the end of your Catch series, to capture unexpected exceptions.*

Using the When Clause

The previous example used the Exception class and classes derived from the Exception class. Using the Exception object as a filter is one method of error catching. Another way involves filtering by using the When clause within the Catch statement. The expression after the When keyword evaluates to a Boolean. Only when the expression returns a True will the exception be trapped by the Catch clause.

Let's add some exception handling to a different subroutine, NWShoppingCartControl_Load, which currently does not contain exception handling. You would need to trap the Fill()method of your DataAdapter. Modify the code within this subroutine to match Listing 11.14.

LISTING 11.14: USING THE WHEN CLAUSE IN THE CATCH STATEMENT

```
Try
   SqlDataAdapter3.Fill(DsCustomers1, "Customers")
   cboCustomers.DataSource = DsCustomers1.Tables("Customers")
   cboCustomers.DisplayMember = "CompanyName"
   cboCustomers.ValueMember = "CustomerID"
Catch excServerStopped As SqlClient.SqlException _
   When excServerStopped.Number = 17
            Console.WriteLine("Please start SQL Server.")
Catch excSqlError As SqlClient.SqlException
   Console.WriteLine _
   ("Message is " & excSqlError.Message & _
    " Error number is " & excSqlError.Number)
End Try
```

Place a breakpoint on the Try statement within the NWShoppingCartControl_Load subroutine and click F5 to execute the code. The code will pause execution at the Try statement. At this point, stop the SQL Server so that you can generate an exception. Click F11 to walk through the code. At the first Catch block, the exception is trapped because it fulfills the When condition, where the exception number is 17. This enables you to specify exception-handling code that is specific to only this exception.

TIP   Try not to rely on error messages or numbers as your conditional logic within your Catch *statement. Error numbers and error messages might differ between different versions of the object that you are working with. Using constants is a better choice because they are less susceptible to changes.*

MULTIPLE *TRY* BLOCKS

You are not limited to only a single Try...Catch block. You can code multiple Try blocks, which enable you to write highly specialized logic for different functionalities. For example, you can write one Try block that handles any errors with your connection, and another block for trapping errors related to filling a DataSet.

You can even nest multiple Try blocks within one another. This is useful when you think that an exception in one Try block might generate a new exception. You can handle the latter by embedding another Try block within the original.

The ability to use multiple and nested Try blocks is yet another compelling reason why you should use structured exception handling over unstructured error handling.

USING THE *FINALLY* STATEMENT

The Finally statement is optional if you already have supplied a Catch block. However, if your Try block doesn't contain a Catch section, you will have to supply the Finally structure. The Finally structure is useful for writing cleanup code, whether you use the Catch clause or not. You don't want to leave loose ends such as open connections in the event of an error. Listing 11.15 shows a sample of how the Finally statement fits inside the Try block.

LISTING 11.15: USING THE FINALLY STATEMENT

```
Try
    ' Data manipulation logic
Catch excConnection as System.Exception
    ' Add exception handler here
Finally
    SqlConnection1.Close()
End Try
```

You can't rely on the Try block to do your cleanup. If an error occurs before the cleanup code, the cleanup code might never get a chance to execute. Carefully construct your Finally logic, taking into consideration what state your application might be in. You don't want to close a connection that might not exist.

TIP   You must have either a Catch or a Finally block for every Try block.

Regardless of what happens inside the Try block, the Finally code will always execute. This makes the Finally block powerful and flexible enough to handle many scenarios. The Finally clause isn't limited to cleanup code. If you feel that your code can recover from an exception, you could write some code within the Finally structure to gracefully bounce back from the error. Alternately, you can take advantage of the Finally block to execute special error logging or debugging code.

The Exception Object

The System.Exception base class provides information regarding the cause of an exception. The Exception object comes with many base properties and methods that you can examine to take appropriate actions based on events that occur.

Most often, you will find the Exception object referenced within the Catch filter:

```
Catch excFill As System.Exception
```

Alternately, you can use any class that derives from the System.Exception object as a Catch filter:

```
Catch excSql As SqlClient.SqlException
```

The System.Exception class comes with several helpful properties that you can examine for more information regarding the exception that was generated. Classes that inherit from the base System.Exception class will also have these properties, but might choose to supplement them with additional properties that are specific to that type of Exception.

THE *STACKTRACE* PROPERTY

The StackTrace property enables you to traverse up the stack of methods that were executed, up until the moment the exception occurred. The stack is listed as a string, with the most recent method call listed first. The most recent method is the one in which the exception was thrown. It might not necessarily be the method in which the exception was generated. This is an important point to consider when you are debugging.

If you add the following line of code to the NWShoppingCartControl_Load subroutine's Catch section, you will see the list of methods that were called before an exception was generated:

```
Console.WriteLine("Stack contains: " & _
         excServerStopped.StackTrace)
```

As you did last time, stop the SQL Server in order to examine the contents of the stack. Listing 11.16 shows the results from the stack. As you can see, this information is quite useful for debugging, especially when you are working with complicated loops and the execution might have taken any branch.

LISTING 11.16: EXAMINING THE RESULTS OF A STACK TRACE

```
Stack contains:
at System.Data.SqlClient.SqlConnection.Open()
at  System.Data.Common.DbDataAdapter.QuietOpen
(IDbConnection connection, ConnectionState& originalState)
at System.Data.Common.DbDataAdapter.Fill
(Object data, Int32 startRecord, Int32 maxRecords,
 String srcTable, IDbCommand command,
 CommandBehavior behavior)
at System.Data.Common.DbDataAdapter.Fill
(DataSet dataSet, Int32 startRecord, Int32 maxRecords,
  String srcTable, IDbCommand command,
  CommandBehavior behavior)
at System.Data.Common.DbDataAdapter.Fill
(DataSet dataSet, String srcTable)
at NWShoppingCart.NWShoppingCartControl.
NWShoppingCartControl_Load
(Object sender, EventArgs e) in
C: \Code\NWShoppingCart\NWShoppingCartControl.vb:line 417
```

THE *SOURCE* PROPERTY

The Source property contains the name of the object in which the exception was generated. In the previous example, in which the SQL Server was not running, use the following line to return the Source property:

```
Console.WriteLine("Source is " & _
         excServerStopped.Source)
```

This returns a string containing the following:

```
Source is SQL Server Managed Provider
```

If you have worked with previous versions of Visual Basic, you should find this property much like the `Err.Source` property.

THE *MESSAGE* PROPERTY

The `Message` property is one of the most useful properties. It is similar to the `Err.Description` property that was often used with previous versions of Visual Basic.

THE *INNEREXCEPTION* PROPERTY

The `InnerException` property is a great way to work with multiple exceptions that occur. This property chains together all the exceptions that occur, enabling you to reference the properties of one exception from another. This way, you can specialize how your exceptions are treated by taking advantage of additional information from other exceptions.

THE *HELPLINK* PROPERTY

The `HelpLink` property contains a Uniform Resource Locator (URL) or Uniform Resource Number (URN), which contains help information regarding the exception that occurred.

THE *TARGETSITE* PROPERTY

The `TargetSite` property returns an object typed as a MethodBase. This object contains the method that generated the exception.

Throwing Exceptions

In this section, we review the options you have for notifying calling code that an error has occurred in your method. We focus on the latest methodology for handling exceptions with Visual Basic: throwing exceptions by using VB .NET's structured error handling.

UNSTRUCTURED ERROR HANDLING

You didn't always have to write code that caught errors with VB, because exception throwing (that is, error raising) was not as prevalent as it is with the .NET platform. With previous versions of VB, you had several choices of how to handle errors within a method:

◆ Don't handle the error at all.

◆ Quietly handle the error internally to the method and continue running.

◆ Return an API-style error code by using the output parameter or return value of a method. The calling code will check for this return value and act appropriately.

◆ Raise an error. The calling code would catch this error by using its error handler.

Again, it wouldn't serve much use to talk about the first option. The second option should already be familiar to you; it uses the `On Error` statement.

The third option used to be quite popular, especially in the heyday of Win32 API programming. This involved returning an HRESULT, Integer, Boolean, or Long as a return value or output parameter from a method. The value of this variable indicated the status of the activity. For example, you could return a zero to indicate a success condition (which, like zero, occurs only once) and any negative number to indicate an error code. This option is quite cumbersome because the calling code often contains intricate conditionals checking for each error code by using an `If...Then` or `Select...Case` construct. On top of this, the error codes are usually nonstandard values that are proprietary to each application. This forces the calling code to write custom error-trapping logic by using conditionals. This leads to nuances between calling code modules regarding how they trapped the errors that were returned. Additionally, there is the burden of where to store the error codes and message mapping tables. Storing the error codes in a centralized place leads to performance degradation because all calling code would need to look up the messages from the centralized location. Alternately, you could store the error mappings in each module, but this becomes a maintenance nightmare. When one mapping changes, each module has to be updated. It's difficult, if not impossible, to have a universal error-handling mechanism or standard with API-style methodology.

The last option is the most desirable one with past versions of Visual Basic, and it conceptually fits in with the .NET Framework's structured error handling. In past versions of VB, you would raise an error. In the .NET Framework, you throw an error.

STRUCTURED EXCEPTION HANDLING

Throwing exceptions is a new concept to Visual Basic. In past versions of Visual Basic, you would use the `Raise()` method of the Error object to notify calling code that an error has been generated. The calling code would capture this error in its internal error handler. The same concept is true for VB .NET; however, instead of the `Raise()` method, you use the `Throw()` statement.

Using structured exception handling with the .NET Framework, you have several choices when an exception occurs within a method:

◆ Don't handle the exception at all.

◆ Handle the exception quietly in the method it was generated, by using the `Try...Catch...Finally` block.

◆ Throw the exception back to the caller so they have to deal with it.

It doesn't make much sense to discuss the first option (not handling the exception at all), because, after all, this section is about handling exceptions. The second option, using the `Try...Catch...Finally` block, was discussed at length earlier in this chapter. The last option, throwing the exception back to the caller, is what you will focus on in this section.

THE *THROW* STATEMENT

You might not know it, but you've already seen an example of code that throws the exception back to the caller. Refer to Listing 11.13 and pay particular attention to this line:

```
Throw excFill
```

The `Throw` statement tosses the exception back to the code that called it and says, "Hey, you deal with this error. After all, you asked for it." This brings us to an important point: any code you write that calls another method should always contain internal exception handlers in case an error is thrown to it.

In your Northwind Shopping Cart project, the `LoadOrderGrid()` method throws the `excFill` exception in the event of a generic `System.Exception`. You can write some error-trapping logic from the calling code to handle this exception when it is thrown. The `Button1_Click` subroutine calls this method. At this point, this subroutine does not contain any exception-handling code. Modify the code in the `Button1_Click` subroutine to match that in Listing 11.17.

LISTING 11.17: CATCHING THROWN EXCEPTIONS

```
Private Sub Button1_Click _
    (ByVal sender As System.Object, _
    ByVal e As System.EventArgs) _
    Handles Button1.Click
        Try
            LoadOrderGrid()
        Catch excLoad As System.Exception
            Console.WriteLine _
            ("Message is " & _
            excLoad.Message & _
            " Stack contains: " & _
            excLoad.StackTrace)
        End Try
End Sub
```

The code in the exception handler is simple. You just added a generic `Try…Catch` block to handle any error. As you can see, location is transparent to the generic `Try…Catch` block. It doesn't care where the error came from. It could be an internal error within the method itself, or it could come from an external method that was called. All the exception handler cares about is testing the logic within the `Try` block, regardless of where it executes. Before you can try out your new exception handler, you must add some temporary code to force an error condition.

The exception in the `LoadOrderGrid()` method is called only when the `Catch excSql As SqlClient`
`.SqlException` block is unable to catch the error. To throw the exception, you are going to have to generate an error that is not captured by the first `Catch` block. Add some temporary logic to the `LoadOrderGrid()`method to force a non-SQL-related error. Within the `Try` block, before the `Fill()` method is called, add the following line of code:

```
SqlDataAdapter1 = Nothing
```

By attempting to fill a nonexistent DataAdapter, you will generate an error. Add a breakpoint to the `Try` block in the `LoadOrderGrid()` method and press F5 to execute your code. The code should halt at the breakpoint you had set. Click F11 to step through the code and watch how the error is thrown from the `LoadOrderGrid()` method and captured within the `Button1_Click` subroutine. As soon as the exception is thrown in the `LoadOrderGrid()` method, the next line of code jumps to the `Catch` block in the `Button1_Click` subroutine. This is referred to as *exception bubbling*. The exception travels up the stack until it finds code that traps it.

Examine the console to examine the properties of the exception that was generated. As you can see, the `Message` property indicates the following:

```
Value null was found where an instance of an object was required.
```

The `StackTrace` property results are shown in the console, as depicted in Listing 11.18.

LISTING 11.18: RESULTS OF STACKTRACE

```
Stack contains:
 at NWShoppingCart.NWShoppingCartControl.
LoadOrderGrid()
in C:\ Code\NWShoppingCart\
NWShoppingCartControl.vb:line 347
 at NWShoppingCart.NWShoppingCartControl.
Button1_Click(Object sender, EventArgs e) in C: \Code\NWShoppingCart\
NWShoppingCartControl.vb:line 363
```

Rethrowing Exceptions

You can also use the `Throw` statement to rethrow the error again, supplementing it with additional information. You can do so by throwing a `New` error, different from the one that was caught.

To do this, you modify the `Catch` block by adding a line of code at the end of the block that catches the `System.Exception`. The `Catch` block should look like the code in Listing 11.19.

LISTING 11.19: THROWING A NEW EXCEPTION

```
Catch excLoad As System.Exception
        Console.WriteLine _
        ("Message is " & _
        excLoad.Message & _
        " Stack contains: " & _
        excLoad.StackTrace)
Throw New System.Exception("You never set the DataAdapter")
```

If an exception that matches the `System.Exception` is thrown, this `Catch` block will be activated. The `Throw` statement will generate a new `System.Exception`, supplementing the default message with exception-specific information.

Exception Handling with SQL Server

In classic ADO, when you work with SQL Server, you either raise an event directly from SQL Server or you work with custom error codes that are housed in the ADO library. Each of these error codes maps to an ADO error constant. For example, the `adErrNoCurrentRecord` maps to error number 3021, which maps to a description:

```
Either BOF or EOF is True; or the current record has been
   deleted; or the operation requested by the application
   requires a current record.
```

To handle ADO errors, you insert an `On Error Goto` statement to redirect program control to an error handler. ADO serves as a database access layer, and it sits between your application and a provider. Different databases come with different OLE DB providers. Because each database has different capabilities, ADO's role is to make all databases look the same to your application. This is especially difficult because each provider raises different errors. In addition to provider-specific errors, ADO itself can raise errors. This means that there are two types of errors you must handle: ADO errors and provider-specific errors.

ADO errors are reported to VB and generate runtime errors, which you can trap in your VB code and handle as usual. *Provider-specific errors* are stored in the Errors collection of the Connection object. This means that as you code, you should know which operations cause ADO errors and which ones cause provider-specific errors. This is especially important because not all provider-specific errors raise runtime errors in VB. Most provider-specific errors cause VB runtime errors, but the Err object contains information about the most recent error, whereas the Errors collection of the Connection object might contain multiple errors raised by the same operation. Most ADO errors are handled through Visual Basic's Err object and the error-trapping mechanism built into the language. In complicated situations, you might have to examine the Errors collection to find out exactly what has happened.

In the .NET Framework, the exception-handling mechanism is centralized. As you know, the `System.Exception` is the base class from which all exceptions are derived. One particular class that inherits from this object is the SqlException class. This exception is generated from SQL Server itself. When the .NET data provider can't handle the error, the SqlException class extends the properties and methods of the `System.Exception` class with attributes and behavior specific to SQL Server itself. To understand the SqlException interface, you must first understand how SQL Server handles errors. After you examine SQL Server's error-handling mechanism, you will explore how the .NET Framework maps to it.

SQL SERVER NATIVE ERROR HANDLING

We reviewed different ways to handle errors by using SQL Server earlier in the book. In Chapter 5, we mentioned that you can use the `RETURN` statement to return custom or native SQL error codes. Additionally, we discussed the `RAISERROR` command, which enables you to fire errors that occur in your stored procedures or SQL statements. In this section, you will examine supplementary error information that enables you to build tighter error-handling code in your applications. You will see that most of these attributes map to the SqlClient .NET data provider error properties.

ERROR NUMBER

The Error Number attribute is a unique identifier that comes from the system table `master.dbo`
`.sysmessages`. As we showed you in Chapter 5, you can use a special stored procedure to add your
own error numbers and data to the `sysmessages` table:

```
sp_addmessage errorNum, severity, errorDescription
```

The error number provides a unique identifier for a particular SQL Server error.

ERROR MESSAGE

The Error Message attribute is a string containing information about an error.

SEVERITY

Severity levels indicate the seriousness of an error generated from SQL Server. The range for severity
begins at 1, which is the lowest, and ends at 25.

Errors with a severity of 10 usually occur when there are errors within the data passed to SQL
Server. These errors are non-fatal errors and indicate the status of a particular operation.

The ADO.NET SqlConnection object can handle errors with a severity of 19 or less. However,
when severity is greater than 19, the SqlConnection will close, generating a SqlException. We discuss
the SqlException class later in this section.

STATE CODE

The State Code helps you identify the condition under which the error occurred. Many different situations can raise the same error. To troubleshoot, you can use the State Code to identify exactly what
caused the error.

PROCEDURE NAME

If the error was caused by a stored procedure, you can use this attribute to retrieve the name of the
stored procedure in which the error occurred.

LINE NUMBER

Again, if the error occurred in a stored procedure, this attribute gives you the line number where the
error occurred.

HANDLING SQL SERVER ERRORS BY USING THE .NET FRAMEWORK

Unlike classic ADO, ADO.NET doesn't have its own independent error-handling mechanism.
Instead, it relies on the .NET Framework `System.Exception` class and its derivations to capture,
identify, and handle any errors that are generated from your data source.

There are two main .NET data providers that you use with ADO.NET: SqlClient and OleDb. Each of these data providers comes with their own implementation of the System.Exception object. The SqlClient data provider uses the SqlError objects, whereas the OleDb data provider uses the OleDbError. Both work in a similar fashion, as do any of the Exception objects in the .NET Framework. After you learn how to work with one, it doesn't take much to apply that knowledge to other objects.

NOTE *Our examples focus on a SQL Server database as the back-end system. All the conceptual knowledge with the SqlClient data provider can be applied to the OleDb provider. You should refer to the documentation for any other .NET data provider, such as ODBC.NET, in regards to their mechanism for exception handling.*

As we mentioned earlier in this chapter, the Connection object's InfoMessage event contains information regarding the error that occurs at the data source layer. If you are using the SqlClient .NET data provider, this will return error information created by SQL Server. When you are working with SQL Server exceptions, the main objects that you will work with in exception handling are the SqlException and SqlError classes. Many of the SqlError class attributes are wrapped within the SqlException class.

TIP *ADO.NET also enables you to create custom errors that you can assign to the DataSet object.*

The SqlException Class

The SqlException class is part of the System.Data.SqlClient namespace. Like other exception classes, it inherits from the System.Exception base class, augmenting the base properties and methods with SQL-specific properties and methods. Some of the System.Exception base properties are overridden with SQL Server–specific information, such as the Message and Source properties.

The Class Property   The Class property maps to the severity level generated from SQL Server. We reviewed the severity level earlier when we discussed the SQL Server error mechanism. Unfortunately, ADO.NET is a bit limited in the errors that it captures, catching only those with a severity of 10 or lower. As we said earlier, the higher the severity number, the more serious the error. Thus, ADO.NET does not catch the more serious errors.

The Errors Property   The Errors property exposes a collection of SqlError object types. As you review the properties of the SqlException property, you will see how the different attributes and behaviors of the SqlError class are wrapped within the SqlException class.

The LineNumber Property   The LineNumber property corresponds to the Line Number attribute generated from the SQL Server error-handling mechanism, which we discussed earlier in this section. The LineNumber property is useful in debugging because it enables you to pinpoint the exact line number in the stored procedure or SQL statement in which the error occurred. The LineNumber property comes from the SqlError object, indicating the line number of the error in the Errors collection.

The Number Property   The Number property corresponds to the Error Number attribute of the SQL Server error-handling mechanism. It indicates the unique error code from the master.dbo .sysmessages table in SQL Server. You saw the Number property in action in a previous example using this property to check for an error condition when an instance of SQL Server was not running.

The* Procedure *Property The Procedure property provides the name of the stored procedure in which the error was generated. Again, this is a useful property to examine when you are debugging.

The* Server *Property As you might gather from its name, the Server property contains the name of the SQL Server from which the error was generated.

The* State *Property The State property comes from the specific error in the SqlError collection. It provides additional information regarding the exception that has occurred.

As you can see, most of the ADO.NET SqlClient errors nicely map back to the errors originating from SQL Server itself. Using these properties, you can build robust applications that anticipate possible error conditions, handling them with grace.

Summary

In this chapter, you've learned many advanced concepts involving data access with the .NET Framework. By no means does this chapter completely cover all advanced functionality; however, you should now at least have a solid foundation for building threaded applications by using solid event programming logic. The reactive members of the ADO.NET objects, such as events, should now be familiar to you, enabling you to build solid applications that anticipate exceptions, events, and data access activity.

Chapter 12

Integration with XML

- ◆ XML tools and technologies
- ◆ Walk-through
- ◆ SQL Server 2000 integration with XML

XML's PREVALENCE IN INTEGRATING many technologies has led to the formation of satellite technologies that further enhance XML capabilities. These satellite technologies use XPath expressions and queries, XML templates, and XSL Transformations (XSLT). These technologies magnify the power of XML. They ensure that XML data is accessible and reusable across platforms, industries, and generations. These technologies continue to emerge as de facto standards with integration into development tools, such as VS .NET, as well as DBMSs such as SQL Server 2000.

Think of the Internet as a result of a unification between computer networks. This unification led to the emergence of languages and specifications to describe this new phenomenon. HTML provides the means to describe and communicate the information from one computer to another. URLs provide a specification to navigate from machine to machine, or within HTML pages on a single machine.

The need for unification among discrete data sets used by industries and organizations has also led to new languages and specifications. Like HTML, XML provides a structure and container to describe and package data items for communication between one computer and another. Much like URLs, the XPath language enables users to navigate from machine to machine, or within XML pages on one machine. Additionally, XPath patterns can be used for XSL Transformations to display reusable XML data with different presentation logic, based on devices, industries, or applications. XPath's usefulness doesn't end there. With SQL Server 2000's support for the XPath language, you can now query SQL Server databases directly from URLs by using HTTP. You'll explore all these options in this chapter.

There are books the length of this one that focus only on XSLT or XPath, so we don't expect to cover every aspect in a single chapter. However, after reading this chapter, you should have a conceptual overview of these technologies and be able to integrate these technologies into your database applications.

IS XML THE NEW OLE DB?

Both XML and OLE DB share common strategies: First, they attempt to unify data access across heterogeneous platforms in order to simplify code. Second, they promote code reuse by supplying common interfaces for either describing or manipulating data. Figure 12.1 shows you just how similar XML and OLE DB are in concept. Both technologies provide a universal interface for accessing data, regardless of the source. As you can see from the figure, XML can even be directly displayed to the browser.

FIGURE 12.1

OLE DB and XML for universal data access

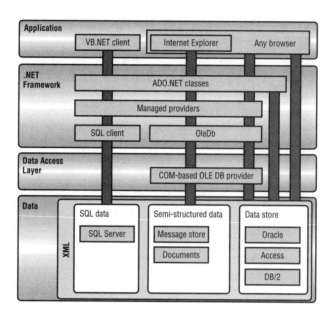

OLE DB had the right idea in theory, but didn't quite make it in practice, whereas XML and XML-related technologies are spreading like wildfire. What happened?

XML, along with its related tools and technologies, offers the same benefits as OLE DB. You can map existing data sources to XML schema and data, enabling heterogeneous data access. OLE DB tried to do the same thing, asking vendors to write OLE DB providers for their data sources and using OLE DB APIs as the mapping mechanism. However, OLE DB has two major stumbling blocks. First, unlike XML, the OLE DB API is messy to program against. Second, OLE DB never gained the widespread industry acceptance of XML. This is because OLE DB is based on COM, a proprietary and binary protocol. XML is text based and easy to transport and interpret across multiple platforms.

After your data and schema are stored as XML, universal data access becomes simple. Technologies such as XPath and XSLT promote this concept, enabling you to query and process the XML to suit your purposes. Instead of using OLE DB API calls and providers, you can use XML-related technologies to reach any data source.

The main advantage of XML is that you don't need to have an OLE DB provider to access a data source. Unlike OLE DB, XML is easy to program, making it faster than writing an OLE DB provider to hook into a specific data source.

In this chapter, you will concentrate on the new languages and developments that support and surround XML. First, we explain each of the technologies so that you can understand when, where, and why they should be used. Then we explain how the different technologies can be implemented by providing a walk-through that will ultimately enable you to retrieve SQL Server data, transform it, and render it via HTTP and XML.

We spent a significant amount of time on XML in Chapter 10, "The Role of XML." However, we didn't nearly cover the myriad of topics related to XML, such as XPath and XSLT. In Chapter 10, we covered XML's role with SQL Server, as well as its role with ADO.NET. We reviewed the SQL Server OPENXML statement, which enabled you to pass XML data from VB .NET to SQL Server for insertion. We worked with the FOR XML function, which enables SQL Server to return query results as XML. With ADO.NET, we programmed with the DataSet's ReadXml() and WriteXml() methods, which enabled you to process XML data and schema. Now we are going to build on that foundation, and show you more advanced techniques for working with relational data by using XML.

In this chapter, you expand your knowledge of XML. You are not just going to read and return results as XML, but actually transform the data by using the satellite technologies that we mentioned earlier. By the end of this chapter, you should be able to answer the following questions:

- How does XPath work with XSL Transformations?

- How can you use XSL stylesheets to transform your XML data?

- How do XSL templates work?

- How does XPath enable you to query SQL Server 2000 databases directly?

XML Tools and Technologies

It's no doubt that after a language has gained prevalence, many satellite technologies evolve from it. In the case of XML, there emerged a need for technologies that not only describe and transport the data, but also format and parse the data. The Extensible Stylesheet Language (XSL) provided a specification for formatting XML data. Specifically, XSL provided a mechanism to specify subsets of an XML document, identify formatting instructions and operations, and incorporate them into a final output document. XSL was originally created as a way to format XML in a purely cosmetic fashion. However, the process for identifying and transforming the source file soon became useful for more than just formatting. This process could also be used for transformation, such as data manipulation, structure creation, and conditional operations. Thus, XSLT emerged as a language in its own right.

Because XSL enables you to manipulate data and the structure of data, you can relate it to the SQL language itself. In fact, much of what you can do with SQL statements can be done with XSL and XPath directives. You'll soon see examples of this capability as you step through the examples in this chapter. XSL can completely restructure an XML document, creating a brand new result document based on logic and conditions that you specify.

NOTE *The XSL specification branches into two main technologies: XSLT and XSL Formatting Objects (XSL-FO). Although XSL-FO is quite useful for defining how an XML document should be displayed, it is a formatting technology and is not meant to handle structured data. This book focuses primarily on the manipulation of data, rather than formatting, so we do not discuss XSL-FO further in this book. You can find more information on this standard on MSDN online at* http://msdn.microsoft.com.

XSL Transformations emerged from the Cascading Stylesheet (CSS) language, along with a related specification, XPath. Both are languages that provide formatting, processing, and manipulation of XML documents. XSLT is used to write stylesheets, which contain processing rules for creating output documents from XML. XPath is used to match patterns by using functions, location paths, and conditionals.

First, you'll spend some time examining these technologies in their own right. After you understand how these technologies work, you'll be able to use them within integrated web and database solutions.

Before you begin, you need some sample XML data to work with. VS .NET makes it easy for you to generate XML data from a data source. As you remember from Chapter 7, "ADO.NET Programming" (see the section "Generating an XML File from an Existing DataSet"), the WriteXml() method is a great way to write to an XML file by using a DataSet.

Let's create a Windows Application that will create a sample XML file for you to work with. Again, this is very similar to the steps that you followed in Chapter 7, so feel free to refer to that chapter.

NOTE *Alternately, you can load this project from the companion CD. The code is listed under the solution file* Generate XML file.sln.

After you've created the project, open the Server Explorer and choose the Customers table in the Northwind database. Drag the table onto the designer window. From the properties window of the Data Adapter, launch the Data Adapter Configuration Wizard by selcting The Configure Data Adapter link. This will launch the Data Adapter Configuration Wizard. Follow the wizard's steps, using the default values to create SqlConnection and SqlDataAdapter objects. From the properties window of the DataAdapter object, choose the Generate DataSet option. Name your newly created DataSet **dsCustomers1**. After you have completed the data access configuration, add a button to the form and place the following code in its click event:

```
SqlDataAdapter1.Fill(DsCustomers1)
DsCustomers1.WriteXml("customers.xml")
```

This code might seem familiar to you. It is almost identical to the code you used in Chapter 7. For simplicity, we chose not to write the schema inline by omitting the XmlWriteMode.WriteSchema parameter.

Execute the project by clicking F5 and then click the button. This is a one-time step to create an XML file, customers.xml, which will be stored within the bin directory of your solution.

After the XML file is created, you are going to have to massage its contents a little bit. To make the sample more generic, replace the root element node, which had been named after the DataSet, with the <NWCustomers> element.

Now that you've generated some sample XML data, you can explore the various technologies related to XML.

XPath

The Extensible Markup Language Path (XPath) is a language for navigating and traversing through an XML document. It leverages the path structure used to access directories, files, or Uniform Resource Locators (URLs). By specifying a path, XPath traverses down the hierarchical nature of an XML document, homing in on a specific subset, or *node-set*, of the document.

XPath is not specific to any development platform, but a language in itself. As a language, it is quickly gaining prevalence. Many development tools support it. Both SQL Server 2000 and VS .NET provide support for XPath-querying expressions.

NOTE *We focus on the SQL Server 2000 integration in this chapter; however, you can find information on VS .NET support within the VS .NET documentation.*

XPath uses the InfoSet model to determine the construction of XPath expressions. The *InfoSet* identifies a series of abstract, syntax-independent terms to describe the information architecture of a well-formed XML document. In its simplest form, the InfoSet for a well-formed XML document contains at least two items: the document and the element item. This information architecture can be expanded to include attributes, comments, namespace declarations, and so on. Additionally, the InfoSet provides the structure for relationships between these items. XPath takes advantage of the InfoSet-implied relationship to navigate within hierarchical items in an XML document. For example, imagine you are working with an XML document whose excerpted data looks similar to Listing 12.1.

NOTE *The full code listing for this sample is listed on the companion CD that comes with this book.*

LISTING 12.1: CUSTOMERS.XML

```xml
<NWCustomers xmlns="http://www.tempuri.org/dsCustomers.xsd">
  <Customers>
    <CustomerID>ALFKI</CustomerID>
    <CompanyName>Alfreds Futterkiste</CompanyName>
    <ContactName>Maria Anders</ContactName>
    <ContactTitle>Sales Representative</ContactTitle>
    <Address>Obere Str. 57</Address>
    <City>Berlin</City>
    <PostalCode>12209</PostalCode>
    <Country>Germany</Country>
    <Phone>030-0074321</Phone>
    <Fax>030-0076545</Fax>
  </Customers>

  <Customers>
    <CustomerID>KOENE</CustomerID>
```

```
                <CompanyName>Königlich Essen</CompanyName>
                <ContactName>Philip Cramer</ContactName>
                <ContactTitle>Sales Associate</ContactTitle>
                <Address>Maubelstr. 90</Address>
                <City>Brandenburg</City>
                <PostalCode>14776</PostalCode>
                <Country>Germany</Country>
                <Phone>0555-09876</Phone>
            </Customers>
        </NWCustomers>
```

You can specify an XPath expression that retrieves child Country elements for all customers:

```
NWCustomers/Customers/Country
```

Clearly, the syntax for XPath expressions is straightforward. It's no different from navigating to a file within a directory structure, or to a web page within a website. A *location path*, such as this, is the most common use of XPath expressions. Each child element is separated by a forward slash. Any nodes that match the pattern make up a *node-set*. A node-set is not the same thing as a node branch, because it might not match the original structure of nodes. Figure 12.2 indicates the node-set for the following XPath expression:

```
NWCustomers/Customers/
```

NOTE *One thing you might find interesting is that XPath relies on a different representation for its specifications than other technologies, such as XSLT or XSD. Whereas XSLT and XSD rely on XML to describe their structure, XPath uses a notation similar to file path directives.*

FIGURE 12.2

Understanding node-sets

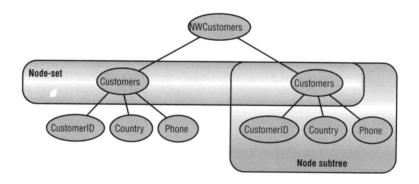

As you can see, a node-set might not necessarily include its logical subtree. If you choose, you can retrieve all the child elements of the Customers element by using the asterisk (*) wildcard operator:

```
NWCustomers/Customers/*
```

This will retrieve all the child elements below the Customers node, getting the values for `CustomerID`, `CompanyName`, `City`, and so on.

IMPORTANCE OF XML SCHEMA

XML schema is vitally important to both the XSL Transformations and XPath technologies. Each language relies on well-formed XML schema in order to process XML documents efficiently, without error.

Although XML schema is becoming more prevalent as industries define common business vocabularies, there is a transitory phase before all companies agree upon a single industry standard. XSL Transformations step in at the point where XML schema implementation subsides. Without a base schema to provide the foundation, mapping the transformation elements would be awkward, if not impossible. A well-defined XML schema is crucial to executing efficient and reusable XSL Transformations.

Throughout this book, we've stressed the importance of both sides of XML: the data itself and the schema that describes its structure. A distinct separation exists between data and schema. VS .NET completely solidifies this concept, creating a schema behind every DataSet that is separate from the data it describes. Well-formed schema definition is paramount to designing robust systems that leverage XML technology. XPath is a prime example of why XML schema is so important.

Without the structural metadata that defines the relationship between data elements, XPath directives would not work. XPath treats an XML document in a hierarchical fashion, traversing through the various nodes of the tree. How could you find a specific location path if your data is not well organized and is stored in an arbitrary fashion? Although XSL Transformations can help by creating well-formed schema out of random XML fragments, as more developers create XML schema properly in the first place, the less transformation code other developers will have to write.

An XPath expression is not limited only to specifying a navigational path. It can contain method calls, variables, Boolean comparisons, mathematical operations, and more. You can narrow your node-set by using brackets to specify search criteria. If you wanted to retrieve all customers from the United States, for example, you could use this XPath expression:

```
NWCustomers/Customers[Country='USA']/CompanyName
```

As you can see, you can embed search criteria within your path directive. This expression retrieves the values specified in the `CompanyName` element for U.S. customers.

How would you work with attributes? They work the same way as elements, separated with forward slashes, with one minor exception. You need to prefix the attribute name with an at symbol (@). The sample XML in Listing 12.1 does not contain any attributes. Here's a small segment of an XML document that uses attributes:

```
<Customers CustomerID="ALFKI" CompanyName="Alfreds Futterkiste" </Customers>
```

If you wanted to retrieve the values in the `CompanyName` attribute, your XPath expression would look like this:

```
Customers/@CompanyName
```

Imagine that you had a website from which a customer could edit their user profile information. You don't want them to see other people's information, so you would create a filter on the XML document to retrieve only their information. Again, you can use square brackets to home in on nodes that match specific search criteria. If you wanted to return only the customer whose `CustomerID` matches the value `ALFKI`, you would use

```
Customers/[@CompanyName= "ALFKI"]
```

NOTE   *We purposely use double quotes in this example to illustrate the point that either single or double quotes can be used with attributes.*

Filtering expressions in the square brackets are known as *predicates*. Predicates enable you to retrieve a subset of information within a specific XPath location path.

Think about the implications of this ability to search, or filter, within your XML document. You can even build your security model by using XPath! Imagine that you have elements or attributes that store security information, such as:

```
<CreditCardInfo AccessLevel="2"
<CardNumber = "1234 567 8901"
</CardNumber>
</CreditCardInfo>
```

The `AccessLevel` attribute indicates the degree of confidentiality of XML data. Imagine that a value of 1 indicates open access data, whereas 2 indicates data with high sensitivity, such as credit card information. You can build an XPath filter that shows only data that is unsecured:

```
CreditCardInfo /[@AccessLevel = "1"]
```

As you can see, XPath is based on relativity. You navigate within node-sets by using relational directives, such as location paths. Additionally, you can use variables and functions to create new data items.

In summary, XPath expressions provide ways to do the following:

- Specify node-sets
- Filter within a node-set by using conditions
- Create text values for the result document
- Create new data by applying functions to modify source data

We realize that this information is a bit hard to digest without a context. You might wonder how you program with XPath expressions. Where do you place the logic? In the "Walk-through" section, we will show you how XPath expressions fit into XSL stylesheets and how you can use them with both XML files and SQL Server 2000 databases.

XSLT

As we have said earlier, XSL Transformations (XSLT) is yet another language that has emerged from the prevalence of XML. In fact, the language itself is based on XML. XSLT enables you to recast an existing XML source document into a new XML result tree. XSLT enables you to restructure the source XML hierarchy and data by applying different filters, structures, or formats. You can think of it as a translation engine that translates your source XML into your desired outcome. It does this with the use of templates and stylesheets.

Stylesheets can store one or more templates. *Templates* contain patterns and processing rules. The *patterns* are used to home in on a node and, potentially, its subtree within the source document. The matching node and its children are then processed by using the instructions within the template.

Before we continue our discussion of XSL Transformations, you should have a solid understanding of the vocabulary used with this technology. To enable easier referencing, we've listed some of the more common terms here:

◆ An XSL *stylesheet* provides the information regarding a transformation, such as mappings between the source and target schema and data. A stylesheet can contain more than one template.

Continued on next page

XSL TRANSFORMATIONS GLOSSARY *(continued)*

◆ The *root* of a stylesheet is the stylesheet itself. It's a virtual reference, from which the root element is spawned.

◆ A *root element* is also known as the *document element*. All elements within an XML document fall under the root element as child elements.

◆ A *node-set* is a specific subset of an XML document that can contain one or more node structures. A node-set is not the same as a node subtree. Its children are not considered part of the node; however, if directed, each node can contain multiple child elements and/or attributes.

◆ *XSL templates* are contained within a stylesheet and provide mapping information between the source and target XML document. A template contains the rules for the transformation. These rules can contain XSLT instructions or literal element transfers, which are elements that are often copied "as is" into the target document.

◆ *Template fragments* enable you to map subsets of an XML document by using specific source and target node-sets. This enables you to dynamically construct a target document.

◆ *Patterns* enable you to navigate to a specific subnode, by using XPath functions, location paths, and processing instructions.

◆ *Predicates* are XPath filtering expressions that enable the retrieval of a subset of data within a specified location path.

THE PURPOSE OF XSLT

To fully reuse and take advantage of XML data, you need a mechanism to manipulate, interrogate, restructure, and share the data. The purpose of XSLT is to do the following:

◆ Unify vocabularies

◆ Present, rather than represent, structured data

◆ Reuse data

The first goal of XSLT is to *unify vocabularies*. As XML becomes more established, businesses hope to unify the shared vocabularies within their industries. This unification would make it easier for one business to understand the data from another. However, industry standards do not form overnight, and no one expects businesses to unanimously agree on specific business term definitions. In the meantime, there is XSLT, which provides a mapping mechanism for data that is inconsistently labeled between organizations.

XML is a great way to represent data. An XML tree's hierarchical structure makes navigation and identification simple and intuitive. However, XML alone is not a great tool for determining how to present data on different devices or applications. If you look at raw XML directly through a browser, it's definitely not the prettiest thing you've ever seen. XML's lack of concern with presentation is its salient point—separation between presentation and data provides for greater reusability.

What about HTML? HTML is a great presentation format, albeit not one for representing structured data. If you could combine the two, you would end up with a way to *present structured data.* XSLT enables you to do exactly that; it combines both HTML and XML elements so that you can create a structure that best suits your needs, while gaining maximum reuse out of your XML data.

The capability of XSLT to interrogate, manipulate, and ultimately transform XML data creates a strong path for data reuse. You no longer have to store the data in multiple formats and structures based on application, industry, or presentation needs. Instead, you store the data once as XML, independent of any format, structure, or presentation. Then you choose the appropriate transformation and apply it to the central data, rendering the structure that best suits your needs. In this way, XSLT provides a robust *mechanism for data reuse.*

BENEFITS OF XSLT

XSLT makes it possible to convert XML to any text-based format such as HTML. XSLT enables you to:

- Convert XML to an alternative format

- Reorder, modify, or filter source data

- Gather, restructure, and redefine schema

You can leverage XSLT to create a brand new XML document from existing source structure. You can reorder data elements or bring back only subsets of data. You can create an entirely different schema. XSLT is a full-fledged language that uses variables and functions, as do other languages such as VB .NET. An XSL Transformation is made up of two core elements: a template and the stylesheet in which it exists.

XSL Templates

XSL templates contain the rules on how your data is going to be transformed. You can think of a template as a road map, which specifies the data source and the route it will take to its final destination. The source is specified with the use of a *pattern.* Patterns specify criteria by using paths, algorithms, literals, or conditions. An XSL Transformation takes a pattern and matches it to a node-set within the source XML document. Most often, a template will use the XPath language to identify the appropriate node-set.

After a node-set is identified, it is directed through the appropriate transformation. The transformation occurs with the help of processing instructions. These instructions execute against the source node-set. Processing occurs for each node-set. Each transformed node-set is built into a resulting XML tree. In the end, you will have a result tree that displays all the post-transformation node-sets. Figure 12.3 illustrates a sample transformation.

Although you can have more than one template embedded within a stylesheet, realize that a single template is very powerful. It can identify multiple node-sets from multiple XML documents and use them to create an arbitrary structure as simple or as complex as you like. If a single template is so powerful, why would you ever want to use more than one? Multiple templates come in handy if any of your transformations depend on the result node-set as it is being processed. That way, you can layer one template after the other to refine and advance your final XML result tree.

FIGURE 12.3

A simple XSL
Transformation
example

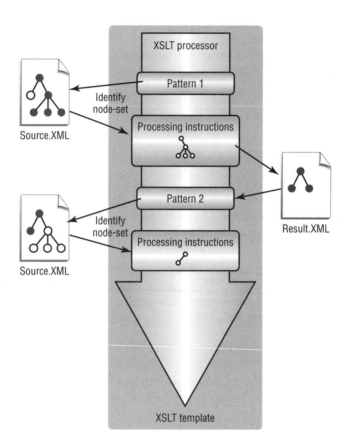

Syntax

Those of you who have worked with traditional object-oriented languages, such as C++, might find XPath and XSLT daunting due to unfamiliarity with their syntax. This section provides a reference guide to some of their key elements, attributes, and symbols. Again, we can't cover every aspect of the languages; however, these samples should give you an idea of how to program with XSLT and XPath.

SPECIAL XSL ELEMENTS AND ATTRIBUTES

An XSL document comprises <xsl> elements and attributes, which specify conditional logic, processing instructions, or directives. Within these element tags, you specify parameters that indicate transformation information, such as XPath query expressions or literal values.

Table 12.1 contains a short list of some of the more common XSLT and XPath elements, attributes, and functions. By no means can we cover all of them, but by learning some common ones, you can have a foundation for building rudimentary XSL stylesheets and templates.

TABLE 12.1: COMMON XSLT RESERVED ATTRIBUTES AND FUNCTIONS

TAG	DESCRIPTION
`select`	Is often referred to as the *pattern*, because it often contains the XPath directive to the current node-set.
`xsl:value-of`	Copies the value of the specified node as text.
`xsl:for-each`	Iterates through a node-set.
`xsl:copy`	Performs a literal transformation by directly copying the current node in the source file to the result tree.
`xsl:choose`	Similar to a `Select` statement in VB .NET. Provides the evaluation criteria for conditional case logic.
`xsl:when`	Similar to the `Case` keyword in VB .NET. Provides the comparison expressions for an `xsl:choose` statement.
`xsl:if`	Similar to the `If…Then` structure in VB .NET. Enables you to evaluate conditional Boolean logic.

NOTE As you will see in the code examples in this chapter, the XSLT namespace URI, `http://www.w3.org/1999/XSL/Transform` is typically referred to in your XSL code files. You should check the `http://www.w3.org` website for the latest XSLT standards.

The `select` attribute provides the location path or pattern for the specific node-set you wish to retrieve. For example, the `select` attribute could specify `select = NWCustomers/Customers` to drill down into the `NWCustomers` element to retrieve the child `Customers` nodes.

The `xsl:value-of` element returns the data within a node. You should specify the `select` attribute along with this element to indicate the name of the node whose value you wish to retrieve. If you wanted to retrieve the value of the `CustomerID`, you would specify

```
<xsl:value-of select="CustomerID"/>
```

The `xsl:for-each` element iterates through a specified element, applying any logic within the `for-each` loop. You'll soon see this function in action.

The `xsl:copy` element copies a specified node (not its children) from a source document to the result document. If you wanted to do a hierarchical copy of the node and its descendants, you would use the `xsl:copy-of` element instead.

The `xsl:choose` element is used in conjunction with one or more `xsl:when` clauses in order to evaluate multiple conditions. The `test` attribute is used with the `xsl:when` clause to specify the condition that you wish to evaluate.

The order of `xsl:when` elements is important. After the condition in an `xsl:when` element is met, the conditional processing stops. Most likely, you will want to specify narrower criteria first, with the generic conditions at the end. That way, your comparison criteria can fall through until it's caught by the appropriate level of specification. For example, if you were looking for an order price that was less than 2, you wouldn't want your `xsl:when` condition

```
<xsl:when test = "Orders/Price < 100">
</xsl:when>
```

to come before

```
<xsl:when test="Orders/Price < 2">
</xsl:when>
```

If you didn't order these expressions properly, the execution would stop on the first `xsl:when` clause, and you would end up with all prices under 100, not just those that are less than 2.

Like the `xsl:when` clause, the `xsl:if` is also used with the test attribute in order to evaluate conditional logic. You will see the `xsl:if` instruction used in the examples later in this chapter.

SPECIAL XPATH SYMBOLS

So far we've worked only with absolute location paths in our XPath expressions, which always use the root element as its context. Alternately, you can use relative location paths, which rely on the concept of a *current*, or *context*, *node*. The current node provides the starting point from which the navigation will occur. To support the concept of relative location paths, special relative navigation symbols are provided in the XPath language. These come as a series of shortcuts that enable you to shorten the lines of code you use to retrieve XML data. Some of these shortcuts are listed in Table 12.2.

NOTE   For brevity, our examples use abbreviated notation. The unabbreviated syntax can get quite lengthy and cumbersome. For example, the XPath location path to retrieve an attribute called `customerid` *is abbreviated from* `attribute: customerid` *and becomes* `@customerid` *instead.*

TABLE 12.2: SPECIAL XPATH ABBREVIATIONS

SYMBOL	MEANING
. (period)	Selects the current node
.. (double period)	Selects the parent of the current node
// (double slash)	Specifies wildcard parent node
* (asterisk)	Selects all the children of the current node
@ (at symbol)	Is the prefix for an attribute name

Here are some scenarios where you might want to use these abbreviations:

You could use the period (`.`) operator with the `xsl:value-of` element to retrieve the value of the current node. For example, if you were iterating through a document and wanted to retrieve the values of each current node, you could use this line within your looping construct:

```
<xsl:value-of select="." />
```

The double slash (//) enables you to directly navigate to a specific node by using its name. For example, if you wanted to retrieve the first name of a customer, instead of using

```
customers/firstname
```

you could specify

```
//firstname
```

Be warned that this will retrieve all the nodes that are named `firstname`, regardless of whether they fall under the `customers` parent node. If you have `firstname` listed under the `employees` node, then these values will be retrieved as well.

XSL Stylesheets

XSLT works with patterns within templates to identify source elements for processing in an XML document. These source elements are used for transformation into the target document. These patterns and templates are stored within an XSL stylesheet.

The `xsl:stylesheet` element is the container for all the child elements within an XSL stylesheet. XSL stylesheets are simply well-formed XML documents with XSL processing instructions embedded within `xsl` tags. Instead of elaborating on the concept of a stylesheet, you'll understand how they work by creating one of your own.

Walk-through

The best way to understand how something works is to experiment with it. Here comes the fun part. In this section, you'll walk through multiple steps showing you how to implement the various XML-related technologies that you learned about earlier in this chapter. You will create a template that will serve as a foundation for an XSL stylesheet. One of the most common requests for an XSL Transformation is to convert XML data into HTML so that it displays nicely in a browser. Your first walk-through will be to take a simple XML document and render it via HTML.

Later in this chapter, we expand upon this example. You will not only transform XML to HTML, but also transfer relational data from SQL Server into HTML with the help of the XML technologies in SQL Server, XSLT, and XPath. In the upcoming "SQL Server 2000 Integration with XML" section, you will use the stylesheet you create here to transform data that you return from the Northwind SQL Server database.

You don't have to specify the entire XML document for conversion. This is where XPath comes into play. XSLT leverages XPath expressions to target specific subsets of an XML document. XPath guides an XSLT processor as it navigates through an XML document. XPath enables you to highly specialize your XSL Transformation; only certain subnodes are marked for conversion. This way, you transform only the data and structure that you need.

As we indicated earlier, XPath fits into a variety of different technologies, including XSL Transformations. You can embed XPath expressions within your XSL Transformations code:

```
<xsl:value-of select="Customers/Orders" />
```

This expression indicates that the xsl:value-of transformation should pull the values from the Customers/Orders XPath navigational directive. You'll use XPath in conjunction with XSL directives as you create your template.

Creating a Template

Templates consist of both literal XML elements and processing instructions. The literal elements contain regular HTML and XML data copied "as is" into the result document. The processing instructions are enclosed in a set of xsl tags, such as xsl:if, which you reviewed earlier in this chapter. Altogether, a template provides directives for where the XML data should be placed.

In this example, you will construct a template by using HTML and comments as placeholders for where you will embed your xsl tags. This way, you can see how a stylesheet is built from the bottom up, beginning with a template shell.

NOTE *All the code for these examples is contained on the CD that accompanies this book.*

To start, our HTML template will look similar to Listing 12.2. If you want to follow along, copy this code by using Notepad or Visual Studio .NET and save the file as **Creating a Template Step1.html**.

LISTING 12.2: *CREATING A TEMPLATE STEP1.HTML*

```
<HTML>
  <HEAD>
    <TITLE>Northwind Customer Template</TITLE>
  </HEAD>
  <BODY>
    <TABLE BORDER="3" BGCOLOR="Cyan">
      <TR>
        <TD>Customer ID</TD>
        <TD>Company Name</TD>
        <TD>City</TD>
        <TD>Country</TD>
      </TR>

      <!-- For each customer-->
      <TR BGCOLOR = "White">
        <!-- Display customer information-->
        <TD><!-- insert CustomerID  --></TD>
        <TD><!-- insert CompanyName --></TD>
        <TD><!-- insert City        --></TD>
        <TD><!-- insert Country     --></TD>
      </TR>
      <!-- End of customer loop-->
```

```
    </TABLE>
  </BODY>
</HTML>
```

NOTE   *Notice that the HTML in this code example is well formed, with proper nesting and paired start and end tags.*

The HTML code is simple. All it does is create a table with four columns. Feel free to examine it within your browser. At this point, there are placeholders for the details that will go in the table rows. To list each customer within the table, you will need to iterate through all customers, adding them one customer at a time to the table.

Now it's time to replace the commented code with the XSL elements you learned about earlier.

NOTE   *Commented code is indicated by using* `<!--` *and* `-->` *tags.*

As you remember, the `xsl:for-each` element enables you to loop through XML elements that match a specified path. The line

```
<xsl:for-each select="NWCustomers/Customers">
```

provides the looping statement you need to iterate through the XML document that you created earlier in this chapter. The `select` attribute specifies an XPath expression that retrieves the node-set specified within the path directive: `NWCustomers/Customers`. Make sure you terminate your `xsl:for-each` element with a closing tag:

```
</xsl:for-each>
```

Next, you need to replace the table row placeholders with actual data from the XML document. For the `CustomerID`, `CompanyName`, `City`, and `Country`, the code looks like the following, respectively:

```
<TD><xsl:value-of select="CustomerID"/></TD>
<TD><xsl:value-of select="CompanyName"/></TD>
<TD><xsl:value-of select="City"/></TD>
<TD><xsl:value-of select="Country"/></TD>
```

You use the `xsl:value-of` element to specify that you wish to return the value for the element indicated in the `select` attribute. The `select` attribute uses a simplistic XPath traversal to locate the specific element.

When you are finished, you should have an HTML file that looks like Listing 12.3. To make reviewing it easier, we've highlighted the changes from Listing 12.2 in bold.

LISTING 12.3: CREATING A TEMPLATE STEP 2.HTML

```
<HTML>
  <HEAD>
    <TITLE>Northwind Customer Template</TITLE>
  </HEAD>
  <BODY>
```

```
<TABLE BORDER="3" BGCOLOR="Cyan">
  <TR>
    <TD>Customer ID</TD>
    <TD>Company Name</TD>
    <TD>City</TD>
    <TD>Country</TD>
  </TR>

  <!-- For each customer-->
  <xsl:for-each select="NWCustomers/Customers>

      <TR BGCOLOR = "White">
        <!-- Display customer information-->
        <TD><xsl:value-of select="CustomerID"/></TD>
        <TD><xsl:value-of select="CompanyName"/></TD>
        <TD><xsl:value-of select="City"/></TD>
        <TD><xsl:value-of select="Country"/></TD>
      </TR>

  <!-- End of customer loop-->
  </xsl:for-each>

  </TABLE>
 </BODY>
</HTML>
```

The next step is to wrap the template code by using the xsl:template element. This element encapsulates a template rule. A *template rule* provides the processing information for a specific subnode transformation. Add the start and end element as a child of the xsl:stylesheet element, right after the stylesheet element:

```
<xsl:template match="/">
</xsl:template>
```

The match attribute specifies an XPath expression that indicates the nodes on which the template should be applied. By specifying a slash (/), you indicate that the entire document should be processed from the root. Using the XML segment in Listing 12.1, if you want to home in on the Customers node, you would use the attribute value match="Customers". This would process only the nodes named Customers. Alternately, you can use any valid XPath pattern. The XML files are processed for nodes matching this XPath expression or pattern. After the nodes are found, the template is applied. If no nodes match the expression, the template is not used.

TIP   By default, processing stops when a match is found. If you want to continue processing child elements, you would need to specify the <xsl:apply-templates> instruction.

Creating a Stylesheet

Now you're ready to take your template and turn it into a stylesheet. It is simple to embed a template into a stylesheet. The process requires only a few steps:

1. Modify the file extension to `.xsl`.

2. Declare the XML version.

3. Wrap the template with the stylesheet element.

4. Link the XML file to the stylesheet by adding processing instructions to the XML document.

First, you have to modify the extension from `.html` to `.xsl`. Rename the file and supply an XML stylesheet extension. The code from the CD was renamed, from `Creating a Template Step 2.html` to `Creating a Template Step 2.xsl`.

Next, at the top of the file, you need to specify the XML version. Usually, only processing instructions are enclosed within `<? ?>` tags. However, in this case, the line serves as a declaration rather than a processing instruction:

```
<?xml version="1.0"?>
```

The next step requires that you embed the template within a stylesheet element. Inside the file, encapsulate the template with the start and end tags:

```
<xsl:stylesheet>
</xsl:stylesheet>
```

NOTE *Alternately, you can use the `<xsl:transform>` element. Both serve as a document root element for the stylesheet.*

Within your `xsl:stylesheet` element, you should specify some attributes that point it to the appropriate stylesheet guidelines. Most often, you will also indicate additional attributes of the `xsl:stylesheet` element:

```
Xmlns:xsl= "http://www.w3.org/1999/XSL/Transform" version="1.0"
```

Although `xsl:stylesheet` appears as the first element, it is not the root. The root is the actual stylesheet itself. Both the `<?xml version="1.0"?>` and the `xsl:stylesheet` element serve as children of the root. All other parts of the stylesheet are descendants of the `xsl:stylesheet` element. You can consider the `xsl:stylesheet` as the document root.

Now you need to link the XML file to the appropriate stylesheet. Open the source XML document and add this processing instruction:

```
<?xml-stylesheet type="text/xsl" href="Creating a Template Step 2.xsl"?>
```

Add this line immediately following the `<?xml version="1.0"?>` processing instruction. Save the file as **Customers2.xml**.

NOTE *You will find the `Customers2.xml` file on the CD. The file is the result of adding the directive to the `Customers.xml` file used earlier in Listing 12.1.*

The final .xsl file should contain the code in Listing 12.4.

LISTING 12.4: CREATING A TEMPLATE STEP 3.XSL

```
<?xml version="1.0"?>
<xsl:stylesheet xmlns:xsl="http://www.w3.org/1999/XSL/Transform" version="1.0">

  <xsl:template match="/">

    <HTML>
      <HEAD>
        <TITLE>Northwind Customer Template</TITLE>
      </HEAD>
      <BODY>
        <TABLE BORDER="3" BGCOLOR="Cyan">
          <TR>
             <TD>Customer ID</TD>
             <TD>Company Name</TD>
             <TD>City</TD>
             <TD>Country</TD>
          </TR>

          <!-- For each customer-->
          <xsl:for-each select="NWCustomers/Customers">

             <TR BGCOLOR = "White">
             <!-- Display customer information-->
        <TD><xsl:value-of select="CustomerID"/></TD>
        <TD><xsl:value-of select="CompanyName"/></TD>
        <TD><xsl:value-of select="City"/></TD>
        <TD><xsl:value-of select="Country"/></TD>
             </TR>


             <!-- End of customer loop-->
          </xsl:for-each>

        </TABLE>
      </BODY>
    </HTML>
  </xsl:template>
</xsl:stylesheet>
```

At this point, you can examine the results by viewing the `Customers2.xml` file within your browser. The results should look like Figure 12.4.

FIGURE 12.4
Viewing the results of an XSL Transformation

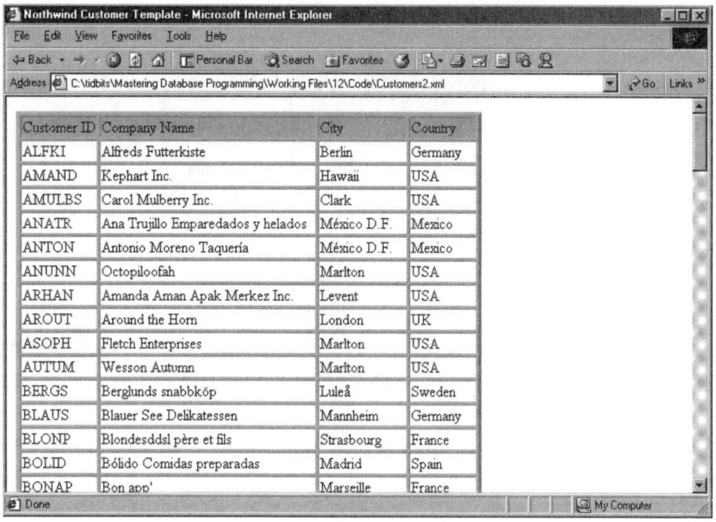

Customer ID	Company Name	City	Country
ALFKI	Alfreds Futterkiste	Berlin	Germany
AMAND	Kephart Inc.	Hawaii	USA
AMULBS	Carol Mulberry Inc.	Clark	USA
ANATR	Ana Trujillo Emparedados y helados	México D.F.	Mexico
ANTON	Antonio Moreno Taquería	México D.F.	Mexico
ANUNN	Octopiloofah	Marlton	USA
ARHAN	Amanda Aman Apak Merkez Inc.	Levent	USA
AROUT	Around the Horn	London	UK
ASOPH	Fletch Enterprises	Marlton	USA
AUTUM	Wesson Autumn	Marlton	USA
BERGS	Berglunds snabbköp	Luleå	Sweden
BLAUS	Blauer See Delikatessen	Mannheim	Germany
BLONP	Blondesddsl père et fils	Strasbourg	France
BOLID	Bólido Comidas preparadas	Madrid	Spain
BONAP	Bon app'	Marseille	France

Working with Functions

So far, the code you've written uses simple absolute positioning and XPath to return customer data. What if you wanted to further refine your target XML document, by applying a filter to the data? As we mentioned earlier, XPath expressions aren't limited to only location paths or patterns. You can also supply conditionals and XPath functions to apply a filter. This example uses the `xsl:if` element as well as the XPath function `contains()`. To return only German customers, add a conditional **`xsl:if`** structure within the `xsl:for-each` block, adding a filter to the `test` attribute:

```
<xsl:if test = "Country[contains(., 'Germany')]">
</xsl:if>
```

The `test` attribute is required and contains the Boolean expression for evaluation. In this case, you are testing whether the `Country` element contains the value `Germany`.

NOTE *When nesting quotes, keep in mind that you can use both double and single quotes as long as you alternate between them.*

In this example, you use the `contains()` function, which is part of the XPath core function group. This function returns a Boolean indicating whether a substring was found within a given string. The syntax looks like the following:

```
contains(string, substring)
```

In our example, the period specifies the current node, which is used as the search string. In lieu of the period, you could specify any valid XPath expression. The criteria is specified in the second parameter, in which you are looking for matches on the value Germany. The final xsl:for-each looping structure should look similar to Listing 12.5.

LISTING 12.5: CREATING A TEMPLATE STEP 4.XSL

```
<!-- For each customer-->
    <xsl:for-each select="NWCustomers/Customers">
        <xsl:if test = "Country[contains(., 'Germany')]">
        <TR BGCOLOR = "White">
        <!-- Display customer information-->

            <TD><xsl:value-of select="CustomerID"/></TD>
            <TD><xsl:value-of select="CompanyName"/></TD>
            <TD><xsl:value-of select="City"/></TD>
            <TD><xsl:value-of select="Country"/></TD>
        </TR>
        </xsl:if>

    <!-- End of customer loop-->
    </xsl:for-each>
```

SQL Server 2000 Integration with XML

As you remember from Chapter 10, SQL Server 2000 integrates tightly with XML. By specifying FOR XML in your SELECT statement, you can compose your results into an XML document. You also learned how to transfer binary data via XML. You used the OPENXML function to insert XML documents into a SQL Server database.

There's more to SQL Server's integration with XML that expands upon these features. Using SQL Server 2000, you can query a database over HTTP by using XPath directives. You can specify XPath queries directly in a URL, or encapsulate them into templates, which are stored in special virtual directories. This enables you to use XML as you would the SQL language to query relational databases.

In this section, you are going to explore some of these more advanced XML features of SQL Server. SQL Server 2000 enables you to submit XML-based commands to SQL via HTTP and SQL OLE DB, as well as submit XPath queries. SQL Server 2000 supports querying virtual XML data files with the XPath language. This enables you to submit XPath queries within XML templates and return SQL Server data without using the SQL language at all. This is a great semantic advantage for XML programmers who are unfamiliar with SQL. The XPath queries are received by SQL stored procedures that contain the FOR XML clause.

Let's begin by configuring SQL Server for HTTP support.

HTTP and XML in SQL Server

As you know, XML works closely with HTTP to relay data via a browser. SQL Server 2000 provides the ability to access SQL Server data through a URL. This gives you the ability to query SQL Server data by using XPath queries that are specified either directly in the URL, or indirectly, by encapsulating the XPath query within a template. In the latter case, the template is then called from the URL.

To query SQL Server 2000 in this fashion, you must first define a virtual root on a Microsoft Internet Information Server (IIS), which enables you to query the data via HTTP by using the native XML functionality of SQL Server 2000.

First, you must enable XML support in IIS for SQL Server. Click the Start button and select Programs ➤ Microsoft SQL Server ➤ Configure SQL XML Support In IIS. This launches the management console for virtual directory management in SQL Server, as shown in Figure 12.5.

FIGURE 12.5

IIS virtual directory management for SQL Server

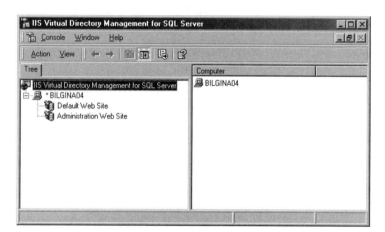

Next, create a new virtual directory. Right-click the Default Web Site node and select New ➤ Virtual Directory. This launches the New Virtual Directory Properties dialog box, which prompts you for information regarding the virtual directory that you wish to create. The first tab prompts you for the name and location path. Name the virtual directory **NorthwindCustomers** and specify a path where you wish the files to be created. We used `C:\temp\NwCustomers`, as you can see in Figure 12.6.

WARNING *The physical path must be an existing folder on your system. The Browse button will take you to a dialog box that enables you to create new folders, should you wish to do so.*

FIGURE 12.6

Specify virtual
directory name
and path

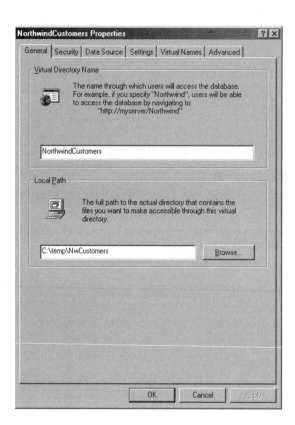

Now you need to configure the security settings, which are listed on the second tab. Specify the login information specific to your connection to the Northwind database. We used Windows Integrated Authentication.

The next tab contains information regarding the data source. Choose the name of the SQL Server that you wish to connect to and then select the Northwind database from the drop-down box. We used (local) for our connection because our SQL Server database is installed on the same machine as our IIS server.

The next tab contains settings indicating how you wish to access this virtual root. Make sure the options shown in Figure 12.7 are selected. Let's examine the choices that you select: The Allow URL Queries option enables you to execute SQL queries directly through the URL. Generally, you would not want to specify this option in a production environment because it doesn't give you the degree of isolation you get with using a template. You probably don't want users directly executing queries against your database. The Allow Template Queries option gives you the level of indirection by allowing execution of queries only from the template, rather than directly against the database. The Allow XPath option enables the execution of XPath expressions.

FIGURE 12.7

Virtual directory
settings

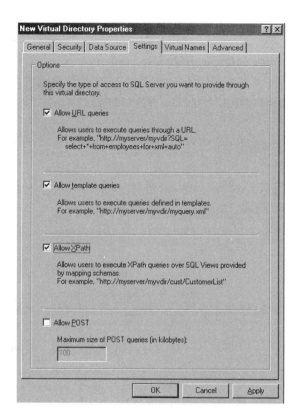

Next, you need to configure your virtual template names. Templates contain both the XML and SQL instructions for manipulating a SQL Server database. Before you configure the settings on this tab, you must first create a physical directory under the directory that you created earlier (we used `C:\temp\NwCustomers`). Unfortunately, you will have to do this through Windows Explorer because the tab doesn't provide this option. Create a directory called **Templates**, and return to the Virtual Names tab. Click the New button to create a new virtual path, specifying the settings shown in Figure 12.8. When you are finished, click the Save button.

The Advanced tab does not contain any settings that need to be changed. As a side note, it references the `sqlisapi.dll` file, which serves as an Internet Server API (ISAPI) filter from which the XPath queries are executed. In fact, XML support is not only relegated to the SQL Server database engine, but is also supported within the SQL OLE DB driver itself. The `sqlisapi.dll` ISAPI filter calls the SQL OLE DB driver, passing it the information to execute the XPath query.

Click Apply and then OK to close the dialog box. When you click the Default Web Site node, you should see the newly created virtual directory, `NorthwindCustomers`. That's it! That's all you have to do to set up XML support in IIS for SQL Server.

FIGURE 12.8

Specify template virtual directory

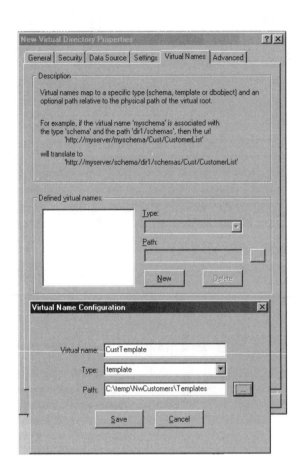

Querying SQL Server via HTTP by Using *FOR XML*

At this point, you can directly query the SQL Server. Take the statement

```
SELECT * from Customers
FOR XML AUTO
```

and convert it to an HTTP request, by concatenating it with plus-sign (+) delimiters into

```
SELECT+*+FROM+CUSTOMERS+FOR+XML+AUTO
```

NOTE *You learned how to work with the* FOR XML *statement earlier in this book. Refer to Chapter 10 if you need to be refreshed on this material.*

Now append that onto the URL for the virtual directory that you've created, by using the `sql` querystring parameter:

```
http://localhost/NorthwindCustomers?sql= SELECT+*+FROM+CUSTOMERS+FOR+XML+AUTO
```

This will generate an error message:

```
Only one top level element is allowed in an XML document.
```

This happens because the FOR XML AUTO statement does not automatically create a root element for you. As you remember from Chapter 10, the FOR XML AUTO clause does not create well-formed XML data, which causes errors when displayed in the browser. All well-formed XML documents must contain exactly one root element. Why does SQL Server allow this to happen? Shouldn't it automatically generate well-formed XML? After all, when wouldn't you want your XML well formed?

SQL Server does this to enable you to execute multiple queries that return XML. When there is no root element, it is easy for you to combine multiple result sets into a single document, specifying your own root element. It's actually a feature of SQL Server, not a bug. To avoid this error in your browser, you will need to specify a root element:

```
http://localhost/NorthwindCustomers?sql=SELECT+*+FROM+CUSTOMERS+FOR+XML+AUTO&root=root
```

The **root** parameter enables you to designate a root element, which allows the document to render correctly in the browser, as you can see in Figure 12.9.

FIGURE 12.9

Displaying SQL
Server data via
HTTP by using
FOR XML

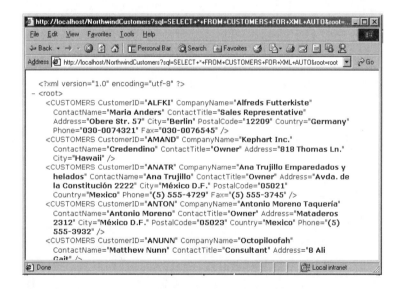

Using Simple XPath Queries with SQL Server

Earlier in this chapter, you saw the importance of XPath as a mechanism for transforming data. Now you will see its value when querying data. You can specify XPath directives in two ways:

◆ Embed the XPath query directly into the URL.

◆ Put the XPath query in a template and specify the template in the URL.

The first method is quite cumbersome as it requires you to create a lengthy URL containing the XML and XPath information that you can more elegantly store in a template. It's not efficient, and we honestly don't see much use for it. Instead, we will work with creating a template, which encapsulates the XPath query inside a file. Storing the query in a file provides greater security and control than if you embedded the query within the URL itself.

WARNING *Keep in mind that SQL Server 2000 has a few nuances from the traditional W3C XPath query standards. For example, SQL Server does not interpret a slash as representing the root query. You must specify a specific element within your XPath location path. The SQL Server Books Online contains documentation regarding its subset of XPath support.*

First, you will have to create a template file, which is a simple XML file that contains the SQL query that you wish to execute. The query is encapsulated within `<sql:query>` tags. Launch Notepad and copy the code in Listing 12.6. Save the file as **NWCustomer.xml** into the physical directory that you created to store your templates. We chose `C:\temp\NwCustomers\Templates` for our template directory.

LISTING 12.6: CREATING A SIMPLE TEMPLATE (*NWCUSTOMER.XML*)

```
<NWCustomers xmlns:sql="urn:schemas-microsoft-com:xml-sql">
    <sql:query>
      SELECT  CustomerID, CompanyName, City, Country
      FROM    Customers
      FOR XML AUTO, ELEMENTS
    </sql:query>
</NWCustomers>
```

As you can see, this template file is a well-formed XML file that contains a SQL query. The NWCustomers element serves as the root element. The SQL query uses the FOR XML function to return XML data. As you remember from Chapter 10, the ELEMENTS clause returns the XML data nested into elements, rather than as attributes. To call this template, you specify the virtual template directory within your URL, as well as the filename of your template:

```
http://localhost/NorthwindCustomers/CustTemplate/NWCustomer.xml
```

If you examine the results in your browser, you'll see they are not very pretty. To present the data nicely, you can use an XSL Transformation to format the XML data.

Using XSL Transformations with SQL Server

The template that you created in Listing 12.6 is rudimentary and not much better than displaying raw XML data. You have the option to include XSL file definitions inside your template file. After the namespace declaration in the root element, add the following attribute:

```
sql:xsl="Creating a Template Step 3.xsl"
```

Rename the template to **NWCustomerStyled.xml** and save it in the template directory. To apply the transformation, you'll need a stylesheet. Fortunately for you, you already have one from the example earlier in this chapter. Copy the XSL stylesheet file you created earlier in this chapter, `Creating a Template Step 3.xsl`, into the template directory. Viewing the NWCustomerStyled.xml file in your browser by using the URL

```
http://localhost/NorthwindCustomers/CustTemplate/NWCustomerstyled.xml
```

will generate an error:

```
The XML page cannot be displayed
Cannot view XML input using XSL style sheet.
```

This is because your stylesheet renders HTML data combined with the XML data. For the content to render appropriately, you will have to append the `contenttype` parameter to the end of your URL:

```
http://localhost/NorthwindCustomers/CustTemplate/NWCustomerstyled.xml?contenttype=
text/html
```

Now if you view the file in your browser, you will see the XML data displayed directly from the SQL Server Northwind database, transformed according to the stylesheet that you've specified.

Summary

In this chapter, you've experimented with more advanced XML functionalities such as XPath and XSL Transformations. You've not only seen how to use these technologies in and of themselves, but you've also seen how they work natively with SQL Server 2000.

You learned how to transform data and structure for different presentations by using different data sources, whether it was an XML file or a relational database. The focus in this chapter was on the back-end and user interface. Next, we are going to switch gears and examine what lies between the back end and the user interface: the middle tier, which encapsulates business logic.

Chapter 13

The Middle Tier

◆ Why use components?

◆ .NET component concepts

◆ Developing components for the middle tier

THE BEST-DESIGNED SYSTEMS CAN support a model of organic growth, by constantly evolving in an ever-changing climate and environment. Business logic changes. Network environments change. Integration with legacy systems might become a requirement. Your system should be able to gracefully handle these fluctuations and be able to grow without affecting its stability or quality. The core of this mutable logic is found in the middle tier.

Although we reviewed the importance of the middle tier in Chapter 1, "Database Access: Architectures and Technologies," up until now we haven't specifically written any code to implement one using VB .NET. You worked with both the back end and front end of a system. For the back end, you saw how to use stored procedures, triggers, and user-defined functions. For the front end, you saw how to program a user interface by using data-aware controls as well as by implementing presentation logic with XML. However, so far, you have yet to program a middle-tier VB .NET component.

This chapter is not meant to be a tutorial on the .NET Framework, but a way to show you how to create a Business layer. If you are new to the .NET Framework, you shouldn't feel lost, as we explain the relevant .NET concepts that you need to efficiently build your middle tier. The focus of this chapter is to present the concepts and benefits of a middle tier, not the actual business logic itself. This doesn't mean that the business logic isn't useful. In fact, in many situations you might want to implement a search engine, and the example we provide shows you how to use a search engine to retrieve titles based on user-supplied search criteria. The component can be centralized on an application server and be used the same way from a traditional Windows Form–based application as it would from a web application.

Although this chapter isn't rich in examples of business logic, the concepts and implementation presented here should give you a solid foundation for building your own custom business components. Ultimately, you should have a firm grasp of how to implement a middle tier to perform data access.

Why Use Components?

The benefit of working with components is that they isolate the front-end application from the database. After you connect to the appropriate database, you don't have to worry about low-level details. The data access implementation logic can be changed without affecting the front end. Additionally, you get a greater degree of reuse when you create a middle tier. If you centralize logic into a component, multiple client applications can use that logic, without rewriting any of the code.

Now you might be wondering: What about XML? Who needs a middle tier when you can have SQL Server directly return the data as XML and then apply XSL transformations to present the data the way you want it? After all, you just spent the preceding chapter learning about the power of XSLT and its ability to transform your data by using business logic. It's easy to maintain and deploy. Why bother with another compiled tier?

The answer is related to the flow of data. Think about it. The data not only has to go from the back end to the front end for presentation, which XML and XSLT are very good at doing, but the data also might need to be manipulated and transferred back to the database from the front end. Most likely, you'll need those modifications to go through some business logic, perhaps even validate against an external system, before the data is permanently stored in the database. Additionally, components offer another benefit by providing accessibility and reusability through their ability to be published as a WebService. A WebService is simply a middle-tier component that is available over the Internet. This accessibility opens the market for business-to-business collaborations and provides an environment that fosters reuse. WebServices aren't merely limited to external access via the Internet. Alternately, organizations can use WebServices to group together internal business logic for access from internal applications.

The Need for a Middle Tier

As you remember from Chapter 1, the middle tier serves as a logical layer that encapsulates the business rules of an application. A *business rule* is a procedure specific to an entity, such as a corporation, industry, or application. In this regard, the middle tier is often referred to as the *Application layer*, because it houses much of the application logic. Centralizing your business logic in an Application layer has several advantages, including maintainability, extensibility, and interoperability.

The biggest advantage of a middle tier stems from its capability to isolate functionality. Because business rules change often, there is a strong need to shield the rest of the system from the mutable logic. This way, when you have to modify a business rule, only the most atomic and isolated part of the code has to change. This decreases the effect on the rest of the application, reduces the time you have to spend testing, and makes the business logic much more maintainable. If the mutable logic were spread throughout the system, then each area would have to be tested when a modification occurred.

A middle tier also gives your system extensibility. You get this extensibility in two ways. First, future versions of your system can expand upon existing functionality by inheriting or extending the existing interface. Imagine that your system is a shipment tracking system. In the first release, you could write functionality that enables shipments to be tracked online. In a next release, you could extend this functionality by adding an alerting system to proactively notify users via e-mail should a shipment be delayed. Second, external systems can extend the functionality encapsulated in your middle tier, enhancing its functionality. FedEx, for example, could hook into your shipment application and supplement its tracking information with additional information regarding a shipment.

Not only does this provide your application with extensibility, but also with interoperability between other applications. You can leverage the services-based .NET Framework model, which facilitates communication between systems. Cross-language inheritance and debugging simplifies integration between systems. Interoperability between languages and applications is further enhanced by the .NET Framework embracing industry-accepted standards such as XML and HTTP as well as providing backward compatibility with COM.

Architectural Considerations

Before creating your Business layer, you must first design it. You need to acknowledge several important considerations so your business logic is readily consumable by any calling code. This is especially important when designing .NET services that you wish to expose to external systems. You need to make sure that your Business layer is as solid as possible.

NOTE   *We can't cover every architectural minutiae in this chapter; however, we can point out several important concepts that will help you design a more stable and robust system.*

First, you should identify the interface of your class. An *interface* serves as your contract to the outside world. It exposes the methods, properties, and events that can be used by calling code. To provide backward compatibility to any calling code, you should ensure that your interface signature does not change over time. An *interface signature* consists of the names, input parameters, and return values of your interface. This doesn't mean that you can't supplement your interface with new methods or properties; you just can't change existing ones that external code might rely on. Because it is important to keep your interface as immutable as possible, you should take the time to anticipate how your interface will be used now and in the future.

Another consideration when designing your interface is to scope wisely. Determine which methods should be hidden and which methods and properties should be publicly exposed. The best way to do this is to assume that they are private until you see a need for them to be used by external components. Your goal is to keep your interface as simple as possible. Hiding implementation details from calling code gets you closer to this goal.

You should ensure that your components contain only logic relevant to the application or business rules. Do not mix presentation logic or rely on how the data should be displayed on the user interface. This way, your components have a greater potential for reuse. If you need to swap out your user interface or render your logic to a different device, such as a cell phone, your application logic can still be used without modification.

Finally, you should ensure that your methods and properties are as atomic as possible. Keep your logic concise and simple. If you find that a block of code contains related functionality, you should create a separate method for it. For example, consider the subroutine in Listing 13.1.

LISTING 13.1: A NON-ATOMIC SUBROUTINE

```
Public Sub AddNewCustomer(ByVal strFirstName As String, _
    ByVal strLastName As String)
    Dim strCustomerName As String
    ' Format customer name
    strCustomerName = strFirstName + strLastName
    strCustomerName = UCase(strCustomerName)
                ' Add new customer using the
                ' insert command member variable
                m_SqlInsertCommand1.Parameters(0).Value = _
        strCustomerName
End Sub
```

This method proposes to add a new customer, as you can surmise from its name, AddNewCustomer(). However, it also does a bit more than that. It applies some formatting logic to the customer name, first concatenating the first and last name, and then uppercasing the results. What does this have to do with adding a new customer? It definitely complicates debugging a bit. If you are looking for an error in the customer addition process, you would have debug through irrelevant formatting logic. Additionally, what happens if any of this formatting logic changes? Because the formatting logic isn't isolated in its own method or property, you would be forced to dissect code that might not apply to pure formatting issues.

By moving the formatting logic into a separate method, you make the code simpler and much easier to debug. Additionally, you hide the implementation details from the calling code. You can set the scope of the method to be private and hidden from the calling code, as shown in Listing 13.2.

LISTING 13.2: ENCAPSULATING BUSINESS LOGIC

```
Public Sub AddNewCustomer(ByVal strName As String)
    ' Add new customer using the
    ' insert command member variable
    m_SqlInsertCommand1.Parameters(0).Value = _
    strName
End Sub

Public Function FormatName(ByVal strFirstName As String, _
    ByVal strLastName As String) As String
    Dim strCustomerName As String
    ' Format customer name
    strCustomerName = strFirstName + strLastName
    strCustomerName = UCase(strCustomerName)
     FormatName = strCustomerName
End Sub
```

Now the `AddNewCustomer()` method does exactly what its name implies, concentrating only on adding a new customer. The `FormatName()`method can be called prior to the `AddNewCustomer()` method, with its results passed to the `AddNewCustomer()` method:

```
Dim strName as String
strName = FormatName("Carol","Mulberry")
AddNewCustomer(strName)
```

You get an additional bonus by separating your logic: reusability. Let's say you want to display your customer name by using the same formatting rules. Instead of writing duplicate formatting logic inside your calling code, you can just call the `FormatName()` method. Then your logic remains centralized and maintainable, as well as reusable. The benefits just keep adding up.

In summary, when you design your Application layer, you should take the following points into consideration:

♦ Identify and clearly define your interface.

♦ Manage scope wisely.

♦ Encapsulate business logic separately from presentation logic.

Moving from a Component-Based to a Services-Based Model

If you've worked with previous versions of Visual Basic, you most likely understand the concept of .NET components. Components, or dynamic link libraries, package together related pieces of logic. For example, your system could consist of three .NET components: a shipment component that tracks shipments, a customer component that tracks customer information, and an order component, which tracks customer orders. Although component-based architecture has many advantages, such as extensibility, adaptability, and reusability, there's one big issue: How do you discover these components and use them from external systems?

COM-based components make integration challenging. Because they are based on COM, a proprietary technology, external systems would have to be COM compliant in order to use them. Additionally, the binary-based DCOM communication protocol makes communication between company firewalls difficult.

Microsoft improves this model with the formalization of a services-based model presented with .NET. This services-based model enables heterogeneous applications services to talk by using industry-accepted, nonproprietary standards such as HTTP and XML.

Designing services-based applications in Visual Basic .NET really hasn't changed much from previous versions. Although the implementation has changed quite a bit, the concepts are very similar. Once you grasp the concepts, the implementation will follow.

.NET Component Concepts

Before you begin to examine how to implement components for the middle tier, you should first have an understanding of some of the concepts and vocabulary introduced with the .NET Framework. There are quite a few new features to grasp, such as assemblies and manifests.

If you are familiar with building .NET assemblies, feel free to skip to the example in the "Developing Components for the Middle Tier" section. However, even if you are familiar with the process of building components, an overview of the concepts probably won't hurt.

The crux of any .NET DLL is in the assembly. An *assembly* is a self-describing package of information that contains all the data and files necessary to run your application. The information regarding this assembly is stored in a *manifest*, which is also referred to as *metadata* for that assembly. Both concepts are explained in this section.

What Is an Assembly?

You can think of an assembly as a logical DLL, containing the versioning, security, type, dependency, and scope information. All this information will be used in the deployment and execution of your code base.

Although an assembly can be a dynamic link library (DLL) or portable executable (PE) file, our focus in this chapter is on DLLs. Do not confuse PE files, which have the extension .exe, with the standard stand-alone executables you've written with previous versions of VB. They are not the same thing, because PE files contain Intermediate Language (IL) code, which requires the .NET runtime.

An assembly doesn't have to be solely contained in a single DLL. If you'd like, you can partition the contents of your assembly into multiple DLLs. Why would you want to do this? If you feel that part of your code can be logically broken out into a separate entity, it might make sense to physically separate it so that when the logic changes, you can redeploy only that particular DLL.

WHY USE ASSEMBLIES?

Why do you need assemblies? Why learn something completely new? There are many reasons. First and foremost, the goal of the assembly model is the elimination of DLL Hell. Under the current COM/COM+ model, a catalog of DLLs is centralized in the Windows Registry. When a new version of a DLL is published, the Registry re-references the catalog to point to the new DLL. Ideally, any new version of a DLL is supposed to be backward compatible with previous versions. Is there any penalty if it isn't? No. If you have any experience writing DLLs with previous versions of VB, you've probably experienced the pains of system failures because your application relied on a specific version of a third-party DLL that was overwritten. This centralized registration paradigm makes it challenging for multiple applications to depend on the same DLL. Most often, the application would bind to a DLL in a centralized location, rather than running multiple versions of a component by using side-by-side execution.

The .NET Framework makes it easy to run multiple versions of a component because it stores assemblies in local application directories by default. This isolates the assembly from use by any other application and protects the assembly from system changes. You should always keep your assembly application private as the default. To keep your assembly private to the application, you deploy it within the directory structure of that application. The CLR will then *probe* this directory to map the referenced assembly name to the manifest file.

SHARED ASSEMBLIES

Although assemblies can be private to an application, this doesn't mean that assemblies can't be shared between applications. The Global Assembly Cache (GAC) stores shared assemblies. If an assembly isn't found in the local application directory, the GAC will be queried. This doesn't mean that the components are listed in the Registry. Indeed, they are not. Instead of using the Registry, an assembly's self-describing nature identifies the relevant attributes, such as name and versioning information.

Side-by-side execution is not limited to local assemblies. You can still place multiple versions of the same component in the GAC at the same time. You have control over whether you want the new version to run side by side or to serve as an upgrade to the previous version. What happens if it isn't found in the GAC? You can specify a codebase hint in your configuration file to let the CLR know that the assembly should be downloaded.

Of course, for shared assemblies to peacefully coincide within multiple applications and other shared components, they must abide by certain rules. For example, shared assemblies have stricter naming requirements. For example, you must ensure that the shared assembly name is globally unique. We aren't going to cover shared assemblies in further detail in this book; however, there's plenty of information in the documentation that ships with VS .NET.

What Is a Manifest?

As we've just said, the beauty of assemblies is that they no longer rely on the Windows Registry. This independence comes from the existence of a manifest. In the COM/COM+ world, there's nothing that enables components to describe themselves. They have to depend on a centralized mechanism, such as the Windows Registry, in order to be cataloged. This dependency goes away with the .NET Framework.

The purpose of a manifest is to store self-describing metadata for an assembly. A manifest contains information about the assembly, such as the name, version number, and list of files that make up the assembly. Additionally, a manifest contains the references and dependencies for the assembly. Security information is also contained in the manifest.

Why do you need self-describing components? So that the CLR can efficiently manage your components. When your code needs to take advantage of the services offered by the CLR, it is considered managed code. To understand how to work with specific managed code, the CLR looks for the metadata in order to locate and load classes, as well as generate native code and provide security. The runtime handles your object lifetime and manages the object's references to objects, garbage collecting them like an in-memory PacMan when the references are no longer needed. For your component to use all the benefits offered by the CLR, you must allow the CLR to find your component via metadata.

The biggest advantage of self-describing components is installation. The manifest simplifies the deployment model. Because it contains so much information about the assembly, you can simply XCOPY the assembly onto another computer, along with its related manifest. Removing applications is a snap. Just delete the application directory and it's gone!

Classes

A *class* is a special type of programming unit that has no user interface. Classes in the .NET Framework still work similarly to those in previous versions of VB. If you worked with classes in the past, you should know that a class defines the properties, methods, events, and public variables of an object. This functionality is exposed through the component's interface. In the .NET Framework, because everything is an object, everything is a class. If you look at the auto-generated code behind a Windows application, you will see that the user interface itself, the Windows Form, is actually a class.

As you can guess, a component doesn't function on its own; it needs an application to invoke it and request its services. To access the functionality of a class, you must reference the class in the calling application. You do so by declaring one or more object variables and using their members to access the functionality of the class. These object variables represent *instances* of the class.

In previous versions of VB, one or more classes within the same project file were referred to as a *COM component*. Realize that in the .NET Framework, you no longer refer to these as COM components; instead, they are called *class libraries*. Class libraries can contain more than one class and are compiled into an assembly. Although multiple classes can be contained within a single class library, you can still use the classes much as you do with previous versions of Visual Basic.

NOTE *Classes provide a way to expose component functionality. In previous versions of VB, classes provided the only way to expose component functionality. VB .NET lifts those restrictions and permits you to use structures and modules as well. Classes have the advantage of being able to be passed by reference, which structures do not allow. Our focus in this chapter is on classes; however, you can find more information on modules and structures in the VS .NET Help documentation.*

The code that implements the class (usually a DLL) need not reside on the same computer as the application that uses it. In other words, you can install the class on a single machine on the network and have all clients on the network access it through a properly declared variable. If your class contains a public function named the `BestCustomers()` method, all client applications will be able to retrieve the names of the best customers. They don't need to know the rules that classify customers.

Component Classes

In VS .NET, there's a big difference between a regular class and a component class. A regular class can be added to project by right-clicking on the project and selecting Add Class. A component class can be added to a project by right-clicking on the project and selecting Add Component. What's the difference?

By default, a regular class doesn't follow any particular convention or standard in terms of how it interacts with other components. Component classes, on the other hand, abide by certain rules:

- Inherits from `System.ComponentModel.Component`, which enables the Component Designer that you can use to drag and drop components

- Contains a public default constructor, which is usually implemented with the `Public Sub New()` method

You could add these features by hand, but there's a better technique. The easiest way to abide by these rules is to have VS .NET auto-generate the logic for you by adding the Component class to your project. The Component class is a great feature of VS .NET. It even comes with its own designer interface. You can drag and drop components, such as a DataSet, onto the designer from the Toolbox. Additionally, it automatically generates the prerequisite default constructor for you.

Your classes do not have to be Component classes to be created by client applications. Whether you inherit from the `System.ComponentModel.Component` namespace or have a default constructor doesn't affect the ability of client applications to access the properties and methods of your class. Think of a Component class as a template that enables you to build standardized components quickly. We won't be using the Component Designer in this chapter because our logic doesn't require a visual designer. However, feel free to experiment with adding a new component to see the type of code generated by the Component Designer.

Developing Components for the Middle Tier

You are going to build a publication manager component that retrieves titles from the Pubs database based on user-supplied search criteria. The search criteria contains the last names of authors whose titles you wish to see. As you will see, the SQL statements for retrieving the qualifying rows are anything but trivial. By implementing the search operation in the middle tier, you free the client from having to build complicated SQL statements. Moreover, the same component can be used by multiple applications. You can change the actual implementation of the search method, recompile the class, and all applications will use the new code.

All the work is done in the middle tier. This is exactly what the class library will buy you: all client applications that need to search the Pubs database will go through the custom component, and developers need not be concerned with the structure of the database, SQL optimization issues, and so on. Let's go ahead and begin creating your first class library.

Creating a Class Library

Launch VS .NET and select File ➤ New ➤ Project from the menu. Select the Class Library project type from the `Visual Basic Projects` folder, within the New Project dialog box. This Class Library template is similar to the ActiveX DLL project type that you might have used with VB6. Choose a file path for your project and name the class library **PubsManager**. Click OK to create the project.

NOTE   The code for this example can be found on the accompanying CD.

When you are creating class libraries, it's important to name your class library as you create the new project. This way, you can take advantage of VS .NET's auto-generation feature, which automatically sets the root namespace and assembly name based on the name of your project. You can examine these attributes by right-clicking on the solution in the Solution Explorer and selecting Properties from the shortcut menu. You will see that the assembly name and root namespace are automatically chosen for you, as shown in Figure 13.1.

FIGURE 13.1

Project properties window

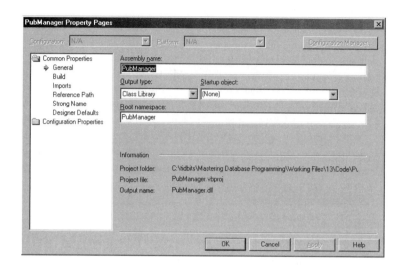

Working with Classes

By default, a single empty class, Class1, will be created for you. As with previous versions of VB, you can have more than one class in your project. If you look at the Solution Explorer, you will notice a difference from VB6. In VB6, classes have a .cls extension, whereas in VB .NET, you'll see that the Class1 file has a .vb extension. Why change the extension? Because in VB .NET, you can store more than one class inside the .vb file. So it doesn't make much sense to give it a .cls extension. You can add additional classes inside the .vb file by encapsulating the code inside a Class...End Class structure. You'll see this structure inside the code window for the default class:

```
Public Class Class1
End Class
```

In the code designer, rename the Class1 to **Titles**. If you look in your Solution Explorer, you will see that this doesn't automatically rename the file for you. For consistency, rename the Class1.vb file to **Titles.vb** via the Solution Explorer by right-clicking the file and selecting Rename. This changes the name of the file that can hold one or more classes.

You'll notice that an AssemblyInfo.vb file was automatically created for you. This is the manifest for the assembly. If you like, you can double-click the file to view the source code for the manifest.

Working with Functions

Now let's add a public function to your class. Double-click the Titles.vb file to launch the code designer window. First, import the namespaces that you will use in this class:

```
Imports System.Data
Imports System.Data.SqlClient
```

Next, declare the public function, GetTitles():

```
Public Function GetTitles _
    (ByVal AuthorName As String) As DataSet
End Function
```

This function expects a string containing the author names for which you wish to retrieve the titles. It returns a DataSet object, which can be cached for local manipulation. The DataSet will contain the results of the search.

Before you code logic into your function, you need to first create a stored procedure that will execute the search logic on the database server. Conveniently, you can do this without leaving the VS .NET IDE.

In the Server Explorer, expand the Servers ➤ SQL Servers ➤ pubs node and right-click the Stored Procedures folder. Select the New Stored Procedure option from the shortcut menu. This launches the code designer and generates placeholder logic for your new stored procedure. Replace the placeholder code with the code in Listing 13.3 to create a new SearchTitlesByAuthorLastName stored procedure.

LISTING 13.3: SEARCHTITLESBYAUTHORLASTNAME.SQL

```
CREATE PROCEDURE dbo.SearchTitlesByAuthorLastName
@AuthorLName nvarchar(20)
AS
SELECT    titles.title,authors.au_id, authors.au_lname
 + ' ,' + authors.au_fname as AuthorName
FROM        titles, titleauthor, authors
WHERE
titleauthor.title_id = titles.title_id AND
titleauthor.au_id = authors.au_id AND
(authors.au_lname LIKE '%' + @AuthorLName + '%')
```

This stored procedure expects a single variable that contains the search criteria for the author's last name. The search engine will then scour the author's last name field in the database for any last names that contain the search criteria. After a match is found, the relevant titles will be retrieved from the titles table, along with the author ID and name. Save the stored procedure by clicking Ctrl+S. This will add the stored procedure to the Pubs database. Now let's return to the GetTitles() method.

Using ADO.NET

First, set up your ADO.NET variables that you will use to manipulate the Pubs database. Listing 13.4 shows you the declarations.

LISTING 13.4: SET UP ADO.NET VARIABLES

```
Dim cnPubs As New SqlConnection _
      ("data source=(local);initial catalog=pubs;" & _
       "integrated security=SSPI;" & _
       "persist security info=False;" & _
       "workstation id=BILGINA04;packet size=4096")
Dim cmdSelect As New SqlCommand()
Dim daTitles As New SqlDataAdapter()
Dim dsTitles As New DataSet()
```

The cnPubs variable references the SqlConnection object for the Pubs database. Notice that we took advantage of the overridden constructor to pass in the connection string. Make sure you replace the connection string with one that works with your environment. The cmdSelect variable contains the SqlCommand object that you will use as the SelectCommand for the SqlDataAdapter, daTitles. Finally, you need to create a new DataSet object that will contain the data returned as a result of the search criteria.

Next, set up the SqlCommand object by using the code in Listing 13.5.

LISTING 13.5: SET UP THE ADO.NET SQLCOMMAND OBJECT

```
With cmdSelect
   .CommandText = "SearchTitlesByAuthorLastName"
   .CommandType = System.Data.CommandType.StoredProcedure
   .Connection = cnPubs
   .Parameters.Add _
     ( New SqlParameter("@AuthorLName", _
       SqlDbType.VarChar, 20, _
       ParameterDirection.Input, _
       True, CType(10, Byte), _
       CType(0, Byte), "", _
       DataRowVersion.Current, Nothing))
   .Parameters("@AuthorLName").Value = AuthorName
End With
```

NOTE Notice that you can take advantage of the With...End With block to shorten your code lines. This is one of the benefits of using VB .NET that you don't have when using C#.

In this code, you set the CommandText property to the name of the stored procedure that you created earlier. Next, you specify that the type of command is a stored procedure. You set the Connection property to the variable that you created earlier. Notice that you never opened the connection. After you pass the reference of the Command object to the SqlDataAdapter, the SqlDataAdapter will be smart enough to realize that the connection has not been opened yet. It will then open the connection, gracefully restoring it back to the closed state in which the connection was found.

You then work with the Parameters collection, adding a new SqlParameter to the collection. This parameter maps to the @AuthorLName input parameter that you created in your stored procedure. Notice that you need to ensure that the data type maps back to the SQL variable. In this case, you specified a varchar with a length of 20. Additionally, you should ensure that your ParameterDirection is set correctly as an Input parameter. Otherwise, you will get an error that a value for the parameter was not supplied. Finally, all you need to do is set the value of your newly created parameter to match the AuthorName input parameter for the GetTitles() method.

The next block configures the SqlDataAdapter, as shown in Listing 13.6.

LISTING 13.6: SET UP THE SQLDATAADAPTER

```
With daTitles
    .SelectCommand = cmdSelect
    .Fill(dsTitles, "Titles")
End With
GetTitles = dsTitles
```

As we mentioned earlier, you need to map the SqlCommand object to the SqlDataAdapter, by using the SelectCommand property. Because this is purely a data retrieval method, you don't need to set up any of the other Command objects, such as the InsertCommand and UpdateCommand properties. By now, you must be familiar with the Fill() method of the SqlDataAdapter object, as you've used it so many times before. In this case, you populate the DataSet with a DataTable called Titles. Finally, you set the return value of the GetTitles() method to the newly populated DataSet. Of course, you should enclose all this code in a Try…End Try block, adding the appropriate exception-handling code. In the end, your final code should look like Listing 13.7.

LISTING 13.7: THE FINAL GETTITLES ( ) METHOD

```
Public Function GetTitles _
    (ByVal AuthorName As String) As DataSet
        Dim cnPubs As New SqlConnection _
        ("data source=(local);initial catalog=pubs;" & _
        "integrated security=SSPI;" & _
        "persist security info=False;" & _
        "workstation id=BILGINA04;packet size=4096")
        Dim cmdSelect As New SqlCommand()
        Dim daTitles As New SqlDataAdapter()
        Dim dsTitles As New DataSet()

  Try
    With cmdSelect
      .CommandText = "SearchTitlesByAuthorLastName"
      .CommandType = System.Data.CommandType.StoredProcedure
      .Connection = cnPubs
      .Parameters.Add _
```

```
                (New SqlParameter("@AuthorLName", _
                 SqlDbType.VarChar, 20, _
                 ParameterDirection.Input, _
                 True, CType(10, Byte), _
                 CType(0, Byte), "", _
                 DataRowVersion.Current, Nothing))
               .Parameters("@AuthorLName").Value = AuthorName
          End With

          With daTitles
            .SelectCommand = cmdSelect
            .Fill(dsTitles, "Titles")
          End With

          GetTitles = dsTitles
        Catch excSQL As SqlException
          ' Add exception handling
        End Try

      End Function
```

Testing Your Code

Now you need to test your code by adding a test harness to the solution. To do so, right-click the solution file in the Solution Explorer and select Add ➤ New Project. Select the Windows Application project type. Name this project **TestHarness**. After the project has been created, right-click on the project and chose the Set As StartUp Project option so that this will be the first project to load after you execute your solution.

You will have to set a reference to the PubManager project so that the TestHarness project can use it. Right-click the TestHarness project and select the Add Reference option. This launches the Add Reference dialog box. Choose the Projects tab. You will see the PubManager project name listed at the top of the form. Click the Select button to reference the project, as shown in Figure 13.2. This will add your project to the Selected Components list.

Now you need to set up your test project. From the Toolbox, add a new TextBox, DataGrid, and Button control, leaving the default names as is. The TextBox will be used to accept the search criteria—the author's last name. The Button will be used to call the Titles class, which will ultimately populate the DataGrid with the results. In the form declarations, import the data access namespaces that you will use when calling your class library:

```
Imports System.Data
Imports System.Data.SqlClient
```

FIGURE 13.2

Add a project
reference

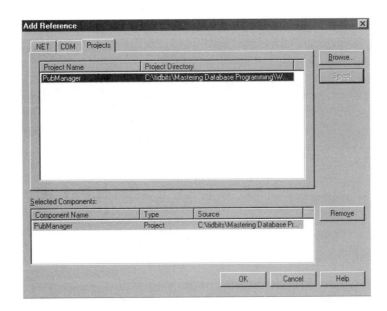

Next, add the code in Listing 13.8 to the click event of the button.

LISTING 13.8: CALLING A CLASS LIBRARY

```
Dim objPubManager As New PubManager.Titles()
Dim dsTitles As DataSet
dsTitles = objPubManager.GetTitles(TextBox1.Text)
DataGrid1.DataSource = dsTitles
```

As you can see from the code, you first have to create a reference to your class library. You do this by using the objPubManager variable and creating a new reference to the PubManager.Titles class. Next, you need to create a DataSet to store the results of the GetTitles() method. You then use this DataSet to populate the DataGrid by using the DataSource property. It's that easy!

Walk through the code execution by pressing F11. As you can see, the debugger steps from your test harness into your class library, as it did in previous versions of VB. After you are satisfied with testing the class library, you can go ahead and compile it.

When you compile your code, the source code is generated into the Microsoft IL. As your code is executed, the CLR appropriately processes the IL and translates it to binary code at runtime. In the past, your applications would be compiled directly into binary code. This is no longer the case. In the .NET Framework, the IL and the metadata together compose the assembly, which is your unit of deployment.

You have two choices when you build your application into IL: Debug or Release. You can choose the Debug configuration if you want your code to contain full symbolic debug information, which doesn't optimize it for a production release. Alternately, if you feel your application is production-ready, you can choose to build by using the Release build option. You can chose either option from the VS .NET toolbar, as shown in Figure 13.3.

FIGURE 13.3

Selecting the Build option

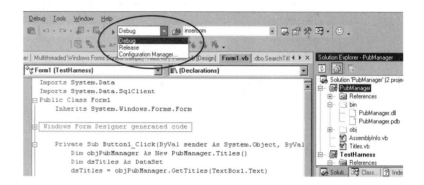

Select the PubManager project within your Solution Explorer. Choose the Release option from the drop-down menu. You can compile your project by right-clicking the PubManager project in the Solution Explorer and choosing Build. Alternately, you can opt to compile it from the Build PubManager option in the Build menu. You'll notice this is different from the File ➢ Build location in VB6. You can now deploy this file and use it from external applications, such as Windows or web applications. We'll review these options in Chapter 18, "VS .NET Deployment Considerations."

Summary

The middle tier can be the most challenging and thought-consuming tier to design. To provide for scalability, extensibility, and maintainability in an ever-changing world of business rules and system environments, you must anticipate how your application will grow and evolve. The more carefully you design your middle tier, the fewer headaches you will have when your application must change.

The release of .NET has the most impact on the Application-layer architecture within a distributed system. .NET evolves the object-oriented paradigm by providing developers with a language-independent, CLR-based framework of libraries. The libraries are fully viewable and extensible. By now, you should have a solid understanding of how to design a middle tier, which will enable you to take advantage of the class libraries offered within the .NET Framework.

Chapter 14

Advanced SQL Server 2000 Features

- ◆ Replication
- ◆ Query Optimizer
- ◆ SQL Profiler
- ◆ Index Tuning Wizard
- ◆ Database Maintenance Planner

No DATABASE PROGRAMMING BOOK would be complete without a discussion of advanced optimizations and features that you might want to apply to your database. We've selected a few techniques that you might want to consider incorporating into your database design.

Of course, this is not a book on database administration, and we can't hope to cover every topic. Instead, this chapter provides an overview of some important administrative features so that when the time comes, you have the knowledge to evaluate whether any of them make sense for your solution.

The purpose of this chapter is twofold: to provide pre- and post-implementation information about these features, and to help you improve system performance.

The pre-implementation material comes in the form of design knowledge about some of the more advanced features available in SQL Server 2000. The post-implementation section provides ways to tune and optimize your database so that it runs efficiently and smoothly. Both sides of implementation are important to ensuring that your system takes advantage of everything SQL Server has to offer, in terms of providing a robust database system. But, remember, don't use these features just because they are there. Otherwise, you might end up with overkill that adds complexity to your database design, increases your maintenance costs, and might hinder performance if you aren't judicious in your choices.

This leads to the second purpose of this chapter: improving performance. One of the key objectives of a well-designed database system is enhanced performance. You should always take performance into account when you are designing your database, and there is a lot to be learned from how your database is used in production. For example, you can identify which searches are conducted most often and configure indexes to retrieve the results faster. We covered indexes in Chapter 2, "Basic Concepts of Relational Databases." Indexes maintain the data or data references in some specific order. This works just like the index at the back of this book, which uses page numbers as references. Proper indexing means that the order of your references loads data the fastest based on the information requested.

Another means of squeezing out extra performance lies in the way your database is normalized. In some situations, denormalizing your data helps. *Denormalizing* reduces the number of tables by placing commonly used data items in a single table. For example, if you find that your queries are often retrieving publisher names along with book titles, it might make sense to denormalize your data and place the publisher data in the same table as the book data. This way, your queries don't have to go through multiple layers of abstraction. By querying a single table, you will have faster performance. There's an opportunity cost with performance tweaks of this nature. The penalty is that you will end up with redundant data. Generally, denormalization occurs with OLAP systems, rather than OLTP systems, so you should give serious thought before denormalizing your data.

After you've designed and implemented your database structure, look for ways to optimize and improve your system indexes. SQL Server 2000 comes with an arsenal of tools to help you analyze and tune your database. Tools such as the Index Tuning Wizard and Query Optimizer can help you pinpoint trouble spots in your system and prompt you with ways to improve your database design so that your system runs like a well-oiled machine.

Altogether, the features and tuning information in this chapter provide tips that you can use in your database architecture. Some of these tweaks are subtle, whereas others require fundamental architectural changes. However, when you apply them correctly, you should end up with a solid, scalable database design that meets your business requirements.

We'll begin our exploration with the topic of replication, which is generally a pre-implementation consideration.

Replication

Back in Chapter 1, "Database Access: Architectures and Technologies," we discussed the advantages of distributed *n*-tier architecture. One of the advantages is reusability. By building a distributed data network, you can take advantage of existing systems. Why reinvent the wheel? If you need customer information and a contact management database is already in place, then you can use replication to reuse that data and schema in your application. Replication enables you to build a sophisticated distributed data network.

This section is not an intensive, detailed exploration into the inner workings of SQL Server replication. Instead, it provides conceptual design information on when, where, and why to use replication. Additionally, it covers the different replication models as well as SQL Server 2000's various implementations of these models. After reading this section, you should be able to determine whether you should incorporate replication into your database design.

Replication is not a new concept to SQL Server, and those of you who have worked with previous versions of SQL Server might be familiar with replication scenarios. SQL Server 2000 has improved some of the replication features and provides several replication wizards that hold your hand as you step through the configuration process. In this section, we show you some of these wizards, such as the Configure Publishing and Distribution Wizard. This way, you not only get a conceptual understanding of how replication works, but you can also see how to implement it within your own system.

Before you explore exactly how SQL Server 2000 implements replication, you should first understand the advantages and disadvantages of using replication. Then you can determine which type of replication topology, if any, best suits your needs.

When to Use Replication

When should you use replication? There are a couple of scenarios where replication can come in handy:

- Unifying a distributed database system
- Synchronizing data with another system

DISTRIBUTED DATABASE ARCHITECTURE

Most often, your application will not be a stand-alone application. Because database programming has been around for quite some time, the chances are that you will have to hook into a legacy data source. Many times, this requires a one-time pull of data into your system, with the legacy system deprecated and retired. Other times, the legacy system is very much alive and kicking and contains valid and up-to-date information. It is this latter case where replication is most applicable.

Replication can also be useful within the boundaries of your own application. If you want to distribute your database system across multiple locations, you might want to use a publisher-subscriber metaphor, in which a single database serves as the central repository for all data. The subscriber databases push data up to the centralized server.

Advantages of Distributed Database Architecture

Why bother to distribute your database? Doesn't this add unnecessary complexity? There are many cases where you would want to distribute your system: many disconnected users, geographic disparity in your user base, or situations where user groups don't need to access the complete data source.

Disconnected users can gain a lot from a distributed database architecture. These gains include:

- Increased availability
- Enhanced performance
- Redundancy

For example, imagine a sales-force automation system where the sales team is out in the field most of the time. They use laptops to update contact information into a database. Because they are disconnected most of the time, you need a place to temporarily house their updates. You could create a mini-version of the database system on their laptops, where the updates would reside. When they directly connect to the LAN with a high-speed connection, they commit their changes back to the central database store.

ADO.NET DataSets could be a good choice to store this cached information; however, if you want to fully take advantage of the capabilities of a robust DBMS, you might want to consider partitioning a segment of the database schema and data. Although DataSets are useful for caching information, at times the size and complexity of your data network needs the capabilities of a database management server.

WHAT IS PARTITIONING?

Partitioning filters data, so that only a subset of data is published for replication. Partitioned data comes in two flavors: horizontal and vertical. *Horizontal partitioning* results in publishing only a subset of all available rows. You can do this by applying a filter, which returns only a smaller subset of the rows. For example, you could apply a horizontal partition that returns only customers for a specific city. In this way, horizontal partitioning works much like the WHERE clause of a SELECT statement. *Vertical portioning*, on the other hand, slices up the data by removing columns from the data set. For example, you can choose to withdraw address information from your customer data set, vertically portioning it by the address columns.

When you determine your data partition model, use natural partitioning wherever possible. For example, divvy your customer data by geographic region, city, or customer type, rather than by arbitrary criteria such as alphabetic order of customer names (for example, splitting into A–K and L–Z). By choosing natural partitioning, such as city, the chances are that your data will be manipulated within these logical subsets. For example, if you choose to partition your data by the customer city, then those customers will likely be used as a group by the specific office location that deals with those customers.

By distributing your system for disconnected users, you increase the availability of your system. On-the-field sales teams don't have to wait until they are connected to the network to make updates to their contact information. You can even take advantage of heterogeneous devices, replicating data to their Personal Digital Assistants (PDAs) or Pocket PCs.

Additionally, the sales team stands to gain enhanced performance. They might use a slow dial-up connection to connect to the network. Data transfer, especially in high volumes, could be slow due to restricted bandwidth. By providing a local copy of the data store, you enable them to quickly retrieve and update data with nominal performance penalties. Searches that retrieve large data sets can truly benefit from local storage.

Performance gains can accrue from the way you partition your replicated system. Multiple systems use the same data; however, each system might need different optimization on retrieving that data. You can have a subset of data that is optimized for quick customer name searches and another subset that is optimized for invoice searches. Partitioning your data enables you to cater your data to the individual needs of a business unit or group. Another way to partition your data would be to drop only a subset of the data onto each local system. This regionalizes your data and improves performance not only because the data access is local, but also because the local users are now working with only a small amount of data. This makes querying the data much faster than working with the entire system. When the local database is updated, the changes can be propagated back up to the main server. In turn, the centralized server can synchronize the changes onto the other remote servers.

Another advantage replication offers is redundancy. If you have multiple copies of the same data, you have a safety net in case one system goes down. For example, imagine that you have a customer database in your Philadelphia office that fully replicates the one in your New York office. These databases are used locally by each office as a back end to a contact management system. If your New York database server goes down, you can point the New York contact management system to the Philadelphia database and continue working with minimal, if any, interruption. When the New York database comes back up, you can replicate the changes from the Philadelphia database over and re-point the New York system to the New York database. There's safety in numbers.

Disadvantages of Distributed Database Architecture

Make sure you are judicious when deciding to use a replicated, distributed database architecture. There are disadvantages to a distributed database system.

The main disadvantage is that data can soon become dated. If a salesperson doesn't connect to the network for a while, their local data can soon become old and inaccurate. Additionally, other users will not be able to see the changes made by the salesperson, which might lead to inaccuracy and inconsistency. These risks might lead you to implement secondary architectural models, such as expiry, to your system. For example, to avoid having data that is out of date, you might opt to implement an expiration policy on the data, preventing the user from operating and manipulating their local data store until they synchronize with the centralized data store.

This leads to another potential problem: concurrency. If multiple users are making changes to the data while disconnected from the centralized data store, the DBMS faces a challenge in managing concurrency. Just because a data modification has occurred after another does not necessarily mean that the data is more accurate. You might need to implement a concurrency management service with custom business rules that determine which data update "wins" over another.

As you can see, replication is no small topic, and you must seriously consider the implications of a distributed database system, such as outdated data and concurrency.

EXTERNAL SYNCHRONIZATION

Another use for replication comes from a need to link to an external database. Let's say you need to synchronize a New York–based sales-force automation system with an external accounting system. The accounting system resides in San Francisco. Bandwidth is tight, and live connections to the accounting system are very slow from New York. You could opt to schedule nightly replication, which pulls data into the New York system. Now your sales team can quickly access the accounting data without any latency issues.

What Is Replication?

In this section, we explain how SQL Server 2000 implements replication. Each server that participates in replication plays a specific role. After you understand these roles, you'll be able to determine which replication strategy best meets your needs. Additionally, you'll review the different models that you can apply for data replication.

REPLICATION ROLES

Each database within your replication topology plays a different role: Publisher, Subscriber, or Distributor.

Publisher

The *Publisher* role consists of a database that allows other databases to connect to it and access its data. The data is made available via a *publication*. A Publisher server can have more than one publication, which consists of a logical subset of data contained within *articles*. These subsets can include, but are not limited to, the following:

◆ A result set from a stored procedure

◆ A result set from a view definition

◆ A whole table

◆ Part of a table vertically partitioned by using column sets

◆ Part of a table horizontally partitioned by using row sets

◆ A result set from a user-defined function

Don't think of the Publisher as only a static repository of data that other databases hook into. Additionally, a Publisher tracks changes that occur during transaction replication, which we discuss shortly.

Subscriber

The *Subscriber* role can be applied to a database that receives replicated data via a publication. Keep in mind that Subscribers do not subscribe to individual articles within a publication, but to the publication itself. Most often, Subscribers are discretionary about which publications they subscribe to and they don't necessarily subscribe to all the publications that are available on the Publisher. This way, they are not overburdened with excessive or unnecessary data, and can be streamlined to contain only the data that they need.

The Subscriber can choose to update the data that they receive in a publication. These changes can then be propagated back up to the Publisher, which, in turn, can republish the data to other Subscribers.

Distributor

The *Distributor* role entails a server that acts as a manager for the entire replication process. The Distributor server can reside on the same server as a Publisher, which makes it a *local Distributor*. If the Distributor resides on a separate machine, it is considered a *remote Distributor*. The reason why the Distributor can be separated from the Publisher is to balance the processing that occurs during replication. By off-loading some of the workload onto a separate machine, you can greatly improve your replication performance. Additionally, you can create a replication architecture that has a single, central Distributor database for multiple Publishers. The Distributor hosts a database, which contains historical data, transactions, and metadata regarding the replication architecture.

REPLICATION MODELS

SQL Server supports three replication models: Snapshot, Transactional, and Merge. It is important to understand the nuances of each model because each is suited for specific scenarios. By understanding what each model does, you will be able to design your replication topology for maximum performance, data integrity, and efficiency.

SQL Server 2000 has made some serious improvements to the replication architecture it supports. In this section, we point out these improvements as we explain the different models.

Snapshot

As the term *snapshot* suggests, Snapshot replication captures the data and database objects as they are at a specific moment in time. The synchronization is not performed incrementally; instead, it is done in one fell swoop. This means that you don't have to continuously log and track all the transaction changes that have occurred. Each Subscriber to a Snapshot replication architecture will receive a complete data set. With each replication, the entire data set is refreshed in its entirety, once again.

Snapshot replication has an advantage over Transaction replication in terms of reduced processing overhead. Because Snapshot replication occurs at a moment in time, the database system does not have to continuously synchronize the changes that occur to the data with each activity. Realize, though, that there is an opportunity cost to decreased processor overhead. This opportunity cost is incurred with the performance degradation for creating the snapshot. Snapshot replication means that all the changes are submitted at once, rather than as a subset of the data in the form of a deltagram. As you can imagine, Snapshot replication might incur performance penalties because the entire data set is replicated, rather than a small portion of the data. To mitigate this problem, you should set up your Snapshot replication schedule so that the synchronization is done as seldom as you can risk. Additionally, you should try to keep your snapshots as small as you possibly can, so that you maximize performance.

When should you use Snapshot replication? You should use it when you expect that your data will be mostly read-only, such as reporting data. Also, if your system isn't concerned with a constantly fresh data set, then the rarity of synchronizations won't be a problem.

Transactional

Transactional replication is a popular model that is used for many systems requiring a high degree of data synchronization for frequently updated data.

Initially, Transactional replication begins with a single snapshot of data, which is distributed to all Subscribers. This way, each Subscriber has a foundation from which to apply changes. After this initial snapshot is applied, incremental changes to the data are stored as transactions. These transactions are then propagated to the appropriate servers within a distributed data network.

What are these changes that are recorded as transactions? Changes consist of the following:

♦ Data insertions

♦ Data deletions

♦ Data updates

These changes are tracked by using the relevant INSERT, UPDATE, and DELETE SQL statements and stored procedures. Direct updates to tables and views are also monitored and recorded as transactions. The changes can occur within the Publisher database, which stores the changes as transactions and replicates them to all Subscribers. You can opt to propagate the changes immediately or on a scheduled basis.

Not surprisingly, Transactional replication also supports the concept of transactions. This means that either *all* the changes in a transaction are committed, or *none* of the changes in a transaction are committed.

When should you use Transactional replication? Transactional replication (using the queued updating option) and Merge replication are best for disconnected users. You should use Transactional replication if you expect frequent updates to the data and you need all Subscribers to be as current as possible with these changes. Additionally, if your system contains a large number of transactions, you might want to use this model.

Another reason to use Transactional replication is to avoid long wait times, which are not supported by your application and which you might get with the bulky Snapshot replication. Transactional replication is atomic and fast, and your system performance does not have to suffer as you wait for replication to occur. Transactional replication is a viable choice for high-performance environments.

The disadvantage of Transactional replication is that it requires higher connectivity. Because replication occurs more frequently, your Publisher and Subscriber should be connected as often as possible.

As we mentioned earlier, Transactional replication does not have to be immediately synchronized. You have the option to queue the modifications. Realize that queued updating does not ensure real-time updates of data. If a remote database is offline for an amount of time, the updates made to that server can be queued until the database reconnects to the network. At that time, the changes can be pushed back up to the distributed data network or central database server.

Merge

Merge replication was introduced with SQL Server 7. Under this model, multiple databases can be updated simultaneously with changes merged into a single result set.

As with Transactional replication, an initial snapshot of data is applied to all Subscribers to provide a foundation for future modifications. Changes can occur on both the Publisher and Subscriber databases. These changes are synchronized on a schedule or on demand.

The disadvantage of Merge replication is that the same data can be updated at the same time on different databases. This increases the chances of conflicts to occur. When a conflict occurs, there must be some decision-support processing to determine which update "wins."

If Merge replication is laden with risks, such as conflicts, why use it? When should you use Merge over Transactional or Snapshot replication? You should use Merge replication if your Subscribers need to update their local data stores simultaneously and you need the Publisher and other Subscribers to receive the data. The best situation is when the Subscribers are fairly independent of one another, and the chances of conflict are small.

Here's a good scenario for Merge replication: Imagine a system with multiple, regionalized Subscribers that update their local customer data. These Subscribers update only customer data that belongs to their city; however, they run reports on all customers as a whole. They need the national customer data to be as current as possible. By using Merge replication, you can enable each city to update its local customer data, which is then merged and published to the other Subscribers. The chances for conflict are low because each city is responsible for only their local customers.

Even if you have a low-conflict scenario, you should still define the rules for conflict resolution in case one should occur. The resolution is enforced by a Merge Agent, which is executed to determine what changes should be accepted and which conflicts should be rejected.

Working with Replication

SQL Server 2000 makes it fairly intuitive to set up your replication topology, by providing various wizards to walk you through the configuration process. However, you might encounter hazards if you are setting up replication for the very first time. In this section, we try to point out the common errors that you might encounter. We help you troubleshoot and resolve them so that you can have a smooth path to your replication configuration. If you don't encounter any of these errors, good for you! You can skip the troubleshooting information and move on through the rest of the configuration process.

Let's set up a simple Transactional replication model, which synchronizes data from the Northwind database. You will be replicating changes that are applied via tables and stored procedures. You are going to create a publication that enables Subscribers to receive updates by using transactions in the publication.

Most likely, you will want to specify different Publisher and Subscriber database servers; however, in case you don't have an environment with multiple SQL Servers, this example uses the same server for the Publisher and Subscriber. It's simple to select an alternate server for either role, should you have this capacity.

THE CONFIGURE PUBLISHING AND DISTRIBUTION WIZARD

Begin by launching the SQL Server Enterprise Manager. First, you are going to set up your Publisher. Expand the SQL Server Group node and drill down to the `Replication` folder. Expand the `Replication` folder to expose the `Publications` folder. Right-click the `Publications` folder and select the Configure Publishing, Subscribers, and Distribution option, as shown in Figure 14.1. This launches the Configure Publishing and Distribution Wizard.

NOTE   *Alternately, you can launch this wizard from the Tools ➤ Replication menu.*

If you've registered your SQL Server by using (`local`) as the server name, you will encounter the error shown in Figure 14.2. SQL Server replication is unable to interpret (`local`) as the machine name. You will have to delete the SQL Server registration and reregister the SQL Server by using the actual server name.

FIGURE 14.1

Launching the
Configure
Publishing and
Distribution Wizard

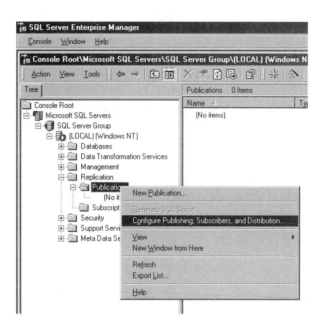

FIGURE 14.2

Error with
unresolved SQL
Server name

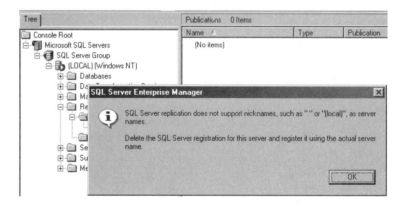

The first screen you will see is an introductory screen telling you what the wizard is capable of doing for you. Click Next to continue onto the following screen.

The next screen prompts you for information regarding the Distributor. By default, the Distributor will be physically located on the same server as the Publisher. Alternately, you can specify a pre-configured Distributor on a separate server. Keep things simple: stick with the default option, which places the Distributor on the same server. Click Next to continue.

At this point, you might encounter an error with the account under which the SQL Server Agent runs, as shown in Figure 14.3. The SQL Server replication engine relies on the SQL Server Agent, which must run under an account that is not the system account. If you get this error, click the OK button to change the startup account. This launches the SQL Server Agent Properties dialog box. In the Service Startup Account field, specify the appropriate account and password, as shown in Figure 14.4. Click Apply and you will be asked whether you are sure that this is a valid account. If you are sure, click OK and then click OK again to close the SQL Server Agent Properties dialog box.

FIGURE 14.3

Error with SQL Server Agent startup account

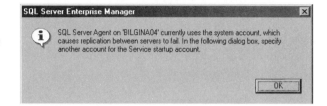

FIGURE 14.4

Configure the SQL Server Agent properties

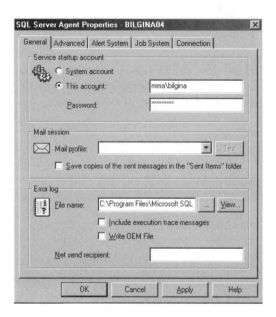

   The next screen that pops up is the Configure SQL Server Agent dialog box. You have two choices: to run the agent automatically or manually. Keep the default setting to run the agent automatically. Click the Next button to continue through the wizard.
   Now you will be presented with the Specify Snapshot Folder dialog box, as illustrated in Figure 14.5. By default, the snapshot will be stored under the applications folder in which you've installed SQL Server. Accept the default value and click Next. You will be prompted to verify that this is a valid path. Click Yes to accept it. Next, you will be presented with another warning regarding the accessibility of this shared path. Because the path is using the special C$ sharing convention, it is accessible only to those accounts that have administrative rights. Because you aren't configuring your replication architecture for remote services, you don't have to worry about this option. Click Yes to agree to use this path.

FIGURE 14.5

Specify Snapshot
Folder dialog box

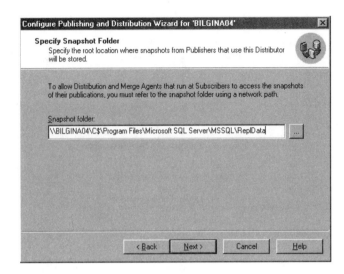

Finally, the Customize the Configuration dialog box appears, which gives you the last-minute option to tweak the settings configured by the wizard. For simplicity, leave the default option of No, whose configuration should look similar to Listing 14.1.

LISTING 14.1: CONFIGURATION SETTINGS GENERATED BY THE CONFIGURE PUBLISHING AND DISTRIBUTION WIZARD

```
Configure 'BILGINA04' as a Publisher. Use 'BILGINA04' as
   the Distributor.

Configure the SQL Server Agent service on 'BILGINA04' to
   start automatically when the computer is started.

Use '\\BILGINA04\C$\Program Files\Microsoft SQL
   Server\MSSQL\ReplData' as the root snapshot folder for
   Publishers using this Distributor.

Store the distribution database 'distribution' in
   'C:\Program Files\Microsoft SQL Server\MSSQL\Data'.

Store the distribution database log file in 'C:\Program
   Files\Microsoft SQL Server\MSSQL\Data'.

Enable the following servers as Subscribers to publications
   on 'BILGINA04':   BILGINA04
```

Click the Next button, which will take you to the Finish dialog box. Click the Finish button to enable the wizard to set up your Publisher.

If this is your first time setting up replication, you will receive a message informing you that the Replication Monitor will be added to your Enterprise Manager. The Replication Monitor enables you to manage schedules, status, alerts, and history involving the Publishers, Distributors, and Subscribers within your replication topology. To view this folder, select the Tools ➤ Replication ➤ Show Replication Monitor Group option. The Replication Monitor relies on SQL Server Agent to run. Go ahead and expand the Replication Monitor. You should see your newly created Publisher within the `Publishers` folder, as shown in Figure 14.6.

FIGURE 14.6

The Replication Monitor

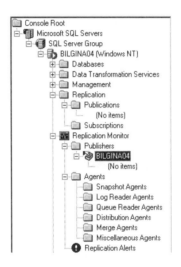

Now that you have a Publisher, you need to create a publication.

THE CREATE PUBLICATION WIZARD

As you did earlier, right-click the `Publications` folder beneath the `Replication` folder. Select the New Publication option, as shown in Figure 14.7. This launches the Create Publication Wizard. The first screen is an introductory screen. Notice on the very bottom of the dialog box is an option, Show Advanced Options In This Wizard. Check this box and click Next.

The next screen is the Choose Publication Database dialog box. Select the Northwind database for the publication and click Next.

Now you will see the Select Publication Type dialog box, as depicted in Figure 14.8. Because you want to use Transactional replication, choose the middle option and then click Next.

FIGURE 14.7

Creating a new
publication

FIGURE 14.8

The Select
Publication Type
dialog box

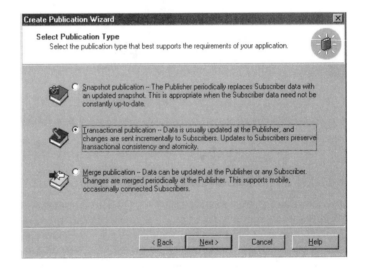

The next screen is the Updatable Subscriptions dialog box, as illustrated in Figure 14.9. This is where you can choose immediate or queued updates, as we described earlier. Check both options, which will enable Immediate and Queued Updating Subscribers, and then click Next. This sets up your replication so that changes are immediately reflected in the Publisher and queued on the Subscribers.

FIGURE 14.9

The Updatable
Subscriptions
dialog box

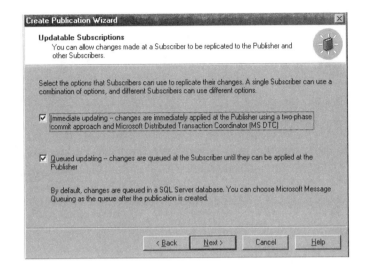

The Specify Subscriber Types dialog box will pop up, which enables you to indicate the DBMS, such as SQL Server 7, Oracle, or Access, that you wish to support as Subscribers. In this example, you want to support only SQL Server 2000 servers, so check only that option. Click Next to continue.

The next screen is a bit more complicated. It's the Specify Articles dialog box, which enables you to specify articles for your publication. This is where you specify the database objects you wish to include in this replication architecture. You want to include both tables and stored procedures. Each table and stored procedure will be treated as a separate article. Altogether, this collection of articles will make up your publication.

Select the Show And Publish All options for both tables and stored procedures. After you select these check boxes, the objects in the right-hand list will automatically be checked, as shown in Figure 14.10. You will notice an Article Defaults button. If you click this button, you can further optimize your article for a specific object type. You should leave the default value, which is Table articles. Click Next to move on to the next screen.

WARNING *Any tables that do not contain primary keys are ignored for publication. The primary key provides a unique and consistent value for data rows. This enables SQL Server to identify a modified row even if all non-key columns are altered.*

You might see a screen that informs you of any potential article issues, such as object references and unique identifiers. For the purposes of this exercise, you can ignore this screen and click Next to continue.

Now you will see the Select Publication Name and Description dialog box. You can opt to leave the default values, or specify new values, as we did in Figure 14.11. We chose to name this publication NWA11.

FIGURE 14.10

The Specify Articles dialog box

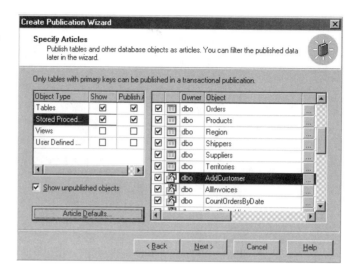

FIGURE 14.11

The Select Publication Name and Description dialog box

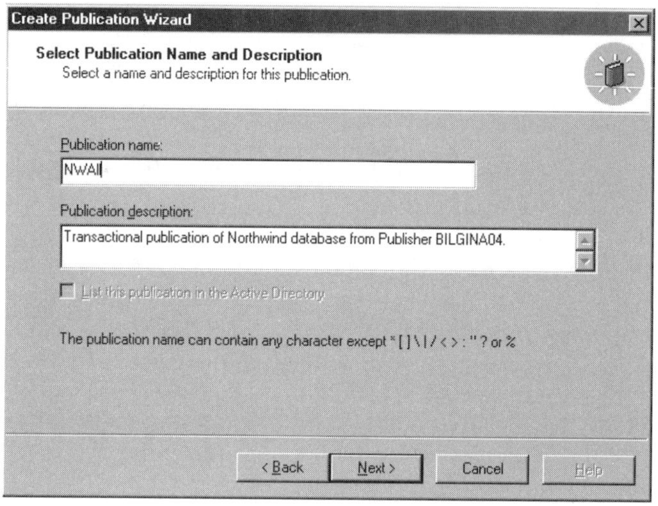

The final screen gives you a last-minute chance to tweak the configuration options created by the wizard. Feel free to examine the configuration options in Listing 14.2 to get a better feel for what the wizard will do behind the scenes.

LISTING 14.2: CONFIGURATION SETTINGS FOR CREATING A NEW PUBLICATION

```
Create a transactional publication from database 'Northwind'.

Allow immediate updating subscriptions.
```

Allow queued updating subscriptions.

The following types of Subscribers may subscribe to this publication:
   Servers running SQL Server 2000

Publish the following tables as articles:
   'Categories' as 'Categories'
   'CustomerCustomerDemo' as 'CustomerCustomerDemo'
   'CustomerDemographics' as 'CustomerDemographics'
   'Customers' as 'Customers'
   'Employees' as 'Employees'
   'EmployeeTerritories' as 'EmployeeTerritories'
   'Order Details' as 'Order Details'
   'Orders' as 'Orders'
   'Products' as 'Products'
   'Region' as 'Region'
   'Shippers' as 'Shippers'
   'Suppliers' as 'Suppliers'
   'Territories' as 'Territories'

Publish the following stored procedures as articles:
   'AddCustomer' as 'AddCustomer'
   'AllInvoices' as 'AllInvoices'
   'CountOrdersByDate' as 'CountOrdersByDate'
   'CustOrderHist' as 'CustOrderHist'
   'CustOrdersDetail' as 'CustOrdersDetail'
   'CustOrdersOrders' as 'CustOrdersOrders'
   'DeleteOrder' as 'DeleteOrder'
   'Employee Sales by Country' as 'Employee Sales by Country'
   'GetCustomersByCountry' as 'GetCustomersByCountry'
   'InsertCustomerRequired' as 'InsertCustomerRequired'
   'InsertOrder' as 'InsertOrder'
   'NewOrder' as 'NewOrder'
   'OrderInterval' as 'OrderInterval'
   'Sales by Year' as 'Sales by Year'
   'SalesByCategory' as 'SalesByCategory'
   'SelectOrdersByCustomer' as 'SelectOrdersByCustomer'
   'SelectOrdersByOrderID' as 'SelectOrdersByOrderID'
   'Ten Most Expensive Products' as 'Ten Most Expensive Products'
   'UpdateOrder' as 'UpdateOrder'

The name of this publication is 'NWAll'. The description is 'Transactional publication of Northwind database from Publisher BILGINA04.'.

Do not filter data in this publication.

Do not allow anonymous subscriptions to this publication.

```
Run the Snapshot Agent at the following scheduled times:
Occurs every 1 day(s), at 10:18:00 PM., ending 11/15/2001
Run the Snapshot Agent as scheduled.
```

That's it! Click Next and then Finish to complete the wizard. Be patient, because it might take a little while to add each of the articles to the publication. You have just set up a basic Transactional replication model using the Northwind database. Feel free to examine the replication settings by using the Replication Monitor.

Query Optimizer

Besides learning the different features, such as replication, which provide pre-implementation design considerations, you should think about post-implementation issues, mainly performance. Even the best-designed system could fail if it isn't tuned for optimal performance. After all, who wants a nicely normalized database system that runs as slow as a slug?

SQL Server 2000 does its best to preempt any performance issues with its self-tuning mechanism, Query Optimizer. However, you might want to dig a little deeper and tweak your database system to squeeze out every last drop of optimization.

Before we begin any discussion of performance tuning, you should understand how the SQL Server Query Optimizer works. There is a great amount of granularity in this topic, such as how the Query Optimizer uses algorithms to determine which index to use. However, we aren't going to attempt to get into this level of detail. Instead, our purpose is to provide a high-level overview so that you can conceptually understand the purpose of the Query Optimizer. We highly recommend that you spend more time exploring this topic within the SQL Server Books Online and on MSDN.

Indexes are one of the primary sources of performance degradation. When you construct your indexes on a table, it doesn't mean that the Query Optimizer will choose to use them. Instead, the Query Optimizer first determines whether using the index will be more efficient than not using it at all. It gauges this on the number of input/output operations that need to be performed to retrieve the desired data. Selectivity is one of the main criteria in measuring index efficiency. *Selectivity* calculates the number of rows returned by a query as compared to the total number of rows in the table. If a query returns a higher percentage (more than 10–20 percent) of rows, it is considered not very selective. Queries with low selectivity might not end up using the index because the query would be faster using a table scan. So many results are returned anyway, so why bother to divvy up the data with indexes? On the other hand, highly selective queries, such as those that return less than 5 percent of the data, generally are faster with an index.

The Query Optimizer determines selectivity by capturing index statistics for each table. These statistics are expensive to run and are cached. They are generated when an index is first built, rebuilt, or refreshed (by using the UPDATE STATISTICS statement). You can examine the statistics yourself with the DBCC SHOW_STATISTICS command. You can examine the density of an index, to determine its selectivity. Try it on the Northwind database:

```
USE Northwind
DBCC SHOW_STATISTICS (Orders, ShippedDate)
```

Type this statement into the Query Analyzer and examine the results, specifically paying attention to the Density column. Our results returned a Density value of 1.5144314E-3. Don't be daunted by this number. Basically, all you need to know is if it is less than 1 percent, which it is. This means that less than 1 percent of the data is returned for this index, which means that it is highly selective, and thus, useful.

Ineffectual indexes waste space and can severely hinder the performance of your application. Index maintenance is not cheap, and your goal should be to streamline your database design so that every element increases the efficiency of your system.

As you might surmise, index analysis is not a trivial task. It's a good thing for you that SQL Server comes with analysis tools to help you choose the appropriate indexes. Both the SQL Profiler and Index Tuning Wizards are excellent tools to help you with this process. We present both next.

SQL Profiler

As SQL Server processes database information, it generates a series of events. Using this integrated event model, you can monitor the activity imposed on your database. This way, you can gather event statistics to help tune your database. After you identify frequent access requests, you can optimize the retrieval of this data to enhance the responsiveness of your system. The biggest way to gain performance advantages is by choosing the most efficient indexes.

If you're not familiar with SQL Profiler, you are certainly missing out on one of the most powerful performance-tuning utilities that you can use. SQL Profiler was released with SQL Server 7, as a very enhanced upgrade to the SQL Trace utility. Those of you who have been working with SQL Server for a while might have used SQL Trace to help identify performance trouble spots. SQL Trace is useful for tracking which SQL statements and stored procedures were executed, but when it comes to anything deeper than that, it doesn't make the cut. When you need to know more granular details about connections, locks, or intra-stored procedure calls, you need to look no further than the SQL Profiler.

To analyze your system, the Profiler uses traces to monitor the various events generated by your SQL Server. A *trace* enables you to track various events, such as client requests or server events. For example, you can track what activities occurred inside a stored procedure so that you can identify any statements that might lead to deadlock conditions.

In addition to tracking events, you can examine specific data points within these events that enable you to create custom statistic reports. You can later use these reports to analyze your database performance and identify any bottlenecks.

Although SQL Profiler records event data, it is not just a tracking tool. SQL Profiler enables you to not only monitor and analyze the behavior of your SQL Server, but also to tune it by using this information. The SQL Profiler has been seriously upgraded from SQL Server version 7 to 2000. We focus on the SQL Server 2000 implementation in this section.

Configure a Simple Profiler Trace

The best way to understand a tool is to work with it. In this walk-through, you are going to create a trace file that you will later use to help optimize your index strategy.

Begin by selecting the SQL Profiler from the Tools menu in the Enterprise Manager. This launches a separate window containing the SQL Profiler console, which is not very interesting at first.

To work with the SQL Profiler, you must first create a trace definition. You have several choices for creating this definition: use an existing trace template "as is," modify an existing trace template, or create a new trace definition by using the Trace Wizard. For this example, you will modify an existing trace template and use it to create a trace workload file. However, before you step into this example, first you should be able to answer the question: What is a trace definition?

WHAT IS A TRACE DEFINITION?

A *trace definition* is the cross-product of results from tracking the events and data generated from SQL Server processing. A trace definition contains the following information:

◆ The events you wish to track.

◆ The data you wish to capture. You track this data across any event that you have selected.

◆ The filters that you wish to apply in order to track events based on specific conditions.

◆ The location where the results should be sent or stored.

You can combine the events and data points you wish to track for each event. This enables you to create a magnitude of permutations that make the SQL Profiler quite a versatile, flexible, and powerful tool for tracking any variety of statistics.

USING EXISTING TRACE TEMPLATE PROPERTIES

One way to create a trace definition is to use an existing trace template. SQL Server provides many sample traces that you can use as they are, or customize for your needs. Go ahead and examine one of these sample trace definitions by selecting File ➢ Open ➢ Trace Template from the menu. You'll see a list of templates, as shown in Figure 14.12.

The template files have the .tdf extension. You can create your own template files and save them for reuse. The templates contain the trace definition information: events, data points, and filters that you wish to use in your trace. The template can then by applied for your trace.

Examine one of the simpler templates, the SQLProfilerTuning.tdf template. This template comes with predefined settings that provide statistics to help you troubleshoot a slow-running query. By double-clicking the file, you will launch the Trace Template Properties dialog box. If you'd like, you can modify the attributes of this template and save it as a different file. Then you can leverage a foundation of events and data points to customize them further for your needs. You'll see how to do this shortly. Now, step through the dialog box's four tabs and examine the various settings that you can modify for any given template.

The General tab simply shows you the path where the .tdf is saved. After you alter any of the settings for the template, you can choose to save the file with a different name.

The second tab, the Events tab, enables you to browse through different event categories and drill down within them to select events that you want to monitor. As you can see in Figure 14.13, in the case of this template, only two events have been chosen: RPC: Completed for the Stored Procedures event class and SQL: BatchCompleted for the T-SQL event class. The former indicates that a remote procedure call to a stored procedure has completed, and the latter event is raised when a batch of SQL statements has completed execution.

FIGURE 14.12

Available trace templates

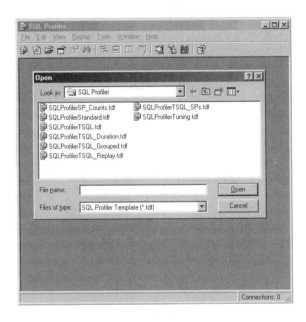

FIGURE 14.13

The Events tab of the Trace Template Properties

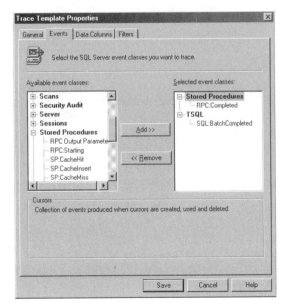

As you can see, there are almost a hundred events to pick and choose from. At this point, you can further customize this template by using this tab to add or remove events.

The next tab, Data Columns, is shown in Figure 14.14. This is where you can select various data points to track across the chosen events. Keep in mind that some data points might not be valid for all events. A full discussion of all the valid permutations of events and data columns is beyond the scope of this chapter; however, the SQL Books Online provides information regarding the choices you have with both events and data columns.

FIGURE 14.14

The Data Columns tab of the Trace Template Properties

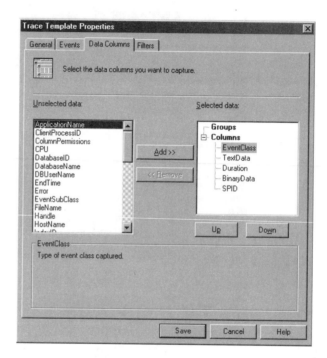

Finally, the last tab, Filters, enables you to return only a subset of events by blocking out events that meet certain filter criteria. For example, you can choose to block specific database or user login activity. In this case, the activity generated from the SQL Profiler application is blocked. It's a good idea to apply filters as often as you can, because your traces will execute faster with streamlined event data.

A useful filter that you can specify will limit the events to a specific database, by using the database ID as the filtering criteria. Modify the existing template by adding another filter using the Northwind database ID, which is 6. This filter setting is displayed in Figure 14.15.

NOTE   *You can determine the Northwind database ID by running the SQL statement, which is listed on the CD in the* `Determining the Northwind database ID.sql` *file:*

```
USE Northwind
SELECT DB_ID()
```

FIGURE 14.15

The Filters tab of the Trace Template Properties

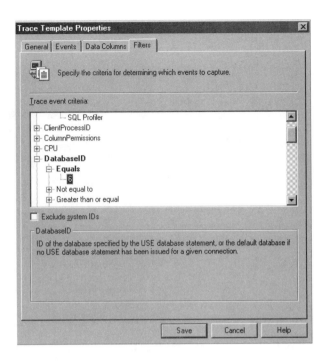

Now that you've made your modifications, it's time to save your template. Select the Save As option in the General tab, and save the template as **NorthwindSQLProfilerTuning.tdf**. Close the Trace Template Properties window by clicking the Save button.

Now you need to configure the Profiler to begin recording activity by using this template. Select Tools ➤ Options to open the Trace Options dialog box and select your newly created template for the default, as illustrated in Figure 14.16. Check the Start Tracing Immediately After Making A Connection option, so that you can start recording your workload.

NOTE *In addition to working with existing templates, you can create a new one from scratch by using the File ➤ New ➤ Trace Template option from the SQL Profiler menu.*

A good use for the Profiler is to simulate loads on your server. For example, you could write SELECT statements and run them to monitor the effect on the trace results. To begin recording a trace file, select the File ➤ New ➤ Trace option. This brings up a dialog box prompting you for the SQL Server whose activities you wish to track. Select your SQL Server, along with the appropriate authentication credentials.

Next, you'll need to set the trace template properties so that the results are saved into a file. Later in this chapter, you are going to use the Index Tuning Wizard to help identify appropriate indexes for the Northwind database. These trace results will serve as your workload file. Don't worry about what this means now; it will all come together when we describe the Index Tuning Wizard. For now, all you need to know is how to save the results of your trace to a file. To do this, select File ➤ Properties from the SQL Profiler menu. This launches the Trace Properties dialog box. Name the trace **SalesTotalsByAmount** and click OK. If you'd like, you can take a peek at the other tabs, where you will see the events, data columns, and filters that were specified by the base template that you created earlier.

FIGURE 14.16

Select the default
template

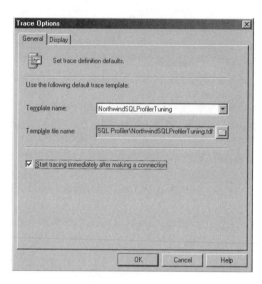

Next, you'll need to save the results of the trace. Stop the trace in order to set this path. You can stop the trace by clicking the Stop icon in the SQL Profiler toolbar. To set the trace file path, select File ➢ Properties from the SQL Profiler menu. Check the option Save To File, which brings you to a browse dialog box. Specify a directory in which you wish to store the SQL Profiler trace file, which has a .trc extension. Use the default name **SalesTotalsByAmount.trc**, as shown in Figure 14.17.

FIGURE 14.17

Saving the trace
results to a file

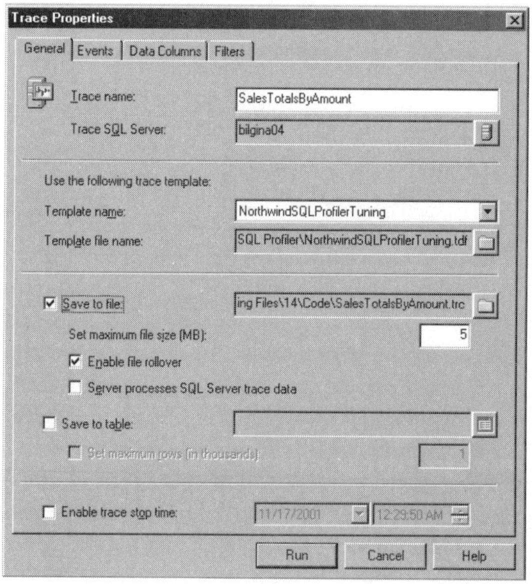

Although we aren't going to examine every single attribute of a trace, there are a couple notable settings in the General tab. The Set Maximum File Size option should be set with an appropriate file size, up to 1000MB. If you additionally set the Enable File Rollover option, SQL Server continues with a new trace file when the maximum file size is reached. There can be more than one rollover file. The new files will be suffixed by using a sequential numbering schema (for example, SalesTotalsByAmount_1.trc).

New!   Another useful option is the Server Processes SQL Server Trace Data. Server-side tracing is a new feature to SQL Server 2000. In previous versions, SQL Trace would run on the client side and there would be no guarantee that it would capture all the events that executed on the server. By running the trace on the server, you are guaranteed that all requested events will be tracked. For this example, leave this option unchecked because you don't want to overtax the server with a basic trace scenario such as this one. At this point, click the Run button to resume trace execution.

Now you'll need to run some queries against the Northwind database so that some events can be generated. We have selected to use the results returned from the Sales Totals By Amount view. Ideally, you'd want to record against a live database, or prepare a carefully designed workload script in advance.

TIP   *With SQL Server 2000, you can index views.*

The WHERE clause of an SQL statement, view, or stored procedure is where the filtering occurs, and is your best bet for identifying the appropriate index strategy. Consequently, we've chosen a view with a more intricate WHERE clause. You can examine the definition of the Sales Totals By Amount view in Listing 14.3.

LISTING 14.3: THE SALES TOTALS BY AMOUNT VIEW DEFINITION

```
create view "Sales Totals by Amount" AS
SELECT "Order Subtotals".Subtotal AS SaleAmount,
       Orders.OrderID, Customers.CompanyName,
       Orders.ShippedDate
FROM   Customers INNER JOIN
       (Orders INNER JOIN "Order Subtotals" ON
       Orders.OrderID = "Order Subtotals".OrderID)
ON Customers.CustomerID = Orders.CustomerID
WHERE ("Order Subtotals".Subtotal >2500) AND
      (Orders.ShippedDate BETWEEN '19970101' And '19971231')
```

Notice that we've also selected a view with some computed logic, which comes from the join on the Order Subtotals view, whose definition is detailed in Listing 14.4.

TIP   *SQL Server 2000 can now also apply indexes on computed columns.*

LISTING 14.4: THE ORDER SUBTOTALS VIEW DEFINITION

```
create view "Order Subtotals" AS
SELECT "Order Details".OrderID,
```

```
SUM(CONVERT(money,(
"Order Details".UnitPrice*Quantity*
(1-Discount)/100))*100) AS Subtotal
FROM "Order Details"
GROUP BY "Order Details".OrderID
```

Launch the Query Analyzer and return the results from the Sales Totals By Amount view by entering:

```
USE Northwind
SELECT * FROM [Sales Totals by Amount]
```

Press F5 to execute the SQL statement and return to the SQL Profiler to examine the trace results. The trace will still be running, but you don't want to record any more results. Click the red Stop button to halt the trace. You'll see the SQL: BatchCompleted event logged in the Profiler window. If you click this event record, the underlying trace activity detail displays in the window below, similar to Figure 14.18.

FIGURE 14.18

Trace activity in the SQL Profiler

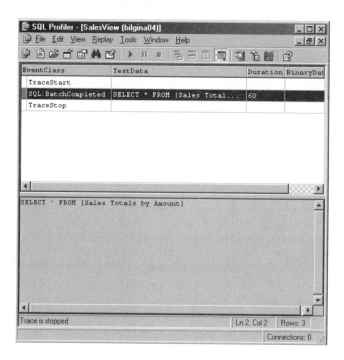

One of the most important uses of a trace file is with the Index Tuning Wizard. A trace file can be used as a workload file, which is loaded into the wizard for analysis. You'll see for yourself when you use this trace file next.

Index Tuning Wizard

As you by now realize, designing an optimal index strategy is crucial to a well-behaved database. Analyzing the database use over time to determine the appropriate indexes can be a daunting, if not time-consuming, task. SQL Server provides a powerful tool, the Index Tuning Wizard (ITW), to help facilitate your analysis.

The ITW analyzes a database by using a specified workload file. A *workload file* is an SQL script or trace that contains information on how the database is used over a period of time. By using this file, the ITW can determine the appropriate indexes based on normal usage data. It's important to give some thought to your workload file so that you accurately capture how the database is used—for example, it's not a good idea to use workload data that was generated in the middle of the night when no one is using the database. After the ITW analyzes the workload, the ITW makes recommendations on appropriate index strategies. Should you like these suggestions, you can have the ITW implement the indexes for you.

To launch the ITW, select the Tools ➤ Wizards option from the Enterprise Manager menu. Expand the Management node in the Select Wizard dialog box and select the Index Tuning Wizard option, as shown in Figure 14.19. Alternately, because the ITW goes hand in hand with the SQL Profiler, you can launch the wizard directly from the Tools menu of the SQL Profiler. Either way, selecting the ITW launches the configuration dialog boxes that you can use to analyze your current indexes.

FIGURE 14.19

Launching the Index Tuning Wizard

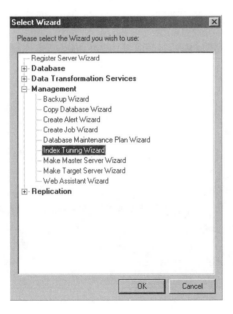

The first screen of the wizard is an introductory screen. Click Next to move on. The next screen brings you to a dialog box where you select the database that you wish to analyze, as well as the level of intensity for the analysis.

NOTE   You might be prompted to connect to a database server prior to selecting the database. If so, select the server and appropriate authentication method, which will bring you back to the wizard.

Select your server and choose the Northwind database. The Keep All Existing Indexes option can be unchecked if you want the ITW to potentially drop and re-create any existing indexes that you have on the Northwind database. In this walk-through, you want the ITW to find only those indexes that aren't in place, rather than re-create existing ones, so leave this option checked.

New! The Add Indexed Views option is new to SQL Server 2000. The ability to index views greatly enhances their performance because it forces the data generated from the view to be stored in the database. A normal view is not stored in the database, and is instead dynamically created on the fly by using the view definition SQL statement.

If you want to seriously analyze your indexes, use the Thorough option for the Tuning mode. We strongly recommend creating a copy of the database onto a test server before you choose this level of intensity so that you don't overly tax your production server. For now, leave the default value of Medium selected. Click Next to continue through the wizard.

The next dialog box prompts you for a workload file or an SQL Server table to use for trace results. For the My Workload File field, use the **SalesTotalsByAmount.trc** file that you created earlier in this chapter. Additionally, this screen enables you to specify Advanced Options, which we aren't going to get into here. Click Next to continue.

The next screen provides a list of tables that you would like the ITW to analyze. You will improve your performance if you can narrow this list to only the specific tables that you wish to tune. If you examine the view definitions from earlier, you will see that only the Customers, Orders, and Order Details tables were used. Select these tables from the list, as shown in Figure 14.20.

FIGURE 14.20

Select tables to tune.

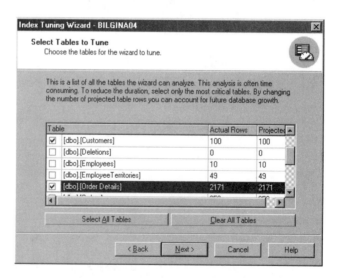

When you click the Next button, the ITW begins its analysis by using the workload. This might take some time. After the analysis is complete, you will see an Index Recommendations dialog box. Most of the recommended indexes you see are existing ones, denoted by an icon of a table with a green arrow. However, if you scroll down, you will see a new index recommendation for the Order Details table, on the OrderID column. A small star on the table icon indicates a new index recommendation, as shown in Figure 14.21.

FIGURE 14.21

Index
Recommendations
dialog box

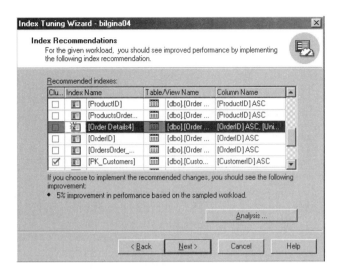

NOTE   *The results in your Index Recommendations dialog box might vary.*

The wizard also notes the percentage of performance improvement that you would gain by implementing this index. In this case, accepting these recommendations would result in a 5 percent performance improvement.

The Analysis button takes you to a screen where you can examine nine reports that summarize various statistics regarding the workload queries. It is beyond the scope of this chapter to go through each of these reports here; however, the SQL Books Online can help you decipher those that might not be as intuitive. You can save these reports if you would like by pressing the Save button.

After you return to the wizard, click the Next button. You will be presented with a screen that prompts you to Schedule Index Update Job. You can accept the recommendations here immediately, or schedule a time for the index implementation to take place. Alternately, you can save the index recommendations to a script file, which you can later examine or tweak to meet your needs. Select the Apply Changes box with the Execute Recommendations Now option. Click Next and Finish to execute the ITW recommendations. That's all you need to do to tune your database with the Index Tuning Wizard.

Of course, realize that you should never arbitrarily accept recommendations from any wizard without fully understanding the implications.

Database Maintenance Planner

Another tool that's worth pointing out is the Database Maintenance Planner. After you design, implement, and optimize your database, there's always maintenance to consider. To maximize the lifetime of your production system, you should always have a maintenance plan in mind. A maintenance plan is not reactive, but proactive. It mitigates risks and problems before they occur. That way, your system can hum along smoothly with minimal downtime.

A maintenance plan should be as automated as possible. Traditionally, a maintenance plan consists of the following four steps:

1. Validate database integrity.

2. Optimize the database.

3. Back up database data.

4. Back up transaction logs.

SQL Server 2000 comes with a Database Maintenance Planner that you can launch from the Tools menu in the Enterprise Manager. This wizard enables you to automate optimization tasks, such as updating statistics using sample data, reorganizing data pages, and compressing your database to remove unused space. The wizard is quite intuitive and enables you to select the maintenance tasks that best meet your needs.

QUICK TIPS FOR MAINTAINING AN EXISTING SYSTEM

Here is a quick overview of specific activities you should keep in mind when creating your database maintenance plan:

◆ Use the Database Maintenance Planner to optimize your database.

◆ Analyze database use to determine which WHERE clauses are executed most frequently. These are likely candidates for indexes. The SQL Profiler is an excellent tool for this purpose.

◆ Drop unnecessary or infrequently used indexes. They just waste space and slow down performance.

◆ Update statistics frequently so that query execution is optimized by using the freshest usage data.

◆ Run the maintenance tasks during off-peak hours.

◆ Schedule regular backups of the data and transaction logs.

Summary

As evident in Microsoft's certification path and various database books, SQL Server development and administration are two separate topics. However, you need to realize that each cannot exist without the other. Certainly, as a database programmer, you are not always expected to be an expert in both development and administration; however, the more knowledge you have of database administration, the better you can design your systems. If you know in advance how to fiddle with tuning optimizations, you'll be able to spot performance bottlenecks ahead of time, and avoid the pitfalls in your system design before a single line of code is implemented.

This is certainly not a book on database administration, which would be a voluminous tome in itself. However, we do hope that you have learned a bit more about the techniques you can employ, such as replication and optimization, to build a distributed database architecture that is scalable, reusable, and efficient.

Part 4

Data Access From the Web

In this section:

Chapter 15

Introducing ASP.NET

- ◆ Overview of ASP.NET
- ◆ Building Web Forms
- ◆ Maintaining state in web applications
- ◆ Caching and configuration
- ◆ Accessing databases from ASP.NET

YOU'VE PROBABLY HEARD A lot about the web features of the .NET platform. But so far in this book, we haven't covered that side of .NET. The key component of the .NET web strategy is ASP.NET. As you can guess from the name, ASP.NET is an upgrade to Microsoft's server-side ASP environment for web page development. Although ASP.NET can use all the ADO.NET code that you've seen so far, it also has some unique connections to ADO.NET built into its programming and user interface model.

In this chapter, we introduce ASP.NET and show you some of its unique features. At the end of the chapter, we show you how to use database-driven web pages on your web server. In the next couple of chapters, you'll drill into ASP.NET data in more detail by looking at some of the specialized data controls that are available for Web Forms, as well as the concept of WebServices.

By the end of this chapter, you should be able to answer the following questions:

- ◆ How does ASP.NET deliver content in standard HTML while still allowing you to use the .NET Framework and languages?
- ◆ What are the advantages of Web Forms and server controls?
- ◆ How can you maintain state in a web application, and when should you avoid doing so?
- ◆ What caching and configuration features can you use to optimize your ASP.NET applications?
- ◆ How do you connect ASP.NET to ADO.NET?

ASP.NET is a huge topic that deserves (and gets) entire books of its own. Our goal in this chapter is to visit the major areas of ASP.NET web page design so that you can get an overall impression of its capabilities. After you've finished working through the concepts and examples in this chapter, you should have a good sense of how to use ASP.NET to move your applications to a web browser interface. Let's start by discussing the general ASP.NET architecture.

NOTE　*To use ASP.NET code, you'll need to have a web server available. In our examples, we've used a copy of Microsoft Internet Information Server running on the same computer as the code, enabling us to use the shorthand name of* `localhost` *for the IIS server. The* `readme.htm` *file from Visual Studio .NET includes detailed instructions on setting up a web server for use with Visual Studio .NET. You will find all the source code for the examples in this chapter on the accompanying CD, as well as our own* `readme.txt` *file that details how to install the samples on your own server.*

Overview of ASP.NET

ASP.NET web applications are superficially very similar to the Windows applications that you've been working with. Both feature a user interface with controls, both can use any .NET language, and both can include live data from a database. But there are also some substantial differences between the two. Most of these differences come about because the code in ASP.NET applications is actually executed on your web server, not on the user's computer. This means, for example, that you'll find a different set of controls in the Toolbox for ASP.NET forms than you will for Windows Forms. That's because only controls that can be converted to HTML can be used on ASP.NET pages.

In this section, you'll explore some of the key features of ASP.NET. Understanding these features will help you write effective ASP.NET applications.

Understanding Server-based Execution

The original design of the World Wide Web implemented static data delivered from a server to a client. This data was (and still is) delivered by using Hypertext Markup Language (HTML). An HTML page goes from the server to the client without changing its form at all, in response to a Hypertext Transfer Protocol (HTTP) request.

Adding programmability to HTML pages was an obvious step in the evolution of the Web. By delivering code, as well as data, to the web browser, designers could add increased interactivity to their HTML pages. This code, hidden in HTML `<script>` tags, enabled client-side programming. That means that the server delivers HTML containing both static elements and code to the web browser, and then the code is executed on the client computer.

This client-based execution scheme has several problems:

◆　Adding code to the page to be downloaded results in larger (and hence slower) web pages.

◆　Anyone can view the client-side code by looking at the web page's source. This makes securing information such as database passwords difficult.

◆　Not every browser knows what to do with source code on the client side, making it difficult to write pages that would perform well in different browsers on different platforms.

As these drawbacks became clear, server-based execution of code became more popular. With server-based execution, the code is executed on the web server, and only the results of the code (which can then be HTML with no scripting) are delivered to the client. The result is better speed, security, and compatibility than is possible with client-based execution.

Active Server Pages (ASP) were Microsoft's original solution for server-side web server development. With ASP, the client sends an HTTP request to the server for a page. The server, however, does not deliver the page to the client in its original form. Instead, it loads the page into the ASP interpreter, which reads through the whole page, executing scripting code as it goes along. Parts of the page that aren't code are sent to the client as is, but any scripting code is replaced by the results of that code before the page is sent out.

ASP.NET is the completely rearchitected version of ASP included in the .NET Framework. Indeed, ASP code won't even run in ASP.NET, because the VBScript language used in ASP is not supported by ASP.NET. However, this doesn't mean that installing ASP.NET on a computer that's running with IIS will break existing ASP pages. That's because ASP.NET pages use .aspx as an extension. Only ASPX files are handled by the new ASP.NET processor; existing ASP pages continue to go through the ASP interpreter. Over the long run, you'll probably want to rewrite existing ASP pages to use ASP.NET, but there's no need to do so just to use ASP and ASP.NET on the same server.

ASP.NET offers enhanced performance compared to ASP. That's because ASP.NET is actually built on top of the .NET CLR, so that it offers all the CLR benefits, including just-in-time compilation, type safety, and early binding. By contrast, the older ASP engine was strictly an interpreter, and required all the variables within its code to be late-bound variants. Code for ASPX pages can be written in any .NET-compatible language (we'll use Visual Basic .NET for our examples).

The first time that a client requests an ASPX file, the ASP.NET processor parses and compiles the file into a .NET Framework class. This class then dynamically processes incoming requests for the ASPX page. The compiled instance is reused across multiple requests, so that the time taken to compile the page is not significant after the first request for the page.

As you'll see later in this chapter, Microsoft also offers an excellent development environment for ASP.NET. Building ASPX pages and the other parts of an ASP.NET application is integrated directly into the Visual Studio .NET IDE, and shares many of the same tools with other Visual Studio .NET applications.

Web Forms

ASP.NET introduces Web Forms. *Web Forms* are text files with the .aspx extension. Although they are text files "under the covers," Visual Studio .NET includes a designer that lets you work with Web Forms just as you can with Windows Forms (which are also text files when viewed outside of the Visual Studio IDE), complete with a Toolbox, moving and sizing of controls via the mouse, settable properties, and so on. We'll be using the Web Form Designer extensively later in this chapter.

There are two programming models for Web Forms. The first follows the traditional ASP programming model, in which HTML is intermingled with code. In this model, your code is set off within script blocks within the web page. The second model, *code-behind Web Forms*, associates a class module with each web form. In this model, the ASPX file contains the HTML and control declarations for the web form, while a separate language file (for example, a .vb file if you're coding in Visual Basic .NET) contains the code that will handle events on the form. The Visual Studio

.NET Web Form Designer makes it easy to write code-behind Web Forms, and we find the separation of code from markup to be an aid to understanding. All our examples in this chapter will use code-behind Web Forms.

We dig into the details of building Web Forms later in this chapter.

Server Controls

In the older ASP model, controls on an HTML page (that is, elements such as anchors, buttons, text boxes, or drop-down lists) are not directly accessible to the code that's being executed by the ASP interpreter. As far as ASP is concerned, there's no distinction between a control on a web page and any other piece of literal text or markup. They're simply sent directly to the web browser without any processing. This makes it difficult to perform common tasks such as generating the target for a hyperlink programmatically.

ASP.NET introduces server controls to remove this limitation. A *server control* is a piece of HTML markup with the addition of the `runat="server"` attribute. For example, a hyperlink rendered as a server control might look like this:

```
<a id="A1" href="TBD" runat="server">
```

Server controls are still delivered to the client for display. But before that happens, they're also available to the server for additional processing. For example, an ASP.NET application could replace the `href` attribute of the control defined in the previous code example by running this code:

```
A1.href="http://www.microsoft.com"
```

TIP *Many controls can be used as either traditional HTML client-side controls or as server controls in ASP.NET. For example, you could include a traditional hyperlink in an ASP.NET page and it would work just fine. However, you can't use code to alter the properties of client-side HTML controls as you can with server controls.*

Disconnected Data Architecture

One of the key design goals of ASP.NET is to deliver excellent support for a disconnected data architecture. That is, when a client needs to display data, that data can be retrieved from a server and delivered to the client without needing to hold a connection open to the database. When the client requests more data, the web server simply renders the page anew with additional data from its own cache.

Of course, by now you'll recognize this as a description of how a DataSet works. By integrating tightly with ADO.NET, ASP.NET can use the DataSet object as the center of its data strategy. Data is retrieved from your database into a DataSet, and at that point it exists on the web server. Whatever piece of the data is needed on the client can be delivered without a continuing connection to the database. And, of course, if there are changes to be made from the client to the database, the DataSet can be reconnected to make those changes.

ASP.NET can also transmit an entire DataSet from one component to another. When it does this, ASP.NET automatically converts the DataSet to its XML representation at the sending end, and then back into a DataSet at the receiving end. By using XML as the data transmission protocol for data, ASP.NET can successfully operate through most firewalls.

WebServices, XML, and SOAP

WebServices provide a way for a client application on one computer to use an object provided by a server application on another computer, even if the only connection between those two computers is via the Internet. ASP.NET provides WebServices support by saving objects to XML and implementing the Simple Object Access Protocol (SOAP). SOAP is a means to call an object by sending a properly formatted XML message over HTTP.

By using HTTP as its transport mechanism, SOAP eliminates many of the connectivity problems of other remote object protocols, such as DCOM. HTTP messages can travel almost anywhere on the Internet and cross most firewalls without problems.

NOTE   You'll learn more about WebServices in Chapter 17, "Working WebServices."

Deployment in ASP.NET

If you have your development computer set up as a web server, it's easy to test ASP.NET applications during the development cycle. When you create a new ASP.NET application, Visual Studio .NET will automatically create a virtual root on your local web server that references this application.

ASP.NET was designed for ease of deployment to production servers after the development cycle is finished. You can FTP, XCOPY, or otherwise copy all the files in the application to the production server, set up a virtual root pointing to the files, and everything will simply work. ASP.NET also enables you to designate an assembly cache directory on your production server. When you copy an assembly into this directory, ASP.NET automatically registers it. There's no need to log on to the server or register the assembly.

When users interact with an application, ASP.NET makes shadow copies of the files in the application and runs from the shadow copies. You can upgrade an application at any time by copying new files into the application's directory. ASP.NET monitors the files in an application for changes and loads newer versions as they are detected. The end result is that you should never have to shut down a web server to upgrade an ASP.NET application.

Building Web Forms

Let's start working with ASP.NET by building a simple Web Forms–based application. To get started, follow these steps:

1. Launch Visual Studio .NET and create a new ASP.NET Web Application project. You'll notice that when you name the application, you're actually specifying a URL location on your local web server (or another server where you have development permissions).

2. The project will open, displaying `WebForm1.aspx` in the Visual Studio .NET IDE. Right-click anywhere on this ASP.NET page and select Properties to open the DOCUMENT Property Pages dialog box shown in Figure 15.1.

3. Set the Page Title to be **Hyperlink Demo** and the Page Layout to be **FlowLayout**. Click OK to close the dialog box. You'll see that this changes the title and `pageLayout` properties of the DOCUMENT object in the Properties window.

FIGURE 15.1

Properties for an
ASP.NET page

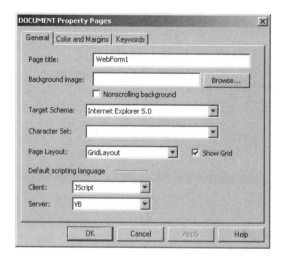

4. Use the Solution Explorer to change the name of the Web Form to **HyperlinkDemo.aspx**.

5. With the page in FlowLayout mode, you can simply start typing to add text to the page. Type the text **Choose a destination** and press Enter. Open the Web Forms tab in the Toolbox and drag a DropDownList control to the form. Use the Properties window to set the ID property of this control to **dd1URL**.

6. Click the builder button for the Items property of the DropDownList to open the ListItem Collection Editor. Click the Add button to add a new ListItem. Use the ListItem Properties window to set the Selected property of this ListItem to False, the Text property to Microsoft and the Value property to http://www.microsoft.com/. Use the same technique to add two other text-value pairs to the list:

   ◆ Yahoo — http://www.yahoo.com/

   ◆ CNN — http://www.cnn.com

7. Click OK to add the list to the web page you're developing. At this point, your page in the designer will look like Figure 15.2.

FIGURE 15.2

Web page in the
Visual Studio .NET
designer

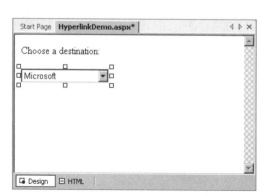

Now you can click the Start button on the Visual Studio .NET toolbar (or select Debug ➤ Start, or press F5). This launches an instance of your default browser and delivers the page to it. You'll see the text and the drop-down list box, and be able to select items from the drop-down. Of course, nothing happens when you select an item from the drop-down...yet.

TIP   *You can choose a particular ASP.NET page to load from a solution by right-clicking on the page in the Solution Explorer and selecting Set As Start Page.*

Adding Code-Behind

Let's add a little code to the web page you just built. First, you'll need to close the browser window and return to the Visual Studio .NET IDE. Double-click the DropDownList control to open the `HyperlinkDemo.aspx.vb` code in the Code Designer. This is the code-behind class for the web page you've been working with.

Visual Studio .NET will generate some default code for the page. You'll need to add one line of code to the `SelectedIndexChanged` event procedure for the DropDownList to make the page navigate to the selected site when the user makes a selection in the DropDownList. The full code of the code-behind class at this point is shown Listing 15.1.

LISTING 15.1: CODE-BEHIND FOR AN ASP.NET PAGE (HYPERLINKDEMO.ASPX.VB)

```vb
Public Class WebForm1
    Inherits System.Web.UI.Page
    Protected WithEvents ddlURL As System.Web.UI.WebControls.DropDownList


#Region " Web Form Designer Generated Code "

    'This call is required by the Web Form Designer.
    <System.Diagnostics.DebuggerStepThrough()> _
     Private Sub InitializeComponent()

    End Sub

    Private Sub Page_Init(ByVal sender As System.Object, _
     ByVal e As System.EventArgs) Handles MyBase.Init
        'CODEGEN: This method call is required by the Web Form Designer
        'Do not modify it using the code editor.
        InitializeComponent()
    End Sub

#End Region

    Private Sub Page_Load(ByVal sender As System.Object, _
     ByVal e As System.EventArgs) Handles MyBase.Load
        'Put user code to initialize the page here
    End Sub
```

```
      Private Sub ddlURL_SelectedIndexChanged(ByVal sender As System.Object, _
        ByVal e As System.EventArgs) Handles ddlURL.SelectedIndexChanged
          Response.Redirect(ddlURL.SelectedItem.Value)
      End Sub
   End Class
```

Save your project and start it again. You'll find that, despite the code, the page still doesn't redirect when you choose an item from the drop-down list. What's going on here?

The answer is that events for server controls behave a bit differently from events that you're used to for Windows Forms. Remember, the web page is running in the user's browser when the user interacts with the control. To trap a particular event, you need to tell the browser to send that event back to the server. You do this by setting the **AutoPostBack** property of the control to True.

Try it: close the browser to stop the application and then set the DropDownList's **AutoPostBack** property to True. Run the application again and select an item from the drop-down list. Your browser should navigate to the selected page.

Of course, there's nothing magical about **AutoPostBack**. Listing 15.2 shows the HTML code that this ASP.NET page sends to the user's browser when you have **AutoPostBack** enabled. As you can see, this functionality is managed by JavaScript code that runs in the user's browser. The great advantage to this scheme is that you don't have to write any of the code yourself. On the other hand, you need to be aware that this won't work with an older browser that doesn't support JavaScript.

TIP   An alternative to using **AutoPostBack** *is to add a submit button to the web page that posts the contents of the page back to the server. All the control events will fire when the user clicks this button.*

LISTING 15.2: *AUTOPOSTBACK* IN THE BROWSER

```
<!DOCTYPE HTML PUBLIC "-//W3C//DTD HTML 4.0 Transitional//EN">
<HTML>
   <HEAD>
      <title>Hyperlink Demo</title>
      <meta content="Microsoft Visual Studio.NET 7.0" name="GENERATOR">
      <meta content="Visual Basic 7.0" name="CODE_LANGUAGE">
      <meta content="JavaScript" name="vs_defaultClientScript">
      <meta content="http://schemas.microsoft.com/intellisense/ie5"
 name="vs_targetSchema">
   </HEAD>
   <body>
      <form name="Form1" method="post" action="WebForm1.aspx" id="Form1">
<input type="hidden" name="__EVENTTARGET" value="" />
<input type="hidden" name="__EVENTARGUMENT" value="" />
<input type="hidden" name="__VIEWSTATE"
value="dDwtMTM2ODg2MTk2NDs7Pg==" />

<script language="javascript">
<!--
```

```
   function __doPostBack(eventTarget, eventArgument) {
      var theform = document.Form1;
      theform.__EVENTTARGET.value = eventTarget;
      theform.__EVENTARGUMENT.value = eventArgument;
      theform.submit();
   }
// -->
</script>

        <P>Choose a Destination:</P>
        <P><select name="ddlURL" id="ddlURL"
onchange="__doPostBack('ddlURL','')" language="javascript"
style="width:139px;">
   <option value="http://www.microsoft.com/">Microsoft</option>
   <option value="http://www.yahoo.com/">Yahoo</option>
   <option value="http://www.cnn.com/">CNN</option>

</select></P>
      </form>
   </body>
</HTML>
```

NOTE   *You'll look at those strange hidden input tags, including* __VIEWSTATE, *later in this chapter, in the "Maintaining State in Web Applications" section.*

The ASP.NET Server Controls

You'll find two sets of HTML controls in the Toolbox when you're working in the ASP.NET Web Form Designer. The HTML tab of the Toolbox holds standard HTML controls, including such controls as a submit button, a drop-down list box, a check box, and so on. By default, these controls are available only to client-side code. You can turn these controls into server controls by adding the runat="server" attribute to their HTML. (You can also do this from the user interface by right-clicking the control and selecting Run As Server Control.) When you convert one of these HTML controls to a server control, the properties of the control become available to server-side code at runtime. There are 18 standard HTML controls in the Toolbox:

◆ Label

◆ Button

◆ Reset Button

◆ Submit Button

◆ Text Field

◆ Text Area

- ◆ File Field
- ◆ Password Field
- ◆ Checkbox
- ◆ Radio Button
- ◆ Hidden
- ◆ Table
- ◆ Flow Layout Panel
- ◆ Grid Layout Panel
- ◆ Image
- ◆ Listbox
- ◆ Dropdown
- ◆ Horizontal Rule

While the standard HTML controls are useful for quickly constructing a web interface, they're not well-suited for ASP.NET programming. That's because, even when they're run as server controls, these controls do not have a rich event model. They also do not support `AutoPostBack`. You need to wait for the user to click a submit button (or otherwise post the form to the server) in order to see any events from these controls.

In most ASP.NET applications, you'll find the ASP.NET server controls to be more useful. These controls are located on the Web Forms tab in the toolbox, and are most easily considered in three groups:

- ◆ User interface controls
- ◆ Data controls
- ◆ Validation controls

USER INTERFACE CONTROLS

ASP.NET supplies 21 user interface server controls. In this section, you'll take a brief look at each of them.

NOTE   *In addition to the events listed in this section, each ASP.NET server control supports several standard events:* `DataBinding`, `Disposed`, `Init`, `Load`, `PreRender`, *and* `Unload`. *These events are fired at various points in the life cycle of the control, and you're unlikely to need them in most ASP.NET applications.*

The most useful ASP.NET user interface controls provide events to enable your code to interact with the user. These controls are listed in Table 15.1.

TABLE 15.1: ASP.NET USER INTERFACE CONTROLS THAT PROVIDE EVENTS

CONTROL	PURPOSE
TextBox	Provides a data entry area analogous to a text box on a Windows Form. This control implements a TextChanged event that is fired whenever the contents of the text box change. Even if you turn on AutoPostBack for the text box, this event is not fired once for every character typed. Rather, it is fired whenever the user posts the form or when the focus leaves the text box after at least one character has been typed.
Button	Renders as an HTML button. The button supports several events, including click and command. The click event occurs when the user clicks the button. The command event also occurs when the button is clicked. The difference between the two is mainly one of intent. The click event is intended for buttons that don't specify a command, whereas the command event is intended for buttons that do. For example, a submit button should generally be hooked up to the click event, whereas a filter button should generally use the command event. The button does not have an AutoPostBack property; button events are always sent to the server.
LinkButton	Has the same functionality as the Button control, but it is visually rendered as a hyperlink rather than a button. Despite looking like a hyperlink, the LinkButton doesn't automatically implement linking behavior. It's up to you to write code to handle clicks in the way that you prefer.
ImageButton	Displays an image and implements click and command events just as the Button control does. The events for an ImageButton include additional information: the X and Y coordinates of the click. This enables you to use an ImageButton control as a clickable image map in your applications.
DropDownList	Creates a combo box on a web page. Its key event is SelectedIndexChanged that you used earlier in this chapter.
ListBox	Creates a list box on the web page. It has the same programmatic interface as the DropDownList control, including a collection of Items and a SelectedIndexChanged event.
CheckBox	Creates a check box on the web page. This control fires a CheckedChanged event whenever the state of the check box changes.
CheckBoxList	Renders as a list or array of check boxes. Programmatically, it's another ListBox-like control, with a collection of Items and a SelectedIndexChanged event.
RadioButton	Creates a radio button on the web page. Radio buttons are designed to be grouped into sets, and only one of the set can be selected at any given time. The GroupName property of the radio button dictates which other RadioButton controls are considered to be a part of the same group. Like a check box, a radio button raises a CheckedChanged event when its state changes.
RadioButtonList	Is yet another analog of the ListBox control, this one rendered as a list or array of radio buttons. All the radio buttons in a RadioButtonList are treated as a single mutually-exclusive group.

Continued on next page

TABLE 15.1: ASP.NET USER INTERFACE CONTROLS THAT PROVIDE EVENTS *(continued)*

CONTROL	PURPOSE
Calendar	Renders as an entire collection of HTML controls that represent, of course, a calendar. It includes script to enable the user to navigate from month to month and to select a particular day. The Calendar control implements a VisibleMonthChanged event and a SelectionChanged event.
AdRotator	Shows a random ad from an XML file of ads. It supplies an AdCreated event that is posted when a new ad is displayed to the page.

A second set of user interface controls provide design capabilities but no events. These controls are listed in Table 15.2.

TABLE 15.2: USER INTERFACE CONTROLS WITHOUT EVENTS

CONTROL	PURPOSE
Label	Provides a way to represent static text on the web page. It has no AutoPostBack property.
HyperLink	Implements a standard hyperlink on your web page, with the control's NavigateUrl property dictating where the user should be redirected when they click the hyperlink.
Image	Inserts an image into the web page. If you want a clickable image map, use an ImageButton control instead.
Panel	Is a container for other controls. The panel is useful for grouping controls and changing their properties as a group. For example, if you hide or show a panel, all the controls that it contains are hidden or shown at the same time.
PlaceHolder	Like the Panel control, is a container for other controls. The difference is that the PlaceHolder is designed to hold controls that are dynamically added at runtime by calling the Add() method of its Controls collection.
Table	Gives you a designer for HTML tables.
Literal	Is similar to the PlaceHolder control, except that it's designed to receive simple text at runtime rather than entire controls.

A third set of user interface controls are best thought of as specialized viewers. They're listed in Table 15.3.

TABLE 15.3: USER INTERFACE CONTROLS—SPECIALIZED VIEWERS

CONTROL	PURPOSE
Xml	Displays an XML document as a part of the web page without applying any formatting to the document
CrystalReportViewer	Displays a Crystal Report as part of the web page

Figure 15.3 shows examples of most of the user interface controls in the Web Form Designer. Figure 15.4 shows the same controls as they're rendered to the browser.

FIGURE 15.3

User interface server controls in the Web Form Designer

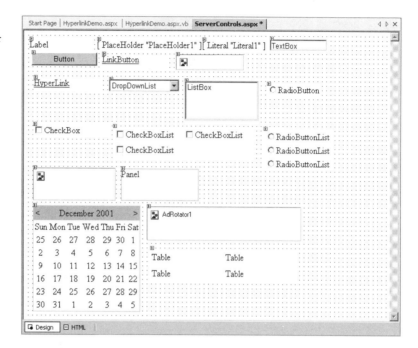

FIGURE 15.4

User interface server controls in the browser

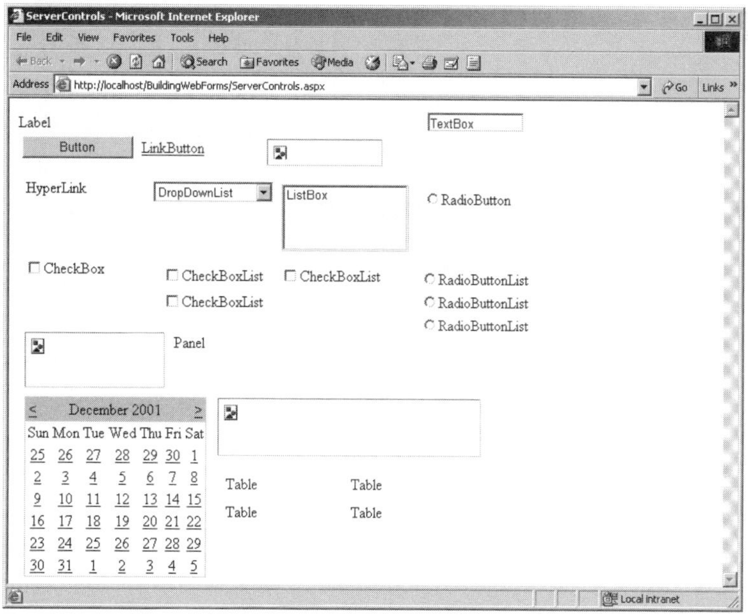

DATA CONTROLS

Although the user interface server controls we've already discussed can be bound to data (and you'll see some examples of this later in the chapter), there's a second set of ASP.NET controls that are designed specifically for displaying large amounts of data. They're listed in Table 15.4.

TABLE 15.4: ASP.NET CONTROLS FOR DISPLAYING LARGE AMOUNTS OF DATA

CONTROL	PURPOSE
DataGrid	Is similar to a DataGrid control you've already seen on Windows Forms
DataList	Provides a flexible display of an entire list of items by implementing template-based formatting
Repeater	Provides another way of using templates to display a list of items

These controls are so important to database programming that we've given them an entire chapter of their own, Chapter 16, "The Web Data Controls." To give you one example of the visual presentation that can result from using these controls, Figure 15.5 shows a DataGrid control displaying data from the Northwind Customers table.

FIGURE 15.5

DataGrid in action

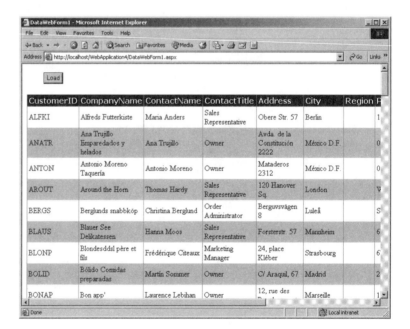

VALIDATION CONTROLS

The third group of ASP.NET server controls has no close analog in either Windows Forms or HTML design. These are the validation controls, designed to simplify a common task: making sure that the user enters reasonable data on a Web Form before you try to process the data. There are six validation controls, listed in Table 15.5.

TABLE 15.5: ASP.NET VALIDATION SERVER CONTROLS

CONTROL	PURPOSE
RequiredFieldValidator	Validates that a control's value has been changed
CompareValidator	Validates that two controls have the same value
RangeValidator	Validates that a control's value falls within a specified range
RegularExpressionValidator	Validates that a control's value matches a specified regular expression
CustomValidator	Validates a control by using custom code
ValidationSummary	Displays a list of all validation errors on a page

The validation controls work by being bound to another control through their `ControlToValidate` property. This property holds the ID of another control on which the validation control should act.

As an example of validation, take a look at the `Validation.aspx` Web Form shown in Figure 15.6. The error messages that you can see here in design mode are individual validation controls. The selected control, displaying a bulleted list of errors, is a ValidationSummary control.

FIGURE 15.6

Designing a Web Form with validation controls

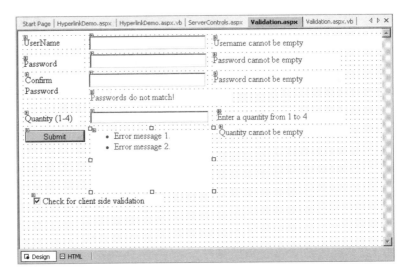

Consider the RequiredFieldValidator control at the top right of the form. This control's properties are set as follows:

◆ (ID)—val1

◆ ControlToValidate—txtUserName

- ◆ `EnableClientScript`—True

- ◆ `ErrorMessage`—Username cannot be empty

When the user clicks the Submit button, this particular control looks at the value in the `txtUserName` control. If that value is the same as it was when the form was first created, then the validation control's error message is displayed, and the data is not submitted to the user.

The other validation controls are similar. This sample form contains four RequiredFieldValidator controls (one for each text box), a single CompareValidator control (which makes sure that the password was typed the same way in both boxes), and a single RangeValidator control (which checks that the value in the `txtQuantity` text box is between 1 and 4).

The form also contains a single ValidationSummary control. When the user submits the form, this control collects validation errors for all the other validation controls on the form and adds them to a list. If the control's `ShowSummary` property is True, this list is displayed on the form. If the control's `ShowMessageBox` property is True, the list is also displayed to the user in a message box.

Figure 15.7 shows how the form might look at runtime if the user made several errors while filling in the required information.

FIGURE 15.7

Validation errors at runtime

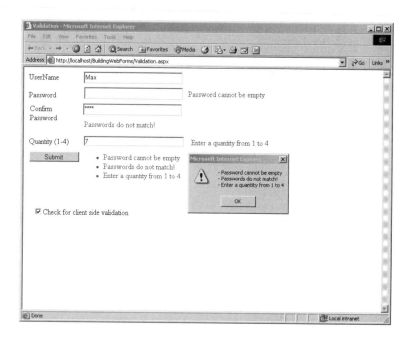

By default, validation is performed twice: once by client-side JavaScript code, and once by ASP .NET on the server. These two validations have different purposes. The client-side validation can catch errors without needing a round-trip to the server, and so keeps processing time and server load at a minimum. But a malicious user could craft an HTTP request that appeared to come from this form and so bypassed client-side validation. In that case, the server-side validation will catch the problem.

The sample form (saved as `Validation.aspx` in the `BuildingWebForms` project) enables you to optionally turn off the client-side validation by unchecking the Check For Client Side Validation check box. This check box executes the following code:

```
Private Sub chkValidateClient_CheckedChanged(ByVal sender As System.Object, _
  ByVal e As System.EventArgs) Handles chkValidateClient.CheckedChanged
    val1.EnableClientScript = chkValidateClient.Checked
    val2.EnableClientScript = chkValidateClient.Checked
    val3.EnableClientScript = chkValidateClient.Checked
    val4.EnableClientScript = chkValidateClient.Checked
    val5.EnableClientScript = chkValidateClient.Checked
    val6.EnableClientScript = chkValidateClient.Checked
    val7.EnableClientScript = chkValidateClient.Checked
End Sub
```

If you uncheck the box and experiment with the page, you'll see that server-side validation has the same visual effects as client-side validation. Still, in most cases you'll want to leave client-side validation active so as to catch as many errors as possible without a round-trip to the server.

Validation on the server takes place after the `Page Load` event but before any control events. You can check whether any particular validation control is reporting a problem by retrieving the `Page.IsValid` property. However, you should be aware that this property will always return True in the `Page Load` event, unless you first explicitly call the `Page Validate` method from within the `Page Load` event.

Maintaining State in Web Applications

If you've never worked with web applications, the notion of maintaining state might be foreign to you. That's because Windows applications simply maintain state without bothering us, and we can take that for granted. For example, if you fill in a value in a text box on a Windows Form and then run code that alters some other controls on the form, the value in the text box will remain unchanged. That's what we mean by maintaining state.

With web applications, you can't take this behavior for granted. That's because web pages are, in general, stateless. If you fill in some fields on a Web Form and click Submit, the form doesn't remain in your browser with the fields filled in. Instead, it is re-created when the response from the server arrives. Unless you take some special measures, the data you entered will be gone at that point.

In older ASP applications, you had to take special care to work around this problem. Typically, you'd add all the values that you care about to the query string sent to the server when the form was posted. Then the server could extract these values and use them to rebuild the new page. The result was typically a great deal of code just to maintain state.

ASP.NET takes care of maintaining state for you automatically. It does this through a property called `ViewState`. You might recall seeing this in the HTML in Listing 15.2. The `ViewState` property is stored as a hidden form field and sent to the server whenever the form is posted. The server then uses this information to rebuild the form on the way back. It's the same system that we used in old-style ASP, but all the pieces are automated by ASP.NET.

What gets stored in `ViewState`? By default, all the values of all the controls on the page. This includes not just values typed in by the user, but things such as the `Text` property of a hyperlink control, which you could have set in code. You can also add arbitrary information to ViewState as a part of running code. For example, this code creates a new ViewState element named Flavor and assigns it a value:

```
ViewState("Flavor") = "Sour"
```

Later you can retrieve the value from the ViewState into a string variable:

```
strFlavor = CStr(ViewState("Flavor"))
```

You can selectively turn off ViewState processing for an entire ASP.NET page or for individual controls. You do this by setting the EnableViewState property of the document or the control to False. Storing the ViewState is necessary only if a page posts back to itself. You should turn off ViewState if a page posts its information to another page, because the ViewState values won't do any good there.

Remember, too, that the information stored in ViewState is sent to the server and back every time you post a page. Although the information is compressed, it still represents additional bulk (and thus delay) for loading the page. ViewState is not a good choice for storing huge amounts of information.

When you're considering the amount of data that gets moved around, you need to remember to check the AutoPostBack properties of your controls. If every control on your form has AutoPostBack set to True, and ViewState is enabled throughout, then you'll be sending the most possible data every time the focus changes on your form. This is very likely to slow down your application. You should reserve the AutoPostBack setting of True for controls where you need to trap events while the user is still working with the page and before they've submitted it back to the server.

Caching and Configuration

ASP.NET includes some advanced management features designed to make your Web Applications faster and more flexible. Two areas where you should be aware of ASP.NET's capabilities are caching and configuration. *Caching* refers to saving frequently-used data in memory so that it can be reused. *Configuration* refers to setting the values that control your Web Application's behavior. Let's look at each of these in turn.

Caching

Some dynamic web pages are relatively expensive to generate, but do not change rapidly. That's the situation that makes caching worthwhile. For example, suppose you have an ASP.NET page that creates an employee directory by querying servers around the world. It might take considerable time to create the directory page, but it wouldn't change very quickly. In that case, you might want to create the page once and then hand it out in response to all requests made within 24 hours, rather than re-creating the page in response to every request.

ASP.NET supports three types of caching:

◆ Page output caching

◆ Page fragment caching

◆ Page data caching

PAGE OUTPUT CACHING

Page output caching stores an entire page in the ASP.NET cache. When you place a page in the cache, you specify a time (in seconds) that the page should be considered "live." All requests for the page that come in over that time will be served by the cached page. At the end of the specified time, the page will be removed from the cache until the next time that it is requested, at which point it will be cached again.

To implement page output caching for a page, you need to insert a server directive directly into the page's HTML:

```
<@ OutputCache Duration="120" VaryByParam="none"%>
```

That particular directive would cause the page that contains it to be cached for two minutes after it was directed. The `VaryByParam` value indicates that there is no dependence on any parameter in the query string that created the page. If, for example, you were caching a page that showed all employees in a particular state, you might have a varying parameter named `State`:

```
<@ OutputCache Duration="120" VaryByParam="State"%>
```

With this directive, a cached page of California employees would not be handed out in response to a request for New York employees, but would be served from the cache in response to a second request for California employees.

PAGE FRAGMENT CACHING

Page fragment caching extends the `OutputCache` directive to parts of a web page. Page fragment caching works by enabling you to include the `OutputCache` directive within a UserControl. For example, you might have a stock price indicator that's changed only once every 10 minutes included as part of a larger page of news data. You could encapsulate the stock price data within a UserControl and use the `OutputCache` directive to cache only that portion of the page.

PAGE DATA CACHING

Finally, page data caching lets you add your own information to the ASP.NET cache and retrieve it programmatically. With page data caching, you can specify your own expiration date for information, or link a cached item to a disk file so that the cache expires if the file is changed. Cached information lasts for the lifetime of a web application.

Configuration

ASP.NET is designed to allow configuration data to be stored in an external file named `web.config` instead of being hard-coded into your application. For example, suppose you're developing an application that uses a test database server during development but that will use a production server after it's been deployed. Rather than store the server name in a variable on a Web Form, you could store the name in a configuration file. This gives you one central repository for configuration information and makes it easier to locate all the items that might need changing.

ASP.NET configuration files are XML files, which means that they can be read by both humans and machines. You can place a `web.config` file in any directory managed by your web server, and its settings apply to applications in and below that directory. For example, a `web.config` file in the `inetpub\wwwroot` folder would apply to all web applications on your server, whereas one in `inetpub\wwwroot\customers` would affect only the Customers application (and would override any settings made in the root configuration file).

TIP   There are other ways for administrators to change the configuration of .NET on a wider scale. For example, a `machine.config` file can be used to dictate settings for every .NET application running on a computer. Refer to the .NET Framework SDK for more information on configuration files in general.

You can add items to and retrieve items from a configuration file programmatically. ASP.NET also uses these files for its own information. Listing 15.3 shows a sample `web.config` file created by ASP.NET.

LISTING 15.3: A *WEB.CONFIG* FILE

```
<?xml version="1.0" encoding="utf-8" ?>
<configuration>

  <system.web>

    <!-- DYNAMIC DEBUG COMPILATION
         Set compilation debug="true" to insert debugging
         symbols (.pdb information)
         into the compiled page. Because this creates a
         larger file that executes
         more slowly, you should set this value to true
         only when debugging and to
         false at all other times. For more information,
         refer to the documentation about
         debugging ASP.NET files.
    -->
    <compilation defaultLanguage="vb" debug="true" />

    <!-- CUSTOM ERROR MESSAGES
         Set customErrors mode="On" or "RemoteOnly" to enable
         custom error messages, "Off" to disable.
         Add <error> tags for each of the errors you want to handle.
    -->
    <customErrors mode="RemoteOnly" />

    <!-- AUTHENTICATION
         This section sets the authentication policies of the
         application. Possible modes are "Windows",
         "Forms", "Passport" and "None"
    -->
```

```
<authentication mode="Windows" />


<!-- AUTHORIZATION
     This section sets the authorization policies of the
     application. You can allow or deny access
     to application resources by user or role.
     Wildcards: "*" mean everyone, "?" means anonymous
     (unauthenticated) users.
-->
<authorization>
    <allow users="*" /> <!-- Allow all users -->

        <!-- <allow     users="[comma separated list of users]"
                         roles="[comma separated list of roles]"/>
              <deny      users="[comma separated list of users]"
                         roles="[comma separated list of roles]"/>
        -->
</authorization>


<!-- APPLICATION-LEVEL TRACE LOGGING
     Application-level tracing enables trace log output
     for every page within an application.
     Set trace enabled="true" to enable application
     trace logging.  If pageOutput="true", the
     trace information will be displayed at the
     bottom of each page.  Otherwise, you can view the
     application trace log by browsing the "trace.axd"
     page from your web application
     root.
-->
<trace enabled="false" requestLimit="10" pageOutput="false"
 traceMode="SortByTime" localOnly="true" />


<!-- SESSION STATE SETTINGS
     By default ASP.NET uses cookies to identify which
     requests belong to a particular session.
     If cookies are not available, a session can be
     tracked by adding a session identifier to the URL.
     To disable cookies, set sessionState cookieless="true".
-->
<sessionState
        mode="InProc"
        stateConnectionString="tcpip=127.0.0.1:42424"
        sqlConnectionString="data source=127.0.0.1;user id=sa;password="
        cookieless="false"
```

```
                        timeout="20"
        />

        <!-- GLOBALIZATION
             This section sets the globalization settings of the application.
        -->
        <globalization requestEncoding="utf-8" responseEncoding="utf-8" />

    </system.web>

</configuration>
```

Accessing Databases from ASP.NET

You saw in Chapter 7, "ADO.NET Programming," that ADO.NET data binding is pervasive: columns of information from a database can be bound to any property of any control on a Windows Form. As you'll see in this section, you can also bind data to controls on Web Forms. In this section, you'll build up a simple application that lets you retrieve and display some information from the Northwind sample database on a series of Web Forms.

To get started, create a new Web Application project and rename the default form **CustomerList.aspx**.

Retrieving Data

Before you can display data, of course, you need to retrieve it from the database. To do this, you can use all the ADO.NET tools that you've seen in previous chapters. Using ADO.NET for data access in a Web Form is no different from using it for data access in a Windows Form. The database code is the same either way.

You'll use the rapid application development (RAD) features of Visual Basic .NET to quickly build the objects that you need for your application. Start by opening Server Explorer and connecting to a copy of the Northwind sample database. Then expand the TreeView until you can see the columns in the **Customers** table. Click **CustomerID**, then Ctrl+click **CompanyName**. This results in both fields being highlighted. Drag the fields and drop them on the Web Form.

TIP   Depending on which fields you choose to drag and drop, you might receive an error from Visual Studio .NET, informing you that update and delete statements could not be created. This happens when you don't include the primary key of the table in the fields you're using. This won't cause any problems if you only want to display the data without editing it.

This operation will create a SqlConnection object and a SqlDataAdapter object, just as it does on a Windows Form. As far as possible, the Visual Studio .NET designers have made Web Forms and Windows Forms behave identically in the designer. Because you selected two columns rather than the entire table, the command properties of the SqlDataAdapter use only those two columns. Listing 15.4 shows the code that creates these two objects.

LISTING 15.4: DATA OBJECTS CREATED FROM TWO COLUMNS (*CUSTOMERLIST.ASPX.VB*)

```vb
Protected WithEvents SqlSelectCommand1 As System.Data.SqlClient.SqlCommand
Protected WithEvents SqlInsertCommand1 As System.Data.SqlClient.SqlCommand
Protected WithEvents SqlUpdateCommand1 As System.Data.SqlClient.SqlCommand
Protected WithEvents SqlDeleteCommand1 As System.Data.SqlClient.SqlCommand
Protected WithEvents SqlConnection1 As System.Data.SqlClient.SqlConnection
Protected WithEvents SqlDataAdapter1 As System.Data.SqlClient.SqlDataAdapter
Me.SqlSelectCommand1 = New System.Data.SqlClient.SqlCommand()
Me.SqlInsertCommand1 = New System.Data.SqlClient.SqlCommand()
Me.SqlUpdateCommand1 = New System.Data.SqlClient.SqlCommand()
Me.SqlDeleteCommand1 = New System.Data.SqlClient.SqlCommand()
Me.SqlConnection1 = New System.Data.SqlClient.SqlConnection()
Me.SqlDataAdapter1 = New System.Data.SqlClient.SqlDataAdapter()
'
'SqlSelectCommand1
'
Me.SqlSelectCommand1.CommandText = "SELECT CustomerID, CompanyName FROM
➥ Customers"
Me.SqlSelectCommand1.Connection = Me.SqlConnection1
'
'SqlInsertCommand1
'
Me.SqlInsertCommand1.CommandText = "INSERT INTO Customers(CustomerID,
➥ CompanyName) VALUES (@CustomerID, @CompanyName)" & _
"; SELECT CustomerID, CompanyName FROM Customers
➥ WHERE (CustomerID = @CustomerID)" & _
""
Me.SqlInsertCommand1.Connection = Me.SqlConnection1
Me.SqlInsertCommand1.Parameters.Add(New System.Data.SqlClient.SqlParameter(
➥ "@CustomerID", System.Data.SqlDbType.NVarChar, 5, "CustomerID"))
Me.SqlInsertCommand1.Parameters.Add(New System.Data.SqlClient.SqlParameter(
➥ "@CompanyName", System.Data.SqlDbType.NVarChar, 40, "CompanyName"))
'
'SqlUpdateCommand1
'
Me.SqlUpdateCommand1.CommandText = "UPDATE Customers SET CustomerID =
➥ @CustomerID, CompanyName = @CompanyName WHERE (" & _
"CustomerID = @Original_CustomerID) AND (CompanyName =
➥ @Original_CompanyName); SE" & _
"LECT CustomerID, CompanyName FROM Customers WHERE (CustomerID = @CustomerID)"
Me.SqlUpdateCommand1.Connection = Me.SqlConnection1
Me.SqlUpdateCommand1.Parameters.Add(New System.Data.SqlClient.SqlParameter(
➥ "@CustomerID", System.Data.SqlDbType.NVarChar, 5, "CustomerID"))
Me.SqlUpdateCommand1.Parameters.Add(New System.Data.SqlClient.SqlParameter(
➥ "@CompanyName", System.Data.SqlDbType.NVarChar, 40, "CompanyName"))
Me.SqlUpdateCommand1.Parameters.Add(New System.Data.SqlClient.SqlParameter(
➥ "@Original_CustomerID", System.Data.SqlDbType.NVarChar, 5,
```

```
➥ System.Data.ParameterDirection.Input, False, CType(0, Byte), CType(0, Byte),
➥ "CustomerID", System.Data.DataRowVersion.Original, Nothing))
Me.SqlUpdateCommand1.Parameters.Add(New System.Data.SqlClient.SqlParameter(
➥ "@Original_CompanyName", System.Data.SqlDbType.NVarChar, 40,
➥ System.Data.ParameterDirection.Input, False, CType(0, Byte), CType(0, Byte),
➥ "CompanyName", System.Data.DataRowVersion.Original, Nothing))
'
'SqlDeleteCommand1
'
Me.SqlDeleteCommand1.CommandText = "DELETE FROM Customers WHERE (CustomerID =
➥ @Original_CustomerID) AND (CompanyName " & _
"= @Original_CompanyName)"
Me.SqlDeleteCommand1.Connection = Me.SqlConnection1
Me.SqlDeleteCommand1.Parameters.Add(New System.Data.SqlClient.SqlParameter(
➥ "@Original_CustomerID", System.Data.SqlDbType.NVarChar, 5,
➥ System.Data.ParameterDirection.Input, False, CType(0, Byte), CType(0, Byte),
➥ "CustomerID", System.Data.DataRowVersion.Original, Nothing))
Me.SqlDeleteCommand1.Parameters.Add(New System.Data.SqlClient.SqlParameter(
➥ "@Original_CompanyName", System.Data.SqlDbType.NVarChar, 40,
➥ System.Data.ParameterDirection.Input, False, CType(0, Byte), CType(0, Byte),
➥ "CompanyName", System.Data.DataRowVersion.Original, Nothing))
'
'SqlConnection1
'
Me.SqlConnection1.ConnectionString = "data source=(local)\NetSDK;
➥ initial catalog=Northwind;integrated security=SSPI;per" & _
"sist security info=False;workstation id=SEESAW;packet size=4096"
'
'SqlDataAdapter1
'
Me.SqlDataAdapter1.DeleteCommand = Me.SqlDeleteCommand1
Me.SqlDataAdapter1.InsertCommand = Me.SqlInsertCommand1
Me.SqlDataAdapter1.SelectCommand = Me.SqlSelectCommand1
Me.SqlDataAdapter1.TableMappings.AddRange(
➥ New System.Data.Common.DataTableMapping()
➥ {New System.Data.Common.DataTableMapping("Table", "Customers",
➥ New System.Data.Common.DataColumnMapping()
➥ {New System.Data.Common.DataColumnMapping("CustomerID", "CustomerID"),
➥ New System.Data.Common.DataColumnMapping("CompanyName", "CompanyName")}})
Me.SqlDataAdapter1.UpdateCommand = Me.SqlUpdateCommand1
```

Select the SqlDataAdapter1 object and click the Generate Dataset link in the Properties window. Name the DataSet **dsCustID**, include the Customers table, and add it to the designer.

Now you're ready to display this data on the user interface. Drag a ListBox control from the Web Forms tab in the Toolbox to the form and size it to show a fair number of rows. Assign properties to the ListBox as shown in Table 15.6.

TABLE 15.6: PROPERTIES FOR A BOUND LISTBOX

PROPERTY	VALUE
(ID)	lboCustomers
AutoPostBack	True
DataSource	DSCustID1
DataMember	Customers
DataTextField	CompanyName
DataValueField	CustomerID

This set of properties will result in a ListBox that displays company names, but returns Customer ID values when you retrieve its value property.

Using the *DataBind ( )* Method

Although the ListBox is now set up to display the data that you want, there still remains the issue of actually retrieving that data. Double-click the Web Form to open its code module and add code to the Page_Load procedure:

```
Private Sub Page_Load(ByVal sender As System.Object, _
  ByVal e As System.EventArgs) Handles MyBase.Load
    If Not IsPostBack Then
        SqlDataAdapter1.Fill(DsCustID1, "Customers")
        DataBind()
    End If
End Sub
```

One piece of this code should look familiar to you: the call to the Fill() method of the SqlDataAdapter1 object. That's the method, of course, that tells the SqlDataAdapter to go out to the database and actually retrieve the requested data for you.

The check of IsPostBack makes sure that you're not retrieving the data more often than you need it. In the next section, you're going to post this page back to itself in order to open detailed information on a particular customer. When that happens, there's no need to retrieve the list of customer information a second time. ASP.NET maintains the IsPostBack variable to tell you whether you're in the middle of a postback operation. On the initial load of the page, this variable will be False, and the code inside the If statement will be executed.

The last thing in this code is the DataBind() method. Although you can use the Web Form Designer in the IDE to set up data binding by setting the appropriate properties (as you did in the previous section), no data is actually bound until you call this method. You can call DataBind() on the page level (as is done in this code example), or on individual controls.

By splitting the DataBind() method from the user interface and making it a manual operation, the ASP.NET designers gave you finer control of the data binding process. This is essential in a distributed environment that might involve slow links between components. Using `DataBind()` on a control level means that you can load data only when it's needed. For example, you might choose to bind address controls only if the user indicates that they need to see address information.

Figure 15.8 shows the `CustomerList` Web Form, with the addition of an explanatory label for the user's benefit.

FIGURE 15.8

Listing customers on a Web Form

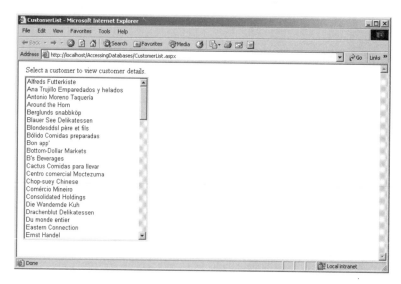

Using User Input as a Parameter

Now you'll create a second Web Form to display detailed information on the selected customer. This time, we'll do everything in code, rather than using the drag-and-drop method. As always, you can work with the user interface or with code, whichever way you find to be more comfortable.

Create a new Web Form in your application and name it **CustomerDetail**. Add Label and TextBox controls to it to hold customer data, as shown in Figure 15.9. Of course, you can add controls for the rest of the columns in the table if you like. We've just done enough here to show you how this works.

FIGURE 15.9

Designing a form for customer detail

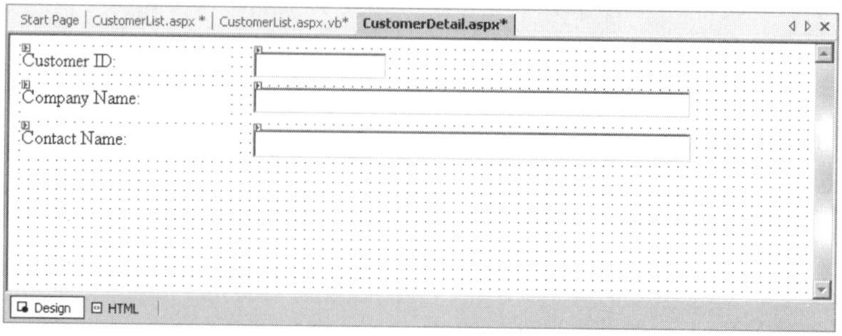

The first problem is how to pass the selected customer from the first Web Form to the second. You'll take an approach that uses a custom property of the first Web Form. Because Web Forms (like everything else in .NET) are classes, they can have custom properties. The trick is in the code that reads the property value, because Web Forms cease to exist when you navigate away from them. But the .NET designers took this into account and provided the necessary tools.

Start by adding code to the `CustomerList` Web Form to implement a custom property:

```
Public ReadOnly Property CustomerID() As String
    Get
        Return lboCustomers.SelectedItem.Value
    End Get
End Property
```

Next, add code to the `CustomerList` form to tell it to open the `CustomerDetail` form when the user selects an item in the ListBox:

```
Private Sub lboCustomers_SelectedIndexChanged( _
 ByVal sender As System.Object, ByVal e As System.EventArgs) _
 Handles lboCustomers.SelectedIndexChanged
    Server.Transfer("CustomerDetail.aspx")
End Sub
```

The `Server.Transfer()` method performs a server-side redirect of the web page's output. That is, it tells the server to deliver the specified page, instead of the original page, when it's invoked.

Now it's time to write the code in the `CustomerDetails` page that will read the value of the `CustomerID` property from the source page. To start, you need to declare a global variable that uses the class of the original page:

```
Public listpage As CustomerList
```

Then, add this code to the `Page Load` procedure of the `CustomerDetails` page:

```
Dim strCustID As String

If Not Page.IsPostBack Then
    listpage = CType(Context.Handler, CustomerList)
    strCustID = listpage.CustomerID
End If
```

The key to this code is the `Context.Handler` object. This object represents the part of the ASP .NET engine that handles the HTTP headers, information that is passed to the server when the user makes a request for a page. Within that object, it's not too late to retrieve the source page where the request came from.

After you have a `CustomerID` value to work with, the rest of the code is fairly straightforward. You'll use a strongly typed DataSet to hold the columns of interest. Select Project ➢ Add New Item, choose the DataSet item, and name it **CustomerDetails.xsd**. Click the Open button to open the .xsd file in the designer. Open Server Explorer and drag the columns of interest to the XSD Designer. Save your project to make sure that the corresponding DataSet class is ready to use.

Listing 15.5 shows the completed `Page Load` procedure.

LISTING 15.5: RETRIEVING INFORMATION ON A PARTICULAR CUSTOMER (*CUSTOMERDETAIL.ASPX.VB*)

```vb
Public listpage As CustomerList
Dim ds As New CustomerDetails()

Private Sub Page_Load(ByVal sender As System.Object, _
  ByVal e As System.EventArgs) Handles MyBase.Load
    Dim strCustID As String
    Dim cnn As New SqlClient.SqlConnection()
    Dim cmdSelect As New SqlClient.SqlCommand()
    Dim da As New SqlClient.SqlDataAdapter()

    If Not Page.IsPostBack Then
        listpage = CType(Context.Handler, CustomerList)
        strCustID = listpage.CustomerID

        cnn.ConnectionString = "data source=(local)\NetSDK;" & _
          "Initial Catalog=Northwind;Integrated Security=SSPI"

        cmdSelect.CommandText = "SELECT CustomerID, CompanyName, " & _
          "ContactName FROM Customers WHERE (CustomerID = @CustomerID)"
        cmdSelect.Connection = cnn
        cmdSelect.Parameters.Add( _
        New System.Data.SqlClient.SqlParameter( _
        "@CustomerID", System.Data.SqlDbType.NVarChar, 5, "CustomerID"))
        cmdSelect.Parameters(0).Value = strCustID

        da.SelectCommand = cmdSelect
        da.Fill(ds, "Customers")

        DataBind()

    End If

End Sub

Private Sub txtCustomerID_DataBinding(ByVal sender As Object, _
  ByVal e As System.EventArgs) Handles txtCustomerID.DataBinding
    Dim r As CustomerDetails.CustomersRow
    r = ds.Customers(0)
    txtCustomerID.Text = r.CustomerID
End Sub

Private Sub txtCompanyName_DataBinding(ByVal sender As Object, _
  ByVal e As System.EventArgs) Handles txtCompanyName.DataBinding
    Dim r As CustomerDetails.CustomersRow
    r = ds.Customers(0)
```

```
        txtCompanyName.Text = r.CompanyName
End Sub

Private Sub txtContactName_DataBinding(ByVal sender As Object, _
  ByVal e As System.EventArgs) Handles txtContactName.DataBinding
      Dim r As CustomerDetails.CustomersRow
      r = ds.Customers(0)
      txtContactName.Text = r.ContactName
End Sub
```

If you trace through the code in Listing 15.5, you'll see that hooking data to controls at runtime is a multistep process:

1. Retrieve the data somehow. In this particular instance, we used a DataSet to retrieve the data. You could also use a DataReader, or even execute a command that returned just the data of interest.

2. Call the page's `DataBind()` method.

3. The `DataBind()` method call will trigger the `DataBinding` event of each bindable control on the page. In this event, you can run code to display the data by retrieving appropriate values from the data structure that you're using.

Summary

This chapter introduced you to the basics of ASP.NET. By now, you should be able to see that most of the features of Web Forms running in ASP.NET are very similar to features of Windows Forms running in Visual Basic .NET. Because ASP.NET (like all other .NET development environments) uses the Common Language Runtime for code execution, you can use any .NET language to develop ASP.NET pages.

You've seen how you can use Web Forms and server controls to build flexible and programmable user interfaces in the user's web browser. By implementing `AutoPostBack` and `ViewState`, you can make sure that information is preserved even in the usually-stateless browser environment. You've also been introduced to the caching and configuration features that enable you to tune ASP.NET applications.

Finally, this chapter showed you that hooking up ADO.NET data to an ASP.NET user interface is not fundamentally different from doing the same with a Windows Forms interface in a traditional application. There are some new bits of syntax to learn (such as the `DataBind()` method), but the overall approach is quite similar.

Now it's time to drill into the use of ADO.NET from ASP.NET a bit deeper. Although individual controls are useful for an occasional bit of data display, most serious database applications in ASP.NET will benefit from using the DataGrid, DataList, or Repeater controls for their user interface. Programming the flexible interface of these controls is the subject of our next chapter.

Chapter 16

The Web Data Controls

◆ The DataGrid web control

◆ The DataList web control

AMONG THE NEW WEB controls introduced with ASP.NET are the DataGrid and DataList controls. They're both data-bound controls and they can be used both for displaying and editing data on the browser. We'll start this chapter with a few remarks you should bear in mind as you build web applications with the data-bound controls. Both the DataGrid and the DataList controls are server-side controls. They exist only while you design a page. You can set their properties and bind them to a data source, but what the user sees at his monitor is an HTML table.

Figure 16.1 shows a page that displays data about the customers of the Northwind database. The page is based on the DataList control, but if you looked at the source file that created this page, you'd see plain HTML. Notice that one of the customers is in edit mode. The edit boxes are HTML TextBox controls, and the entire grid is an elaborate HTML table. The client is a browser, and browsers haven't changed drastically in the last few years. All they can handle is HTML, and your Web application must interact with the client by sending HTML code and getting HTTP requests. The .NET platform has introduced some powerful tools for designing data-driven web applications, but the final stage is the production of HTML code that can be viewed on any browser.

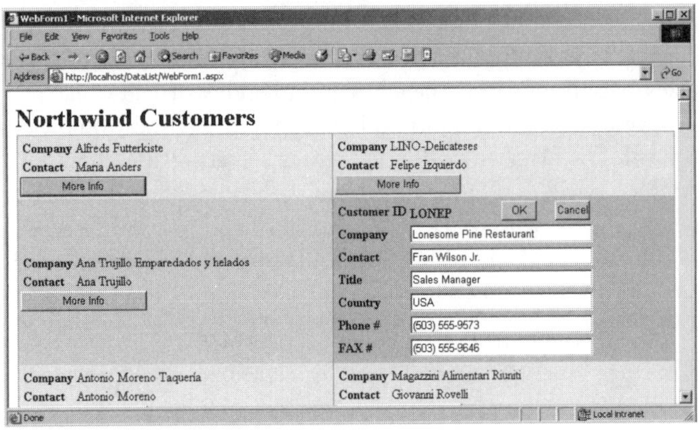

FIGURE 16.1

Editing a customer's fields on a DataList control

Later in this chapter, you'll build the web application you see in Figure 16.1. First, we'll start with a few simpler topics and then move on to more advanced ones, such as displaying relational data (master/detail forms) and building data-bound pages that can be edited.

The DataGrid Web Control

The DataGrid web control is the basic tool for displaying data. It's equivalent to the Windows DataGrid control. The process of displaying a table or a view on a DataGrid web control is no different from setting up a DataGrid control in a Windows application. You can create the necessary DataSet object(s) with visual tools and then bind the DataSet to the control by setting the `DataSource` and `DataMember` properties. Alternately, you can create the DataSet in your code and bind it to the control.

The first difference between the two controls is that the web DataGrid control doesn't allow you to edit its data. To edit the data on the data-bound web control, you must add a bit of code to your application, and you'll see how this can be done later in the chapter. To build a data-bound web page, start a new web application and place an instance of the DataList control on the Form. Then drop a database table on the designer, configure the DataAdapter, and create a DataSet. Open the Property Browser of the DataList control and set its `DataSource` property to the name of the DataSet, and the `DataMember` property to the name of one of the tables in the DataSet.

To actually load the data-bound control to the DataSet, you must call its `DataBind()` method. This takes place usually from within the page's `Load()` event handler. This event takes place every time the page is loaded, even when the page is refreshed. To avoid rebinding the data to the control with every postback, you can examine the property `IsPostBack`. This property is True every time the page is posted back (a postback occurs after a page is loaded for the first time; that is, when a page is refreshed).

```
Private Sub Page_Load(ByVal sender As System.Object, _
                    ByVal e As System.EventArgs) Handles MyBase.Load
    If Not Me.IsPostBack Then
        DACategories.Fill(Categories1)
        DataGrid1.DataBind()
    End If
End Sub
```

In this example, `DACategories` is the name of the DataAdapter in the project, and `Categories1` is the name of the DataSet. When a page is posted back, there's no reason to bind the DataSet to the control. If you refresh the DataSet, you must also rebind the control to the DataSet. This usually takes place from within the Click event handler of a button.

Notice that the DataSet is filled explicitly, as you would do with the Windows version of the control. The DataSet resides on the web server—the computer that executes the Load event handler. ASP.NET will extract the data from the DataSet and it will create an HTML table, which will be sent to the client. To test your page, run the project and Internet Explorer will pop up with the data. If you examine the HTML document (open the View menu and select Source), you'll see an HTML table. You will also see a large section with seemingly random data, such as the following:

```
<input type="hidden" name="__VIEWSTATE"
value="dDw3MjE3MDkzMTE7dDw7bDxpPDE+Oz47bDx0PDtsPGk8MT47aTwyPjs+Oz4w8dDxAM
```

Dw7Ozs7Ozs7Ozs7Pjs7PjtOPEAwPHA8cDxsPFBhZ2VDb3VudDtfIUl0ZW1Db3VudDtfIURhd
GFTb3VyY2VJdGVtQ291bn" />

This is a small section of the contents of a hidden control, which contains the state of the control. This section contains the DataSet encoded as text. You can't spot event the text fields in this string, but this is your data. The data is stored in a hidden control and it's posted back to the control every time the page is refreshed, which explains why you need not call the `DataBind()` method repeatedly. When the page is posted back, the control's data is sent to the server, and the web application can use it to build the page again. You need not provide any code for this; ASP.NET will re-create the page from the posted data.

Close the Internet Explorer window to return to the designer. Open the control's Property Browser again, locate the `EnableViewState` property, and change its setting from True to False. Run the project again, look at the page's source code, and this time you won't see the large data section. The `EnableViewState` property determines whether the control automatically saves its state during round-trips to the server. Here's what this means to your application: When the page is created, the entire DataSet is encoded and embedded into the page. When the page is posted back, (when the user presses F5 for instance), the data is sent back to the web server, where it's used to create another page. The same data is sent to the client again, and so on. As you understand, a large DataSet can place quite a bit of burden on the web server, in addition to making a slow-loading page.

You can turn off this property to conserve bandwidth, but then you must explicitly re-create the DataSet and bind it to the data-bound control with every postback. This means that you must also reload the DataSet, because web applications don't maintain any state. The DataSet is filled with data in the page's `Load()`event handler, ASP.NET creates the web page, and this is it. No state is maintained between sessions, and the DataSet must be filled again when the page is reloaded. Of course, you can make this process more efficient by caching the page.

Customizing the Appearance of the DataGrid

The web page you created in the first example was as plain as it gets. The DataGrid control is highly customizable, and it's fairly easy to create professional-looking web pages with this control. The process of customizing the DataGrid is substantially different from the process of customizing the Windows version of the control; we'll go through the steps in this section.

The DataGrid control in Figure 16.2 was generated by the `DataGrid1` project, which you will find on the CD. To use it, you must copy the entire folder with the project to your web server's root folder and then open it with Visual Studio. The control was customized with visual tools, and you should follow the instructions in this section to re-create it. You should also experiment with properties and settings not mentioned in this chapter.

Create a new web application, open the Server Explorer, and drop the `Categories` table of the Northwind database on the design surface. Rename the DataAdapter object that will be automatically created to **DACategories** and create a DataSet with the following SQL statement:

```
SELECT CategoryID, CategoryName, Description FROM Categories
```

While you configure the DataSet, in the Advanced Options screen of the wizard, clear the option titled Generate Insert, Update And Delete statements. You will not update the DataSet, so there's no need to include Insert, Update and Delete statements. Create the DataSet and bind the DataGrid control to it.

FIGURE 16.2

Displaying the product categories on a DataGrid control

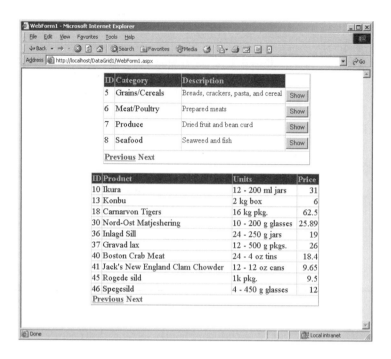

Right-click the DataGrid control and from the pop-up menu select Property Builder. The DataGrid Properties dialog box appears, and there are five tabs on this dialog box. The General tab, shown in Figure 16.3, displays the data-binding properties of the control and some basic characteristics of the control, such as whether the control will have a header and a footer, and so on.

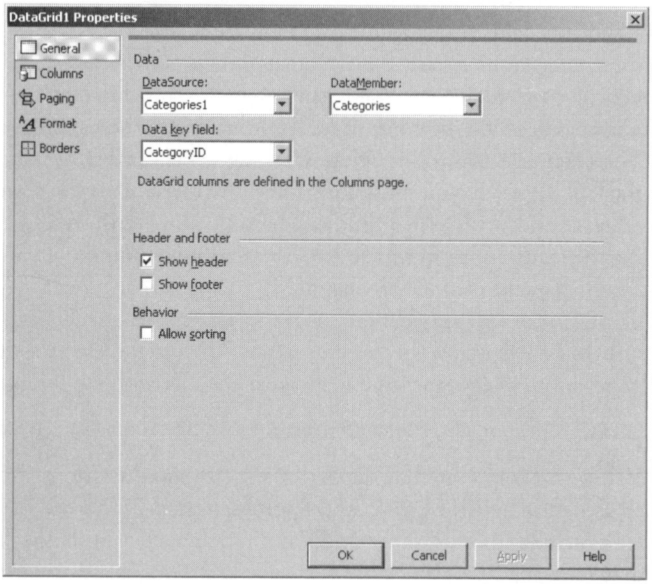

FIGURE 16.3

The General tab of the DataGrid Properties dialog box

Click Columns on the left pane to see the Columns tab, shown in Figure 16.4. Here you can specify the columns that will appear on the control. Start by clearing the option Create Columns Automatically At Run Time. This option is set by default. It instructs ASP.NET to include all the columns of the DataSet, in the order in which they appear in the SELECT statement. In the Available Columns list, you can select the columns you want to display. In addition, you can select one or more generic column types (for example, a column with buttons). Select the data columns in the order you want them to appear on the control and click the button with the arrow to add them to the Selected Columns list.

FIGURE 16.4

Columns tab

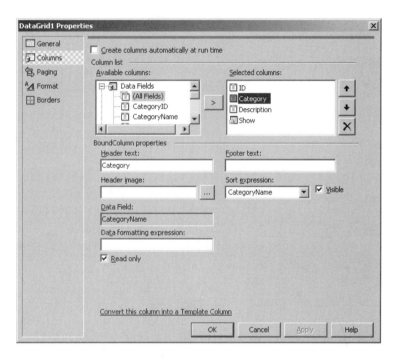

Then select each one of the columns in the Selected Columns list and set their properties. The Header text is the column's header, and the Footer text is the string that will appear at the bottom of the column, after the last item. The Data formatting expression is where you specify how the column will be formatted; you will supply an expression for numeric and data fields. The formatting expression is the same one you would use with the ToString() method. The expression {0: #,###.00} signifies that the amount must be formatted with a thousand separator and two decimal digits. The value 14302.5785 will be formatted as 14,302.58, and the value 14.48 will be formatted as 14.50, for example. You can also apply formatting masks to dates. The specification {0:dd MMM yyyy} will format the date 13/3/2002 as 13 March 2001.

The next tab, Paging, is where you specify how to create paged DataSets. A paged DataSet is displayed in pages with a fixed number of rows, along with the appropriate navigational buttons at the bottom of the control. You'll examine the paging features of the data-bound controls in detail later in this chapter.

The next tab, Format, is where you specify how each item will appear on the control (see Figure 16.5). Let's go through each of the items in the Objects list. The first four items, DataGrid, Header, Footer, and Pager, determine the appearance of the corresponding object of the grid. To set the foreground/background color and the font of the entire grid, select the DataGrid item in the list and then set the various properties on the tab.

FIGURE 16.5

Format tab

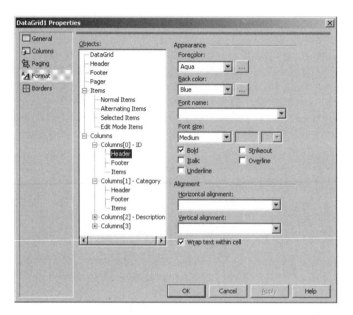

In the Items section of the list, there are four items: Normal Items, Alternating Items, Selected Items, and Edit Mode Items. These are templates that apply to various types of items. All the rows of a DataGrid control contain items, and so do the cells of a DataList control. You can format the even-numbered rows differently from the odd-numbered rows, to make a dense grid easier to read. Select the appropriate item in the list and then set its properties. When an item on the control is selected at runtime, it becomes the selected item and its appearance is determined by the Selected Items template. Finally, when an item is placed in Edit mode at runtime (if the control allows the editing of its rows), the appearance of the item being edited is determined by the last template.

The Columns branch of the Objects list contains an entry for each column in the control. Each one of these entries has three elements: the column's header, footer, and item. This is where you set the appearance of the corresponding element of the grid. You can customize the foreground/background colors, the font, and the alignment of the text.

The last tab, Borders, is where you specify the spacing and padding of the grid's cells (remember, the DataGrid control will be rendered as an HTML table) and whether there will be borders, and how thick, around the cells.

Set the corresponding properties on the DataGrid Properties dialog box to make your DataGrid control look like the one shown in Figure 16.2. Ignore the column with the buttons for now; you'll design it in the following section. Then run the project and experiment with setting the grid's appearance.

If you switch to the control's Property Browser, you will see properties for all the items you've set up in the Property Builder. However, these settings apply only to items that haven't been individually customized through the Property Builder.

Displaying Paged DataSets

One of the problems with HTML tables is that they can't be scrolled. If the DataSet you bound to the control contains too many lines, the DataGrid control will grow in length, perhaps overlapping other elements of the page. It's imperative that the control's height doesn't exceed a maximum value. To ensure that this doesn't happen, you break the DataSet into pages of the same size (more or less).

A *page* is a group of rows that are displayed on the same form. The bottom of the form usually has links for the next and previous page, or links to all the pages that make up the DataSet. The user can click a link and jump to any other page of the DataSet. Paged DataSets are useful when they contain a relatively small number of pages. A DataSet with 300 pages isn't very practical, even though you're not displaying all the rows at once. How the user supposed to figure out which page contains the row they're interested in? Very large DataSets aren't appropriate for typical web applications altogether. If a search returns more than a couple of hundred rows at most, you should probably ask users to be more specific.

The data-bound web controls have built-in support for paging. They provide properties and recognize events that simplify the display of the page numbers at the bottom of the control and the display of the appropriate page when a page hyperlink is clicked. To enable paging, you must set the control's `AllowPaging` property to True and the `PageSize` property to the number of rows per page. The `PagerStyle` property determines the layout of the paging section of the control. This property is an object that exposes a number of properties for setting the foreground/background color of the paging section, the font, and so on. One of the properties it exposes is the `Mode` property, which can have one of two values: `NextPrev` and `NumericPages`. These are the two paging modes that are supported automatically. You can also turn on `AllowCustomPaging`, in which case you must provide your own mechanism for paging through the DataSet. These properties can be set in the Paging tab of the Property Builder, shown in Figure 16.6.

After you've enabled paging, the control will receive the `PageIndexChanged()` event every time one of the paging links is clicked. These links might be the previous/next arrows or page numbers. In this event's handler, you must set the page to jump to and refill the DataSet. Listing 16.1 is a typical `PageIndexChanged()` event handler.

LISTING 16.1: HANDLING PAGING EVENTS

```
Private Sub DataGrid1_PageIndexChanged(ByVal source As Object, _
           ByVal e As System.Web.UI.WebControls.DataGridPageChangedEventArgs) _
           Handles DataGrid1.PageIndexChanged
    DataGrid1.CurrentPageIndex = e.NewPageIndex
    DACategories.Fill(Categories1)
    DataGrid1.DataBind()
End Sub
```

FIGURE 16.6

Paging tab

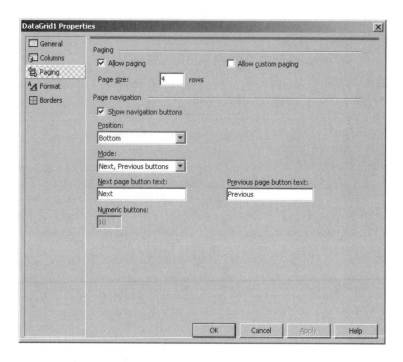

The property `e.NewPageIndex` is the page number selected by the user on the control. The transition to the new page isn't automatic; you must explicitly set the `CurrentPageIndex` property and then reload the DataSet and bind the control to it again to force its contents to change.

Paging is a technique used widely in web design, and many designers go overboard. You might have seen web pages with hyperlinks to the other 299 pages with the results. This is clearly overkill. If a query returns too many rows, use the SQL `TOP` keyword to limit the number of rows returned, and display a message to this effect, so that users can narrow their search. When you use the built-in paging capabilities of the data-bound controls, you should be aware that the control doesn't know how to retrieve the rows of the current page from the database. Instead, it retrieves all the qualifying rows and then displays the appropriate subset, taking into consideration the current paging settings. Every time you click the Next button, for example, you read all the qualifying rows to the client, display a small subset of the rows, and discard the rest. A public web application might accept a very large number of requests; moving a lot of data out of the database to use a small percentage of them is clearly an unacceptable practice. The simplest, most efficient, and most convenient approach is to limit the number of rows you retrieve from the database. If you absolutely have to page a very large DataSet, you should look into custom paging techniques.

Building A Master/Detail Page

In this section, you'll build a web page to display the product categories of the Northwind database on one DataGrid control and the products in the selected category on another DataGrid. The information on the first control can be considered the master, while the second control contains the details.

You can use this arrangement to display orders and their details, or customers and their orders, and so on. You used the master/detail user interface when you built the shopping cart project in Chapter 8, "Data-Aware Controls." It's a typical interface in many business applications, and you can apply the same techniques to create functional web pages to present data to your users.

Continuing the previous example, you're going to add a column with buttons to your DataGrid, as shown in Figure 16.2. When a button is clicked, the products of the selected category will be displayed on another DataGrid control, at the bottom of the page. Start by adding the column with the buttons to your grid. Select the `DataGrid1` control in the designer and from the pop-up menu select Property Builder. In the dialog box that pops up, select the Columns tab and expand the Button Column item in the Available Columns list. There are three types of buttons you can add to the grid: Select buttons, Edit/Update/Cancel buttons, and Delete buttons. The Select button triggers an event that indicates the selection of an item in the grid. The Edit/Update/Cancel buttons handle the editing actions of the control's data. Initially, an Edit button is displayed. When the user clicks this button, the current row's cells switch to edit mode (they're replaced by TextBox controls, where you can edit them). At the same time, the Edit button is replaced by the Update/Cancel buttons, and users can either commit the changes to the database by clicking the Update button, or cancel the operation by clicking the Cancel button. The Delete button deletes the current row.

Click the Select button and add it to the Selected Columns list. Select the new column and set its properties in the control on the lower part of the dialog box. Set its Text property to Show (this is the caption on the control) and its type to PushButton. That's all there is to it. A new column will be added to the control and it will be filled with buttons. Now you must add a few statements to display a second DataGrid control with the products of the selected category. But first, you must create the appropriate DataAdapter and DataSet objects.

Drop the `Products` table from the Northwind database in the Server Explorer onto the design surface and configure it with the following SQL statement:

```
SELECT ProductID, ProductName, QuantityPerUnit, UnitPrice
FROM   Products WHERE (CategoryID = @catID)
```

This statement selects the products in a category whose ID is passed as an argument. Name the new DataAdapter **DAProducts** and create the **SelectedProducts** DataSet to store the rows returned by the query. Place the second DataGrid control on the form, bind it to the `SelectedProducts` DataSet, and configure its appearance. The ID of the selected products must be retrieved from the top DataGrid control. Select this control and locate its `DataKeyField` property. This property specifies the column with the keys of the table shown on the control. Expand its settings box and select CategoryID. The IDs of all categories will be stored in the DataKeys collection, which you'll access from within your code to retrieve the ID of the selected category.

At this point, you can connect the two DataGrid controls by programming the event of the selection of a different category. When one of the Show buttons on `DataGrid1` is clicked, the `ItemCommand` event is fired. This event is fired when you click any item on the DataGrid control, including the headers/footers and even the items in the paging section of the control. The declaration of the `ItemCommand` event handler is as follows:

```
Private Sub DataGrid1_ItemCommand(ByVal source As Object, _
            ByVal e As System.Web.UI.WebControls.DataGridCommandEventArgs) _
            Handles DataGrid1.ItemCommand
```

The e argument exposes the ItemType property, which is one of the members of the ListItem-Style enumeration: AlternatingItem, EditItem, Footer, Header, Item, Pager, SelectedItem, Separator. When the user clicks the button of an Item or AlternatingItem row, you must populate the SelectedProducts DataSet, whose rows will appear in the second DataGrid control. Enter the following statements in the ItemCommand event handler of the DataGrid1 control:

```
Private Sub DataGrid1_ItemCommand(ByVal source As Object, _
                ByVal e As System.Web.UI.WebControls.DataGridCommandEventArgs) _
                Handles DataGrid1.ItemCommand
    If e.Item.ItemType = ListItemType.AlternatingItem Or _
                    e.Item.ItemType = ListItemType.Item
        Dim categoryID As Integer = DataGrid1.DataKeys(e.Item.ItemIndex)
        DAProducts.SelectCommand.Parameters("@catID").Value = categoryID
        DAProducts.Fill(SelectedProducts1)
        DataGrid2.DataBind()
    End If
End Sub
```

The DAProducts DataAdapter expects the ID of a category (it's the @catID parameter in the SQL statement) as a parameter. To extract this value, you retrieve the row index value of the selected item in the top DataGrid control. All the keys of the DataTable to which the DataGrid control is bound are retrieved through the DataKeys collection. This collection is indexed by the number of the row. The expression DataGrid1.DataKeys(e.Item.ItemIndex) returns the key of the selected category. The expression e.Item.ItemIndex is the number of the selected row.

After you've obtained the ID of the selected category, you pass it as a parameter to the Select-Command object of the DataAdapter object. The DataAdapter will return the products in the selected category, and the DataGrid2 control is bound to this DataSet.

Run the application now and see how you can search the Products table hierarchically, by viewing the products in a selected category. Set the DataGrid1 control's EnableViewState property to False and run the project. If you don't want to move the control's state back and forth, you must comment out the If and End If statements in the page's Load() event handler, so that the DataSet will be refilled with every postback. You should also try to disable paging on the two controls. If you display all the categories on the top DataGrid control, it will expand vertically and cover part of the second DataGrid. Even if you move the second control lower to make room for the top one, adding a few rows to the Categories table will result in a longer table, overlapping the control with the products. For your reference, Listing 16.2 shows the entire listing of the DataGrid1 project.

LISTING 16.2: THE CODE OF THE DATAGRID1 PROJECT

```
Private Sub Page_Load(ByVal sender As System.Object, _
                    ByVal e As System.EventArgs) Handles MyBase.Load
    'Put user code to initialize the page here
    If Not Me.IsPostBack Then
        DACategories.Fill(Categories1)
        DataGrid1.DataBind()
    End If
End Sub
```

```
    Private Sub DataGrid1_ItemCommand(ByVal source As Object, _
                ByVal e As System.Web.UI.WebControls.DataGridCommandEventArgs) _
                Handles DataGrid1.ItemCommand
        If e.Item.ItemType = ListItemType.AlternatingItem Or _
                        e.Item.ItemType = ListItemType.Item Or _
                        e.Item.ItemType = ListItemType.SelectedItem Then
            Dim categoryID As Integer = DataGrid1.DataKeys(e.Item.ItemIndex)
            DAProducts.SelectCommand.Parameters("@catID").Value = categoryID
            DAProducts.Fill(SelectedProducts1)
            DataGrid2.DataBind()
        End If
    End Sub


    Private Sub DataGrid1_PageIndexChanged(ByVal source As Object, _
                ByVal e As System.Web.UI.WebControls.DataGridPageChangedEventArgs) _
                Handles DataGrid1.PageIndexChanged
        DataGrid1.CurrentPageIndex = e.NewPageIndex
        DACategories.Fill(Categories1)
        DataGrid1.DataBind()
    End Sub


    Private Sub DataGrid2_PageIndexChanged(ByVal source As Object, _
                ByVal e As System.Web.UI.WebControls.DataGridPageChangedEventArgs) _
                Handles DataGrid2.PageIndexChanged
        DataGrid2.CurrentPageIndex = e.NewPageIndex
        DAProducts.Fill(SelectedProducts1)
        DataGrid2.DataBind()
    End Sub
```

Maintaining State

As you already know, web applications don't maintain their state. In other words, you can't declare a global variable and expect it to maintain its value between executions. Every time the page is posted back, the code behind the page is executed, it creates a new page, and then it terminates. There's absolutely no relation between two successive executions of the same page. Aside from using session variables, the same page is executed for all users and it just doesn't know which client invoked it. This is also why ASP.NET stores the values of the controls into the page itself. Even a DataGrid's rows are stored in the HTML file that's sent to the client on a hidden control. Notice that the same is also used to create the page, which is an HTML table that represents the DataGrid control on the client. This is the state needed by ASP.NET to create the page, and you can't access the hidden data from within your code, even though the data is moved back and forth.

To maintain state between postbacks, you can use the Session object. Every time a new user connects to the application, ASP.NET creates a new Session object for the specific client. This object is always available to your code, and you need not track and maintain the current user data from within your code. ASP.NET takes care of maintaining a separate Session object for each client and makes the proper Session object available to your code.

The Session object is a repository for variables, and you can store anything in this object—not exactly *anything*, just enough information for your application's needs. A text file uploaded by the user, for example, need not be stored in the Session object. You store the contents to a disk file and the file's name to the Session object. In the following section, you'll see how to use the Session object to store a shopping cart.

Let's say your site enables users to select items and place them in their cart. The items can be located in various pages, so you must keep track of the items ordered so far. To implement a shopping cart, you can create a collection, add a new element for each item ordered, and store the collection in the Session object. As long as the same user shops at your site, the items ordered will remain in their cart. If they disconnect before placing the order, the cart's contents will be lost, because the Session object ceases to exist when the session terminates. Of course, you can store the items ordered to cookies at the client (use the Cookies collection of the Response object to send the cookies to the client and the same collection of the Request object to read the cookies). Alternately, you can store the collection to a database table and prompt users to identify themselves, so that you can retrieve their saved cart. Or, you can combine both approaches: store the cart to a local database and a unique ID to the client as a cookie. When a user connects, request the value of this cookie on the client computer and, if it exists, retrieve automatically the contents of the user's cart from the table and store it in the Session object.

The Session object can store all types of objects. To add a parameter to the Session object, specify the name of the parameter in a pair of parentheses following the Session object's name and set it to the desired value:

```
Session("UserID") = "Guest"
```

The values stored in the Session object need not be simple types such as strings or integers. You will most likely use a collection to store related data. An appropriate structure for implementing a shopping cart is the HashTable collection. If you haven't explored the new collections of VB .NET yet, a *HashTable* is an array with values and keys. Instead of accessing its elements with an index value, you can access them with a meaningful key. For the shopping cart, you can create a HashTable with the IDs of the selected products as keys and their quantities as values. The contents of this collection are pairs such as the following:

```
{SW1080, 1}
{SW1003, 1}
{HW843, 4}
```

where SW*xxx* and HW*xxx* are product IDs, and the numeric values are the corresponding quantities. In the following section, you'll see this technique in action; we will discuss the details as we go along.

Getting Orders on the Web

The GridOrders application, shown in Figure 16.7, is quite similar to the previous application. You display the categories of the Northwind database in a DataGrid control and allow the user to select a category with the View button. The selected category's items appear on the second DataGrid control. The Buy button places the selected item in the user's shopping cart. If the cart contains a selected item already, the quantity is increased by one. If not, a new element is created and added to the cart.

FIGURE 16.7

The `GridOrders`
web application

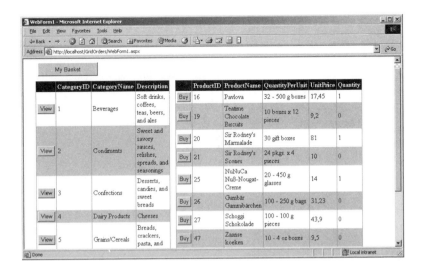

The main page of the `GridOrders` application looks awkward, but you already know how to customize the appearance of the DataGrid control, and you can improve the appearance of the application considerably. In this section, we'll focus on the basic operations of updating the items of the DataGrid control: taking orders and maintaining the user's shopping cart. If you decide to improve the appearance of the two DataGrid controls, you should start by making the two ID columns invisible. The IDs are needed by the application code, but users don't care about IDs. You should also change the default width of the remaining columns and set the format of the prices. Finally, you should create paged DataSets to enable the results of the DataSet to be spread among multiple web pages, because certain categories contain quite a few products. As a reminder, a DataGrid control can be customized through its Property Pages (right-click the control and select Property Builder). In the Columns tab of the Property Pages, clear the option Create Columns Automatically At Run Time and then add the appropriate columns to the control and set each column's properties.

The interface of the `GridOrders` application is very similar to that of the `DataGrid1` application, and you know how to bind the two DataGrid controls on the main page. You also know how to add a column with buttons to the DataGrid control. The two DataAdapters we used in this project are called `DACategories` and `DAProducts`, and the corresponding DataSets are the `Categories` and `Products` DataSets (they store the categories and products of the Northwind database). The DataGrid control with the categories is bound to the `Categories` DataSet, and the DataGrid control with the products is bound to the `Products` DataSet.

Let's look at the code of the application. When the page is loaded, the following statements are executed to fill the `Categories` DataSet: bind it to the `DataGrid1` control, and create a new Session variable, the `Basket` variable. Notice that the `Basket` variable is declared outside any procedure and it's a HashTable object. The fact that it's declared at the form's level doesn't mean that it maintains its value between executions; it just enables it to be available for use between different methods.

NOTE   *In the code, the term basket refers to the user's shopping cart.*

LISTING 16.3: POPULATING THE DATAGRID CONTROL WITH PRODUCT CATEGORIES

```
Private Basket As New Hashtable()
Private Sub Page_Load(ByVal sender As System.Object, _
                      ByVal e As System.EventArgs) Handles MyBase.Load
    'Put user code to initialize the page here
    If Not IsPostBack Then
        DACategories.Fill(Categories1)
        DataGrid1.DataSource = Categories1
        DataGrid1.DataMember = "Categories"
        DataGrid1.DataKeyField = "CategoryID"
        DataGrid1.DataBind()
        Session("Basket") = Basket
    End If
End Sub
```

The control is bound to a DataSet programmatically. You could have done the same declaratively by using the control's properties at design time.

When the Show button is clicked on the DataGrid1 control, you want to retrieve the matching products and display them on the second DataGrid control. To populate the second DataGrid control with the products in the selected category, you must retrieve four columns from the Products names: the product's ID, the product's name, the QuantityPerUnit column, and the price. All the rows you will retrieve from the Products table must belong to the same category as the Show button that was clicked on the left DataGrid control. In short, you must retrieve the ID of the selected category from the first DataGrid control, use it in building a fairly simple SELECT statement, execute this statement against the Northwind database, and use the rows returned by the query to populate the second DataGrid control.

The second DataGrid displays an additional column with the quantity ordered from each product. This column doesn't exist in the Products table, so you must add it to the Products DataSet from within your code. To add a new column to a table of a DataSet, create a DataColumn object, set its properties, and add it to the Columns collection. The following statements add the quantity column to the first table of the DataSet object:

```
Dim qtyCol As New DataColumn()
qtyCol.DataType = GetType(Integer)
qtyCol.DefaultValue = 0
qtyCol.Caption = "Qty"
qtyCol.ColumnName = "Quantity"
Products1.Tables(0).Columns.Add(qtyCol)
```

The extra column must display the quantity of each product in the shopping cart—if the item has been placed in the cart. This information is stored in the Basket collection. Each time the DataGrid2 control is populated, you must iterate through its rows. For each row, you must look up the product's ID in the Basket collection. If it's there, the corresponding quantity must be copied to the last cell of the current row (the quantity column). When the DataGrid with the products is bound to the Products DataSet, the quantities will be zero by default, so the process of looking up the quantities must be repeated every time a new category is selected. The ItemCommand event handler for the DataGrid control with the categories is shown in Listing 16.4.

LISTING 16.4: COMBINING PRODUCTS AND QUANTITIES FROM THE SHOPPING CART

```
Private Sub DataGrid1_ItemCommand(ByVal source As Object, _
                ByVal e As System.Web.UI.WebControls.DataGridCommandEventArgs) _
                Handles DataGrid1.ItemCommand
    DAProducts.SelectCommand.Parameters("@catID").Value = _
                DataGrid1.DataKeys(e.Item.ItemIndex)
    Response.Write(DataGrid1.DataKeys(e.Item.ItemIndex))
    DAProducts.Fill(Products1)
    Dim qtyCol As New DataColumn()     qtyCol.DataType = GetType(Integer)
    qtyCol.DefaultValue = 0
    qtyCol.Caption = "Qty"
    qtyCol.ColumnName = "Quantity"
    Products1.Tables(0).Columns.Add(qtyCol)
    Dim i As Integer     Dim BSKT As New Hashtable()
    BSKT = CType(Session("Basket"), Hashtable)
    For i = 0 To Products1.Tables(0).Rows.Count - 1
        If BSKT.ContainsKey(Products1.Tables(0).Rows(i).Item(0)) Then
            Products1.Tables(0).Rows(i).Item(4) = _
                        BSKT.Item(Products1.Tables(0).Rows(i).Item(0))
        End If
    Next
    DataGrid2.DataBind()
End Sub
```

The Basket collection is extracted from the Session object and stored in the BSKT local variable, which is a HashTable. Then the code iterates through all the rows of the first table in the Products DataSet—the table with the selected category's products. The Products1.Tables.Rows collection holds the rows of the table in the DataSet, and its Item property returns a specific cell's value. The first cell in each row is the ID of the product. If this value exists as a key in the HashTable (the ContainsKey method returns True), the corresponding quantity is extracted and stored in the last cell of the same row (the Quantity column). After populating the last column of the table, the code binds the DataSet to the DataGrid2 control. Capturing the quantities of the products in the cart wasn't very difficult.

Now let's look at the code that places a new item into the shopping cart. When a Buy button is clicked, the ItemCommand() event of the DataGrid2 control is raised. In this event's handler, you update the contents of the Basket Session variable. You extract the ID of the selected product and use it as a key to access the collection. If the key exists, you increase the corresponding quantity by one. If not, you add a new element to the collection with this key and set its value to 1.

LISTING 16.5: ADDING AN ITEM TO THE SHOPPING CART

```
Private Sub DataGrid2_ItemCommand(ByVal source As Object, _
                    ByVal e As System.Web.UI.WebControls.DataGridCommandEventArgs) _

                    Handles DataGrid2.ItemCommand
    DataGrid2.Items(e.Item.ItemIndex).Cells(5).Text = _
                        Val(DataGrid2.Items(e.Item.ItemIndex).Cells(5).Text) + 1
    Dim BSKT As New Hashtable()
    BSKT = CType(Session("Basket"), Hashtable)
    If BSKT.ContainsKey(CInt(DataGrid2.Items(e.Item.ItemIndex).Cells(1).Text)) Then
        BSKT(CInt(DataGrid2.Items(e.Item.ItemIndex).Cells(1).Text)) = _
                        Val(DataGrid2.Items(e.Item.ItemIndex).Cells(5).Text)
    Else
        BSKT.Add(CInt(DataGrid2.Items(e.Item.ItemIndex).Cells(1).Text), _
                        Val(DataGrid2.Items(e.Item.ItemIndex).Cells(5).Text))
    End If
    Session("Basket") = BSKT
End Sub
```

NOTE *Keep in mind that the index values for your Cell items may vary depending on your choice for column order and display. In our code, we use* `Cells(5)` *to refer to the quantity column.*

To access the contents of a DataGrid control from within your code, use the control's Items collection. To access a specific row, specify the row's index in parentheses. The selected row's index is given by a property of the event handler's argument, and it's `e.Item.ItemIndex`. The following expression is the ID of the selected product:

```
DataGrid2.Items(e.Item.ItemIndex).Cells(1).Text)
```

and the following expression is the current quantity of the selected product (the value in the last cell of the row):

```
DataGrid2.Items(e.Item.ItemIndex).Cells(5).Text
```

The code first increases the value of the quantity cell of the current row. Then it updates the items of the collection to include the newly ordered product. Finally, it stores this collection back to the `Basket` Session variable.

The My Basket button on the form redirects the user to another page with the contents of the cart. The IDs stored in the cart are converted to actual product names and they're displayed along with their values and ordered quantities, as shown in Figure 16.8. This is a simple table, but it demonstrates how to access the items in the shopping cart, retrieve the corresponding rows from the `Products` table, and prepare some sort of online invoice. You can add more HTML code to enhance the appearance of the table, or even build a new DataSet and bind it to another DataGrid control.

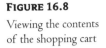

FIGURE 16.8

Viewing the contents of the shopping cart

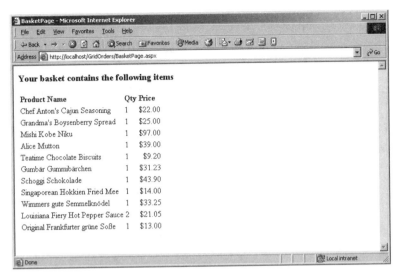

When the My Basket button is clicked, the following statement is executed, which redirects the user to another page with the contents of the shopping cart:

```
Private Sub Button1_Click(ByVal sender As System.Object, _
                    ByVal e As System.EventArgs) Handles Button1.Click
    Response.Redirect("BasketPage.aspx")
End Sub
```

The BasketCartPage.aspx is another web page, which is generated on the fly with the Response .Write() method. This method sends its output to the client, and you can use it to build pages on the fly. The code of the BasketPage.aspx page resides in the page's Load() event handler, which is shown in Listing 16.6.

NOTE   *Keep in mind that the settings for the Connection object should be altered to suit your environment. You will need to change the name of the database server as well as the security credentials. Realize that you should never deploy a database into production with the default* sa *username and password.*

LISTING 16.6: DISPLAYING THE CONTENTS OF THE CART

```
Private Sub Page_Load(ByVal sender As System.Object, _
                    ByVal e As System.EventArgs) Handles MyBase.Load
    Dim BSKT As New Hashtable()
    BSKT = CType(Session("Cart"), Hashtable)
    Dim itm As Integer
    Dim SelIDs As String
    For Each itm In BSKT.Keys
        SelIDs = SelIDs & itm.ToString & ", "
    Next
```

```
        SelIDs = Left(SelIDs, Len(SelIDs) - 2)
        Dim sql As String
        sql = "SELECT ProductID, ProductName, UnitPrice FROM Products " & _
              " WHERE ProductID IN (" & SelIDs & ")"
        Dim conn As New SqlClient.SqlConnection()
        conn.ConnectionString = "initial catalog=Northwind;user id=sa;"

        conn.Open()
        Dim sqlCMD As New SqlClient.SqlCommand()
        sqlCMD.Connection = conn
        sqlCMD.CommandText = sql
        sqlCMD.CommandType = CommandType.Text
        Dim DataIn As SqlClient.SqlDataReader
        DataIn = sqlCMD.ExecuteReader()

        Response.Write _
    ("<h3>Your cart contains the following items</h3>")
        Response.Write("<table font name='Verdana'>")
        Response.Write("<tr><td font size=4><b>Product Name</b></td>")
        Response.Write("<td font size=4><b>Qty</b></td>")
        Response.Write("<td font size=4><b>Price</b></td>")
        While DataIn.Read
            Response.Write("<tr>")
            Response.Write("<td>" & DataIn.Item("ProductName") & "</td>" & _
                    "<td>" & BSKT(DataIn.Item("ProductID")) & "</td>" & _
                    "<td align=right>" & _
                    Format(DataIn.Item("UnitPrice"), "$###.00") & "</td>")
            Response.Write("</tr>")
        End While
        Response.Write("</table>")
End Sub
```

The code starts by extracting the IDs of all products in the cart with the Keys property of the HashTable collection. These keys are placed next to each other with a comma between them, and the result is the IN clause of a SELECT statement. The final SELECT statement is something like the following:

```
SELECT  ProductID, ProductName, UnitPrice FROM Products
WHERE   ProductID IN (12, 39, 4, 22)
```

When this statement is executed, it returns the names and prices of the products in the user's cart. The code then goes through each product, retrieves the corresponding quantity from the cart by using the product's ID as the key, and builds the table, one line at a time.

The order hasn't been saved to the database yet. In the following chapter, you'll see the code that commits the order to the database, and it does so in a transaction. Another limitation of this application is that it doesn't allow the user to edit the quantities of the products in the shopping cart.

In Appendix A, you will find the Online sample application, which maintains a shopping cart, allows the user to edit the quantities, and commits the order to the database. The Online application demonstrates many of the features of a web application skipped in this chapter. The focus in the chapter is on customizing the appearance and manipulating the advanced data-bound controls, and not how to create fully functional Web applications.

So far, you've seen how to use the DataGrid control as a presentation tool, how to select items, and even how to manipulate the control's items from within your code at runtime. It's also possible to edit the rows of the DataGrid control. The other data-bound web control, the DataList control, is better suited for editing operations. You'll see how to set up a DataList control and edit its contents in the following section. The principles are similar, and you can apply the same principles to add edit functionality to the rows of a read-only web-based DataGrid as well.

The DataList Control

The DataList control is conceptually similar to the DataGrid control, but it displays each item in a small rectangle instead of a row. It's more flexible than the DataGrid control because it enables you to customize the appearance of the rectangle by using HTML.

Figure 16.9 shows the customers of the Northwind database on a DataList control. You can arrange the rectangles in rows and columns, have items and alternating items, and customize the appearance of the selected item as well. You can also edit the contents of a DataList control.

FIGURE 16.9

The customers of the Northwind database on a DataList control

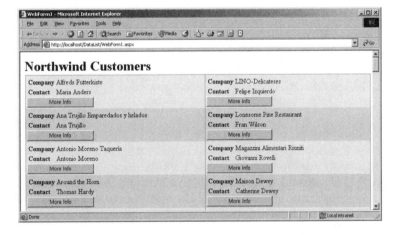

Unlike the DataGrid control, the DataList control doesn't auto-generate its items based on the columns of its data source. You'll have to step in and actually add a few lines of HTML code. There's a tiny visual designer for setting up the appearance of the control's items, but you will have to edit the HTML code it generates. Most often you will build an HTML table to display the fields in each rectangle. You can also add buttons or other HTML controls to each rectangle, and you will see how to do this in the following sections.

To use a DataList control in a project, place an instance of the control on the form and bind it to a table or view as usual. To customize the appearance of the control, right-click the control and select Edit Templates from the pop-up menu. From the submenu that appears, select Item Templates. The Item Templates designer is shown in Figure 16.10. You see a segment of the designer here, and you can scroll it up and down.

FIGURE 16.10

Customizing the appearance of a DataList control

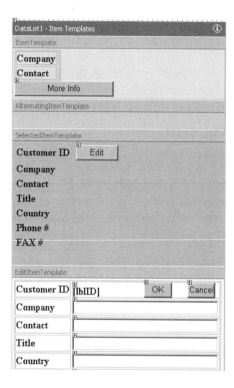

The designer has four sections, which are templates; they determine the appearance of the items of the corresponding type. The available templates are ItemTemplate, AlternatingItemTemplate, SelectedItemTemplate and EditItemTemplate. Their names indicate when they're applied to an item. If you don't want to display alternating items, you need not specify the AlternatingItem-Template, and if you don't want to allow users to edit the control's data, you need not specify an EditItemTemplate.

Usually, you will set up the SelectedItemTemplate, so that selected items stand out. It's also customary to display more information about the selected item. Figure 16.11 shows the same DataList control as Figure 16.9, with one of the customers selected. To select a customer, the user can click the appropriate More Info button. This button is part of the ItemTemplate, and you must program the event it raises when you click it.

FIGURE 16.11

Viewing more fields of the selected customer with the DataListView control

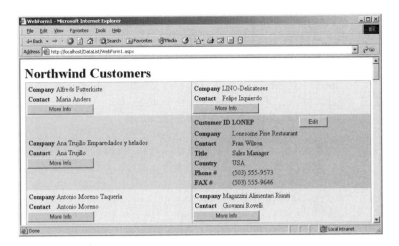

All items display the customer's company and contact names. The selected item displays additional fields, uses a different background color, and provides an Edit button. When clicked, this button will display the fields in TextBox controls so that they can be edited. When an item is placed in edit mode, you must also supply the appropriate buttons to either commit or cancel the edits and return either to selection mode or normal viewing mode. Figure 16.12 shows the customer selected in Figure 16.11 in edit mode.

FIGURE 16.12

Editing a customer on a DataList control

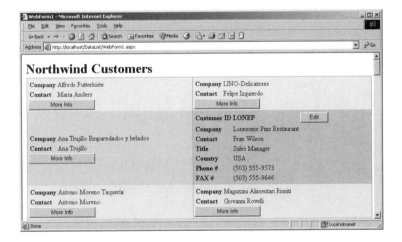

You already know what the DataList project does. It displays a few fields for each customer on a DataList control, displays additional fields of the selected customer, and allows users to edit a customer's fields on the browser. As you can see, the interface isn't as elegant as the interface of a Windows application, but this application runs on the browser and the interface must be translated into HTML. In addition, every operation (for example, selecting an item or switching to edit mode) requires a trip to the server.

Let's review the design process for the DataList project. Create a new web application project, place an instance of the DataList control on the form, and drop the `Customers` table of the Northwind database on the design surface. Create the `DSCustomers` DataSet and bind it to the DataList control. To do so, set the DataList control's `DataSource` property to **DSCustomers1**, its `DataMember` property to **Customers**, and its `DataKeyField` property to **CustomerID**. The last step isn't necessary for this project, but you might have to access the selected customer's ID through the DataKeys collection, as you did with the DataGrid control.

Now you can customize the appearance of the control. Right-click the control and select Edit Template ➤ Item Template from the pop-up menu. You can edit the various templates with visual tools (enter text, drop HTML or web controls from the Toolbox on the template's area, and so on). This process is rather cumbersome, and you will end up editing the HTML source code anyway. At the very least, you will have to remove the <P> (paragraph) tags inserted liberally by the designer.

We have found it helpful to type a few strings (the titles of the fields to be displayed) in the designer, switch to the HTML view of the templates, and use these strings as guides. At the bottom of the form, you see two tabs, the Design and HTML tabs. Switch to the HTML tab to see the HTML code of the various templates. Each template's section is delimited by a pair of tags:

```
<ItemTemplate>
.  .  .
</ItemTemplate>
<SelectedItemTemplate>
.  .  .
</SelectedItemTemplate>
```

All you have to do is insert the appropriate HTML code in each template. Let's start with the regular and alternating items. To display the company and contact name of each customer, as well as the More Info button, insert the following statements between the `<ItemTemplate>` and `</ItemTemplate>` tags:

```
<ItemTemplate>
   <TABLE>
      <TR>
            <TD vAlign="top"><B>Company</B></TD>
            <TD vAlign="top">
            <%# databinder.Eval(Container.DataItem, "CompanyName") %></TD>
      </TR>
      <TR>
            <TD vAlign="top"><B>Contact</B></TD>
            <TD vAlign="top">
            <%# databinder.Eval(Container.DataItem, "ContactName") %></TD>
      </TR>
   </TABLE>
   <asp:Button id="Button1" runat="server" Width="160px"
            CommandName="Selected" Text="More Info"></asp:Button>
</ItemTemplate>
```

This is straight HTML, except for the expression that retrieves the value of the corresponding field. The `DataBinder` object represents the mechanism that binds the data-bound controls on the form to the data source. Its `Eval()` method returns the value of the specified field for one of the items. The first argument is the item (row) to which the field belongs. The expression `Container .DataItem` is the current item. The second argument is the name of the field whose value you want to extract. To extract the value of the `CompanyName` field on the current item of the control, use the following expression:

```
databinder.Eval(Container.DataItem, "CompanyName")
```

Don't forget to enclose all ASP.NET expressions with the <%# and %> tags. Everything that appears between these two tags is evaluated, and the entire expression, including the tags, is replaced by its value. The last element in the ItemTemplate is a button control, whose `CommandName` property is `Selected`. This value is passed to the subroutine that handles the event of an item's selection.

So far, you've created the template for the control's items and alternating items. You'll use the same template for the alternating items, so you need not design another template. The items will differ from alternating items in their background color only, and this is something you can specify in the control's Property Browser.

Expanding the Selected Item

Now you must tell your control how to handle the selection of an item. Locate the tag for the DataList control, which is a very long template near the beginning of the file. Here's what it looks like:

```
<asp:datalist id=DataList1 style="Z-INDEX: 101; LEFT: 14px; POSITION:
    absolute; TOP: 10px" runat="server" DataMember="Customers"
    DataSource="<%# DsCustomers1 %>" DataKeyField="CustomerID"
    Width="839px" Height="242px" RepeatColumns="2" BorderColor="#999999"
    GridLines="Vertical" BorderWidth="1px" BorderStyle="None"
    BackColor="White" CellPadding="3">
```

Add the following attribute to this tag:

```
OnItemCommand="ItemSelected"
```

This attribute tells the control to invoke the `ItemSelected` subroutine when an item is clicked. The `ItemSelected` subroutine is, in effect, an event handler for the selection of an item on the DataList control, and you must supply it in the application's class. Switch to the code module and enter the following event handler:

```
Sub ItemSelected(ByVal sender As Object, ByVal e As DataListCommandEventArgs)    If
e.CommandName = "Selected" Then
        DataList1.SelectedIndex = e.Item.ItemIndex
        DACustomers.Fill(DsCustomers1)
        DataList1.DataBind()
    End If
End Sub
```

Do you see now why you had to set the `CommandName` property? This value is passed to the Item-Selected subroutine, and you can use it to find out where the event originated. We'll get to the code for the SelectedItemTemplate a bit later. To select an item from within your code, you set the Data-List control's `SelectedIndex` property to the current item's index. This action will apply the Selected-ItemTemplate to the selected item. Then you fill the DataSet again and bind the DataList control.

All the items will have the same appearance, except for the selected one, which will be formatted differently.

Now you must specify the template to be applied to the selected item. Switch back to the designer, right click the DataList control, and select Edit Template ➤ Item Template. In the SelectedItemTemplate section, you will create another small table similar to the one you created for the regular items, only this one will have more fields (and their appropriate labels), as shown in Figure 16.11. You'll enter some HTML code similar to the one that created the ItemTemplate. This time, you'll specify more fields, and you'll add an Edit button next to the customer's ID field. Listing 16.7 shows the HTML code for the SelectedItemTemplate.

LISTING 16.7: THE DATALIST CONTROL'S SELECTEDITEMTEMPLATE

```
<SelectedItemTemplate>
    <TABLE>
        <TR>
            <TD><B>Customer ID</B></TD>
            <TD><B><%# databinder.Eval(Container.DataItem, "CustomerID")
%></B></TD>
            <TD>
            <asp:Button id="Button2" runat="server" Width="68px"
                CommandName="Edit" Text="Edit"></asp:Button></TD>
        </TR>
        <TR>
            <TD><B>Company</B></TD>
            <TD vAlign="top">
                <%# databinder.Eval(Container.DataItem, "CompanyName") %></TD>
        </TR>
        <TR>
            <TD><B>Contact</B></TD>
            <TD vAlign="top">
                <%# databinder.Eval(Container.DataItem, "ContactName") %></TD>
        </TR>
        <TR>
            <TD><B>Title</B></TD>
            <TD vAlign="top">
                <%# databinder.Eval(Container.DataItem, "ContactTitle") %></TD>
        </TR>
        <TR>
            <TD><B>Country</B></TD>
            <TD vAlign="top">
                <%# databinder.Eval(Container.DataItem, "Country") %></TD>
        </TR>
        <TR>
            <TD><B>Phone #</B></TD>
            <TD vAlign="top">
                <%# databinder.Eval(Container.DataItem, "Phone") %></TD>
        </TR>
```

```
    <TR>
        <TD><B>FAX #</B></TD>
        <TD vAlign="top">
            <%# databinder.Eval(Container.DataItem, "FAX") %></TD>
                </TR>
    </TABLE>
</SelectedItemTemplate>
```

Again, notice that the button's `CommandName` property is `Edit`. Locate the tag of the DataList control and insert the attribute as follows:

```
OnEditCommand="ItemEdit"
```

Then implement the `ItemEdit()` subroutine. This subroutine applies the `EditItemTemplate` to the item specified with the `EditItemIndex` property of the DataList control. Then it fills the `DSCustomers` DataSet as usual and binds the control to it.

```
Sub ItemEdit(ByVal sender As Object, ByVal e As DataListCommandEventArgs)
    DataList1.EditItemIndex = e.Item.ItemIndex
    DACustomers.Fill(DsCustomers1, "Customers")
    DataList1.DataBind()
End Sub
```

As you can guess, you must now create yet another template for the item being edited. This template should display the fields of the selected item on TextBox controls, so that users can edit them. The Edit template should also contain buttons to commit or cancel the edit operation, as shown in Figure 16.12.

Editing the Selected Item

The EditItemTemplate is a bit more complicated than the other two, because it involves TextBox controls. To edit an item, you must copy its fields onto text boxes, let the user edit them, and provide the means to end the edit operation. An edit operation can end either by committing the edits to the database, or by canceling it, with the usual Update and Cancel buttons.

To create the EditItemTemplate, open the template editor and add a Label and TextBox control on the EditItemTemplate's section. You don't have to align them now or get their sizes right. It's much easier to create a table in HTML and embed the TextBox controls into the table's cells. You'll use the Label control to display the customer's ID (you won't allow the user to edit the IDs) and a TextBox control for each of the remaining fields. In addition, you must copy the values of the fields onto the text boxes so that users can edit them. Listing 16.8 shows the HTML code of the EditItemTemplate.

LISTING 16.8: THE DATALIST CONTROL'S EDITITEMTEMPLATE

```
<EditItemTemplate>
<TABLE>
    <TR>
        <TD><B>Customer ID</B></TD>
```

```
        <TD><B>
            <asp:Label id=lblID runat="server" Width="114px"
                    Text='<%# container.dataitem("CustomerID") %>'>
            </asp:Label>
            <asp:Button id="Button3" runat="server" Width="45px"
                    CommandName="Update" Text="OK">
            </asp:Button>     
            <asp:Button id="Button4" runat="server" Width="45px"
                    CommandName="Cancel" Text="Cancel">
            </asp:Button></B>
        </TD>
    </TR>
    <TR>
        <TD><B>Company</B></TD>
        <TD vAlign="top">
            <asp:TextBox id=txtCompany runat="server" Width="235px"
                    Text='<%# container.dataitem("CompanyName") %>'>
            </asp:TextBox></TD>
    </TR>
    <TR>
        <TD><B>Contact</B></TD>
        <TD vAlign="top">
            <asp:TextBox id=txtContact runat="server" Width="235px"
                    Text='<%# container.DataItem("ContactName") %>'>
            </asp:TextBox></TD>
    </TR>
    <TR>
        <TD><B>Title</B></TD>
        <TD vAlign="top">
            <asp:TextBox id=txtTitle runat="server" Width="235px"
                    Text='<%# container.DataItem("ContactTitle") %>'>
            </asp:TextBox></TD>
    </TR>
    <TR>
        <TD><B>Country</B></TD>
        <TD vAlign="top">
            <asp:TextBox id=txtCountry runat="server" Width="235px"
                    Text='<%# container.DataItem("Country") %>'>
            </asp:TextBox></TD>
    </TR>
    <TR>
        <TD><B>Phone #</B></TD>
        <TD vAlign="top">
            <asp:TextBox id=txtPhone runat="server" Width="235px"
                    Text='<%# container.DataItem("Phone") %>'>
            </asp:TextBox></TD>
    </TR>
    <TR>
```

```
            <TD><B>FAX #</B></TD>
            <TD vAlign="top">
                <asp:TextBox id=txtFAX runat="server" Width="235px"
                            Text='<%# container.DataItem("Fax") %>'>
                </asp:TextBox></TD>
        </TR>
    </TABLE>
</EditItemTemplate>
```

All the elements are table cells, so that they'll be nicely aligned on the browser. The two buttons, Update and Cancel, invoke the `Update()` and `Cancel()` subroutines or event delegates, which are serviced by the `UpdateItem()` and `CancelEdit()` subroutines in the code. Add the following two attributes to the DataList control's tag:

```
OnCancelCommand="CancelEdit" onUpdateCommand="UpdateItem"
```

Notice the expression that assigns each field's value to the `Text` property of the TextBox control. This time we're not using the `DataBinder` object, but the `Container` object. The `Container` object represents the control that contains the TextBox control, which is an item of the DataList. As such, it exposes the `DataItem` property, and you can request the value of any field by calling the `DataItem` property passing the field's name as argument.

Updating the Database

The last step is to commit the changes made by the client to the database. When the Update button is clicked, the `UpdateItem()` subroutine is invoked on the server, and you must supply the code for this event handler as well. In the `UpdateItem()` subroutine, you must extract the new values of the fields from the text boxes, build the appropriate SQL statement, and execute it through an SqlCommand object. The text boxes belong to the current item, and you can retrieve them with the `FindControl()` method. The following expression returns a reference to the `txtCompany` TextBox control:

```
e.Item.FindControl("txtCompany")
```

where `e` is the subroutine's second argument. Then you can cast this object to the TextBox type and call its `Text` property. The control's value is then used to create an UPDATE statement. Listing 16.9 presents the complete `UpdateItem()` subroutine:

LISTING 16.9: COMMITTING THE EDITS TO THE DATABASE

```
Sub UpdateItem(ByVal sender As Object, ByVal e As DataListCommandEventArgs)
    Dim cmd As New System.Text.StringBuilder()
    Dim objTBox As TextBox
    cmd.Append("UPDATE Customers SET ")
    objTBox = CType(e.Item.FindControl("txtCompany"), TextBox)
    cmd.Append(" CompanyName = '" & objTBox.Text & "'")
    objTBox = CType(e.Item.FindControl("txtContact"), TextBox)
    cmd.Append(", ContactName = '" & objTBox.Text & "'")
```

```
        objTBox = CType(e.Item.FindControl("txtTitle"), TextBox)
        cmd.Append(", ContactTitle = '" & objTBox.Text & "'")
        objTBox = CType(e.Item.FindControl("txtCountry"), TextBox)
        cmd.Append(", Country = '" & objTBox.Text & "'")
        objTBox = CType(e.Item.FindControl("txtPhone"), TextBox)
        cmd.Append(", Phone = '" & objTBox.Text & "'")
        objTBox = CType(e.Item.FindControl("txtFAX"), TextBox)
        cmd.Append(", FAX = '" & objTBox.Text & "'")
        cmd.Append("WHERE CustomerID='" & _
                    CType(e.Item.FindControl("lblID"), Label).Text & "'")
    SqlConnection1.Open()
    SqlCommand1.CommandText = cmd.ToString
    SqlCommand1.CommandType = CommandType.Text
    SqlCommand1.ExecuteNonQuery()
    SqlConnection1.Close()
    DataList1.EditItemIndex = -1
    DataList1.SelectedIndex = -1
    DACustomers.Fill(DsCustomers1)
    DataList1.DataBind()
End Sub
```

This code assumes that you have placed an instance of the SqlCommand object on the form. By using the Text properties of the controls, the code concatenates strings to create the UPDATE statement for the SqlCommand object. The cmd variable is the SqlCommand object's command (property CommandText) and it's executed with the ExecuteNonQuery() method, because the UPDATE statement doesn't return any rows. This method returns an integer value, which is the number of rows affected by the command, and this value should always be 1 for this example. If not, the update operation has failed.

After committing the changes to the current item, you can return the DataList control to its initial state by setting the EditItemIndex and SelectedItemIndex properties to −1. Run the project, change the values of a few customers, and check out the editing features of the DataList control.

The code in Listing 16.9 doesn't do anything about possible update errors. You should examine the value returned by the ExecuteNonQuery() method, which should be 1 (the SQL statement updates a single row in the Customers table). If it's 0, you know that the original row couldn't be changed (because a field has an invalid value, or the row itself has been removed from the table) and you should display another page with the appropriate message.

The CancelEdit() subroutine, finally, cancels the edits on the control. It doesn't execute any SQL statements against the database; it simply resets the EditItemIndex to −1 to cancel the edit operation and then places the current item into select mode, as shown in Listing 16.10.

LISTING 16.10: CANCELING AN EDIT OPERATION

```
Sub CancelEdit(ByVal sender As Object, ByVal e As DataListCommandEventArgs)
    DataList1.EditItemIndex = -1
    DataList1.SelectedIndex = e.Item.ItemIndex
```

```
        DACustomers.Fill(DsCustomers1)
        DataList1.DataBind()
    End Sub
```

Summary

In this chapter, you've learned how to use the two most flexible data-bound web controls. The DataGrid and DataList controls are nothing more than design tools that enable you to create elaborate HTML tables. Both the DataGrid and the DataList controls are rendered on the client as HTML tables and they interact with the user in a rather limited way.

In the following chapter, you'll see one more advanced use of the DataGrid control. You will build a WebService that can accept orders and you'll bind a DataGrid control to this service. This time, you won't use buttons to add one more item of the selected product to the cart; you'll allow users to edit a table with product names and prices and then submit their order to the database.

Chapter 17

Working with WebServices

- ◆ Building a WebService

- ◆ Building a data-bound WebService

WEBSERVICES ARE THE single most advertised, and most promising, feature of the .NET platform. A *WebService* is a class that resides on a web server, and its methods can be called over the Internet. Unlike a web application, however, the methods of this class don't return an HTML page. Instead, they return one or more values, packaged as XML documents. As a result, any application that can handle XML can call these methods and use their results. The idea is that every application, no matter its language or operating system, can access WebServices; conversely, any web server can expose functionality in the form of WebServices. What makes it all possible is that everything is based on a (soon to become) universal standard, the XML standard.

You don't have to develop WebServices for a typical application, and there are hardly any WebServices around to use from within your code. Companies that provide stock quote services will most likely expose their services as WebServices, but the Web isn't going to flood with WebServices. However, many corporations will expose WebServices to share information with other corporations.

When would you use a WebService? WebServices are another step, probably the most important one so far, toward providing software services. Consider for a moment why you're spending so much time on the Internet today. You locate information, which arrives at your computer in the form of static pages (text and images). You can either read the information or save it to a local file and read it later. The form of information that arrives to the client computer is suitable for consumption by humans, but you can't reuse it from within your applications. You can write applications to parse HTML documents and extract the information you're interested in, but if the structure of the page changes, you'll have to modify your applications accordingly.

By using a WebService, you can provide information in a form that can be easily reused by another application. You can also charge for this information, if there are people willing to pay for it—or if the information you provide is worth any money. Different applications can access your WebService and use the same information in different ways. Initially, WebServices will be used almost exclusively in business-to-business (B2B) scenarios.

Later in this chapter, you'll write a WebService to accept orders over the Web. This WebService consists of a method that provides product information (product IDs, names, and prices) and a method that accepts an order made up of product IDs and quantities. The consumers of this WebService are free to set up their own interface, which can be incorporated into their applications. The client applications don't access your database directly; they can retrieve only the information you provide and can submit information to the server. They don't have to know how you store your data nor do they have to maintain a local list of the products. They can retrieve your products at any time and submit an order. Some client applications might be Windows applications; some others might be web applications. Their interfaces will be totally different, but they all provide the same functionality, use the same data (the data you post through your webservices), and place orders with your company.

Building a WebService

Building a WebService with Visual Studio is as simple as writing a class. The class inherits from System.Web.Services, and this base class includes all the plumbing necessary to make the functions (methods) of the class available on the Web. Basically, if you can write a function, you can write a web method; it's that simple. The difference between a class and a WebService is that the members of the WebService can be called remotely, over the Internet.

Building a Web Application is almost trivial with Visual Studio .NET. You start a new project of the WebService type and enter the definition of one or more functions. Then you prefix the names of the functions with the following keyword to turn them into web methods:

```
<WebMethod()>
```

The following is a web method that translates a sentence from German into English (provided you have the appropriate software installed on your computer):

```
<WebMethod()> Public Function TranslateGE(ByVal strGerman As String) As String
' call the appropriate methods to translate the argument into English
' and store the translated text into the string strenglish
Return(strenglish)
End Function
```

Any client application that has access to the Internet can call this method, passing a string in German, and retrieve the same text in English. Instead of translating the text, we'll simply change the order of the words in the strGerman argument. Let's build the WebService that exposes the TranslateGE() method and then test it. Let's say that TranslateGE() is a method of the Translate WebService, which belongs to the MyServices project. After you post this service to your web server, others can access it through their browsers by specifying a URL such as the following:

```
http://www.yourservices.net/MyServices/Translate.asmx/
TranslateGE?strGerman=Say+it+in+German
```

Note that the argument to the method (the string to be translated) is URL encoded. MyServices is the name of the WebService and Translate is the name of the web method. To access the same method through a Windows application, you must add a reference to this service and then access its methods as you would with any other class. You'll see how this is done shortly.

Creating the *SimpleWebService* Project

Create a new WebService project and name it **SimpleWebService**. WebServices don't have a visible interface, so the designer's surface is empty. You can place components on it, such as DataAdapters and DataSets, and use them in your code. However, you can't use any components with a visual interface. The Service1 item will be automatically added to the project, and this is a class that contains all the code that implements the web methods. This is actually the name of the WebService; it's named after the class and not after the project. Notice that a project can contain multiple WebServices, each one implemented by a different class.

Double-click the designer's surface to open the code window. Then enter the code of the TranslateGE() web method. The WebService template contains a sample web method, which is commented out; you can delete or ignore it. Then enter the code shown earlier; the code of the new WebService is shown in Listing 17.1 (we have omitted the code generated automatically by the WebServices Designer, which you need not even look at).

LISTING 17.1: YOUR FIRST WEBSERVICE

```
Imports System.Web.Services

Public Class Service1
    Inherits System.Web.Services.WebService
    <WebMethod()> Public Function TranslateGE(ByVal strGerman As String) As String
        ' call the appropriate methods to translate the argument into English
        ' and store the translated text into the string strenglish
        Dim strEnglish As String
        strEnglish = StrReverse(strGerman)
        Return (strenglish)
    End Function
End Class
```

NOTE   *The class's name is* Service1. *If you want to change its name, you must rename the* Service1 *item in the Solution Explorer's window, as well as the name of the class in the code.*

TESTING THE WEBSERVICE

Now press F5 to run the WebService. The WebService doesn't have a visible interface. How do you test it? The CLR will create a small site that enables you to test each method. If you press F5 to run the project, Internet Explorer will come up, displaying the page shown in Figure 17.1. This page displays all the methods of the WebService you're testing and a warning to the effect that it uses the default namespace. After you decide to make the WebService available to others on the Internet, you should change the namespace to something like http://*yourServer*.com/ (where *yourServer* is the name of the Web Server where the code resides). Because the name of the WebService's name is prefixed by the URL of the server on which it resides, many companies can create identically named methods, but clients will always access the correct service. In other words, you needn't do anything special to make your WebService's name globally unique.

FIGURE 17.1

Viewing the methods of a WebService in Internet Explorer

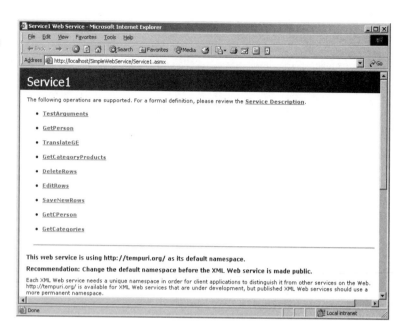

The page shown in Figure 17.1 contains additional methods, which you will add to the WebService shortly. On your screen you will see only the `TranslateGE()` method. Click this hyperlink and you will see the page shown in Figure 17.2, which prompts you to enter the `strGerman` argument (the string to be processed). Enter a string in the text box and click the Invoke button to call the method. If the method accepted more arguments, they'd all be listed here.

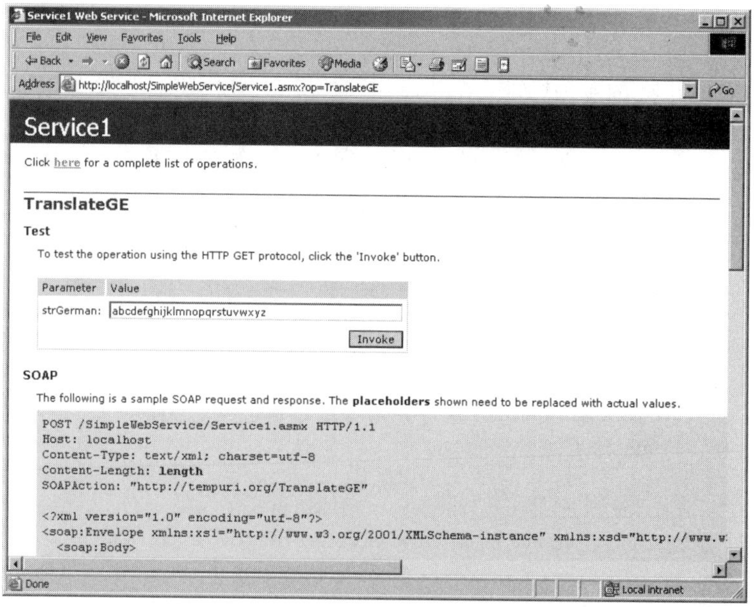

FIGURE 17.2

Supplying the value for the argument of the `TranslateGE()` method

The result will be returned in XML format, as shown here:

```
<?xml version="1.0" encoding="utf-8" ?>
<string xmlns="http://tempuri.org/">zyxwvutsrqponmlkjihgfedcba</string>
```

The actual value of the result appears in bold. It's the string surrounded by the two `<string>` tags. Everything between the two tags is the string returned by the web method. You can try throwing off Internet Explorer by supplying the value `</string>` backward. If you pass the value `>gnirts<` to the method, you'll get back the following response:

```
<?xml version="1.0" encoding="utf-8" ?>
<string xmlns="http://tempuri.org/"></string></string>
```

Internet Explorer isn't thrown off by the two identical delimiters. To understand why, open the View menu and choose Source to see the HTML document sent to the client:

```
<?xml version="1.0" encoding="utf-8"?>
<string xmlns="http://tempuri.org/">&lt;string&gt;</string>
```

The string is HTML encoded, and the browser had no problem figuring out the text from the tags. Even though the result is transmitted to the client in XML format, there's nothing special you have to do to extract it.

Using the WebService in Your Apps

Let's write a Windows application that uses the WebService. Start a Windows Application project and design a form with a single button on it. Name the project **Test WebService** or something similar.

First, you must include in your new project a reference to the `SimpleWebService` WebService. Open the Project menu and select Add Web Reference. You will see the Add Web Reference dialog box, as shown in Figure 17.3. On the left pane there are three hyperlinks: one to the UDDI (Universal Description Discovery Integration) Directory, another one to Microsoft's UDDI, and a third one to the Web References on the local machine. The first two links lead to directories of WebServices on Microsoft sites. The first one is intended for real, practical WebServices and the second one for testing purposes. You can post your own WebServices either to the test directory or to the UDDI directory with the "real" services, if you think it's of interest to other developers.

Your task is to test the newly created WebService. Click the last hyperlink and you will see a list of all WebServices installed on the local machine (you will most likely see a single service name in the right pane of the dialog box). Select the `SimpleWebService` item in the right pane and you will see two new hyperlinks on the right pane, as shown in Figure 17.4. Click the View Documentation hyperlink to view a list of the names of the web methods provided by the `SimpleWebService`. Figure 17.4 shows a number of web methods, which we'll explain in the following section. At this point, click the Add Reference button on the dialog box to add a reference to the specific WebService to the current project.

FIGURE 17.3

The Add Web
Reference dialog box

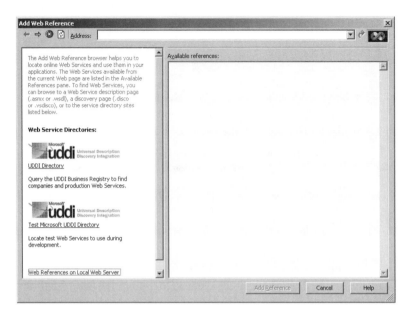

FIGURE 17.3

The Add Web
Reference dialog box

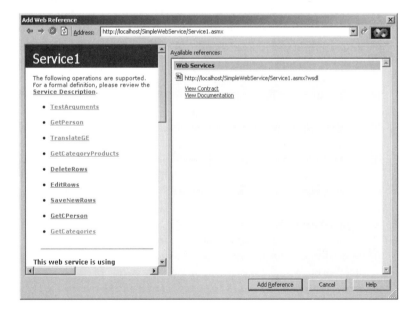

FIGURE 17.4

Viewing the
methods exposed
by a WebService

A new item will be added to the Solution Explorer, the Web References item. Under that, you will see the `localhost` item, and under that, the `Service1` item. Then switch to the code window and enter the following statements in the button's click event handler:

```
Private Sub Button1_Click(ByVal sender As System.Object, _
```

```
                               ByVal e As System.EventArgs) Handles Button1.Click
        Dim WS As localhost.Service1
        MsgBox(WS.TranslateGE("Enter your German text here"))
    End Sub
```

This code creates an instance of the WebService and then calls its `TranslateGE()` method. Run the project, and a few seconds later a message box with the "translated" (reversed) string will pop up. The Windows application contacts the web server, requests the URL of the `TranslateGE()` method, and retrieves the result. The result is returned to the client in XML format and it's presented to the application as a string. You don't have to deal with decoding the value; you don't even have to know what goes on behind the scenes. As far as your code goes, it's like calling a method of any class on the local machine. The same will happen regardless of the location of the web server on which the WebService is running. It could be the same machine (as in your tests), another server on your LAN, or any web server on the Internet.

Writing a fictitious WebService that does nothing really useful is fairly easy. As we mentioned earlier, writing a web method is as simple as writing a function. Before we move on to a practical web method that interacts with a database, let's experiment a little with passing arguments to and retrieving values from a web method. As with regular VB .NET functions, there are two ways to pass an argument to a web method: by value, which is the default mechanism, and by reference. If you want to pass multiple values from your web method to the caller, you can write a web method that accepts one or more arguments by reference and sets their values, and then you can read the values of the reference arguments in the client application's code. Web methods accept base data types as arguments, as well as arrays.

The web method in Listing 17.2 accepts three arguments: an integer, a date, and an array of integers. All three arguments are passed by reference, and the web method's code sets their values: it doubles the integer, adds three days to the Date argument, and negates all the elements of the array. The return value is a string.

LISTING 17.2: EXPERIMENTING WITH A WEB METHOD'S ARGUMENTS AND RETURN VALUES

```
<WebMethod()> Public Function TestArguments(ByRef arg1 As Integer, _
                        ByRef arg2 As Date, ByRef arg3() As Integer) As String
    arg1 = 2 * arg1
    arg2 = arg2.AddDays(3)
    Dim i As Integer
    For i = 0 To arg3.GetUpperBound(0)
        arg3(i) = -arg3(i)
    Next
    Return "Done!"
End Function
```

On the client, you can use the statements indicated in Listing 17.3 to call this method and display the values of the arguments after the return of the web method. `TestArguments()` is a method of the `SimpleWebService` project.

LISTING 17.3: USING THE TESTARGUMENTS ( ) WEB METHOD IN A WINDOWS APPLICATION

```
Private Sub Button2_Click(ByVal sender As System.Object, _
                          ByVal e As System.EventArgs) Handles Button2.Click
    Dim WS As New localhost.Service1()
    Dim ints(9) As Integer
    Dim i As Integer

    For i = 0 To 9
        ints(i) = i
    Next

    Dim D As Date = Now()
    Dim Int As Integer = 999
    Dim Str As String
    Str = WS.TestArguments(Int, D, ints)
    Console.WriteLine("Return value = " & Str)
    Console.WriteLine("Integer argument = " & Int)
    Console.WriteLine("Date argument = " & D)
    For i = 0 To 9
        Console.Write(ints(i) & vbTab)
    Next
End Sub
```

If you run the test application again and click the Call TestArguments Web Method button, these lines will appear in the Output window:

```
Return value = Done!
Integer argument = 1998
Date argument = 11/29/2001 6:38:46 PM
0    -1   -2   -3   -4   -5   -6   -7   -8   -9
```

REFERENCE AND VALUE ARGUMENTS

If you want to retrieve multiple values from the web method, you can pass arguments by reference. The web method will marshal back the arguments passed by reference, which are presumably set in the method's code. Notice that the ByRef and ByVal keywords work a little differently with web methods than they do with regular VB .NET functions. All arguments are passed by value; the WebService's code can't access the memory of the client computer and directly alter the values of the arguments. Instead, it marshals back the values of the arguments passed by reference. In other words, the ByRef and ByVal keywords are used as tags, telling the WebService whether it should pass the arguments' values back to the caller.

Arrays, for example, are passed to regular functions by reference even if you specify the ByVal keyword in front of their names. When a function changes the elements of an array passed as an argument, the caller sees the modified values of these elements. If you pass an array to a web method by value, the WebService won't marshal back the array to the caller. Change the keyword ByRef in front of the `arg3` argument of the `TestArguments()` method to `ByVal` and run the client application. The values you will see in the Output window will be the same as the ones you passed to the method (this wouldn't happen with a VB .NET function).

USING STRUCTURES WITH WEB METHODS

Beyond simple data types, web methods also support custom structures. Of course, the fields of the structure used by the web method must be known to the client application. Let's say the WebService contains the following structure:

```
Public Structure Person
    Dim Name As String
    Dim Age As Integer
    Dim SSN As String
    Dim BDate As Date
End Structure
```

This declaration must appear in the WebService's file, outside any method. Using this structure in a web method is straightforward: you assign values to its fields and return an object of this type. The following web method does exactly that:

```
<WebMethod()> Public Function GetPerson() As Person
    Dim p As Person
    p.Name = "My Name"
    p.Age = 35
    p.SSN = "555-66-0009"
    p.BDate = #9/9/1999#
    Return (p)
End Function
```

The structure is exposed by the WebService because it's public, which means that you can declare a variable of the `localhost.Person` type to represent a `Person` object. Then you can call the `GetPerson()` method, assign its return value to the proper variable, and access the values of the structure's fields as properties. The following statements call the `GetPerson()` method and display the fields it returns in the Output window:

```
Dim WS As New localhost.Service1()
Dim p As localhost.Person

p = WS.GetPerson
Console.WriteLine("NAME = " & p.Name)
Console.WriteLine("AGE  = " & p.Age)
Console.WriteLine("SSN  = " & p.SSN)
Console.WriteLine("BDATE= " & p.BDate)
```

If you test the WebService by pressing F5 and invoke the `GetPerson()` method from the test page, you will see the following XML description of the result:

```
<?xml version="1.0" encoding="utf-8" ?>
```

```
- <Person xmlns:xsi="http://www.w3.org/2001/XMLSchema-instance"
xmlns:xsd="http://www.w3.org/2001/XMLSchema" xmlns="http://tempuri.org/">
  <Name>My Name</Name>
  <Age>35</Age>
  <SSN>555-66-0009</SSN>
  <BDate>1999-09-09T00:00:00.0000000-04:00</BDate>
  </Person>
```

This is a simple schema description. An object variable set to this schema exposes the four attributes as properties. Notice that you don't have to parse the XML document in your client application's code to extract the names of the attributes and their values. The CLR uses XML behind the scenes, and you need not even be aware of this.

If you're wondering how the client application knows about the `Person` structure, the answer is in the `Service1.wsdl` file. If you open this file (you must first activate the Show All Files button at the top of the Project Explorer), you will find the following lines:

```
<s:complexType name="Person">
  <s:sequence>
    <s:element minOccurs="0" maxOccurs="1" name="Name" type="s:string" />
    <s:element minOccurs="1" maxOccurs="1" name="Age" type="s:int" />
    <s:element minOccurs="0" maxOccurs="1" name="SSN" type="s:string" />
    <s:element minOccurs="1" maxOccurs="1" name="BDate" type="s:dateTime" />
  </s:sequence>
</s:complexType>
```

The WSDL file is read into the client application when you add a reference to the WebService. Then the CLR creates a class for you, which resides in the file `Reference.vb`. To view this file's contents, expand the `localhost` branch under Web References in the Solution Explorer and then expand the `Reference.map` branch. The class generated by the CLR is shown next:

```
Public Class Person

    '<remarks/>
    Public Name As String

    '<remarks/>
    Public Age As Integer

    '<remarks/>
    Public SSN As String

    '<remarks/>
    Public BDate As Date
End Class
```

Even a trivial structure like the one used in this example can be also implemented as a class. To complete the demonstration, we've added the `CPerson` class to the `SimpleWebService`. The implementation of the `CPerson` class is just as trivial:

```
Public Class CPerson
```

```
        Public Name As String
        Public Age As Integer
        Public SSN As String
        Public BDate As Date
    End Class
```

The current implementation of WebServices doesn't support properties. In other words, there's no `WebProperty` attribute, and you can't add property procedures in your WebService.

The Properties of the `<WebMethod>` Attribute

The `<WebMethod>` attribute supports a few properties. These properties must appear in the angle brackets of the `WebMethod` qualifier as a name/value pair, and multiple attributes must be separated with commas:

```
<WebMethod() Description = "This is a test WebService", BufferResponse = False>
```

The properties of the `<WebMethod>` attribute are the following:

BufferResponse   A Boolean value that determines whether to buffer the method's response.

CacheDuration   The duration (in seconds) to keep the method's response in the cache. The default value is 0 (the result isn't buffered). A method that returns its argument translated into another language shouldn't be cached, because this method will be called with a different argument every time. A method that returns the products in a specific category, on the other hand, should be cached, because it will be called many times before a new product is added.

Description   A string with additional information about the web method. The method's description appears in the test pages created by the CLR when you test the WebService.

EnableSession   A Boolean value that enables or disables session state. It's True by default. Turn it off for a marginal performance improvement if you don't need to maintain state. When this attribute is True, the web method maintains session IDs for each client accessing the method.

MessageName   Web methods can't be overloaded like regular functions and classes. If you have a class with overloaded functions that you want to convert to a Web class, you can still use the same name for multiple functions, but you must provide an alternate name, which will be different for each function. The alternate name is specified with the `MessageName` property. The clients see the method's `MessageName` and, in effect, each method in the WebService has a different name.

TransactionOption   The `TransactionOption` attribute can be one of following values, which determine whether the web method participates in a transaction: `Disabled`, `NotSupported`, `Supported`, `Required`, or `RequiresNew`. Web methods can be only the root objects in a transaction, so both the `Required` and `RequiresNew` options create a new transaction. The other three settings do not create a transaction.   The `TransactionOption` is used with distributed transactions—such as updating two different databases, or updating a single database and placing a message into a transactional message queue. The database's built-in transactional capabilities (T-SQL transactions for SQL Server, for example) or ADO.NET transactions should be adequate for all but rare occasions, and you shouldn't have to use the `TransactionOption` attribute on a web method.

So far you've seen the basics of building a WebService and how to use it in your applications. In the following section, you'll build a couple of data-bound WebServices to move data in and out of a database. These services can be used with remote clients running Windows and web applications.

Building a Data-Bound WebService

In this section, you'll create a WebService that returns DataSets, and later you'll revise it so that it can accept DataSets from the client and update the database. It's quite simple to retrieve data from a database and pass it to the client as a DataSet. Updating the database is a bit more complicated, because there's no wizard to generate any code for you. You must select the modified rows (or the deleted, or the new ones), store them to a new DataSet, and pass it to the WebService as an argument. In the WebService's code, you must perform the updates and then pass the DataSet with the error information to the client. If a row fails to update the database, you can't display a message from within the WebService. You must reject the changes and send back the DataSet to the client, and the client application will handle these rows (most likely, with the user's interaction).

Among the data types a web method recognizes is the DataSet. You can write a function that returns a DataSet and turn it into a web method. The DataSet will be encoded in XML format, which means that it's usable by any client (Windows or otherwise). Using the DataSet with Windows applications, however, is no different from what you've learned so far.

To retrieve data from a database, the WebService must execute an SQL statement against the database. Any parameters must be passed to the service as arguments, and it will return to the calling application a DataSet object. The DataSet might contain multiple tables, and even relations between them. The WebService you'll build in this section exposes two methods, the `GetCategories()` and `GetCategoryProducts()` methods. As you might have guessed, the first method returns the categories of the Northwind database, and the second method returns the products in a specific category, whose ID is passed to the WebService as an argument.

The two methods of the WebService are simple functions that return a DataSet object. You can implement the two methods entirely in code, or use the visual database tools to set up the appropriate Connection and DataAdapter objects. Let's add on to the `SimpleWebService` project; you can also create a new WebService project from scratch.

Return to the `SimpleWebService` project, open the Server Explorer, locate the tables of the Northwind database, and drop the `Categories` and `Products` tables on the design surface of the WebService. Rename the DataAdapter objects to **DACategories** and **DAProducts** and configure them. The `DACategories` adapter uses the following SQL statement to retrieve the category IDs and names:

```
SELECT CategoryID, CategoryName
FROM   Categories
```

Likewise, the `DAProducts` adapter uses the following SQL statement to retrieve the products of a category, which is specified with the `@category` parameter:

```
SELECT ProductID, ProductName, UnitPrice
FROM   Products WHERE (CategoryID = @category)
```

You should let the wizard generate the `INSERT`, `DELETE`, and `UPDATE` statements for the `Products` table. In the following section, you'll build a client that enables the user to edit the rows of the table and you'll pass the edited DataSet to another method of the WebService, which will update the underlying table in the database.

For now, create two DataSets, one for each DataAdapter, and add them to the project. The first DataSet, **DSCategories**, should contain the `Categories` table, and the second one, **DSProducts**, should contain the `Products` table (even though it contains a small section of the table). With the DataAdapters and the DataSets in place, you can easily implement the `GetCategories()` and `GetCategoryProducts()`methods, as shown in Listing 17.4.

LISTING 17.4: THE GETCATEGORIES ( ) AND GETCATEGORYPRODUCTS ( ) METHODS

```
<WebMethod()> Public Function GetCategories() As DataSet
    DACategories.Fill(DsCategories1)
    Return (DsCategories1)
End Function

<WebMethod()> Public Function GetCategoryProducts(ByVal categoryID As Integer) _
            As DataSet
    DAProducts.SelectCommand.Parameters("@category").Value = categoryID
    DAProducts.Fill(DsProducts1)
    Return (DsProducts1)
End Function
```

To test the new WebService, just press F5 to run the application. Visual Studio .NET starts Internet Explorer and displays the usual test page with the names of all methods of the WebService. This page isn't part of the project; it was generated on the fly by Visual Studio .NET for testing purposes. If you select the GetCategories hyperlink on the first page, you will see the XML description of the DataSet with the categories. If you select the GetCategoryProducts hyperlink, you will see another page that prompts you to enter the ID of a category. Enter a category's ID (a value from 1 to 7) and then click the Invoke button. A new Internet Explorer window opens, and you will see on it the XML description of the DataSet. This description consists of two sections, the schema section and the diffgram section. The schema section contains information about the structure of each row in the Products table.

The *diffgram* is the XML representation of the data. The data section is called the diffgram because it contains the initial data, but after editing the DataSet it will store the modified data as well. The following lines are two product descriptions:

```
- <Products diffgr:id="Products5" msdata:rowOrder="4">
  <ProductID>59</ProductID>
  <ProductName>Raclette Courdavault</ProductName>
  <UnitPrice>55</UnitPrice>
  </Products>
- <Products diffgr:id="Products6" msdata:rowOrder="5">
  <ProductID>60</ProductID>
  <ProductName>Camembert Pierrot</ProductName>
  <UnitPrice>34</UnitPrice>
  </Products>
```

If you change the price of the first product to 55.95, the corresponding entry in the diffgram will become:

```
<Products diffgr:id="Products6" msdata:rowOrder="5" diffgr:hasChanges="modified">
<ProductID>59</ProductID>
<ProductName>Raclette Courdavault</ProductName>
<UnitPrice>55.95</UnitPrice>
</Products>
```

The new tag contains an attribute indicating that the row has changed. Additionally, another element has been added to the diffgram:

```
<diffgr:before>
  <Products diffgr:id="Products6" msdata:rowOrder="5"
                xmlns="http://www.tempuri.org/DSProducts.xsd">
    <ProductID>59</ProductID>
    <ProductName>Raclette Courdavault</ProductName>
    <UnitPrice>55</UnitPrice>
  </Products>
</diffgr:before>
```

The `before` element contains the row's original values. When this DataSet is submitted to the server, it contains enough information for a DataAdapter object to update the underlying tables. If the operation fails, the DataSet can be restored to its original state.

You have tested the methods of your new WebService, and they behave as expected. In the following section, you'll consume them in a Windows application.

How about editing the DataSet on the client? As you will see in the following section, it's possible to edit the data on the client and then submit the changes to the server. Because the DataSet retains the original values of its fields, you can write a method that accepts the modified DataSet and call its `Update()` method to update the underlying table. Chances are that a small percentage of the DataSet's rows will be modified, so you should write a separate web method for the edited rows, another one for the deleted rows, and a third one for the added rows. This way, you will not move the unchanged rows to the server.

You must construct three new methods: the `SaveNewRows()`, `DeleteRows()`, and `EditRows()` web methods. Their code is quite simple. Each method accepts a DataSet with the appropriate rows (the new, deleted, and edited rows) of the original DataSet and calls the `Update()` method of the corresponding DataAdapter. The `ContinueUpdateOnError` property is True (the default value is False), so that the `Update` method will continue updating the underlying rows even if some of the updates will fail. See Listing 17.5.

LISTING 17.5: THE SAVENEWROWS ( ), DELETEROWS ( ), AND EDITROWS ( ) WEB METHODS

```
<WebMethod()> Public Function SaveNewRows(ByVal DS As DataSet) _
                    As DataSet
    DAProducts.Update(DS)
    Dim row As DataRow
```

```
        For Each row In DS.Tables("Products").Rows
            If row.HasErrors Then
                row.RejectChanges()
            Else
                row.AcceptChanges()
            End If
        Next
        Return DS
    End Function

    <WebMethod()> Public Function EditRows(ByVal DS As DataSet) As DataSet
        DAProducts.Update(DS)
        Dim row As DataRow
        For Each row In DS.Tables("Products").Rows
            If row.HasErrors Then
                row.RejectChanges()
            Else
                row.AcceptChanges()
            End If
        Next
        Return DS
    End Function

    <WebMethod()> Public Function DeleteRows(ByVal DS As DataSet) _
                        As DataSet
        DAProducts.Update(DS)
        Dim row As DataRow
        For Each row In DS.Tables("Products").Rows
            If row.HasErrors Then
                row.RejectChanges()
            Else
                row.AcceptChanges()
            End If
        Next
        Return DS
    End Function
```

The code attempts to update all the rows. Then it goes through the rows in the DataSet and examines their HasErrors property. Depending on the value of this property, the code calls either the AcceptChanges() or the RejectChanges() method. The rows of the DS DataSet that have errors are restored to their original values. This DataSet is then returned to the client application, where the errors will be handled.

CONSUMING THE WEBSERVICE

The pages generated by Visual Studio for testing a new WebService's methods are quite convenient, but this isn't how you use WebServices, obviously. A WebService can be used in a Windows application to exchange information with a web server, or in a web application to interact with a web server. To consume a WebService from within either type of application, you follow the same steps:

1. Add a reference to the WebService. This means that the server on which the WebService is running must be accessible, so that your project can retrieve information about the WebService's members.

2. Create an instance of the WebService in your code by declaring a variable of the appropriate type. To the application, the WebService is like another class that exposes methods. It just happens that the class's code is executed on another machine, and your application contacts it through the Internet.

To test the data-bound methods of the `SimpleWebService` project, you'll add another form to the `TestSimpleWebService` project. The new form is called `TestForm2`, and you must change the properties of the test project to make the new form the Startup object for the project. The new test form is shown in Figure 17.5.

FIGURE 17.5

Testing the
data-bound
methods of the
`SimpleWebService`
project

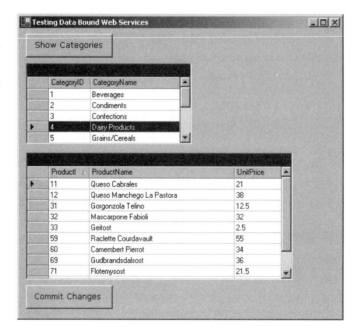

First, declare the following variables: `WS` and `DS`. `WS` represents the WebService—you need it to access the WebService's methods—and `DS` represents a DataSet. You'll use this variable to store the data you want to send to the server.

```
Dim WS As New localhost.Service1()
Dim DS As DataSet
```

Then enter the following code behind the Show Categories button. This button calls the `GetCategories()` web method and then uses the DataSet returned by the method to populate the top DataGrid control.

```
Private Sub Button1_Click(ByVal sender As System.Object, _
                          ByVal e As System.EventArgs) Handles Button1.Click
    DataGrid1.DataSource = WS.GetCategories
    DataGrid1.DataMember = "Categories"
End Sub
```

To view the products in a specific category, click the category's row in the upper DataGrid and the lower one will be populated. The action of selecting a category is signaled to the application through the `CurrentCellChanged()` event, whose handler is shown in Listing 17.6. The code in this handler retrieves the value of the first cell in the selected row, which is the ID of the corresponding category. Then it passes it as an argument to the `GetCategoryProducts()` web method, which in turn returns a DataSet. You can configure the DataGrid control so that the first column is hidden, because IDs don't convey any useful information to the user. This DataSet becomes the data source for the lower DataGrid control.

LISTING 17.6: POPULATING THE GRID WITH THE PRODUCTS OF A SELECTED CATEGORY

```
Private Sub DataGrid1_CurrentCellChanged(ByVal sender As Object, _
            ByVal e As System.EventArgs) Handles DataGrid1.CurrentCellChanged
    Dim id As Integer
    id = DataGrid1.Item(DataGrid1.CurrentRowIndex, 0)
    DS = WS.GetCategoryProducts(id)
    DataGrid2.DataSource = DS
    DataGrid2.DataMember = "Products"
End Sub
```

After the products appear in the lower DataGrid, you can edit their names and prices. To commit the changes to the `Products` table in the database, you must create three different DataSets, with the modified, deleted, and added rows, and submit these DataSets to the server through the `EditRows()`, `SaveNewRows()`, and `DeleteRows()` methods, as shown in Listing 17.7.

LISTING 17.7: SUBMITTING THE MODIFIED ROWS TO THE SERVER

```
Private Sub Button2_Click(ByVal sender As System.Object, _
                          ByVal e As System.EventArgs) Handles Button2.Click
    Dim DSEdit As DataSet
    ' Uncomment the following two statements to save the Dataset's rows
    ' to a local XML file:
    'DS.WriteXml("c:\ProductDiffgram.xml", XmlWriteMode.DiffGram)
    'Exit Sub
    ' EDITED ROWS
    DSEdit = DS.GetChanges(DataRowState.Modified)
```

```
        Dim returnedDS As DataSet
        If Not DSEdit Is Nothing Then
            returnedDS = WS.EditRows(DSEdit)
        End If
        AcceptRejectRows(returnedDS)
        '   NEW ROWS
        Dim DSNew As DataSet
        DSNew = DS.GetChanges(DataRowState.Added)
        If Not DSNew Is Nothing Then
            returnedDS = WS.SaveNewRows(DSEdit)
        End If
        AcceptRejectRows(returnedDS)
        '   DELETED ROWS
        Dim DSDel As DataSet
        DSDel = DS.GetChanges(DataRowState.Deleted)
        If Not DSDel Is Nothing Then
            returnedDS = WS.DeleteRows(DSEdit)
        End If
        AcceptRejectRows(returnedDS)
    End Sub
```

The few commented lines at the beginning of the code save the DataSet to an XML file. You can uncomment these lines to see what the DataSets you submit to the server look like. You can click the update button as soon as the DataGrid control is loaded with the products of the selected category. No changes will be submitted to the server, but the XML representation of the DataSet will be saved to the `ProductDiffgram.xml` file. After making a few changes, you can click the Commit Changes button to update the `Products` table and save the same XML file with the changes. Open the XML files generated by the code and look at the description of the DataSet.

The code creates three smaller DataSets with the edited, deleted, and added rows. Each time it calls the `GetChanges()` method of the DataSet object and passes the appropriate constant as an argument. If the corresponding DataSet contains one or more rows, it's submitted to the WebService through the appropriate web method. After sending each DataSet to the client, the `AcceptRejectRows()` subroutine is called to reject the changes that couldn't be committed to the database.

The `AcceptRejectRows()`subroutine, shown in Listing 17.8, goes through each row of the DataSet returned by the server and examines its `HasErrors` property. If True, it rejects the changes (restores the row's fields to the values that were originally read from the database) and displays a message in the Output window. The rows that fail to update are also marked on the DataGrid control with a red icon. If the row has no errors, the changes are accepted. If you don't reject the rows in error, the changes will be rejected by the database, but no visual indication will appear on the DataGrid control.

LISTING 17.8: REJECTING CHANGES THAT COULDN'T BE COMMITTED TO THE DATABASE

```
    Sub AcceptRejectRows(ByVal newDS As DataSet)
        Dim row As DataRow
        For Each row In newDS.Tables(0).Rows
```

```
            If Not row.HasErrors Then
                Console.WriteLine("Product " & row.Item("ProductID").ToString & _
                                " accepted")
                row.AcceptChanges()
            Else
                Console.WriteLine("Product " & row.Item("ProductID").ToString & _
                                " has errors")
                Dim col As DataColumn
                For Each col In row.GetColumnsInError
                    Console.WriteLine("   " & row.GetColumnError(col))
                Next
                row.RejectChanges()
            End If
        Next
        DS.Merge(newDS)
    End Sub
```

Placing an Order

OK, you can bind a DataGrid control to a DataSet to display data to the client. Let's build a new WebService that will accept orders over the Web. You aren't going to build a web application, just a WebService that other developers can use to build their own front ends, either as web applications or as Windows applications. The client that uses this WebService must provide an interface that will enable users to add quantities to the list of products and then submit the modified DataSet to the server, where a new order will be placed. You'll build a new WebService with two methods: the GetAllProducts() method and the NewOrder() method.

The GetAllProducts() method will return a DataSet with all the rows of the Products table. You don't need to send all the columns to the client, just the product's ID, name, and price. You also need a new column to store the quantities and allow the client application to edit this column's cells. We'll get to this soon, but let's start by adding a method to your WebService to accept the modified DataSet and insert a new order to the Northwind database.

As you know by now, a new order requires a new row in the Orders table, and a number of new rows (one for each product ordered) in the Order Details table. The row added to the Orders table will be automatically assigned an order ID. This numeric value is the foreign key in the Order Details table, and the ID of the new order must be repeated in every line of the order that will be placed in the Order Details table. You also need the ID of the customer that placed the order, which will be passed as an argument to the new method. You can add even more arguments, such as the shipping address, the ID of the salesperson, and so on. This example uses only the ID of the customer (the shipping address is the one stored in the Customers table).

The signature of the new method is as follows:

```
<WebMethod()> Public Function NewOrder(ByVal custID As String, _
                             ByVal details As DataSet) As Integer
```

The `custID` argument is a string argument with the customer's ID, and the `details` argument is a DataSet with the product IDs, names, prices, and quantities. The `NewOrder()` method inserts the proper rows to the `Orders` and `Order Details` tables. You already know how to add a new order to the Northwind database, but let us repeat the two stored procedures that add a new order and the order's details—see Listings 17.9 and 17.10.

LISTING 17.9: THE NEWORDER STORED PROCEDURE

```
CREATE PROCEDURE NewOrder
@custID nchar(5)
AS
INSERT INTO Orders (CustomerID, OrderDate) VALUES(@custID, GetDate())
RETURN (@@IDENTITY)
GO
```

LISTING 17.10: THE NEWORDERLINE STORED PROCEDURE

```
CREATE PROCEDURE NewOrderLine
@OrderID integer, @ProductID integer, @quantity integer
AS
DECLARE @ProductPrice money
SET @ProductPrice=(SELECT UnitPrice FROM Products WHERE ProductID=@ProductID)
INSERT INTO [Order Details] (OrderID, ProductID, Quantity, UnitPrice)
VALUES (@OrderID, @ProductID, @Quantity, @ProductPrice)
GO
```

To test the application, you must attach these two stored procedures to the Northwind database. The web method that adds a new order to the Northwind database is shown next. It adds all the necessary rows as a transaction, so that even if one of the insertions fails, the entire order will be rolled back. If the transaction is rolled back, an exception is also raised. This exception can be handled at the client with a structured exception handler. Alternately, you can comment out the line in the `NewOrder` web method that throws the exception and uncomment the following line that returns the value −1 for the web method. Then modify the client application so that it examines the value returned by the web method and displays the appropriate message. You will see shortly how to handle the exception at the client (it's shown in Listing 17.14). Listing 17.11 shows the code of the `NewOrder()` web method.

NOTE   *The connection string should be changed to match your individual environment.*

WARNING   *A username of* sa *and a blank password is not advisable in a production system.*

```
<WebMethod()> Public Function NewOrder(ByVal custID As String, _
                                   ByVal details As DataSet) As Integer
    Dim CMD As New SqlClient.SqlCommand()
    CMD.CommandText = "NewOrder"
    CMD.CommandType = CommandType.StoredProcedure
    Dim sqlParam As New SqlClient.SqlParameter()
    sqlParam.SqlDbType = SqlDbType.Char
    sqlParam.Size = 5
    sqlParam.ParameterName = "@CustID"
    sqlParam.Direction = ParameterDirection.Input
    CMD.Parameters.Add(sqlParam)

    sqlParam = New SqlClient.SqlParameter()
    sqlParam.ParameterName = "RETURN"
    sqlParam.SqlDbType = SqlDbType.Int
    sqlParam.Direction = ParameterDirection.ReturnValue
    CMD.Parameters.Add(sqlParam)
    CMD.Parameters("@custID").Value = custID

    Dim CNstr As String
    Dim CN As New SqlClient.SqlConnection()
    CNstr = "server=localhost;database=northwind;uid=sa;pwd=;"
    CN.ConnectionString = CNstr
    CN.Open()
    Dim DetailTrans As SqlClient.SqlTransaction
    DetailTrans = CN.BeginTransaction()
    CMD.Connection = CN
    CMD.Transaction = DetailTrans
    Dim orderID As Integer
    Dim totalItems As Integer
    Dim retValue As Integer
    Try
        CMD.ExecuteNonQuery()
        orderID = CMD.Parameters("RETURN").Value
        CMD.CommandText = "NewOrderLine"
        CMD.CommandType = CommandType.StoredProcedure
        CMD.Parameters.Clear()
        sqlParam = New SqlClient.SqlParameter()
        sqlParam.SqlDbType = SqlDbType.Int
        sqlParam.ParameterName = "@OrderID"
        sqlParam.Direction = ParameterDirection.Input
        CMD.Parameters.Add(sqlParam)

        sqlParam = New SqlClient.SqlParameter()
        sqlParam.SqlDbType = SqlDbType.Int
        sqlParam.ParameterName = "@ProductID"
```

```
                sqlParam.Direction = ParameterDirection.Input
                CMD.Parameters.Add(sqlParam)

                sqlParam = New SqlClient.SqlParameter()
                sqlParam.SqlDbType = SqlDbType.Int
                sqlParam.ParameterName = "@quantity"
                sqlParam.Direction = ParameterDirection.Input
                CMD.Parameters.Add(sqlParam)

                sqlParam = New SqlClient.SqlParameter()
                sqlParam.ParameterName = "RETURN"
                sqlParam.SqlDbType = SqlDbType.Int
                sqlParam.Direction = ParameterDirection.ReturnValue
                CMD.Parameters.Add(sqlParam)

                Dim row As DataRow
                For Each row In details.Tables(0).Rows
                    CMD.Parameters("@OrderID").Value = orderID
                    CMD.Parameters("@ProductID").Value = row.Item(0)
                    CMD.Parameters("@quantity").Value = row.Item(3)
                    ' this  variable isn't used in the code,
                    ' but you can return the number
                    ' of the items ordered if the order is registered successfully
                    totalItems = totalItems + row.Item(3)
                    CMD.ExecuteNonQuery()
                Next
                DetailTrans.Commit()
                retValue = orderID
            Catch exc As Exception
                DetailTrans.Rollback()
                Throw exc
                ' retValue = -1
            Finally
                CN.Close()
            End Try
            Return retValue
        End Function
```

The code starts by setting up a Command object for the NewOrder stored procedure. This stored procedure accepts a single argument, the customer's ID, and returns the ID of the new row it adds to the Orders table. The order's ID is an integer value generated by the database, and you'll need it when you add the details to the Order Details table. Notice that the stored procedure isn't executed immediately. Instead, the code creates a Transaction object and executes the NewOrder stored procedure in the context of this transaction (in the Try…Catch statement, later in the code). After executing the NewOrder stored procedure, the code sets up the parameters of the NewOrderLine stored procedure and calls it once for each row in the DataSet (each detail line). The For Each…Next loop commits all the detail rows to the database. If all updates succeed, the connection is closed and the function exits. If one of them fails, the transaction is rolled back, an exception is thrown, and the function exits.

The `GetAllProducts()` method is shown in Listing 17.12. Instead of using the visual tools of the designer, we've implemented everything in code. The web method creates a SqlDataAdapter object and uses it to execute a `SELECT` command against the Northwind database. The resulting DataSet is passed back to the client, but not before setting the DataSet's rows to read-only. This way, the user won't be allowed to edit product names or prices.

LISTING 17.12: THE GETALLPRODUCTS ( ) WEB METHOD

```
<WebMethod()> Public Function GetAllProducts() As DataSet
    Dim CNstr As String
    Dim CMDstr As String
    CNstr = "server=localhost;database=northwind;uid=sa;pwd=;"
    CMDstr = "SELECT ProductID, ProductName, UnitPrice FROM Products"
    Dim DA As New SqlClient.SqlDataAdapter(CMDstr, CNstr)
    Dim Orders As New DataSet()
    DA.Fill(Orders, "Products")
    Orders.Tables(0).Columns(0).ReadOnly = True
    Orders.Tables(0).Columns(1).ReadOnly = True
    Orders.Tables(0).Columns(2).ReadOnly = True
    Return Orders
End Function
```

Let's switch our attention to the client application now. You'll first build a Windows application that uses the `GetAllProducts()` and `NewOrder()` methods and later you'll do the same with a web application. The Windows application is called `TestOrder` and it calls the `GetAllProducts()` method to retrieve all the products from the database. The DataSet will be displayed on a DataGrid control, as shown in Figure 17.6. Northwind happens to be a small database with fewer than 100 products, so you can afford to download the entire product list to the client. In a real database, you'd have to limit the number of rows transferred to the client. One way to do this would be to download only the products in a specific category or only the products from a specific supplier.

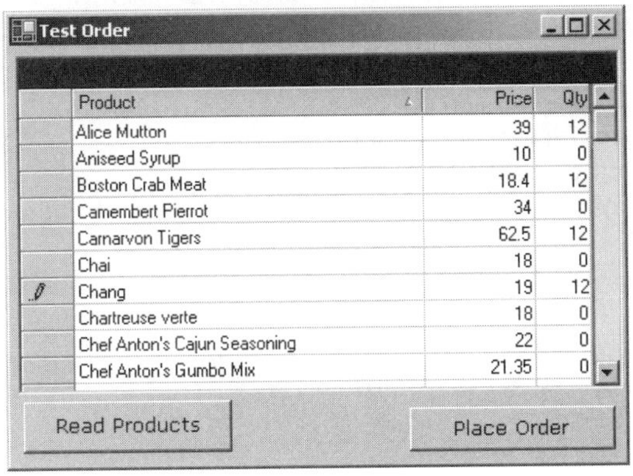

FIGURE 17.6

The `TestOrder` Windows application uses the `Orders` WebService's methods to place an order

The information will be sent to the client in the form of a DataSet, and you'll display it on a DataGrid control. You can build all kinds of different interfaces for the application, but the DataGrid is the most convenient method of displaying a table. To allow the users to place orders, you must provide a new column, where they can type the quantity of each item they wish to order. This will be a numeric column (its cells must be aligned to the right) and editable (its `ReadOnly` property set to False). The remaining columns must be read-only; there's no reason to allow users to edit the product IDs or names.

First, you must retrieve the DataSet with the products by calling the `GetAllProducts()` method:

```
NewOrder = WS.GetAllProducts
```

Then you can add the extra column with the following statements:

```
Dim qtyCol As New DataColumn()
qtyCol.DataType = GetType(Integer)
qtyCol.DefaultValue = 0
qtyCol.Caption = "Qty"
qtyCol.ColumnName = "Quantity"

NewOrder.Tables(0).Columns.Add(qtyCol)
```

`qtyCol` is the name of a new DataColumn object, which is added to the Columns collection of one of the tables in the DataSet. Our DataSet just happens to contain a single table, and you can access it as `NewOrder.Tables(0)`. The new column holds the quantity ordered for each product and it must be editable and aligned to the right. You must also specify a header for this column. The remaining columns of the table can be set up at design time with visual tools. The new column, however, must be set up from within your code.

Finally, you create a `DataGridTableStyle` object for the table in the DataSet. Each column in the `DataGridTableStyle` has its own style, which is specified with a `DataGridTextBoxColumn` object. This object represents the style of a specific column and the column itself. Listing 17.13 shows the code of the Read Products button's `Click()` event handler.

LISTING 17.13: DISPLAYING THE PRODUCT LIST ON A DATAGRID CONTROL

```
Private Sub Button1_Click(ByVal sender As System.Object, _
                          ByVal e As System.EventArgs) Handles Button1.Click
    NewOrder = WS.GetAllProducts

    Dim qtyCol As New DataColumn()
    qtyCol.DataType = GetType(Integer)
    qtyCol.DefaultValue = 0
    qtyCol.Caption = "Qty"
    qtyCol.ColumnName = "Quantity"

    NewOrder.Tables(0).Columns.Add(qtyCol)

    Dim tbl As New DataGridTableStyle()
    tbl.MappingName = "Products"
```

```
        Dim col As New DataGridTextBoxColumn()
        col.MappingName = "ProductID"
        col.ReadOnly = True
        col.Width = 0
        tbl.GridColumnStyles.Add(col)

        col = New DataGridTextBoxColumn()
        col.MappingName = "ProductName"
        col.HeaderText = "Product"
        col.ReadOnly = True
        col.Width = 150
        col.Alignment = HorizontalAlignment.Left
        tbl.GridColumnStyles.Add(col)

        col = New DataGridTextBoxColumn()
        col.MappingName = "UnitPrice"
        col.HeaderText = "Price"
        col.Width = 60
        col.ReadOnly = True
        col.Alignment = HorizontalAlignment.Right
        tbl.GridColumnStyles.Add(col)

        col = New DataGridTextBoxColumn()
        col.MappingName = "Quantity"
        col.HeaderText = "Qty"
        col.Width = 30
        col.Alignment = HorizontalAlignment.Right
        tbl.GridColumnStyles.Add(col)
        DataGrid1.TableStyles.Add(tbl)
        DataGrid1.SetDataBinding(NewOrder, "Products")
    End Sub
```

As you realize, this code does what you'd normally do in the DataGridTableStyle Collection Editor of the DataGrid control. Because you can't bind the data to the control before the actual execution of the project and the insertion of the additional column, you can't use the visual tools of the IDE.

The last step is to submit the new order to the server. You need not transmit the entire DataSet, only the rows that were edited. You can isolate these columns with the DataSet's GetChanges() method. Because all the rows are not editable, users can't add or delete rows, and you need not care about deleted or inserted rows; you need only submit the modified rows. The code in Listing 17.14 is executed when the Place Order button is clicked and submits the edited rows of the original DataSet to the NewOrder() web method.

LISTING 17.14: SUBMITTING AN ORDER THROUGH A WEB METHOD

```
Private Sub Button2_Click(ByVal sender As System.Object, _
                        ByVal e As System.EventArgs) Handles Button2.Click
    Try
```

```
                            NewOrder = NewOrder.GetChanges(DataRowState.Modified)
                            Dim newOrderID As Integer
                            newOrderID = WS.NewOrder("ALFKI", NewOrder)
                            ' The NewOrder method will never return a negative value for the order ID
                            ' Change the Web Method so that it doesn't throw an exception and returns
                            ' a negative value if it can't successfully complete the transaction
                            ' See the code of the SimpleWebService for more details
                            If newOrderID > 0 Then
                                MsgBox("Your order's number is " & newOrderID)
                            Else
                                MsgBox("There was an error in processing your order, please try again")
                            End If
                        Catch exc As Exception
                            MsgBox(exc.Message)
                        End Try
                    End Sub
```

Run the `TestOrder` project, load the products, and enter some quantities in the last column of the grid. The other columns are locked, and you can't change product IDs or names. You might notice that the application submits the product descriptions along with the IDs and the quantities. To avoid sending the descriptions to the server (which aren't used in any way), you can create a new DataSet at the client, store product IDs and quantities, and submit that DataSet to the server.

NOTE   *While developing a project that consumes a WebService, you might have to switch back to the WebService project and edit it. The client application won't see the new WebService automatically. You must first build the WebService with the Build ➤ Build <project_name> command, then switch to the client application and select Update Web References from the pop-up menu of the Web References ➤ localhost item in the Solution Explorer window. Every time you test a WebService by pressing F5, the WebService is rebuilt, but you still have to update the web references of the client application. You can create a solution that contains both the WebService and the test project, in which case you won't have to update the web references and you also won't have to run multiple instances of Visual Studio .NET. In a production environment, where the WebService will be running on the web server, you shouldn't forget to refresh the web references in the client project every time you edit the WebService.*

THE *TestOrder* WEB APPLICATION

Now you'll build a web application that uses the same WebService to place orders through the browser. The web version of the application shouldn't be much different from the equivalent Windows application, right? In this case, it's a totally new application. You will find some interesting techniques in this example, which will also help you understand and use the DataGrid web control a little better. First let's discuss how this application differs from the previous one.

The web version of the DataGrid control doesn't have nearly as much functionality as the Windows DataGrid control. As you recall from the previous chapter, the DataGrid is rendered on the client as an HTML table and it doesn't provide any editing features. To edit a row, you must notify the DataGrid that it should prepare a row for editing and then end the operation by clicking another button. Moreover, the web DataGrid control can't be scrolled. You must either settle for a very long table, which is out of the question for all but trivial applications, or use the paging feature of the control. Users should be able to edit any row of any page on the control, and you'll see how this is done.

But what do you think will happen when the user switches to another page of the DataSet? The current page will be posted back to the server, and the application will request another page of the DataSet without storing the quantities ordered to the database. The application will request another page, but in reality it will retrieve the entire DataSet from the database and ignore the rows it doesn't need. In other words, every page will arrive with its quantities reset to zero.

After the new DataSet arrives to the application, you must find out whether any of the items contained on the current page have been ordered already and display the appropriate quantity. This means that the orders must be stored somewhere. Obviously, you can't store them in the Order Details table before the entire order has been finalized. Another approach is to set up a new table and store there all partial orders (the current user's shopping basket). Because your application is running in a business-to-business environment, you can safely assume that there won't be hundreds or thousands of concurrent users. As a result, you can use the application's Session object to store the items ordered and their quantities. This is what you'll do in our example, because it will enable you to reuse the existing WebService without modifying the database. You could also develop an application for storing the basket's contents to another table in the database. This means that you would have to change the WebService as well, so that it would accept a DataSet with quantities and store it in this intermediate table.

To summarize, your application will create a paged DataSet for each request by calling the GetProducts() method of the WebService. Then it will place the DataSet's rows (the products) on a DataGrid and send the page to the client. The DataGrid should have an extra column with the quantities and a column with buttons that users can click to signify their intention to edit the quantity of the current row, as shown in Figure 17.7. When a button is clicked, the product name of the corresponding row is displayed on a Label control at the top of the form, and the row's current quantity is displayed on a TextBox control. The user can enter the desired quantity and then click the Add to Basket button to confirm the new quantity, or click another row's Buy button. You can use the techniques described in the previous chapter to edit the grid in place, but we found this approach a little simpler. The selected product appears near the top of the form in blue, and users can confirm the new quantity with the Add to Basket button.

The code of the TestOrder web application is fairly similar to the code of the equivalent Windows application. You call the same web method to retrieve the DataSet with the products; you add a new column for the quantities to the DataSet, as well as a column with the Buy buttons. However, the column with the quantities must be populated from within your code. With every postback, the code extracts the quantities and updates the corresponding Session variables. Each item is stored in a Session variable, whose name is the ID of the product prefixed with the *P* character. The product IDs are numeric values, and the variable names must be strings; that's why the prefix is necessary. When a new page of the DataSet is prepared to be submitted to the client, the code goes through the DataSet's rows and tries to find out whether the current product has been ordered. If a quantity for the current product is stored in the Session object, this quantity is copied to the last column of the same row in the DataSet—the column with the quantities. The modified DataSet is then submitted to the client.

Let's start with the simpler parts of the application. The DataGrid control has been set up to accommodate paged DataSets with the following statements, which appear in the subroutine that sets up and loads the control:

```
DataGrid1.AllowPaging = True
DataGrid1.PageSize = 10
DataGrid1.PagerStyle.Mode = PagerMode.NumericPages
```

FIGURE 17.7

The TestOrder web application demonstrates how to receive an order through the browser by using the methods of the Orders WebService.

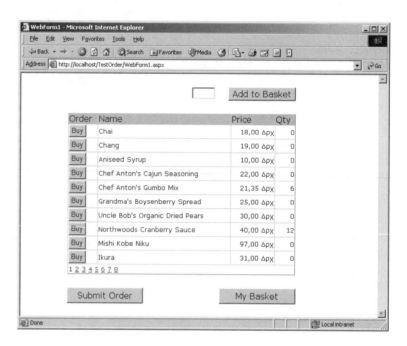

In addition to specifying some properties, you must also provide some code to handle the selection of another page. This is signaled to your application with the PageIndexChanged() event, whose handler is shown next:

```
Private Sub DataGrid1_PageIndexChanged(ByVal source As Object, _
            ByVal e As System.Web.UI.WebControls.DataGridPageChangedEventArgs) _
            Handles DataGrid1.PageIndexChanged
    DataGrid1.CurrentPageIndex = e.NewPageIndex
    LoadDataSet()
End Sub
```

When the page is loaded, the following statement calls the LoadDataSet() subroutine from within the page's Load event handler:

```
Private Sub Page_Load(ByVal sender As System.Object, _
                ByVal e As System.EventArgs) Handles MyBase.Load
    'Put user code to initialize the page here
```

```
        LoadDataSet()
    End Sub
```

The `LoadDataSet()` subroutine is the heart of the application. First, it retrieves a DataSet with all the products in the database. Then it adds two columns: the `Order` column, which contains the Buy buttons, and the `Quantity` column, which contains the quantity of each item. Notice that the first column is of the ButtonColumn type and the second is of the DataColumn type. All other columns are of the BoundColumn type and they'll be bound to a column of the DataSet.

After adding the `Quantity` column, the code populates it with the corresponding quantities. The DataSet with the products is created new with every postback, so you must add the quantities from within your code. When an item is ordered, a new Session variable is created to hold the product's ID and quantity. The `For…Next` loop in the code goes through all the products in the DataSet and finds out whether there's a Session variable for the current product. If so, it sets the value of the last cell in the row. If not, this cell's value is set to zero.

In the last section, the code adds to the DataGrid a BoundColumn for each column in the DataSet, binds it to the appropriate column of the DataSet, and then sets some properties. The column that's bound to the `ProductID` field, for example, has its `Visible` property set to False. The numeric columns are right-aligned with the `HorizontalAlign` property. Listing 17.15 shows the `LoadDataSet()` subroutine.

LISTING 17.15: CREATING THE DATASET WITH PRODUCTS AND QUANTITIES

```
Public Sub LoadDataSet()
    Dim WS As New localhost.Service1()
    Dim neworder As DataSet
    neworder = WS.GetAllProducts

    ' CLEAR THE STRUCTURE OF THE DATAGRID TO AVOID
    ' ADDING MULTIPLE COLUMNS WITH BUTTONS
    DataGrid1.Columns.Clear()

    Dim editcol As New ButtonColumn()
    editcol.ButtonType = ButtonColumnType.PushButton
    editcol.CommandName = "SelectItem"
    editcol.HeaderText = "Order"
    editcol.Text = "Buy"
    DataGrid1.Columns.Add(editcol)

    Dim qtyCol As New DataColumn()
    qtyCol.Caption = "QTY"
    qtyCol.DataType = GetType(System.Int16)
    qtyCol.DefaultValue = 0
    neworder.Tables(0).Columns.Add(qtyCol)
    neworder.Tables(0).Columns(3).ColumnName = "Quantity"
    neworder.Tables(0).Columns(3).Caption = "QTY"

    Dim iRow As Integer
```

```
            Dim itm As Integer
            Dim qty As Integer
            For iRow = 0 To neworder.Tables(0).Rows.Count - 1
                itm = Val(neworder.Tables(0).Rows(iRow).Item(0))
                If Session("P" & itm.ToString) Is Nothing Then
                    qty = 0
                Else
                    qty = Val(Session("P" & itm.ToString))
                End If
                neworder.Tables(0).Rows(iRow).Item(3) = qty
            Next
            DataGrid1.AllowPaging = True
            DataGrid1.PageSize = 10
            DataGrid1.PagerStyle.Mode = PagerMode.NumericPages

            Dim col As New BoundColumn()
            col.HeaderText = "ID"
            col.DataField = "ProductID"
            col.Visible = False
            DataGrid1.Columns.Add(col)

            col = New BoundColumn()
            col.HeaderText = "Name"
            col.DataField = "ProductName"
            DataGrid1.Columns.Add(col)

            col = New BoundColumn()
            col.HeaderText = "Price"
            col.DataField = "UnitPrice"
            col.ItemStyle.HorizontalAlign = HorizontalAlign.Right
            DataGrid1.Columns.Add(col)

            col = New BoundColumn()
            col.HeaderText = "Qty"
            col.DataField = "Quantity"
            col.ItemStyle.HorizontalAlign = HorizontalAlign.Right
            DataGrid1.Columns.Add(col)

            DataGrid1.DataSource = neworder
            DataGrid1.DataMember = "Products"
            DataGrid1.DataBind()

        End Sub
```

When the user clicks one of the Buy buttons, the ItemCommand event is raised at the server and the following code is executed. This code prepares the controls at the top of the form to accept the new quantity for the selected product, as shown in Listing 17.16.

LISTING 17.16: THE BUY BUTTON'S CLICK EVENT HANDLER

```
Private Sub DataGrid1_ItemCommand(ByVal source As Object, _
                    ByVal e As System.Web.UI.WebControls.DataGridCommandEventArgs) _
                    Handles DataGrid1.ItemCommand
    If e.Item.ItemType = ListItemType.Item Or _
        e.Item.ItemType = ListItemType.AlternatingItem Then
        Label1.Text = e.Item.Cells(2).Text
        Label2.Text = e.Item.Cells(1).Text
        TextBox1.Text = e.Item.Cells(4).Text
    End If
End Sub
```

The action of clicking one of the buttons on the DataGrid control is signaled to the application through the control's `ItemCommand()` event. This event takes place when clicking just about any part of the control, including the paging buttons, and that's why the code examines the `Item.ItemType` property and reacts only if an item (or an alternating item) was clicked.

The Add to Basket button updates the appropriate Session variable, or creates a new one with the specified quantity. Then it clears the controls at the top of the form as an indication of the completion of the edit operation. The handler of the Add to Basket button is shown in Listing 17.17. Notice that after collecting and saving the data (the quantity of a product), it calls the `LoadDataSet()` subroutine to populate the DataGrid control. If you let the CLR handle the postbacks on its own, you won't see the new quantity on the grid after clicking the Add button. Instead, you will see the new quantity the next time the control is populated, which will happen the next time you click a Buy button. Comment out the last statement in Listing 17.17 and observe how the application behaves.

LISTING 17.17: HANDLING THE ADD TO BASKET BUTTON

```
Private Sub Button1_Click(ByVal sender As System.Object, _
                        ByVal e As System.EventArgs) Handles Button1.Click
    If Label2.Text = "" Then Exit Sub
    If Session("P" & Label2.Text) Is Nothing Then
        Session("P" & Label2.Text) = Val(TextBox1.Text)
    Else
        Session("P" & Label2.Text) = Session("P" & Label2.Text) +
Val(TextBox1.Text)
    End If
    Label1.Text = ""
    Label2.Text = ""
    TextBox1.Text = ""
    LoadDataSet()
End Sub
```

The application behaves as expected. The quantities are maintained through the Session variables, and the proper quantities are displayed on each page of the DataSet. You can add the necessary logic to the application to maintain a running total and display it on another Label control on the same form.

When the user is finished entering quantities, they can click the Submit Order button to post the DataSet with the quantities to the server. The NewOrder() web method accepts the ID of a customer and the DataSet with the order. The sample code uses the same customer ID for all orders, but you can prompt the user for an ID through a new Web Form. Listing 17.18 is the handler of the Submit Order button.

LISTING 17.18: SUBMITTING AN ORDER THROUGH THE NEWORDER () WEB METHOD

```
Private Sub Button3_Click(ByVal sender As System.Object, _
                          ByVal e As System.EventArgs) Handles Button3.Click
    Dim DS As DataSet
    DS = DataGrid1.DataSource
    DS.AcceptChanges()
    Dim iRow As Integer
    For iRow = 0 To DS.Tables(0).Rows.Count - 1
        If Val(DS.Tables(0).Rows(iRow).Item(3)) = 0 Then
            DS.Tables(0).Rows(iRow).Delete()
        End If
    Next
    DS.AcceptChanges()
    Dim WS As New localhost.Service1()
    Response.Write(WS.NewOrder("BLAUS", DS))
End Sub
```

The code goes through the rows of the DataSet and deletes all the rows that have a zero quantity. Then the AcceptChanges() method is called to actually remove the deleted lines from the DataSet. The new DataSet is submitted to the server by calling the New Order() web method, as shown Listing 17.18.

Calling Web Methods Asynchronously

When you contact a WebService from within an application, unexpected delays might occur. A slow connection, a busy server, even an overloaded database can introduce substantial delays between the moment you call a web method to the moment the result arrives to the application. The application can't complete before the web method returns, but there might be other tasks that you can perform before the response arrives. When the web method is called synchronously, your application can't react to any event before the method returns (just like calling a local function), so it's a good idea to call the web method asynchronously.

An *asynchronous call* initiates an action but doesn't wait for the action to complete. It relinquishes control to your application, and an event is raised when the specific action completes. If your application calls multiple web methods, you can initiate them at once and then continue with other tasks while you're waiting for the results to arrive from the web server.

At the very least, your application won't appear frozen to the user. Even trivial web methods should be called asynchronously to enhance the responsiveness of your application. As you will see in this section, it is possible to call a web method asynchronously with very little extra code. The infrastructure is there, and all you have to do is to provide the event handler that will be invoked when the method returns.

To learn how to call web methods asynchronously, you'll build a WebService that exposes a single method, the `PrimeNumber()` method. The `PrimeNumber()` method calculates prime numbers with a brute force method. The only reason we've chosen to use a prime number calculator is because the algorithm is simple, yet it involves many calculations. The `PrimeNumber()` method accepts an integer as an argument and returns the prime number that corresponds to the specified order. If you pass the value 1000 as an argument, it will return the 1000th prime number (it took several seconds to do so on our system). The program starts with the number 1 and increases it by one. Each number is divided repeatedly by 1, 2, 3 and so on, until you find a number that can't be divided by any other number other than itself and 1. This is a prime number. You don't really need to understand anything about prime numbers or how they're calculated. The `PrimeNumber()` method you'll build in this section takes an integer argument and returns a value, which is also an integer. You can substitute the `PrimeNumber()` function's code with any algorithm that involves many calculations. The method takes a while to calculate the result, and you'll see how you can call the method asynchronously, perform other tasks, and retrieve the result when it becomes available.

The form of the test application is shown in Figure 17.8. The two buttons at the top call the `PrimeNumber()` method synchronously and asynchronously, respectively. The Label control below the two buttons displays the current time and is updated every 500 milliseconds, with the help of a Timer control. When the method is called synchronously, the Label isn't updated for a while. As soon as you call the method synchronously, the interface will freeze and the time will be updated several seconds later, when the web method returns its result. When the method is called asynchronously, the Label is updated every half a second and you will not notice anything unusual, except that you will have to wait a while before you see the result on a message box.

FIGURE 17.8

The `TestPrime-Numbers` application calls the same method synchronously and asynchronously.

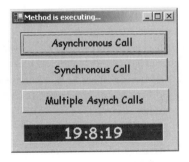

The `PrimeNumbers` WebService exposes a single method, and its implementation is shown in Listing 17.19. The code is quite trivial, and you need not even understand how it works. Just notice that it's a very simple function you could have used in any other project. The method's code is the same, regardless of how you call it.

LISTING 17.19: THE PRIMENUMBER ( ) WEB METHOD

```
Imports System.Web.Services

Public Class Service1
    Inherits System.Web.Services.WebService

    <WebMethod()> Public Function PrimeNumber(ByVal upper As Integer) As Integer
        If upper = 1 Then Return 1
        Dim iNum As Integer = 1
        Dim IsPrime As Boolean
        Dim i As Decimal = 1
        Dim N As Decimal = 2
        While True
            IsPrime = True
            For i = 2 To N - 1
                If N Mod i = 0 Then
                    IsPrime = False
                    Exit For
                End If
            Next
            If IsPrime Then
                iNum = iNum + 1
                If iNum = upper Then Return N
            End If
            N = N + 1
        End While
    End Function
End Class
```

Now you'll build the client application for the PrimeNumber() web method. Create a new Windows application project, design the form shown in Figure 17.8, and add a reference to the PrimeNumber WebService. In the Solution Explorer, click the Show All Files button to see all the files of the project. Under Web References ➤ localhost, there's a node called Reference.map. Expand this node and you will see the file Reference.vb. Double-click this file, and you will see the code of a class, with a method for each of the methods of the WebService. The method for the PrimeNumber() web method is shown next:

```
Public Function PrimeNumber(ByVal upper As Integer) As Integer
    Dim results() As Object = Me.Invoke("PrimeNumber", New Object() {upper})
    Return CType(results(0),Integer)
End Function
```

In addition, there are two more methods for each web method, the BeginXXX() and EndXXX() methods (where XXX is the name of the corresponding web method). The two methods for the PrimeNumber() web method are the BeginPrimeNumber() and the EndPrimeNumber() methods:

```
Public Function BeginPrimeNumber(ByVal upper As Integer, _
                ByVal callback As System.AsyncCallback, _
```

```
                ByVal asyncState As Object) As System.IAsyncResult
        Return Me.BeginInvoke("PrimeNumber", New Object() _
                {upper}, callback, asyncState)
    End Function

    Public Function EndPrimeNumber( _
                ByVal asyncResult As System.IAsyncResult) As Integer
        Dim results() As Object = Me.EndInvoke(asyncResult)
        Return CType(results(0),Integer)
    End Function
```

To call the `PrimeNumber()` method asynchronously, call the `BeginPrimeNumber()` method of the variable that references the WebService in your code, passing the arguments you would normally pass to the `PrimeNumber()` method (plus two additional arguments that are discussed next). Notice that the `BeginInvoke()` method doesn't report the return value of the web method it's calling—it couldn't possibly return any values created by the web method, because it doesn't wait for the web method to complete its execution.

In addition to the arguments needed by the web method, the `BeginPrimeNumber()` method also expects an event delegate and a variable that represents the WebService whose method you're calling. When the web method completes, the event handler you specified is invoked automatically. To retrieve the web method's return value, you must assign the return value of the `EndPrimeNumber()` method to a variable.

First, you must create a variable to reference the WebService in your code, so that you can call its methods, as usual. Insert the following statement at the beginning of the code (outside any procedure):

```
Dim WSprime As New localhost.Service1()
```

To initiate the `PrimeNumber()` procedure, you will call the `BeginPrimeNumber()` method and pass the *upper* argument of the `PrimeNumber()` method, followed by an `AsyncCallback` object, which represents the handler that will be automatically invoked when the web method completes its execution. An object of the `System.AsyncCallback` type is a delegate: a reference to a method that resides in the client application and is invoked when the asynchronous call to the web method finishes. The last argument is an instance of the WebService. Assuming there's a subroutine called `primeCallback` in your project (which we'll write shortly), the following lines initiate the web method:

```
Dim cback As New AsyncCallback(AddressOf primeCallback)
WSprime.BeginPrimeNumber(500, cback, WSprime)
```

The last argument of the `BeginPrimeNumber()` method associates a local variable with the asynchronous call. The `EndPrimeNumber()` method is used to retrieve the web method's return value, and you call it when you know that the method has completed its execution. In other words, the `EndPrimeNumber()` method must be called from within the `primeCallback` delegate's code. Listing 17.20 shows how to call the `PrimeNumber()` web method asynchronously.

LISTING 17.20: CALLING THE PRIMENUMBER ( ) METHOD ASYNCHRONOUSLY

```
Private Sub Button1_Click(ByVal sender As System.Object, _
                    ByVal e As System.EventArgs) Handles Button1.Click
    Dim cback As New AsyncCallback(AddressOf primeCallback)
```

```
            Console.WriteLine("Will call WebService asynchronously")
            Me.Text = "Method is executing..."
            Dim ord As Integer
            ord = InputBox("Enter the order of the prime number you wish to calculate")
            WSprime.BeginPrimeNumber(ord, cback, WSprime)
    End Sub
```

You need to implement an event handler to handle the completion of the web method. The `primeCallback` delegate will be invoked automatically when the web method completes its execution, and you'll use this event to retrieve the return value. Enter the subroutine in Listing 17.21 in the code window.

LISTING 17.21: RETRIEVING THE RESULTS OF AN ASYNCHRONOUS CALL

```
Sub primeCallback(ByVal ar As IAsyncResult)
    Console.WriteLine("Service completed at " & Now.TimeOfDay.ToString)
    Dim prm As localhost.Service1
    prm = CType(ar.AsyncState, localhost.Service1)
    Dim primeNum As Integer
    primeNum = WSprime.EndPrimeNumber(ar)
      Me.Text = "Calling Web Methods"
    MsgBox("The prime number is " & primeNum.ToString)
End Sub
```

This method receives an `IasyncResult` object as an argument, creates a reference to the WebService (variable `prm`), and uses this reference to call the `EndPrimeNumber()` method. The `EndPrimeNumber()` method returns the same result as the original web method that was called asynchronously.

To demonstrate the nature of the asynchronous call, the form of the client application displays the current time on a Label control and updates it every half a second. If you request the prime number of an unusual order (the 1000th prime number, for instance), it will take the `PrimeNumber()` method a while to calculate and return the result. If the call is made synchronously, the application will freeze and the time won't be updated. When the result becomes available, everything will return to normal—the client application will react to the usual events, and the Label will display the correct time again. If the call is made asynchronously, the client application will continue reacting to the events and the time will continue being updated every half a second. The web method is running in the background and it steals CPU cycles (quite a few of them). Keep in mind that this is a test environment. If the method is executing on a remote computer (which will be the case in a production environment), there will be no process running in the background. Between the time you call the method and the time it returns the result, your computer is free to carry out other tasks.

The top two buttons on the client application demonstrate how to call the `PrimeNumber()` method synchronously and asynchronously. The last button calls the `PrimeNumber()` method three times, one after the other. All the calls are asynchronous, and as each method completes its calculations and returns a value to the client application, a message box with the corresponding prime number will appear. The code behind this button is shown in Listing 17.22.

LISTING 17.22: CALLING MULTIPLE INSTANCES OF THE SAME WEB METHOD ASYNCHRONOUSLY

```
Private Sub Button3_Click(ByVal sender As System.Object, _
                         ByVal e As System.EventArgs) Handles Button3.Click
    Dim WSprime1 As New localhost.Service1()
    Dim WSprime2 As New localhost.Service1()
    Dim WSprime3 As New localhost.Service1()
    Dim cback As New AsyncCallback(AddressOf primeCallback)
    Console.WriteLine("Will call WebService asynchronously")
    Me.Text = "Method is executing..."
    WSprime1.BeginPrimeNumber(1200, cback, WSprime1)
    Console.WriteLine("Will call WebService asynchronously")
    WSprime2.BeginPrimeNumber(600, cback, WSprime2)
    Console.WriteLine("Will call WebService asynchronously")
    WSprime3.BeginPrimeNumber(300, cback, WSprime3)
End Sub
```

Notice that we've used three different instances of the `Service1` WebService? The three instances will be executing in parallel, and you will get back the results of the methods that take the least time to execute first. If you use the same instance of the WebService to call all three methods, then the results will arrive in an unpredictable order. The three methods are executing on the same CPU, which doesn't reduce the total time. If you called three methods on three different servers, however, the three processes would be running in parallel and you'd get the results much sooner.

Summary

WebServices are the single most advertised and talked about feature of Visual Studio .NET and they're certainly one of the best-implemented features of the new platform. As you have seen in the examples of this chapter, building WebServices with Visual Studio .NET is as simple as building classes that expose methods. Consuming a WebService is also straightforward. After you've added a WebService reference to a Windows application, you can use it as if it were another Framework object. The difference is that the class doesn't execute on your computer, but on a remote computer. You've also learned how to execute WebServices asynchronously, so that the delay introduced by the round-trip to the remote server won't freeze your application.

This chapter was an introduction to WebServices, targeted for database programmers. You saw how to use WebServices to move DataSets between computers over the Internet and how to provide data services to a large number of clients. You've also seen how to send information to a client in the form of a DataSet (which is in effect an XML file) and then receive the edited DataSet and use it to update the database.

Chapter 18

VS .NET Deployment Considerations

◆ Understanding the importance of deployment design

◆ Designing your deployment strategy

◆ Implementing deployment settings

◆ VS .NET deployment tools walk-through

DID ANYONE EVER TELL you that Buddhism is not a religion, but a way of life? Well the same applies for .NET—it's not just a language or a platform, but a way of programming. You have to completely rethink how you do the most basic tasks in programming, such as object model design, debugging, testing, and, yes, deployment. Which bring us to why we are here—how does deployment work under the .NET paradigm?

Clearly, deployment with VS .NET has made much progress since previous versions of Visual Studio. Many of these changes are tactical changes, such as improved file packaging, Registry management, and virtual root installations. However, more importantly, many strategic changes have emerged with the release of the .NET Framework. The distribution of Microsoft WebServices enables organizations and businesses to strategically reuse functionality and content from one another, without going through the pains of local installation. The strategy of leveraging the Internet as a distribution platform enables applications to mesh together organically. Both these technical and strategic advances should give you pause on how you design your deployment approach.

In this chapter, we take a two-pronged approach. In the first part, you'll review the considerations that go into a well-thought-out .NET deployment strategy. You'll review the various angles from which you should examine your project in order to prepare for deployment. You'll learn to ask important questions: Will your components be shared with other applications? How will uninstallations and upgrades work?

In the second half of this chapter, we take a tactical approach. You will focus on the deployment tools available with VS .NET. You'll examine the deployment options available with a web application, as well as a Windows application. This chapter is not intended to be a thorough exploration of every deployment configuration setting; instead, it should give you a firm foundation from which to begin packaging your application. You will begin by exploring the importance of deployment design.

Understanding the Importance of Deployment Design

Like any other process of the software development cycle, deployment should be designed before it is implemented. You can't just package an application and install it on another machine without understanding how you want your application to work now and how you want it to scale in the future. You need to envision how it will work with existing applications and how reinstallation and upgrades will be done.

There are certain considerations that you should take into account during each phase of your project. All play a part in how your application is deployed. The traditional phases of the software development cycle are shown in Figure 18.1. As you step through each phase, you can ask yourself questions that pertain to how the application will be deployed.

FIGURE 18.1

Software
development phases

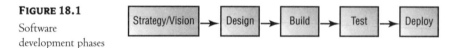

In the Strategy/Vision phase, you discover and identify business requirements and the features that belong in each release. This is a good time to identify scalability and integration issues. Will you need to connect to external systems? Do you plan for incremental versioning? If so, how will your upgrade policy work? All these considerations need to go into your deployment strategy.

During the Design phase, you create the system architecture. At this point, you incorporate the scope of your components into your design. Do you expect your components and services to be shared in the future? If so, do you need to design your components as WebServices or as shared components? You'll need to identify which components should be grouped together in a single assembly or namespace. What is the physical architecture of the servers? Will you have a web farm with multiple servers? If so, you'll need to identify how you want to install your virtual root onto the web server. Most likely, you'll want to simplify the process by using a Windows Installer package, which you will learn how to build in this chapter.

During the Build phase, you begin the tactical implementation of your deployment strategy. You'll need to identify how often you want to do your builds and begin testing the deployment process in your development environment.

The Test phase will further solidify deployment implementation. More than likely, you will have a Quality Assurance (QA) environment that mimics the production environment. Here you can address issues such as remote debugging, communication through firewalls, and system integration. The Test phase also includes User Acceptance Testing (UAT). In UAT, a sample user base is selected to work with the application during a pilot period. The sample user base, or pilot group, will use the application in real-life business scenarios so they can pinpoint any features that hinder productivity. Feedback from UAT is crucial to ensuring the quality of an application and helps secure its acceptance within the end user community.

After you've been though all these phases of the software development life cycle, you finally arrive at the Deployment stage. By this time, you should have fully designed, tested, and finalized your delivery strategy. This way, you can eliminate all foreseeable risks and therefore ensure a more successful and timely rollout. As you can see, proper deployment planning takes place in every stage of the software development process. After you understand the importance of deployment design, you can create a deployment strategy that best meets the needs of your system.

Designing Your Deployment Strategy

Before a single file is deployed, you must first design how you want the deployment process to occur. For example, you must determine which components you wish to keep local to the application and which you wish to share. You should examine whether you want your installation to be formalized with a package file, rather than simply using the lazy XCOPY distribution that's possible with .NET (and other) applications.

In this section, we present the different questions that you should consider before preparing your deployment package.

What Type of Project Are You Deploying?

VB .NET has advanced the concept of deployment by treating deployment packages as projects in their own right. Before you actually deploy your system, you must first determine which of these projects is applicable to your needs. You can find the projects by choosing File ➤ New ➤ Project from the VS .NET menu and selecting the `Setup and Deployment Projects` folder, as shown in Figure 18.2.

FIGURE 18.2

Setup and Deployment Projects

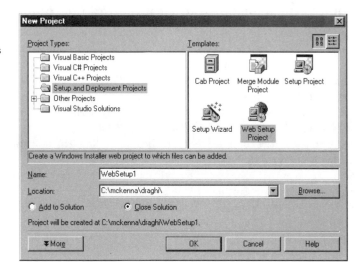

Table 18.1 briefly outlines the different deployment packages. Later, in the "Implementing Deployment Settings" section, we'll review the specifics of where and when to implement each type of deployment package.

TABLE 18:1: DEPLOYMENT PROJECTS	
DEPLOYMENT PROJECT TYPE	**DESCRIPTION**
Cab Project	Creates a cabinet file (best for when your user base is using old browser versions)
Merge Module Project	Packages shared components as subsets of a single application
Setup Project	A Windows-based application—installs files to the `Program Files` directory on a local computer
Web Setup Project	Builds an installer for a web application—installs files onto a virtual root on a web server

There is one last item included with the deployment projects: the Setup Wizard is not really a project, but an overarching guide to help you determine the appropriate deployment project options to meet your needs. It can direct you through the setup options of the four project templates listed in Table 18.1. We aren't going to focus on the wizard in this chapter. When you learn about the four deployment projects, you'll be able to work with the wizard, which really just helps you identify which project best meets your needs. It's fairly intuitive, and you should have no trouble using it.

What Is the Scope of Your Application Components?

One of the main benefits of the .NET platform is the ability to isolate components at the application level, thus preventing the pains of DLL Hell. You can guarantee that your application runs with the appropriate version of your component and enable side-by-side execution of multiple versions of the same component. Granted, this means that there might be redundant components on any given system; however, the opportunity cost of disk space seems trivial compared with the debugging and mainten-ance costs of ensuring version compatibility between shared components.

However, this isn't to say that shared components have no place in the .NET Framework. It just means that you have to make an explicit decision to implement component sharing. Component sharing is not the default behavior with the .NET platform.

Component sharing works differently than it did with previous versions of VB. Rather than cata-loging shared components in the Windows Registry, they maintain their self-describing nature. The difference is in the deployment. Local components are stored within the application directory. Shared components are deployed to the global assembly store, which is generally found in the `C:\WINNT\ Assembly` directory.

Before you begin coding your application, you should first determine the scope of your compo-nents. This enables you to ascertain where they will be deployed and to mitigate any risks caused by sharing components.

What Are Your Dependencies?

More often than not, your system will rely on external utilities or systems to provide additional functionality or content. This makes sense because you don't want to reinvent the wheel when you can use an existing technology. However, you should consider how you will manage your dependencies to external systems. For example, what will you do when new versions of external assemblies emerge? What if they are not compatible with the version that you use?

Fortunately, the .NET Framework helps alleviate the management of dependencies by ensuring that your application will always work with the right version of any dependent component. When you package your files, the dependencies are also packaged along with them and stored in the local application directory. Should your user upgrade that assembly within their system directory, your application will remain unscathed.

This doesn't mean that you can forget about dependencies altogether. The .NET Framework opens the doors to tighter integration between systems, especially with WebServices. You'll need to build exception-trapping code to handle any incompatibility issues in case an external system does not upgrade gracefully. Additionally, you should take care to ensure that your own shared components abide by proper versioning and compatibility standards, so that external systems can continue to leverage your systems.

Where Should You Deploy the Files?

Where to deploy files? This seems like a silly consideration. Of course, you are going to deploy the files onto the machine where they'll be used. Obviously, ASP.NET files are distributed on the web server, and SQL stored procedures are loaded onto the database server. This is logical enough; however, there is a deeper level of granularity that you should consider when determining the physical distribution of your files.

Keeping all your files within a single directory is a good practice to follow when deploying your application. That way, uninstallation is quick and painless, requiring only the deletion of the parent directory. Within the parent directory, you can choose to distribute your ASP.NET files and your VB .NET files into two subdirectories.

The best way make sure your files are distributed properly lies with the packaging. A good rule of thumb would be to split your application into multiple package files that match the number of logical servers that are hosting your application. For example, if you have four servers, two web servers and two application servers, then logically you have two different server roles. In this scenario, you would have two package files: one containing the assembly components for your middle-tier, the other containing the ASP.NET files.

How Will You Distribute Your Files?

All you really have to decide in this step is how you plan on distributing your files. You have several options for this: FTP, cabinet files, Windows Installer package, or third-party packaging software.

Sometimes, to save time, you might choose to copy your ASP.NET and web files onto the web server by using Windows Explorer. This might suit your needs for a one-time demo, but what if you are preparing for a production installation onto multiple web servers? In this case, it might make sense to use a Windows Installer package to deploy your files, as well as to configure installation settings. In this chapter, you will explore the options you have with VS .NET. This information will help you gauge which delivery mechanism is best for you.

XCOPY DEPLOYMENT

You might have heard the term *XCOPY deployment*. This term symbolizes the nirvana of deployment scenarios, where nothing beyond simply copying the files needs to be done—no registration, no fuss, no mess, no coupling between the file and the Registry—the end of DLL Hell. You get closer to this nirvana with the .NET platform, where some of the simpler applications can be deployed by simply copying a file directory. However, it might not be that easy for more advanced applications that have external dependencies or shared components.

.NET certainly doesn't solve all your deployment woes; in fact, some argue that the reliance on the Common Language Runtime (CLR) prevents an ideal deployment scenario. However, the .NET Framework makes XCOPY deployment more feasible by eliminating the centralized cataloging of components in the Windows Registry as well as advocating self-describing components.

Deploying a .NET Framework application is very simple. After you determine your method of distribution, all that remains is copying the files into the appropriate application directory.

There are many ways to copy your application files to the destination directory. You can copy the directory contents by using Windows Explorer, browsing to the appropriate machines. You can copy the files directly from the source directory to the target directory by using FTP. You can zip up all the files, using a compression utility, and unzip them onto the target server. Or you can use the DOS command XCOPY, from which the term XCOPY deployment originates. You can leverage the XCOPY syntax to copy entire directory trees:

```
XCOPY source_directory destination_directory /s
```

What type of files can you copy? HTML, XML, local assemblies (DLLs and EXEs), and ASP.NET files can all be directly copied into the file system. All these file types can be copied by using any of the techniques we've just mentioned. In fact, VS .NET provides native copying functionality within its IDE. For example, you can deploy the project right from Visual Studio .NET. To do so, select the Project ➤ Copy Project option from the VS .NET menu. Alternately, you can use Windows Explorer to copy the files from the source directory and paste them to the web server.

Implementing Deployment Settings

After you've determined your deployment design, it's time to turn to how you are going to implement your application's installation package. Deployment in the VS .NET is powerful and flexible. By the end of this chapter, you might even call it easy and painless.

"Painless" is not the word to describe deployment in previous versions of Visual Studio. More often than not, you had to revert to manually installing the application, especially for server-side components. When you are deploying onto a COM+ server, manually copying and registering files and manually setting up packages and connections is a lot faster than building a custom installer to distribute your application. The Package and Deployment Wizard, which comes with VB6, was always an option, but often you would still need to do some manual tweaking.

VS .NET has tried to simplify this installation packaging by providing some deployment project templates, which can absolve you from some of the custom scripting you had to do with previous versions of Visual Studio.

Working with the VS .NET Deployment Project Templates

As you remember from Figure 18.2, you can create a deployment project template by choosing File ➤ New ➤ Project from the VS .NET menu and selecting the Setup and Deployment Projects folder. Alternately, you can add a deployment project to an existing solution by selecting File ➤ Add Project ➤ New Project.

In Table 18.1, we outlined the deployment templates that are available with VS .NET. Now you are going to see when and where they should be used.

USING A CAB PROJECT TEMPLATE

The Cab Project template is the most straightforward deployment choice. It simply compresses your application files into a single file with a .cab extension. If you have built web applications in the past, you should know that the .cab files can then be downloaded via a web browser, for installation on the client machine.

Most often, you use this deployment option for intranet sites, where the network administrators permit you to download local application files, and for times when you are dealing with an environment that supports only legacy browsers.

USING A MERGE MODULE PROJECT TEMPLATE

The Merge Module Project is an interesting deployment template, introducing a new technology to the way you deliver applications. It enables to you to easily distribute shared components. This promotes the reuse of your component-specific installation scripts. That way, other systems synchronize their delivery mechanism for a shared component.

The Merge Module Project hinges upon the creation of a *merge module*, which logically packages a component and its related files. This logical grouping creates a stand-alone module, which can be reused from other deployment projects.

Merge Module Projects enable you to share setup code between applications. You can think of them as templates for deployment projects. Merge modules are a single file with an .msm extension. They are used with the Windows Installer in conjunction with an .msi file. The best time to use merge modules is when you want to package a shared component; then multiple installation programs can share the merge module, enabling each application to be consistent with the way it deploys the same shared component. We aren't going to get into much detail on merge modules in this chapter, but feel free to explore this topic in more detail by reading the VS .NET documentation.

USING A SETUP PROJECT TEMPLATE

The Setup Project template works much like the Packaging and Deployment Wizard in VS6, and creates a setup package. It leverages the Windows Installer as its delivery mechanism. You should use this option when you want to deploy a standard Windows Forms–based application onto a client machine. Generally, when you create a Windows Application project type, you would use this deployment template to package your application. The default installation for this type of project is into the `Program Files` directory. You will be exploring this project later in this chapter.

USING A WEB SETUP PROJECT TEMPLATE

The Web Setup Project template is designed as the obvious choice for installing VS .NET web applications. You should choose this template when you want to install a web application into a virtual root on a web server. This deployment option is most appropriate when you are working with a web application that contains files such as ASP.NET, XML, and HTML files. Like the Setup Project template, the Web Setup Project template leverages the Windows Installer as its delivery mechanism.

In the next section, you will experiment with the various tools and editors available when working with a deployment project. Additionally, you'll learn more about the Web Setup Project template.

VS .NET Deployment Tools Walk-through

In this section, you will explore the various options available to you within deployment projects. You will review the tools by using both a Windows and a web application.

Deploying a Windows Application

Begin by creating a Windows Application project and then add a Setup Project to it. Keep the default project names, `WindowsApplication1` and `Setup1`, respectively. After this, your Solution Explorer should look similar to Figure 18.3.

NOTE   To keep things simple, instead of using one of the applications we built earlier in this book, we are going to create a new Windows application. If you'd like, you can load this project from the CD.

FIGURE 18.3

Adding a deployment project to an existing solution

There are many deployment tools and utilities that come with a deployment project. Right-click the `Setup1` project and select the View option from the shortcut menu. You will see a list of all the available deployment editors, as shown in Figure 18.4. Alternately, you can launch these editors from the View ➤ Editor menu in VS .NET.

FIGURE 18.4

Deployment editors

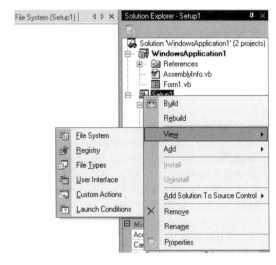

There are six editors:

The File System Editor enables you to work with a virtual representation of the file directory on the target machine.

The Registry Editor enables you to work with a virtual representation of the Windows Registry on the target machine.

The File Types Editor enables you to associate different file extensions with specific actions.

The User Interface Editor gives you the ability to tweak the installation dialog boxes that present the steps in the installation wizard.

The Custom Actions Editor is for advanced installs. It enables you to specify the execution of scripts, actions, or programs upon various installation events (such as Install or Uninstall).

The Launch Conditions Editor enables you to specify criteria that must be met before your application can be successfully deployed onto the target machine. For example, you can use this editor to define searches for certain files or Registry keys on the target machine.

In this section, you will take a closer look at many of these tools. This chapter focuses on more common deployment practices, so we won't review the Custom Actions Editor or the Launch Conditions Editor; however, you can find more information about these tools in the Help documentation that ships with VS .NET. Now, let's go back to the `Setup1` project that you have just created and review how the Windows Installer packages your application.

WINDOWS INSTALLER

The `Setup1` project represents the `.msi` file that will be generated after your deployment project is compiled. A file with an `.msi` extension is a Windows Installer file. It contains the necessary files and instructions for deploying files onto a target machine.

The Windows Installer is a service that is part of Windows 2000 and ships with some software packages, such as Office 2000. The Windows Installer is not a traditional packaging program that enables you to install your system files. Instead, it serves more as a tracking system. It works with the operating system as a centralized repository for application information, such as file locations, Registry keys, and dependencies. It's capable of detecting if a dependency or file is missing, automatically repairing the installation on the fly, or ensuring that a system file is not overwritten with an older version.

You can use the Windows Installer to build your application deployment package. All you need to do is create a Windows Installer Package file, which, again, has an `.msi` extension. Inside this file, you specify the instructions for your application installation. After you distribute this file, all the user needs to do is double-click the `.msi` file to install the application.

The installation instructions for an application should be split into three logical subsets: features, components, and products. This enables the Installer to group functional subsets to provide customizable granularity in the install.

Products consist of one or many features and components. One or many components can make up a feature. Components are the most granular level of the installation. Within each of these hierarchies, you can select what you want to install. For example, you can elect to install only certain components within a feature. You've probably seen this yourself when installing products. When you install Excel, for instance, you can select specific features, as shown in Figure 18.5.

FIGURE 18.5

Installing features

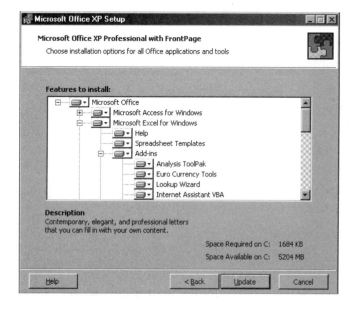

Within the Microsoft Excel for Windows product, you can choose the Help component. This is the lowest level of granularity and consists of one or many files that must be installed together to install the Help component. The Add-ins feature contains many components, such as the Euro Currency Tools, which you can select for your custom installation.

You have this option with VB6, by using the Visual Studio Installer, which was released as an add-on for Visual Studio 6. What about .NET applications? VS .NET heavily leverages the Windows Installer, which is different from the VS Installer, for almost all its deployment packages. As we mentioned earlier, the Windows Installer enables you to build packages to distribute application files.

WARNING   *Keep in mind that the VS .NET Windows Installer is not compatible with previous versions of the Visual Studio Installer.*

Now let's examine the different types of output files that can be generated for your deployment project.

DEPLOYMENT PROJECT OUTPUTS

When you examine the `Setup1` deployment project, you will see that it doesn't contain any files, by default. You will have to add the necessary external assemblies, merge modules, and other application files by choosing the Add option from the shortcut menu for the deployment application. From the submenu of the Add selection, you will see four choices: Project Output, File, Merge Module, and Assembly. The latter three are quite obvious in what they do, but what about Project Output? What does that add to your deployment project?

By default, the deployment package doesn't know that it needs to reference the existing Windows application. Select the Add ➤ Project Output option to add the output of your Windows application to the deployment package. This launches the Add Project Output Group dialog box, as illustrated in Figure 18.6.

FIGURE 18.6

Add Project Output Group dialog box

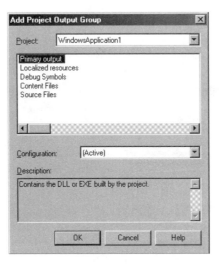

The Add Project Output Group enables you to select files to add to the deployment project. The drop-down list at the top of this dialog box lists the various projects that are available for packaging. Of course, it will list only those projects that are not deployment projects. You have only a single project in this solution, `WindowsApplication1`, so this is what you see listed.

Below the combo box is an Outputs List, containing several packaging options. Technically, this dialog box serves as a wizard, with these options serving as the various paths you can take in the wizard. Oddly, the dialog box doesn't take the form of a traditional wizard, so it can be a bit confusing to understand what happens after you hit the OK button. Depending on the option you select in the box below the project name, different files will be added to your deployment project. You can select more than one output from the Outputs List:

Primary Output specifies the project DLL or EXE as well as its dependency tree. To avoid DLL Hell, copies of all the dependencies and children dependencies are deployed along with the application. This way, the application doesn't have to depend on the presence or reliability of external DLLs on the target machine.

Localized Resources is used for specifying country-, language-, or culture-specific files.

Debug Symbols enables you to specify that the project should be compiled with debugging information.

Content Files pertains to Web Applications, where you can specify the resource files such as HTML and graphic files.

Source Files enables you to add all the source code for a project, not including the solution file.

Finally, the Configuration setting combo box enables you to specify whether you want debug code or release code compiled. Choosing the (Active) option indicates that you want to use the existing configuration specified within that project.

Choose the Primary Output choice and click OK. You will see that the `Detected Dependencies` folder in the Solution Explorer now contains two references, as shown in Figure 18.7.

The first reference is a merge module, called `dotnetfxredist_x86_enu.msm`. You can see that it's a merge module based on its extension, `.msm`. We discussed merge modules earlier and as you remember, merge modules contain independently distributable components. In this case, `dotnetfxredist_x86_enu.msm` contains the .NET Framework's CLR. The second dependency is the `mscorlib.dll`, which contains the type definitions used within the .NET Framework.

FIGURE 18.7

Detected
Dependencies
folder

FILE SYSTEM EDITOR

After VS .NET adds your deployment project to your solution, you will be able to launch the File System Editor tab within your designer pane. You can launch the File System Editor by right-clicking the `Setup1` project and choosing View ➤ File System from the shortcut menu. The editor should look similar to Figure 18.8.

FIGURE 18.8

File System tab

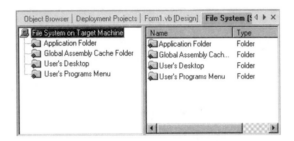

You can use this tool to determine where you want your application files distributed. The File System Editor is a virtual representation of the file directory on the target installation machine. For example, by default the `Application` folder is within the `Program Files` subdirectory for your specific Windows application. The application will be installed in subdirectories named after the manufacturer and the project. You can set the manufacturer and project name values from the properties for the project. Based on the settings shown in Figure 18.9, the application will be stored within the `C:\Program Files\Neslihan\Setup1` directory.

FIGURE 18.9

Project properties

If you'd like, you can add custom folders, files, or shortcuts to this virtual file system. After you are finished tweaking your deployment settings, you can compile the deployment project by selecting Build ➤ Build Setup1 from the VS .NET menu.

Deploying a Web Application

Let's continue our exploration of the deployment tools. This time you will use a web application. Create a new project by using the ASP.NET Web Application project template. Name your project **WebDeployment**. Add a new project by using the Web Setup deployment project template. Use the default name **WebSetup1**. In the end, you should have a solution file containing two projects, as shown in Figure 18.10.

FIGURE 18.10

Deploying a web application

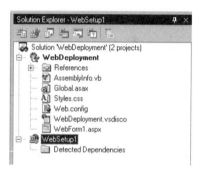

Although web applications also use an .msi file for deployment, the installation works a bit differently than Windows applications. Web applications install via a virtual root, rather than within a `Program Files` directory. Regardless, you can still specify how you would like the files packaged. In the Project Properties dialog box for the deployment, under the Build page, you can specify whether you would like the files to be compressed in a cabinet file or within a Windows Installer package (.msi) file.

Aside from the files being installed into a virtual root, the deployment packaging of a web application works much like that of a Windows application. The deployment tools, such as the File System Editor and the Registry Editor, are used almost the same way.

After your deployment project is created, there will be no files or dependencies. As with Windows applications, you have to add the Project Output for your web application to the deployment project. You can do this the same way you did earlier with the Windows application. Right-click the `WebSetup1` file in the Solution Explorer and choose Add ➤ Project Output from the shortcut menu. From the Add Project Output Group dialog box, select the `WebDeployment1` application and choose the Primary Output option to add `WebDeployment1` to the deployment project.

Unlike the Windows application project, you couldn't compile and distribute your deployment project as it stands now. Web applications contain content files, such as HTML and graphics, which also need to be packaged with the deployment application. Repeat the same steps to add another project output to the deployment project. This time, choose the Content Files option from the Outputs List. If you examine your File System Editor, you will see a reference to the content files listed within the Web Application folder.

REGISTRY EDITOR

The Registry Editor can be accessed from the View ➤ Editor menu. This editor presents a virtual representation of the hives in the Windows Registry of the target machine. You can right-click any of these hives to add custom keys to the Registry. Alternately, you can choose to import an existing Registry file by selecting the Action ➤ Import menu from VS .NET.

FILE TYPES EDITOR

The File Types Editor enables you to associate actions to specific file types. You identify these file types by using the Extensions property to specify the extension. Experiment with this editor by adding a file type called Special File. You can add this file type by choosing Add File Type from the Action menu of VS .NET. In the properties window for this file type, you can set the Extensions property to what you would like, such as .spc. (This is an arbitrary extension we chose for the purpose of illustrating the point.) By default, the Open action will be associated with this file type. You can choose to associate a specific application that will be opened when the file system encounters a file with the extension you specified.

USER INTERFACE EDITOR

The User Interface Editor enables you to modify the installation steps for your application. As you know, most installation programs follow a wizard metaphor, and the VS .NET deployment project is no different. The steps within the wizard are displayed in a hierarchical format, as shown in Figure 18.11.

FIGURE 18.11

The User Interface Editor

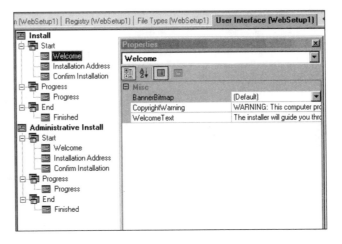

The TreeView is broken out into two installation options: the regular user installation and the administrative installation. The former is intended for the typical end user. The latter is for a network installation by a system administrator, and can be executed by appending the /a parameter to the command line call for msiexec.exe, as such:

```
Msiexec.exe /a package_name.msi
```

You can click on any of these nodes and modify its properties. You can drag and drop the nodes to change the order of the steps. Additionally, if you'd like, you can add additional steps to the wizard. To add another dialog box, you select the Action ➤ Add Dialog option from the VS .NET menu. Fortunately, VS .NET provides some predefined dialog box templates that you can choose from.

Summary

Now that you've read this chapter, you should understand how to plan your deployment strategy. Part of understanding deployment is to be aware of issues such as the scope of your components, your delivery mechanism, and how you want your application to scale and grow. Additionally, this chapter provides a high-level overview of the various editors and tools available for deployment projects in VS .NET.

Appendix A

Sample Projects

THIS APPENDIX CONTAINS TWO projects that demonstrate several of the topics discussed in this book. These projects also show how to combine some techniques discussed already to build a complete application, like the ones you'll be paid to write. We've selected two typical types of applications for this appendix: an invoicing application and an online store. We've written similar applications with several of the earlier versions of Visual Basic (and ADO), and they incorporate design features that make them almost intuitive to use.

The invoicing application consists of a single form that enables the user to enter product IDs and adds the invoices to the database. It's the type of application that runs all day long at a cash register of a retail store. If you allow users to select a customer name, shipping address, and discount (either for all items, or individual discounts for each item), you have a complete invoicing application.

The second application is the core of a web application for selling the items of the Northwind database on the Internet. It enables users to specify the products they're interested in, view them, and add individual items to their baskets. Users can view their baskets at any time and edit the quantities. When they're ready, they can place the order. As with the invoicing application, the order is registered to the same customer. If you add a form for users to specify a shipping address and a payment method, the form can be converted to a flexible invoicing application. The most interesting segment of the application is the part that indicates how to maintain a shopping basket, edit it, and update it anytime.

The Invoice Project

The Invoice project consists of a single form, which is shown in Figure 1. Users can enter detail lines on the TextBox controls at the top of the form. Each detail line is automatically added to the DataGrid control that takes up most of the form when the user presses the Enter key in the last TextBox, which corresponds to the Quantity field. The focus on the design of the interface of the Invoice project is to enable keyboard operations, without requiring the user to reach for the mouse. Users should be able to simply type the ID of the selected product in the first TextBox, press Enter to see the product's description and price in the next two TextBoxes, and then type its quantity (or accept the default). There's no reason for the pointer to ever stop at the description or price of the product. The corresponding TextBoxes are read-only and they don't belong to the form's tab order (in other words, their TabStop property is False).

FIGURE 1

Preparing an invoice

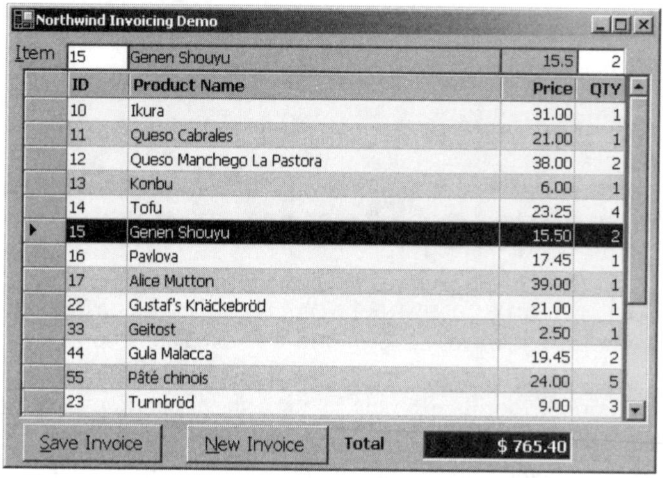

You need a data structure to store the invoice as it's being edited. This structure is a DataSet, which you must create from scratch. The simplest method to create a new DataSet in code is to add an XML schema component to the project and then add one or more elements with the designer's visual tools. The XML schema in the project is called Details.xsd and its XML description is shown in Listing 1.

LISTING 1: THE *DETAILS.XSD* SCHEMA

```
<?xml version="1.0" encoding="utf-8" ?>
<xs:schema id="Details" targetNamespace="http://tempuri.org/Invoice.xsd"
  elementFormDefault="qualified" xmlns="http://tempuri.org/Invoice.xsd"
  xmlns:mstns="http://tempuri.org/Invoice.xsd"
  xmlns:xs="http://www.w3.org/2001/XMLSchema">
  <xs:element name="DetailLine">
    <xs:complexType>
        <xs:sequence>
            <xs:element name="ID" type="xs:integer" />
            <xs:element name="Description" type="xs:string" />
            <xs:element name="Price" type="xs:decimal" />
            <xs:element name="Quantity" type="xs:integer" />
        </xs:sequence>
    </xs:complexType>
  </xs:element>
</xs:schema>
```

To create this schema, drop an Element object from the Toolbox onto the designer's surface, call it **DetailLine**, and then add an element for each field of the detail lines:

Element	Type
ID	Integer
Description	String
Price	Decimal
Quantity	Integer

After completing the design of the schema, right-click somewhere on the designer's surface and select Generate DataSet to create a DataSet based on this schema. This is a very simple DataSet with a single table, the **DetailLine** table, which in turn holds the detail lines of an invoice.

Return to the project's form and add the controls you see in Figure 1. The boxes at the top of the form are TextBoxes, in which the user can enter (or view) the fields of the current detail line. Place a DataGrid control on the form and bind it to the newly created DataSet. Its **DataSource** property should be set to the name of the DataSet, **Details1**, and its **DataMember** property to the name of the single table in the DataSet, the **DetailLine** table.

To configure the DataGrid control, open the TableStyles collection and add a new table. The new table's **MappingName** property should be **DetailLine**. Then add a **GridColumnStyle** for each field and set their **MappingName** properties to the names of the columns of the **DetailLine** table, as shown in Figure 2. Don't forget to set the width and header of each column in the DataGrid, as shown in Figure 3. Depending on your monitor's resolution, the controls on the project's form might not be perfectly aligned when you open the project on the CD. Notice that the **Anchor** and **Dock** properties aren't going to help you in designing the form of Figure 1. This form requires that you align the controls to the columns of the DataGrid control. We have done it manually, but you can insert the appropriate code in the form's Load event handler.

FIGURE 2

Setting the style of the **DetailLine** table in the DataGridTableStyle Collection Editor of the DataGrid control

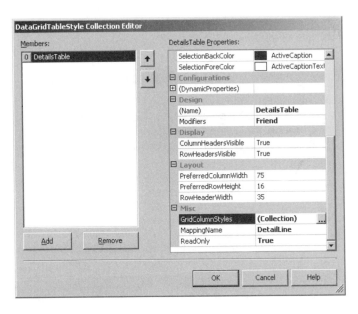

FIGURE 3

Setting the styles of
the DetailLine
table's columns in the
DataGridColumn-
Style Collection
Editor of the
DataGrid control

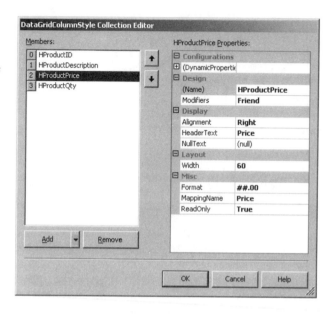

So far, you've created the visual interface of the application. The DataSet is bound to the DataGrid control, and every time you add/remove or edit a row in the DataSet, the result will be reflected on the control. Your code will manipulate the DataSet, rather than the DataGrid control. In the following section, we'll discuss the code behind the various controls of the form.

Let's assume a detail line has been filled—all TextBoxes at the top of the form have been set to some values. The product's description and unit price are read from the database, and you shouldn't allow users to edit these boxes. Later in this section, you'll see the code that enables users to supply the appropriate data. The subroutine in Listing 2 adds a new detail line to the DataGrid control on the form.

LISTING 2: ADDING A DETAIL LINE TO THE CURRENT INVOICE

```
Sub InsertDetailLine()
    Dim PRow As Integer
    Dim DRow As Details.DetailLineRow
    DRow = CType(Details1.Tables(0).NewRow, Details.DetailLineRow)
    DRow.ID = CInt(txtProductID.Text)
    DRow.Description = txtProductName.Text
    DRow.Price = CDec(txtProductPrice.Text)
    DRow.Quantity = CInt(txtQuantity.Text)
    For PRow = 0 To Details1.Tables(0).Rows.Count - 1
        If CInt(Details1.Tables(0).Rows(PRow).Item(0)) = _
                CInt(Trim(txtProductID.Text)) Then
            If CInt(txtQuantity.Text) = 0 Then
                Details1.Tables(0).Rows.RemoveAt(PRow)
                Exit For
```

```
                End If
                Details1.Tables(0).Rows(PRow).Item(0) = DRow.Item(0)
                Details1.Tables(0).Rows(PRow).Item(1) = DRow.Item(1)
                Details1.Tables(0).Rows(PRow).Item(2) = DRow.Item(2)
                Details1.Tables(0).Rows(PRow).Item(3) = _
                        CInt(Details1.Tables(0).Rows(PRow).Item(3)) + _
                        CInt(txtQuantity.Text)
                Exit For
            End If
        Next
        If PRow = Details1.Tables(0).Rows.Count Then
            Details1.Tables(0).Rows.Add(DRow)
        End If
        ClearFields()
        ShowTotal()
    End Sub
```

The program creates a new row for the first (and single) table of the Details DataSet and assigns the values entered by the user in the TextBoxes at the top of the form to the fields of the new row. This row isn't added immediately to the DataSet's table. The code is "intelligent" enough to increase the quantity of an item if it's already in the invoice. It does so by scanning all the rows of the Data-Grid control and comparing their IDs to the new ID. If a match is found, then it increases the quantity of the existing row instead of adding a new one. If the new ID isn't found in the existing detail lines, the new row is added to the table Details1.Tables(0).

The ClearFields subroutine clears the TextBoxes at the top of the form, in anticipation of the next detail line, while the ShowTotal subroutine updates the total displayed at the bottom of the form. The ClearFields subroutine is shown in Listing 3.

LISTING 3: THE CLEARFIELDS SUBROUTINE

```
Sub ClearFields()
    txtProductID.Clear()
    txtProductName.Clear()
    txtProductPrice.Clear()
    txtQuantity.Text = "1"
    txtTotal.Text = "$ 0.00"
End Sub
```

The subroutine that displays the order's current total at the bottom of the form iterates through the rows of the DetailLine table of the DataSet and sums the products of quantities and prices for each row. See Listing 4.

LISTING 4: THE SHOWTOTAL SUBROUTINE

```
Sub ShowTotal()
    Dim R As Integer
    Dim total As Decimal
    For R = 0 To Details1.Tables(0).Rows.Count - 1
        total = total + CDec(DataGrid1.Item(R, 2)) * CDec(DataGrid1.Item(R, 3))
    Next
    txtTotal.Text = total.ToString("$ ##.00")
End Sub
```

Let's look now at how the application handles user input. The user must provide the ID of an item and its quantity. As soon as the user enters an ID in the first TextBox, the program should look it up in the Products database and return the matching product's description and price. These two fields are displayed in two of the TextBoxes at the top of the form, and the focus is moved to the last TextBox, where the user can enter the quantity for the item. Listing 5 shows what happens as soon as the user presses Enter in the first TextBox.

NOTE   *Keep in mind that the setting for the Connection object should be altered to suit your environment. You will need to change the name of the database server as well as the security credentials. Realize that you should never deploy a database into production with the default* sa *username and password.*

LISTING 5: RETRIEVING THE DESCRIPTION AND PRICE OF A PRODUCT

```
Private Sub txtProductID_KeyPress(ByVal sender As Object, _
                    ByVal e As System.Windows.Forms.KeyPressEventArgs) _
                    Handles txtProductID.KeyPress
    If e.KeyChar <> vbCr Then Exit Sub
    If Not IsNumeric(txtProductID.Text) Then
        MsgBox("Invalid Product ID!")
        Exit Sub
    End If
    SqlConnection1.ConnectionString = _
            "initial catalog=Northwind;user id=sa;workstation id=POWERTOOLKIT"
    SqlConnection1.Open()
    SqlCommand1.CommandText = _
                "SELECT ProductID, ProductName, UnitPrice FROM Products " & _
                "WHERE ProductID=" & txtProductID.Text
    SqlCommand1.Connection = SqlConnection1
    Dim SReader As SqlClient.SqlDataReader
    SReader = SqlCommand1.ExecuteReader()
    If Not SReader.Read Then
        MsgBox("Invalid Product ID")
        SReader.Close()
        SqlConnection1.Close()
```

```
        Exit Sub
    End If
    txtProductName.Text = SReader.Item("ProductName").ToString
    txtProductPrice.Text = SReader.Item("UnitPrice").ToString
    SReader.Close()
    SqlConnection1.Close()
    txtQuantity.Focus()
End Sub
```

To retrieve the row of the product with the ID specified by the user in the first TextBox, the program executes the following SQL statement:

```
SELECT ProductID, ProductName, UnitPrice
FROM    Products
WHERE   ProductID= xxx
```

where *xxx* is the specified ID. The corresponding row is returned to the application through an SqlDataReader object. If no matching ID is found in the database, the Read() method of the SqlDataReader returns False and the program displays an error message and exits. If the ID is found, the fields of the matching row are displayed in the appropriate TextBoxes on the form and the focus is moved to the last TextBox, where the user can enter the quantity of the current item—or press Enter to accept the default quantity of 1.

You can use this application with a bar code reader as well. The bar code reader scans the bar code and returns the characters read, followed by one or more Enters. If you configure your bar code reader to emit a single Enter, the pointer will wait at the last TextBox for the quantity. If all the items have a bar code, you need not supply a quantity; it's quicker to scan all the items. In this case, you should configure the bar code reader to emit two Enter characters. The program will bring in the description and the price of the item after the first Enter and then accept the default quantity of 1 with the second Enter. Users will be entering new detail lines by simply scanning the bar code of the item.

When the Enter key is pressed in the Quantity TextBox, the program calls the InsertDetailLine subroutine, as shown in Listing 6.

LISTING 6: ACCEPTING THE QUANTITY AND INSERTING A NEW DETAIL LINE

```
Private Sub txtQuantity_KeyPress(ByVal sender As Object, _
                    ByVal e As System.Windows.Forms.KeyPressEventArgs) Handles _
                    txtQuantity.KeyPress
    If e.KeyChar <> vbCr Then Exit Sub
    If Not (IsNumeric(txtQuantity.Text) And Val(txtQuantity.Text) >= 0) Then
        MsgBox("Quantity must be a numeric value greater than zero!")
        Exit Sub
    End If
    InsertDetailLine()
    txtProductID.Focus()
End Sub
```

The `InsertDetailLine` subroutine adds the new line to the `Details` DataSet and then moves the focus to the first TextBox, to accept the ID of the next item.

The New Invoice button clears the DataSet and prepares the TextBoxes for a new detail line. Here's the code behind this button:

```
Private Sub bttnClear_Click(ByVal sender As System.Object, _
                        ByVal e As System.EventArgs) Handles bttnClear.Click
    Details1.Tables(0).Rows.Clear()
    ClearFields()
    txtProductID.Focus()
End Sub
```

The last button on the form, the Save Invoice button, commits the new order to the database in a transaction. First, it adds a new order to the `Orders` table by calling the `NewOrder` stored procedure. To test the application, you must add the following stored procedure to the database (see Listing 7).

LISTING 7: THE NEWORDER STORED PROCEDURE

```
CREATE PROCEDURE NewOrder
@custID nchar(5)
AS
INSERT INTO Orders (CustomerID, OrderDate) VALUES(@custID, GetDate())
RETURN (@@IDENTITY)
GO
```

This stored procedure was also used in the examples of Chapter 17, "Working with WebServices." It adds a new row to the `Orders` table and returns the ID of the new order. After that, you must add the detail lines to the `Order Details` table. Each detail line includes the ID of the order to which it belongs (the value returned by the `NewOrder` stored procedure). Listing 8 shows the `NewOrderLine` stored procedure, which adds a new row to the `Order Details` table for each detail in the invoice.

LISTING 8: THE NEWORDERLINE STORED PROCEDURE

```
CREATE PROCEDURE NewC.derLine
@OrderID integer, @ProductID integer, @quantity integer
AS
DECLARE @ProductPrice money
SET @ProductPrice=(SELECT UnitPrice FROM Products WHERE ProductID=@ProductID)
INSERT INTO [Order Details] (OrderID, ProductID, Quantity, UnitPrice)
VALUES (@OrderID, @ProductID, @Quantity, @ProductPrice)
GO
```

After adding the two stored procedures to the Northwind database, you're ready to commit the invoices. The code behind the Save Invoice button starts a new transaction and adds the appropriate lines to the Orders and Order Details tables. The value returned by the NewOrder stored procedure is the ID of the new order (a value generated by the database) and it's used to identify this order's details. Each row in the Order Details table that belongs to this order has its OrderID field set to the ID of the order.

If all actions complete successfully, the transaction is committed. If one of them fails, then the entire transaction is aborted. Not much can go wrong in this application, because the data is validated as it's entered. You can't enter negative quantities or change the prices of the products. To force the transaction to abort, you must enter a line, switch to the database and delete from the Products table the item you just added to the invoice, and then attempt to commit the invoice. This is a highly unlikely situation in a production environment (items might go out of stock, but you rarely remove rows from a table). Listing 9 shows the code of the Save Invoice button.

LISTING 9: COMMITTING AN INVOICE

```
Private Sub bttnSave_Click(ByVal sender As System.Object, _
                           ByVal e As System.EventArgs) Handles bttnSave.Click
    SqlCommand1.Parameters.Clear()
    SqlCommand1.CommandText = "NewOrder"
    SqlCommand1.CommandType = CommandType.StoredProcedure
    Dim sqlParam As New SqlClient.SqlParameter()
    sqlParam.SqlDbType = SqlDbType.Char
    sqlParam.Size = 5
    sqlParam.ParameterName = "@CustID"
    sqlParam.Direction = ParameterDirection.Input
    SqlCommand1.Parameters.Add(sqlParam)

    sqlParam = New SqlClient.SqlParameter()
    sqlParam.ParameterName = "RETURN"
    sqlParam.SqlDbType = SqlDbType.Int
    sqlParam.Direction = ParameterDirection.ReturnValue
    SqlCommand1.Parameters.Add(sqlParam)
    ' Replace this customer ID with the ID of the <retail> customer
    ' or prompt user for the ID of an existing customer
    SqlCommand1.Parameters("@custID").Value = "ALFKI"

    SqlConnection1.Open()
    Dim DetailTrans As SqlClient.SqlTransaction
    DetailTrans = SqlConnection1.BeginTransaction()
    SqlCommand1.Connection = SqlConnection1
    SqlCommand1.Transaction = DetailTrans
    Dim orderID As Integer
    Dim totalItems As Integer
    Dim retValue As Integer
    Try
        SqlCommand1.ExecuteNonQuery()
        ' STORE THE ID OF THE NEW ORDER
        orderID = CInt(SqlCommand1.Parameters("RETURN").Value)
```

```
            SqlCommand1.CommandText = "NewOrderLine"
            SqlCommand1.CommandType = CommandType.StoredProcedure
            ' SET UP THE PARAMETERS COLLECTION OF THE SQLCOMMAND OBJECT
            SqlCommand1.Parameters.Clear()
            sqlParam = New SqlClient.SqlParameter()
            sqlParam.SqlDbType = SqlDbType.Int
            sqlParam.ParameterName = "@OrderID"
            sqlParam.Direction = ParameterDirection.Input
            SqlCommand1.Parameters.Add(sqlParam)
            ' SET UP THE PRODUCT-ID PARAMETER
            sqlParam = New SqlClient.SqlParameter()
            sqlParam.SqlDbType = SqlDbType.Int
            sqlParam.ParameterName = "@ProductID"
            sqlParam.Direction = ParameterDirection.Input
            SqlCommand1.Parameters.Add(sqlParam)
            ' SET UP THE QUANTITY PARAMETER
            sqlParam = New SqlClient.SqlParameter()
            sqlParam.SqlDbType = SqlDbType.Int
            sqlParam.ParameterName = "@quantity"
            sqlParam.Direction = ParameterDirection.Input
            SqlCommand1.Parameters.Add(sqlParam)
            ' SET UP THE RETURN_VALUE PARAMETER
            sqlParam = New SqlClient.SqlParameter()
            sqlParam.ParameterName = "RETURN"
            sqlParam.SqlDbType = SqlDbType.Int
            sqlParam.Direction = ParameterDirection.ReturnValue
            SqlCommand1.Parameters.Add(sqlParam)

            Dim row As DataRow
            For Each row In Details1.Tables(0).Rows
                ' ASSIGN VALUES TO ALL PARAMETERS AND EXECUTE THE QUERY
                SqlCommand1.Parameters("@OrderID").Value = orderID
                SqlCommand1.Parameters("@ProductID").Value = row.Item(0)
                SqlCommand1.Parameters("@quantity").Value = row.Item(3)
                totalItems = totalItems + CInt(row.Item(3))
                SqlCommand1.ExecuteNonQuery()
            Next
            DetailTrans.Commit()
            retValue = orderID
        Catch exc As Exception
            DetailTrans.Rollback()
            MsgBox(exc.Message)
        Finally
            SqlConnection1.Close()
        End Try
        bttnClear_Click(sender, e)
    End Sub
```

All invoices are registered to the same customer. The application uses the customer ID of "ALFKI" (the first row in the Customers table). You should add a new customer to the table, a customer with a name such as "RetailCustomer," and use this customer's ID for all orders. Or, you can design another form, where users can locate the desired customer, or specify a new one, enter the shipping address, and so on.

Before ending this example, we should point out a few of the editing features of the application. The most important feature is that the data entry takes place with the help of the keyboard. You can use the mouse, but this is optional. Because this is the type of application you'll deploy in a production environment, it can also be used with a bar code reader, as we noted earlier. Configure your device to read the product's ID and then produce two Enter keystrokes. Users won't have to press a single key to enter the details of an invoice. When done, they can press Control+S to save the invoice. Of course, you must add the code to print the invoice.

To edit a line, just select it. Switch to the DataGrid control by pressing Tab a few times and then use the arrow keys to select the desired line. The fields of the current line in the DataGrid are displayed on the TextBox controls at the top of the form, and you can edit them at will. To delete the current detail line, enter the value **0** in the quantity box.

Notice that when you edit a line, the new quantity is added to the existing quantity. The application is programmed to facilitate entering single items, not for editing invoices. You can also remove the section of the code that goes through the current lines of the invoice to locate a line with the same item. Depending on the type of products sold, you could have multiple lines with the same product ID. The simplest way to use this application is to delete an item and then enter a new line.

You can also customize the application. For example, you can add some code to intercept certain keystroke that removes the most recently added item. To remove an item, the user would enter its ID (or scan its bar code) and then press a function key. Your code should keep track of the most recently added item and then delete the corresponding line from the invoice. Usually, this is how a program at the cash register works: you scan the item you want to remove from the invoice and press a key to indicate that the item should be removed from the invoice.

The OnlineStore Project

The second example of this appendix is a web application. The OnlineStore project consists of two forms: a form on which you can select products and place them in your basket, and another form that displays the current contents of the basket and enables you to edit the quantities. Entering zero as the quantity effectively removes the item from the basket. Figures 4 and 5 show the two forms of the application.

Let's review the basic operations of the application. On the first form of the application, the user can select items by specifying part of their name, by selecting a category, or both. If your database contains many products, users will probably specify part of the name, as well as a category.

The selected products are displayed on a DataList control, along with a column of buttons. Each Buy button places the corresponding item into the basket. To add multiple items of the same product to the basket, the user can either click the corresponding Buy button multiple times, or view the basket and edit the quantities.

FIGURE 4

Selecting products
by name or category

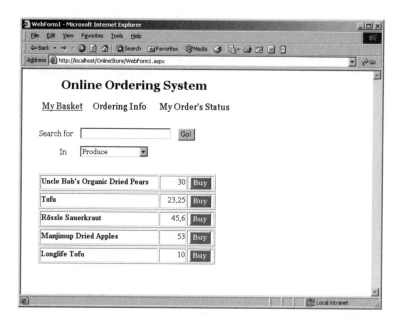

FIGURE 5

Editing the basket's
contents

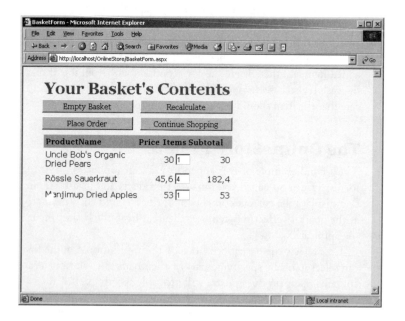

The application doesn't display the basket every time the user clicks the Buy button, nor a confirmation form. It simply adds the selected item to the basket. To view the contents of the basket, click the My Basket hyperlink at the top of the form. The other two links, Ordering Info and My Order's Status, are just fillers; they don't lead to any form.

The form with the shopping basket displays all the items selected so far, along with their quantities. The quantities are displayed in TextBoxes so the user can edit them. After changing the quantities, the user must click the Recalculate button. The editing of the quantities takes place at the client, and they won't be stored to the basket unless the user clicks the Recalculate button. This button will post the page to the server, where the basket's contents are updated through the appropriate code.

To return to the main form, click the Continue Shopping button. To empty the basket and start over, click the Empty Basket button. The code behind these two buttons is rather trivial. The last button, Place Order, creates a new order and inserts it into the database. The code is the same as the one we used in the previous example to create a new invoice, and it even uses the same stored procedures: `NewOrder` and `NewOrderLine`.

Start a new web application project and place the controls you see in Figure 4 on the main form of the application. Then add another form to the project, the `BasketForm`, and add the controls shown in Figure 5 on it. The control that displays the categories is a DropDownList control, and the other two data-bound controls that display the products and the basket's contents are DataList controls.

To populate the data-bound controls on the main form, drop the `Categories` and `Products` table on the designer's surface. The first DataAdapter object should use the following query to select the categories:

```
SELECT  CategoryID, CategoryName FROM Categories
```

You should also disable the generation of the Update, Insert, and Delete commands. The second DataAdapter, which retrieves the qualifying products, is another simple query that retrieves the products of a category:

```
SELECT  ProductID, ProductName, QuantityPerUnit, UnitPrice
FROM    Products
WHERE   (CategoryID = @categoryID)
```

As you will see, this query will never be used in the code. We specified it here so that you can bind the DataList control to a DataSet with the desired fields. In your code, you will generate a query that will take into consideration the data supplied by the user on the two controls (the TextBox and the DropDownList controls).

Now generate a DataSet for each DataAdapter and name them **DSCategories** and **SelectedProducts**. Bind the DropDownList control to the instance of the `DSCategories` DataSet and the DataList control to the instance of the `SelectedProducts` DataSet.

The next step is to configure the DataList control on the main form. The process of configuring a DataList control was described in detail in Chapter 16, "The Web Data Controls." Each row of the DataList is formatted as a table. The cells of the table have the same width, so that the columns will be aligned. Notice how you retrieve the current row's field values through the `DataBinder.Eval()` method. This method accepts two arguments, the current row (`Container.DataItem`) and the name of the field whose value you want to read, as shown in Listing 10.

LISTING 10: THE DATALIST CONTROL'S ITEMTEMPLATE DEFINITION

```
<ItemTemplate>
  <TABLE border="all">
    <TR>
```

```
            <TD vAlign="top" width="240"><B>
<%# databinder.Eval(Container.DataItem, "ProductName") %></B></TD>
            <TD vAlign="top" align="right" width="50">
<%# databinder.Eval(Container.DataItem, "UnitPrice") %></TD>
            <TD vAlign="center" align="middle" width="50">
                <asp:Button id=bttnBuy runat="server" Font-Bold="True"
Text="Buy" Font-Name="Georgia" ForeColor="#ffffcc"
BackColor="#cc6666" CommandArgument=
'<%# databinder.Eval(Container.DataItem, "ProductID") %>'>
                </asp:Button></TD>
        </TR>
    </TABLE>
</ItemTemplate>
```

The last column contains a button. It is placed there with the `<asp:Button>` tag, which includes the `CommandArgument` attribute. The `CommandArgument` attribute is set to the ID of the product displayed on the current row. Here's the definition of the `<asp:Button>` tag:

```
<asp:Button id=bttnBuy runat="server" Font-Bold="True" Text="Buy"
Font-Name="Georgia" ForeColor="#ffffcc" BackColor="#cc6666"
CommandArgument='<%# databinder.Eval(Container.DataItem, "ProductID") %>'>
</asp:Button></TD>
```

Note how the value of the `CommandArgument` is specified, and that the entire expression is delimited by single quotes. When this button is clicked, it invokes the `OrderItem` subroutine in your code. This must be specified in the declaration of the DataList control, which is as follows:

```
<asp:datalist id=DataList1 style="Z-INDEX: 106; LEFT: 34px; POSITION: absolute;
TOP: 206px" runat="server" Width="394px" DataSource="<%# SelectedProducts1 %>"
DataMember="Products" DataKeyField="ProductID" Height="128px"
OnItemCommand="OrderItem">
```

The `OnItemCommand` attribute must be added manually and it must be set to the name of a subroutine, which will be invoked automatically when an item is selected on the DataList control. The `OrderItem` subroutine adds the current row's item to the shopping basket. Listing 11 shows its implementation.

LISTING 11: ADDING THE SELECTED ITEM TO THE BASKET

```
Public Sub OrderItem(ByVal sender As Object, _
                ByVal e As System.Web.UI.WebControls.DataListCommandEventArgs)
    Dim productID As Integer = e.CommandArgument
    ShoppingBasket = Session("UserBasket")
    If ShoppingBasket.ContainsKey(productID) Then
        ShoppingBasket(productID) = Val(ShoppingBasket(productID) + 1)
    Else
        ShoppingBasket.Add(productID, 1)
```

```
        End If
        Session("Basket") = ShoppingBasket
    End Sub
```

The selected product's ID is passed to the subroutine through the e argument, and it's the value of the CommandArgument property. If the product's ID exists in the basket, the corresponding quantity is increased by one. If not, it's added to the basket and the corresponding quantity is set to 1.

When the application is first loaded, the main form's Load event handler is executed, as shown in Listing 12.

LISTING 12: DISPLAYING THE CATEGORIES

```
    Private Sub Page_Load(ByVal sender As System.Object, _
                          ByVal e As System.EventArgs) Handles MyBase.Load
        'Put user code to initialize the page here
        If Not Page.IsPostBack Then
            If Session("UserBasket") Is Nothing Then
                ShoppingBasket = New Hashtable()
                Session("UserBasket") = ShoppingBasket
            End If
            DACategories.Fill(DsCategories1)
            Dim newRow As DSCategories.CategoriesRow
            newRow = DsCategories1.Tables(0).NewRow
            newRow.CategoryID = "999"
            newRow.CategoryName = "All"
            DsCategories1.Tables(0).Rows.InsertAt(newRow, 0)
            DropDownList1.DataSource = DsCategories1
            DropDownList1.DataMember = "Categories"
            DropDownList1.DataTextField = "CategoryName"
            DropDownList1.DataValueField = "CategoryID"
            DropDownList1.DataBind()
        End If
    End Sub
```

The code creates a new HashTable, where the basket's contents will be stored. The shopping basket is stored in the UserBasket Session variable. This variable is a HashTable, and each item is stored as two numeric values. The product's ID is the key, and the quantity is the value.

Then the code fills the DSCategories DataSet with the rows of the Categories table and binds the DropDownList control to the Categories table of the DSCategories DataSet. It also adds a new row to the table, the "All" category, which includes all the categories. The ID of this category is 999, and you'll soon see how it's used in the code.

The Go button retrieves the qualifying products from the database and populates the Selected-Products DataSet. The code behind this button, which is shown in Listing 13, takes into consideration the values entered on the form by the user and it executes the appropriate SELECT statement against the database.

LISTING 13: DISPLAYING THE SELECTED PRODUCTS ON A DATALIST CONTROL

```
Private Sub bttnGO_Click(ByVal sender As System.Object, _
                     ByVal e As System.EventArgs) Handles bttnGO.Click
    If DropDownList1.SelectedItem.Value = 999 Then
        DAProducts.SelectCommand.CommandText = _
                    "SELECT ProductID, ProductName, UnitPrice " & _
                    "FROM Products WHERE ProductName LIKE '%" & _
                    txtProductName.Text & "%'"
    Else
        DAProducts.SelectCommand.CommandText = _
                    "SELECT ProductID, ProductName, UnitPrice " & _
                    "FROM Products WHERE CategoryID=" & _
                    DropDownList1.SelectedItem.Value & _
                    " AND ProductName LIKE '%" & txtProductName.Text & "%'"
    End If
    DAProducts.SelectCommand.Parameters("@categoryID").Value = _
                    DropDownList1.SelectedItem.Value
    DAProducts.SelectCommand.Parameters("@productName").Value = txtProductName.Text
    DAProducts.Fill(SelectedProducts1, "Products")
    DataList1.DataBind()
End Sub
```

The ShowBasket subroutine displays the basket's contents on a DataList control. The code, shown in Listing 14, creates a new DataSet, the DSBasket DataSet, and adds five columns to it: ProductID, ProductName, ProductPrice, Quantity, and Subtotal. These are the items shown in the DataList control that displays the contents of the basket, except for the ProductID column. This column isn't displayed, but you need to know each product's ID to update the basket.

Then the code iterates through the contents of the basket, collects their IDs, and retrieves the related information from the Products table. The results are returned to the application through an SqlDataReader object, and then the DSBasket DataSet is populated. After the DataList control is bound to the DataSet, the basket's contents are displayed on the control.

LISTING 14: DISPLAYING THE BASKET'S CONTENTS ON A DATALIST CONTROL

```
Sub ShowBasket()
    'Put user code to initialize the page here
    Dim DSBasket As New DataSet()
    DSBasket.Tables.Add("BASKET")
    DSBasket.Tables("BASKET").Columns.Add("ProductID")
    DSBasket.Tables("BASKET").Columns.Add("ProductName")
    DSBasket.Tables("BASKET").Columns.Add("ProductPrice")
    DSBasket.Tables("BASKET").Columns.Add("Quantity")
    DSBasket.Tables("BASKET").Columns.Add("Subtotal")
    Dim prodRow As DataRow
    Dim UserBasket As New Hashtable()
    UserBasket = Session("UserBasket")
```

```
    Dim itm As Integer
    Dim SelIDs As String
    If UserBasket.Count = 0 Then
        Label1.Text = "Your basket is empty"
        Exit Sub
    End If
    For Each itm In UserBasket.Keys
        SelIDs = SelIDs & itm.ToString & ", "
    Next
    SelIDs = Left(SelIDs, Len(SelIDs) - 2)
    Dim sql As String
    sql = "SELECT ProductID, ProductName, UnitPrice FROM Products " & _
        "WHERE ProductID IN (" & SelIDs & ")"
    Dim conn As New SqlClient.SqlConnection()
    conn.ConnectionString = "initial catalog=Northwind; " & _
"persist security info=False;user id=sa; " & _
"workstation id=POWERTOOLKIT;packet size=4096"
    conn.Open()
    Dim sqlCMD As New SqlClient.SqlCommand()
    sqlCMD.Connection = conn
    sqlCMD.CommandText = sql
    sqlCMD.CommandType = CommandType.Text
    Dim DataIn As SqlClient.SqlDataReader
    DataIn = sqlCMD.ExecuteReader()
    While DataIn.Read
        prodRow = DSBasket.Tables("BASKET").NewRow
        prodRow.Item(0) = DataIn.Item(0)
        prodRow.Item(1) = DataIn.Item(1)
        prodRow.Item(2) = DataIn.Item(2)
        prodRow.Item(3) = UserBasket(DataIn.Item(0))
        prodRow.Item(4) = CDec(prodRow.Item(2)) * CDec(prodRow.Item(3))
        DSBasket.Tables("BASKET").Rows.Add(prodRow)
    End While
    DataList1.DataSource = DSBasket
    DataList1.DataMember = "BASKET"
    DataList1.DataKeyField = "ProductID"
    DataList1.DataBind()
End Sub
```

You must also configure the DataList control, as explained in Chapter 16. The control's
`ItemTemplate` and `HeaderTemplate` sections are shown here:

```
<HeaderTemplate>
    <TABLE>
        <TR>
            <TD width="180"><b>ProductName</b>
            </TD>
```

```
                            <TD align="right" width="50"><b>Price</b>
                            </TD>
                            <TD align="right" width="50"><b>Items</b>
                            </TD>
                            <TD align="right" width="70"><b>Subtotal</b>
                            </TD>
                    </TR>
                </TABLE>
        </HeaderTemplate>
        <ItemTemplate>
            <TABLE>
                <TR>
                        <TD width="200">
                                <%# databinder.Eval(Container.DataItem, "ProductName") %></TD>
                        <TD align="right" width="70">
                                <%# databinder.Eval(Container.DataItem, "ProductPrice") %></TD>
                        <TD align="right">
                            <asp:TextBox id="txtQuantity" Width="30" runat="server"
                            text='<%# databinder.Eval(Container.DataItem, "Quantity") %>'>
                            </asp:TextBox></TD>
                        <TD align="right" width="80">
                                <%# databinder.Eval(Container.DataItem, "Subtotal") %></TD>
                </TR>
            </TABLE>
        </ItemTemplate>
```

The TextBox control that enables users to edit the quantities was inserted with the `<asp:TextBox>` tag, and its value is the current product's quantity. To retrieve this value from the control's DataSet, you use the `DataBinder.Eval()` method, as before.

The user can edit all the quantities on the form, or remove a product from the basket by setting its quantity to zero. Then, the Recalculate button must be clicked to update the contents of the basket (see Listing 15).

LISTING 15: RECALCULATING THE BASKET'S TOTAL

```
Private Sub bttnRecalc_Click(ByVal sender As System.Object, _
                            ByVal e As System.EventArgs) Handles bttnRecal.Click
    Dim UserBasket As New Hashtable()
    Dim newUserBasket As New Hashtable()
    UserBasket = Session("UserBasket")
    Dim currentRow As Integer
    Dim qty As Integer
    Dim key As IEnumerator
    Dim keys As ICollection
    keys = DataList1.DataKeys
    key = keys.GetEnumerator
    Dim itm As Integer
    While key.MoveNext
```

```
        itm = key.Current
        qty = CType(DataList1.Items(currentRow).FindControl("txtQuantity"), _
                TextBox).Text
        If qty > 0 Then
            newUserBasket.Add(itm, qty)
        End If
        currentRow = currentRow + 1
    End While
    Session("UserBasket") = newUserBasket
    ShowBasket()
End Sub
```

This is an interesting section of the application. The code goes through the IDs in the basket with the While loop. At each iteration, it extracts a product ID from the basket and stores it in the itm variable. To find the quantity of this product on the control, it calls the current item's FindControl() method. The current item on the control is given by the expression DataList1.Items(currentRow), where currentRow is an index that is increased by one at each iteration. This expression returns one of the control's items. If the item contains one or more controls, you can retrieve a reference to these controls through the FindControl() method, which accepts as an argument the control's name. After you have a reference to the TextBox control with the revised quantity, you can cast it to the TextBox type and request its Text property. The product IDs and the matching quantities are added to a new HashTable, which is then assigned to the UserBasket Session variable.

Why did we have to introduce a second HashTable and not manipulate the original HashTable directly? If you remove an item from a collection while you iterate it with its Enumerator, the results are unpredictable. The safest approach is to copy the elements with positive quantities to another HashTable and then use the new HashTable as the shopping basket.

To store the order to the database, the Place Order button initiates a transaction, calls the NewOrder and the NewOrderLine stored procedures, and then either commits or aborts the transaction. The key portion of the code behind the Place Order button goes through each item in the HashTable that stores the items of the shopping basket. The code calls the NewOrderLine stored procedure for each item, passing the product's ID and its quantity as arguments. It also passes a third argument, which contains the ID of the order to which the detail line belongs (this is the value returned by the NewOrder stored procedure).

As with the invoicing demo, the web application doesn't prompt the user for additional information, such as the shipping address and payment method. For this, you'll need to display yet another form and display it before committing the order to the database. Listing 16 shows the code behind the Place Order button.

LISTING 16: STORING AN ORDER TO THE DATABASE

```
Private Sub bttnCommit_Click(ByVal sender As System.Object, _
                            ByVal e As System.EventArgs) Handles bttnCommit.Click
    Dim UserBasket As New Hashtable()
    UserBasket = Session("UserBasket")
```

```vb
Dim CMD As New SqlClient.SqlCommand()
CMD.CommandText = "NewOrder"
CMD.CommandType = CommandType.StoredProcedure
Dim sqlParam As New SqlClient.SqlParameter()
sqlParam.SqlDbType = SqlDbType.Char
sqlParam.Size = 5
sqlParam.ParameterName = "@CustID"
sqlParam.Direction = ParameterDirection.Input
CMD.Parameters.Add(sqlParam)

sqlParam = New SqlClient.SqlParameter()
sqlParam.ParameterName = "RETURN"
sqlParam.SqlDbType = SqlDbType.Int
sqlParam.Direction = ParameterDirection.ReturnValue
CMD.Parameters.Add(sqlParam)
CMD.Parameters("@custID").Value = "ALFKI"

SqlConnection1.Open()
Dim DetailTrans As SqlClient.SqlTransaction
DetailTrans = SqlConnection1.BeginTransaction()

CMD.Connection = SqlConnection1
CMD.Transaction = DetailTrans
Dim orderID As Integer
Dim totalItems As Integer
Dim key As IEnumerator
Dim keys As ICollection
keys = DataList1.DataKeys
key = keys.GetEnumerator
Dim itm, qty As Integer
Try
    CMD.ExecuteNonQuery()
    orderID = CMD.Parameters("RETURN").Value
    While key.MoveNext
        itm = key.Current
        qty = UserBasket(itm)
        If qty > 0 Then
            CMD.CommandText = "NewOrderLine"
            CMD.CommandType = CommandType.StoredProcedure
            CMD.Parameters.Clear()

            sqlParam = New SqlClient.SqlParameter()
            sqlParam.SqlDbType = SqlDbType.Int
            sqlParam.ParameterName = "@OrderID"
            sqlParam.Direction = ParameterDirection.Input
            CMD.Parameters.Add(sqlParam)
```

```
                sqlParam = New SqlClient.SqlParameter()
                sqlParam.SqlDbType = SqlDbType.Int
                sqlParam.ParameterName = "@ProductID"
                sqlParam.Direction = ParameterDirection.Input
                CMD.Parameters.Add(sqlParam)

                sqlParam = New SqlClient.SqlParameter()
                sqlParam.SqlDbType = SqlDbType.Int
                sqlParam.ParameterName = "@quantity"
                sqlParam.Direction = ParameterDirection.Input
                CMD.Parameters.Add(sqlParam)

                sqlParam = New SqlClient.SqlParameter()
                sqlParam.ParameterName = "RETURN"
                sqlParam.SqlDbType = SqlDbType.Int
                sqlParam.Direction = ParameterDirection.ReturnValue
                CMD.Parameters.Add(sqlParam)

                CMD.Parameters("@OrderID").Value = orderID
                CMD.Parameters("@ProductID").Value = itm
                CMD.Parameters("@quantity").Value = qty
                CMD.ExecuteNonQuery()
            End If
        End While
        DetailTrans.Commit()
    Catch exc As Exception
    Finally
        SqlConnection1.Close()
    End Try
End Sub
```

Finally, there's a little bit of code behind the other two buttons. The Continue Shopping button redirects the user to the main form of the application with the following statement:

```
Response.Redirect("WebForm1.aspx")
```

The Empty Basket button empties the basket with the following statements:

```
        Dim Basket As New Hashtable()
        Basket = Session("UserBasket")
        Basket.Clear()
        Session("UserBasket") = Basket
```

Index

Note to the Reader: Throughout this index **boldfaced** page numbers indicate primary discussions of a topic. *Italicized* page numbers indicate illustrations.

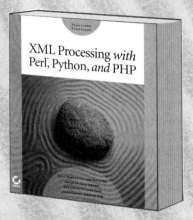
 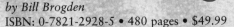

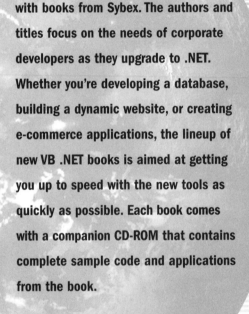